LANDMARK CASES IN CONSUMER LAW

This book analyses the history of the common law foundations of consumer law, and encourages readers to rethink the role that consumer law plays in our society.

Consumer law is often constructed as purely statute-based law. However – as this collection will demonstrate – this is far from the truth. Much of the history of the common law concerns consumer transactions and markets. Case law has often established or modified the ground rules of consumer markets, has had a patterning effect on the economic organisation of markets, and has expressed cultural visions of the market and consumers. An analysis of landmark cases of consumer law allows many traditional cases to be viewed through a new and distinct lens, providing significant academic and intellectual value.

The collection also includes a unique socio-legal perspective, considering the role that consumer law has played in addressing racial discrimination, LGBTQ challenges and the rights of women.

This collection of landmark cases demonstrates the theoretical and practical significance of consumer law through a wide range of contributions by distinguished authors from the United Kingdom, Europe, the United States, Australia and New Zealand.

Landmark Cases in Consumer Law

Edited by
Jodi Gardner
and
Iain Ramsay

·HART·
OXFORD · LONDON · NEW YORK · NEW DELHI · SYDNEY

HART PUBLISHING

Bloomsbury Publishing Plc

Kemp House, Chawley Park, Cumnor Hill, Oxford, OX2 9PH, UK

1385 Broadway, New York, NY 10018, USA

29 Earlsfort Terrace, Dublin 2, Ireland

HART PUBLISHING, the Hart/Stag logo, BLOOMSBURY and the Diana logo are trademarks of Bloomsbury Publishing Plc

First published in Great Britain 2024

Copyright © The editors and contributors severally 2024

The editors and contributors have asserted their right under the Copyright, Designs and Patents Act 1988 to be identified as Authors of this work.

All rights reserved. No part of this publication may be reproduced or transmitted in any form or by any means, electronic or mechanical, including photocopying, recording, or any information storage or retrieval system, without prior permission in writing from the publishers.

While every care has been taken to ensure the accuracy of this work, no responsibility for loss or damage occasioned to any person acting or refraining from action as a result of any statement in it can be accepted by the authors, editors or publishers.

All UK Government legislation and other public sector information used in the work is Crown Copyright ©. All House of Lords and House of Commons information used in the work is Parliamentary Copyright ©. This information is reused under the terms of the Open Government Licence v3.0 (http://www.nationalarchives.gov.uk/doc/open-government-licence/version/3) except where otherwise stated.

All Eur-lex material used in the work is © European Union, http://eur-lex.europa.eu/, 1998–2024.

A catalogue record for this book is available from the British Library.

A catalogue record for this book is available from the Library of Congress.

Library of Congress Control Number: 2023944560

ISBN: HB: 978-1-50995-229-8
ePDF: 978-1-50995-231-1
ePub: 978-1-50995-230-4

Typeset by Compuscript Ltd, Shannon

To find out more about our authors and books visit www.hartpublishing.co.uk. Here you will find extracts, author information, details of forthcoming events and the option to sign up for our newsletters.

Contents

List of Contributors vii
Table of Cases xi
Table of Legislation xxvii

1. *Key Themes in Landmark Consumer Law Cases* 1
   Iain Ramsay and Jodi Gardner

PART I
COMMON LAW FOUNDATIONS OF CONSUMER LAW

2. *Earl of Chesterfield v Janssen*: Equitable Foundations 23
   Benjamin Douglas

3. *Gardiner v Gray* 39
   David Ibbetson

4. Incorporation and Exemption Clauses in Consumer Contracts:
   Parker v South Eastern Railway Company 55
   Stelios Tofaris

5. Quackery and Contract Law: The Case of the *Carbolic Smoke* Ball 79
   AWB Simpson

6. *Helby v Matthews*: The 'Great Test Case'? 115
   Iain Ramsay

7. *Blacker v Lake and Elliot*: (closing and opening) a Path for Injured
   Consumers in Tort before *Donoghue* 135
   Emily Gordon

8. *Jarvis v Swans Tours*: Can Holidays be a Human Right? 153
   Jodi Gardner

9. The Foundations of Corporate Criminal Responsibility in Consumer Law:
   Tesco Supermarkets Ltd v Nattrass in Perspective 169
   Peter Cartwright

10. *Lloyds Bank Ltd v Bundy*: The Influence of the Omnibus Principle of
    Unequal Bargaining Power 189
    Jeannie Marie Paterson and Elise Bant

11. *Erven Warnink Besloten Vennootschap v J Townend & Sons (Hull) Ltd*: Consumer Welfarism by the Back Door?..............................207
John Murphy

PART II
RETHINKING THE ROLE OF CONSUMER LAW

12. Of Marginal Gains and Opportunities Missed: The Lost Landmark of *Constantine v Imperial Hotels Ltd* 225
Toni Williams

13. Abortion and the 'Right to Choose': The Consumer Rights Implications of *Roe v Wade* 245
Stevie Martin

14. *Virginia State Board of Pharmacy v Virginia Consumer Citizens Council, Inc*: Commercial Speech: Advancing the Rights of Consumers or Enhancing the Rights of Corporations?..265
Mary Spector

15. *A v National Blood Authority*: An Experiment in Radical Consumer-centric Strict Liability for Products 283
Jacob Eisler

16. Failure to Protect the Vulnerable: *Office of Fair Trading (Respondents) v Abbey National Plc and Others (Appellants)* 299
Christine Riefa

17. Bankruptcy, Housing, 'Have Nots', and the Limits of Legal Landmarks: *Places for People Homes Ltd v Sharples* 315
Joseph Spooner

18. European Integration after *Mohammed Aziz*................................333
Irina Domurath and Hans-W Micklitz

19. *Plevin v Paragon*: Undisclosed PPI Commissions Give Rise to an Unfair Credit Relationship..351
Nicola J Howell

20. Cake, Conflict and Consumer Law: The Significance of *Masterpiece Cakeshop v Colorado Civil Rights Commission* and *Lee v Ashers Baking Company Ltd*..369
Sarah Brown

21. Small Claims, Big Challenges: *Merricks v Mastercard*....................387
Simone Degeling, Jodi Gardner and Josh McGeechan

Index 403

List of Contributors

Elise Bant is Professor of Private Law and Commercial Regulation at the University of Western Australia, a Professorial Fellow at the University of Melbourne and a Fellow of the Australian Academy of Law. With Professor Jeannie Marie Paterson, Elise has held Australian Research Council Discovery grants for research into misleading and unconscionable conduct in trade and commerce. She was appointed an ARC Future Fellow to examine corporate liability for serious civil misconduct, including fraud and predatory trading practices.

Dr Sarah Brown is one of the contributing authors to Goode: *Consumer Credit Law and Practice*. She is a qualified solicitor (non-practising), and until recently, an Associate Professor at the School of Law, University of Leeds, UK. She has published primarily in the field of consumer protection, more particularly the provision of credit, and personal insolvency from both national and comparative perspectives.

Peter Cartwright is Professor of Consumer Protection Law in the School of Law at the University of Nottingham, UK. His books include *Consumer Protection and the Criminal Law* (Cambridge University Press) and *Banks Consumers and Regulation* (Hart Publishing). He is a member of the University of Nottingham Commercial Law Centre and is currently researching in the area of exploitative technology, vulnerability and consumer protection.

Simone Degeling is a Professor in the Faculty of Law & Justice, University of New South Wales, Australia.

Irina Domurath is Adjunct Professor at the Universidad Adolfo Ibañez in Chile and Visiting Researcher at University of Trento, Italy. Previously, she has held positions at the University of Amsterdam, the University of Copenhagen, and the University of Iceland. She researches European Private Law in the fields of consumer debt, housing, and data.

Jacob Eisler is the James Edmund and Margaret Elizabeth Corry Professor at Florida State University College of Law, US. He previously served as College Lecturer and Yates Glazebrook Fellow in Law at Jesus College, University of Cambridge, UK. He received his JD and PhD in political science from Harvard University.

Jodi Gardner is the Brian Coote Chair in Private Law at the University of Auckland and a Senior Research Fellow at the Centre for Banking & Finance Law at the National University of Singapore. Her research focuses on the intersection between private law and social policy, analysing the impact of legal doctrines on inequality and vulnerability.

Dr Emily Gordon is a Lecturer in Law at UCL, who teaches and researches in the areas of legal history and tort. Emily is originally from Perth, Western Australia, but came to the UK for postgraduate study (LLM, PhD) at the University of Cambridge. She was a Fellow and Director of Studies in Law at Lucy Cavendish College, Cambridge, before taking up her current post at UCL.

Nicola J Howell is a Senior Lecturer at the Law School, Queensland University of Technology, Australia. Her teaching responsibilities include commercial, consumer, banking and finance, and insolvency law, and her research focuses on legal and policy issues in consumer financial services, consumer credit and other consumer transactions, and personal insolvency. She has published widely on these topics and is also a regular contributor to relevant policy and law reform processes.

David Ibbetson is the Emeritus Regius Professor of Civil Law at the University of Cambridge, UK.

Dr Stevie Martin is a College Lecturer in Law at Fitzwilliam and King's Colleges at the University of Cambridge, UK. Stevie's research sits at the interface of human rights and medicine, with a particular focus on end-of-life care and reproductive autonomy.

Joshua McGeechan is a senior specialist in the civil litigation team at the Australian Securities and Investments Commission, Australia. He is a graduate of the University of Queensland and the University of Oxford.

Hans-W Micklitz is part-time professor at the Robert Schuman Centre of Advanced Studies, European University Institute, Florence Italy. Previously he held positions at the law department of the European University Institute and the University of Bamberg. His research fields are – European private and economic law, consumer law, private law theory.

John Murphy is a Professor of Law at Hong Kong University.

Jeannie Marie Paterson is a Professor of Law and the founding co-director of the Centre for AI and Digital Ethics at the University of Melbourne, Australia. Jeannie's research interests are in the areas of consumer protection, consumer credit and data protection law, as well as emerging digital technologies, AI and robotics. She is interested in regulatory design for fair safe and accessible consumer contracts and products, with a particular focus on consumers experiencing vulnerability.

Iain Ramsay is Emeritus Professor of Law, Kent Law School, University of Kent, Canterbury, UK.

Christine Riefa is a Professor of Law at the University of Reading, UK. Her research specialises in consumer law enforcement and policy. She notably serves on the United Nations Working Group on Consumer Protection in E-Commerce as part of the UNCTAD Inter-Governmental Group of Experts.

Mary Spector is Professor of Law and Associate Dean for Experiential Learning at SMU Dedman School of Law, US. Her research combines theory and practice to advance the rights of consumers and tenants. She currently serves on a Texas Access to Legal Services Working Group and previously served as an official observer to the Uniform Law Commission's drafting committee on consumer debt collection and as an expert on consumer debt to the US Department of Justice.

Dr Joseph Spooner is an Associate Professor at LSE Law School, UK. He researches issues of law, policy, and politics relating to household debt. He also takes particular interest in issues of dispute resolution, access to justice, and how law serves low-income groups. Joseph has published articles on the law and politics of bankruptcy in leading journals including the *Journal of Law and Society* and the *Modern Law Review*, and is the author of *Bankruptcy: the Case for Relief in an Economy of Debt*.

Stelios Tofaris is Associate Professor at the University of Cambridge, UK.

Toni Williams is Fellow and the Senior Tutor of Girton College, Cambridge, UK, and Honorary Professor at the University of Kent, UK, where she served as Professor of Law, Head of Kent Law School and Director (Executive Dean) of the Division for the Study of Law, Society and Social Justice before moving to Girton College in October 2022.

Table of Cases

A v National Blood Authority [2001] EWHC QB 446, (2001)
65 BMLR 1 .... 16, 19, 283–97
Aannemersbedrijf PK Kraaijeveld BV ea v Gedeputeerde Staten van
Zuid-Holland (Case 72/95)[1996] ECLI:EU:C:1996:404 340
Abanca Corporación Bancaria SA v Alberto García Salamanca Santos
and Bankia SA v Alfonso Antonio Lau Mendoza and Verónica Yuliana
Rodríguez Ramírez (Joined Cases C-70/17 and C- 179/17) [2019]
EU:C:2019:250, CJEU (Grand Chamber) 346
Abbey National Plc & Others v The Office of Fair Trading [2009]
EWCA Civ 116, [2009] 2 WLR 1286 .... 299, 302, 303,
304, 305, 309
Abbey National Plc & Others v The Office of Fair Trading [2009]
UKSC 6, [2010] 1 AC 696 .... 2, 300, 301, 302, 303, 304,
305, 306, 307, 308, 309,
310, 311, 312, 313
Abouzaid v Mothercare (UK) Ltd [2000] EWCA Civ 348, [2000]
All ER (D) 246 287
ACCC v Chrisco Hampers Australia Ltd [2015] FCA 1204, 239 FCR 33 356
Addiko Bank (Case C-407/18) ECLI:EU:C:2019:537, CJEU 346
AG Spalding & Bros v AW Gamage Ltd (1915) 32 RPC 273, HL 207
Alakaya / New Mansions Hotels case (1932), Cty Ct 233–4
Alec Lobb (Garages) Ltd v Total Oil (GB) Ltd [1985] 1
WLR 173, CA 189, 196, 197, 198
Allcard v Skinner (1887) 36 Ch D 145, CA 192
American Hospital Association v Azar, 983 F.3d 528, 541 (D.C. Cir. 2020) 279
Antuzis & Ors v DJ Houghton Catching Services Ltd & Ors [2019]
EWHC 843 (QB), [2019] Bus LR 1532 161
Antuzis & Ors v DJ Houghton Catching Services Ltd & Ors [2021]
EWHC 971 (QB), [2021] 4 WLUK 249 161
Ardglasse v Muschamp and Pitt (1682) 1 Vern 76, (1684) 1 Vern 237,
(1684) 2 Ch Rep 266 .... 31, 32, 33
Arlene's Flowers v Washington. See State v Arlene's Flowers, Inc
Armitage v Nurse [1998] Ch 241, CA 26
Ashdown v Samuel Williams & Sons Ltd [1957] 1 QB 409, CA 74
Asturcom Telecomunicaciones SL v Cristina Rodrıguez Nogueira (C-40/08),
EU:C:2009:615, [2009] ECR I-9579, ECJ (First Chamber) 342
Attorney General's Reference (No 2 of 1999) [2000] 2 Cr App R 207, CA 184

Austin v Manchester, Sheffield and Lincolnshire Railway Co (1850)
  10 CB 454, 138 ER 181, Ct of Common Pleas 59
Australian Competition and Consumer Commission v CG Berbatis
  Holdings Pty Ltd [2003] HCA 18, (2003) 214 CLR 51 198
Australian Competition and Consumer Commission v Samton
  Holdings Pty Ltd [2002] FCA 62, (2002) 117 FCR 301..................................198
Australian Securities and Investments Commission v Kobelt [2019]
  HCA 18, (2019) 267 CLR 1 202
Aziz (Mohamed) v Caixa d'Estalvis de Catalunya, Tarragona i Manresa
  (Catalunyacaixa) (Case C-415/11) [2014] ECLI:EU:C:2013:164,
  [2013] 3 CMLR 5..4, 11, 19, 333–42,
                                                                 344, 346, 347, 348
B (A Child) v DPP [2000] 2 AC 428, HL...174
Bailey v Bullock [1950] 2 All ER 1167, KBD..157
Baldry v Marshall [1925] 1 KB 260, CA..49
Baldwin v Rochford (1748) 1Wils KB 229, 95 ER 589..37
Banco Primus SA v Jesús Gutiérrez García (Case C-412/14) [2017]
  ECLI:EU:C:2017:60, ECJ (Second Chamber) 340
Banesto – Banco Español de Crédito SA v Joaquín Calderón Camino
  (Case C-618/10) ECLI:EU:C:2012:349, ECJ (First Chamber) 342, 346
Banif Plus Bank Zrt v Csipai (Case C-472/11) EU:C:2013:88, [2013] 2
  CMLR 42, [2013] WLR(D) 76, ECJ (First Chamber).....................................342
Barclays Bank v O'Brien [1993] UKHL 6, [1994] 1 AC 180...................... 12, 189, 194
Barclays Bank plc v Various Claimants [2020] UKSC 13, [2020] AC 973...............293
Barney v Beak (1682) 2 Ch Cas 136, 22 ER 883 ....31–2, 33
Barney v Tyson (1672) 2 Vent 359, 86 ER 485... 31, 33
Bates v Batey & Co Ltd [1913] 3 KB 351, KBD 145, 149
Bates v State Bar of Arizona, 433 US 350 (1977) 279
Batty v Lloyd (1682) 1 Vern 141, 23 ER 374...32
Beckett v Kingston Brothers (Butchers) Ltd [1970] 1 QB 606, QBD.....................170
Beckett v Tower Assets Co Ltd [1891] 1 QB 638, CA 121
Berney v Pitt (1680) 2 Swanst 142n..33
Bigelow v Virginia, 421 US 809 (1975)...269
Bigge v Parkinson (1862) 7 H & N 955, 31 L J Ex 301 47
Blacker v Lake and Elliott Ltd (1912) 106 LT 533 .... 19, 135, 136–8, 139,
                                                                 140, 147, 149, 150, 151–2
Blackwell v Blackwell [1943] 2 All ER 579, CA..142
Blades v Higgs (1844) 6 Man & G, 142 ER 634 124
Bluett v Osborne (1816) 1 Stark 384, 171 ER 504, Assizes....................................44
Blu-Sky Solutions Ltd v Be Caring Ltd [2021] EWHC 2619 (Comm),
  [2022] 2 All ER (Comm) 254 73
Bolger v Youngs Drug Prod Corp, 463 US 60 (1983) 274
BOM v BOK [2018] SGCA 83 .... 190, 197, 198, 199
Bosanquet v Dashwood (1734) Forr 38...34
Brass v Maitland (1856) 6 El & Bl 470, 119 ER 940 136

Brasserie du Pêcheur SA v Bundesrepublik Deutschland and the Queen v
  Secretary of State for Transport, ex parte: Factortame Ltd and others
  (Joined Cases 46/93 and C-48/93) [1996] ECLI:EU:C:1996:79, ECJ 339
Breard v Alexandrea 341 US 622 (1951) 272
Bridge v Campbell Discount Ltd [1962] AC 600, HL 116
Bristol Conservatories Ltd v Conservatories Custom Built Ltd [1989]
  RPC 455, CA 220
British Telecommunications Plc v One In A Million Ltd [1999] 1 WLR
  903, CA 211
Broadway v Morecraft (1729) Mos 247, 25 ER 377 30
Brown v Edgington (1841) 2 Man & G 279, 2 Scott NR 496, 1 Drink 106,
  10 LJCP 66 47
Burke v South Eastern Railway Co (1879) 5 CPD 1 72
Burton's case (1590) 5 Co Rep 69a, 77 ER 159 30
Butler v Heane (1810) 2 Camp 415, 170 ER 1202 58
Cadbury Schweppes Pty Ltd v Pub Squash Co Pty Ltd [1981] RPC 429,
  PC (Aus) 207
Cadogan v Kennett (1776) 2 Cowp 432, 98 ER 1171 29
Camelo Case (1920) 149 LT 397 .... 145, 146, 151
Canada Square Operations Ltd v Potter (Rev 2) [2020] EWHC 672 (QB),
  [2020] 4 All ER 1114 362
Cano v Baker, 435 F.3d 1337 (11th Cir Court, 2006); Docket No 05-11641
  US Sup Ct 250
Carlill v Carbolic Smoke Ball Company [1893] 1 QB 256, CA; [1892]
  2 QB 484, QBD 6, 8, 9, 50, 79, 87, 89,
                                                              93–5, 99, 100, 103, 104,
                                                                  105, 106, 107, 112
Carr v Lancashire & Yorkshire Railway Co (1852) 7 Ex 707, 155 ER 1133,
  Ct of Exch 59, 60
Cassis de Dijon case. See Rewe-Zentral AG v Bundesmonopolverwaltung
  für Branntwein
Cavendish Square Holding BV v Talal El Makdessi; ParkingEye Ltd v
  Beavis [2015] UKSC 67, [2016] AC 1172 .... 1, 133, 204
Centennial Northern Mining Services Pty Ltd v Construction, Forestry,
  Mining and Energy Union [2015] FCAFC 100, 231 FCR 298 161
Central Hudson Gas & Elec. Corp. v Public Serv Comm'n, 447 US 557
  (1980) 274, 275
Chanter v Hopkins (1838) 4 M & W 399, 1 H & H 377 .... 47, 49
Chapelton v Barry UDC [1940] 1 KB 532, CA 75
Charge Card Services, Re [1986] 3 All ER 289, ChD 1
Charles of the Ritz Distribution Corp v FTC 143 F 2d 676 (2nd Circuit 1944) 6, 9
Cheltenham & Gloucester Building Society v Norgan [1995] EWCA Civ 11,
  [1996] 1 WLR 343 325
Christie v York Corp [1940] SCR 139, 1939 CanLII 39 (SCC) 381
CILFIT v Ministry of Health (Case 283/81) [1982] ECR 3415, ECJ 306
Citizens United v Federal Election Comm'n 558 US 310 (2010) 275

City of Cincinnati v Discovery Network, Inc., 507 US 410 (1993) 274
Clark v Malpas (1862) 4 De GF & J 401, 45 ER 1238 198
Clarke v Army and Navy Co-operative Society Ltd [1903] 1 KB 155, CA 136, 137
Clayton v Hunt (1811) 3 Camp 27, 170 ER 1294, Assizes...58
Clayton's case (1594) 5 Co Rep 70b, 77 ER 160...30
Clifford Davis Management Ltd v WEA Records Ltd [1975] 1 WLR 61, CA 196
Coco v AN Clark (Engineers) Ltd [1969] RPC 41, ChD...27
Cole v Gibbons (1734) 3 P Wms 290, 24 ER 1070 32
Colt v Woollaston (1723) 2 P Wms 154, 24 ER 679...27
Commercial Bank of Australia Ltd v Amadio [1983] HCA 14, (1983)
  151 CLR 447... 190, 197, 198, 199
Commission Decision C(2007) 6474 final (COMP/34.579 – MasterCard,
  COMP/36.518 – EuroCommerce, COMP 38.580 – Commercial Cards) 389
Constantine v Imperial Hotels Ltd [1944] KB 693, (1944) The Times,
  29 June, KBD..3, 11, 19, 225–7,
                                                                                                                234–243
Cooke v T Wilson Sons & Co (1915) 85 LJKB 888 72
Courage Ltd v Crehan (Case C-453/99) EU:C:2001:465, [2002] QB 507,
  ECJ...397
Crabb v Arun DC [1976] Ch 179, CA 26
Craig and Mullins v Masterpiece Cakeshop, Inc 370 P.3d 272
  (Colo App 2015) 372
Cray v Mansfield (1749) 1 Ves Sen 379, 27 ER 1093 37
Creative 6F.4th 1160 (10th Circ 2021) 381
Creative LLC v Elenis 600 US ____ (2023)..373–4, 383
Crédit Lyonnais SA v Fesih Kalhan (Case 565/12) [2014] ECLI:EU:
  C:2014:190, CJEU..336
Cresswell v Potter [1978] 1 WLR 255, ChD 197
Crooks & Co v Allan (1879) 5 QBD 38, QBD 75
CTN Cash and Carry Ltd v Gallaher Ltd [1994] 4 All ER 714, CA 199
Davis v Willan (1817) 2 Stark 279, 171 ER 646, Assizes...58
Denton v Great Northern Railway Co (1856) 5 E & B 860, 119 ER 701................105
Dimmock v Hallett (1866) LR 2 Ch App 21 104
Director, Fair Work Building Industry Inspectorate v Foxville Projects
  Group Pty Ltd [2015] FCA 492..161
Director General of Fair Trading v First National Bank plc [2001]
  UKHL 52, [2002] 1 AC 481..302, 303
Director of Consumer Affairs Victoria v Scully [2013] VSCA 292, (2013)
  303 ALR 168...203
Dobbs v Jackson Women's Health Organisation 597 US 66 (2022)...........7, 246, 249,
                                                                                                    250, 251, 252, 253, 254,
                                                                                                    256, 258, 259, 260, 263, 264
Dobbs v Jackson Women's Health Organisation, Sup Ct of the US,
  No 19-1392, Oral Arguments, 1 December 2021 252
Dobbs v Jackson Women's Health Organisation, US Sup Ct, No 19-1392,
  Brief of Respondents, 38–39 254

Doe v Bolton, 410 US 179 (1973) 250
Domestic and General Group Ltd v Bank of Scotland Plc [2018] EWHC
   3604 (QB), [2018] 12 WLUK 68 211
Dominion Natural Gas Co Ltd v Collins [1909] AC 640, PC (Can) 139
Donoghue v Stevenson [1932] AC 562, HL (Scot) 1, 3, 6, 16, 135, 136,
                                                                                                139, 140, 145, 146,
                                                                                                147, 149, 151, 284
Doran v Paragon Personal Finance Ltd [2018] 6 WLUK 518 (26 June 2018,
   Manchester Cty Ct) 363, 366
Downer v Pitcher [2017] NLCA 13, Newfoundland and Labrador CA 200
Drapers' Co v Davis (1742) 2 Atk 295, 26 ER 580 35
Dune Group Ltd v Mastercard Inc [2022] CAT 14, [2022] 3 WLUK 551 390
Earl of Aylesford v Morris (1872-73) LR 8 Ch App 484 32
Earl of Chesterfield v Janssen (1750) 2 Ves Sen 125; 1 Atk 301; 1 Wils
   KB 286 .... 3, 5, 19, 23–31,
                                                                                                33, 34, 37
Earl of Oxford's Case in Chancery (1615) 1 Ch Rep 1, 21 ER 485 27
Earl v Lubbock [1905] 1 KB 253, CA 137, 138
Elane Photography LLC v Vanessa Willock 309 P3d 53 (NMSC 2013) 373, 383
Elder v Koppe (1974) 53 DLR (3d) 705 158
Ellesden v Oetzmann *London and Provincial Music Trades Review*,
   15 February 1890, 25 124
Employment Div, Dept of Human Resources of Ore v Smith 494 US
   872 (1990) 372
EMW Women's Surgical Center v Daniel Cameron, Jefferson Cir Ct,
   Division Three, No 22-CI-3225 .... 260, 261
Erven Warnink Besloten Vennootschap v J Townend & Sons (Hull) Ltd
   [1979] AC 731, [1979] FSR 397, HL; [1978] FSR 1, HC................... 3, 10–11, 18,
                                                                                                19, 207–221
Escola v Coca Cola Bottling Co, 150 P.2d 436, 441 (Cal. 1944) 285
Expressions Hair Design v Schneiderman, 581 US 37 (2017) 266
Farrant v Barnes (1862) 11 CBNS 553, 142 ER 912 136
Fenty v Arcadia Group Brands Ltd (No 2) [2015] EWCA Civ 3, [2015]
   1 WLR 3291, CA 219
Financial Ombudsman Service – Decision DRN3040152 (23 March 2019) 363
Financial Ombudsman Service – Decision DRN – 3532010 (14 June 2019) 361
Financial Ombudsman Service – Decision DRN1671473 (5 June 2020) 366
Financial Ombudsman Service – Decision DRN-1886455 (15 June 2020) 361
Financial Ombudsman Service – Decision DRN-3029312 (5 October 2021) 361
FOS Decision DRN-3029132 (5 October 2021) 366
First National Bank of Boston v Bellotti 435 US 765 (1979) 275
Food and Drug Administration v American College of Obstetricians and
   Gynecologists 141 S.Ct. 578 262
Foreman v Great Western Railway Co (1878) 42 JPN 648 73
Formula One Autocentres Ltd v Birmingham City Council (1999) 163
   JP 234, DC 176

Forstater v CGD Europe [2022] ICR 1, [2021] IRLR 706, EAT..................382
Foster v Midland Railway Co *Cambridge Independent Press*, 13 May 1876, 8 65
Freiburger Kommunalbauten GmbH Baugesellschaft & Co KG v Ludger
    Hofstetter und Ulrike Hofstetter (Case 237/02) [2004] ECLI:EU:
    C:2004:209 ....340, 341
Fry v Lane (1888) 40 Ch D 312, ChD 197
Gabell *The Times*, 15 November 1876, 11; *Reynolds's Newspaper*,
    19 November 1876, Common Pleas 65
Gale v Lindo (1687) 1 Vern 475, 23 ER 601 34
Garcia v National Australia Bank Ltd [1998] HCA 48, (1998) 194 CLR 395 .... 193, 194–5
Gardiner v Gray (1815) 4 Camp 144, 171 ER 46 .... 3, 8, 19, 39, 40–1, 43, 44, 46, 47
Gee v DePuy International Ltd [2018] EWHC 1208 (QB), [2018] Med
    LR 347 .... 283, 284, 290, 291–2, 293, 294
George v Skivington (1869-70) LR 5 Ex 1..................................5, 135, 136, 137, 138, 139, 140, 141, 149, 152
George Mitchell (Chesterhall) Ltd v Finney Lock Seeds Ltd [1983]
    QB 284, CA 73
GH Myers & Co v Brent Cross Service Co [1934] KB 46, KBD 143
Gibaud v Great Eastern Railway Co [1920] 3 KB 689, KBD 73
Gibbon v Paynton (1769) 4 Burr 2298, 152 ER 763 58
Gillespie Bros & Co Ltd v Roy Bowles Transport Ltd [1973] QB 400, CA 75
Gillette UK Ltd v Edenwest Ltd [1994] RPC 279, ChD 207
Gómez del Moral Guasch v Bankia (Case 125/18) [2020] ECLI:EU:
    C:2020:138, CJEU...346
Grand Trunk Railway Co of Canada v Robinson [1915] AC 740, PC (Can)...........73
Gray v Cox 1 C & P 184 (nisi prius), 4 B & C 108, 6 D & R 200 ....44–5, 46
Greater New Orleans Broadcasting Assn v United States, 527 US
    173 (2014)...274
Griswold v Connecticut, 381 US 479 (1965)... 269, 271
Gutmann v South Western Trains Ltd [2021] CAT 31, [2021] 10 WLUK 594 391
Hall v Potter (1695) 2 P Wms 392n; Show Parl Cas 76, 1 ER 52, HL......................34
Hamilton v Mohun (1710) 1 P Wms 118, 24 ER 319......................................34
Hamlin v Great Northern Railway Co (1856) 1 H & N 408, 156 ER 1261 158
Harpur Trust v Brazel [2022] UKSC 21, [2023] 2 All ER 113................................161
Harris v Great Western Railway Co (1876) 1 QBD 515, QBD 63, 67, 69
Harris v McRae, 448 US 279 (1979) 257
Harrison v Black Horse Ltd [2011] EWCA Civ 1128, [2012] Lloyd's
    Rep IR 521.. 353, 354, 357, 362
Hawkins v Crook (1729) 2 P Wms 556, 24 ER 860...36
Heathcote v Paignon (1787) 2 Bro CC 167, 29 ER 96.....................................31
Heaven v Pender (1883) 11 QBD 503, CA...136, 138
Helby v Matthews [1895] AC 471, HL 1, 3, 12, 15, 19, 115–6, 121, 124, 125, 128, 129, 130, 131, 132, 133

Henderson v Stevenson (1875) LR 2 Sc 470, HL (Scot) 62–3, 64, 66, 67, 69
Henningsen v Bloomfield Motors 161 A 2d 69 (NJ 1960) 15
Himmelspring v Singer Manufacturing Co (29 July 1898) 124
HL Bolton (Engineering) Co Ltd v TJ Graham & Sons Ltd [1957]
   1 QB 159, CA 171
Hobbs v London & Southern Western Railway Co (1875) 157
Hodes & Nauser, MDs, PA v Schmidt No 114, 153 (26 April 2019)
   Kansas Sup Ct 261
Hood v Anchor Line (Henderson Brothers) Ltd [1918] AC 837,
   HL (Scot) 66, 71, 72
HP Bulmer Ltd and Showerings Ltd v J Bollinger SA and Champagne
   Lanson pére et fils [1974] EWCA Civ 14, [1974] Ch 401, [1974] 3
   WLR 202, [1974] 2 All ER 1226 337
Hylton v Hylton (1754) 2 Ves Sen 547, 28 ER 349 37
Ingham v Emes [1955] 2 QB 366, CA 143
Interfoto Picture Library Ltd v Stiletto Visual Programmes Ltd [1989]
   QB 433, CA 75, 76
Investors Compensation Scheme Ltd v West Bromwich Building Society
   [1998] 1 WLR 896, HL 26
Ipstar Australia Pty Ltd v APS Satellite Pty Ltd [2018] NSWCA 15, (2018)
   356 ALR 440 203
Irvine v Talksport Ltd [2002] EWHC 367 (Ch), [2002] 1 WLR 2355 219
Irwell Valley Housing Association Ltd v Docherty [2012] EWCA Civ 704,
   [2012] 5 WLUK 413 331
J Bollinger v Costa Brava Wine Co Ltd (No 2) [1961] 1 WLR 277 208
J Spurling Ltd v Bradshaw [1956] 1 WLR 461, CA 75
J van der Weerd and others (Joined Cases 222/05 to 225/05) [2007]
   ECLI:EU:C:2005:797 340
Jack v Azucar Bakery, Charge No P20140069X (24 March 2015), Colorado
   Civil Rights Commission 373
Jack v Gateaux, Ltd, Charge No P20140071X (24 March 2015), Colorado
   Civil Rights Commission 373
Jack v Le Bakery Sensual Inc, Charge No P20140070X (24 March 2015),
   Colorado Civil Rights Commission 373
Jackson v Horizon Holidays Ltd [1975] 3 All ER 92, CA 159
Jackson Women's Health Organisation v Dobbs, US Court of Appeals
   for the Fifth Circuit, No 18-60868, 13 December 2019 .... 251, 258
Jarvis v Swans Tours Ltd [1973] 1 QB 233 .... 2, 3, 11, 18, 19, 153,
                                                                                154–9, 167, 168, 240
Jeroen van Schijndel and Johannes Nicolaas Cornelis van Veen v
   Stichting Pensioenfonds voor Fysiotherapeute (Joined Cases 430/93
   and C-431/93) [1995] ECLI:EU:C:1995:441 340
John St John Long / Catherine Cashin, Old Bailey Sessions Papers (1830),
   case no 1952 at 856 108
John St John Long / Mrs Colin Campbell Lloyd, Old Bailey Sessions
   Papers (1831) at 283 109

John Walker & Sons Ltd v Henry Ost & Co Ltd [1970] 1 WLR 917, ChD 208
Jolly v Rees (1864) 15 Common 628, 143 ER 931 117
Jones v Bowden (1813) 4 Taunt 847, 128 ER 565 41
Jones v Bright (1829) 5 Bing 533, 3 Moo & P 155, 7 LJCP 213, 1 Dan &
 L 304 45–6
Jones v Just (1868) LR 3 QB 197, Times, 18 February 1868 47–8
Jones v Westside Buick Co, 93 S.W.2d 1083 (Mo. Ct. App. 1936) 273
Joseph v Davis *Furniture Gazette*, 1 September 1886, 2 August 1886, QBD 124
Joseph Beete v Henry Fisher Bidgood (1827) 7 B&C 453, 108 ER 792 119
Junior Sports Magazines Inc v Bonta, 2022 WL 14365026, Case
 No 2:22-cv-04663-CAS (C.D. Cal., 22 November 2022) 275
Kamil Dziubak and Justyna Dziubak v Raiffeisen Bank International AG,
 prowadzący działalność w Polsce w formie oddziału pod nazwą
 Raiffeisen Bank International AG Oddział w Polsce, anciennement
 Raiffeisen Bank Polska SA (Case 260/18) [2019] EU:C:2019:819 346
Kàsler and Kàslerné Rábai v OTP Jelzálogbank Zrt (Case C26/13)
 ECLI:EU:C:2014:282 .... 312, 343, 346, 347
Keks v Esquire Pleasure Tours Ltd [1974] 3 WWR 406 158
Kemp v Coleman (1707) 1 Salk 156, 91 ER 144 34
Kerr v Willan (1817) 2 Stark 53, 171 ER 570, Assizes 58
Kerr v Willan (1817) 6 M & S 150, 105 ER 1199, Ct of KB 58
Kerrigan v Elevate Credit International Ltd (t/a Sunny) (In Administration)
 [2020] EWHC 2169 (Comm), [2020] CTLC 161 357
Kleinwort Benson Ltd v Lincoln City Council [1999] 2 AC 349, HL 308
Kranz v National Australia Bank Ltd (2003) 8 VR 310 .... 193, 195
Kušionová (Monika) v SMART Capital (Case 34/13) [2014] ECLI:EU:
 C:2014:2189, CJEU 336
Lamplugh v Smith (1688) 2 Vern 77, 23 ER 660 31
Laing v Fidgeon (1815) 6 Taunt 108, 128 ER 974 .... 41, 45, 48
Lambert v Lewis [1982] AC 225, HL 212
Lamont v Postmaster General, 381 US 301 (1965) 271
Lancashire Loans Ltd v Black [1934] 1 KB 380, CA 23
Langridge v Levy (1837) 2 M & W 519, 150 ER 863 136
Lawley v Hooper (1745) 3 Atk 278, 26 ER 962 27
Lee v Ashers Baking Co Ltd [2015] NICty 2; [2015] 5 WLUK 483 374–5
Lee v Ashers Baking Co Ltd [2018] UKSC 49, [2020] AC 413 .... 7, 19, 369, 370,
 371, 374, 380, 381,
 382, 383, 384, 385
Lee v Butler [1893] 2 QB 318, CA 126, 127, 129
Lee v Lancashire and Yorkshire Railway Co (1871) 25 LT 77 71
Lee v McArthur [2016] NICA 39, [2016] 12 WLUK 629 375
Lee v United Kingdom (App no 18860/19) [2022] IRLR 371, ECtHR 376
L'Estrange v F Graucob Ltd [1934] 2 KB 394, KBD 73, 75
Levison v Patent Steam Carpet Cleaning Co Ltd [1978] QB 69, CA 75
Lewis v M'Kee (1868-69) LR 4 Ex 58 66

Lintner Györgyné v UniCredit Bank Hungary Zrt (Case C-511/17)
    [2020] ECLI:EU:C:2020:188, CJEU 343
Liquormart, Inc v Rhode Island, 517 US 484 (1996) 274
Liu v Adamson (2003) 12 BPR 22,205 195
Lloyd v Google LLC [2019] EWCA Civ 1599, [2020] QB 747 399
Lloyds Bank v Bundy [1974] EWCA Civ 8, [1975] QB 326, CA 5, 10, 19, 189–93,
    195–9, 201, 203, 204, 206
Lorillard Tobacco Co v Reilly, 533 US 525 (2001) 266, 274
Lukey v O'Donnel (1805) 2 Sch & Lef 466 25
Luna, The [1920] P 22, PD&A 73
Lyons & Co v Caledonian Railway Co 1909 SC 1185, Ct of Sess (IH, 1 Div) 72
Maher v Roe 432 US 464 (1977) 257
Makdessi (Talal El) and ParkingEye Ltd v Beavis [2015] UKSC 67,
    [2016] AC 1172 .... 1, 133, 204
Malaysian Airline System Berhad v Tarn Chin Siong & Ors [2009]
    9 CLJ 435 158
Manchester, Sheffield and Lincolnshire Railway Co v Brown (1883)
    8 App Cas 703, HL 75–6
Martin-Smith v Welcome Finance Ltd (Manchester Cty Ct, 18 December
    2019) 363
Mason v Abdy (1689) Comb 125, 90 ER 383 30
MasterCard and others v Commission (Case T-111/08) EU:T:2012:260,
    General Ct 389
MasterCard and others v Commission (Case C-382/12P) EU:C:2014:2201,
    CJEU 389
Masterpiece Cakeshop v Colorado Civil Rights Commission 584
    US (2018) 4, 7, 19, 369, 370, 371–3,
    375, 378, 380, 381,
    382, 383, 384, 385
MacPherson v Buick 111 NE 1050 (NY) 16
Marcolongo v Chen [2011] HCA 3, (2011) 242 CLR 546 29
Marriott v Yeoward Bros [1909] 2 KB 987, KBD 72
Martin v City of Struthers, 319 US 141 (1943) 269
McCorvey v Hill, 385 F.3d 846 (5th Cir. 2004); Docket No 04-967 US
    Supreme Court 250
McCutcheon v David MacBrayne [1964] 1 WLR 125 74
McGuffick v Royal Bank of Scotland plc [2009] EWHC 2386 (Comm),
    [2010] 1 All ER 634 324
McEntire v Crossley Bros Ltd [1895] AC 457, HL (Ire) 131
McKenzie v Bank of Montreal (1975) 55 DLR (3d) 641 199
McMullon v Secure the Bridge Ltd (Rev 1) [2015] EWCA Civ 884, [2015]
    8 WLUK 51 359
McWilliam v Norton Finance (UK) Ltd (in liquidation) [2015] EWCA
    Civ 186, [2015] 2 BCLC 730 362
Merchant Interchange Fee Umbrella Proceedings [2022] CAT 31, [2022]
    7 WLUK 212 390

Merck & Co v Health and Human Services, 962 F.3d 532 (D.C. Cir. 2020) 279
Meres v Ansell (1771) 3 Wils KB 275, 95 ER 1053 40
Meridian Global Funds v Management Asia Ltd [1995] 2 AC 500, PC 183–5
Merricks v Mastercard Inc [2019] EWCA Civ 674, [2019] Bus LR 3025 ...... 15, 17, 19,
387–8, 392–3, 395
Merricks (Walter Hugh CBE) v Mastercard Inc Case No 1266/7/7/16,
   18 May 2022, CAT 388
Merricks (Walter Hugh CBE) v Mastercard Inc, Mastercard International
   Inc and Mastercard Europe SPRL [2017] CAT 16, [2017] 5
   CMLR 16 .... 388, 389, 391, 392,
393, 394, 395
Merricks (Walter Hugh CBE) v Mastercard [2020] UKSC 51, [2021]
   3 All ER 285 .... 15, 17, 19, 387, 388, 390,
391, 393–5, 396, 398,
399, 400, 401, 402
Meyer v Everth (1814) 4 Camp 22, 171 ER 8, Assizes 41
Mohamud v Wm Morrison Supermarkets plc [2016] UKSC 11, [2016]
   AC 677 293
Montague v Bath (1693) 3 Ch Cas 55, 22 ER 963 34
Mullen v AG Barr & Co Ltd 1929 SC 461, Ct of Sess (IH, 2 Div) 146, 151, 152
National Australia Bank Ltd v Satchithanantham [2009] NSWSC 21,
   affd [2009] NSWCA 268 195
National Westminster Bank plc v Morgan [1985] 1 AC 686, HL 189, 193–4,
196, 201
Nelmes v Nram Plc [2016] EWCA Civ 491, [2016] CTLC 106 366
New York Times v Sullivan, 376 US 254 (1964) 269, 272, 275
NG and OH v SC Banca Transilvania SA (Case 81/19) [2020] ECLI:
   EU:C:2020:532, CJEU (First Chamber) 337, 341
Nocton v Lord Ashburton [1914] AC 932, HL 26
Nott v Hill (1683) 1 Vern 167, 2 Ch Rep 120, 1 Eq Ca Abr 275 32
Nunan v Southern Railway Co [1923] 2 KB 703, KBD 72
NV Algemene Transport-Expedite Onderneming Van Gend en Loos v
   Nederlandse Administratie der Belastingen (1963) Case 26/62, ECJ 338
Office of Fair Trading v Abbey National Plc [2008] EWHC 875
   (Comm), [2008] 2 All ER (Comm) 625 .... 299, 302, 303, 305
Office of Fair Trading v Abbey National Plc [2009] UKSC 6, [2010]
   1 AC 696 .... 4, 10, 19
Office of Fair Trading v Ashbourne Management Services [2011]
   EWHC 1237 (Ch), [2011] ECC 31 .... 302, 312
Office of Fair Trading v Foxtons Ltd [2009] EWHC 1681 (Ch), [2009]
   CTLC 188 302
Office of Fair Trading v Purely Creative Ltd [2011] EWHC 106 (Ch),
   [2011] ECC 20 8
Okell v Smith (1815) 1 Stark 107, 171 ER 416, Assizes 44
Ollivant v Bayley (1843) 5 QB 288, D & M 223 47
Osmond v Fitzroy (1731) 3 P Wms 129, 24 ER 997 34–5

Ottília Lovasné Tóth v ERSTE Bank Hungary Zrt (Case 34/18) [2019]
  ECLI:EU:C:2019:764..343
OTP Bank Nyrt and OTP Faktoring Követeléskezelő Zrt v Teréz Ilyés
  and Emil Kiss (Case 51/17) [2018] EU:C:2018:750.......................... 337, 341, 343
Palmer v Grand Junction Railway Co (1839) 4 M & W 749, 150 ER 1624...............59
Pannon GSM Zrt gegen Erzsébet Sustikné Győrfi (Case 243/08)
  [2009] ECLI:EU:C:2009:350 .... 340, 343, 346
Pao On v Lau Yiu Long [1980] AC 614, PC (Hong Kong) 189, 196
Paquin v Beauclerk [1906] AC 148, HL 142
Parker v South Eastern Railway Co *Standard*, 28 January 1876, 2;
  York Herald, 31 January 1876, 3... 3, 15, 19, 55–7, 61,
  62, 63–4, 65
Parker v South Eastern Railway Co (1876) 1 CPD 618; 11 LJNC 106;
  25 WR 97 ....64, 66
Parker v South Eastern Railway Co; Gabell v South Eastern Railway
  Co (1877) 2 CPD 416; 41 JP 644; 46 LJQB 768; 36 LT 540;
  25 WR 564, CA... 65–72, 73, 74, 75, 76, 77
ParkingEye Ltd v Beavis [2015] UKSC 67, [2016] AC 1172 .... 1, 133, 204
Parkinson v Lee (1802) 2 East 314, 102 ER 389 .... 41, 44
Patterson Drug Co v Kingery, 305 F. Supp. 821 (W.D. Va, 1969)............................270
Payne v Wilson (October 1894), Whitechapel Cty Ct..128
Peek v North Staffordshire Railway Co (1863) 10 HL Cas 473,
  11 ER 1109, HL 59, 60, 61, 65
Peekay Intermark Ltd v Australia and NZ Banking Group Ltd [2006]
  EWCA Civ 386, [2006] 2 Lloyd's Rep 511...73
Penton v Southern Railway [1931] 2 KB 103, KBD 72
Perry v Truefitt (1842) 5 Beav 66, 49 ER 749 208
Peterbroeck, Van Campenhout & Cie SCS v Belgian State (Case 312/93)
  [1995] ECLI:EU:C:1995:437 340
Photo Production Ltd v Securicor Transport Ltd [1980] AC 827, HL 76
Pickering v Dowson (1813) 4 Taunt 779, 128 ER 537 41
Pierce v Waring (1745) 1 P Wms 120n, 1 Ves Sen 379 37
Pittsburgh Press Co v Pittsburgh Comm on Human Relations, 413
  US 376 (1973) 269, 272
PKO Bank Polski (Case C-632/17) ECLI:EU:C:2018:963, CJEU 346
Places for People Homes Ltd v Sharples; A2 Dominion Homes Ltd v
  Godfrey [2011] EWCA Civ 813, [2011] HLR 45, CA 13, 19, 315–21,
  324–9, 331
Planned Parenthood v Casey, 505 US 833 (1992) 245, 250, 251, 254,
  257, 258, 263
Planned Parenthood of Southwest and Central Florida v State of Florida,
  Cir Ct of the Second Judicial Circuit in and for Leon County, Florida,
  Case No 2022 CA 912...260
Planned Parenthood of Wisconsin Inc v Schimel, 806 F. 3d 908 (CA7 2015)..........258
Plevin v Paragon Personal Finance Ltd (Manchester Cty Ct,
  4 October 2012) 352, 353, 364, 367

Plevin v Paragon Personal Finance Ltd; Conlon v Black Horse Ltd
[2013] EWCA Civ 1658, [2014] Bus LR 553............................... 353, 354, 355, 362
Plevin v Paragon Personal Finance Ltd [2014] UKSC 61, [2014] 1
WLR 4222 .... 3, 5, 17, 19, 351–68
Plevin v Paragon Personal Finance Ltd [2017] UKSC 23, [2018] 1
All ER 292...353, 367
Poland – Case K/3/21, Constitutional Ct..344
Pratt v South Eastern Railway Co [1897] 1 QB 718, QBD 73
Profi Credit Polska SA v QJ (C-84/19), ECLI:EU:C:2020:631, CJEU 346
Proof v Hines (1735) Forr 111...35
Queen, The v Secretary of State for Transport, ex parte Factortame
Ltd and others (Case 213/89) [1990] ECR I-2433, ECJ................................339
R v A Ltd, Re [2016] EWCA Crim 1469, [2016] 4 WLR 176.............................. 185
R v v British Steel [1995] 1 WLR 1356, CA.. 182
R v K (Age of Consent: Reasonable Relief) [2001] UKHL 41, [2002]
1 AC 462.. 174
R v Lord Chancellor, ex parte Lightfoot [2000] QB 597, CA........................324, 326
R v St Regis Paper Co Ltd [2011] EWCA Crim 2527, [2012] PTSR 871................176
R (Cooper and Payne) v Secretary of State for Work and Pensions [2010]
EWCA Civ 1431, [2011] BPIR 223 317
Raj Properties Ltd v James Walter John Wallace-Jarvis [2010] EWLandRA
2009_1095 155
Randall v Newson (1877) 2 QBD 102, CA... 48, 49
Razzaq v Pala [1997] 1 WLR 1336, QBD..328
Redhead v Westwood (1878–88) 4 Times Law Reports 671................................. 121
Redman v Redman (1685) 1 Vern 348, 23 ER 514 34
Regency Villas Title Ltd v Diamond Resorts (Europe) Ltd [2018]
UKSC 57, [2019] AC 553 159
Reproductive Health Services v Strange, 3 F.4th 1240 (11th Cir. 2021) 245
Rewe-Zentral AG v Bundesmonopolverwaltung für Branntwein
(Cassis de Dijon) (Case 120/78) [1979] ECLI:EU:C:1979:42, ECJ..... 333, 338, 348
Richardson, Spence and Co Ltd v Rowntree [1894] AC 217, HL 72
Riley v Horne (1828) 5 Bing 217, 130 ER 1044...59
Roberts v Roberts (1730) 3 P Wms 66, 24 ER 971 33
Roberts (George) case (1944), Liverpool Recorder 239–40, 241
Robertson v DiCicco [1972] RTR 431, DC.. 6
Roe v Wade 410 US 113 (1973).. 4, 6, 7, 19, 245–64
Rogers v Clarence Hotel [1940] 3 DLR 583 242
Rothfield v North British Hotel 1920 SC 805, Ct of Sess (IH, 2 Div) 239
Rousk v Sweden App No 27183/04 (25 July 2013), ECtHR 336
Royal Bank of Scotland plc v Etridge (No 2) [2001] UKHL 44, [2002]
2 AC 773... 13, 189, 190, 193, 194
Rubin v Coors Brewing Co, 514 US 476 (1995) 274
RWE Vertrieb AG v Verbraucherzentrale Nordrhein-Westfalen eV
(Case 92/11) [2013] EU:C:2013:180, CJEU 337, 341

Sainsbury's Supermarkets Ltd & Ors v MasterCard Inc & Ors [2018]
    EWCA Civ 1536, [2019] 1 All ER 903 389
Sainsbury's Supermarkets Ltd v Mastercard Inc [2016] CAT 11, [2016]
    Comp AR 33 389
Sainsbury's Supermarkets Ltd v Visa Europe Services LLC; Sainsbury's
    Supermarkets Ltd v Mastercard Inc [2020] UKSC 24, [2020] Bus
    LR 1196 .... 389, 390, 397
Sánchez Morcillo (Juan Carlos) und María del Carmen Abril García
    gegen Banco Bilbao Vizcaya Argentaria SA (Case 169/14) [2014]
    ECLI:EU:C:2014:2099, CJEU (First Chamber) 336, 342
Saunderson v Glass (1742) 2 Atk 296 .... 27, 37
Scardina v Masterpiece Cake Shop Inc 19CV32214 (D Colo 2019) 373
Schneider v New Jersey, 308 US 147 (1939) 268
Schroeder (A) Music Publishing Co Ltd v Macaulay [1974] 1 WLR 1308,
    [1974] 3 All ER 616, HL 74, 196
Scotland v British Credit Trust Ltd [2014] EWCA Civ 790, [2014] Bus
    LR 1079 357
Semler v Oregon State Board of Dental Examiners, 294 US 608 (1935) 270, 271
Series v Poole [1969] 1 QB 676, DC 170
Serious Fraud Office v Barclays Plc [2018] EWHC 3055 (QB), [2020]
    1 Cr App R 28 .... 184–5, 187
Shaw v York and North Midland Railway Co (1849) 13 QB 347,
    116 ER 1295 59
Shenstone & Co v Hilton [1894] 2 QB 452, QBD 128
Shepherd v Pybus (1842 3 Man & G 868, 4 Scott 434, 11 LJCP 101 46
Sherras v De Rutzen [1895] 1 QBD 918, QBD 173
Simmenthal (Case 106/77) [1978] ECR 629, ECJ 338
Singer Manufacturing Co v Clark (1879) 5 Ex D 37 121
Singer Manufacturing Co v London and South Western Railway Co
    [1894] 1 QB 833, QBD 61
Small v Nairne (1849) 13 QB 840, 116 ER 1484 39
Smith v Hughes (1871) LR 6 QB 597 63
Smith v Royal Bank of Scotland plc (Burrell v Royal Bank of Scotland plc)
    [2021] EWCA Civ 1832, [2022] 1 WLR 2136; [2022] WLR(D) 69 .... 351, 362
Spain – Tribunal Constitucional Order no 113/2011, ECLI:ES:TC:
    2011:113A 342
Spain – Tribunal Supremo Judgment no 681/2006, ECLI:ES:TS:
    2006:681 342
Spencer v Harding (1870) LR 5 CP 561 105
State v Arlene's Flowers, Inc 441 P 3d 1203 (Wash 2019) 370, 373
Stedman v Swan's Tours (1951) 95 SJ 727, CA 156
Stewart v London and North Western Railway Co (1864) 3 Hurl &
    C 135, 159 ER 479 .... 62, 68, 69
Stuart v Wilkins (1778) 1 Doug KB 18, 99 ER 15 41
Stubbings v Jams 2 Pty Ltd [2022] HCA 6, (2022) 399 ALR 409 .... 198, 202
Sugar v London, Midland & Scottish Railway Co [1941] 1 All ER 172 .... 72, 74

Suisse Atlantique Société d'Armement Maritime SA v NV Rotterdamsche
  Kolen Centrale [1967] 1 AC 361, HL..74
Sweet v Parsley [1970] AC 132, HL 174
Telescope MediaGroup v Lucero 936 F3d 740 (8th Circ 2019)...........................373
Tesco Stores Ltd v Brent LBC [1993] 1 WLR 1037, DC.................................. 181–4
Tesco Stores Ltd v Pollard [2006] EWCA Civ 393, (2006) 150 SJLB 537................287
Tesco Supermarkets Ltd v Nattrass [1972] AC 153, HL 17, 19, 169–85, 187
Thomas v Collins, 323 US 516 (1945)..269
Thomas v Winchester (1852) 6 NY 397, New York Sup Ct....................................139
Thompson v London, Midland & Scottish Railway Co [1930]
  1 KB 41, CA 72, 73
Thorne v Kennedy [2017] HCA 49, (2017) 263 CLR 85.................. 190, 197, 198, 199
Thornton v Shoe Lane Parking Ltd [1971] 2 QB 163, CA......................................74
3 Glocken GmbH and Gertraud Kritzinger v USL Centro-Sud and
  Provincia asutonoma di Bolzano [1988] ECLI:EU:C:1988:401 348
Times Travel (UK) Ltd v Pakistan International Airline Corp
  [2021] UKSC 40, [2021] 3 WLR 727.................................. 197, 198, 199, 201, 210
Toll (FGCT) Pty v Alphapharm Pty Ltd [2004] HCA 52, (2004)
  219 CLR 165..201
Toomey v London, Brighton & South Coast Railway (1857) 3
  CBNS 146, 140 ER 694..65
Torfaen Borough Council v B&Q plc (Case 145/88) [1989] ECLI:EU:
  C:1989:593 348
Tots Toys v Mitchell [1993] 1 NZLR 325 211
Towers v Affleck [1974] 1 WWR 714, BCSC...199
Trenchard v Wanley (1723) 2 P Wms 166, 24 ER 685 34
Turton v Benson (1718) 2 Vern 764, 1 P Wms 496...33
Twisleton v Griffith (1716) 1 P Wms 310, 24 ER 403..32
Twyne's case (1601) 3 Co Rep 80b; Hawarde 125; Hudson 96 28–9
Uber Technologies Inc v Heller 2020 SCC 16, 447 DLR 4th 179 .... 190, 196, 197,
                                                                    198, 200, 202, 204
UBS AG (London Branch) v Kommunale Wasserwerke Leipzig
  GmbH [2017] EWCA Civ 1567, [2017] 2 Lloyd's Rep 621 359
UK Trucks Claim Ltd v Fiat Chrysler Automobiles NV [2019] CAT 26,
  [2019] 10 WLUK 722..400
United States v Kras 409 US 434 (1973) 326
Valentine v Chrestenson 316 US 52 (1942).. 269, 270, 271, 272
Van Gend en Loos. See NV Algemene Transport-Expedite Onderneming
  Van Gend en Loos v Nederlandse Administratie der Belastingen
Van Toll v South Eastern Railway Co (1862) 12 CBNS 75,
  142 ER 1071 .... 62, 66, 69, 73
Various Claimants v Catholic Child Welfare Society. See Various
  Claimants v Institute of the Brothers of the Christian Schools
Various Claimants v Institute of the Brothers of the Christian Schools;
  sub nom Various Claimants v Catholic Child Welfare Society [2012]
  UKSC 56, [2013] 2 AC 1...178, 293

VB Pénzügyi Lízing Zrt v Ferenc Schneider (Case 137/08) [2010]
   ECLI:EU:C:2010:659 340
Verrin v Welcome Financial Services Ltd [2017] ECC 7, [2016] 5 WLUK 671,
   Plymouth Cty Ct 363
Vine Products Ltd v Mackenzie & Co Ltd [1969] RPC 1, ChD 208
Virginia Citizens Consumer Council v State Board of Pharmacy 373 F
   Supp 683 (ED Va 1974)..270, 271
Virginia State Board of Pharmacy v Virginia Citizen Consumer
   Council (1976) 425 US 748 .... 1, 3, 8, 9, 19, 265–81
Vyse v Foster (1872) LR 8 Ch App 309 29
Walker v York & North Midland Railway Co (1853) 2 El and Bl 750,
   118 ER 948 59–60
Waller v Dale (1676) 1 Ch Cas 276; Rep t Finch 295 31
Wallis, Son and Wells v Pratt and Haynes [1911] AC 394, HL 50
Walter Hugh Merricks CBE v Mastercard Inc. See Merricks
   (Walter Hugh CBE) v Mastercard Inc
Watkins v Rymill (1883) 10 QBD 178, QBD 72
Watt v Grove (1805) 2 Sch & Lef 492..29
Weeks v Tybald (1605) Noy 11, 74 ER 982..105
Western Canadian Shopping Centres Inc v Dutton 2001 SCC 46,
   [2001] 2 SCR 534 14
White v Blackmore [1972] 2 QB 651, CA 74
White v Steadman [1913] 3 KB 340, KBD 149, 151
Whole Women's Health v Hellerstedt 579 US 582 (2016) 256, 258
Wiggins v Kent, *The Times* Tuesday, 26 May 1895, 13 124
Wilkes v DePuy International Ltd [2016] EWHC 3096 (QB), [2018]
   QB 627 .... 283, 284, 290, 291,
                                                                                        292, 293, 294
Williams v Carwardine (1833) 5C & P 566, 172 ER 1101, 4 B and
   Ad 621, 110 ER 590, 1 Nev & MKB 418, 2 LJKB 101 105–6
Williams v Walker Thomas Furniture Co 350 F.2d 445 (1965) 121
Williamson v Lee Optical of Oklahoma, 348 US 483 (1955).......................270, 271
Williamson v North of Scotland and Orkney and Shetland Steam
   Navigation Co 1915 2 SLT 165, Ct of Sess (OH)..75
Williamson v North of Scotland and Orkney and Shetland Steam
   Navigation Co 1916 SC 554, Ct of Sess (IH, 2 Div) 71, 72
Wilson v First County Trust Ltd [2003] UKHL 40, [2004] 1 AC 816 119
Wimbish v Tailbois (1550) 1 Plow 38, 75 ER 63 27
Wings Ltd v Ellis [1985] AC 272, [1984] WLR 965, HL................................. 17, 178
Winterbottom v Wright (1842) 10 M&W 109, 152 ER 402................. 136, 137, 138,
                                                                                    139, 145, 148, 151
Wiseman v Beake (1690) 2 Vern 121, 23 ER 688...33
Witley v Price (1688) 2 Vern 78, 23 ER 660...31
WM Morrison Supermarkets plc v Various Claimants [2020] UKSC 12,
   [2020] AC 989...293
Wood v Letrick Ltd (1932)..113

Woodman v Photo Trade Processing Ltd (1981) 3
Yates and Lorenzelli v Nemo Personal Finance (14 May 2010), Manchester
    Cty Ct 362
Yeats v Pim (1816) 2 Marsh 141 44
Yerkey v Jones [1939] HCA 3, (1940) 63 CLR 649 194
Zauderer v Office of Disciplinary Counsel of Supreme Court of Ohio,
    471 US 626 (1985) 276, 279
Zsolt Sziber v ERSTE Bank Hungary Zrt (Case C-438/16) ECLI:EU:C:
    2018:367 343
Zunz v South Eastern Railway Co (1868-69) LR 4 QB 539, QB 62

Table of Legislation

Statutes

37 Hen VIII, c 9 (Usury 1545)	29
21 Jac I, c 17 (Usury 1624)	29
12 Car II, c 13 (Usury Act 1660)	29
12 Ann, c 16 (Act to Reduce the Rate of Interest 1713)	29
14 Geo 3, c 48 (Life Assurance Act 1774)	93
Act to Reduce the Rate of Interest 1713, 12 Ann, c 16	29
Adulteration of Food and Drink Act 1860	50
Adulteration of Food Act 1872	50
Bills of Sale Act	121, 131
Bills of Sale Act 1878	119
Bills of Sale Act (1878) Amendment Act 1882	116, 119, 131
Canada Act 1982	
Sch B	275
Cancer Act 1939	113
Carriers Act 1830	58, 59
Competition Act 1998	390, 394, 398
s 2(1)	397
s 47A	390
s 47B	14, 387, 391, 398, 399, 400
s 47B(4), (5)	391
s 58A(2)	390
Consumer Credit Act 1974	116, 194, 351, 357, 359, 365
s 127	119
s 129	18
s 140A	351, 353, 354, 355, 356, 357, 359, 360, 361, 362, 363, 364
s 140A(1)	353
s 140A(1)(c)	355, 358
s 140B	353, 356, 359
s 140B(1)	353
s 140C	353, 356, 359
s 140D	356
s 189(1)	116

Consumer Protection Act 1987 .... 19, 283, 286, 287, 288, 289, 290,
                                                                291, 292, 293, 294, 295, 296, 297
   s 3 286
   s 3(1) 286, 292
   s 3(2) 295
   s 4 ....294, 295
   s 4(1)(e) 288
Consumer Rights Act 2015 .... 76, 205, 305, 311, 312, 378, 398
   Pt 2 .... 190, 203, 312
   s 2(3) 153, 400
   ss 61, 62 204
   s 64 312
   s 64(1), (2) 204
Criminal Law Act 1977
   s 13(2) 124
   s 65 124
   Sch 13 124
Data Protection Act 2018 205
   s 15 205
   s 155(1) 205
Enterprise Act 2002
   Pt 8 356
Enterprise and Regulatory Reform Act 2013 300
Equality Act 2010
   s 10 374
European Withdrawal Act 2018
   ss 2–4 378
Evidence Act 1851 61
Factors Acts 126
Factors Act 1889 129
   s 9 .... 126, 127, 128, 130
Financial Services and Markets Act 2000 359
   s 228 361
Food Safety Act 1990
   s 15 214
Forcible Entry Act 1381 24
Habeas Corpus Act 1640 29
Health and Safety at Work Act 1974 182
   s 3(1) 182
Hire Purchase Act 1938 .... 50, 121, 131
   s 8(3) 50
   s 90 131
   ss 99–100 131
Hire Purchase Act 1964 52

Housing Act 1988 (c 50) 319
　s 117(1) 319
　Sch 2, ground 8 318
Human Rights Act 1998
　s 3 374
　s 6 374
Insolvency Act 1986
　s 251G 316
　s 251G(2) 319
　s 283(3A) 319
　s 285 319
Law Reform (Married Women and Tortfeasors) Act 1935 142
Legal Aid, Sentencing and Punishment of Offenders Act 2012 322
Life Assurance Act 1774, 14 Geo 3, c 48 93
Married Women's Property Act 1870 141
Married Women's Property Act 1882 141
Married Women's Property Act 1893 141
Married Women's Property Act 1964 142
Moneylenders Act 1900 .... 116, 119
Pharmacy Act 1868 50
　s 2 97
Public Health (Regulations as to Food) Act 1907 .... 50, 151
Race Relations Act 1965 c 73 .... 225, 226, 227
Railway and Canal Traffic Act 1854 .... 60, 61, 63
Railway Regulation Act 1844 61
Road Traffic Act 1930
　s 97 74
Sale of Food and Drugs Act 1875 .... 50, 151
Sale of Goods Act 1893 .... 8, 16, 48, 49, 51, 52
　s 13 53
　s 14 .... 8, 48, 51, 53, 143
　s 14(1) 48, 49, 50, 51, 52, 112
　s 14(2) 48, 51, 52
　s 14(2)(a), (b) 52
　s 14(3) 53
　s 15 53
　s 55 50
　s 55(4) 53
Small Business, Enterprise and Employment Act 2015
　s 37 379
Statute of Frauds
　s 17 40
Statute of Fraudulent Conveyances 13 Eliz I, c 5 28
Statute of Fraudulent Conveyances 27 Eliz I, c 4 28
Statutes of Usury 25, 27, 29, 30

Supply of Goods (Implied Terms) Act 1973 52
    ss 3, 4 53
    s 7(2) 53
Trade Descriptions Act 1968 ....5, 17, 52, 169, 173, 176, 178, 183
    s 1 176
    s 11 175
    s 11(2) 170, 171
    s 14 .... 175, 176, 181
    s 20 179
    s 23 179
    s 24 ....170, 171, 176, 177, 180, 181
    s 24(1) 171, 173
    s 24(1)(a) 170, 171
    s 24(1)(b) 170
Transport Act 1947
    s 76 74
Unfair Contract Terms Act 1977 76
Usury Act 1545, 37 Hen VIII, c 9 29
Usury Act 1624, 21 Jac I, c 17 29
Usury Act 1660, 12 Car II, c 13 29
Venereal Disease Act 1917 113
Video Recordings Act 1984 181
    s 11(2)b 181
Wages Attachment Abolition Act 1870 119

Statutory Instruments

Air Passenger Rights and Air Travel Organisers' Licensing (Amendment)
    (EU Exit) Regulations 2019, SI 2019/278
        reg 261 159
CAT Rules. See Competition Appeal Tribunal Rules 2015, SI 2015/1648
Civil Procedure Rules 1998, SI 1998/3132
    Pt 19 – Parties and group litigation
        r 19.6 399
        rr 19.10, 19.11 399
Competition (Amendment etc) (Eu Exit) Regulations 2019, SI 2019/93 390
Competition Appeal Tribunal Rules 2015, SI 2015/1648 ('CAT Rules') 391, 394
    r 78 399
    r 78(1)(b) 400
    r 78(2) 400
    r 78(2)(b) 399
    r 78(3) 400
    r 78(3)(c) 396
    r 79 ....391, 399
    r 79(2) 391
    r 81 399

r 93 401
r 94(3) 401
r 115(3) 400
Consumer Contracts (Information, Cancellation and Additional Charges)
  Regulations 2013, SI 2013/3134 379
Consumer Protection Amendment Regulations 2014, SI 2014/870 379
Consumer Protection from Unfair Trading Regulations 2008,
  SI 2008/1277 .... 169, 178, 180, 183, 185,
                                                                            187, 201, 205, 356, 379
  Pt 2 190
  reg 2(1), (2) 201
  reg 3 201
  reg 3(1) 356
  reg 3(3)(a), (b) 183
  reg 4 201
  reg 7 202
  reg 7(1)(a) 202
  reg 8(1) 181, 183
  regs 9–12 181
  reg 17(1) 180
Debt Respite Scheme (Breathing Space Moratorium and Mental Health Crisis
  Moratorium) (England and Wales) Regulations 2020, SI 2020/1311 18
Equality Act (Sexual Orientation) Regulations (Northern Ireland)
  Order 2006, SR 2006/439 .... 374, 375
Fair Employment and Treatment (Northern Ireland) Order 1998,
  SI 1998/3162 (NI 21) 374
Financial Services and Markets Act 2000 (Regulated Activities)
  (Amendment) (No 2) Order 2013, SI 2013/1881
  art 20(40) 356
  art 60L 116
Unfair Terms in Consumer Contracts Regulations 1999, SI 1999/2083 .... 299, 301,
                                                                            302, 305, 308, 309
  reg 5 356
  reg 5(1) 302
  reg 6(2) (former art 3(2)) 299, 300, 301, 302,
                                                                            303, 304, 305, 312
  reg 6(2)(b) 306
  reg 8(1), (2) 301
  Sch 2 303

Australian Federal Legislation

Australian Securities and Investments Commission Act 2001 (Cth)
  s 12CB(1) 356
  s 12CB(4) 356
  s 12CC 195, 202, 356

Competition and Consumer Act 2010 (Cth)
    Sch 2, s 21 (Australian Consumer Law) 190, 202, 205
        s 21(4)(a), (b) 202
        s 22 202
        s 22(1)(a), (b) 203
        s 22(1)(d) 203
        s 22(1)(j) 203
        s 22(2)(a), (b) 203
        s 23(4) 204
        s 224 205
    Australian Consumer Law, pts 2–3 .... 190, 203
Australian Unfair Contract Terms Law 204
National Consumer Credit Protection Act 2009 (Cth)
    Sch 1 – National Credit Code
        s 17(15) 367
        s 76 195
        s 145 367

Canada

Constitution Act, 1982
    Pt 1: Canadian Charter of Rights and Freedoms 275
        s 1 275
        s 2(b) 275

Germany

Abzahlungsgesetz, 1894 (German Repayment Act) 116

Poland

Code of Civil Procedure 347

Singapore

Consumer Protection (Fair Trading) Act 2003
    s 4 201
    Sch 2, p 1 (13) 203

Spain

Code of Civil Procedure
    Art 698 .... 334, 335

Law 1/2013 concerning measures to protect mortgage debtors and
    provide for debt restructuring and social rents 342
Law 42/2015 342
Ley 5/2019, de 15 de marzo, reguladora de los contratos de crédito
    inmobiliario establece las normas de protección para las personas
    físicas que sean deudoras de préstamos hipotecarios 342
Royal Decree 11/2014 342

US Federal Legislation

Affordable Care Act (aka Obamacare) 279
Consumer Bill of Rights 1962 377
Constitution 246, 247, 249, 261
    First Amendment 265, 266, 268, 269, 270, 271, 272,
                                                                    273, 274, 275, 279, 372, 373
        Fourteenth Amendment 245, 247, 248, 250,
                                                                    251, 256, 257, 263
42 US Code 1981 Equal Rights Under the Law 242
Equal Credit Opportunity Act 1974 15 U.S.C. §§ 1691–91f 267
Fair Credit Reporting Act 1970 15 U.S.C. §§ 1681–81x 267
Fair Debt Collection Practices Act 1978 15 U.S.C. §§ 1692–92p 268
Food, Drug and Cosmetic Act 1938 267
Magnuson Moss Warranty Federal Trade Commission Improvements
    Act 1975, 15 USC §§2301-2312 (Supp. 1975) 378
Presidential Executive Order on Promoting Competition in the
    American Economy (9 July 2021) 376
Pure Food and Drugs Act 1906 .... 111, 266
Restatement (Second) of Torts (American Law Institute, 1977)
    § 402A 285
Truth in Lending Act 1968 15 U.S.C. §§ 1601–07 267
Truth in Lending Act, 15 U.S.C. § 1601(a) 273
US Uniform Commercial Code 378
    Art 9 131
Women's Health Protection Act 2022 .... 262, 263

US State Legislation

Colorado

Anti-Discrimination Act 1957 Colo Rev Stat § 24-34-60(2) 371, 373

Kansas

Constitution 261

xxxiv *Table of Legislation*

Kentucky

Constitution 261
    s 2 260

New Mexico

Human Rights Act 373

Virginia

Vir. Code Ann. § 54-524.35(3) (1974) 270

EU and International

Charter of Fundamental Rights of the European Union [2012] OJ C326/391
    Art 7 336
    Art 47 .... 335, 336, 337, 342
Directive 85/374/EEC of 25 July 1985 on the approximation of the laws,
    regulations and administrative provisions of the Member States
    concerning liability for defective products [1985] OJ L210/29 .... 16, 286
Directive 93/13/EEC of 5 April 1993 on Unfair Terms in Consumer
    Contracts, [1993] OJ L95/29 .... 13, 300, 304, 305, 306,
                                                            307, 308, 309, 334, 336, 337,
                                                            338, 340, 343, 345, 346, 348
    Art 3(1) 335
    Art 3(3) 335
    Art 4(2) 301, 305, 306, 309, 343
    Art 6 .... 301, 336
    Art 6(1) 343
    Art 7(1) 335
Directive 2005/29/EC of the European Parliament and of the Council of
    11 May 2005 concerning unfair business-to-consumer commercial
    practices in the internal market and amending Council Directive 84/450/EEC,
    Directives 97/7/EC, 98/27/EC and 2002/65/EC of the European Parliament
    and of the Council and Regulation (EC) No 2006/2004 of the European
    Parliament and of the Council ('Unfair Commercial Practices Directive')
    [2005] OJ L149/22 4
Directive (EU) 2015/2302 of the European Parliament and of the Council of
    25 November 2015 on
package travel and linked travel arrangements [2015] OJ L326/1 .... 18, 158
EC Treaty
    Art 81(1) EC 389

European Convention for the Protection of Human Rights and Fundamental
  Freedoms, as amended by Protocols Nos 11 and 14, 4 November 1950,
  ETS 5 (ECHR) 275, 374, 375, 376, 380
    Art 8 375
    Art 9 .... 374, 375, 382
    Art 10 .... 9, 275, 374, 375
    Art 10(2) 275
    Art 14 375
International Covenant on Economic, Social and Cultural Rights (1976) 159
    Article 7(d) 154, 160
Regulation (EC) No 261/2004 of the European Parliament and of the
  Council of 11 February 2004 establishing common rules on compensation
  and assistance to passengers in the event of denied boarding and of
  cancellation or long delay of flights [2004] OJ L46/1 158
Regulation (EU) 2016/679 of the European Parliament and of the Council
  of 27 April 2016 on the protection of natural persons with regard to the
  processing of personal data and on the free movement of such data,
  and repealing Directive 95/46/EC (General Data Protection Regulation)
  [2016] OJ L119/1 205
Treaty of Amsterdam (1997) 338
Treaty on European Union (TEU)
    Arts 1, 2 344
    Art 19 .... 339, 344
Treaty on the Functioning of the European Union (TFEU) [2016] OJ C 202/152
    Art 101 .... 389, 390
    Art 234 (ex Art 201 TEC) 306
Unfair Commercial Practices Directive. See EC Directive 2005/29/EC
United Nations Convention on the Rights of the Child 160
    Art 31(1) 160
Universal Declaration of Human Rights 159, 160
    Art 24 160

Table of Guidance, Protocols etc

ABTA
  Code of Conduct 1973 .... 18, 158
American Medical Association
  Code of Ethics, Opinion 9.6.1 280
Association of Litigation Funders of England and Wales, Code of
  Conduct for Litigation Funders
(January 2018) ('ALF Code') 401
    [9] 401
    [9.1] 401
    [10] 401
    [11]–[13] 401

Competition and Markets Authority
  'Guidance on the functions of the CMA after the end of the
    Transition Period' 1 December 2020 CMA125 390
Competition Appeal Tribunal
  Guide to Proceedings 400
    [6.30] 396, 400
    [6.33] 400
Financial Conduct Authority
  Decision Procedure and Penalties Manual (July 2022)
    para [6.2.1]..205
  'FCA Handbook' (1 January 2022)
    EG 7.1.2..205
  Guidance for Firms on the Fair Treatment of Vulnerable Customers
    (2021)...310
  Handbook
    DISP 1.4.1R..360
    DISP 2.8.9R..364
    DISP App 3.1.2G; 3.1.3G 360
    DISP App 3.1.4A 360
    DISP App 3.3A.2 360
    DISP App 3.3A.4(1), (2) 360
    DISP App 3.3A.5 ....360, 363
    DISP App 3.3A.5(3) 366
    DISP App 3.3A.6 360
    DISP App 3.6.1...361
    DISP App 3.6.4...361
    DISP App 3.7A.3, 3.7A.4 360
    DISP App 3.10.3.7A.3 360
    Principle 2.1.1(6), CONC 2.2.22, 7.3 18
    PRIN 2.1.1 (Principle 6) 356
  High Cost Credit Review: Overdrafts Policy Statement, Policy
    Statement PS19/16 (June 2019) 313
  Overdraft Pricing and Competition Remedies, Policy Statement
    PS19/25 (2019)...312
  Policy Statement: Payment protection insurance complaints: feedback
    on CP16/20 and final rules and guidance (PS 17/3, March 2017) 359
    6 (paras 1.8, 1.9) 359
    34 364
    36 359
    85 ....362, 363
    86 .... 362, 366, 367
  Previously rejected PPI complaints and further mailing requirements –
    Feedback on CP18/33 and final rules and guidance (Policy Statement
    PS 19/2, January 2019) 359

Rule Book, CONC 3 & 4 131
   Rules and guidance on payment protection insurance complaints
      (Consultation Paper CP15/39, November 2015), 52 (para 5.53)..................362
Insolvency Service
   'Insolvency Service Technical Manual, Pt 4: Tenancies' (18 July 2012)
      para 30.70 318
Insurance Conduct of Business (ICOB) Rules................................ 354, 355, 358, 362
Office of Fair Trading Unfair Relationships: Enforcement Action
   under Part 8 of the Enterprise Act 2002 (OFT854Rev, May 2008,
   updated August 2011)
      4..356
      para 3.32 357
Opinion of the European Central Bank of 18 July 2019 on the
   conversion of Swiss franc loans (CON/2019/27) 347
Pre-action Protocol for Possession Claims by Social Landlords............................327

1

Key Themes in Landmark Consumer Law Cases

IAIN RAMSAY AND JODI GARDNER*

A LANDMARK CASES in *Consumer Law* contribution may be considered a surprising addition to the series. Consumer law is often constructed as statutory law, a policy-based incursion into common law principles with statute law playing a larger part than case law in the modern development of UK consumer law.[1] However, as this collection highlights, an analysis of the landmark cases in consumer law is a valuable tool to fully understand this area. These cases have often established or modified the ground rules of consumer markets,[2] had a patterning effect on the economic organisation of consumer markets,[3] and expressed cultural visions and critiques of the market and consumers.[4] Case law may often have the first word and the last word. Judges decide whether a new technology will be recognised, or a new contract form will be enforced.[5] Many examples can be provided. *Helby v Matthews*, a test case between two trade associations, legitimised the contract of hire-purchase, a dominant form of twentieth century credit,[6] demonstrating the long term political and social importance of such decisions. *In re Charge Card Services* delineated the obligations associated with credit card transactions,[7] while more recently the UK Supreme Court in *Cavendish Square Holding BV (Appellant) v Talal El Makdessi (Respondent)* and *ParkingEye Limited (Respondent) v Beavis*[8] legitimised a controversial model of parking charges.

---

* We would like to thank Elliot Wright for his research assistance with finalising this chapter.
[1] See, eg, Sir G Borrie, *The Development of Consumer Law and Policy – Bold Spirits and Timorous Souls* (The Hamlyn Lectures 36th Series) (Stevens 1984) 1.
[2] Eg, *Donoghue v Stevenson* [1932] AC 562, E Gordon, ch 7 in this volume.
[3] *Helby v Matthews* [1895] AC 471 (HL), ch 5.
[4] Eg, *Virginia State Board of Pharmacy et al v Virginia Citizen Consumer Council* (1976) 425 US 748, M Spector ch 13.
[5] See D Kennedy, 'The Stakes of Law, or Hale and Foucault!' in D Kennedy (ed), *Sexy Dressing etc: Essays on the Power and Politics of Cultural Identity* (Cambridge, MA, Harvard, 1993) 110: I Ramsay, 'Consumer Credit Law, Distributive Justice and the Welfare State' (1995) 15 *Oxford Journal of Legal Studies* 177.
[6] See Ramsay (n 6) ch 5.
[7] *In re Charge Card Services* [1986] 3 All ER 289 (CA).
[8] *Talal El Makdessi (Respondent)* and *ParkingEye Limited (Respondent) v Beavis* [2015] UKSC 67, [2016] AC 1172.

Many of the cases considered in this collection revolve around key pieces of legislation. An analysis of these decisions show that, even where a legislature acts, courts will play a key role. Judges determine the scope and ultimate success or failure of statutory schemes.[9] Judicial decisions may be part of a continuing political battle over regulation,[10] a signal of the failure of regulation, or a demand for new regulation.[11] Law is both an ideological structure of thought as well as a technology, and an examination of elite judicial doctrine is therefore significant to thinking about its relation to dominant social values.[12]

This book analyses the common law foundations of consumer law, and encourages readers to rethink the role that consumer law plays in our society. The common law developed by the judiciary establishes the ground rules of consumer markets. These may be rules of permission or prohibition. A rule of permission might be a 'no duty to disclose' or the court might characterise a transaction as at-arms-length with no duty on one party to act in the interests of the other. These rules of permission and prohibition will have distributional effects on the nature and structure of markets, shaping market outcomes and contractual culture. They are not a natural consequence of concepts such as freedom of contract but may be shaped by bargaining power. This was recognised in Coase's classic article which highlighted the importance of transaction costs in establishing market ground rules.[13]

A central argument of consumer law is that consumers face high bargaining and enforcement costs in attempting to shape the terms of consumer transactions. While market forces may be significant at a general level, individuals rarely have bargaining power or are in a position to bargain with potential tortfeasors. Thus, the ground rules matter. The recognition that the judiciary are engaged in working and re-working the ground rules undermines the commonplace distinction between a natural, non-political world of the market and political intervention in the market through the legislature. The judiciary has long been involved in elaborating and reworking the rules of the market, which has in turn influenced directly and indirectly the nature of the market and market outcomes. Judicial decisions in consumer law may have distributional effects. For example, rules permitting high overdraft fees by banks combined with a 'free if in credit rule' represent a cross-subsidisation of a majority of more affluent consumers by lower income consumers, a form of 'reverse Robin Hood'.[14]

---

[9] See A Burrows, *Thinking About Statutes: Interpretation, Interaction, Improvement* (Cambridge, Cambridge University Press, 2018), as well as chapters by P Cartwright (ch 9) and J Murphy (ch 11) in this volume.

[10] Eg, in relation to: overdraft charges, see C Riefa, ch 16 in this volume; unfair terms and housing rights, see I Domurath and HW Micklitz, ch 18 in this volume.

[11] Eg, greater protection for holiday disruptions following *Jarvis v Swans Tours* see J Gardner, ch 8 in this volume.

[12] See R Gordon, 'Critical Legal Histories', 1984 36(1/2) *Stanford Law Review* 57. See I Ramsay, 'Consumer Law and Structures of Thought: A Comment' (1993) 16 *Legal Journal of Consumer Policy* 79.

[13] R Coase, 'The Problem of Social Cost' (1960) 3 *Journal of Law & Economics* 1. The importance of market ground rules was a central theme of the institutional economists. See, eg, R Hale, 'Coercion and Distribution in a Supposedly Non-Coercive' State (1923) 38 *Political Science Quarterly* 47; 'Bargaining Duress and Economic Liberty' (1943) *Columbia Law Review* 286: J Commons, *The Legal Foundations of Capitalism* (1924).

[14] *Abbey National Plc & Others v The Office of Fair Trading* [2009] UKSC 6, [2010] 1 AC 696 [2] (Walker SCJ) and see further discussion in C Riefa, ch 16 in this volume.

Determining what cases to include in this collection was a challenging but rewarding experience, which required us to think deeply about the nature of consumers and the role of consumer law. A study of landmark cases might suggest that these represent 'leading cases' in consumer law, from which an individual might distil the principles of this area. Christopher Columbus Langdell based the case method for teaching contract law at Harvard on this model.[15] This is not the objective of this book. Studies of landmark cases either analyse the intrinsic merits of the case, its reasoning, relation to precedent and principle, or provide a rich context to the decision, often illustrating the contingency and idiosyncrasies of the decision.[16] A further approach has analysed the role of subsequent courts in constructing its importance.[17] This book contains examples of all three approaches.

The concept of a landmark case in consumer law is complicated. First, much consumer law is 'low law', occurring in county courts, small claims courts, police courts etc, and is often unreported,[18] and even when reported, classified under a variety of categories. This causes difficulties for understanding the development of consumer law and its role in society. For example, Emily Gordon demonstrates that in the decades before *Donoghue v Stevenson*, plaintiffs often succeeded against the manufacturers of products such as potentially dangerous hair dyes under expansive theories of an inherently dangerous product. Second, significant consumer law developments have often been a sidewind of commercial litigation or cases classified under more traditional categories of law.

The cases in this collection highlight that it is uncommon for an 'everyday' consumer to take on a business and create a landmark case.[19] Rather, the consumer bringing the action may be a person of significant wealth or power, as occurred in (footnotes refer to chapters in this volume) *Earl of Chesterfield v Janssen*,[20] *Gardiner v Gray*,[21] *Parker v South Eastern Railway*,[22] and *Constantine v Imperial Hotels Ltd*.[23] Alternatively, the parties may have a personal knowledge of the law, as in *Jarvis*[24] where the claimant was a solicitor. In other situations, a consumer law issue is litigated through two businesses, where the outcome has significant impact on consumers (*Helby v Matthews*;[25] *Erven Warnink BV v J Townend & Sons (Hull) Ltd*[26]). More frequently, a regulatory body or interest group will take a case on behalf of consumers, such as *Virginia State Board of Pharmacy v Virginia Citizens*

---

[15] CC Langdell, *A Selection of Cases on the Law of Contracts* (Little Brown, 1871).
[16] See AW Brian Simpson, *Leading Cases in Common Law* (Oxford, OUP, 1996).
[17] See E Lim, 'Of 'Landmark' or 'Leading' Cases: *Salomon* 's Challenge' (2014) 41(4) *Journal of Law and Society* 523.
[18] See, eg, the test case brought by the Consumers Association in *Woodman v Photo Trade Processing Ltd* (1981) extracted in I Ramsay, *Consumer Law and Policy: Text and Materials on Regulating Consumer Markets* (Oxford, Hart Publishing, 2012) 308.
[19] There are, however, exceptions, such as *Plevin*, discussed by N Howell, ch 19 in this volume.
[20] B Douglas, ch 2.
[21] D Ibbetson, ch 3.
[22] S Tofaris, ch 4.
[23] T Williams, ch 12.
[24] J Gardner, ch 8.
[25] I Ramsay, ch 6.
[26] J Murphy, ch 11.

Council[27] and *Office of Fair Trading v Abbey National plc*.[28] On rare occasions, a consumer law issue can align with an interest group, and therefore litigants receive financial support in order to use the case as a way to advocate for the perspective of a particular interest or group: *Masterpiece Cakeshop v Colorado Civil Rights Commission*[29] and *Roe v Wade*.[30] An analysis of landmark cases in consumer law allows many traditional cases to be viewed through a new and distinct lens, providing significant academic and intellectual value. Many cases included in this collection, such as the controversial *Roe v Wade*, whilst not traditionally viewed as related to consumer law, fundamentally impact the rights of everyday citizens to access goods and services. This collection therefore also includes a unique socio-legal perspective, considering the role that consumer law has played in addressing racial discrimination, LGBTQ+ challenges, and the rights of women.

The cases included in the collection cover multiple jurisdictions and appellate levels. They include cases involving contract, tort, land, equity, criminal, public, competition, human rights, and constitutional law. This is both a blessing and a curse. The wide variety of cases covered highlights the broad and important nature of consumer law – it goes far beyond the standard consumer law statutes so often taught to undergraduate students and touches so many different aspects of our legal system. It can however feel like there is no clear 'end' – what is consumer law and how should it be defined is an ongoing question. This introductory chapter therefore draws together the themes raised in the collection. It addresses questions of who a consumer is, the impact of freedom of contract, the role of access to justice, how the law responds to technological change and risk bearing, and finally the role of judges and the regulatory state.

I. WHO IS THE CONSUMER? CLASS, RACE, GENDER, AND SEXUALITY

The law conceptualises the consumer as the reasonable or vulnerable person, or sometimes 'the weaker party',[31] and a substantial literature exists on these distinctions.[32] However, much of consumer law retains the discourse of liberal individualism with consumer law providing the means of attaining the norm of the rational chooser or, to paraphrase a senior EU official, 'rational economic operators'.[33]

---

[27] M Spector, ch 14.
[28] C Riefa, ch 16.
[29] S Brown, ch 20.
[30] S Martin, ch 13.
[31] See, eg, the European Court of Justice in *Aziz v Caixa d'Estalvis de Catalunya* (2013) Case C-415/11, 3 CMLR 5, discussed by H Micklitz and I Domurath in ch 18 in this volume.
[32] See, eg, references in HW Micklitz, J Stuyck and E Terren (eds) *Cases Material and Text on Consumer Law Jus Commune Casebooks for the Common Law of Europe* (Oxford, Hart Publishing, 2010) 1–3, 10–19, 110–113; C Riefa, ch 16 in this volume: P Cartwright, Understanding and Protecting Vulnerable Financial Consumers (2015) 38 *Journal of Consumer Policy* 119: R Incardona and C Poncibò, 'The average consumer, the unfair commercial practices directive, and the cognitive revolution' (2007) 30 *Journal of Consumer Policy* 21.
[33] G Abbamonte, 'The Unfair Commercial Practices Directive and its General Prohibition' in S Weatherill & U Bernitz (eds) *The Regulation of Unfair Commercial Practices under EC Directive 2005/29: New Rules and Techniques* (Oxford, Hart Publishing, 2007).

Consumers are too often portrayed as a homogenous class of individuals, and this picture often occludes inequalities of social class, gender and race.

'Weakness' justifying protection can come in many shapes and forms. For example, the claimant in the *Earl of Chesterfield v Janssen* was Mr John Spencer, the favoured grandson of Sarah, the Dowager Duchess of Marlborough. John was the primary beneficiary to a vast fortune worth over £400,000 in land and £25,000 in investments. On first glance, he does not appear to be someone needing protection on the basis of vulnerability. The court however set aside a usurious contract with a moneylender on the basis of an expanded notion of fraud in equity. As Benjamin Douglas outlines, this was based on a policy of protecting both certain institutions (notably in this period, marriage and family structures) and certain persons with weakness from being taken advantage of by those in positions of strength or trust.

To the extent that courts have taken account of issues of identity in consumer law, they have sometimes drifted towards misleading and damaging stereotypes. In the classic case of *Lloyds Bank v Bundy*,[34] 'old Herbert Bundy' is characterised as lacking the capabilities of a normal rational contractor, reinforcing ageist stereotypes and downplaying the fact that he seems to have been a successful farmer. Protection under this approach to inequality of bargaining power is limited to a few (*sic*) 'presumptive sillies' such as expectant heirs and seamen identified in Arthur Leff's famous article on the unconscionable provisions of article 2 of the Uniform Commercial Code.[35] This approach maintains the norm of equality of bargaining power in contract, with consumer law as an exception. Consumer law can within this approach be hived off without challenging the dominant norm of parties bargaining at arm's length. This approach also displaces a more structural analysis of the power relations, for example, between banks and consumers, a fact acknowledged if not developed by Sumption J in *Plevin v Paragon Finance*. Sumption recognises that 'the great majority of relationships between commercial lenders and private borrowers are probably characterised by large differences of financial knowledge and expertise. It is an inherently unequal relationship'.[36] However for Sumption J, the regulation of this generally unequal relationship is for Parliament to decide, a classic English judicial trope for denying the distributional and political role of the judiciary. Consumer law represents the preserve of the legislature, representing the sometimes transient political compromises between consumer and producer groups rather than the supposedly neutral, rational and coherent basic principles of contract law.

Women have been the primary consumers, notwithstanding historical legal limitations on their capacity to contract or sue in tort[37] in many jurisdictions, and practical barriers to their full participation in markets. Those constructed as 'credulous consumers' have often been women, such as Mrs Walker in a well-known Trade Descriptions Act case who believed that the description by a salesperson of a car as

---

[34] *Lloyds Bank v Bundy* [1974] EWCA 8; see below E Bant and J Patterson, ch 10 in this volume.
[35] AA Leff, 'Unconscionability and the Code: The Emperor's New Clause' (1967) 115(4) *University of Pennsylvania Law Review* 485.
[36] *Plevin v Paragon Personal Finance* (2014) UKSC 61 [10]; see below N Howell, ch 19 in this volume.
[37] Eg, *George v Skivington* (1869-70) L.R. 5 Ex. 1, where Emma George suffered injury from a hair wash and sued the manufacturer in tort, but her husband was joined for conformity.

'beautiful' implied that it was mechanically sound.[38] The central cases establishing the 'credulous consumer' test in the US in the 1930s concerned women's cosmetics,[39] perhaps with the underlying message that such consumers lacked the masculine virtues of objectivity and rationality. Louisa Carlill, in the celebrated case of the Carbolic Smoke Ball, represented for some of the contemporary press the gullible consumer, with the *Spectator* indicating that no man would have pressed the claim, but that Mrs Carlill had shown 'all that patient determination of which only a woman is capable'.[40] In *Charles of the Ritz v FTC*, the court held that a cosmetic cream advertised as 'Rejuvenescence' might mislead a consumer into thinking that it could actually retard the ageing process. Clark J commented

> while the wise and worldly may well realize the falsity of any representations that the present product can roll back the years there remains that vast multitude of others who like Ponce de Leon, still seek a perpetual fountain of youth…, the average woman conditioned by talk in the magazines and over the radio of vitamins, hormones, and God knows what might take rejuvenescence to mean that this is one of the modern miracles.[41]

Women appear as claimants in several cases in this volume,[42] and Emily Gordon documents the significant numbers of women who suffered injuries from potentially dangerous cosmetic products in the 1920s,[43] foreshadowing the principled breakthrough in manufacturer liability in *Donoghue v Stevenson*. Women often act as guarantors for a male partner's business, with potentially devastating consequences for her should the business fail, leading to one writer describing the situation as 'sexually transmitted debt'.[44] In the post-second-world-war economy, credit card companies openly discriminated against women by insisting for example that a married woman's husband should be legally responsible for any credit card account, and adopting a practice where divorced or separated women would be left with no credit rating.[45] Consumer bankruptcy and over-indebtedness certainly raise gender issues.[46] Women, often single parents, comprise the majority of individuals filing for a Debt Relief Order in England and Wales, a remedy designed for individuals with little income and few assets, dubbed by the press as the 'poor person's bankruptcy'.[47]

The intersection between gender and access to consumer services was central in the US case *Roe v Wade*. As Stevie Martin highlights, whilst this case is most often discussed for the impact that it had on abortion rights around the world, it has important ramifications on consumers' access to health services. The more recent

---

[38] *Robertson v DiCicco* [1974] RTR 431.
[39] *Charles of the Ritz Distribution Corp v FTC* 143 F 2d 676 (2nd Circuit).
[40] Quoted in I Ramsay, *Advertising, Culture and the Law: Beyond Lies, Ignorance and Manipulation* (London, Sweet & Maxwell, 1996).
[41] *Charles of the Ritz Distrib. Corp. v FTC*, 143 F.2d 676 (2d Cir. 1944), 680.
[42] Eg, *Plevin* (N Howell, ch 19), *Sharples* (J Spooner, ch 17), *Roe* (S Martin, ch 13) in this volume.
[43] E Gordon ch 7 in this volume.
[44] B Fehlberg, *Sexually Transmitted Debt: Surety Experience and English* Law (Oxford, OUP, 1997).
[45] L Cohen, *A Consumers' Republic: The Politics of Mass Consumption in Postwar America* (New York, Vintage, 2004) 147.
[46] E Warren, 'What is a Women's Issue? Bankruptcy, Commercial Law and other Gender Neutral Topics' (2002) 25 *Harvard Women's Law Journal* 19.
[47] See Insolvency Service Statistics 2021, where women file 54% of Debt Relief Orders. www.gov.uk/government/statistics/individual-insolvencies-by-location-age-and-gender-england-and-wales-2021.

case of *Dobbs v Jackson Women's Health Organisation* however overturned *Roe v Wade* and fundamentally altered the power dynamic between individuals, the state, and the medical profession. *Dobbs* also highlights that the courts can 'wind back' hard fought-for rights, often disproportionately impacting the rights of those already vulnerable.

Consumer law is traditionally used as a mechanism for allowing individuals to escape unfair contracts, or to obtain compensation when things go wrong. This collection however also highlights that consumer law can be a vehicle to allow marginalised groups to enforce their rights by attempting to prohibit businesses from refusing to enter into contracts with people. An example of this was addressed by Sarah Brown in her analysis of the USA-based *Masterpiece Cakeshop v Colorado Civil Rights Commission*[48] and the UK equivalent *Lee v Ashers Baking Company Ltd*.[49] Both of these cases concerned the refusal of a bakery to provide cakes to a homosexual individual/couple on the basis of the owners' religious beliefs. The claimant used access to markets and contracts to challenge the actions of the businesses, therefore these cases represented (an unfortunately unsuccessful) attempt to utilise consumer law to protect against discrimination on the grounds of sexuality.

Authors are increasingly excavating and illustrating the significance of race in shaping and restricting consumer choice. In the US, the post-war consumer society which promised democratic equality through consumption largely excluded black consumers. Policies promoting consumption such as subsidised mortgages, operated racist criteria and 'redlined' many areas where blacks hoped to buy.[50] In the UK, many black immigrants in post-second-world-war Britain faced discrimination in housing and credit, forcing them to establish their own credit unions.[51] Even a renowned cricket star such as Sir Learie Constantine suffered direct racial discrimination in being refused accommodation at a well-known London hotel during the Second World War, continuing a disgraceful tradition which included the denial of service at the Savoy to Paul Robeson, and against a background of substantial discrimination against the black population in cities such as Liverpool, Bristol and Cardiff.[52]

The landmark cases discussed in this collection highlight the difficulty of defining a 'consumer' and the use of unhelpful stereotypes in this process. They also show that treatment of consumers has not been uniform, and that consumer law can – but sometimes chooses not to – play a role in protecting already marginalised groups of people.

II. FREEDOM OF CONTRACT, CHOICE AND FAIRNESS

English private law is grounded in strong notions of 'freedom', particularly freedom of contract, which is often equated with ideas of an unregulated market.[53] Establishing

---

[48] *Masterpiece Cakeshop v Colorado Civil Rights Commission* 584 U.S. (2018).
[49] *Lee v Ashers Baking Company Ltd* [2018] UKSC 49.
[50] Cohen, see above n 45.
[51] See discussion in S O'Connell, *Credit and Community* (Oxford, OUP, 2009) 227 et seq.
[52] See T Williams, ch 12 in this volume.
[53] See discussion in J Gardner, *The Future of High-Cost Credit: Rethinking Payday Lending* (Oxford, Hart Publishing, 2022) ch 3.

the ground rules of a market however often involves difficult normative questions. For example, *caveat emptor* is supposedly a fundamental principle in English law. Briggs J stated confidently in 2011 that 'the starting point under English common law in relation to pre-contractual negotiations is "*caveat emptor*"'.[54] Indeed this proposition is so obvious that rarely are any supporting citations provided. The phrase has the virtues of being 'brief and compact, an easy focus for judicial thought, the benefit of being in Latin and therefore smacking of classical thought and centuries of experience, [and] an easy guide to follow when the going gets difficult'. But as the same author notes 'its pedigree is not easy to pin down'.[55]

Analysis of the complexities of the law of misrepresentation and the subtleties of distinctions between silence, half-truths, statement of opinion, and facts, suggest a world of competing principles rather than a dominant norm of *caveat emptor*, subject to legislative exceptions. As outlined by David Ibbetson, sales cases such as *Gardiner v Gray* (1815) concerning sellers quality obligations in the goods, and its subsequent interpretation in the nineteenth century[56] demonstrate the increasingly limited nature of this principle in English sales law. By the end of the nineteenth century, *caveat emptor* was effectively the norm only in face-to-face transactions where individuals had an opportunity to examine the goods, a fact obscured by Mackenzie Chalmers in section 14 of his 1893 English codification. Chalmers claimed that its origin was that 'in early times' most sales were in 'market overt', a claim unsupported by historical evidence, but he admitted that the distinct tendency of modern cases was to limit its application.[57] The sidebar to the section: 'rule of *caveat emptor*' might suggest that there was more ideology than scientific restatement of the law in the codification.[58]

Establishing the ground rules of a consumer market may entail different visions of that market and assumptions about consumers. Almost all first-year law students are aware of *Carlill v Carbolic Smoke Ball Company*,[59] where the Smoke Ball Company had offered £100 to anyone who contracted influenza after using the smoke ball as directed. The offer was made in the shadow of an international influenza epidemic and in a contemporary context of medical quackery with little regulation of advertising of patent medicines.

The court in that case was not impressed by arguments that no one would take such promises seriously. In a damning cultural criticism of the exaggerated and often misleading ads proliferating at this time, Bowen J commented in the Court of Appeal that

> 'if a person chooses to make extravagant promises … he probably does so because it pays him to make them, and, if he has made them, the extravagance of the promises is no reason in law why he should not be bound by them.'[60]

---

[54] *OFT v Purely Creative* [2011] EWHC 106 (Ch), [2011] ECC 20 Briggs J at [73].
[55] See W Hamilton, The Ancient Maxim Caveat Emptor (1931) 40 *Yale Law Journal* 1135.
[56] See D Ibbetson, ch 3 in this volume.
[57] M Chalmers, *Sale of Goods Act 1893* (London, Butterworth & Co, 1963) 21.
[58] See R Ferguson, 'Legal Ideology and Commercial Interests' (1977) 4(1) *British Journal of Law and Society* 18.
[59] *Carlill v Carbolic Smoke Ball Company* [1893] 1 QB 256, see A Simpson, ch 5 of this volume.
[60] ibid 268.

Notwithstanding this comment, consumer law has had difficulty in dealing with advertising images which often invite consumers to associate products with often fantasised personal, social, or sexual success.[61] Even though we 'know' that such images manipulate reality, the success of such advertising is convincing sufficient numbers of people to 'buy into' these images and the relationships implied in the images. The difficulties of addressing the potentially damaging nature of advertising images, for example in cases of sexual and racial stereotyping, through traditional categories of truth and falsity suggest that they may be best addressed through issues of dignitary harm and human rights.

The patrician disdain for advertising exaggeration expressed in *Carlill* contrasts with the 1976 US Supreme Court judgment in *Virginia State Board of Pharmacy et al v Virginia Citizens Consumer Council* which heralded the constitutionalisation of commercial speech.[62] Mary Spector highlights how, in an action brought by consumer groups to ensure better information for a vulnerable group of consumers, the Court elevated advertising which 'merely proposes a commercial transaction' to constitutional protection, and underlined consumerism as a fundamental aspect of life. Justice Blackmun opined that individuals had a greater interest in marketplace information than in the most urgent political debates, and that society has a strong interest in the free flow of commercial information, which was indispensable to a market economy. 'Advertising, however tasteless and excessive it sometimes may seem, is nonetheless dissemination of information as to who is producing and selling what product, for what reason and at what price.'[63] This information theory of advertising, supported by neo-classical economic analysis,[64] contrasted with an earlier theory of advertising as preference manipulation in cases such as *FTC v Charles of the Ritz*,[65] and with a more sceptical view of advertising in English policy documents of the 1960s which concluded that advertising was primarily persuasive and not factual 'without giving the consumer any truly helpful information'.[66]

The rationale in *Virginia Pharmacy* was consumerist: price advertising restrictions reduce competition, preventing consumers from shopping around for the best buy, with the hardest hit being the aged, sick and poor consumers who faced high search costs. Ironically, an important legacy of *Virginia Pharmacy* does not seem to have been a more transparent market for prescription drugs in the US.[67] However, the constitutionalisation of advertising spread internationally, being recognised for example, under article 10 of the European Convention of Human Rights, and often providing an initial barrier to regulation of dangerous products such as cigarettes.[68]

---

[61] See generally I Ramsay, *Advertising, Culture and the Law: Beyond Lies, Ignorance and Manipulation* (London, Sweet & Maxwell, Modern Legal Studies, 1996).
[62] *Virginia State Board of Pharmacy et al v Virginia Citizens Consumer Council* (1976) 425 US 748; see further M Spector, ch 14 in this volume.
[63] ibid.
[64] See, eg, P Nelson, 'Advertising as Information' 82(4) *Journal of Political Economy* 729: R Pitofsky, 'Beyond Nader: Consumer Protection and the Regulation of Advertising' (1977) 90 *Harvard Law Review* 661: I Ramsay, *Advertising Culture and the Law* (London, Sweet & Maxwell, 1996) ch 2.
[65] *FTC v Charles of the Ritz* 143 F.2d 676 (1944); see further discussion in Ramsay, ibid.
[66] Final Report of the Committee on Consumer Protection (The Molony Committee) Command 1781 (1962) para 732.
[67] M Spector, ch 14 in this volume.
[68] See R Shiner, *Freedom of Commercial Expression* (Oxford, OUP, 2003).

The rise of commercial speech coincided with a gradual shift away from consumer protection from the market to a policy paradigm of empowering consumer choice through information – an approach compatible with the increasing influence of neo-liberalism.[69] Christine Riefa discusses the impact of this in her analysis of *Office of Fair Trading v Abbey National Plc*, which was a test case brought by the regulator concerning the fairness of bank overdraft charges.[70] In this case, Lady Hale stated that 'As a very general proposition, consumer law in this country aims to give the consumer an informed choice rather than to protect the consumer from making an unwise choice.'[71] This raises the question as to whether distinct visions of consumer law exist in Anglo-American law and in other jurisdictions such as the EU. A consumerist vision, sometimes associated with the US, is that consumers should have access to a wide variety of goods and services at the lowest possible prices, and easy access to credit to finance such purchases.[72] Broad access to consumer markets provided the possibility for achieving an egalitarian society, and a justification for both attacking discrimination in access to consumer markets and nesting advertising within protected constitutional speech. A contrasting vision is one where consumers as 'the weaker party' need protection from the market. For example, Bant and Paterson's chapter highlights protection of the weak was an important factor in the court's consideration of *Lloyds Bank v Bundy*.[73]

Consumer choice implies a reasonable menu of choices, underlining the close relationship between competition policy and consumer law. Unfair competition may harm both consumers and competitors, and much consumer protection of consumers' economic interests developed from unfair competition law, such as the Merchandise Marks Acts in the UK or unfair competition law in European jurisdictions. In Germany, for example, small businesses – the *Mittelstand* – are an important political constituency, and unfair competition law often seemed to protect their interests. Thus, German unfair advertising laws restricted 'eye-catching' advertisements even if the advertisement contained correct information. While this might protect small traders and some consumers, other consumers might lose the opportunity to investigate the product advertised. These complexities are illustrated by John Murphy in *Erven Warnink Besloten Vennootschap v J Townend & Sons (Hull) Ltd*[74] where Lord Diplock claimed to add a consumerist twist to the common law tort of passing off. The Dutch manufacturer of Advocaat brought a passing off action against an English supplier of a drink sold as 'Old English Advocaat', which sold at a significantly lower

---

[69] See, eg, R Reich, 'Towards a New Consumer Protection' (1979) 128 *University of Pennsylvania Law Review* 1: Pitofsky (n 20): G Howells, 'The Potential and Limits of Consumer Empowerment by Information' (2005) 32(3) *Journal of Law and Society* 349. I Ramsay, 'Ordoliberalism and Opportunism: The Making of Consumer Law in the UK 1950-85' in HW Micklitz (ed), *The Making of Consumer Law and Policy in Europe* (Oxford, Hart Publishing, 2021) ch 9.
[70] C Riefa, ch 16 in this volume.
[71] *The Office of Fair Trading v Abbey National Plc & others* [2009] UKSC 6, [2010] 1 AC 696, ibid.
[72] See J Whitman, 'Consumerism Versus Producerism: A Study in Comparative Law' (2007) 117 *Yale Law Journal* 340.
[73] See discussion by P Cartwright, ch 9 in this volume.
[74] *Erven Warnink Besloten Vennootschap v J Townend & Sons (Hull) Ltd* [1979] AC 731; see J Murphy, ch 11 in this volume.

price because its ingredients included fortified wine rather than spirits. Warnink sought an injunction to prevent the company marketing its product under the description 'Advocaat'. The House of Lords granted the injunction based in part on potential consumer confusion as to the ingredients of the product. The case therefore seemed to further the consumer interest. However, the two products differed little in taste, so that those consumers who were happy to consume 'fake' Advocaat lost that choice, and the elimination of competition may have permitted the Dutch manufacturer to maintain higher prices than would be possible in a more competitive market.

As discussed above, a commonplace comment is that consumer protection law interferes with or restricts freedom of contract. But freedom of contract may be subdivided into *freedom to* contract and *freedom from* contract. The latter freedom protects individuals from being subject to obligations without their consent, but may also have a dark side where freedom from contract limits other individuals' freedom to contract. If practiced on a widespread basis, such freedom may result in systemic social disadvantage. The common law recognised historically the potential of suppliers to restrict supply through the common callings which imposed obligations to serve on carriers and innkeepers. Toni Williams discusses how the common law attempted, with only modest success, to grapple with direct racial discrimination in services in the case of Sir Learie Constantine, the famous cricketer, refused accommodation in a London hotel during the Second World War.[75] She also indicates that Constantine's experience was hardly unique. Celebrity did not protect against discrimination, with other famous black artists such as Paul Robeson being refused service at the Savoy hotel, and wealthy African students being denied hotel accommodation. Her chapter indicates a blind spot in the development of consumer law in the UK, where the *Constantine* case is absent from histories of consumer law or consumer and contract law case books.

The rise of international human rights law poses the question of the extent to which consumer rights might be subsumed within a human rights discourse.[76] Jodi Gardner, in discussing the extension of contractual damages to include the disappointment of a spoiled holiday in *Jarvis v Swans Tours*, raises its relationship to the international recognition of rights to a vacation.[77] The Eurozone crisis following the financial recession of 2008 resulted in widespread mortgage foreclosures in countries such as Spain which have strict creditor-oriented laws, and private litigation became a method for groups attempting to halt foreclosures and bring about political change. The 2014 judgment of the Court of Justice of the European Union in *Mohamed Aziz v Caixa d'Estalvis de Catalunya*, discussed by Irina Domurath and Hans Micklitz,[78] not only forced the amendment of Spanish mortgage foreclosure law, but also promoted reflection on the role of housing as a human right and what that might mean in practical protections against repossession. But a human rights approach can

---

[75] T Williams, ch 12 in this volume.
[76] See generally 'Consumer Protection and Human Rights' in G Howells, I Ramsay and T Wilhelmsson (eds), *Handbook of Research on International Consumer Law* 2nd edn (Cheltenham, Elgar, 2018) ch 2.
[77] J Gardner, ch 8 in this volume.
[78] H Micklitz and I Domurath, ch 18 in this volume.

III. CONSUMER LAW AND ACCESS TO JUSTICE: CONSUMER LITIGATION AS A FAIR FIGHT?

Law and Society scholarship demonstrates how legal systems work in practice, and the complex relationship between social practices and the law. Socio-legal studies have challenged ideologies of law as being a rational and non-political science. Many early socio-legal studies focused on consumer law to illustrate the gap between law's promise – for example of litigation as a fair fight – and the realities of law in action.[79] Marc Galanter, in a famous article, drew a distinction between Repeat-Players (RPs) and One-Shotters (OSs).[80] Repeat players are 'a unit which has had and anticipates repeated litigation, which has low stakes in the outcome of any one case, and which has the resources to pursue its long-run interests.' They are able to structure transactions in advance (eg, through the form contract), develop expertise and have access to specialist advice, develop valuable informal relationships with institutional officials, play the odds by a strategy which maximises gains over a series of cases, and play for rules in litigation rather than immediate gains. RPs may therefore settle cases where they expect unfavourable outcomes, while selecting or appealing those cases with an expectation of a favourable rule change. RPs may be in a better position to determine whether legal precedents will have a long-term impact in practice and be able to invest in resources to ensure that this occurs.

The One-Shotter in contrast is likely to be interested in immediate tangible gains rather than long term rule change. Galanter concludes that given the divergent characteristics of RPs and OSs, the weight of precedent is likely to be skewed towards RPs.[81] Certainly, the great bulk of consumer litigation occurs within the Repeat Player v One Shotter category of debt claims by institutional creditors against consumer debtors. This 'assembly-line' litigation[82] has a long history in Anglo-American law. Recent empirical research indicates that consumer finance companies have a 'track record' of intervening in credit litigation and playing for rules,[83] and Hugh Collins describes how the UK banks, in the wake of their defeat in *Barclays Bank v O'Brien*,[84] engaged

---

[79] See, eg, M Cain's survey of early socio-legal work in the UK in M Cain, 'Rich Man's Law or Poor Man's Law?' [1975] *British Journal of Law & Society* 61, noting the predominance of welfare, housing and consumer protection in the research topics of graduate students. See also R Cranston, *Regulating Business: Law and Consumer Agencies* (London, Macmillan, 1979) an empirical study of local authorities' approaches to the enforcement of consumer law: S Macaulay, 'Lawyers and Consumer Protection Laws' (1979) 14(1) *Law & Society Review* 115–71.

[80] M Galanter, 'Why the Haves Come out Ahead: Speculations on the Limits of Legal Change' (1974) 9 *Law & Society Review* 95.

[81] ibid 102.

[82] D Wilf-Townsend, 'Assembly line Plaintiffs' (2022) 135(7) *Harvard Law Review* 1704.

[83] See L Mulcahy, 'Are Litigants, Trials and Precedents Vanishing After All?' (2002) 85(2) *Modern Law Review* 326: *Helby v Matthews* (I Ramsay, ch 6 in this volume) is an early example.

[84] *Barclays Bank v O'Brien* [1993] UKHL 6.

in continuing strategic litigation to reduce its impact, ultimately succeeding in *Royal Bank of Scotland Plc v Etridge*.[85]

Strategies to upgrade the status of the OS include introducing the role of lawyers as specialists. However, access to legal advice will not necessarily provide the one-shot consumer with the advantages of the repeat player. Public advice agencies with often limited resources must often engage in individual 'firefighting' which will often involve negotiating a settlement rather than pursuing a point of principle, illustrated in Joseph Spooner's discussion of *Places for People Homes Ltd v Sharples*[86] where Citizens Advice[87] attempted to prevent an individual bankrupt from being evicted.

A further method of upgrading the One-Shotter is through the creation of a government agency with responsibility for consumer protection. In the UK this role was played by the Office of Fair Trading (now the Competition and Markets Authority and Financial Conduct Authority) and local Trading Standards Authorities. During the noughties, thousands of individual cases were brought by UK consumers in the lower courts claiming that banks' overdraft terms, generally borne by lower income consumers, were unfair under the relevant regulations implementing the EU Unfair Terms in Consumer Contracts Directive. The banks often filed lengthy standard defences, then settled claims on the day of the hearing[88] (a standard ploy of repeat players attempting to avoid uncomfortable precedents). Given this upsurge of consumer claims and the potential diversity of lower court outcomes, the Office of Fair Trading brought a test case against the major UK financial institutions.[89] Although the Supreme Court ultimately upheld the arguments of the banks, continuing pressure for regulation has resulted in some further changes to the manner in which overdraft charges are imposed. The Supreme Court case was therefore part of a continuing battle over regulation. In a similar vein, the Supreme Court intervened in cases where consumers were seeking compensation in relation to the scandal of Payment Protection Insurance, where UK financial institutions had for many years sold consumers useless and often unwanted additional insurance on credit products, resulting in an ultimate compensation bill of over £40 billion. The search for compensation included both alternative dispute resolution through the Financial Ombudsman service and the courts, and Nicola Howell analyses the relationship between these distinct forms of consumer redress.[90]

Government agencies are often subject to financial constraints. Thus, the overdraft charges test case was brought on the basis that each side would bear its own costs. In addition, there is always the danger that regulators may be captured by the regulated. A further method of upgrading consumers is therefore through class actions, which roll up many small individual actions into a single group action.

---

[85] *Royal Bank of Scotland plc v Etridge (No 2)* [2001] UKHL 44; H Collins, 'Regulating Contract Law' in C Parker, C Scott, N Lacey and J Braithwaite (eds), *Regulating Law* (Oxford, OUP, 2004) 21.

[86] *Places for People Homes Ltd. v Sharples: A2 Dominion Homes Ltd v Godfrey* [2011] HLR 45.

[87] Citizens Advice in the UK is the largest free advice service in Europe. See Annual Report 2021-22. assets.ctfassets.net/mfz4nbgura3g/5piAqpbrv71hBujORjhM9r/b578b9b5057e545e91ec38076ece/Annual_Report_2021_22.pdf (last accessed 25 February 2023).

[88] R Mulheron, Reform of Collective Redress in England and Wales: A Perspective of Need (2008) Civil Justice Council of England and Wales commissioned report 124.

[89] C Riefa, ch 16 in this volume.

[90] N Howell, ch 19 in this volume.

A characteristic of many violations of consumer laws is that consumer losses may be small individually but large in the aggregate. This means that many individuals would not consider it worthwhile bringing an action, even in a Small Claims Court with reduced fees. Nicola Howell notes for example that although Mrs Plevin's PPI claim was approximately £5,000, the legal costs even at the County Court level were £320,000.[91] As a consequence, these barriers to litigation mean that individuals absorb the costs of consumer law violations and companies may not be deterred from future violations. Thus, the private law system may fail to ensure performance in a mass consumption economy. The US model of the class action offers a potential solution. An individual representative claimant is permitted to sue on behalf of a potentially large group of similarly-situated consumers to claim compensation on behalf of that class. A class action permits an action where joinder of actions would not be feasible because of the large number of individual claimants. A distinct feature of the US model is that potential members of the class do not need to opt-in to the class but must receive 'adequate notice' to permit them to opt out.

Class actions might be a valuable method to ensure that businesses internalise costs of failures in contract performance, thereby guaranteeing that private costs equal social costs. As the Supreme Court of Canada has stated:

> class actions serve efficiency and justice by ensuring that actual and potential wrongdoers do not ignore their obligations to the public. Without class actions, those who cause widespread but individually minimal harm might not take into account the full costs of their conduct.[92]

They may also permit the development of substantive consumer law by exposing the courts to legal arguments which would not otherwise be advanced.

The US model of the class action is controversial, with opponents claiming that it leads to 'organised blackmail' where unfair settlements are extorted from defendants afraid of the high costs of litigation, and that the primary beneficiaries are lawyers. Given these controversies, a hesitation has existed in other jurisdictions such as the EU to introduce European-wide class actions, and some jurisdictions, for example, Sweden requires consumers to opt-in to any class action. One English judge feared that it would stoke a 'compensation culture'.[93] Commonwealth jurisdictions such as Australia and Canada now have significant experience of class action laws, but England and Wales hesitated to introduce class actions, so that only group actions (where all parties must be before the court) or representative actions were possible, the latter suffering from restrictive conditions such as the requirement for parties have the 'same interest' so that individual parties with different contracts and individual damage claims could not be aggregated within a common representative action. As part of encouraging private enforcement of EU Competition Law, the UK enacted section 47B of the Competition Act which permits a 'follow on' opt-out class action for damages caused to consumers by a breach of Competition Law. Walter Merricks,

---

[91] ibid.
[92] *Western Canadian Shopping Centres Inc. v Dutton* 2001 SCC 46, [2001] 2 SCR 534, McLachlin CJ [29].
[93] Steyn J quoted in R Mulheron, 'Some Difficulties with Group Litigation Orders – And Why a Class Action is Superior' (2005) 24 *Civil Justice Quarterly* 40, 59.

formerly the Financial Ombudsman, instituted a class action against Mastercard on behalf of 46 million UK Mastercard holders claiming an estimated £14 billion in losses caused by Mastercard's uncompetitive practices. Degeling, Gardner and McGeechan analyse the implications of this development for consumer law in their chapter on *Merricks v Mastercard*.[94] The authors highlight how, on one hand, class actions can be used to enhance consumer welfare and provide an effective mechanism for rights enforcement. On the other hand, they are fertile ground for exploitation and advantage-taking of consumers who have little understanding and limited choices.

One advantage for the Repeat Player noted by Galanter is the ability to structure the transaction in advance. The standard form consumer contract, dubbed more negatively by Saleilles as the *contrat d'adhesion*, is an obvious example. But the process of consumer contract development seems to have had greater contingency, not representing a clear linear development. The development of the hire-purchase contract as an important form of credit selling in the late nineteenth century represented a continuing experiment, as different trades tried distinct types of contract intended to provide them with security, and to defeat any opportunistic activity by a buyer. The courts also took differing attitudes to hire purchase with a few judges viewing it as a fraud. *Helby v Matthews* provided legitimacy to the contract, and the consumer finance industry grew around this contract. Iain Ramsay shows that undoubtedly *Helby* was a judgment of significant economic and social importance, but made without any input from consumers, being a test case between two finance trade associations.[95] Stelios Tofaris emphasises that *Parker v South Eastern Railway Co* and the 'ticket cases' introduce a novel manner of ensuring that consumers were bound to a company's terms through business taking reasonable efforts to inform them that there are terms and conditions.[96] Technological developments have harnessed this approach; through digitalisation, the ubiquitous 'T & Cs apply' on almost all advertisements and the online tick-box 'I have read and understood' have permitted the inclusion of a vast number of conditions and terms.

IV. TECHNOLOGY AND RISK BEARING

Modern consumer protection in the US was kickstarted by Ralph Nader's claim that the Corvair was a dangerous automobile in *Unsafe at Any Speed*, and the landmark case of *Henningsen v Bloomfield Motors*[97] in 1960 extended implied warranties of suitability from an automobile manufacturer to a consumer not in privity with the manufacturer. Technological innovations have been a central aspect of modern consumer economies. While these bring benefits, they may also create risks, both of physical injury as in the Corvair and thalidomide scandals, but also financial harm as seen in with PPI and payday lending. The question is therefore raised – who should bear the risk of innovation in consumer markets?

---

[94] S Degeling, J Gardner and J McGeechan, ch 21 in this volume.
[95] I Ramsay, ch 6 in this volume.
[96] S Tofaris, ch 4 in this volume.
[97] *Henningsen v Bloomfield Motors* 161 A 2d 69 (NJ 1960).

Compensation and deterrence represent two objectives of tort law. Private law provided theories of liability in relation to products causing physical injuries. The implied conditions in the Sale of Goods Act 1893 represented a model of strict liability in the sense that it is not a defence to an action that the seller took all reasonable care in the manufacture and supply of the product. These conditions provided the historical precedent for the general concept of strict liability for defective products, but were limited by the doctrine of privity in relation to manufacturer liability to the ultimate consumer. Tort law has developed clear duties of care for actions causing physical harm to claimants, but a complicated and piecemeal regime exists in relation to products and services that cause financial harm.[98]

The advent of the automobile in the early 1900s posed the question of who would bear the risks of consumer injury caused by defective production and design. Manufacturers of automobiles tried to protect their interests by ensuring that dealers were not their agents, and by creating the dealer franchise model of automobile distribution.[99] An important breakthrough for consumers, therefore, was *MacPherson v Buick*[100] where the New York Court of Appeals upheld a claim in negligence by a driver injured by a defective wheel, notwithstanding the lack of privity between the plaintiff and the automobile manufacturer. Cardozo J expanded the existing concept of inherently dangerous products equating an automobile to a product that 'is reasonably certain to place life and limb in peril when negligently made'.

Donoghue v Stevenson is often considered the starting point of modern product liability in the UK. It was however the Thalidomide scandal of the 1960s which stimulated product liability reform, ultimately resulting in the EU Directive of 1985. The Products Liability Directive has had a modest impact on product liability law in action.[101] In the UK, the case of *A v National Blood Authority* raised the application of the Directive to the tragedy of consumers contracting Hepatitis C from receiving infected blood transfusions in the National Health Service. The judgment in the case upheld liability on the Service for infected blood, and provided a strong pro-consumer interpretation of both the test of defectiveness and the development risks defence under the Directive. As Jacob Eisler notes, however, this judgment has been downplayed or ignored by subsequent judgments. It also raises questions about the role of the courts in achieving the goals of compensation and deterrence associated with tort law, given the arbitrary exclusion of victims who cannot find a 'defect', the long delay in obtaining compensation, and the high expenses in bringing claim. A no-fault compensation scheme, such as that implemented in New Zealand, may have been more appropriate.

Technological developments in financial products also raise risks, albeit to consumers' economic welfare as opposed to physical health. The courts, regulators

---

[98] See E Warren, 'Unsafe at Any Rate: If It's Good Enough for Microwaves, It's Good Enough for Mortgages' [Summer 2007] *Democracy* 8; J Stapleton, 'Comparative Economic Loss: Lessons From Case-Law-Focused "Middle Theory"' (2002) 50 *UCLA Law Review* 531.

[99] SH Clarke, 'Unmanageable Risks: *MacPherson v. Buick* and the Emergence of a Mass Consumer Market' (2005) 23(1) *Law and History Review* 1.

[100] *MacPherson v Buick* 111 NE 1050 (NY).

[101] See M Reimann, 'Product Liability in a Global Context: The Hollow Victory of the European Model' (2003) 11(2) *European Review of Private Law* 128.

and legislature face challenges associated with these developments, and this is reflected in *Plevin v Paragon Personal Finance Ltd* and the 'multilateral interchange fee' associated with *Mastercard v Merricks*. Due to the power and knowledge imbalances, it is important for the law to respond to the challenge and ensure that the risks associated with these developments are borne by the organisation and not the consumers; this is a key objective of, and change for, consumer law.

V. CONSUMER LAW, JUDGES AND THE REGULATORY STATE

Consumer law is a form of regulation, and judicial decisions play several important roles. These include determining the scope and impact of regulation, and signalling the need for regulation, or indeed the failure of regulation.

Much has been written on the relationship of statutes to the common law,[102] with key questions being the approach to interpretation and the interaction between statutes and common law. Consumer law certainly raises these questions. There may be different values or ideologies lurking in distinct judicial approaches to questions of interpretation. For example, the use in the UK of the hybrid regulatory offence – strict criminal liability with a statutory defence – as the typical technique of public enforcement of consumer law, posed the question as to whether it should be interpreted strictly like a criminal statute or given a more purposive approach in light of the public welfare aspect of many consumer statutes. Judges differed on these issues so that in *Wings v Ellis*,[103] a case dealing with potentially misleading holiday brochures under the Trade Descriptions Act 1968, Lord Scarman emphasised the important economic objective of maintaining trading standards while Lord Hailsham thought it unfortunate that the criminal law was being involved in this situation, potentially criminalising the 'owners of a decent business'.

In *Tesco v Nattrass*, the House of Lords had to determine whether a corporate supermarket retailer should be held liable under the Trade Descriptions Act 1968 for the mistakes of a manager which resulted in misleading pricing of goods. This involved analysis of the nature of corporate liability for regulatory offences. Peter Cartwright indicates how the willingness of the court to accept the statutory defence that the manager could not be identified since he was not a person of sufficient status within the company and senior management had not delegated their powers to him, seemed based on a conception of individual fault out of keeping with the contemporary organisational complexity of corporate decision making. Although some later decisions have departed from the relatively strict identification doctrine outlined in *Tesco*, the case remains significant in highlighting both differences in judicial approaches to the use of strict criminal liability in regulation and the difficulties

---

[102] See, eg, P Atiyah, 'Common Law and Statute Law' [1985] *Modern Law Review* 1; Lord Hodge, 'The scope of judicial law-making in the common law tradition' (2020) 84 *Rabels Zeitschrift für ausländisches und internationales Privatrecht* 211, 222; K Barker, 'Private Law as a Complex System: Agendas for the Twenty-First Century' in K Barker et al (eds), *Private Law in the 21st Century* (Oxford, Hart Publishing, 2017); A Burrows, 'The Relationship Between the Common Law and Statute in the Law of Obligations' (2012) 128 *Law Quarterly Review* 232; J Stapleton, *Three Essays on Torts* (Oxford, OUP, 2021).
[103] *Wings Ltd v Ellis* [1984] WLR 965.

in using criminal law to control corporate conduct. The case may also have created difficulties in enforcing consumer protection law against larger organisations, leading to a focus on smaller firms.

Signalling the need for regulation is represented by *Jarvis v Swans Tours*, where Lord Denning introduced the idea of experiential damages for lost enjoyment from a sub-standard holiday. This decision occurred at a time when package holidays were becoming common in the UK, and further regulation of this sector occurred both through self-regulatory approaches[104] and later EU requirements.[105] A private law case such as *Jarvis* discovers possible new areas for regulation.[106] The case also identified a limitation in existing common law rules on damages for breach of contract, which only permitted damages for 'lost feelings' as an exception to the traditional contract damages rule that damages compensate foreseeable financial losses. However, case law development since *Jarvis* indicates an increasing recognition of the personal value which an individual may expect from a contract, not recognised in the contract price, whether or not phrased in the economic language of the consumer surplus.[107] Indeed, the increasing recognition of experiential damages suggests that it should no longer be regarded as an exceptional remedy.[108]

The traditional view that the common law represents basic principles and that statutes are ad hoc political interventions has meant that consumer regulations are not generally seen as a source of common law principles. For example, several statutory provisions provide the opportunity to adjust a credit contract if an individual has suffered from an unfortunate change of circumstance such as loss of employment.[109] The courts in England and Wales have however been unwilling to recognise an underlying principle of social force majeure. Such a principle could have significant symbolic impact. Lord Diplock suggested in *Erven Warnink* that where a steady trend in legislation can be seen which reflects successive Parliament's view of what the public interest requires in a field of law, the courts ought to develop the common law in those parts of the field not covered by legislation in a parallel rather than divergent course.[110]

VI. STRUCTURE OF THE COLLECTION

As outlined above, it was a difficult but rewarding process to decide what cases to include in this collection. So much of the common law, covering a wide variety of

---

[104] See, eg, ATOL (Air Travel Organisers Licence) introduced in 1973: ABTA Code of Conduct www.abta.com/about-us/code-of-conduct (last accessed 25 February 2023).
[105] Directive (EU) 2015/2302 on package travel and linked travel arrangements.
[106] See T Wilhelmsson, 'The Paradox of the Risk Society and the Fragmentation of Consumer Law' in I Ramsay et al (eds) *Choice and Risk in Consumer Society* (Sakkoulas, 2007).
[107] See D Harris, A Ogus and J Phillips 'Contract Remedies and the Consumer Surplus' (1979) 95 *Law Quarterly Review* 581; J Wightman, *Contract: A Critical Commentary* (London, Pluto, 1996).
[108] Z Zlatev, 'Recoverability of Damages for Non-pecuniary Losses Deriving from Breach of Contract' (2021) 41(3) *Oxford Journal of Legal Studies* 638.
[109] See, eg, the relevant rules of the Financial Conduct Authority, FCA Handbook at Principle 2.1.1(6), CONC 2.2.22, 7.3; The Debt Respite Scheme (Breathing Space Moratorium and Mental Health Crisis Moratorium) (England and Wales) Regulations 2020; Consumer Credit Act 1974, s 129.
[110] *Erven Warnink Bv v J. Townsend and Sons (Hull) Ltd* [1979] Fleet Street Reports 397, 406.

subjects, addresses the rights of individuals when accessing goods and services from the market. Part I of this collection 'the common law foundations of consumer law', highlights the breadth and range of cases in this area. It shows that consumer law issues are raised in multiple topics, including contract law (*Gardiner v Gray, Parker v South Eastern Railway, Helby v Matthews* and *Jarvis v Swan Tours*), equity (*Earl of Chesterfield v Janssen*), tort law (*Blacker v Lake and Elliott* and *Erven Warnink BV v J Townend & Sons (Hull) Ltd*), land law (*Lloyds Bank v Bundy*), and criminal law (*Tesco v Nattrass*).

The second part of the collection 'rethinking the role of consumer law' engages with the socio-legal aspects of consumer law. This includes its relationship with a variety of statutes, such as the Consumer Protection Act (*A v National Blood Authority*), unfair contract terms provisions (*Office of Fair Trading v Abbey National plc*), EU legislation (*Aziz v Catalunyacaixa*), and responsible lending regulations (*Plevin v Paragon Personal Finance Ltd*). Part II also explores consumer law's intersection with different aspects of vulnerability, such as race (*Constantine v Imperial Hotels Ltd*), gender (*Roe v Wade*), sexuality (*Masterpiece Cakeshop v Colorado Civil Rights Commission*; *Lee v Ashers Baking Company Ltd and Others*), constitutionalising commercial speech (*Virginia State Board of Pharmacy v Virginia Citizens Council*), and bankruptcy (*Sharples v Places for People Homes Ltd*). The collection concludes with a chapter analysing the important – but often overlooked – procedural aspects of consumer law, using the landmark case of *Merricks v Mastercard* as an opportunity to explore the benefits and disadvantages of class actions in enforcing consumer rights.

Whilst the cases have been divided into these two parts, it is important to recognise that the cases and issues raised intersect. For example, many cases in Part I also raise issues of vulnerability and protection of the weak (for example, *Earl of Chesterfield v Janssen* and *Lloyds Bank v Bundy*), and Part II highlights that consumer law issues are raised in public law (*Roe v Wade, Virginia State Board of Pharmacy v Virginia Citizens Council*) and competition law (*Merricks v Mastercard*). This intersection highlights the richness and diversity of the cases and topics. We hope that readers will come away from this collection with a newfound appreciation for the importance, variation, and appeal of consumer law.

Part I

Common Law Foundations of Consumer Law

2

Earl of Chesterfield v Janssen: Equitable Foundations

BENJAMIN DOUGLAS

IF THE CONCEPT of consumer law could be explained to a lawyer of the eighteenth century, they would surely nominate *Earl of Chesterfield v Janssen*[1] as the leading case on consumer law. It has all the elements of a leading case. Grand parties, unusual facts, and a famous judgment where Lord Hardwicke set forth a list of four species of fraud, that continued to be cited into the twentieth century[2] as a leading authority on the nature of 'fraud' in equity. It is from this wide notion of fraud that the equitable roots of modern consumer law can be traced. This chapter explores the concept of fraud explained in *Chesterfield v Janssen* from a historical perspective, charting the developments that led to Lord Hardwicke's famous statement of principle, and the cases and policy concerns that animated the Chancery in developing the law to this stage.

I. THE CASE

The central character in *Chesterfield v Janssen* was Mr John Spencer, the favoured grandson of Sarah, the Dowager Duchess of Marlborough. Sarah was one of the leading forces in British Politics for more than half a century, being at one time the favourite[3] of Queen Anne, the wife of one of the leading generals of the day, and a political force in her own right.[4] She had over that time amassed a vast fortune worth over £400,000 in land and £25,000 in investments.[5] John was the primary beneficiary under her will.[6]

John had an income of £7,000 per annum plus considerable personal estate,[7] but was about £20,000 in debt to tradesmen. He needed to borrow £5,000 to pay

---

[1] *Earl of Chesterfield v Janssen* (1750) 2 Ves Sen 125; 1 Atk 301; 1 Wils KB 286.
[2] *Lancashire Loans Ltd v Black* [1934] 1 KB 380, 403 ff.
[3] See the film *The Favourite* (2018), although its historical accuracy seems to vary inversely with its degree of humour. The film, sadly, does not cover the events in *Chesterfield v Janssen*.
[4] See generally F Harris, *A Passion for Government: The Life of Sarah, Duchess of Marlborough* (Oxford, OUP, 1991) and O Field, *The Favourite: Sarah, Duchess of Marlborough* (London, Weidenfeld & Nicolson, 2018).
[5] Harris (n 4) 349.
[6] Field (n 4) ch 14.
[7] The facts are taken from the report at 2 Ves Sen 125.

his immediate debts, but wished to keep it secret from Sarah.[8] John engaged a Mr Blackwell to put it about in the market that he wished to borrow £5,000 on terms that if he survived his grandmother he would repay £10,000, but if she survived him he would repay nothing. John was aged 30, 'originally of a hale constitution but impaired' because he was 'addicted to several habits prejudicial to his health, which he could not leave off'. Sarah was aged 78, 'of a good constitution for her age and careful of her health'. This proposal was rejected by several people in the market as 'not sufficiently advantageous'. Eventually, although he first rejected it, Mr Abraham Janssen accepted the bargain and lent the £5,000. The bond was drawn up in the usual post-obit bond terms: a penalty of £20,000 payable unless the debt of £10,000 was repaid on a certain condition, and with a warrant of attorney confessing judgment on the debt (so that the creditor could proceed immediately to execution of the debt without needing judgment).

Abraham Janssen was not an unrespectable person. He was the son of a Baronet and had served briefly as a member of Parliament, but his family fortunes were heavily tied up with the South Seas Company and fell when that company crashed.[9] Ironically, one of the properties in Sarah's estate was Wimbledon Manor, which Abraham's father, Sir Theodore Janssen, had by financial necessity sold to Sarah upon the collapse of the South Seas Company, and had passed to John.[10]

Sarah died six years and three months after the bond. Two months after Sarah died, after John's expectancy had vested, John executed a new bond confirming the arrangement (although it was antedated to the day after Sarah's death so that it would carry interest from then). He then made two payments of £1,000 to Janssen, showing Janssen preference from among his creditors because Janssen had treated him 'like a gentleman'. John knew that Chancery generally relieved against post-obit bonds from expectant heirs, but executed the confirmation anyway. John died one year and eight months after Sarah. His executor, the Earl of Chesterfield, brought a bill in Chancery to set the transaction aside.

The argument for the executor was that this arrangement was usurious, or in the alternative a fraudulent or unconscionable bargain, and that the confirmation was a continuation of the original fraud. The argument was that John Spencer was an expectant heir caught by a catching bargain. An expectant heir was one who was very likely to inherit a large estate from an elderly relative. The heir, being desirous of immediate money, and short on patience, would find a moneylender to lend cash on the expectancy of the inheritance. The moneylender would demand exorbitant repayment terms, well above the ordinary commercial rates of interest. The usual arrangement would be a post-obit bond, where repayment was not to start until after the death of the elderly relative if the heir survived.[11] It had been common practice for at least three centuries for bargains like this to be set aside by the Chancery. Counsel for the plaintiff also argued that the very terms of the bargain were so unequal as to suggest fraud in themselves.

---

[8] Nevertheless, Sarah was aware of John's indebtedness, but ignored it: Harris (n 4) 326–7.
[9] S Campbell, 'The Economic and Social Effect of the Usury Laws in the Eighteenth Century' (1933) 16 *Transactions of the Royal Historical Society* 197.
[10] Harris (n 4) 255–6.
[11] L Sheridan, *Fraud in Equity: A Study in English and Irish Law* (London, Pitman, 1957) 133–45.

Like many leading cases, the facts of *Chesterfield v Janssen* are highly unusual. They are not a typical instance of equity's intervention for fraudulent bargains. In fact, they are so untypical and so obviously unmeritorious that, to a modern eye, it is surprising that there is an arguable case that this bond could be set aside, especially in view of the following:

- The borrower/heir, though much younger than the testator, was in poor health, so that the contingency of him predeceasing the testator was real.
- The borrower initiated the transaction and set the terms to the market.
- The borrower had been refused by other lenders as an undesirable bargain in their assessment of the contingency.
- The borrower had a great personal estate of his own, even without the expectancy.
- The borrower then confirmed the arrangement when he came into his inheritance, in full knowledge of its terms and the practice of the Chancery.

The case was heard by Lord Chancellor Hardwicke, who summoned the Master of the Rolls, the two Chief Justices and Burnett J to provide opinions.[12] Their reasoning all coincided. First, the bargain was held not to be usurious, because wagers over real hazards or contingencies were outside the Statutes of Usury. In this case, the poor health of John meant there was a real possibility that Janssen would lose all the money, and so the contingency was not just a colourable device to evade the Statutes of Usury. Second, after a general discussion on the chancery practice in relieving against fraudulent and unconscionable bargains, it was held that the confirmation, done freely, without compulsion and in full knowledge, rendered the transaction free from objection.[13]

The best known part of the case is a passage in the judgment of Lord Hardwicke where he describes the basis on which a court of equity intervenes to set aside contracts. Lord Hardwicke said:

This court has an undoubted jurisdiction to relieve against every species of fraud.

1. Then fraud, which is *dolus malus*, may be actual, arising from facts and circumstances of imposition; which is the plainest case.

2. It may be apparent from the intrinsic nature and subject of the bargain itself; such as no man in his senses and not under delusion would make on the one hand, and as no honest and fair man would accept on the other; which are unequitable and unconscientious bargains; and of such even the common law has taken notice …

A 3d kind of fraud is, which may be presumed from the circumstances and condition of the parties contracting: and this goes farther than the rule of law; which is, that it must be proved, not presumed; but it is wisely established in this court to prevent taking surreptitious advantage of the weakness or necessity of another: which knowingly to do is equally

---

[12] This was common Chancery practice when a common law element was present or the case was thought particularly important.
[13] Nevertheless, Lord Redesdale thought that the bargain might have been set aside without the confirmation: *Lukey v O'Donnel* (1805) 2 Sch & Lef 466, 472. See also JL Barton, 'The Enforcement of Hard Bargains' (1987) 103 *LQR* 118, 135–6.

against the conscience as to take advantage of his ignorance: a person is equally unable to judge for himself in one as the other.

A 4th kind of fraud may be collected or inferred in the consideration of this court from the nature and circumstances of the transaction, as being an imposition and deceit on the other persons not parties to the fraudulent agreement …

The last head of fraud, on which there has been relief, is that, which infects catching bargains with heirs, reversioners, or expectants, in the life of the father, &c, against which relief always extended. These have been generally mixed cases, compounded of all or several species of fraud …[14]

To a modern eye this may not seem a particularly useful classification. There are four types of fraud, but there is no single organising principle behind the list or determinate of the precise order.[15] It is a loose list based upon methods of proving fraud, with a slight decrease in the amount of proof needed in the second, third and fourth types of fraud.[16] The third type in particular speaks of a *presumption* of fraud, which goes further than at least the first two types of fraud. What is abundantly clear was that equity had moved quite a bit beyond the first type of fraud in types two, three and four. There have been attempts to organise the modern grounds of equitable intervention in contracts around this classification, notably Sheridan's Treatise on Fraud.[17] It would be of limited utility to attempt to fit the modern law under the four heads. The modern law has largely dispensed with the use of the term 'fraud' altogether.[18] If it is referred to as fraud, it is called 'constructive fraud' or 'equitable fraud'.[19] This chapter will instead explore how historically equity got to this state of the law under Lord Hardwicke. In particular, looking at the way in which the established jurisdictions over fraud originated in equity and other common law courts, and then expanded under equity, particularly in the eighteenth century. In doing this we will see the policy concerns that animated the courts and, through the changing nature of the cases, the elements of human behaviour that equity was concerned to regulate.

It has been customary to praise Lord Hardwicke's judgment as containing a particularly lucid explanation of the principles of equity in analysing intervention in contracts.[20] But for a long time this was all that there was in terms of self-analysis by a leading judge in equity.[21] Perhaps part of its appeal is that the principles are set out in a numbered list, which imparts an extra air of authority to statements of principle.[22] Most other times the Chancery explicitly reflected on its jurisdiction to

---

[14] *Chesterfield v Janssen* (1750) 2 Ves Sen 125, 155–6. Of the three reports of the case (see n 1), Vesey is closest to Lord Hardwicke's manuscript draft: see G Harris, *Life of Lord Chancellor Hardwicke* vol 2 (London, E Moxon, 1847) 425, 427–8.

[15] *Cf* P Birks, 'Equity in the Modern Law: An Exercise in Taxonomy' (1996) 26 *University of Western Australia Law Review* 1.

[16] The last head is a combination of the other types of fraud, not a type in itself.

[17] Sheridan, *Fraud in Equity* (n 11). See also W Swain 'Reshaping Contractual Unfairness in England 1670–1900' (2014) 35 *JLH* 120.

[18] *Crabb v Arun DC* [1976] Ch 179, 195.

[19] *Nocton v Lord Ashburton* [1914] AC 932, 953–4; *Armitage v Nurse* [1998] Ch 241, 250–2.

[20] Eg, W Holdsworth, *A History of English Law*, vol 12 (London, Methuen, 1938) 262; EP Hewitt & JB Richardson (eds), *White & Tudor's Leading Cases in Equity*, 9th edn, vol I (London, Sweet & Maxwell, 1928) 267.

[21] See W Kerr, *Fraud and Mistake* (London, W Maxwell, 1868) 3.

[22] Eg, *Investors Compensation Scheme Ltd v West Bromwich Building Society* [1998] 1 WLR 896, 912–13.

relieve against contracts, it would simply state that it was based on fraud and then add that fraud was undefinable. The most famous statement is by Lord Hardwicke in a letter to Lord Kames:

> as to relief against frauds, no invariable rules can be established. Fraud is infinite; and were a Court of Equity once to lay down rules, how far they would go, and no farther, in extending their relief against it, or to define strictly the species or evidence of it, the jurisdiction would be cramped, and perpetually eluded by new schemes which the fertility of man's invention would contrive.[23]

Two centuries earlier, Coke had described fraud (he used the term 'covin'[24]) as encompassing 'All covins, frauds and deceits, for the which is no remedy by the ordinary course of law.'[25] Despite a lack of formal definition, fraud was said to be the 'great subject of relief'[26] in equity. Lord Hardwicke in *Chesterfield* speaks of Chancery as having a 'jurisdiction' to relieve against every 'species' of fraud, and a rhyming couplet attributed to Sir Thomas More LC[27] said: 'Three things are helped in conscience: fraud, accident and things of confidence' [ie, trusts[28]].

The refusal to define fraud has meant that the core meaning of the juridical term has stayed firmly rooted to an intuitive conception of fraud. Samuel Johnson defined fraud as 'Deceit; cheat; trick; artifice; subtilty; stratagem'[29] and a contemporary text defines fraud similarly as 'comprehend[ing] all manner of unfair means to cheat another.'[30] We can see an element of dishonesty and moral turpitude in these ideas of fraud. Equity, however, had slowly gone further and had begun to label certain types of transactions and conduct as 'fraudulent' based on the consequences of a particular behaviour, rather than a mental state.[31] The growth of the jurisdiction over fraud can therefore only be seen by charting the growth of the equity jurisdiction and seeing the policy concerns that motivated successive Chancellors to intervene in contractual arrangements under the expanded notion of fraud. This chapter will examine:

- the antecedents to the equitable jurisdiction: the Star Chamber and Usury Laws;
- the early common instances of fraud with a strong policy element: catching bargains and marriage brocage contracts; and then
- the formal abandonment of the requirement to prove a fraudulent intention in the growth of undue influence.

---

[23] P Yorke, *The Life and Correspondence of Lord Hardwicke*, vol ii (Cambridge, CUP, 1913) 554; *Lawley v Hooper* (1745) 3 Atk 278.
[24] Coke defined covin as 'a secret assent, determined in the hearts of two or more to the defrauding and prejudice of another.' Co Litt 357 (taken from *Wimbish v Tailbois* (1550) Plow 38).
[25] 4 Co Inst 84.
[26] *Colt v Woolaston* (1723) 2 P Wms 154. See also *Earl of Oxford's Case* (1615) 1 Ch Rep 1, 6–7.
[27] 1 Roll Abr 374. See *Coco v AN Clark (Engineers) Ltd* [1969] RPC 41, 46.
[28] *Saunderson v Glass* (1742) 2 Atk 296.
[29] S Johnson, *A Dictionary of the English Language*, vol 1 (London, W Strahan, 1755) tit F, 'FRA-FRE'.
[30] *Grounds and Rudiments of Law and Equity*, 2nd ed (London, T Osborne, 1751) 89. (The reference given for this statement is Nels 439, which is well beyond the page count in Nelson's reports.).
[31] *Nocton* (n 19); J Story, *Commentaries on Equity Jurisprudence*, vol i (Boston, Hilliard, Gray, & Co, 1836) 258.

II. STAR CHAMBER

The Chancery was not the first court to take up fraud as a ground of intervention. Centuries before, local courts had exercised a jurisdiction over fraud which had both a penal and civil element.[32] With the rise of the prerogative courts, the penal and civil elements were taken up separately by the Star Chamber and the Chancery respectively, with the Star Chamber punishing fraud as one of its seven criminal jurisdictions,[33] and the Chancery setting aside fraudulent agreements.

A very common sort of fraud prosecuted in the Star Chamber was 'cozenage', where young heirs were tricked into entering into bonds promising to repay large debts. It is essentially what was known in Chancery as a 'catching bargain' with an expectant heir, whereby a lender offered to lend money on the expectancy of the heir's inheritance, to be repaid an exorbitant amount when the heir came into the estate. The Star Chamber was particularly concerned to punish this behaviour on policy grounds. In one case,[34] a broker and solicitor was sentenced to a year's imprisonment, with pillory, whipping and a fine, in the words of Egerton LK, 'for this is a great and common offence; great, because it concerns all the pillars of the land and commonwealth, noble and ignoble; common, because one Williamson has a "bedrolle" of all young gentlemen in the town'. Fraud was being punished, not just because of the harm caused to the victims, but because in general it was viewed as harmful to society. The purpose of the punishment was explicitly to discourage. Lord Burghley, pushing the creative freedom of the Star Chamber in crafting punishment, said that he

> would have those that make the plays to make a Comedy hereof, and to act it with these names, and give good Counsel to their Fathers, that when they send their sons to the Inns of Court to have one or two superintendents over them that may look over them, and certify their Friends of their manner of living, as by experience he had known to be commonly used.[35]

A notable further jurisdiction over fraud was under the Statutes of Fraudulent Conveyances.[36] The meaning of fraud, in the context of a fraudulent deed made to deprive creditors of their assets, was considered in *Twyne's case*.[37] Pierce, indebted to two creditors, made a secret deed assigning all his chattels to one of the creditors (Twyne). The deed was antedated, kept secret, and produced only when the Under-Sheriff came to enforce the writ of execution of the other debtor. Pierce continued to use the goods as his own: he shore his sheep and branded them. In labelling the deed as fraudulent, the Star Chamber identified six[38] 'badges' of fraud: 1) the generality of the gift (covering necessities too, meaning it was highly improbable that the gift was genuine); 2) the intent to defraud third parties (the creditors); 3) the secrecy; 4) that the donor continued to use the goods inconsistently with the deed; 5) that the donor kept the only copy of the deed; and 6)

---

[32] SFC Milsom, *Historical Foundations of the Common Law*, 2nd ed (London, Butterworths, 1981) 362.
[33] W Hudson, 'A Treatise of the Court of Star Chamber' in F Hargrave (ed), *Collectanea Juridica*, vol 2 (London, E & R Brooke, 1791), 95.
[34] *Attorney-General v Howe and East* (1596) Hawarde 47 (spelling modernised). References to Hawarde are to J Hawarde (WP Baildon, ed), *Les Reportes del Cases in Camera Stellata* (London, Privately Printed, 1894).
[35] *Attorney-General v Moulsworth* (1596) Hawarde 59.
[36] 13 Eliz I, c 5; 27 Eliz I, c 4.
[37] *Twyne's case* (1601) 3 Co Rep 80b; Hawarde 125; Hudson 96.
[38] The exact number of badges of fraud differ slightly in each of the reports.

that the deed contained a suspicious clause reciting that 'the gift was made honestly, truly, and bona fide, which clause itself raised suspicions'.

This enumeration of 'badges' of fraud was new to the common law, although it had roots in the civilian concept of *praesumptiones fraudis*.[39] What it shows is that early on the common law was willing to find fraud even when there was a lack of direct evidence of fraudulent intention by looking at the surrounding circumstances of the transaction. In particular, it would look at facts which are out of keeping with the ordinary way in which transactions of the sort purported to be described on paper would usually proceed.[40] In the absence of explanation for those features or badges, the court would infer fraud. Although the cases do speak of 'presuming' fraud, the term is most likely being used as a synonym for inferred, and is more a way in which a fact finder might be justified in finding fraud from limited evidence.[41]

The Star Chamber was abolished midway through the seventeenth century by the Habeas Corpus Act 1640.[42] Upon the abolition of the Star Chamber, while the common law took up some of the criminal jurisdiction developed by that Court,[43] it was the Chancery that was left as the primary court that would seek to reverse and discourage fraud. However, unlike the Star Chamber, the Chancery was not a penal court,[44] having no jurisdiction to slit noses and cut off ears.[45] But in the attempted fulfilment of a policy of discouraging fraud, the Chancery over the eighteenth century developed a willingness to presume fraud when there was a social practice it wanted to discourage. The practice of this began in the Star Chamber, and was accommodated into the civil machinery of the Chancery as best it could.

A. Usury Laws

An important piece of background to the eighteenth-century attitudes towards fraud was the general approach of the common law towards usury. The concept of usury was imported into the common law from canon law. At its most basic, usury was a practice of charging excessively high interest for the use of money, beyond what was allowed by Statute.[46] In 1545, Henry VIII set the legal interest rate at 10 per cent.[47] This was lowered to 8 per cent under James I, 6 per cent under Charles II, and finally 5 per cent under Anne.[48]

The common law and equity shared a concurrent jurisdiction over usurious bargains, and each demonstrated a rigorous approach to examining transactions for usury. What we see from the cases is that the Statutes of Usury provided a substantive

---

[39] C Willems, 'Coke, Collusion, and Conveyances: Unearthing the Roots of *Twyne's Case*' (2015) 36 *JLH* 129.
[40] See, eg, *Watt v Grove* (1805) 2 Sch & Lef 492.
[41] See the recent discussion in *Marcolongo v Chen* [2011] HCA 3, (2011) 242 CLR 546, [10]–[26].
[42] 16 Car I, c 10.
[43] *Cadogan v Kennett* (1776) 2 Cowp 432, 434.
[44] *Vyse v Foster* (1872) LR 8 Ch App 309, 333.
[45] 4 Co Inst 66.
[46] 3 Co Inst 151; 2 Bl Comm 156.
[47] 37 Hen VIII, c 9.
[48] 21 Jac I, c 17; 12 Car II, c 13; 12 Ann, c 16.

basis for a fair transaction. The courts would also examine a transaction in substance, and not just form, to see whether there was usury, and kept exceptions to the Statutes of Usury to a minimum. Thus, counsel for the plaintiff in *Chesterfield v Janssen* described the Statutes of Usury as vesting in the common law courts 'a kind of equitable jurisdiction, to consider the circumstances of the case stated as particularly as in bills in this Court'.[49] An attempt to evade the Statutes by hiding the return in another form, such as charging interest on interest, turning interest into principle upon late payment, and advancing interest, would all be found usurious.[50]

A usual device of lenders to try and evade the Statutes was to insert a contingency in the loan, and argue that the contingency meant that the transaction was not a loan for interest, but a wager on a contingency. In these transactions, the courts would assess the nature of the contingency. If the probability of the contingency occurring in reality was small, the court would hold the contract to be usurious. Thus in *Clayton's case*,[51] a loan of £30 on terms that £33 must be paid if on a certain day the obligee's son was alive and £27 otherwise was held to be usurious. The reason why a mere contingency was not sufficient was explained by Popham CJ in *Burton's case*:[52]

> if A comes to B to borrow £100, B lends it him, if he will give him for the loan of it for a year £20 if the son of A be then alive, this is usury within the statute; for if it should be out of the statute for the incertainty of the life of A, the statute would be of little effect: and by the same reason that he may add one life, he may add many; and so like a mathematical line, which is *divisibilis in semper divisibilia*.

The usual example given of a contract outside the Statutes of Usury was a bottomry bond, which was in the nature of the mortgage of a ship (where the master mortgages the bottom of the ship). There, the contingency exposed the lender to a great risk. The real possibility that the ship could sink, destroying both principal and interest, justified interest rates above the Statutes of Usury.[53]

In *Chesterfield v Janssen*, the executor argued that a contingency that the loan would be lost if the 78-year-old outlived the 30-year-old was a colourable contingency. However, it seemed that the poor health of John Spencer was the material factor in convincing the court that the contingency was more in the nature of a bottomry bond as a genuine wager.

III. CATCHING BARGAINS[54]

After the abolition of the Star Chamber, there were several high-profile cases involving catching bargains in the Chancery. They showed that the court was increasingly willing to infer fraud when transactions had recurring elements, and the exemplar of this was the catching bargain with an expectant heir. In the later seventeenth century, there

---

[49] *Chesterfield v Janssen* (1750) 2 Ves Sen 125, 127.
[50] *Broadway v Morecraft* (1729) Mos 247 and the cases cited.
[51] *Clayton's case* (1594) 5 Co Rep 70b.
[52] *Burton's case* (1590) 5 Co Rep 69a (citations omitted).
[53] *Mason v Abdy* (1689) Comb 125.
[54] The most comprehensive treatment is H Saunders, '"Corrupt Bargains and Unconscionable Practices": The Expectant Heir in The Seventeenth-Century Chancery' (PhD Thesis, Cambridge, 2019).

was an inconsistency in the approach of three Lords Chancellors in finding fraud from the circumstances of a transaction in order to set aside contract. Lord Mansfield, then William Murray, as counsel in *Chesterfield v Janssen* summed up the confusion, saying

> Lord Nottingham ... relieved against many of these contracts on particular evidence. Lord North thought he went too far. Lord Jefferies, that he did not go far enough: which is not to be wondered at; for, judging upon circumstantial evidence, they might draw different conclusions.[55]

The leading case in this period is *Ardglasse v Muschamp and Pitt*.[56] Muschamp had obtained an annuity of £300 from the Earl of Ardglasse by 'debauching' the Earl 'with drink and women'. At the time, the Earl was a young expectant heir, had forsaken his wife and lived in debauchery in London, making the bargain to supply his habits. He had no advice from counsel or his friends. The defendant, who was the Earl's 'companion to those debaucheries' had advanced only one year's purchase (£300) to the Earl. There was also a contingency that if the Earl had children the annuity would be void, but the defendant knew that the Earl was 'disabled to get children' having been informed by his surgeon. When the case first came before Lord Keeper North, he hesitated, and 'though he declared there was a foul practice, yet he doubted it might be too great a violation upon contracts, to set it aside'. But on an amended Bill, he set the transaction aside, after having been shown 'many precedents in the Lord Ellesmere's, Lord Bacon's and Lord Coventry's times ... whereby it appeared, that unconscionable bargains, which had been made with young heirs, had been set aside'. The case continued before Lord Jeffreys, when the plaintiff brought a bill against Sir George Pitt, who had obtained a similar grant using Muschamp as his agent. Pitt argued he knew nothing of the Earl's medical condition and was an innocent purchaser, but Lord Jeffreys held it to be a further instance of fraud because Pitt had knowledge of the fraud, and himself practised similar frauds on others.

Catching bargains might, like usurious transactions, also be hidden in the form of a sale of goods.[57] This type of transaction was designed to look like the defendant was enforcing payment for a sale of goods. Goods were sold to the heir on credit at a great overvalue, who was then to sell them himself (at the true lower value) to raise money. For example, in *Barney v Beak*,[58] the plaintiff, and heir in financial need, wished to raise funds to supplement the meagre allowance given to him by his father. One Stysted offered to sell him wine and told the heir he would not insist upon payment until after the father's death. They went to Beak, the defendant, who sold the plaintiff wine for £1,280, taking a bond under penalty for £2,800 to secure payment of £1,440 within 20 days after the death of the father. The wines were 'flat and dead' and could only fetch £360. Beak alleged he did not know Stysted, but there was evidence that Stysted was Beak's agent and was paid £20 for procuring the transaction. Beak pointed to

---

[55] *Chesterfield v Janssen* (1750) 2 Ves Sen 125, 139.
[56] *Ardglasse v Muschamp and Pitt* (1682) 1 Vern 76 (Lord Nottingham), (1684) 1 Vern 237 (Lord North), (1684) 2 Ch Rep 266 (Lord Jeffreys).
[57] *Barney v Tyson* (1672) 2 Vent 359; *Waller v Dale* (1676) 1 Ch Cas 276; Rep t Finch 295; *Barney v Beak* (1682) 2 Ch Cas 136; *Lamplugh v Smith* (1688) 2 Vern 77; *Witley v Price* (1688) 2 Vern 78.
[58] *Barney v Beak* (1682) 2 Ch Cas 136. As to the inconsistencies between Lords Nottingham, North and Jeffreys, see *Heathcote v Paignon* (1787) 2 Bro CC 167, 172).

the contingency as justifying the high repayment price. Lord Nottingham relieved the plaintiff; Lord North dismissed the bill on a rehearing, saying 'there was no Proof of any Fraud, but it was a hazardous bargain … It may be Stysted put in other Wines or took out of these and filled them again with bad.' But Lord Jeffreys would not make such a charitable inference: for him, the nature of the bargain implied fraud, and he restored Lord Nottingham's decree. We see Lord North's unwillingness to infer fraud from the circumstances compared with Lords Nottingham and Jeffries, who are more typical of the approach of the Chancellors.

Lord North's hesitancy seemed based on a policy of not intervening too much in the market. In *Ardglasse*, presumably without being shown the precedents, he would have refused to provide relief because it was 'too great a violation upon contracts'. On another occasion, he emphasised that necessity alone should not be sufficient to warrant the Chancery's protection; some special necessity was needed: 'What is mentioned of the plaintiff's necessities, is, as in all other cases. One that is necessitous must sell cheaper than those who are not.'[59]

In the case of the expectant heir, the weakness was usually described as a combination of prodigality of the heir and their lack of funds in their father's lifetime.[60] This may seem a rather weak necessity to the modern eye. It vanishes if the heir simply spends a little less.[61] Perhaps because this was too flimsy a basis for robust intervention, the Chancery, as indeed the Star Chamber had done before it, also repeatedly expressed an opinion that transactions *of this sort* should not be able to stand, based upon a policy of protecting great aristocratic estates.[62] Not for nothing has the Chancery been described as 'the court of the landed gentry'.[63] The effect on third parties was emphasised in this policy, particularly the effects on the parents, as well as even on the Crown. Nevertheless, the protection of the expectant heir is very much the forerunner of the necessitous consumer of financial services. The landed gentry were a major category of debtors in a much more limited financial market, and among them the expectant heir is in a particularly weak position and thus liable to form the most disadvantageous bargains. We can see the continuity from the situation of the expectant heir to the consumers we are more familiar with today in the following explanation by Bertrand Russell:[64]

> From Greek times to the present day, mankind … have been divided into debtors and creditors; debtors have disapproved of interest, and creditors have approved of it. At most times, landowners have been debtors, while men engaged in commerce have been creditors. The views of philosophers, with few exceptions, have coincided with the pecuniary interests of their class. Greek philosophers belonged to, or were employed by, the landowning class; they therefore disapproved of interest. Mediaeval philosophers were churchmen, and the property of the Church was mainly in land; they therefore saw no reason to revise Aristotle's opinion. … With the Reformation, the situation changed.

---

[59] *Batty v Lloyd* (1682) 1 Vern 141.
[60] *Nott v Hill* (1683) 1 Vern 167, 2 Ch Rep 120, 1 Eq Ca Abr 275.
[61] *Twistleton v Griffith* (1716) 1 P Wms 310.
[62] See the notes in 2 Swanst 140; C Macmillan, 'Earl of *Aylesford v Morris* (1873)' in C Mitchell and P Mitchell (eds), *Landmark Cases in Equity* (Oxford, OUP, 2012) ch 11; *Cole v Gibbons* (1734) 3 P Wms 290.
[63] D Foster, 'Construction and Execution of Trusts in Chancery, c.1660–1750' (2019) 40 *JLH* 270.
[64] B Russell, *History of Western Philosophy*, 2nd edn (London, Allen & Unwin, 1946) 209–10.

Many of the most earnest Protestants were business men, to whom lending money at interest was essential.

The reports of this period reveal that there was a relatively small circle of people involved in perpetrating these frauds (as in Lord Burghley's time a century earlier). For example, the names of Pitt,[65] Beak,[66] and Tyson[67] recur multiple times.[68] Dislike of the practice of the moneylenders and a desire to shape lending standards seems to be another focus of the Chancery's repeated intervention in catching bargains.

These additional policy factors: the protection of family estates and the need to discourage this sort of financial practice meant that even in a situation where an heir was particularly learned and experienced, such as a Proctor at Doctors' Commons, there might still be relief.[69] It is for this reason that Lord Hardwicke in *Chesterfield*, when he came to speak of catching bargains, treated it as comprised of multiple types of fraud. The richness of the circumstances in the cases, and the combination of general policy and the protection of innocent third parties meant that the catching bargain provided fertile ground on which analogies could be drawn with new situations. So protections based on only one or a few of the circumstances present were able to be analogised as fraud and the extension of Chancery's protection, like a branching tree, was able to evolve over the next century.

IV. MARRIAGE BROCAGE CONTRACTS

The fourth type of fraud identified by Lord Hardwicke was fraud on third parties not privy to the agreement. A prominent example was the Chancery's intervention in marriage brocage contracts. Marriage involved a complex contractual arrangement for the exchange of property between the bride and groom. In the usual marriage contract the bride brought a portion of assets to the groom, and the groom in turn brought to the marriage assets from which he would settle upon his wife a jointure, which would provide for her financially. The usual proportions were that the jointure be 10 per cent of the portion.[70] The negotiations would be conducted by the parties' parents or guardians. Lord Macclesfield went so far as to liken the parents to purchasers: 'the parent as a Purchaser of the Portion to his Child, by settling Lands, or bestowing a pecuniary Advancement upon him on his Marriage ...'.[71] The Chancery actively sought to prevent any private transaction that might deceive the parents in their role in settling the marriage. Thus, any fraudulent design involving one of the parties to the marriage or both might also deceive the families involved in

---

[65] *Berney v Pitt* (1680) 2 Swanst 142n; *Ardglasse v Muschamp and Pitt* (1684) 1 Vern 237.
[66] *Berney v Pitt* (1680) 2 Swanst 142n; *Barney v Beak* (1682) 2 Ch Cas 136; *Wiseman v Beake* (1690) 2 Vern 121.
[67] *Barney v Tyson* (1672) 2 Vent 359; *Berney v Pitt* (1680) 2 Swanst 142n.
[68] In *Ardglasse v Muschamp and Pitt* (1684) 1 Vern 237, Lord Jeffreys is reported as rejecting the idea that Pitt did not know Muschamp, saying he had seen Mr Pitt involved in other unreasonable bargains and that 'it was not to be believed that Mr Pitt would make this bargain without enquiry and knowledge of the condition of the man he dealt with'.
[69] *Wiseman v Beake* (1690) 2 Vern 121.
[70] See *Roberts v Roberts* (1730) 3 P Wms 66.
[71] *Turton v Benson* (1718) 2 Vern 764, 1 P Wms 496.

the marriage contract, and for that reason be a fraud on parties other than the bride and groom.[72] Similarly, contracts for the repurchase of marriage portions after the marriage had taken place were set aside.[73] The reasoning was again a fraud on the parents, who might be deceived into giving property they might not have given.

Apart from the effect on third parties, the Chancellors emphasised general policy grounds of protecting marriage in setting aside these agreements. It was said in the House of Lords that

> Marriages ought to be procured and promoted by the Mediation of Friends and Relations, and not of Hirelings. That not vacating such Bonds, when questioned in a Court of Equity, would be of Evil Example to Executors, Trustees, Guardians, Servants, and other People having the Care of Children.[74]

Thus, it was necessary that contracts of this sort be discouraged by routinely setting them aside when they produced certain effects. In this sort of intervention, the focus was on the *effects* of the contract rather than any fraudulent intention of the parties in making it.

V. PRESUMING FRAUD AND THE ORIGINS OF UNDUE INFLUENCE

The common law rule regarding proof of fraud was that fraud was never to be presumed.[75] The examples of equitable intervention show that equity was prepared to go quite far in finding fraud. But nevertheless there were authorities as late as 1723 that stated that the rule was good in equity as well.[76] Yet in the third ground of fraud laid down in *Chesterfield v Jannsen*,[77] Lord Hardwicke expressly said that equity went further than the law in presuming fraud.[78] In a short period of time, equity suddenly went quite far in developing a new category of fraud, which became the doctrine of undue influence.

There are two early cases involving guardians where the Chancery, reasoning by analogy with the policy behind marriage brocage contracts and expectant heirs, sought to set aside transactions where a guardian had taken advantage of a ward. In *Hamilton v Mohun*,[79] the mother and guardian of the bride insisted on a release in the mother's favour in the marriage articles. Lord Cowper thought that there was no surprise, but that this was a misuse of the 'power' the mother had over the daughter to secure an advantage for the mother: 'to tolerate such an agreement, would be paving a way to guardians to sell infants under their wardship'. The policy of protecting the institutions of marriage and the family and the process of negotiating marriage settlements have been used to justify protecting a ward or child from a guardian or parent, even in the absence of actual fraud.

In *Osmond v Fitzroy*,[80] a servant hired for the care of a young Lord had prevailed on the Lord (aged 27) to make a bond for £1,000 in the servant's favour.

---

[72] This type of transaction was more in the nature of a 'covin' as defined by Coke. See n 24 above.
[73] *Redman v Redman* (1685) 1 Vern 348; *Gale v Lindo* (1687) 1 Vern 475; *Kemp v Coleman* (1707) 1 Salk 156.
[74] *Hall v Potter* (1695) 2 P Wms 392n; Show 76.
[75] See M McNair, *The Law of Proof in Early Modern Equity* (Berlin, Duncker & Humblot, 1999) 273–5.
[76] *Montague v Bath* (1693) 3 Ch Cas 55; *Trenchard v Wanley* (1723) 2 P Wms 166; McNair, ibid 274–5.
[77] Above n 14
[78] A forerunner to this opinion appeared already in *Bosanquet v Dashwood* (1734) Forr 38.
[79] *Hamilton v Mohun* (1710) 1 P Wms 118.
[80] *Osmond v Fitzroy* (1731) 3 P Wms 129.

One of the reasons for setting the bond aside was that the servant was placed in a position of trust and that

> A breach of trust is of itself evidence of fraud, nay, of the greatest fraud: because a man, however careful otherwise, is apt to be off his guard when dealing with one in whom he reposes a confidence.

We can see here that the relationship is characterised as a position of trust, and that the consequences of breaching trust make the transaction fraudulent. By this reasoning, the intention to defraud becomes unnecessary.

An important case was *Proof v Hines*,[81] decided in the brief Chancellorship of Lord Talbot. The plaintiff, a poor and illiterate man, had become entitled through his wife to an estate, and he asked the defendant and his wife to assist in getting proofs of his pedigree to establish his title. The defendant and his wife claimed this could not be done without money, and since the plaintiff had no other means, he borrowed from the defendant and executed a bond for £1,000. Essentially, we have a poor customer purchasing professional services and giving a highly unusual payment. In his judgment, Lord Talbot LC drew an analogy with what a court would do if the same had been done by an attorney:

> Had an Attorney, pending the Suit, taken such a Bond as this upon the same Transaction, Would not the Court set it aside? or would it suffer to stand any farther than as a Security for what was justly and legally due? The Rule, *That a Mischief is rather to be suffered than a general Inconvenience*, does not at all affect this Case: For it would be a much greater Inconvenience to leave Men under Difficulties and Distresses open to all the Oppression that other People may please to make them undergo.

The analogy with attorneys is significant. The practice at both law and equity was for an attorney's bill to be taxed in order to determine whether the attorney had charged proper amounts, and the attorney could not recover beyond the just amount.[82] There was a conceptual fair value and method of taking payment that the court regularly enforced. This provided a substantive yardstick to determine when advantage was taken, similar to the function of the legal rate of interest. The willingness to draw this analogy showed that the court was willing to extend the protection given to a client of an attorney to others in a similar relationship. We see also an explicit recognition that it would be good policy to achieve a general outcome, and any need to find a fraudulent intention is deemphasised.

VI. WALMESLEY V BOOTH

From these two promising threads – cases on guardians and the analogy with attorneys in *Proof v Hines* – Lord Hardwicke took the definitive step in abandoning any requirement of proof of a fraudulent intention in the case of *Walmesley v Booth*.[83] This case concerned a thoroughly disreputable man called Japhet Crook, a notorious

---
[81] *Proof v Hines* (1735) Forr 111.
[82] See *Drapers Co v David* (1742) 2 Atk 295.
[83] *Walmesley v Booth* (1739–1741) 2 Atk 25.

confidence trickster who operated under the pseudonym 'Sir Peter Stranger', and was the subject of a tale, well-known in its time, called *The Unparallel'd Impostor: or, the whole life, artifices and forgeries of Japhet Crook, alias Sir Peter Stranger, Bart with all proceedings against him*.[84] In 1731 he was convicted of forgery in the King's Bench, sentenced to the pillory, the nose slit, ears cut off. Alexander Pope referred to this in his *Epistle to Bathurst*. Pope introduces a stanza 'What Riches give us, let us first enquire'. A few lines later he says: 'What can they give? To dying Hopkins, heirs? To Chartres, vigour? Japhet, nose and ears?'[85] Crook was also personally known to Lord Hardwicke, who was counsel in a case where Crook had forged a will.[86]

In *Walmesley v Booth*, Crook had been prosecuted for perjury and forgery in the King's Bench. Crook employed an attorney, Booth, to find him two people willing to provide surety for bail. During that time, Booth also drew up Crook's will, under which Crook, having promised to give him £1,000, directed a legacy of £1,000 to Booth. Booth also requested that Crook give him a bond for £1,000 to secure the legacy. Later, Crook revoked the will, appointed the plaintiff as executrix, and made her a residuary legatee to £17,000. The executrix sought to be relieved against the bond as obtained by fraud and imposition.

Lord Hardwicke, familiar with Japhet Crook's infamy, initially dismissed the bill. Thought he noted that the court will 'dislike the first appearance' of this type of bond, he insisted that there must be some evidence or circumstances of fraud or imposition to set it aside. The plaintiff's counsel, William Murray, submitted that as Booth was an attorney, he could not entitle himself to the bond. Lord Hardwicke responded, saying 'To be sure it is extremely wrong in an attorney to take bonds for services; but if a client, with his eyes open, will give such a bond, it would be going too far to say such a bond is absolutely void.' He dismissed a comparison with expectant heirs, saying

> for there the court presumes weakness in the person, and upon that consideration relieves; but there is no pretence for it here, for Japhet Crook was *more likely to impose, than to be imposed upon* ... and yet if there had been the slightest evidence of imposition upon Crook, I should make no scruple of relieving against this bond.[87]

Lord Hardwicke essentially dismissed the bill for lack of evidence of actual imposition, whilst conceding that it was an undesirable practice for an attorney to engage in.

Two years passed. Then, remarkably, on the application of Murray, Lord Hardwicke agreed to rehear the case and completely reversed his earlier opinion. He emphasised that Booth was an attorney, subject to rules imposed by the court regulating relations with a client, and that in general 'there is a strong alliance between an attorney and his client, and a great obligation upon the attorney to take care of his client's interest'.[88] He then emphasised Crook's distress from being under the possibility of imprisonment if he could not obtain bail, adding that it was irrelevant

---

[84] J Moore, *The Unparallel'd Impostor* (London, J Wilford, 1731).
[85] Alexander Pope, *Of the Use of Riches, An Epistle to the Right Honorable Allen, Lord Bathurst* (London, J Wright, 1732) 5.
[86] *Hawkins v Crook* (1729) 2 P Wms 556. See 2 Atk 21.
[87] *Walmesley v Booth* (1739) 2 Atk 25, 26 (emphasis in original).
[88] ibid, 27.

whether that distress was brought about by Crook himself. He also drew analogy with catching bargains, stating that there

> the court relieves upon general principles of mischief to the publick, *without requiring particular evidence of actual imposition upon them*, as they are cases of general concern; they also give relief, because the circumstances and situation of the young persons at the time of the agreement make them extremely liable to impositions.[89]

In contrast to his earlier judgment, Lord Hardwicke then treated Crook's infamy in a very different manner:

> It has been said that Japhet Crook was a very cunning fellow, and a very great knave, and I believe it to be true ; but the court must not consider the particular circumstances of the man, *but the case in general* ... for a person may be prosecuted for these very crimes, and yet be innocent; and it would be very mischievous if there was any encouragement given to an undue advantage taken of another under such circumstances.[90]

We see here a clear concern to prevent certain types of transactions from occurring, regardless of whether or not there was fraud. The fact that Crook was in fact himself a knave meant the policy aspect of the case had to carry the outcome. Lord Hardwicke then stated a general principle:

> What is the general rule the court goes upon? why the person's being in such circumstances that any body might have taken advantage of him, and here the court will not allow A any more than B to get an illegal benefit to himself.[91]

A comparison between Lord Hardwicke's first and second judgments show the magnitude of the achievement in this case. The prophylactic policy elements, latent in the cases on catching bargains and marriage brocage contracts, and surfacing earlier in the eighteenth century, were taken to their logical conclusion. Any lingering requirements of intention or actual fraud were discarded, and the principle was framed generally and not limited to solicitors.

The advance made by *Walmesley v Booth* was swiftly consolidated shortly after in cases involving solicitors,[92] guardians,[93] and then extended to 'common sailors',[94] describing their weakness as follows:

> There cannot be a more useful set of men to the public, nor a more unthinking sort of people, than common sailors, who, as soon as ever they get on shore, for the sale of a little immediate pleasure are willing to part with their right to any thing in expectation, for a very little in possession.

By this stage the law of undue influence was ready to be set free from the original jurisdictional notion of 'fraud' from which it had been birthed by a process of analogical reasoning. The term 'fraud' was no longer one of utility, and the statement that

---

[89] ibid, 28–9 (emphasis added).
[90] ibid, 29 (emphasis added).
[91] ibid, 29.
[92] *Saunderson v Glass* (1742) 2 Atk 296.
[93] *Pierce v Waring* (1745) 1 P Wms 120n, 1 Ves Sen 379; *Cray v Mansfield* (1749) 1 Ves Sen 379 (but cf 2 Ves Sen 259); *Hylton v Hylton* (1754) 2 Ves Sen 547.
[94] *Baldwin v Rochford* (1748) 1Wils KB 229.

fraud was presumed showed that actual fraud was in fact unnecessary. In place of a type of conduct was an explicit policy of protecting certain types of people who were involved in disadvantageous contracts.

VII. CONCLUSION

By the time Lord Hardwicke spoke in *Chesterfield v Janssen*, the Chancery had stretched the concept of fraud very far indeed, to the point that it had probably outlived its usefulness. It served only as a term that put beyond doubt the Chancery's jurisdiction. But in terms of the basis of intervention in contracts, the Chancery had long been moving towards establishing doctrines based on a policy of protecting certain institutions (notably in this period marriage and family structures) and protecting certain persons with weakness from being taken advantage of by those in positions of strength or trust. The characteristics that we see in the modern consumer that demand protection by the Chancery are present in the expectant heir, the client of the attorney and the ward of a guardian or parent.

3

Gardiner v Gray

DAVID IBBETSON

GARDINER V GRAY[1] is not a landmark case in the same way that most of the cases in this volume are: an appellate decision, or at least a decision of a senior court, settling a controverted and important point of law. On the contrary, it is a first-instance decision, reaching what may seem to us to be an obvious result without the citation of any authority. Nor is it a case on consumer law: the claimant, if I identify him correctly, was a textile magnate, and the contract on which the action was brought was for goods clearly intended to be used in the course of business.[2] But it is none the less a landmark in the development of consumer law, the source of the implied warranty of merchantability in the modern law, an important exception to the rule of *caveat emptor* and a significant feature of consumer protection.

I. THE DECISION

Changes in the practice of law reporting shed light on the way in which cases like *Gardiner v Gray* gained their significance. Around the end of the eighteenth century there began to appear in England reports of first instance cases at common law: those of Peake (1790-94, with additions to 1812), Espinasse (1793-1810), Campbell (1807-16), Holt (1815-17), and so on into the nineteenth century.[3] These were not always reliable; those of Espinasse in particular got a very bad reputation,[4] but it is not clear that the other sets were of significantly better quality.[5] The commercial focus of these *nisi prius* reports is clear: Campbell noted that his reports were predominantly of such cases, and Oldham's study of the *nisi prius* reports of this period pointed to 46 per cent of reported cases being contractual.[6]

These cases were generally decided very quickly, Oldham estimates in perhaps as little as 15 minutes on average, though there would no doubt have been some

---

[1] *Gardiner* v *Gray* (1815) 4 Camp 144.
[2] See below.
[3] J Oldham, 'Law-Making at Nisi Prius in the Early 1800s' (2004) 24 *Journal of Legal History* 221.
[4] Memorably in *Small v Nairne* (1849) 13 QB 840, 844, per Lord Denman.
[5] JW Wallace, *The Reporters*, 4th edn (Boston 1882), 541–43.
[6] Hardcastle, *Life of John, Lord Campbell*, 1.216 (from his autobiography); Oldham (n 3) 229.

variation.⁷ The brevity of hearings surely reflects and explains the paucity of authorities cited: in fewer than 10 per cent of the cases in Campbell's fourth volume, the volume containing *Gardiner v Gray*, is there any citation of authority. This was not simply a feature of reporting practice, for Lord Ellenborough's trial notes show a similarly low level of citations.⁸ It is on the face of it surprising that cases decided so quickly, largely without the citation of authority, should have any influence at all on the law, but part of the explanation may lie in the use of special juries consisting substantially of merchants.⁹ To the extent that this is so, the reported decisions can be seen as crystallising merchants' practices and expectations into legal rules. *Gardiner v Gray* is probably such a case.

The facts of the case, as they appear from Campbell's report, can be easily stated. A sample of waste silk, then in transit from continental Europe, was shown to the plaintiff's agent. The contract was then made for the plaintiff to purchase twelve bags, and what is described as the sale note was drawn up. Significantly, the note made no reference to the sample. The silk duly arrived in London and was transported to the plaintiff[10] in Manchester where it was discovered that it was not of a good enough quality for the plaintiff's purposes. Witnesses described it as unfit for the purposes of waste silk. The plaintiff sued the defendant in assumpsit for breach of contract.

The judgment in the case was given by Lord Ellenborough. His primary finding was that this could not be a sale by sample. The written sale note, taken to embody the contract, made no reference to the sample and the antecedent oral representation, if there was any, could neither add to nor subtract from the written terms. However, he said, where there was a sale by description, as there was here, the intention of the parties must have been that the goods were of saleable quality, according to the description in the contract.

> The intention of both parties must be taken to be, that it shall be saleable in the market under the denomination mentioned in the contract between them. The purchaser cannot be supposed to buy goods to lay them on a dunghill.¹¹

Here the jury found that the goods were not of a quality which could reasonably be marketed as waste silk, and judgment was accordingly given for the plaintiff.

The first of these findings was hardly surprising. It was well established by the nineteenth century that parol evidence could not be admitted in the face of a document, to qualify the effect of the document, at least if there was no ambiguity.¹² This was yet more obvious in a case like *Gardiner v Gray*, if it involved a sale of goods for more than £10, which was required to be evidenced in writing by section 17 of the Statute of Frauds. It followed that this could not be analysed as a sale by sample, there being no reference to the sample in the written sale note. It might perhaps have been

---

⁷ Oldham (n 3) 245, fn 46.
⁸ *Cf* Oldham (n 3) 227, citing Lord Brougham.
⁹ Oldham (n 3) 228; for background, see J Oldham, 'Special Juries in England: Nineteenth-Century Usage and Reform' (1988) 8 *Journal of Legal History* 148.
¹⁰ The report reads 'defendant', but it is altogether more likely that it should read 'plaintiff'. The Manchester trade directories reveal no textile merchant called Gray, whereas (as appears below) there was a textile manufacturer called Gardner. The emendation is made silently in Addison, *Contract* (1847) 222.
¹¹ At [145].
¹² *Meres v Ansell* (1771) 3 Wils KB 275.

different if the plaintiff had sued in tort, by an action on the case for deceit, though here the purchaser would have had to show fraud by the seller.[13]

The second point was perhaps more troubling. Unfortunately, I have not been able to discover any note of it in Lord Ellenborough's notebooks – I suspect it may have been in a volume that is lost – and Campbell's report is silent on the arguments of counsel, so we can only guess where their focus was. In *Parkinson v Lee*,[14] the King's Bench had held that in a sale by sample of hops there was no implied warranty of merchantability; hence, when it turned out that they had been contaminated by water, unknown to either buyer or seller and without the fault of either, so that they started to rot, no action lay by the buyer for breach of warranty. It is not easy to see what the law had been before *Parkinson v Lee*.[15] Richard Wooddeson, Vinerian Professor in Oxford, said in 1777 that the basic rule had formerly been *caveat emptor*, but by his time this had been replaced by a 'more reasonable' rule that where a fair price was paid there was an implied warranty that the goods were sound.[16] However, according to Grose J in *Parkinson*, Lord Mansfield had found this to be too loose a rule, saying that there needed to be an express warranty or actual fraud in the seller.[17] *Parkinson* would have been distinguishable in *Gardiner v Gray* on the grounds that the latter case was not a sale by sample, but Mansfield's underlying position, as stated by Grose J, would still have favoured the defendant: there would have been no liability in the absence of express warranty or fraud. Lord Ellenborough did not directly address the point of implied warranties, preferring to say that the goods simply did not match the description of what had been sold.[18] Clearly it could not be argued that it had to be of some particular quality or fineness – that would require an express term – but it could not have been difficult to infer that something described as 'waste silk' was meant to be saleable as 'waste silk'. A similar approach to that of Lord Ellenborough in *Gardiner v Gray* was taken in the same year in *Laing v Fidgeon*:[19] 'it resulted from the whole transaction that the article was to be merchantable'.

II. THE FACTS OF THE CASE

Landmark cases typically fix a point of law of general application; but the case itself arises against the background of social, economic and technical conditions and a particular factual matrix. We are given so little detail of *Gardiner v Gray* – and I have found no other contemporary accounts or discussion of it – that some guesswork on

---

[13] *Pickering v Dowson* (1813) 4 Taunt 779 (antecedent representation); *Meyer v Everth* (1814) 4 Camp 22, per Lord Ellenborough CJ (sample).
[14] *Parkinson v Lee* (1802) 2 East 314.
[15] J Oldham, *The Mansfield Manuscripts*, 232–44.
[16] R Wooddeson, *Systematical View of the Laws of England* (1792), 415 (based on lectures of 1777). The basic position of *caveat emptor* was stated by Coke, Co Litt 102a.
[17] 2 East 314, 322. This may have been an oblique reference to *Stuart v Wilkins* (1778) 1 Doug KB 18, though it was not the point of the case.
[18] See too *Jones v Bowden* (1813) 4 Taunt 847, a sale by auction of pimento powder without disclosing that it had been sea-damaged and repacked (which would reduce its value). The case was pleaded as one of fraud, and there was plentiful evidence that the seller knew of the damage and did not disclose it, justifying the jury's verdict for the buyer. However, the judgments get close to saying that the unqualified description as 'pimento' amounted to an assertion that it had not been water-damaged or repacked.
[19] *Laing v Fidgeon* (1815) 6 Taunt 108.

the basis of meagre clues is inevitable. Apart from the names of the parties, the only clues which might help us to penetrate further into the case are that it involved a sale of waste silk sent to Manchester.

I have not been able to identify the seller, Gray; he was probably a middleman of some sort, and may have traded in different commodities. The most plausible candidate for the buyer is Robert Gardner, the only person with a similar name listed in the early nineteenth-century trade directories of Manchester.[20] He was to become a major entrepreneur, with a strong focus on the textile industry, said in 1847, when he had serious cash-flow difficulties, to have assets in real estate of £300,000 or £400,000.[21] He is regarded by some as the progenitor of the Tootal company, named after Edward Tootal, who joined the business in 1842, though it is not at all clear on what evidence this is based.[22] Whether or not his connection with Tootal at this time is made out, by 1815 he was in partnership, it seems, trading as Gardner and Dawson.[23]

The second clue to understanding the case is that it was a sale of silk waste. What was left after the pure thread of the silkworm cocoon had been unravelled, it had traditionally been seen as largely useless, but technological developments from the late eighteenth century onwards had meant that it could be spun and woven and was hence usable.[24] Official figures for its importation show the rapidity of this growth in the second and third decades of the nineteenth century:[25]

Year	Weight (pounds)
1814	27,208
1815	30,457
1816	3,668
1817	48,777
1818	98,604
1819	71,331
1820	67,905
1821	81,298
1822	117,481
1823	58,997
1824	83,665
1825	261,448

[20] ecclesoldroad.uk/person/robert-gardner/. There is a brief obituary in the *Manchester Times*, 30 June 1866. See, eg, *Pigot & Dean's New Directory of Manchester and Salford*, 1821–22, 57.

[21] *Manchester Courier and Lancaster General Advertiser*, 30 October 1847 (assets of £300,000, debts of £100,000); *Cambridge Independent Press*, 30 October 1847 (and other newspapers) (assets of £400,000); *Morning Post*, 28 October 1847; *Lloyds Illustrated Newspaper*, 31 October 1847. After his death, his personal estate was sworn as 'below £350,000'): *Standard*, 30 July 1866.

[22] /www.tootal.co.uk/blog/tootal-scarves-a-brief-history/. Doubt is cast on this by D Tracey, *Silk and Muslin: The Story of Tootal Broadhurst Lee & Co* (typescript in Manchester University Library), suggesting (convincingly in my view) that the founder was Henry Tootal. The Tootal company started to produce silk goods in 1816: J Wheeler, *Manchester, its Political, Social and Commercial History* (Manchester, 1836) 219.

[23] *Manchester Mercury*, 9 May 1815.

[24] F Warner, *The Silk Industry of the United Kingdom, Its Origin and Development* (London, 1921) ch 33, esp 402–03.

[25] *Select Committee on the Silk Trade* (House of Commons, 1832), 10. The figures take no account of domestically produced silk waste.

Silk waste, spun into yarn, was not of a good enough quality to make fine garments for the luxury market, but it was good enough for relatively inexpensive items of haberdashery. As one Coventry silk merchant deposed in 1832, 'Previous to [1820] the bulk of the silks were sold only to persons moving in the better spheres of life: now the lowest class of person wear them ....'[26] Manchester was a major city for the manufacture of these 'inferior' items, commonly of silk mixed with cotton or worsted,[27] traceable back to the first decade of the century.[28] It is a plausible hypothesis, though admittedly a speculative one, that Gardner had seen a business opportunity, and contracted to buy waste silk only to discover that it was not fit for purpose.

The economics of trade in silk waste may help to understand *Gardiner v Gray*. The product came in many forms, of variable quality within each form;[29] prices varied, therefore, as well as being subject to adventitious fluctuations.[30] Given this, the sale note's description merely as 'waste silk', with no reference to its quality or to the sample shown to the purchaser's agent, looks curious. One suspects that it was intended to be a sale by sample, the quality of the sample fixing the price: 10s 6d per pound seems high, a price of 5s per pound being referred to in 1793, 2s 6d or 2s 10d to 3s 6d per pound in 1832[31] but given the possible fluctuation in prices caused by the Napoleonic War we should probably not read too much into that.[32] A second factor, which may have had a part to play, is that in the early nineteenth century the import duty on waste silk was 4s per pound (3s 9d on that imported from British India) until 1824 when it was reduced to 3d, further reduced to 1d in 1826.[33] A verdict that what had been sold as waste silk could not properly be so described might have meant that the 4s per pound duty could be avoided, which would not have been the case if the issue had only been on the quality of the silk.

III. THE RULES IN THE NINETEENTH CENTURY[34]

Bedevilling the whole question of implied warranties of quality was the sale of horses.[35] Almost a century ago Karl Llewellyn wrote that the history of this area of

---

[26] *Select Committee on Silk Trade*, 423 (Mr R Baggalay).
[27] ibid, 22, 419.
[28] For the Manchester silk trade, see Warner (n 24) 149–69; *Select Committee on Silk Trade*, 152–76 (Mr V Royle), 481 (Mr J Ballance), 614–19 (Mr H Tootal), 813 (Mr D Rowbotham).
[29] H Rayner, *Silk Throwing and Waste Silk Spinning* (London, 1903) 36–44; *Select Committee on Silk Trade*, 191.
[30] Warner (n 24) 424–26.
[31] ibid 425; *Select Committee on Silk Trade*, 162, 170, 617.
[32] Italy was the dominant source of silk imports, and the market price of spun silk in Italy rose by 40 to 50% between 1793 and 1815: A De Maddalena, *Prezzi e Mercedi a Milano dal 1701 al 1860* (Milan, 1974) 416, 417.
[33] *Select Committee on Silk Trade*, 11.
[34] K Llewellyn, 'Warranty of Quality and Society' (1936) 36 *Columbia Law Review*; S J Stoljar, 'Conditions, Warranties and Descriptions of Quality in Sale of Goods' (1952) 15 *MLR* 425; P Mitchell, 'The Development of Quality Obligations in the Sale of Goods' (2001) 117 *LQR* 645; M Lobban, *Oxford History of the Laws of England, vol. XII* (Oxford, OUP, 2010) 480–85.
[35] W Swain, 'Horse Sales: the Problem of Consumer Contracts from a Historical Perspective', in J Devenney and M Kenny (eds), *European Consumer Protection* (Cambridge, CUP, 2012) 282.

the law could be divided into horse and non-horse cases, with the non-horse, commercial, cases only really emerging in the early nineteenth century.³⁶ Lord Mansfield's trial notes largely bear out the predominance of horse cases.³⁷ Why this should be so does not matter for present purposes – it may be that merchants preferred to go to merchant courts or arbitration – but as the practice and rule in horse sales was to require an express warranty of soundness, in the absence of which actual fraud had to be proved,³⁸ there may have been something of a gravitational pull from these cases to commercial contracts. The centrality of horse sales is well brought out in Selwyn's *Nisi Prius*, where *Parkinson v Lee* (and in later editions the subsequent non-horse cases too) was dealt with in a lengthy footnote in the section on horse sales.³⁹ *Gardiner v Gray* marks the beginning of the divergence between horse and non-horse cases.⁴⁰ In the following dozen years the focus of the rule was sharpened.

Fundamental to *Gardiner v Gray* was that the buyer had had no opportunity to inspect the silk; it was this that justified the departure from *caveat emptor*. The treatment of the case in the early treatises stressed this,⁴¹ as did the cases.

In *Yeats v Pim*⁴² the defendant had sold to the plaintiff 50 bales of 'prime singed bacon'. Two months after the bacon had been delivered the buyer gave notice to the seller that the bacon was tainted and hence not in accordance with the contract. It was argued that it was a custom of the trade that such merchandise should be examined as soon as possible after delivery and notice of inadequacy be given then. At nisi prius, Heath J rejected this argument: 'the usage could not be set up to countervail the warranty'. In banc, Gibbs CJ took the same approach as Lord Ellenborough had done: 'Where a party undertakes that he will supply goods of a certain description, he must execute his engagement accordingly.'⁴³ So far as can be seen from the report, there had been no allegation of a warranty, simply a failure to match the description; but it was all too easy to slide into the language of warranty. Lord Ellenborough similarly slipped into the language of warranty in *Bluett v Osborne* in the same year: 'A person who sells impliedly warrants that the thing sold shall answer the purpose for which it is sold.'⁴⁴

The separation between the requirement that the goods sold match the description in the contract and the requirement that they be fit for purpose seems to be in place by 1825. In *Gray v Cox*⁴⁵ copper was sold for sheathing a ship, but after one

---

³⁶ Llewellyn (n 34) 711, fn 39.
³⁷ Oldham (n 15) 232.
³⁸ Mitchell (n 34) 647–50.
³⁹ W Selwyn, *Abridgment of the Law of Nisi Prius* (London, 1806) 584–85.
⁴⁰ Mitchell n 34.
⁴¹ G Long, *Treatise on the Law relative to Sales of Personal Property* (London, 1821) 123, 121; S Comyns, *Law of Contracts and Promises*, 2nd edn (London, 1824), 113. Professor Mitchell suggests that it was a re-interpretation of the case to say that there was no opportunity to inspect the goods, on the assumption that they had actually been landed when the contract was made (Mitchell (n 34) 653); but the better reading of the report is that the goods were still in transit at the time.
⁴² *Yeats v Pim* (1816) 2 Marsh 141.
⁴³ (1816) 2 Marsh 141, 143.
⁴⁴ *Bluett v Osborne* (1816) 1 Stark 384. This was an action by the seller for the price of a bowsprit which turned out to be defective. The very short judgment is almost incoherent, and may be misreported. See too *Okell v Smith* (1815) 1 Stark 107, also badly reported, where Bayley J makes the same point.
⁴⁵ *Gray v Cox* 1 C & P 184 (nisi prius), 4 B & C 108, 6 D & R 200.

voyage to the West Indies it was badly corroded and had to be replaced. An action of assumpsit was brought. According to one report of the arguments for the plaintiff in banc, there were two distinct reasons why he should recover: non-conformity with the contractual description, and breach of a warranty that they be fit for purpose.[46] The other report of the argument agrees with this in substance, though is rather different in structure.[47] So far as the warranty was concerned, the real question was whether it arose only on a sale by description, and was hence a warranty that the goods were fit for their ordinary purposes, or whether there was also an implied warranty that they be fit for a special purpose if the seller was aware of the purpose for which they were being bought. Abbott CJ, who had been the trial judge, thought that the implied warranty did arise in the latter situation, but observed that his fellow judges disagreed. In the event, though, since no warranty of fitness for a special purpose had been pleaded the point did not have to be resolved.

Four years later, the Common Pleas in *Jones v Bright* followed the approach of Abbott CJ in recognising the implied warranty of fitness for purpose when the seller was aware of the purpose for which the goods were bought.[48] The three versions of the report treat the arguments very differently, the result of inevitably heavy editing;[49] their substance can be reconstructed by careful comparison of the different texts. There are, too, major variations between the 'unofficial' versions of the judgment and the 'authorised' report.[50] Like *Gray v Cox*, the case involved the sale of copper sheets for sheathing a ship, which turned out to be corroded after a single voyage, this time to Sierra Leone. Unlike *Gray v Cox*, the defendants were not merely vendors but had also (before the contract of sale) manufactured the sheets. Serjeants Wilde and Russell seemingly argued that since they were the manufacturers, a knowledge of its qualities must be implied;[51] more clearly, the fact that the sheets were manufactured goods meant that they could be distinguished from the horse cases.[52] Serjeant Ludlow countered the first of these arguments by showing that the defendants were being sued solely as vendors, not as manufacturers,[53] and the second he countered by ignoring it, simply relying on the horse cases.[54] The second point, and probably the most important one, whether there was an implied warranty of fitness for purpose when the buyer's purpose was known, came down to a pure matter of policy: in favour of liability, 'good policy requires that the seller should be responsible where he sells an article for a specific use;'[55] against liability, it would place too heavy a burden on

---

[46] 4 B & C 108, 110.
[47] 6 D & R 200, 202–05. The transition from the argument of non-conformity to that of breach of warranty is clear at 203 ('Bur, independently of this ground of action …').
[48] *Jones v Bright* (1829) 5 Bing 533, 3 Moo & P 155, 7 LJCP 213, 1 Dan & L 304.
[49] WTS Daniel, *History and Origin of the Law Reports* (London, 1884), 165–67.
[50] Judges might sometimes correct reporters' versions of their judgment, perhaps favouring the so-called authorised reporters: Daniel, *Law Reports*, 66, 102.
[51] 3 Moo & P 161, 5 Bing 538; it was on this basis that *Parkinson v Lee* was distinguishable, for there the vendors were not the growers of the hops: 3 Moo & P 165, 5 Bing 538, 7 LJCP 216.
[52] 3 Moo & P 161, 5 Bing 536 (muted at 7 LJCP 215). *Laing v Fidgeon* (1815) 6 Taunt 108 (sale of saddles) was interpreted as importing a warranty of merchantability into sales of manufactured goods, but the reported judgment does not support this interpretation.
[53] 3 Moo & P 166–67, 5 Bing 539, 7 LJCP 216.
[54] 3 Moo & P 167–69, 7 LJCP 216-217 (compressed almost to extinction in 5 Bing 540).
[55] 5 Bing 535.

sellers.⁵⁶ A third distinction from *Gray v Cox* was that the action was framed in deceit rather than assumpsit. Here, it was said by Ludlow, a uniform series of decisions showed there had to be actual deceit or an express warranty.⁵⁷ Wilde and Russell said little on this; they did not deny that the alleged warranty was implied,⁵⁸ but seemed to be suggesting that the knowledge imputed to the defendant as manufacturer was enough to prove the deceit.⁵⁹

In what we take to be the original form of his judgment, evidenced by Moore and Payne's report and supported by those of Danson and Lloyd and in the Law Journal, Best CJ elided the first two of the arguments. The case could be distinguished from the horse cases since it involved manufactured goods, and the policy arguments were strongly in the buyer's favour because of the propensity of manufacturers to produce shoddy goods with a view to maximising profits. In Bingham's polished version the focus of manufactured goods has all but disappeared,⁶⁰ and the lengthy peroration on the evils of manufacturers has been removed. The focus of the judgment has changed, shifting to the bare point that a sale for a particular purpose imports a warranty of fitness for that purpose, applicable equally to the sale of horses and the sale of manufactured goods. Whether the implication of the warranty was a matter of law or of fact is not wholly clear, but the thrust of the judgment on the need to protect buyers suggests that for Best CJ it was a matter of law. The other three judges dealt with the question of warranty very much as a question of fact. Park J grounded it on the parties' course of dealing; Burrough J said that the evidence showed it was an express warranty; for Gaselee J it did not matter, for the declaration referred simply to a warranty.

Jones v Bright marks a step of the rule in *Gardiner v Gray* towards consumer law. First, though as a matter of pleading all that was alleged was a warranty without further qualification, the slant of the judgment of Best CJ was very much towards its being implied as a matter of law. Second, most obvious in the original versions of the judgments, there was a leaning towards the manufacturer-vendor, effectively a professional, rather than a simple vendor. This was yet clearer in Best CJ's judgment at *nisi prius*, where the defendant's status as manufacturer was stressed;⁶¹ and a commentator in the *Law Magazine* argued that the decision should be restricted to such cases.⁶²

The first of these features of *Jones v Bright* was solidified in *Shepherd v Pybus*.⁶³ Here there was a written contract for the sale of a barge. The writing contained no reference to a warranty of fitness for purpose, and hence the parol evidence rule meant that it could not be implied as a matter of fact. It was held that the parol evidence rule did not apply here, since the warranty was implied by the law.

---

⁵⁶ Most clearly at 5 Bing 540–41.
⁵⁷ 3 Moo & P 166, 5 Bing 539, 7 LJCP 216.
⁵⁸ Citing 3 BL Com 161, on implication in law rather than implication in fact: 3 Moo & P 160, 5 Bing 536, 7 LJCP 215.
⁵⁹ 5 Bing 538 (not in the other reports).
⁶⁰ Compare 3 Moo & P 174 (confirmed by 7 LJCP 219), 'in every contract to furnish manufactured goods … it is an implied term that they be merchantable', with 5 Bing 544, where the sentence is omitted. The point is still just visible at 5 Bing 545.
⁶¹ (1829) 1 Dan & L 304.
⁶² (1830) 3 Law Mag 180, 195–96.
⁶³ *Shepherd v Pybus* (1842 3 Man & G 868, 4 Scott 434, 11 LJCP 101.

A decade or so later, in *Brown v Edgington*,⁶⁴ the Common Pleas pulled back from the suggestion that the manufacturer-vendor was in a special position. There the vendor, described in the pleadings as a dealer in ropes, sold a rope to the plaintiff, knowing what it was to be used for; he obtained it from a rope-maker without specifying the purpose. It proved to be inadequate for the task. The court held there was an implied warranty notwithstanding that the defendant was not the manufacturer. Significantly perhaps, Scott's report of Tindal CJ's judgment specifies that the purchase was from a tradesman, while the other reports merely describe him as a person. But it was Scott's report that was picked up in the next edition of *Chitty on Contracts*;⁶⁵ the implied warranty of merchantability arose on a sale by a tradesman. Chitty's formulation, in its turn, was picked up and approved in the Exchequer Chamber in *Bigge v Parkinson*.⁶⁶

Around the same time, the Court of Exchequer provided some clarity to the law in *Chanter v Hopkins*.⁶⁷ Lord Abinger CB drew the distinction between cases in which the goods sold had failed to match the description in the contract and cases where they lacked some specific quality. In the former situation, essentially that of *Gardiner v Gray*, there was a straightforward breach of contract and no need to use the language of warranty, while in the latter an action would lie if and only if there was an express or implied warranty. Second, he held that there was no implied warranty of fitness for a particular purpose, even where that purpose had been made known to the seller, where there had been a sale of specific goods ('the horse in the third stall from the end', or, as in *Chanter v Hopkins* itself, a 'Chanter's Smoke-Consuming Furnace'), but only when there had been a sale by description.⁶⁸ Behind this, probably, lay the approach already visible in *Brown v Edgington*, that there would be no implied warranty unless the purchaser could be taken to have relied on the judgement of the vendor.⁶⁹

This stage of development culminated in the decision of the Queen's Bench in *Jones v Just*.⁷⁰ Here Mellor J summarised the effect of the case law in a series of propositions:

- Where there was a sale of existing goods open to inspection by the buyer, caveat emptor applied in the absence of fraud by the seller.
- Where there was a sale of a specific chattel open to inspection by either party, caveat emptor applied.
- Where there was a sale of a specific chattel by a manufacturer, known to be wanted for a particular purpose, there was no implied warranty that it was fit for that purpose.

---

⁶⁴ *Brown v Edgington* (1841) 2 Man & G 279, 2 Scott NR 496, 1 Drink 106, 10 LJCP 66.
⁶⁵ 4th edn, 1850, 392. There is no reference to the other reports.
⁶⁶ *Bigge v Parkinson* (1862) 7 H & N 955, 31 L J Ex 301.
⁶⁷ *Chanter v Hopkins* (1838) 4 M & W 399, 1 H & H 377.
⁶⁸ As Professor Mitchell points out ((n 34) 657–58), the boundaries of the terminology here are rather fuzzy.
⁶⁹ See the argument of counsel in *Ollivant v Bayley* (1843) 5 QB 288, D & M 223; the case shows the difficulty of applying the rule to concrete facts.
⁷⁰ *Jones v Just* (1868) LR 3 QB 197. The report in *The Times*, 18 February 1868, is in some respects clearer than that in the official report.

- Where there was a sale by a manufacturer or dealer of non-specific goods for a particular purpose, there was an implied warranty that they were fit for that purpose.
- Where there was a sale of manufactured goods by a manufacturer or dealer, there was an implied warranty that the goods were merchantable.

These rules were approved, after further citation of authorities, by the Court of Appeal in *Randall v Newson*.[71]

The judgment in *Jones v Just* was immediately incorporated into the first edition of Judah Benjamin's treatise on sale, published later in the same year, and reproduced unchanged in the second (1873), third (1883) and fourth (1888) editions of the work.[72] The decision had become the canonical statement of the law.

We may therefore move from *Jones v Just* to the Sale of Goods Act of 1893.[73] In the initial form of the bill, in 1889, the relevant parts of clause 21, read:

> 2 Where the buyer, relying on the seller's skill or judgment, orders goods for a particular purpose known to the seller, and the goods are of a description which it is in the course of the seller's business to supply (whether he be the manufacturer or not), there is an implied warranty that the goods shall be reasonably fit for such purpose.
>
> 3 Where goods are ordered by description from a seller who deals in goods of that description (whether he be the manufacturer or not) and the buyer has no opportunity of examining the goods, there is an implied warranty that the goods shall be of merchantable quality and condition.

The final version the Act, now section 14, was slightly different:

> (1) Where the buyer, expressly or by implication, makes known to the seller the particular purpose for which the goods are required, so as to show that the buyer relies on the seller's skill or judgment, and the goods are of a description which it is in the course of the seller's business to supply (whether he be the manufacturer or not), there is an implied condition that the goods shall be reasonably fit for such purpose, provided that in the case of a contract for the sale of a specified article under its patent or other trade name, there is no implied condition as to its fitness for any particular purpose:
>
> (2) Where goods are bought by description from a seller who deals in goods of that description (whether he be the manufacturer or not), there is an implied condition that the goods shall be of merchantable quality; provided that if the buyer has examined the goods, there shall be no implied condition as regards defects which such examination ought to have revealed:

The former requirement that the goods be manufactured goods, based on the reading of *Laing v Fidgeon*,[74] has disappeared; Story's treatise on the sale of goods had

---

[71] *Randall v Newson* (1877) 2 QBD 102, 109.

[72] *A Treatise on the Law of Sale of Personal Property: with References to the American Decisions and to the French Code and Civil Law* (London, 1868).

[73] On the legislative history of the Act, see Mitchell (n 34) 656–61. For references to the considerable number of cases decided through the 1870s and 1880s, see the notes in W Ker, *Digest of the Law relating to the Sale of Goods* (Oxford 1888) 51–61.

[74] See above.

already noted in 1871 that the requirement was disappearing.[75] We can see three differences of substance between the earlier and the later versions. Most importantly, perhaps, is that the warranty in the earlier version has become a condition in the final text. This was based on a reading of a slightly ambiguous judgment of Brett JA in *Randall v Newson*, taken by Chalmers as indicating that the merchantability or fitness for purpose was fundamental to the contract.[76] The terminological difficulty is well brought out in the note on English law in Moyle's *Contract of Sale in the Civil Law*, describing it as 'an implied warranty, amounting to a condition (for on breach of it the buyer is entitled to reject the goods)'.[77] Second, section 14(1) attempts to sharpen up the circumstances in which there was a condition of fitness for purpose, reflecting the decision in *Chanter v Hopkins*.[78] And third, the final version provided that it was only when there had actually been an examination of goods bought by description that the condition of merchantability did not arise, not simply when there had been an opportunity to examine.

IV. SALE OF GOODS AND CONSUMER LAW

From the standpoint of consumer law, the most important feature of the 1893 Act was the fixing in place of the rule attaching liability only to merchants. But it did not give any rights specifically to non-commercial purchasers, and as businesses in a strong bargaining position began more frequently to use standard-form terms there was nothing to prevent them modifying or excluding altogether the implied terms as to quality. As well, and more subtly, the enactment of the Act reduced the possibility of judicial law-making as a means of adjusting the law in the light of changing practices.

The cases generating the implied warranty rules were substantial commercial claims, though of course the rules applied to consumer sales too.[79] That said, there is very little evidence that they were used by individual consumers. Unless actual injury had been caused, any claim would have been small, and even after the introduction of county courts would hardly have been worth pursuing. Moreover, cases where compensation for injury was sought might be robustly defended, perhaps by a defendant supported by a trade organisation, with a heavy informational imbalance between the consumer and the vendor/manufacturer.[80] Two further barriers faced the consumer, both in the legal rules themselves. First, in the retail environment of the nineteenth and early twentieth centuries the purchaser of an item would commonly

---

[75] WW Story and EH Bennett, *Treatise on the Law of Sales of Personal Property*, 4th edn (Boston 1871) 445, fn 3.
[76] Chalmers, *Sale of Goods* (1890) 22, citing (1877) 2 QBD at [109]. I have found no early suggestion that this was the meaning of Brett JA.
[77] JB Moyle, *The Contract of Sale in the Civil Law* (Oxford, 1892) 218, citing Chalmers and *Randall v Newson*. See too Ker, *Digest of the Law relating to Sales*, 52, explaining (with reference to Story) that the term is a condition but that the language of warranty is used in defence to long usage. Story (n 75) 401–72, clearly treats cases of breach of warranty as entitling the purchaser to reject the goods.
[78] See above.
[79] For an untypical consumer case, see *Baldry v Marshall* [1925] 1 KB 260 (purchase of an 'eight-cylinder Bugatti').
[80] See Dr Gordon's ch 7 in this volume.

have had at least the opportunity to examine the goods. The principal exceptions to this were chemical preparations, especially medicines, and packaged or bottled food and drink; with these there was concern for safety and agitation over the adulteration of foods, but this was dealt with through largely ineffective regulation rather than through private law.[81] Second, the definition of warranty did not extend to 'mere puffs',[82] so mendacious claims as to the effectiveness of quack medicines, for example, did not give rise to legal liability.[83] Moreover, section 55 of the 1893 Act explicitly permitted the exclusion or modification of the implied terms.[84]

The late nineteenth and early twentieth centuries witnessed a shift towards a 'consumer society'.[85] Changes in the distribution of wealth meant that the less well off might nonetheless have access to what might have been seen as luxury goods; the emergence of department stores meant that a greater variety of goods were easily available; and technological advances brought electrical goods, cars and other machines within the reach of individual consumers. Coupled with the imbalance of power between vendor/producer and consumer, the opportunities for the former to exploit the latter were magnified.

The Hire Purchase Act of 1938 took the first explicit steps towards consumer protection. Limited in its effects to relatively small contracts, it imposed a number of implied conditions and warranties into hire purchase agreements along the lines of the Sale of Goods Act, but in addition provided that these terms could not be excluded or modified by the agreement of the parties.[86] It was not for another two decades, however, that attention began to turn to the sale of goods. The essential trigger for this was the founding of the Consumer Association (originally the Association for Consumer Research) and the publication of its magazine *Which?* The same year also saw the appearance of the less successful *Shoppers' Guide*, published by the British Standards Institute.[87] Two years later, in 1959, the government set up a committee to examine the whole subject of consumer protection, the Molony Committee.

The Molony Committee reported in 1962.[88] It noted that since the Sale of Goods Act had been passed there had been a change in the types and methods of manufacture of products, with a marked increase in the complexity of goods which were for sale.[89] It made a number of recommendations relating to such things as uniform standards and advertising, but for present purposes the important section of the report was

---

[81] See, eg, Adulteration of Food and Drink Act 1860, Pharmacy Act 1868, Adulteration of Food Act 1872, Sale of Food and Drugs Act 1875, Public Health (Regulations as to Food) Act 1907.

[82] A Jones, *Law Relating to Advertisements* (London, 1906) 3–6; *Carlill v Carbolic Smoke Ball Co* [1893] 1 QB 257. See A Rosenberg, 'Legal Ridicule in the Age of Advertisements: Puffery, Quackery and the Masas Market' (2021) 61 *American Journal of Legal History* 281.

[83] House of Commons, *Report of the Select Committee on Patent Medicines*, 1914, ix–xix, is replete with shocking (and, with hindsight, amusing) examples.

[84] It was important that the clause as drafted was wide enough to exclude the relevant term: *Wallis, Son and Wells v Pratt and Haynes* [1911] AC 394 (exclusion of guarantees and warranties did not extend to conditions under s 14(1).

[85] J Benson, *The Rise of Consumer Society in Britain, 1880-1980* (London, Longman, 1994).

[86] Hire Purchase Act 1938, s 8(3).

[87] On the rise of the consumer movement, see for example G Borrie and A L Diamond, *The Consumer, Society and the Law* (Harmondsworth, Penguin, 1964) 9–13, reflecting on it as a recent phenomenon.

[88] *Final Report of the Committee on Consumer Protection*, Cmnd 1781 (hereafter *Molony Report*).

[89] *Molony Report*, 14–17, 131–32.

concerned with the implied terms arising under section 14 of the 1893 Act.[90] The principal problems arose with the use of exclusion clauses, ubiquitous in the sale of cars and very common in the sale of electrical goods. Particular criticism was directed towards so-called 'guarantee cards': the purchaser was enjoined to fill in and send to the manufacturer a card, whose effect was to exclude the implied terms of fitness for purpose and merchantable quality, in exchange for a limited undertaking from the manufacturer to repair or replace an unsatisfactory item. Similar terms might also be found in documents incorporating – in small print – the terms and conditions of the sale.[91] These 'guarantees' might not have been legally effective because of the operation of the doctrine of privity of contract, but the important thing was that consumers thought they were. The problem was not with the manufacturers' guarantees as such, but with the fact that they involved the exclusion of the liability of the vendors. The Committee concluded that the interests of consumers were best served by prohibiting the contracting out of the implied terms, noting as well that the consequence would be to bring the law of the sale of goods into line with that of hire purchase.[92]

These recommendations only applied to 'consumer contracts'. These were defined as contracts to acquire goods 'for private use or consumption'.[93] The requirement that the vendor be a dealer, already present in the 1893 Act, was retained, although the requirement that he should have been a dealer in goods of the particular type in question was criticised.[94] There had been some suggestion that sales of consumer goods to retailer from wholesaler, and so on along the chain back to the manufacturer, should similarly have unexcludable terms, but this was rejected on the grounds that it would frequently be impossible to know whether something was destined for sale to a consumer or not; the upshot was that liability might stop with the retailer, where the wholesaler had been able to exclude the implied terms as to quality.[95]

Further amendments to the provisions of the 1893 Act were also recommended. The unexcludable condition of merchantability in section 14(2) should apply to all consumer sales, not only sales by description, though it should not apply to the sale of second-hand goods or goods sold as imperfect.[96] So far as the condition of fitness for purpose under section 14(1) was concerned, it should no longer be disapplied where the goods were sold under a patent or trade name.[97]

The Molony Committee had identified a number of problems relating to consumer protection, and it could hardly have been expected that all would be implemented immediately. Perhaps the most urgent need was to address the problem of consumers' lamentable lack of understanding of their rights, so the first step was to set up a Consumer Council with a function of educating consumers as well as giving advice

---

[90] ibid ch 11.
[91] ibid 127.
[92] ibid 137–42.
[93] ibid 1.
[94] ibid 143–44.
[95] ibid 139–40.
[96] ibid 143–45.
[97] ibid 145–46.

more generally on consumer issues; it was abolished as a cost-cutting measure in 1970. This was followed by reform to the law of hire purchase in the Hire Purchase Act of 1964 and reform to unfair advertising practices in the Trade Descriptions Act of 1968. Partly because of the need to prioritise, the suggested amendments to the Sale of Goods Act were slow in coming. Already in 1964 and 1965 parliamentary questions were being asked about their implementation;[98] and in 1966 a bill was introduced into the House of Lords to outlaw exemption clauses in consumer sales.[99] By this time, however, the subject had been handed over to the newly-created Law Commission and had formed part of their first programme of work.

The Law Commission set up a working party, in conjunction with the Scottish Law Commission, which reported in 1969.[100] The Report accepted the two amendments to section 14(1) which had been proposed by the Molony Committee,[101] but went slightly further in recommending the replacement of the requirement that the buyer should have shown reliance on the seller's skill and judgement with a provision that the seller might avoid liability by showing that the buyer had not relied on their skill and judgement.[102] The Report accepted, too, the recommendations of the Molony Committee on section 14(2),[103] but went slightly further by importing the condition of merchantability into all sales by business sellers and defining what was meant by 'merchantable'.[104] The sharper definition of 'merchantable' removed the need to have any special provisions relating to express sales of second-hand or substandard goods or those whose defects were made clear by the seller.[105] The most important recommendation of the Molony Committee, that exemption clauses in consumer contracts should be void,[106] was accepted, but there was no agreement about the introduction of rules regulating exemption clauses in sales to business customers.[107]

Ten years after the Molony Committee reported a Bill was presented to deal with the problems in the law of sale of goods identified by them, becoming the Supply of Goods (Implied Terms) Act 1973. Largely giving effect to the recommendations of the Law Commissions, the relevant provisions of section 14 of the 1893 Act were amended to read:

(2) Where the seller sells goods in the course of a business, there is an implied condition that the goods supplied under the contract are of merchantable quality, except that there is no such condition—

(a) as regards defects specifically drawn to the buyer's attention before the contract is made; or

(b) if the buyer examines the goods before the contract is made, as regards defects which that examination ought to reveal.

---

[98] 704 Hansard HC, 5th series, 540; 709 Hansard HC, 5th series, 1040.
[99] 275 Hansard HL, 5th series, 397.
[100] *Exemption Clauses in Contracts, First Report: Amendments to the Sale of Goods Act 1893* (Law Com 24).
[101] See above.
[102] Law Com 24, 13–14.
[103] See above.
[104] Law Com 24, 15–175.
[105] ibid 18–19.
[106] See above.
[107] Law Com 24, 24–51.

(3) Where the seller sells goods in the course of a business and the buyer, expressly or by implication, makes known to the seller, any particular purpose for which the goods are being bought, there is an implied condition that the goods supplied under the contract are reasonably fit for that purpose, whether or not that is a purpose for which such goods are commonly supplied, except where the circumstances show that the buyer does not rely, or that it is unreasonable for him to rely, on the seller's skill or judgment.[108]

Merchantable quality was defined, as recommended:

Goods of any kind are of merchantable quality … if they are as fit for the purpose or purposes for which goods of that kind are commonly bought as it is reasonable to expect having regard to any description applied to them, the price (if relevant) and all the other relevant circumstances …[109]

Finally, and most importantly, the power to exclude liability in section 55 of the 1893 Act was stringently modified:

(4) In the case of a contract of sale of goods, any term of that or any other contract exempting from all or any of the provisions of section 13, 14 or 15 of this Act shall be void in the case of a consumer sale and shall, in any other case, not be enforceable to the extent that it is shown that it would not be dair or reasonable to allow reliance on the term.[110]

---

[108] Inserted by Supply of Goods (Implied Terms) Act, s 3.
[109] Supply of Goods (Implied Terms) Act, s 7(2).
[110] Inserted by Supply of Goods (Implied Terms) Act, s 4.

4

Incorporation and Exemption Clauses in Consumer Contracts: *Parker v South Eastern Railway Company*

STELIOS TOFARIS*

When Mr Parker dropped his bag at a cloakroom in Charing Cross station on 5 April 1875, he could never have imagined that a century and a half later his name would feature prominently in newspaper discussions on whether consumers are bound by clickwrap agreements.[1] That it does attests to the status of *Parker v South Eastern Railway Company* as a landmark in consumer law.

Parker is first and foremost a landmark in the law of contract. It is not hard to see why. *Parker* is indispensable to understanding the law on the incorporation of terms into a contract. To this day, it provides the main framework of analysis at common law.[2] The decision significantly influenced the development of the law and remains a staple of contract law curricula and literature.

Parker's canonical status in consumer law follows on from this. The issue of incorporation of terms arises acutely when consumers purport to contract on standard form, and particularly where the terms to be incorporated are exemption clauses.[3] It is only a little exaggeration to claim that the history of judicial efforts to protect consumers against the incorporation of such clauses in recent times is the history of how *Parker* has been interpreted, applied, and expanded, and of how its meaning has been tested and refined as the transactional patterns to which it was applied diversified. *Parker*'s status as a landmark then depends not only on its formulation of authoritative rules, but also on the exposure of the tensions that underlie the issue of incorporation by the judges in their reasoning and the range of suggested solutions. While the understanding of those tensions was shaped by the context of the times, in

---

* The author is grateful to Professors David Ibbetson, John Murphy, and Iain Ramsay for their comments on earlier drafts. The usual caveat applies.

[1] 'Can't Understand Clickable Online Contracts?' *CBS News*, 30 April 2018 (available at www.cbc.ca/news/business/clickable-agreements-contract-law-1.4634780).

[2] H Beale (ed), *Chitty on Contracts*, 34th edn (London, Sweet & Maxwell, 2021) [15-007]–[15-014].

[3] I Ramsay, *Consumer Law and Policy*, 3rd edn (London, Hart Publishing, 2012) ch 6.

the long run it enabled *Parker* to be read in a new light with the result that the tensions were reconfigured and the solutions morphed.

The present chapter explains how this happened. It first situates the case in its historical context with a view to identifying the legal issues, the circumstances in which those issues arose, the procedural and doctrinal framework within which they were analysed, and the broader factors that influenced their resolution. It then examines the aftermath in an effort to trace how and why *Parker* has remained important.

I. FACTS

On 5 April 1875, Halford Parker[4] travelled on South Eastern Railway (SER)'s train from Tunbridge Wells to Charing Cross station. On arriving there, he deposited his portmanteau and black leather bag at the company's cloakroom. He paid 2d and received a paper ticket from the clerk. On the front was printed the office's opening times, information about unclaimed luggage, and at the bottom the words '[See Back.]'. On the back was the following notice:

> This company will not be responsible for articles left by passengers at the station unless the same be duly registered, for which a charge of 2*d* per article will be made, and a ticket given in exchange; and no article will be given up without the production of the ticket, or satisfactory evidence of the ownership being adduced … The company will not be responsible for any package exceeding the value of 10*l*.

A placard, containing a notice to the same effect, hung in a visible part of the cloakroom. Parker returned to the station several hours later. Upon presenting the ticket, he was handed the portmanteau, but not the bag, which was never found. He brought a claim against the company for the value of the bag and its contents, which came to 24l 10s.

On 7 February 1876, Alverstone Gabell, a 24-year-old surgeon-dentist, travelled from Tunbridge Wells to Charing Cross, where he deposited his bag, containing surgical instruments, in SER's cloakroom.[5] He paid 2d and received a ticket with the same writing as Parker. Gabell sought to retrieve his bag the next day, but it could not be found. He claimed 50l 16s for it.

In both cases, the company had a duty as a bailee to take care of the deposited goods. Its argument was that it contracted with Parker and Gabell on the basis of the special conditions on the ticket, consequently, its responsibility was limited to packages worth no more than 10l.

The two cases were eventually heard together by the Court of Appeal. The amount of money involved was modest, but the point at stake was important for the company.[6]

---

[4] The National Archives (TNA): IND/1/9060. Parker appears to have been 26 years old with no known occupation: '1881 England Census', database Ancestry (available at www.ancestry.com).

[5] Gabell was at the time working for Eskell, an established dental practitioner (WE Hitchin, *Surrey at the Opening of the Twentieth Century* (1906) 205; LB Eskell, *The Eskells: The Story of a Family* (Bristol, University of Bristol, 1995).

[6] The SER was formed in 1836 to construct a route from London to south-eastern England. The line to central Tunbridge Wells was opened in 1846. In the 1870s, SER's reputation was moderate at best: see, eg, A Gray, *The South Eastern Railway* (Midhurst, Middleton Press, 1990).

Railway companies operated cloakrooms across the country. This was profitable but exposed them to unknown risks and liabilities; Parker's and Gabell's experiences were not unusual. To guard against those risks, companies wished to know if, and how, they could rely on exemption clauses printed on tickets. Receiving an answer from an authoritative court[7] made expensive litigation worthwhile.[8]

II. BACKGROUND

The framing of the issue in *Parker* operated against a set of backgrounds of economic, social, and legal nature. To appreciate fully the decision, those backgrounds must first be examined.

A. Consumer Society and the Railway

In 1875, Britain had a mass consumer market. The Industrial Revolution brought about large-scale manufacturing. Steady economic growth after 1850 increased wages and improved living standards. The range of available goods therefore grew at a time when more people could buy them. The method by which those goods were bought was also changing, with retail shops becoming more popular. Provision of services to consumers similarly expanded: individuals took out insurance, holidayed at hotels, and travelled on the railway in growing numbers. The net result was a dramatic rise in consumer transactions. This brought a larger section of the population into the domain of contractual relations. It also transformed contract-making practices: consumer contracts were increasingly made in standard form rather than by individual negotiations.

At the heart of the Victorian consumer economy was the railway.[9] The first intercity railway opened in 1830 between Liverpool and Manchester. By the mid-1840s, 'railway mania' had taken over, leading to huge levels of investment. Railway mileage increased from around 125 in 1830 to more than 13,000 in 1871.[10] This revolutionised travel for most of the population: an estimate 423 million passengers travelled on it in 1870.[11]

The claim in *Parker* raised an important issue affecting the everyday life of the Victorian consumer: when, if at all, was he bound by terms issued in standard form? The question had been asked before in other contexts. Exemption clauses and

---

[7] As J Young, solicitor to the Great Western Railway, explained: 'sometimes very important principles are involved where the particular amount is small, and in such a case we wish to have some principle for our future guidance determined by the superior tribunal ...' (Second Report of Judicature Commissioners (1872), C.631, Vol XX, Appendix, q.6254). Railway companies routinely attempted to appeal or have their cases removed into superior courts, partly to discourage litigation against them (P Polden, *A History of the County Court, 1846-1971* (Cambridge, CUP, 1999) 92).

[8] Eg, the costs in the Common Pleas Division in *Parker* were recorded as 79l 0s 8d ((TNA): IND/1/9060).

[9] See, eg, PJG Ransom, *The Victorian Railway and How It Evolved* (London, Heinemann, 1989).

[10] L Shaw-Taylor & X You, 'The Development of the Railway Network in Britain 1825-1911', 11 (available at www.campop.geog.cam.ac.uk/research/projects/transport/onlineatlas/).

[11] P Kelly, 'A Golden Age', *The Railway Magazine*, 4 July 2022.

standard form contracting originated in the commercial world,[12] but by 1875, they were both firmly established in the consumer's world. While railway companies were not the only ones to make use of them, they were among the most visible and consequential to the consumer's life.

B. Common Carriers, the Railway, and Limitations of Liability

Railway companies sought to limit their liability by notices or tickets from their earliest days. This was a legacy of the law on common carriers, of which they were the newest manifestation. Common carriers were obliged to carry the goods of those wishing to use their services and were strictly liable for their loss or damage. When goods of value, such as banknotes, began to be transported in small parcels, the carriers' position became financially precarious. To protect themselves, they adopted the practice of using notices to exclude liability for loss of goods beyond a certain value, unless that was declared and an additional fee paid. The courts upheld the notices but only when brought home to the customer.[13]

This could be done directly or constructively.[14] One way was to display a notice in the carriers' office. This, however, was not brought home where the customer could not read,[15] or, thinking that the board did not contain anything material, did not read it,[16] or where the notice was in small letters.[17] Another way was by means of handbills distributed to customers when they delivered their goods.[18] From this, it was a short step in the lawyers' imagination to suggest that common carriers who complained of the difficulty in showing sufficiency of notice could print the terms on a ticket and give it to the customer.[19]

Following lobbying by the carriers, Parliament passed the Carriers Act 1830. Under this, customers had to declare the value of particular goods if it exceeded £10, otherwise the carrier was not liable. In return, the Act forbade carriers to restrict their liability by a public notice. The Act did not apply to special contracts between carriers and customers, meaning that any future limitations of liability had to be brought about by contract.

It was against this background that railway companies sought to restrict liability by printing terms on tickets. The economic case for using tickets in contracting was obvious. Profit margins depended on efficiency. Individually negotiating terms took time and cost money. Standardising them and putting them on tickets produced savings.

---

[12] O Prausnitz, *The Standardization of Commercial Contracts in English and Continental Law* (London, Sweet & Maxwell, 1937).

[13] *Clayton v Hunt* (1811) 3 Camp 27. For details, see JN Adams, 'The Carrier in Legal History' in EW Ives and AH Manchester (eds), *Law, Litigants and the Legal Profession* (London, Royal Historical Society, 1983) 39.

[14] W Hodges, *The Law Relating to Railways and Railway Companies* (London, Sweet, 1847) 444.

[15] *Davis v Willan* (1817) 2 Stark 279.

[16] *Kerr v Willan* (1817) 2 Stark 53.

[17] *Butler v Heane* (1810) 2 Camp 415.

[18] *Gibbon v Paynton* (1769) 4 Burr 2298.

[19] *Kerr v Willan* (1817) 2 Stark 53, 55 (counsel for consignor); *Kerr v Willan* (1817) 6 M & S 150, 152 (Lord Ellenborough).

From early on, judges acknowledged that the use of tickets, or written memoranda, might help avoid the difficulties with bringing notice home.[20] It was no surprise that railway companies, 'masters of the field'[21] with frequent access to lawyers,[22] sought to explore the new legal possibilities by printing exemption clauses on tickets.

The economic case for controlling liability was equally obvious. The technological advantages of the railway over the horse stagecoach meant that a wider range of valuable goods could be carried in greater quantities. These went far beyond the goods for which protection to carriers was provided under the Carriers Act 1830. Furthermore, the Acts under which railways were created generally required them to provide their services at a reasonable price, and fixing a reasonable price when faced with unknown financial risks was not easy.[23]

The companies' efforts to regulate their risk in this period were treated sympathetically by the courts. These held that tickets, invariably signed, and given to customers on receipt of their goods, operated as special contracts, and were not prohibited by the Act.[24] Accordingly, goods were carried subject to those contracts and the limitations of liability included therein, rather than the general law of carriers. The courts further held that terms excluding liability for any damage however caused ought to be given effect.[25] This made it possible to exclude liability arising from negligence.[26] Reflecting the general attitude of mid-nineteenth century judges, Parke B explained that

> it is very reasonable that carriers should be allowed to make agreements for the purpose of protecting themselves against the new risks and dangers of carriage to which they are in modern times exposed.[27]

The framework of analysis was based on consent.[28] Railway companies were free to exclude their liability as carriers, but the customer had to assent. Signing the ticket, which invariably occurred, was regarded as acknowledging its terms and as proof of assent.[29] It was when there was no signed ticket that the framework of analysis could be seen more transparently. In *Walker v North Midland Railway Company*,[30] a fisherman objected to notices served on him by the railway company that fish would only

---

[20] *Riley v Horne* (1825) 5 Bing 217, 221 (Best CJ).
[21] *Peek v North Staffordshire Railway Company* (1863) 10 HL Cas 473, 556 (Cockburn CJ).
[22] S Jack and A Jack, 'Nineteenth-Century Lawyers and Railway Capitalism: Historians and the Use of Legal Cases' (2003) 24 *JLH* 59.
[23] JN Adams, 'The Standardization of Commercial Contracts or the Contractualization of Standard Forms' (1978) 7 *Anglo-American L Rev* 136, 145.
[24] *Palmer v The Grand Junction Railway Company* (1839) 4 M & W 749; *Shaw v The York and North Midland Railway* Company (1849) 13 QB 347.
[25] Eg, *Carr v The Lancashire and Yorkshire Railway Company* (1852) 7 Ex 707.
[26] Eg *Carr* (n 25); *Austin v The Manchester, Sheffield and Lincolnshire Railway Company* (1850) 10 CB 454; *Peek* (n 21) 494 (Blackburn J).
[27] ibid 712. While judges were not within the direct sphere of the 'railway interest', nor were they entirely immune to its influence, eg, many had shares in railway companies and so were disqualified from hearing appeals against the particular companies. Nevertheless, railway decisions were never one-way traffic: the same judges ruled for and against railway companies depending on the legal issue.
[28] This may have been implicit in the pre-1830 case-law (Adams (n 23) 142).
[29] *Walker v York and North Midland Railway Company* (1853) 2 El and Bl 750, 758 (counsel's concession).
[30] ibid.

be carried subject to exemption clauses and at a reduced rate. He subsequently sent his fish by the railway at the reduced rate. It was held that the notice was the basis of a special contract to which his assent could be inferred from his sending the fish after the notice was brought home to him.

The focus on consent echoed doctrinal developments taking effect at the time. The nineteenth-century conception of contract was primarily based on the will theory.[31] Its essence was that contractual obligations arose from an agreement, understood as a meeting of wills, though as *Walker* nakedly shows, this was subordinated to an objective approach with no insistence on actual will. The corollary was that once the parties established the content of the contract through their will, the courts had to respect that will and refrain from revising the contract even if it appeared unfair to them. In this sense, the will theory largely upheld freedom of contract.[32]

Consent-based analysis masked practical challenges. These were vividly exposed in the real-life experiences of the railway customer.[33] The primary challenge concerned the 'reality' of consent. In mid-nineteenth century Britain, customers contracting with railway companies had little bargaining power: they could either agree to the company's terms or not use the railway. Non-use, however, was becoming unrealistic as railway companies practically enjoyed a monopoly of carriage of goods.[34] Customers were left with no 'real' choice. Railway companies could take advantage of their superior position to impose exemption clauses and other harsh terms. Freedom of contract existed only in name.

It would be wrong to think that judges were unaware of these concerns.[35] The issue was laid bare during the debate on the Railway and Canal Traffic Bill in 1854. Lord Brougham thought the railway companies were trying to evade responsibility by a special contract that was 'forced' upon a customer; a contract 'into which he entered upon compulsion'.[36] A decade later, Cockburn CJ made the same point from the bench.[37] The key, however, is that these concerns were expressed in Parliament or by judges after relevant legislation was enacted. Prior to that, judges by and large felt that it was not their role to disturb contractual terms to protect railway customers so long as their consent had been given voluntarily (understood in a narrow, formalist sense). As Parke B said in *Carr*:[38]

> it is not for us to fritter away the true sense and meaning of these contracts, merely to make men careful. If any inconvenience should arise from their being entered into, that is not a matter for our interference, but it must be left to the legislature, who may, if they please, put a stop to this mode which the carriers have adopted of limiting their liability.

---

[31] DJ Ibbetson, *A Historical Introduction to the Law of Obligations* (Oxford, OUP, 1999) 220–44.
[32] PS Atiyah, *The Rise and Fall of Freedom of Contract* (Oxford, Clarendon Press, 1979).
[33] These included passengers allowed to carry luggage of a particular weight, often at no additional cost.
[34] The railways had mostly exclusive territory.
[35] JH Baker, 'The Freedom to Contract Without Liability' (1971) CLP 53, 61.
[36] Hansard's Parliamentary Debates, 3rd Series, Vol 133 (1854) 609. See also ibid 602 (Earl of Derby); 603–04 (Lord Lyndhurst).
[37] *Peek* (n 21), 555–56.
[38] (n 25) 713–34; ibid, 716 (Martin B). *cf* ibid, 714 (Platt B).

This general belief was formed against the background of increasing state regulation of the railway, most notably, by the Railway Regulation Act 1844.[39]

Public disapproval of railway-friendly decisions led to the enactment of the Railway and Canal Traffic Act 1854. This made railway companies liable for damage to goods they carried due to their negligence or default, notwithstanding any notice to the contrary. It further provided that companies could impose conditions restricting their liability as long as these were 'just and reasonable', and that special contracts between the companies and customers were binding only if signed.[40]

C. Cloakrooms and Limitations of Liability

The 1854 Act did not apply to the facts in *Parker* as the goods in question were not in transit. A solution had to be found under the common law. It is for this reason that *Parker* is significant: its reasoning had to be based on, and eventually absorbed in, the common law. As always, this responded to external developments. Three were of particular importance.

The first was the cloakroom at railway stations. This grew out of the requirement imposed by the Railway and Canal Traffic Act 1854 on railway companies to afford reasonable facilities for receiving, forwarding, and delivering traffic.[41] Within a few decades, the cloakroom was regarded as a crucial service offered to passengers who did not want to carry their bags when they were not on the train.[42] Understandably, railway companies wished to restrict their liability. Covering all deposited goods for an unlimited amount would have driven the fee up and would have required customers storing cheap goods to pay the same high insurance element as those storing expensive goods.

The second development was the pre-printed ticket. In 1839, Thomas Edmondson devised the idea of a pre-printed ticket that was validated on the day of purchase.[43] The gained efficiencies over handwritten tickets made this a feature of railway cloakrooms and passenger travel; signed handbills continued to be used for the carriage of goods. The size of the pre-printed ticket meant it was difficult to print much information on the face of it. Accordingly, the practice arose of referring on the front to conditions on the back or in another document.

The third development was procedural. The Evidence Act 1851 allowed parties in civil cases to act as witnesses. A customer could now deny under cross-examination that he knew about, or consented to, the terms restricting liability even if he was given a ticket.

---

[39] O Kahn-Freund, *The Law of Carriage by Inland Transport*, 4th edn (London, Stevens & Sons, 1965) 775–79.
[40] s 7. In *Peek* (n 21), the House of Lords held that the 'justice and reasonableness' of conditions depended on whether the company had offered the customer a reasonable alternative to those conditions.
[41] *Singer Manufacturing Co v London and South Western Railway Co* [1894] 1 QB 833, 836 (Mathew J).
[42] (1876) 61 Law Times 116.
[43] JB Edmondson, *The Early History of the Railway Ticket* (Manchester, Lancashire and Cheshire Antiquarian Society, 1968).

These issues came to a head in a series of cases preceding *Parker*, all of which were outside the 1854 Act. In *Van Toll v South Eastern Railway Co*,[44] the plaintiff deposited a bag in the defendant's cloakroom and received a ticket, which included a limitation clause on the back. A similar notice was placed in the office. Although the plaintiff testified that she had not seen the notice, the Common Pleas held that the company received the goods as a bailee upon the terms contained on the ticket. According to Erle CJ, what mattered was that she knew from experience that the deposit was made subject to special terms, and that the company had used all reasonable means to make those terms known to customers.[45] Byles J thought that there was implicit assent where the passenger chose to put the ticket in her pocket without reading it. Implicit assent was valid as long as the terms were reasonable, and plain and obvious.[46]

In *Stewart v The London and North Western Railway Company*,[47] an excursion ticket had printed on the front 'ticket as per bill' and on the back words indicating that it was issued subject to terms found in the excursion bills. Those terms excluded liability for personal luggage carried for free. Although the passenger had no knowledge of the terms, the Court of Exchequer drew an inference of fact that he assented to them. According to Pollock CB, the plaintiff was presumed to know what he had the means of knowing, irrespective of whether he availed himself of those means. By choosing not to check the terms, he assented to whatever they turned out to be.[48] Similarly, Bramwell B thought that it was enough that the customer had the opportunity to find out the terms.[49]

Some judges lamented the state of the law. In *Zunz v South Eastern Railway Co*,[50] Cockburn CJ begrudgingly concluded:

> however harsh it may appear in practice to hold a man liable by the terms and conditions which may be inserted in some small print upon the ticket, which he only gets at the last moment after he has paid his money … still we are bound on the authorities to hold, that when a man takes a ticket with conditions on it he must be presumed to know the contents of it, and must be bound by them.

The House of Lords made an effort to restrict the effect of this case law in *Henderson v Stevenson*.[51] It held that an exemption clause printed on the back of a steamboat company's passenger ticket was not incorporated into the contract. This was supported by two lines of reasoning. The first, unanimously adopted, was that the mere handing of a ticket was not enough to bind the passenger to conditions he did not see or know about. There was no evidence that the conditions were brought to the passenger's knowledge and of his having assented to them since no reference was made to them on the front of the ticket.[52] The second, found in Lord Chelmsford's

---

[44] *Van Toll v South Eastern Railway Co* (1862) 12 CB (NS) 75.
[45] ibid 83.
[46] ibid 88–89.
[47] *Stewart v The London and North Western Railway Company* (1864) 3 Hurl & C 135.
[48] ibid 138–39.
[49] ibid 140.
[50] *Zunz v South Eastern Railway Co* (1868-69) LR 4 QB 539, 544.
[51] *Henderson v Stevenson* (1875) LR 2 Sc 470.
[52] ibid 473–76 (Lord Cairns LC).

judgment, was that reference to the terms in the ticket came after the contract was formed and was therefore too late to be effective.[53] The contract was formed when payment of the fare was accepted by the company or when the ticket was delivered to the passenger. Overall, the House of Lords was alive to the underlying policy issue. Lord O'Hagan suggested that if companies wished to ensure that the terms were incorporated, they ought to get the passenger's signature, which would be conclusive evidence of assent. Such a precaution would mirror developments under the Railway and Canal Traffic Act 1854 and help further its policy by protecting 'the ignorant and unwary'.[54]

Following *Henderson*, railway companies wishing to restrict their liability in respect of cloakrooms would have been frustrated. The case law was riddled with inconsistencies and *Henderson* was hostile to their interests. It is unsurprising that in its immediate aftermath, three cases concerning luggage lost in cloakrooms appeared in quick succession. The first was *Harris v Great Western Railway Co*.[55] The ticket stated on its front that luggage was deposited subject to conditions on the back, which included a limitation clause. The plaintiff knew that there were conditions on the back but not what they were. The Queens' Bench held that the contract was made subject to those conditions. Blackburn J took the view that Lord Chelmsford's analysis in *Henderson* was obiter and need not be followed. He explained the underlying principle on the ground of estoppel.[56] Where one assented to a contract reduced to writing, for example, by depositing the goods and taking the ticket, he represented to the other side that he made himself acquainted with the written conditions and assented to them, or was content to be bound without ascertaining them, and in this way induced the other side to act on that representation to contract with him. He was thereby precluded from denying that he made himself acquainted with the conditions.

The remaining two cases were Parker's and Gabell's.

III. LITIGATION

A. Parker: Trial[57]

Parker's claim was tried before Pollock B and a common jury in the Exchequer Division on 27 January 1876. The bag was presumed lost by the negligence of the company's servants. Parker's claim was that the defendant was liable as an ordinary bailee. SER's answer was that they accepted the bag, not as ordinary bailees, but subject to a contract effected by the ticket, and thus subject to the terms included therein. The focus was therefore on the ticket and the limitation clause on the back. Parker testified that when he received the ticket, he put it in his pocket without reading it. The first he found out about the clause was when he threatened to sue the company and they informed him about it.

---

[53] ibid 477. Only Lord Hatherley agreed (ibid 479).
[54] ibid 482.
[55] *Harris v Great Western Railway Co* (1876) 1 QBD 515.
[56] *Cf* his judgment in *Smith v Hughes* (1871) LR 6 QB 597.
[57] *Standard*, 28 January 1876, 2; *York Herald*, 31 January 1876, 3.

Parker was represented by Samuel Prentice QC,[58] but the company did not employ a Queens' Counsel at this stage.[59] Pollock B left the following two questions to the jury: (1) Did the plaintiff read or was he aware of the special condition upon which the luggage was deposited? (2) Was the plaintiff, under the circumstances, under any obligation, in the exercise of reasonable and proper caution, to read or to make himself aware of the condition? The jury answered both questions in the negative, therefore judgment was entered for the plaintiff.

B. Parker: Court of Common Pleas[60]

The defendant obtained an order nisi from the Common Pleas Division for a new trial on the ground that the judge had misdirected the jury. The case was heard on 1 February. Frederick Pollock, who was at the start of his distinguished career as a legal scholar,[61] had now joined Parker's legal team as junior counsel.[62]

Parker's central argument, based on *Henderson*, was that the ticket was not a valid contract as the plaintiff had not assented to it given that his attention was not drawn to the words on the back and he had not read them. The defendant distinguished *Henderson* on the ground that there was no reference on the face of the ticket to the conditions on the back.

The court unanimously discharged the order and refused the motion. In Coleridge CJ's view, it was impossible as a matter of common sense to lay down fixed rules as to whether a customer was bound by a ticket.[63] Following *Henderson*, it depended in each case on whether he was aware of the conditions, and if not, whether this was due to his negligence. This turned on whether the conditions were brought to his knowledge. On the facts of *Parker*, he thought it was reasonable to consider the ticket as a mere voucher for identifying the luggage's owner.[64] Coleridge CJ affirmed that the right questions were left to the jury and their findings were supported by the available evidence. Brett J and Lindley J gave concurring judgments.

The defendant appealed to the Court of Appeal.

---

[58] A member of the South-Eastern circuit with moderate success as silk ((1883) 28 *The Law Journal* 882). Prentice edited Archbold's *Practice of the Courts of Common Pleas and Exchequer*, leading Willes J to proclaim that 'Archbold was his god, and Prentice was his prophet' (*The Biograph and Review*, Vol V (London, Allen, 1881), 37).

[59] Willis, SER's lead counsel, was most likely William Willis, who became a QC in 1877 and an MP in 1880, or Edward Willis, who became a QC in 1882, both of the South-Eastern circuit (J Foster, *Men-at-the-Bar*, 2nd edn (London, Hazell, Watson and Viney, 1885) 511). The junior counsel, Alexander Bremner, was also of the South-Eastern circuit (ibid 53).

[60] (1876) 1 CPD 618; 11 LJNC 106; 25 WR 97. See also, *Pall Mall Gazette*, 2 May 1876, 6; *Alnwick Mercury*, 6 May 1876, 3; *Bury and Norwich Post*, 9 May 1876, 7.

[61] Pollock's first edition of *Principles of Contract at Law and in Equity* was published in 1876.

[62] Pollock is known to have appeared only twice in court: N Duxbury, *Frederick Pollock and the English Juristic Tradition* (Oxford, OUP, 2004) 29.

[63] (1876) 1 CPD 618, 624.

[64] ibid 626.

C. Gabell: Trial[65]

Gabell's claim against SER was heard before Grove J and a special jury in the Common Pleas Division on 13 November 1876. Gabell testified that he had not read what was printed on the ticket. Although he had received such tickets in the past and knew there was writing on them, he thought it was merely evidence that the company received his bag. Gabell used the same QC as Parker. As a sign of the case's importance, SER had secured the services of the celebrated Judah Benjamin QC.[66] Finding the case to be almost identical to *Parker*, Grove J left the same questions to the jury. They answered these in the negative and verdict was entered for the plaintiff at agreed damages of £36. The defendant subsequently obtained an order nisi from the Court of Appeal for a new trial on the ground of misdirection.

D. Court of Appeal[67]

The two cases, by now known as 'cloak-room cases',[68] were heard together by the Court of Appeal, consisting of Mellish LJ, Baggallay LJ and Bramwell LJ, on 6 and 7 February 1877. The case was significant for SER and railway companies. As the *Saturday Review* exaggeratedly claimed, 'the moral of the … [Common Pleas'] decision is that reading is a dangerous accomplishment which had better be forgotten when we enter a railway station. Where ignorance gets damages "tis folly to be wise"'.[69] The safest way to ensure that limitation clauses were effective was to 'convey to every depositor … a verbal intimation', which 'would be … as inconvenient and disagreeable to the public as to the companies' servants.'[70] The case's significance extended beyond the cloakroom, with the Common Pleas' decision already used to decide similar cases.[71] SER's strategy was to get the matter decided as one of law. That would remove inconsistent judicial guidance, but above all remove the matter from the jury, whose bias against railways was well-documented.[72]

Benjamin QC put forward three arguments. The first was that there was no *consensus ad idem* because the parties meant different things. This allusion to a subjective meeting of minds was shot down by Bramwell LJ during argument on the basis that a party 'may so conduct himself as to lead the other to believe that there was a

---

[65] *The Times*, 15 November 1876, 11; *Reynolds's Newspaper*, 19 November 1876, 6.
[66] On his life, see C MacMillan, 'Judah Benjamin: Marginalized Outsider or Admitted Insider?' (2015) 42 *Journal of Law and Society* 150.
[67] (1877) 2 CPD 416; 41 JP 644; 46 LJQB 768; 36 LT 540; 25 WR 564. The interaction between counsel and bench generated several moments of laughter (*The Morning Post*, 8 February 1877, 7).
[68] *The Times*, 8 February 1877, 10.
[69] *Saturday Review*, 6 May 1876, 584.
[70] *Hastings and St Leonards Observer*, 6 May 1876, 4.
[71] *Foster v The Midland Railway Company* (luggage lost on a train running on another company's lines), reported in *Cambridge Independent Press*, 13 May 1876, 8.
[72] *Hastings and St Leonards Observer*, 6 May 1876, 4; *Toomey v London, Brighton & South Coast Railway* (1857) 3 CB (NS) 146, 150 (Williams J); *Peek* (n 21) 510–11 (Blackburn J); RW Kostal, *Law and the English Railway Capitalism, 1825-1875* (Oxford, Clarendon Press, 1994) 63–64, 101–14, 283–308.

contract'.⁷³ The second was that by receiving the ticket when he had the opportunity to read the printed terms, the plaintiff had impliedly assented that those terms were in the contract. *Henderson* was distinguished on the ground that the company in that case, as common carriers, were bound to carry the passenger on terms fixed by law, whereas SER voluntarily provided a cloakroom and so had an absolute right to determine the terms of doing so. The third argument was more practical. It was absurd for a company to be liable for hundreds of pounds in exchange for a charge of 2d. As Bremner added, the company would have to take 4,320 parcels to make up £36.⁷⁴ This amounted to a warning about defensive practices: if the railway companies were to incur indefinite liability in return for 2d, they would shut down the cloakrooms.

Prentice QC for the plaintiffs pursued the line of argument that persuaded the courts below.⁷⁵ Whether a man was bound by the contents of a printed paper given to him was a matter of common sense left to the jury and not a question of law. One would not be bound by terms printed on a turnpike ticket. The same was true of a voucher given to secure the return of the deposited goods to their owner. Pollock asked hypothetically whether the plaintiff would be bound if the ticket had instead stated that goods unredeemed within 24 hours would be forfeited. It was no answer to say that that would be unreasonable if the ticket constituted a contract, nor was a depositor obliged to know what would be reasonable. His point was that if the defendant's argument was accepted, it would become difficult to deal adequately with cases involving wholly unreasonable terms.

The Court of Appeal's judgment, given on 25 April, ordered a new trial on the ground that the judge had misdirected the jury by asking the wrong question. All judges eventually acceded to the order, but not without hesitation.⁷⁶ The leading proponent and most eloquent exponent of the order was Mellish LJ. Baggallay LJ was inclined to find for the plaintiff, while Bramwell LJ's preference was to rule for the defendant. The outcome was a compromise with the judgments including something for everyone.

Mellish LJ's judgment represented the middle view. The question was whether the plaintiff was bound by the conditions in the ticket to modify the ordinary contract of bailment. He cleared the ground by setting out the following propositions. Where a party signs a written agreement, the agreement is proved by proving his signature and in the absence of fraud it is immaterial that he has not read it or does not know its content.⁷⁷ Where, in the process of making a contract, a party delivers a paper with writing on it: (i) if the other party knows that it contains conditions intended to be contractual, he assents to those conditions, despite not reading or knowing them, by

---

⁷³ n 67, 418. Benjamin's argument can be traced to a comment by Willes J in *Van Toll* (n 44) 87 and *Lewis v M'Kee* (1868-69) LR 4 Ex 58, 62, and had already been raised by Willis in the Common Pleas ((1876) 1 CPD 618, 622). Bramwell's reply reflected what Benjamin himself had written in his *A Treatise on the Law of Sale of Personal Property* (London, Street, 1868).

⁷⁴ *The Times*, 8 February 1877, 10.

⁷⁵ No argument was made based on Lord Chelmsford's analysis in *Henderson*. It was unlikely to succeed (n 67, 426 (Bramwell LJ)).

⁷⁶ Bramwell LJ's judgment is often treated as dissent: eg, *Hood v Anchor Line (Henderson Brothers) Ltd* [1918] AC 837, 844 (Viscount Haldane).

⁷⁷ n 67, 421.

receiving and keeping the paper; (ii) if he does not know that there is any writing on the ticket or the back, he is not bound by the conditions. *Harris* fell under (i), while *Henderson* was authority for (ii).[78]

Parker was different because the plaintiff knew there was writing on the back of the ticket, but he swore that he did not read it and did not know or believe that the writing contained conditions. In such a case, the matter was to be decided as a question of fact by the jury. This was because the answer ultimately turned on the type of paper and transaction involved. In some cases, for example, a ticket at a turnpike gate upon paying the toll, it was reasonable to assume that there were no conditions. In other cases, for example, a bill of lading for the carriage of goods by sea, the opposite could be assumed, even where the consignor did not know about bills of lading. The key was what persons involved in those transactions knew in the great majority of cases and therefore what the person putting forward the conditions was entitled to assume. Railway companies were entitled to assume that a person depositing luggage and receiving a ticket could read, understand English and pay attention to what may be reasonably expected from a person in that transaction. Beyond that, their legitimate assumptions depended on whether what they did was sufficient to convey to people in general that the ticket contained conditions. If it was, a particular customer could not rely on his ignorance, stupidity, or carelessness; if not, they received the goods without the customer's consent to the exemption clause.[79] It followed that the proper direction for the jury was as follows:[80]

> if the person receiving the ticket did not see or know that there was any writing on the ticket, he is not bound by the conditions; that if he knew there was writing, and knew or believed that the writing contained conditions, then he is bound by the conditions; that if he knew there was writing on the ticket, but did not know or believe that the writing contained conditions, nevertheless he would be bound, if the delivering of the ticket to him in such a manner that he could see there was writing upon it, was, in the opinion of the jury, reasonable notice that the writing contained conditions.

Mellish LJ held that there ought to be a new trial. The right question to ask the jury was whether SER did what was reasonably sufficient to give the plaintiff notice of the conditions.

Baggallay LJ's judgment was the most consumer friendly. As there was no general practice of issuing cloakroom tickets with binding conditions, customers were entitled to regard them as vouchers for the identification of the deposited articles and their owner.[81] If, however, a particular customer was aware or ought to have been aware that there were binding conditions on the ticket, he was taken to have agreed to them. The same was true if he was aware or had reason to believe there was writing on the ticket intended to affect the parties' rights, but he negligently abstained from acquainting himself with it. This was a question of fact. Had it been up to him, he would have decided it on the available evidence in the plaintiff's favour.[82] In the end,

---

[78] ibid 421.
[79] ibid 423.
[80] ibid 423–24.
[81] ibid 424.
[82] ibid 425–26.

Baggallay LJ was persuaded by Mellish LJ to order a new trial based on the questions Mellish LJ identified.[83] Even so, he thought the same result would follow.

Bramwell LJ's judgment was the most pro-railway. He held that the question was one of law, not fact, and that judgment should have been entered for SER. His judgment was underpinned by two considerations.[84] First, for him the blameworthy party was the plaintiff. This was on the grounds that having not read the ticket when he had the opportunity to do so, he wished to saddle the defendant with liability. He thought it was unjust to allow a man to omit to inform himself when he could and then claim, when he could not have claimed if he had informed himself. Second, he was concerned about the burden on the companies' ability to conduct their business. Putting the ticket into the customers' hands was equivalent to telling them 'Read that'. Companies should not have had to do more;[85] they were entitled to assume that the recipient of a paper was content to deal on its terms. The fact that the 'defendants are a caput lupinum – a railway company'[86] should not make a difference. People in general were happy to take a paper on trust. This was because they were satisfied that the terms included therein were not unreasonable; otherwise, the particular transactions would stop. Bramwell LJ put faith in the market's ability to regulate unreasonable terms,[87] but he was also willing to consider a role for the courts. He answered Pollock's hypothetical question in the negative:[88]

> I think there is an implied understanding that there is no condition unreasonable to the knowledge of the party tendering the document and not insisting on its being read – no condition not relevant to the matter in hand.

Bramwell LJ thought the right question was whether a man could properly omit to inform himself, being able to do so, and then justly claim, when he could not have claimed if he had informed himself. He concluded that because the plaintiffs saw the printing, which common sense suggested that it related to the transaction, they should have been held to consent to its terms even if they had not read it. However, given that a majority did not accept that, he agreed to order a retrial based on Mellish LJ's question.

IV. ANALYSIS

What happened next in *Parker* is not known. Whether the parties settled the claim, or there was a new trial in which the jury was asked Mellish LJ's questions, mattered to the parties. For Mr Parker and Mr Gabell, it determined whether they received

---

[83] Baggallay's reputation was of a respectable judge, but one whose judgments did not exhibit profundity or originality: (1888) 23 *Law Journal* 592. He often deferred to the opinion of senior colleagues: (1888) 86 *Law Times* 77.
[84] n 67, 427–28.
[85] Bramwell made similar comments in *Stewart* (n 47).
[86] n 67, 427.
[87] ibid 428. This form of argument was later embraced by scholars of the Chicago school of thought: R Posner, *Economic Analysis of Law*, 2nd edn (Boston, Little Brown, 1977) 85.
[88] ibid 428.

compensation for their lost bags. For SER and railway companies, it determined whether printing a limitation clause on the back of a ticket with 'see back' on the front was enough. It mattered far less, however, for the development of the law. The key in that connection was the Court of Appeal's decision.

The tensions at the heart of *Parker* were not new.[89] The reasons why railway companies wished to limit their liability by tickets when operating cloakrooms were essentially the same as when carrying goods, with the difference that they could stop the service.[90] The consequences for consumers were familiar. Contracting by ticket had obvious benefits, such as making queues shorter, but the effect of exculpatory clauses could be serious.

The broader framework of analysing those tensions was also not entirely new. *Parker* presents no paradigm shift. The starting point was that railway companies could choose the terms upon which they contracted. This meant that, if they wished, they could restrict their liability. The customer was bound by those terms as long as he assented to them, expressly or impliedly.[91] Mellish LJ's jury question was addressing this point on an objective basis.[92] Within this framework, however, Mellish LJ's formulation of the jury question was distinct, even if it echoed ideas that previous generations of lawyers would recognise.

Mellish LJ's judgment was essentially a compromise;[93] something which in the long run facilitated *Parker*'s significance. First, it was a compromise between the views expressed in the preceding case law. It explained *Henderson* and *Van Toll, Stewart, Harris* in a seemingly coherent manner which had the benefit of simplicity and elegance.[94] It was presented in a form that could easily become the focal point of future analysis – a fresh start which potentially removed the need to continue to examine the extent to which the previous case law was consistent.

Second, it was a compromise between the differing views of Baggallay LJ and Bramwell LJ. Although Mellish LJ's jury question won their support, it did not drown their voices. This was important. It ensured that *Parker* contained the seeds of multiple ideas which could flourish at different times and in different environments.

Third, it was a compromise in outcome. SER's win was narrow. The question remained one of fact, not law, and thus in the hands of the jury. The notion of reasonable notice through which the question was to be answered was malleable, capable of different outcomes depending on the circumstances; as such, it was neither entirely pro-business nor pro-consumer. *Parker* can be regarded as striking a balance in a different sense. On the one hand, it met the practical needs of a railway company

---

[89] (1876) 11 *Law Journal* 645.
[90] Railway companies were under no obligation to provide cloakrooms or others means of storing goods at railway stations.
[91] W Hodges, *A Treatise on the Law of Railways*, 6th edn by JM Lely (London, Sweet and Maxwell, 1876) 617. For a different view, see C MacMillan, 'Legal Development from a Comparative Perspective: English Contract Law in the Nineteenth Century' in JC Tate et al (eds), *Global Legal History* (London, Routledge, 2019) 41.
[92] S Waddams, *Principle and Policy in Contract Law* (Cambridge, CUP, 2011) 37–39.
[93] J Adams and R Brownsword, *Key Issues in Contract* (London, Butterworths, 1995) 68.
[94] Mellish was praised for the 'marvellous faculty of extracting the pith of a case and putting it in the fewest possible words' ((1894) 98 *Law Times* 35, 36).

which could not afford to negotiate each term, orally inform the customer about it, or obtain his signature. Given the difficulty of making customers read every, or indeed any, standard term, it laid down a rule which did not require them to do so. On the other hand, it provided a minimum safeguard for customers by insisting that there was at least an opportunity for a reasonable person in their position to acquaint himself with those terms.[95]

In truth, however, Mellish LJ's judgment was more friendly to the railway companies than it initially appears. First, the formulation of the jury question involved a shift from a customer-based perspective (whether the customer should have reasonably known about the conditions), to a railway-based perspective (whether it gave the customer reasonable notice). The two could be seen as two sides of the same coin: whether the customer ought reasonably to know about the terms depended on whether reasonable notice was given to him. This underpins Baggallay LJ's belief that the answer would be the same under Mellish LJ's question as under Pollock B's one. However, the shift of perspective opened the door for potentially divergent answers, depending on what factors the courts considered relevant to this perspective. A contemporary article took the view that the jury question was 'left charmingly open' but it took 'a form far more calculated to lead them to a decision adverse to [the customer]'.[96]

Second, Mellish LJ's analysis focused on the general customer engaged in a transaction of that type, as opposed to the particular customer.[97] For example, whether the person entering a bill of lading was a businessman or one with no familiarity with bills of lading did not matter; the company could expect them to understand that it would include conditions. Likewise, whether the person using the railway was a commercial traveller or a 'flurried old woman'[98] who had travelled once or twice did not make a material difference. What counted as reasonable notice did not turn on the characteristics of the customer. This was justified on grounds of commercial necessity and effectively gave the company 'the right to deal with the public *as a mass*, making provision for "the general case" at the expense of those who are unusual'.[99] In other words, the company was entitled to make one form fit all.[100]

Third, like in the preceding case law, the analysis did not allude to the limited choice that the customer may have had in many instances, or its causes.

The reasoning in *Parker* was informed by the judges' ideological outlook. Bramwell LJ is a case in point.[101] Bramwell was the high priest of freedom of contract and laissez-faire on the bench.[102] He was an enthusiastic supporter of railway enterprise, indeed a

---

[95] E Macdonald, 'The Duty to Give Notice of Unusual Contract Terms' [1988] *JBL* 375, 382.
[96] *Saturday Review*, 7 July 1877, 15.
[97] See further, Adams (n 23) 150.
[98] (1877) 22 *Solicitors' Journal* 4, 5. The article criticised Mellish LJ's analysis as being 'almost too favourable to the company'.
[99] S Hedley, 'From Individualism to Communitarianism: The Case of Standard Forms' in TG Watkin (ed), *Legal Record and Historical Reality* (London, Hambledon Press, 1989) 239.
[100] ibid 240.
[101] (1877) 22 *Solicitors' Journal* 4, 5.
[102] Atiyah (n 32) 380; collection of articles on Bramwell in (1994) 38 *American Journal of Legal History* 241–373.

shareholder, and delivered speeches in Parliament advocating its causes. In Bramwell's words, the railway was 'not "monopoly" … but an exclusive goodness'.[103] Even so, drawing direct links between individual judges and particular decisions is not only difficult, but potentially distortive.[104] For example, Bramwell also handed down decisions that were hostile to railway companies.[105] Coleridge's name was mentioned in the context of allegations of judicial favouritism towards railway companies when an attempt was made to give him free railway tickets in Canada;[106] he found against SER. Mellish LJ had acted for years for railway companies, and had, by his own admission, defended some questionable practices on their behalf in respect of railway accidents;[107] he found for SER but only in so far as he ordered a retrial.

V. AFTERMATH: THE RECEPTION OF *PARKER* IN COURTS

Parker's significance today lies primarily in the principles it set out, abstracted from their context. What *Parker* stands for transcends the railway, the cloakroom, and the ticket. At the same time, *Parker*'s context has affected the way it has been understood. Transposed into new contexts, *Parker* was simultaneously abstracted from, and conceptualised against, its own context.

The modern context has been dominated by the even greater use of standard form contracts. In the twentieth century, these contracts formed part of almost all aspects of commercial life. It is the judicial preoccupation with standard form contracts that ultimately explains how *Parker* has been received by the courts.

A. Late Nineteenth–mid-Twentieth Century

Within half a century, Mellish LJ's judgment in *Parker* had 'become a *locus classicus*'[108] on the incorporation of terms by ticket. The judgment could be used to cut across the mass of cases on the subject, not all of which were perfectly consistent.[109]

Even so, the courts grappled with the limits of *Parker*'s application.[110] In some cases, these were drawn restrictively: Mellish LJ's jury question only applied where

---

[103] C Fairfield, *Some Account of George William Wilshere, Baron Bramwell of Hever, and his Opinions* (London, Macmillan, 1898) 216. See further, DG Raw, 'Compassion Without Compensation: The Novelists and Baron Bramwell' (PhD thesis, Newcastle University, 2013).
[104] M Lobban, 'The Politics of English law in the Nineteenth Century' in P Brand and J Getzler (eds), *Judges and Judging in the History of the Common Law and Civil Law: From Antiquity to Modern Times* (Cambridge, CUP, 2012) 102.
[105] See, eg, M Wilde, 'Railway Sparks: Technological Development and the Common Law' (2019) 59 *American Journal of Legal History* 444.
[106] (1884) 18 *American Law Review* 94.
[107] *Lee v Lancashire and Yorkshire Railway Company* (1871) 25 LT 77.
[108] *Williamson v North of Scotland and Orkney and Shetland Steam Navigation Company* 1916 SC 554, 562 (Lord Dundas).
[109] *Hood v Anchor Line (Henderson Brothers) Ltd* [1918] AC 837, 846 (Lord Dunedin).
[110] The same was true of some textbook writers: see, eg, F Pollock, *Principles of Contract at Law and in Equity*, 2nd edn (London, Stevens, 1878) 31.

the nature of the transaction was such that the person accepting a document in common form could reasonably suppose that it did not contain relevant terms.[111] In other cases, *Parker*'s jury questions were applied more widely.[112]

The key issue was what constituted reasonable notice. Some cases required consideration of the class of persons addressed.[113] This invited differentiation between consumers and businessmen, and facilitated a fine-tuned application of reasonable notice that could yield more favourable outcomes for consumers. In most cases, however, the potential did not materialise. Printing conditions that sought to restrict liability for property damage on the front of a ticket,[114] or on the back with a reference on the front,[115] counted as reasonable notice. The outcome was similar where the attempt was to limit liability for personal injury. Steamship companies printing conditions to that effect on the face of a ticket gave sufficient notice.[116] Likewise, railway companies issuing tickets with the words 'For conditions see back' on the front and the relevant conditions on the back took adequate steps.[117]

Nowhere was the stark reality facing the consumer more evident than in *Thompson v London, Midland and Scottish Railway Company*.[118] A traveller on a cheap excursion who could not read had the ticket taken for her by her niece. The ticket had the words 'Excursion. For conditions see back' on the front, and a notice on the back that it was issued subject to the conditions in the timetables. These were available for purchase and included an exemption clause on page 552. The Court of Appeal held that the company gave reasonable notice of the conditions. The traveller's inability to read did not affect her legal position.[119] Nor was it decisive that the conditions were in an external document that was harder to find.[120] In effect, the ticket could now be a link in a paper chain which led with difficulty to the actual terms.

Overall, application of Mellish LJ's dictum in *Parker* screened out only the gravest practices: where the ticket was folded so no writing was visible unless opened,[121] where the stamp obstructed the writing,[122] and where the writing was in such small font that it was not readable by most people without spectacles.[123] This left customers losing goods in cloakrooms or suffering injury from the railway's or steamship's negligence in a precarious position, especially when compared with owners of goods damaged in transit.[124]

A possible solution was to reach for Bramwell LJ's dictum in *Parker* that a condition was not binding if unreasonable. This was explored in *Gibaud v Great Eastern*

---

[111] *Watkins v Rymill* (1883) 10 QBD 178; *Burke v The South Eastern Railway Company* (1879) 5 CPD 1.
[112] *Richardson, Spence and Co v Rowntree* [1894] AC 217; *Marriott v Yeoward Brothers* [1909] 2 KB 987.
[113] ibid 221 (Lord Ashbourne); *Marriott* (n 112) 993.
[114] ibid.
[115] *Lyons v Caledonian Railway Company* 1909 SC 1185.
[116] *Cooke v T Wilson Sons & Co* (1915) 85 LJ (KB) 888; *Hood* (n 109).
[117] *Nunan v Southern Railway Company* [1923] 2 KB 703; *Penton v Southern Railway* [1931] 2 KB 103. On the nineteenth century position, see Kostal (n 72) 319.
[118] *Thompson v London, Midland and Scottish Railway Company* [1930] 1 KB 41.
[119] ibid 46 (Lord Hanworth MR).
[120] ibid 55 (Sankey LJ).
[121] *Richardson* (n 112).
[122] *Sugar v London, Midland & Scottish Railway Co* [1941] 1 All ER 172.
[123] *Williamson* (n 108).
[124] (1906) 50 *Solicitors' Journal* 200; (1905) 118 *Law Times* 534.

Railway Company[125] by counsel for a customer whose goods were lost in a railway cloakroom. The argument found little favour with the judges. Bray J said that he was neither bound by, nor in agreement with, Bramwell LJ's dictum in *Parker* or that of Byles J in *Van Toll*. A clause was not prevented from being part of the contract merely because it was unreasonable unless it was so extravagant or irrelevant as to imply fraud.[126]

i. Incorporation by Signature

The rule that a party who signs a contractual document is bound by its terms, irrespective of whether he reads it or knows its content, was cemented during this period. The rule is commonly associated with *L'Estrange v F Graucob Ltd*,[127] but the Divisional Court did little more than affirm Mellish LJ's obiter observations in *Parker* to the same effect.[128] *L'Estrange* made explicit what Mellish LJ's differing analysis of signed and unsigned documents suggested: the need to prove that a party knew or ought to have known the terms applied only to the latter.[129]

Mellish LJ's dictum has been regarded as probably the rule's original source.[130] In truth, Mellish LJ was merely encapsulating ideas found in a more embryonic form in older cases. In those cases, the courts treated the signature as evidence of assent and did not inquire into whether the notice was brought to the customer's attention. Mellish LJ's neat formulation of the underlying idea had the benefit of being able to be presented as a standalone rule.

While fortifying the rule, *L'Estrange* also exposed its potential harshness.[131] It applied with little regard to the realities of consent or negotiation, such as where the clause taking away a party's rights under the contract was buried in small print.[132] *L'Estrange* was one of two cases used by Lord Denning MR in *George Mitchell (Chesterhall) Ltd v Finney Lock Seeds Ltd* to illustrate the 'bleak winter' for the English law of contract.[133] He could have easily cited Mellish LJ's words instead.

B. Mid-twentieth Century Onwards

The second half of the twentieth century brought greater awareness of consumer welfare and a more critical attitude to standard form contracts and exemption

---

[125] *Gibaud v Great Eastern Railway Company* [1920] 3 KB 689.
[126] See further, *Pratt v South Eastern Railway Company* [1897] 1 QB 718; *Grand Trunk Railway of Canada v Robinson* [1915] AC 740, 747 (Viscount Haldane). Cf *Thompson* (n 118).
[127] *L'Estrange v F Graucob Ltd* [1934] 2 KB 394.
[128] ibid 402–03 (Scrutton LJ). Mellish LJ's comments had already been cited in *Foreman v The Great Western Railway Company* (1878) 42 JPN 648, 649; *The Luna* [1920] P 22.
[129] ibid 402–03. The application of this remains a live issue: *Blu-Sky Solutions Ltd v Be Caring Ltd* [2021] EWHC 2619 (Comm), [2022] 2 All ER (Comm) 254.
[130] JR Spencer, 'Signature, Consent, and the Rule in *L'Estrange v. Graucob*' (1973) 32 *CLJ* 104.
[131] PA Landon, 'Note on L'Estrange v Graucob' (1935) 51 *LQR* 272 described it as a 'menace to the community'.
[132] Maugham LJ expressed regret at the outcome: n 127, 405.
[133] *George Mitchell (Chesterhall) Ltd v Finney Lock Seeds Ltd* [1983] QB 284, 297. For justification of the rule, see *Peekay Intermark Ltd v Australia and NZ Banking Group* [2006] EWCA Civ 386, [2006] 2 Lloyd's Rep 511, [43] (Moore-Bick LJ).

clauses.[134] Against the backdrop of piecemeal legislation,[135] the courts took the lead. They recognised that the practical reality in standard form contracts did not match the doctrinal image of a voluntary agreement to be given effect to.[136] Two problems were singled out. First, the courts accepted that large companies took advantage of their greater bargaining power to impose harsh terms on customers, especially when dealing on a 'take-it-or-leave-it' basis. Second, customers signing or taking documents in standard form did not typically read the terms or understand them.[137]

Parker was now seen in a new light. Railway tickets were treated as prototypical standard form contracts, the result of exploitation of monopolistic power.[138] And although the nineteenth century framework of formation of contract, with its focus on consent through offer and acceptance, was not abandoned, its real-life limitations and those of *Parker* were openly acknowledged. As early as 1941, Viscount Caldecote LCJ stated in *Sugar v London, Midland & Scottish Railway Co*, that the atmosphere in which *Parker* was decided was 'rather unreal' and the resulting contract 'of a rather artificial nature'.[139] Likewise, Lord Denning MR in *Thornton v Shoe Lane Parking Ltd*[140] described the theory on which the 'ticket cases' were based as 'fiction'. Moreover, the courts recognised the potentially onerous consequences of *Parker* on consumers. In *McCutcheon v David MacBrayne*,[141] Lord Pearce spoke of 'the protection afforded to defendants by the ticket cases' and of 'some hardship' inflicted 'on ignorant or careless plaintiffs' for 'the reasons … given in *Parker*'.

The consequence was greater judicial willingness to control exemption clauses found in standard form. Paradoxically, many of the attempts at such control were based on *Parker*. In the new era, *Parker* was neither overruled, nor confined to the margins. It continued to be treated as a leading case with prominent place in the analytical framework.[142] *Parker* was at one and the same time the bête noire of judicial attempts to deal with exemption clauses in standard form and the foundation of modern ones. Most of these sought to limit the incorporation of exemption clauses into contracts. Almost all were based on understandings of the judgments in *Parker* which did not reflect their original meaning.

---

[134] I Ramsay, 'Ordoliberalism and Opportunism? The Making of Consumer Law in the UK' in HW Micklitz (ed), *The Making of Consumer Law and Policy in Europe* (Oxford, Hart Publishing, 2021) 235. Consumer bodies and public opinion played a role: G Borrie and AL Diamond, *The Consumer, Society and the Law*, 3rd edn (Middlesex, Penguin, 1973) 61–62.

[135] Eg, Road Traffic Act 1930, s 97; Transport Act 1947, s 76. On the need for legislation of general application, see *Final Report of the Committee on Consumer Protection* (Molony Committee) (Cmnd 1781, 1962).

[136] Academic writing exposed this with penetrating clarity: KN Llewellyn, 'Book Review' (1939) 52 *Harvard LR* 700; F Kessler, 'Contracts of Adhesion – Some Thoughts About Freedom of Contract' (1943) 43 *Columbia LR* 629; HB Sales, 'Standard Form Contracts' (1953) 16 MLR 318.

[137] *Suisse Atlantique Société d'Armement Maritime SA v NV Rotterdamsche Kolen Centrale* [1967] 1 AC 361, 406 (Lord Reid); *Schroeder Music Publishing Co Ltd v Macaulay* [1974] 1 WLR 1308, 1316 (Lord Diplock).

[138] *Schroeder* (n 137) 1316 (Lord Diplock).

[139] n 122, 173.

[140] *Thornton v Shoe Lane Parking Ltd* [1971] 2 QB 163, 169. See also Lord Devlin's reference to the 'world of make-believe which the law has created' in *McCutcheon* (n 141) 133.

[141] *McCutcheon v David MacBrayne* [1964] 1 WLR 125, 139.

[142] Eg, *Thornton* (n 140) 170–71 (Megaw LJ). *Parker*'s impact extended to tort law: *Ashdown v Samuel Williams & Sons* [1957] 1 QB 409, affirmed in *White v Blackmore* [1972] 2 QB 651.

First, in *Chapelton v Barry UDC*,[143] it was held that notice of the conditions must be given in a document intended to have contractual effect. A ticket given in return for hiring a deckchair was a mere non-contractual receipt for the money paid. In so finding, Slesser LJ relied on Mellish LJ's example in *Parker* of the turnpike ticket.[144] Slesser LJ took the view that the reasonable notice requirement did not apply in such a case.[145] This appears inconsistent with *Watkins*. In truth, Mellish LJ's position in *Parker* was not perfectly clear. Either way, it was now understood in a way that protected consumers.

Second, in *J Spurling Ltd v Bradshaw*,[146] Denning LJ famously stated that in deciding whether reasonable steps were taken to give sufficient notice within *Parker*,

> the more unreasonable a clause is, the greater the notice which must be given of it. Some clauses which I have seen would need to be printed in red ink on the face of the document with a red hand pointing to it before the notice could be held to be sufficient.

Returning to this in *Thornton*, Lord Denning explained that, while Mellish LJ mostly referred to 'conditions' in *Parker*, it was more appropriate to speak of 'condition' since it was the exempting condition that mattered.[147] Once the analytical inquiry focused on the individual clause, its character became relevant, affecting the degree of notice to be given.[148] In a receptive environment, Mellish LJ's dictum could be developed to suit modern conditions.[149]

Third, Lord Denning attempted to introduce a common law power to strike down exemption clauses that were unreasonable, especially where there was inequality of bargaining power.[150] His inspiration was Bramwell LJ's dictum in *Parker*.[151] In isolation, the dictum was open to Denning's interpretation, but the effect of that interpretation was very different to what Bramwell intended. Bramwell's threshold of unreasonableness was exceedingly high.[152] This was made clear in *Manchester, Sheffield and Lincolnshire Railway Co v Brown*,[153] where he denied that there was

---

[143] *Chapelton v Barry UDC* [1940] 1 KB 532.
[144] ibid 537–38.
[145] *Cf* ibid, 539 (Mackinnon LJ).
[146] *J Spurling Ltd v Bradshaw* [1956] 1 WLR 461, 466.
[147] n 140, 170.
[148] Precursors of the 'red-hand' rule can be found in *Crooks v Allan* (1879) 5 QBD 38 and, more literally, in *Williamson v The North of Scotland and Orkney and Shetland Steam Navigation Company* 1915 2 SLT 165, 168 where the Lord Ordinary referred to 'the sketch of a hand with index-finger directed to the condition'.
[149] *Interfoto Picture Library Ltd v Stiletto Visual Programmes Ltd* [1989] QB 433, 437 (Dillon LJ). For the view that the 'red-hand' rule's roots lie in Bramwell LJ's judgment, see ibid, 443 (Bingham LJ); R Bradgate, 'Unreasonable Standard Terms' (1997) 60 MLR 582, 589.
[150] Eg, *Gillespie Bros & Co Ltd v Roy Bowles Transport Ltd* [1973] QB 400, 416; *Levison v Patent Steam Carpet Cleaning Co Ltd* [1978] QB 69, 79. While at the bar, Denning acted frequently for a railway company and knew the 'ticket cases' inside out (Lord Denning, 'The Way of an Iconoclast' (1960) 3 *Sydney Law Review* 209, 215). He was successful counsel for the defendant in *L'Estrange* (n 127). By his own admission, Denning undertook a crusade from the bench against exemption clauses in standard form contracts (Lord Denning, *The Family Story* (London, Butterworths, 1981) 174–75).
[151] *Spurling* (n 146) 465.
[152] C Grunfeld, 'Passenger Charges Schemes 1952–3 and the Voice of the Consumer' (1954) 17 *MLR* 119, 123.
[153] *Manchester, Sheffield and Lincolnshire Railway Co v Brown* (1883) 8 App Cas 703, 717–18.

'anything necessarily unreasonable' in railway companies exempting themselves 'from all responsibility even for the wilful default or wilful act of [their] own servants'. For Denning, exemption clauses of this type were anathema and almost invariably unreasonable. Nonetheless, even in the new environment, Denning's approach was deemed to be too violent an assault on freedom of contract and was rejected.[154] Such a general power was ultimately conferred by the Unfair Contract Terms Act 1977 and the Consumer Rights Act 2015.

Fourth, in *Interfoto Picture Library Ltd v Stiletto Visual Programmes Ltd*,[155] Bingham LJ explained Bramwell LJ's judgment in *Parker* as concerned with the question of whether it is fair (or reasonable) to hold a party bound by a condition. In doing so, Bingham LJ was reaching for a 'concept of fair dealing' that was wider than the doctrine of incorporation of terms.[156] Once again, *Parker* was interpreted innovatively to generate principles that went beyond its original scope.

VI. CONCLUSION

Few, if anyone, would doubt the status of *Parker* as a landmark in the law of contract. Its enduring legacy is no doubt a product of the internal workings of the common law and its process of abstraction of principles from context. But it also owes much to the clarity and lucidity with which the lead judgment of Mellish LJ distilled the relevant principles from the existing law, enabling *Parker* to acquire a dominant position in future analysis.

Parker's status as a landmark in consumer law is ostensibly less obvious. *Parker* did not exhibit a distinct conceptualisation of the law for consumers; it applied the ordinary law of contract,[157] and it was through that that the interests of consumers were protected. In that respect, *Parker* had limitations. In line with contemporary contract law, it was primarily concerned with the process of making the contract rather than its content.[158] That process was analysed through the prism of consent in ways that may (anachronistically) appear myopic to modern eyes. As a result, the decision was not particularly consumer friendly. After the mid-twentieth century, *Parker* was understood in a new light. The process of making the contract that it embraced came to be seen as fictional. Yet, abstracted from its context, *Parker* formed the basis of attempts to protect consumers from unfair terms. This was done mainly through a process of strict incorporation of terms, though in the hands of Lord Denning it crossed over into substantive matters. Two specific

---

[154] Eg, *Photo Production Ltd v Securicor Transport Ltd* [1980] AC 827.
[155] n 149, 439–41.
[156] B Rix, 'Lord Bingham's Contributions to Commercial Law' in M Andenas and D Fairgrieve (eds), *Tom Bingham and the Transformation of the Law: A Liber Amicorum* (Oxford, OUP, 2009) 670.
[157] The doctrine of notice also applies to contracts between businesses: eg, *Interfoto* (n 149).
[158] D Foxton, 'The Boilerplate and the Bespoke: Should Differences in the Quality of Consent Influence the Construction and Application of Commercial Contracts?' in C Mitchell and S Watterson (eds), *The World of Maritime and Commercial Law: Essays in Honour of Francis Rose* (Oxford, Hart Publishing, 2020) 262.

aspects of *Parker* contributed to this: first, the flexibility in outcome that Mellish's formulation of the applicable principles allowed; second, the fact that *Parker* was a compromise, offering something for everyone. *Parker* contained the seeds of multiple ideas (reasonable notice, reasonableness of conditions). Some of these flowered into doctrines that were primarily intended to protect consumers. In the process, *Parker* became a landmark in consumer law.

5

Quackery and Contract Law: The Case of the *Carbolic Smoke* Ball*

AWB SIMPSON**

ALL LAWYERS, AND indeed many nonlawyers, are familiar with the case of *Carlill v Carbolic Smoke Ball Company*.[1] Continuously studied though it has been by lawyers and law students for close to a century, it has never been investigated historically. Even the form taken by the celebrated smoke ball itself remains a mystery, as indeed it was in 1892 at least to one of the members of the Court of Appeal who decided the case. For Lord Justice Lindley is reported to have referred to it as 'a thing they call the 'Carbolic Smoke Ball.' What that is, I don't know.'[2]

Happily, a considerable volume of material survives that makes it possible to recreate at least something of the historical background and significance of this landmark in the history of contract law and its relationship to the seedy world of the late nineteenth-century vendors of patent medical appliances.

I. THE INFLUENZA EPIDEMIC OF THE 1890s

The story behind the case begins in Central Asia, in the ancient city of Bokhara.[3] Life in Bokhara in the nineteenth century was, even at the best of times, rugged,

---

* [Reproduced with permission from *Journal of Legal Studies*, vol. XIV (June 1985) ©1985 by The University of Chicago. All rights reserved. 0047-2530/85/1402-0008$01.50. Please note, under the terms of the licence, we could not make amendments to the style or footnotes, so apologies for any inconsistencies between this chapter and the rest of the collection.

** I am greatly indebted to Elizabeth Carlill, a distant cousin of Louisa Elizabeth Carlill, for family information. B. Bracegirdle of the Wellcome Museum of the History of Medicine and W. D. Hackmann of the Oxford Museum of the History of Science have also assisted in attempts, so far unsuccessful, to locate a surviving smoke ball. I am especially grateful to Helmut Coing and the Gerda Henkel Stiftung for a grant to support this research.

[1] [1892] 2 Q.B. 484, before Hawkins J., [1893] 1 Q.B. 256, before the Court of Appeal. The law reports do not report the application to the Court of Appeal (Lord Justices Kay and Bowen) for a stay of execution; this was heard on July 5, and is reported in newspapers the following day. The report in 8 T.L.R. adds further information including Lindley's ignorance of what the object was; other reports do not add anything. The case is reported in The Times for June 20, July 5 and 6, and December 8, 1892, and in other papers such as the Standard, the Daily Telegraph, and the Daily Chronicle, but these add nothing of significance. The Daily News carried a leader on July 5 approving the decision, and there is an article in 69 Spectator 62 (1892). Much the fullest reporting of the case is in the professional journals: the Patent Medicines J. (1892) at 196; 40 Chemist and Druggist 875 (1892), and 41 *id*. 39, 48, 839 (1892).

[2] 41 Chemist and Druggist 843 (1892).

[3] What follows is based on the official Report of the Influenza Epidemic of 1889–90 by Dr. Franklin Parsons, British Parliamentary Papers (H.C.) 1890–91 XXXIV (Cmd. 6387 (1891)) 375.

particularly during the reign of the ferocious Emir Nasrullah, who was, even by the standards of the times, a peculiarly unpleasant piece of work.[4] Although Emir Nasrullah passed on to paradise in 1860, the natural rigors of the place remained, and the winter of 1888–89 was especially grim. According to a contemporary account: 'As the winter had been so severe the Bokhariots were obliged to spend money on firing, instead of food, so that they were weak from want of nourishment'[5] when spring arrived. Being in the main devout Moslems they nevertheless persisted in a resolute observance of the fast of Ramadan. This enfeebled them still further, so that when a severe epidemic broke out in the city during the month of May 1889, they died in large numbers. Since 1868 Bokhara had been a Russian protectorate, or satellite, the imperial government maintaining a legation in the city. The Russians in the legation, less adapted to conditions in Bokhara, suffered particularly severely. At one point all were prostrated, no one remaining in a condition to nurse the invalids. As soon as the sufferers became convalescent, they hurried home to mother Russia to enjoy a change of air and good nursing. Their flight was aided by the newly constructed Transcaspian Railway, completed only in 1888 and terminating, to please the Emir (who disliked such godless things) some eight miles from the ancient city. So it came about that by the end of November influenza had moved out of Central Asia and become so well established in St. Petersburg that half the population had been attacked. This, in all probability was how the great pandemic of influenza, 'Russian' influenza, began.[6]

The outbreak of influenza in Russia, and its movement across Europe, was of course reported in England. *The Times*, for example, on November 30, carried a story from its correspondent in St. Petersburg: 'The epidemic called by the doctors influenza, for want of a better name, continues to rage in St. Petersburg. Several Grand Dukes are affected or are just recovering, and the British Ambassador and members of his staff are nearly all ill. The writer has also just recovered from an attack.' Inevitably the disease continued to spread. Britain had last suffered from epidemic influenza in 1847–48, when, in London alone, 1,739 deaths had been attributed to the disease.[7] Since then there had only been isolated cases and a diminishing record of deaths; the figures reached a record low in 1889. But during late October of that year a new

---

[4] See F. Maclean, A Person from England and Other Travellers (1958) at ch. 1, for an account of this grisly potentate's activities.

[5] This account, taken from Unsere Zeit, is quoted in Parsons, *supra* note 3, at 14.

[6] Dr. Parsons avoided committing himself to any conclusion as to the ultimate source of the infection, and since different strains of the virus exist, there could have been more than one source. One theory, discussed by Parsons, *supra* note 3, at 82, attributed the epidemic to the bursting of the banks of the Chinese river Hoang Ho (see The Times, January 11, 1888) which spread especially malodorous mud over a wide area and caused atmospheric pollution, that some saw as the source of the disease. Other theories located the source in Athabasca in Canada, or in Siberia.

[7] The standard historical study is Theophilus Thompson, Annals of Influenza in Great Britain (1852). The Encyclopaedia Britannica (11th ed. 1910–11) contains a useful unsigned article on the subject, possibly written by Parsons.

wave of infection was quietly establishing itself. By December the disease had become common, though at first this was not generally appreciated. *The Times* published a leading article on the subject on December 3, speculating belatedly on the possibility that the disease might indeed have then reached England, and offering sage advice on the precautions to be taken by its readers. The writer favored warm underclothes, well-ventilated rooms, and breathing through the nostrils. He concluded: 'If people will lead rational lives, they may not indeed be able to bid defiance to an epidemic, the channels of diffusion of which are as yet unknown to us, but they will certainly keep themselves in the best position for resisting its onslaught, or for minimising the consequences of its occurrence.'

But by December 13 even *The Times* had caught up with reality, and rumors of influenza in London were then reported. Soon it became common knowledge that 'Russian' influenza had reached the capital, and by January the disease had reached epidemic proportions. In the city during the first quarter of 1890, 558 deaths were attributed to it. Though depressing and debilitating, influenza, at least in the form it then took, was not a disease with a high mortality rate. In the absence of complications, such as pneumonia, most recovered, and such deaths as did occur mainly came about as an indirect consequence. But a large proportion of the population was temporarily incapacitated.

At this time the nature of influenza was not understood, of course. A widely held view, and one strenuously argued by Dr. Franklin Parsons in the official reports on this and later epidemics,[8] was that microbes, transmitted from person to person, were to blame. But though claims were made from time to time[9] these had not yet been identified microscopically, nor, as we now know, could they have been. Orthodox medicine of the period favored good nursing as beneficial but in general offered no certain cure, though there was some support for the use of quinine as a prophylactic.[10] Quinine, it must be noted, was at the time one of the very few drugs available that actually did cure a disease, but that disease, of course, was not influenza. The absence of a certain cure however in no way inhibited doctors from prescribing a wide variety of drugs to their unfortunate patients; they came to doctors for treatment, and treatment they duly received. A leader in the *Lancet*, published somewhat later in 1892, cautiously concentrated attention merely on the management of the disease, rather than its cure, remarking gloomily that 'there is no disease in which it is so easy to satisfy oneself of the efficacy of a pet remedy and the truth of a plausible theory as influenza.'[11] The less reputable providers of medical care were

---

[8] Franklin Parsons, Further Reports and Papers on Epidemic Influenza, 1889–92, British Parliamentary Papers (H.C.) 1893–94 (Cmd. 7051 (1893)) 529.

[9] As by Dr. Richard Pfeiffer; see The Times, January 5, 8, and 9, 1892.

[10] Dr. Parsons's first report (*supra* note 3, at 119, 232) mentions this possibility, but the second report (*supra* note 8) in the section on prophylaxis (pt. 7 at 78) does not, presumably because its value was doubted. To judge from newspaper advertisements quinine was widely sold and used by the public both for prevention and cure. It was compulsorily administered in January 1890 to the inmates of Birmingham Prison by Dr. Arthur Price, as Parsons records.

[11] 1892 (no. 1) Lancet 320.

not so inhibited, and during the first epidemic of 1889–90 and later a wide variety of supposed cures and prophylactics were placed on the market and widely advertised. Thus in the *Illustrated London News* for December 28, 1889, Brown's Bronchial Troches, formerly advertised for other ailments, were offered as a cure, as were R. Huggins's Ozone Papers; on January 4 Salt Regal featured as a prophylactic under the headline 'The Coming Epidemic! The Coming Epidemic!' and on January 25 Beechams, better known for their liver pills, took a full page of the journal to advertise Beecham's Cough Pills as a specific remedy.

II. THE PATENTING OF THE SMOKE BALL

On October 30, 1889, one Frederick Augustus Roe, 'of 202 Regent St. in the County of Middlesex, Gentleman,' submitted an application to patent what he described as 'An Improved Device for Facilitating the Distribution, Inhalation and Application of Medicated and Other Powder.' The application was handled by the patent agents Haseltine Lake and Company from 45 Southampton Buildings, conveniently adjacent to the London Patent Office. As described in the specification, the improved device 'comprises a compressible hollow ball or receptacle of India Rubber or other suitable elastic material, having an orifice or nozzle provided with a porous or perforated disc or diaphragm consisting of muslin, silk, wire or gauze, perforated sheet metal or the like, through which, when the ball or receptacle is compressed, the powder will be forced *in a cloud of infinitesimally small particles resembling smoke.*'[12] Accompanying drawings (see Figure 1) showed two variant forms of this elegant medical appliance, the beauty of which, so its inventor claimed, lay in the fact that the inrush of air when the ball filled prevented the screen from clogging, thus enabling the user to discharge 'a cloud or diffused stream of powder resulting from each compression of the said receptacle.' When exhausted the receptacle could of course be refilled. Aesthetic claims were also made; the fact that the powder was both put in and puffed out through a single orifice, so Roe argued, greatly improved the appearance of the appliance. The invention also possessed considerable development potential. It could, for example, be modified so as to have two nozzles, or two oval outlets, 'to enable the apparatus to be applied to both nostrils at once' in a swift and concerted assault on the seat of infection. By a fortunate chance the directions for use of the ball as marketed survive in the *Inventor*:[13]

---

[12] Patent No. 17,220 of 1889 (emphasis added); the specification is obtainable from the London Patent Office. The principle of the device was similar to that of the Pulverator, described in 1892 (no. 2) Lancet 313, which forced powder through a cloth screen to emerge so as to 'very closely resemble smoke.' This was an American invention. G. Skinner of the Science Museum, South Kensington, has kindly searched for a surviving specimen, without success; the museum does possess two insufflators, which are in some respects similar (34/1974 and 35/1974), but their date and provenance are not known. The Museum of the History of Science in Oxford possesses an advertising leaflet for the smoke ball, with illustration.

[13] 6 Inventor (1890) at 189. The Inventor appeared from 1885 to 1891, then changed its name to the Inventors' Review (1891–94), finally becoming the Inventors' Review and Scientific Record (1894–1904).

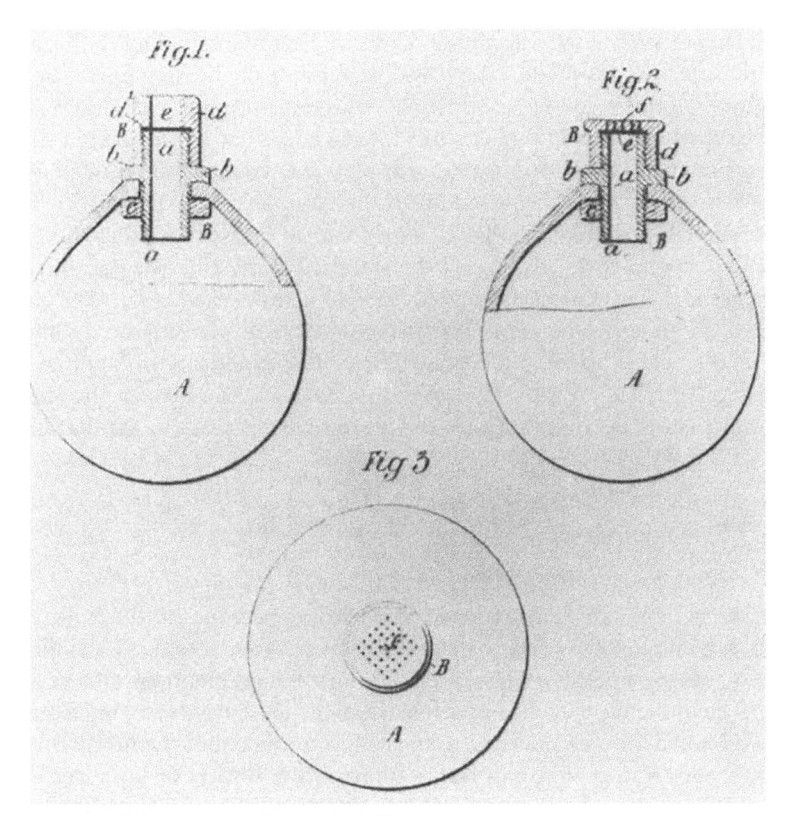

Figure 1 Technical drawings of the smoke ball

Hold the ball by the loose end below the silk floss, with the thumb and forefinger in front of the mouth. Snap or flip rapidly on the side of the ball, on the place marked 'S' and a fine powder resembling smoke will arise. Inhale this smoke or powder as it arises, as shown in the above illustration. This will cause sneezing, and for a few moments you will feel as if you were taking cold. This feeling will soon pass away and the cure has commenced. If you do not feel the effects at the first inhalation by it making you sneeze, take a second in the same manner.

This was not Roe's first invention. He had previously devoted his talents to improving the lot of horses, patenting improvements to a form of horseshoe incorporating springs in 1882, 1885, and 1886, as well as improvements to machines for sharpening calks on horseshoes and grooming horses.[14] Horses attracted considerable mechanical ingenuity at this time – patent 3644 of 1892 was a device to prevent self-abuse in stallions – and Roe's contraptions were related to a patent taken out in 1879 for Messrs. Dewey of San Francisco,[15] a business with which Roe appears to have been involved. It could be that his 'Improved Device,' which was granted patent number

---

[14] Patents 3177 and 4728 of 1882, 8001 of 1885, 6187 of 1886. In 1885 Roe's address for the patent application was given as 42 Fairholme Road, West Kensington. This was presumably his home or lodgings. He was bom in March 1842.

[15] Patent 4424 of 1879.

17,220 on December 7, 1889, was initially conceived in order to reduce the hazards and increase the effectiveness of the established practice of medicating horses by puffing powders through tubes down their throats, a technique fraught with the ever-present danger that the horse would retaliate by blowing back. But in the form in which the device was patented human application was plainly envisaged, and though no doubt other powders could have been used to fill the receptacle (and the patent does not specify) Frederick Roe seems always to have confined himself to using carbolic acid or phenol in powder form, this being the standard germ killer of the time. Patent records also show that Roe was from New York; he is thus described in 1882 and 1885, though in 1885 he was living at 42 Fairholme Road, West Kensington, London, and in 1886 at 10 Duchess Street, off Regents Street. The American origin of the smoke ball is confirmed by an advertising leaflet in the Oxford Museum for the History of Science, which describes it as the 'New American Remedy' and the 'Standard Remedy of America.'[16]

III. THE MARKETING OF THE BALL

Whether the ball was in fact marketed in America, perhaps as 'the Pulverator,' is unknown, but late in 1889 or early in 1890 Roe began to market his Carbolic Smoke Ball in England, moving his premises to 27 Princes Street, Hanover Square, at about this time. The influenza epidemic which had begun, as we have seen, in December of 1889, must have come as a godsend to his new enterprise, but the utility of the ball was by no means restricted to this single ailment. The earliest of his advertisements that I have located appeared in the *Illustrated London News* on January 11, 1890.[17] He claimed that the ball, to be had from the Carbolic Smoke Ball Company at their new premises for a price of ten shillings, 'Will positively cure Influenza, Catarrh, Asthma, Bronchitis, Hay Fever, Neuralgia, Throat Deafness, Hoarseness, Loss of Voice, Whooping Cough, Croup, Coughs, Colds, and all other ailments caused by Taking Cold.' Behind this optimism lay a theory, more fully articulated in some of his later advertisements. It was that all these ailments arose from a single cause, taking cold, and were therefore all amenable to the same single remedy, the Carbolic Smoke Ball. His advertisements exhibited a note of caution in insisting that the ball was to be used for inhalation only. Carbolic acid, though not at the time a scheduled poison, could be fatal if taken internally in more than small amounts. Inhaling the powder through the nostrils must certainly have produced a numbing and astringent effect and been somewhat disagreeable and, as the directions for use indicate, caused sneezing. Messrs. Wilcox and Company, a firm of druggists in business at 239 Oxford Street, seem to have been closely associated with Roe in the promotion of the ball. In late 1889 and early 1890 they offered especially favorable sale or return terms to

---

[16] See note 12 *supra*. In contemporary post office directories Roe turns up at 202 Regents Street in 1889, and at 27 Princes Street, Hanover Square, from 1891–40. He then disappears, but a Frederick A. Roe, LL.D. who could be our man is at 2 Seymour Road, Church End, Finchley. At the time of his death he was at 3 Princes Street, Hanover Square, with his wife, Anna N. Roe.
[17] At 56.

those who would stock it, and a set of twelve free dummies; this, so the *Chemist and Druggist* later reported, was highly successful.[18]

Frederick Roe was only one of many advertisers who made claims to cure or ward off influenza. It was the practice of the patent medicine vendors to adapt their claims, rather than their products, to the current needs of the market, and Roe was merely doing what was normal in the trade. The product remained the same; its function changed.

According to his later claims the ball was widely sold during this epidemic, and gave great satisfaction. There is no particular reason to doubt this. In the catalog of Barclay and Sons, Ltd., published for the trade in 1890, it appears in two obscurely different forms, 'the Carbolic Smoke Ball' and 'the Carbolic Smoke (India Rubber) Ball.' The wholesale prices were eighty-eight shillings and ninety-four shillings a dozen, respectively, with a retail price of ten shillings.[19] During 1890 the appliance does not seem to have been heavily advertised, though a more exhaustive search through the newspapers and journals of the period might reveal advertising that I have missed. During 1891, however, the ball was heavily and imaginatively advertised in the *Illustrated London News* at what must have been considerable expense; a full page at this time cost £100 for one issue.[20] Thus on January 24 a series of very specific claims was made: the ball would cure cold in the head or chest in twelve hours, catarrh in three months, asthma 'in every case' with relief in ten minutes, hoarseness in twelve hours, influenza in twenty-four hours, the bizarre ailment called throat deafness in three weeks, and so on. If used before retiring the ball would also prevent snoring.[21] After running this advertising for three months new copy was inserted on April 4. The list of diseases remained the same, but the theory of the smoke ball was made explicit: 'As all these diseases mentioned above proceed from the same cause – viz. taking cold, they may all be cured by one remedy – viz. the Carbolic Smoke Ball.' An appeal was also made to the snobbery of the readers by providing a list of distinguished people who, it was claimed, used the ball; the use of such testimonials, which could be fraudulent, was standard practice in the quack medicine world. This list included the duchess of Sutherland; the earls of Wharncliffe, Westmoreland, Cadogan, and Leitrim; the countesses Dudley, Pembroke, and Aberdeen; the marchionesses of Bath and Conyngham; a continental count, Count Gleichen; and a brace of run-of-the-mill lords, Rossmore and Norton. Further lists of satisfied customers appeared on April 18, May 2, and May 16. In addition to aristocrats – nine dukes – doctors now began to appear, including the distinguished Sir Henry Acland, K.C.B., a particularly important client; he was at the time Regius Professor of Medicine at Oxford and physician to the Prince of Wales.

---

[18] 40 Chemist and Druggist 142 (January 1892) and 273 (February 1892).

[19] I am grateful to G. Skinner of the Science Museum, Kensington, for supplying this reference and a copy of the circulars. Barclays was a firm established in the 1780s which supplied chemists with an extensive range of drugs, medical appliances, and sundries. Arthur E. Barclay gave evidence to the Select Committee on Patent Medicines (1912–14). See Report of the Select Committee on Patent Medicines, with Proceedings, British Parliamentary Papers, 1912–13 (hereinafter cited as Norman Report) (508) ix 99, 1913 ix 1, 1914 (414) ix 1.

[20] See Sell's Dictionary of the World's Press 1400 (1889). Half pages cost somewhat more than £50.

[21] This advertisement appeared again on February 7 and 21 and on March 7 and 21.

With the coming of spring Roe's advertising changed again; on May 30 the ball was offered as a cure for hay fever, indeed as the only cure for 'a disease that has hitherto baffled the skill of the most eminent physicians.'[22] The approach of winter brought a new advertisement on November 14, with testimonials from, for example, the Reverend Dr. Reade of Banstead Downs, Surrey, and Dr. Colbourne, M.D., of 60 Maddox Street in London. I have not traced Dr. Reade, but a W. W. Colborne does feature in the Medical Directory for 1892, with no address given. Testimonials from clerics and doctors were much favored in quack medicine advertisements, both professions combining respectability and status with a close association with death, and Roe used the names of very eminent doctors indeed.[23] Whether he had their permission it is quite impossible to tell. On December 5 he inserted a much larger advertisement, showing not merely an adult lady using the ball but a child as well; the undated advertising leaflet preserved in Oxford also directed attention to children, who could, it pointed out, be medicated when asleep, thus preserving them from illnesses which 'usually led to fatal results.' The new advertisement embodied further illustrious testimonials: 'as prescribed by Sir Morell Mackenzie, M.D.' The duke of Portland was also quoted as writing 'I am much obliged for the Carbolic Smoke Ball which you sent me, and which I find most efficacious.' And no less than His Grace the bishop of London confessed that 'the Carbolic Smoke Ball has helped me greatly,' though whether spiritually or physically was not made clear. The advertisement in the special Christmas supplement went even further by reproducing the Royal Arms –' By Royal Letters Patent' – with the obvious intention of suggesting that Her Majesty herself had in some way approved the ball. This form of deception was then common in the trade.

IV. THE RECURRENCE OF INFLUENZA, 1891–92

Influenza again became established in London during 1891, first in June and July and again during the winter of 1891–92. According to Dr. Parson's meticulous report, the winter epidemic started in November and reached its peak in the week ending January 23, 1892, when 506 deaths were attributed to it, as a primary cause, in London alone and a further eighty-six as a secondary cause.[24] The dangers of the disease were dramatically illustrated by the death of 'Eddie,' the duke of Clarence and Avondale, son of the Prince of Wales and potentially future king of England, on January 14.

---

[22] See also June 13 and 27, and July 11 and 25.

[23] See also November 28. Of the doctors mentioned during the year in Roe's advertisements, Henry Wentworth Dyke Acland (1815–1900) was one of the leading physicians of the time; he held the chair at Oxford from 1857 to 1894. See Who Was Who 1897–1915 and the Dictionary of National Biography (hereinafter cited as DNB). Sir James Paget, 1st baronet (1814–1899) was sergeant surgeon to Queen Victoria, surgeon to the Prince of Wales and vice-chancellor of London University 1884–95. See DNB and Who Was Who 1897–1915. Sir William Scovell Savory (1826–1895) was surgeon extraordinary to the Queen, 1887, and Hunterian Professor at St. Bartholomews. See DNB. Sir Edward Henry Sieveking (1816–1904) was physician to the Queen and the Prince of Wales. See DNB.

[24] Figures from Parsons, *supra* note 3.

He was to have married Princess May or Mary of Teck (later Queen Mary by marriage to his brother) on February 27; she attended his extremely well-populated death bed. The death provoked Alfred Austin, later, in 1896, to become the poet laureate, to pen these appalling lines:

> O, If she could exchange her lot,
> And now were free to choose,
> With one who in some whitewashed cot,
> Over her baby coos,
> And tend the humblest heart that burns,
> To whose awaiting smile the cherished one returns.

It was a demise which must have produced sighs of relief among the cognoscenti in high circles but one which, so far as the general public was concerned, made it clear that even the highest in the land were not immune.[25] The epidemic died out in February of 1892. At this time Frederick Roe was, as we have seen, advertising heavily. The London post office directory for that year lists him at 27 Princes Street, Hanover Square, described, no doubt by himself, as 'maker of carbolic smoke ball.' He had become a specialist. His premises lay next door to those of Sargent and Smith, Hair Restorers, and the Misses Annie and Selina Marling, Ostrich Feather Manufacturers; it appears a very suitable location. And though no such company had in fact been formally incorporated, Roe, probably with a partner, Henry Teasdale Turner,[26] was trading as the Carbolic Smoke Ball Company, in some association with Messrs. Wilcox and Company.

The advertisement that gave rise to the litigation first appeared not in the *Illustrated London News* but in the *Pall Mall Gazette* on November 13, 1891, and again on November 24 and December 8; apparently it also appeared in substantially the same form in other newspapers, not all of which I have identified.[27] One such was the *Illustrated London News*, which carried the advertisement in substantially the same form on January 30 with a facsimile reproduction of the duke of Portland's handwritten testimonial, dated March 1, 1891, from 2 Grosvenor Square. The *Pall Mall Gazette*, despite its high moral tone, carried at this period many advertisements for dubious remedies. Thus readers on November 11 were exhorted to buy Clarke's World Famous Blood Mixture, 'warranted to cleanse the blood of all impurities,

---

[25] The poem is quoted from the Pall Mall Gazette for January 15, which included a full account of the death bed. Eddie was a very unsatisfactory person, and it has even been suggested that he was in some way implicated in the affair of Jack the Ripper; the closure date on the much-laundered Home Office file is significantly a century from the date of his death. It has also been suggested that his marriage would have been bigamous. For discussion of these speculations see H. Montgomery Hyde, The Cleveland Street Scandal 55–105 (1976).

[26] See text, at note 86 *infra*..

[27] This is noted in the law report's account of the litigation. Roe also advertised in the Idler (see vol. 1, May 10, 1892 at xviii; vol. 2, 1892–93, at xvii); and the Daily Graphic (see issue of June 10, 1892). I have not made a comprehensive search for advertisements. Patent medicines were widely advertised in periodicals of this period, particularly religious ones.

from whatever cause arising. For Scrofula, Scurvy, Eczema, Skin and Blood Diseases, Pimples and Sores of all kinds, its effects are marvellous.' On November 19 Beecham's Pills, 'for regulating the system and for all Bilious and Nervous Disorders such as Headaches, Constipation, Weak Stomach, Impaired Digestion, Disordered Livers etc.,' were advertised together with Towle's Pennyroyal and Steel Pills for Females, a thinly disguised and no doubt wholly ineffective abortifacient ('quickly corrects all Irregularities and Relieves the Distressing Symptoms so Prevalent with the Sex'). Pepsolic, advertised on December 15, was even claimed to prevent divorce, which the copywriter attributed to indigestion: 'Causes Bad Temper, Irritability, Peppery Disposition, Domestic Quarrels, Separation and – The Divorce Court.' Issues of January 8 and 9, 1892, published advertisements for Holloway's celebrated ointment, Dr. Henry Paterson's Electrolytic Pill, Sequah's Prairie Flower, Dr. Durbar's Alkaram Inhalant, and Epp's Glycerine Jube-Jubes. Between them they cured more or less everything.

But if Frederick Roe was typical in his extravagant claims, he was early off the mark in directing his advertising specifically to influenza, and none of his competitors seems to have gone so far as to offer a substantial sum of money to purchasers of the ball if it failed to protect them. The text of the relevant advertisement (a particularly dull example of Roe's advertising) is reproduced in Figure 2.

To the lasting benefit of the law of contract, Mrs. Carlill saw this advertisement on the evening of November 13, 1891.

V. THE CARLILL FAMILY

Her full name was Louisa Elizabeth Carlill.[28] She used the name Elizabeth. Her maiden name was Flamank, and she was born at 10:15 A.M. on October 22, 1845, at West Street, Tavistock, in Devon. Her father was John Walkom Flamank, originally a draper and later a shipping agent, and her mother was Mary (Willcock). She was the third of ten children. On December 17, 1873, at All Saints Church, Clapton Park, she married James Briggs Carlill.[29] He sometimes dropped the name James, becoming simply Briggs Carlill, and according to family tradition he was an actuary. But he was not a member of the Institute of Actuaries, and although the family had connections with insurance,[30] I have not been able to confirm his occupation.

---

[28] Her full name appears from the pleadings in the Public Record Office, J54/740, and the report in the Daily Graphic for June 17, 1892. Her birth certificate reference is Tavistock IX 468 Dec. 1845, and her marriage certificate Hackney 1b 661 Dec. 1873.

[29] (May 24, 1848–Oct. 6, 1930). His death certificate reference is Greenwich 1d 966 Dec. 1930, on which he is described as being 'of independent means.' His marriage certificate is Hackney 1b 661 Dec. 1873. He left no will and perhaps provided for his widow by annuity.

[30] Kelly's Directory of Lincolnshire and the Port of Hull (1885) (hereinafter cited as Kelly's Directory) show Watson Carlill (his uncle) as agent for the Phoenix Fire and Eagle Life Companies, and Edward Howard Carlill (his son) in business as an insurance agent; he later became an Insurance Company secretary, as appears from the will of Sarah Ann Carlill (d. April 27, 1903). Arthur John Hepburn Carlill

Whatever he eventually became, he was originally a solicitor. He was admitted to the roll in 1870, and practiced in Hull until 1882.[31] The Carlill family indeed came from Hull, their prosperity going back to one Briggs Carlill, James Briggs's grandfather, who was a tallow chandler, insurance broker, and general commission merchant.[32] James Briggs moved to London in about 1882 and established a legal practice at 173 Fenchurch Street in partnership with William Crook, under the style of Crook and Carlill. This appears to have come to an end by 1885, when he is back in Hull in partnership with one Simon Crawshaw.[33] This practice does not seem to have continued long, as he is not in later law lists, and at the time of the action the Carlills were living in West Dulwich;[34] what occupation James Briggs then followed is uncertain. There were three children of the marriage, a son and two daughters. The son was Harold Flamank Carlill (June 24, 1875–December 7, 1959),[35] a graduate of Trinity College, Cambridge. He became a distinguished civil servant in the Board of Trade and a writer. Of the daughters one was called Dorothy; as Mrs. Brousson she cared for her mother in old age.[36] The family did have medical as well as legal connections. John Burford Carlill (1814–July 22, 1874),[37] our man's uncle, was a London doctor who practiced at 42 Weymouth Street. The Westminster Hospital has a laboratory named after him, endowed by Arthur J. B. Carlill, a Shanghai merchant and director of Dodwell and Company.[38] Hildred Bertram Carlill (1880–April 16, 1942),[39] father of my informant and cousin to James Briggs, was a very distinguished doctor. As for Mrs. Carlill herself, she was described by counsel in the legal proceedings as 'a literary lady.'[40] This was a slightly mocking expression at the time, but it is clear that she had, as a writer, an income of her own. I have been unable to trace any writings by her either under her own names, Carlill or Flamank, or a pseudonym.[41] The point is one to which I return.

(c. 1844–December 10, 1934), an entertaining character and cousin of James Briggs, who left most of his estate to his mistress, Beatrice Legge, appointed the London Life Association as executors, and may have been connected with it. I have been unable to confirm this.

[31] Information supplied by the Law Society. The firm was Collyer-Bristow and Company.

[32] His will is in Somerset House, and he appears in directories of the period in business at 36 Dock Street and 20 High Street, in, for example, F. White, General Directory and Topography of Kingston upon Hull and the City of York 1851, and Kelly's Directory (the business continuing after his death). He left four sons (John Burford, James Green, Watson, and Stephen) and five daughters (Elizabeth Briggs, Mary, Sarah Ann, Naomi, and Rachel Selina). James Green was our man's father: he was an accountant. Being a relatively affluent family the Carlills are well documented in public records; hence many left wills from which much family detail can be discovered. Many also appear in directories of the time.

[33] See Kelly's Directory *supra* note 30.

[34] The Post Office Directory for 1894 identifies the house as 30 Park Road, West Dulwich. Later the Carlills lived at The Hollies, Main Road, Sidcup (family information, and see directories for 1900–1903).

[35] See Who Was Who 1951–60. His publications were a translation of Plato's Theaetetus and Philebus (1906), and a work on Socrates (1924). His son became Admiral Sir Stephen Hope Carlill.

[36] As appears from her death certificate and from family information.

[37] His will (probate August 6, 1874) is in Somerset House, and he appears in directories of the period.

[38] Information from the family.

[39] He appears in Who's Who, and, of course, Who Was Who 1941–1950.

[40] The reference is made both at the trial and in the Court of Appeal when the application to stay execution is considered.

[41] Nothing is noted in the standard dictionaries of pseudonyms, and the family has not been able to help. I have searched all the standard indices and library catalogs.

Figure 2

[Advertisement reproduction:]

£100 REWARD

WILL BE PAID BY THE

CARBOLIC SMOKE BALL CO.

To any person who contracts the increasing Epidemic,

INFLUENZA,

Colds, or any diseases caused by taking cold, AFTER HAVING USED the BALL 3 times daily for two weeks according to the printed directions supplied with each Ball.

£1,000

Is deposited with the ALLIANCE BANK, REGENT-STREET, showing our sincerity in the matter. During the last epidemic of Influenza many thousand CARBOLIC SMOKE BALLS were sold as Preventives against this Disease, and in no ascertained case was the disease contracted by those using the CARBOLIC SMOKE BALL.

One **CARBOLIC SMOKE BALL** will last a family several months, making it the cheapest remedy in the world at the price—10s., post free. The BALL can be RE-FILLED at a cost of 5s. Address :—

CARBOLIC SMOKE BALL CO.,

27, Princes-street, Hanover-sq., London, W.

Mrs. Carlill saw the advertisement, and on November 20 she purchased a smoke ball from Messrs. Wilcox and Company, who operated a druggist's shop at 239 Oxford Street.[42] She paid for the ball out of her literary earnings. The vendors, as we have seen, were actively promoting the ball at the time. According to her account of the matter, which was given in evidence at the trial and not disputed, she assiduously used the ball three times daily for two weeks, in accordance with the already quoted printed

---

[42] This account of the litigation and the facts of the case is based on the law reports and newspapers cited in note 1 *supra*, and material in the Public Record Office. This consists of J54/740 (pleadings), J54/748 (notice of change of solicitor) and KB25/10 (Court of Appeal Order Book). None of the letters mentioned in the case survives in the public records, but texts can be recovered from the professional journals.

instructions supplied with it: 'In the morning before breakfast, at about 2 o'clock, and again when I went to bed.'[43] Whether she continued to use the ball thereafter does not appear. On January 17, that is, at the height of the epidemic, she contracted influenza. She remained ill under the care of a Dr. Robertson for some two weeks.

On January 20 her husband, James Briggs Carlill, wrote to the Carbolic Smoke Ball Company informing them of what had occurred; possibly her letter was only one of many received at this time:

> Dear Sir,
>
> Seeing your offer of a reward, dated July 20, in the 'Pall Mall Gazette' of November 13, my wife purchased one of your smoke balls, and has used it three times a day since the beginning of December. She was, however, attacked by influenza. Dr. Robertson, of West Dulwich, attended, and will no doubt be able to certify in the matter. I think it right to give you notice of this, and shall be prepared to answer any inquiry or furnish any evidence you require. I am, yours obediently,
>
> J. B. Carlill.[44]

This was ignored. He wrote again, threatening to place the matter in the hands of his solicitors, and received in reply a post card saying the matter would receive attention. He wrote a third time, and received in reply a printed circular, undated, endorsed 'In answer to your letter of January 20.' This remarkable document read:

> Re reward of £100 – The Carbolic Smoke Ball Company, seeing that claims for the above reward have been made by persons who have either not purchased the smoke ball at all, or else have failed to use it as directed, consider it necessary that they should state the conditions in which alone such reward would be paid. They have such confidence in the efficacy of the carbolic smoke ball, if used according to the printed directions supplied to each person, that they made the aforesaid offer in entire good faith, believing it impossible for the influenza to be taken during the daily inhalation of the smoke ball as prescribed. In order to protect themselves against all fraudulent claims, the Carbolic Smoke Ball Company require that the smoke ball be administered, free of charge, at their office, to those who have already purchased it. Intending claimants must attend three times daily for three weeks, and inhale the smoke ball under the directions of the Smoke Ball Company. These visits will be specially recorded by the secretary in a book. 27 Princes St. Hanover Square, London.[45]

Why this gem was not quoted in the law reports must forever remain a mystery, for it goes a long way toward explaining the hostile judicial attitude to the company. It certainly irritated James Briggs Carlill, who replied, insisting his claim was perfectly honest. To this Roe replied that 'the company considered his letter impertinent and gave him the names of his solicitors.' And so it was that on February 15 an action was commenced to claim the £100 promised. It was not apparently the only such action envisaged. The *Chemist and Druggist* for April 30, 1892, records that an application had been made in the previous week in the Chester County Court for an order to

---

[43] 40 Chemist and Druggist 876 (1892).
[44] 41 *id*. 39 (1892); and 1892 Patent Medicine J. 196, which records that seven letters in all passed between the parties.
[45] 41 Chemist and Druggist 39 (1892).

compel the company to give the names of the partners trading under the company style; an action to claim the reward was being taken in the High Court. There may have been others.

The legal proceedings were handled by solicitors, Messrs. Field Roscoe of 36 Lincoln's Inn Fields, acting as agents for J.E. Foster of 10 Trinity Street, Cambridge.[46] The use of a Cambridge firm is curious. The family lived at the time in West Dulwich, and their son did not matriculate at Cambridge until 1894. There is no directory evidence that the Carlills lived in or near Cambridge at any time. Possibly James Briggs's legal career had crossed with one or other of the partners in the Cambridge firm. Nor is there any documentary evidence as to why the suit was brought at all. But the family tradition is that Mrs. Carlill was encouraged to sue by her husband; he was so exasperated by the absurdity of current advertisements that he encouraged the challenging of the company. There is another possibility. On July 1, 1903, Mrs. Carlill's daughter Dorothy (or Dorothea) married Herbert Louis Brousson, son of Louis Maurice Brousson, a well-known Huguenot and journalist.[47] Among other papers he edited the *Inventor*[48] from 1883 to 1892. In April 1890 this published, as an advertisement, Roe's instructions for the use of the ball; this is odd, and suggests the use of the block simply to fill space in a struggling journal. The ball was not subsequently advertised there. It could be that there was some earlier connection between the families, and that the Broussons had some hand in the matter. Another hypothesis, and it is no more, is that Elizabeth Carlill's literary work was associated with Brousson's publications.

The plaintiff s formal statement of claim was delivered on February 24 to the defendant's solicitors, Messrs. Rowcliffe, Rawle Johnstone, and Gregory of 1 Bedford Row, London. It was drafted by W. Baugh Allen, a junior counsel.[49] A reply, drafted also by junior counsel in the person of H. W. Loehnis[50] was delivered on March 24. It was an elaborate document, which set out nine distinct and ingenious objections to the statement of claim. First, it said, the terms of the advertisement had not been accurately stated. Second, the plaintiff had not acted in reliance on the advertisement, used the ball as directed, or even caught influenza. Third, the defendants had received no notice of her having purchased the ball, used it, or caught influenza until after she had succumbed to the disease (which in any event they denied). Fourth, in a more conciliatory way, they conceded that they had indeed published an advertisement

---

[46] Messrs. Foster and Lawrence, solicitors, appear in Spalding's Street and General Directory of Cambridge (1881, 1884, 1887). The partners were Edmond Foster, town clerk, John Ebeneezer Foster, M.A., and William Henry Lawrence. Field Roscoe were their regular London agents, as appears from the Law List for 1892.

[47] See Who Was Who 1916–28.

[48] The name of this journal, which was run in conjunction with a patent agency, changes from time to time; see note 11 *supra*.

[49] A Wilfred Baugh Allen appears in the Law List for 1892; he had been called to the bar at Lincoln's Inn on June 21, 1882, and practiced from 4 Paper Buildings. J. Foster, Men at the Bar (1885), notes his earlier call (1870) at the Inner Temple, and his B.A. from Trinity College, Cambridge. There was also a George Boyce Allen, called 1890, and some confusion between the two men. The copy of the pleadings in the Public Record Office gives the first initial as G., not W.

[50] Herman William Loehnis, son of Herman Loehnis, a Berliner living on Dulwich Common, was an M. A. of Trinity College, Oxford, and had been called to the bar of the Inner Temple in 1882.

in the following terms: '£100 Reward will be paid by the Carbolic Smoke Ball Co. to any person who contracts the increasing epidemic influenza, colds or any disease caught by taking cold after having used the Carbolic Smoke Ball three times a day for two weeks according to the printed directions supplied with each ball. X X X One Carbolic Smoke Ball will last a family several months making it the cheapest remedy in the world at the price 10/- post free.'[51] This was of course not the complete text of the advertisement, as the pleadings indicated by the three crosses. In particular it left out the claim that £1,000 had been deposited with the Alliance Bank as a sign of sincerity; whether this was true or not was never established at the trial. Fifth, they repeated that they had had no communication with the plaintiff until January 20, after, as she claimed, she had contracted influenza on January 17. Sixth, they denied that any valid contract had been made by them to pay the £100 to the plaintiff, and, if there was such a contract, it was a gaming contract or bet, and thus legally unenforceable. Seventh and eighth, they said that if the advertisement was to be regarded as a contractual offer it constituted an offer of an insurance contract, which was never accepted and in any event did not satisfy the statutory requirements for a valid insurance contract.[52] Finally the ingenious Loehnis said that if indeed there were a contract, it was void as contrary to public policy. He did not explain why. Probably what he had in mind was the legal doctrine which forbade the recovery of contractual penalties, as contrasted with genuine preestimates of loss; he would have argued that £100 was a penal sum.

Confronted with this barrage of defenses Allen contented himself with the laconic reply, on behalf of his client, that 'except in so far as the defence consists of admissions she joins issue thereon.'

So it was that *Carlill v. Carbolic Smoke Ball Co.* came on for trial, on June 16, 1892, in court number five at the Royal Courts of Justice in the Strand, built, ironically enough, on the site of the premises of a celebrated maker and advertiser of patent medicines, Thomas Holloway. The judge was Sir Henry Hawkins, assisted by his fox terrier Jack, which always sat on the bench with him,[53] with a special jury. Neither side appears to have been parsimonious in securing the very best legal representation. Indeed the plaintiffs expenditure on counsel supports the suggestion that principle, not money, was at issue. Briefed for her was John Patrick Murphy, Q.C.,[54] assisted by both William Graham[55] and, so the law reports record, one 'Bonner,' in reality W. Baugh Allen.[56] The defense was led by no less than Herbert Henry Asquith, Q.C., future prime minister; his junior was H. W. Loehnis. The costs of this array of

---

[51] Public Record Office J 54/740.
[52] The legislation in question was 14 Geo. 3, ch. 48.
[53] See Richard Harris, The Reminiscences of Sir Henry Hawkins, (1904), especially 2 *id*. 45–64. Two pictures of Jack appear in this work. There is an obituary for the animal in the Illustrated London News for December 15, 1894, at 736.
[54] J. P. Murphy (1831–1907) was a bencher of the Middle Temple who retired from practice in 1897. He is noted in Who Was Who 1897–1915.
[55] Perhaps William Graham (died November 19, 1911), an Inner Temple barrister and professor of jurisprudence at Queen's University, Belfast, but this identification is uncertain, as there were a number of individuals of this name in practice at the time.
[56] 'Bonner' appears in the report in (1892) 2 Q.B. 484. There was a barrister of this name in practice at the time, George Albert Bonner (called June 17, 1885, Inner Temple).

legal talent must have been very considerable indeed. Notwithstanding the formal denials of Loehnis, the facts of the case were not in any real dispute, and a full trial before the special jury would have further inflated the costs. Mrs. Carlill did indeed go into the witness box, and the judge inspected the letters and the document setting out the instructions for use, and showing a lady using the ball – the picture appears in many of Roe's advertisements and in the *Inventor*.[57] Asquith asked her when she used the ball, but did not cross examine as the facts were undisputed. Counsel agreed to leave the decision to the judge, giving him power to enter whatever verdict the jurymen, in his view, ought to have found; the jury was discharged. The case was then adjourned until Saturday June 18, when the judge heard counsels' argument on the points of law involved. He then reserved judgment to consider their arguments, eventually, on July 4, entering a verdict in favor of Mrs. Carlill for the £100 claimed, together with costs, and refusing an application for a stay of execution of the judgment. The form of procedure adopted, which bypassed the jury, was a significant factor in the conversion of the dispute into a leading case, for the judge gave reasons for his decision in a complex written opinion. Had the matter gone to a jury the case would have terminated in a laconic jury verdict, and although there could have been an appeal based on the judge's directions to the jury, it is unlikely that the legal elaboration of the case would have proceeded so far as it did.

Frederick Roe was not prepared to accept this reverse. Notice of appeal was at once given, and on July 5 another queen's counsel, Arthur Cohen, appealed against the trial judge's refusal of a stay of execution of the judgment, pending an appeal, so long as the money was paid into court. This was refused.[58] Arthur Cohen[59] was one of the leading barristers of the period, particularly in demand for appellate work; his entry into the case must indicate yet again a willingness to pay for the best man available, but not necessarily any dissatisfaction with Asquith. For it was the day of the general election, and Asquith was no doubt busy in his constituency of Fifeshire East. But Roe must have been dissatisfied with his lawyers, who may well have advised against an appeal's being taken. His solicitors were sacked and replaced by James Banks Pittman of Basin's House, Basinghall Street.[60] The reason for the attempt to stay execution was principally sexist. Being a married woman Mrs. Carlill might be unable to refund the money if she lost the appeal. The judges rejected this; as a 'literary lady' she had her own earnings, and might indeed make as much as £1,000 a year, so Lord Justice Kay, no doubt slightly frivolously, suggested. For the appeal itself they replaced Cohen by Robert B. Finlay,[61] a future lord chancellor, and Loehnis by Thomas Terrell.[62] Asquith would not in any event have been available, for he had become home secretary on August 18. Mrs. Carlill retained her original solicitors

---

[57] See note 12 *supra*.
[58] See The Times for July 6, 1892, and the professional journals cited in note 1 *supra*.
[59] See DNB. Lord Selborne had offered him a judgeship in 1881, but he declined this at the request of Gladstone to avoid the necessity for a by-election. He became a privy councillor in 1905. See Who Was Who 1897–1915.
[60] Public Record Office J54/748.
[61] Robert Ballantyne Finlay (1842–1929), later Lord Chancellor and Viscount Finlay.
[62] Thomas Terrell (d. 1928) was a member both of Gray's Inn and the Middle Temple; he became a king's counsel in 1895 and treasurer of Gray's Inn in 1904. See Who Was Who 1916–1928.

but leading counsel was also replaced, by Henry Dickens, Q.C., the son of the novelist and future common serjeant of London.[63] A second junior counsel was briefed, George John Talbot, an Oxford double first and future judge and privy councillor.[64] By this time the legal costs must surely have well exceeded the £100 in dispute between the parties. The appeal was heard by Lord Justices Lindley, Bowen, and A. L. Smith on December 7 and the court, without reserving judgment, unanimously upheld the verdict in favor of Mrs. Carlill. For the moment, at least, Frederick Roe accepted defeat, and no attempt was made to carry an appeal to the ultimate tribunal, the House of Lords.

Comical though the facts appear to us today, the decision in favor of Mrs. Carlill excited only limited comment in the press of the time. The *Pall Mall Gazette*, however, published a deeply hypocritical leader on December 8:

> As Mr. Justice Lindley pointed out, for once advertisers have counted too much on the gullibility of the public.... The plaintiff bought the ball and carried out the instructions. Three times a day for two weeks she did it, with faith and with industry and yet the foul fiend gripped her. In vain the ball was smoked in the sight of any germ. Carbolic smoke positively braced the bacilli. But convalescence came, and the plaintiff rose in wrath and smote the company. Mr. Justice Hawkins backed her case, and the Court of Appeal has backed Mr. Justice Hawkins. Smoke is good, but the carbolic smoke, we fear, will have lost its savour.

The *Spectator*'s leader writer, in a piece entitled 'A Novel Breach of Contract,' revealed that he had personally sampled the ball: 'To judge from our own experiences, twenty-five violent sneezes is the least result that can be expected from a single application. Therefore, we may suppose that in the course of these two weeks, this heroic lady suffered forty-two applications of the ball, and sneezed violently more than a thousand times.'[65] He argued that no *man* would have pressed the claim to its conclusion; Mrs. Carlill showed 'all that patient determination and persistent importunity of which only a woman is capable.'

The *Chemist and Druggist*[66] welcomed the decision and took the opportunity to voice disgust on the cynicism of lawyers, in particular Asquith, quoting him as saying: 'We are not discussing the honourable obligation to pay.' In the medical press too the case was noticed, and Sir Henry Hawkins's decision was welcomed in a leader in the *Lancet*, then (and now) one of the leading organs of the legitimate medical profession. This was published on July 9, and the journal did not trouble to repeat its grudging approval when the decision was upheld in December:

> To those amongst our readers who are familiar with the way of the quack medicine vendor the facts proved the other day by Mrs. Carlill in the action she has brought against the Carbolic Smoke Ball Company will occasion no surprise.... We are glad to learn that in spite of the ingenuity of their legal advisers the defendants have been held liable to make

---

[63] Henry Fielding Dickens (1849–1933) was an Inner Temple barrister. His memoirs, rather surprisingly, do not mention this case.

[64] His involvement is noted in the Times Law Reports; it seems to have been slight, since he took no part in the oral argument. Conceivably the reporter was mistaken in including him. George John Talbot (1861–1938) became a judge of the King's Bench 1923–37 and a privy councillor on retirement.

[65] 69 Spectator 62 (July 9, 1892).

[66] 41 Chemist and Druggist 48 (July 9, 1892).

good their promise. People who are silly enough to adopt a medicine simply because a tradesman is reckless enough to make extravagant promises and wild representations as to its efficiency may thank themselves chiefly for any disappointment that ensues. Still for this folly, which is only foolish and nothing worse, it is possible to feel sympathy when the disappointment comes. It is a pleasant alternative to learn that the dupe has been able, in the present instance, to enforce a sharp penalty ....[67]

The doctors at this time were fighting a continuous and not very successful battle against various forms of quack medicine; in particular they took strong exception to the extravagant claims made by advertisers.[68] No doubt there were at the time genuinely satisfied users of the Carbolic Smoke Ball; indeed, initially Mrs. Carlill was one, for in the witness box she explained how she had recommended the ball to her friends. Although the claims made for its efficacy were ludicrously optimistic, the puffing of carbolic powder up the nostrils as a mode of treatment was not in itself any odder than many of the procedures employed at the time by orthodox medicine.

For in the Victorian world the distinction between quackery and legitimate scientific medicine was by no means as clear as it now seems. It depended, at least in part, purely on who was prescribing the treatment. Much of what the doctors did was either useless or positively harmful, except insofar as it may have improved the morale of the patient. Quack medicine was not obviously any worse as a morale booster and could, especially if available on mail order, be considerably cheaper. Considered merely as an appliance the ball was not in itself in any way unorthodox. It was what was and indeed still is known in the business as an insufflator, close cousin to an inhaler. Frederick Roe indeed used 'Inhalations London' as his telegraphic address.[69] The medical press of the period regularly reported on new developments in the field of medical appliances, so long as a regular doctor had invented or approved of them, describing and depicting, for example, contraptions such as Dr. Blenkarne's Improved Insufflator with Adjustable Tongue Depressor, which, it claimed, surpassed the old established insufflator associated with the name of Dr. Osborne.[70] Also advertised in this way in the *British Medical Journal* for 1890 was the more alarming New Vaginal Insufflator.[71] For no human orifice was safe from the assaults of Victorian medical science, and vast ingenuity was expended in perfecting suitable instruments, or even mechanisms for storing them in serried ranks, ready for instant use, such as Reynolds Enema Rack, whose virtues were extolled in the *Lancet* in 1892.[72] The availability of suitable materials encouraged this hideous trade. It was the age of rubber, gutta percha, and vulcanite.[73] It was also the golden age of the enema, which reached the summit

---

[67] 1892 (no. 2) Lancet 102. The British Medical Journal simply carried a law report of the case without comment.
[68] See for example 1889 (no. 2) Lancet 602; 1890 (no. 1) 571, 617; 1890 (no. 2) 188, 429; 1892 (no. 2) 733; 1893 (no. 2) 1138.
[69] This is recorded in the London Post Office Directory for 1895, and the telegraphic address appears on the company notepaper which he used in 1895; one sheet of this survives in the Public Record Office BT 34/895.
[70] 1890 (no. 1) British Medical J. 292.
[71] 1890 (no. 1) British Medical J. 24. See also 1889 (no. 2) Lancet 648, for the J.R.P Insufflator, invented by J. R. Philpot: 'The nozzle is placed in the affected nostril, and a sharp puff given through the mouthpiece.'
[72] 1892 (no. 1) Lancet 318.
[73] The India Rubber, Gutta Percha and Electrical Trades Journal had started publication in 1885.

of its development in America with the invention of the J.B.L. Cascade, promoted by Dr. Charles A. Tyrrell, author of *The Royal Road to Health*, a horrendous and obscene work on the mythical condition of auto-intoxication, which reached, so its author claimed, its thirty-seventh edition in 1901.[74] For those in pursuit merely of the more restrained practice of insufflation, Roe's device was one among many, and, for those desiring elegance there was an abundance of ivory, which Frederick Roe mentioned in his patent specification as a possible material for the orifice.

Nor of course were the external surfaces of the body in any way immune from the products of the mechanical ingenuity of the time; one might, if suffering from hysteria, be set upon with Dr. Andrew Smart's Dermic Punctator, which enabled the medical man to puncture one's skin simultaneously, and with little effort, with large numbers of needles to produce what was euphemistically called counterirritation. If need be, dilute acid could then be applied to the skin to enhance and sharpen the effect.[75] But Frederick Roe never widened his activities to become involved either with the external surfaces or more intimate parts of the Victorian anatomy.

The smoke ball's active ingredient, carbolic acid, is a poison, and from 1882 onward the Pharmaceutical Society had waged a campaign to persuade the Privy Council to add it to the list of scheduled poisons, a campaign which was eventually partially successful in 1900.[76] Earlier it had been freely available, and an article by Dr. Robert Lee in the *Lancet* for 1892[77] indicates that inhaling carbolic acid fumes was a recognized form of treatment for some conditions. We may be fairly confident that it did little more good to his patients than inhaling carbolic dust did for the purchasers of the Carbolic Smoke Ball, but we must not judge Frederick Roe too harshly for his optimism. And, so far as influenza is concerned the use of the ball compares favorably with the heroic measures adopted for the same condition by Dr. J. C. Voight, a product of the medical school at Edinburgh: rectal injections of eucalyptus oil,[78] or the milder methods of Dr. John Crerar, who relied on large and repeated doses of potassium bicarbonate.[79] These were inventive spirits; more typical perhaps was the scatter-gun system followed by Dr. E. C. Barnes, divisional surgeon to the Metropolitan Police: 'I gave all cases carbonate of ammonia early, with citrate of potass, and Liq. Ammon. Acetatis, followed quickly or even accompanied with quinine pills in one grain doses three times a day. For the bilious cases two grains calomel, one grain opium followed in two hours with haust. rhei and a mixture containing sodae bicarb, ammonia and

---

[74] The initials stood for Joy Beauty Life, and in reality Tyrrell was not the inventor of the machine, which was the brainchild of one Henry Child. Tyrrell's medical theories were based on the claim that virtually all illness originated in the colon, and he also sold the Ideal Sight Restorer. See Nostrums and Quackery 311–12 (2d ed. 1912); this volume was published by the American Medical Association, as part of its campaign against quackery.

[75] 1889 (no. 2) British Medical J. 724, 883, 931.

[76] Norman Report (1914), *supra* note 19, questions 12390, 12441–45. The Privy Council was responsible under § 2 of the Pharmacy Act 1868. It was estimated that the inertia of the Privy Council for this period of eighteen years cost some 3,600 avoidable deaths, but the estimate is statistically unsound, the figure including suicides who might well have used some other poison.

[77] 1892 (no. 1) Lancet 1130.

[78] *Id.* at 795.

[79] 1891 (no. 2) Lancet 1385, discussed in an editorial in 1892 (no. 2) *id.* 204.

chlorodyne. I also found liniment of chloroform and belladonna very valuable.'[80] This list excludes the extras for coughs or rheumatic symptoms. To be fair to the good doctor his patients did also receive gruel, beef tea, and brandy, which they surely deserved and needed. But it is perhaps not too surprising that some sufferers preferred the regular use of the Carbolic Smoke Ball.

VI. ROE GOES PUBLIC

The litigation with Mrs. Carlill took from February 15 to December 7, 1892, to wend its way through the courts. A less optimistic man than Frederick Roe might have thought it prudent to lie low during this period or even to flee. The scale of his advertising suggests that many balls had indeed been sold during the epidemic of 1891–92, and the reward had been offered over a period of just under three months, through the peak of the epidemic. Initially at least he must have feared that there would be very many claimants; but perhaps it was this very fear that impelled him to continue his operations boldly during the period when the litigation was being conducted. On February 27, 1892, he was once again advertising the ball from his base at 27 Princes Street: 'SNORING Cured in 1 week. SORE EYES Cured in 2 weeks. INFLUENZA Cured in 24 hours. HAY FEVER Cured in every case. CROUP Relieved in five minutes. WHOOPING COUGH Relieved by first application,' and so on. He quoted numerous testimonials; for example: 'Lady Baker writes from Ranston, Blandford, Jan. 19, 1892 'Please send me another Smoke Ball. I and the children have hitherto escaped influenza, though in the thick of it, owing entirely, I believe, to its good effects, I am recommending it to everyone.' 'Another satisfied customer, quoted in the same advertisement, was Madame Adelina Patti, who wrote from Craig-y Nos Castle; she was a celebrated prima donna of the period. So far as I have been able to check all the names quoted by Roe were of real people, and his testimonials may have been quite genuine.[81]

Though prudently avoiding any further promises of reward, he continued to advertise in the *Illustrated London News* throughout 1892, again directing his copy toward hay fever once the season started. Thus on May 28 he claimed that 'THE CARBOLIC SMOKE BALL will positively cure, and is the only remedy ever discovered which has permanently cured HAY FEVER, a disease which has hitherto baffled the most eminent physicians, who have sought in vain to cure or prevent its annual return.' Testimonials include this touching one from Major Roland Webster: 'The Carbolic Smoke Ball gave me entire satisfaction last summer. I unintentionally got into a field where hay making was going on, and I was not inconvenienced by it. I have not been able to do such a thing for the last twenty years without suffering frightfully.' As for throat deafness, J. Hargreaves wrote to inform the company that

---

[80] 1890 (no. 1) British Medical J. 599–600.
[81] Illustrated London News, February 27, 1892. Madame Patti, or Baroness Rolf Cederstrom (1843–1919) is noted in Who Was Who 1916–1928. Other writers of testimonials included the duke of Portland, the bishop of London and Sir Frederick Milner, Bart., writing from Nice, again a real person; he was the seventh baronet.

'I can hear my watch tick three or four inches away, which I have not done for months.'[82] Similar advertisements appeared in June and July.[83] Then on November 12 Roe redirected his advertising toward winter ailments, with testimonials from such illustrious figures as the Honourable Chandos Leigh, counsel to the Speaker of the House of Commons; the Reverend Canon Fleming, canon residentiary at York Minster; and Generals A. L. Playfair and E. T. Hasken. This advertisement further reveals that the smoke balls, originally, as we have seen, an American invention, were being exported, for it provided the addresses of depots in Paris, New York, and Toronto.[84]

This was not the only development in 1892.[85] On December 16, shortly after the decision had gone against him in the Court of Appeal, Frederick Roe, together with one Henry Edwin Teasdale Turner, agreed to form a limited company to market the ball and another product, a tonic known as 'Sunilla.'[86] Henry Turner was a manufacturing chemist and may have previously been in the business either as a partner or as maker of the ball. The Carbolic Smoke Ball Company, Ltd. was duly incorporated on December 19 with a nominal capital of £5,000 in £1 shares, the incorporation being handled by Morton Cutler, solicitors practising at 99 Newgate Street. The objects of the company were 'to purchase and carry on the business heretofore carried on under the style or firm of The Carbolic Smoke Ball Company in London, Paris, New York, and Toronto, and to carry out the agreement of December 16 to manufacture and sell both the ball and 'Sunilla.' Frederick Roe was appointed managing director for a term of five years at a salary of one fifth of the net profits. The assets of the earlier unincorporated firm were sold for a price of £4,400, £2,000 being paid to Roe in cash and the balance in fully paid-up shares. In addition to Roe and Turner, the original subscribers, to the extent of one share each, were five clerks, no doubt clerks in the solicitor's office. No list of other shareholders of this company exists in the public records, and in all probability there never were any. The object of the incorporation was presumably to secure the benefits of limited liability and to give Turner a larger share in the business, not to raise capital from the public.

Now it might be supposed that December 1892, just after the loss of the action, was hardly the moment for forming the new company. A flood of claims ought surely to have arrived to drive Roe into the bankruptcy court, for his personal liability for the payment of the £100 rewards would in no way be affected by the later acquisition of limited liability. Counsel in the argument before Hawkins indicated that there had

---

[82] The originals of these testimonials were available for inspection at Roe's consulting rooms, or so it was claimed. False testimonials were widely used in the trade, but genuine ones were sent in by satisfied customers, some of whom may have been sent free smoke balls.

[83] On June 18 and July 2 in the Illustrated London News, and on June 4 in the Graphic, with testimonials from persons including the Reverend Dr. Bullock, editor of the Fireside, in which Roe may have advertised. The advertising leaflet in the Museum of the History of Science in Oxford, which probably dates from late 1892, lists Ellen Young and Henry Irvine among grateful users, and the Queen's physician, Dr. Russell Reynolds, F.R.S.

[84] 14 Rue de la Paix, 196 Broadway, 71 and 72 Front Street. I have not had access to directories in which the genuineness of these addresses could be checked, nor searched for advertising in the United States, Canada, or France.

[85] The account which follows of the first company, whose number was 37795, is based on the Board of Trade Records in the Public Record Office BT 31/5463/37795 and BT 34/895/ 37795.

[86] He lived at 12 St. Phillips Road, Surbiton, and had business premises at 3 Cursitor Street.

been other claims, and the *Chemist and Druggist* noted one such, from the Chester area.[87] In the Court of Appeal much was made of this by Finlay: 'At the present there might be 10,000 people watching for the result of this appeal. There might be a swarm of imposters in the industry of smelling smoke-balls who might continue to march in as long as there was anything to be squeezed out of this unfortunate company.'[88] But in fact no flood of claims seems to have occurred. On February 25 we find the managing director of the new company boldly publishing in the *Illustrated London News* a new advertisement, cunningly framed in order to turn the whole affair to his advantage. In it he pointed out that a reward of £100 pounds had recently been promised to anyone who contracted influenza, or eleven other diseases 'caused by taking cold,' after using the ball according to the instructions. The text continues: 'Many thousand Carbolic Smoke Balls were sold on these advertisements, but only three persons claimed the reward of £100, thus proving conclusively that this invaluable remedy will prevent and cure the above mentioned diseases. THE CARBOLIC SMOKE BALL COMPANY LTD. now offer £200 REWARD to the person who purchases a Carbolic Smoke Ball and afterwards contracts any of the following diseases. ...' There followed a list of nineteen ailments: influenza, coughs, cold in the head, cold in the chest, catarrh, asthma, bronchitis, sore throat, hoarseness, throat deafness, loss of voice, laryngitis, snoring, sore eyes, diphtheria, croup, whooping cough, neuralgia, headache (see Figure 3). It will be noted that this offer appears to envisage only a single prize, and the small print went on to restrict the scope of the offer still further in a way which suggests legal advice: 'This offer is made to those who have purchased a Carbolic Smoke Ball since Jan. 1, 1893, and is subject to conditions to be obtained on application, a duplicate of which must be signed and deposited with the Company in London by the applicant before commencing the treatment specified in the conditions. This offer will remain open only till March 31, 1893.'

What these conditions were, or whether anyone succeeded in claiming the reward, does not appear. But no similar offer appears to have been made in later advertisements, so perhaps the experiment proved costly. The ball continued to be advertised enthusiastically in the early part of 1893, and the summer number of the *Illustrated London News* for that year carried one principally directed toward hay fever. In June 1893, however, there took place a curious reorganization of the business, which involved the formation of a second limited liability company and a transfer of control.[89]

The new company, called the Carbolic Smoke Ball Company (1893), Ltd., was incorporated on June 10, 1893, with a nominal capital of £35,000 in £1 shares, the registration again being handled by Morton Cutler. The objects were:

(A) To purchase and carry on the business heretofore carried on by the Carbolic Smoke Ball Company Limited in London and elsewhere, (B) To adopt and carry into effect, with or without modification, an agreement expressed to be made between the Carbolic Smoke

---

[87] 40 Chemist and Druggist 622 (1892), and 41 *id*. 48 (1892), suggesting the action was dropped on counsel's advice. See also 1892 Patent Medicines J. 196 and following, where further claims were mentioned without any specific detail.
[88] 41 Chemist and Druggist 841 (1892).
[89] What follows is based on BT 31/5604/39021 and BT 34/929/39021.

Ball Company Limited of the first part, Frederick Augustus Roe of the second part, the Bankers' Guarantee Society of the third part, and the Company of the fourth part ....

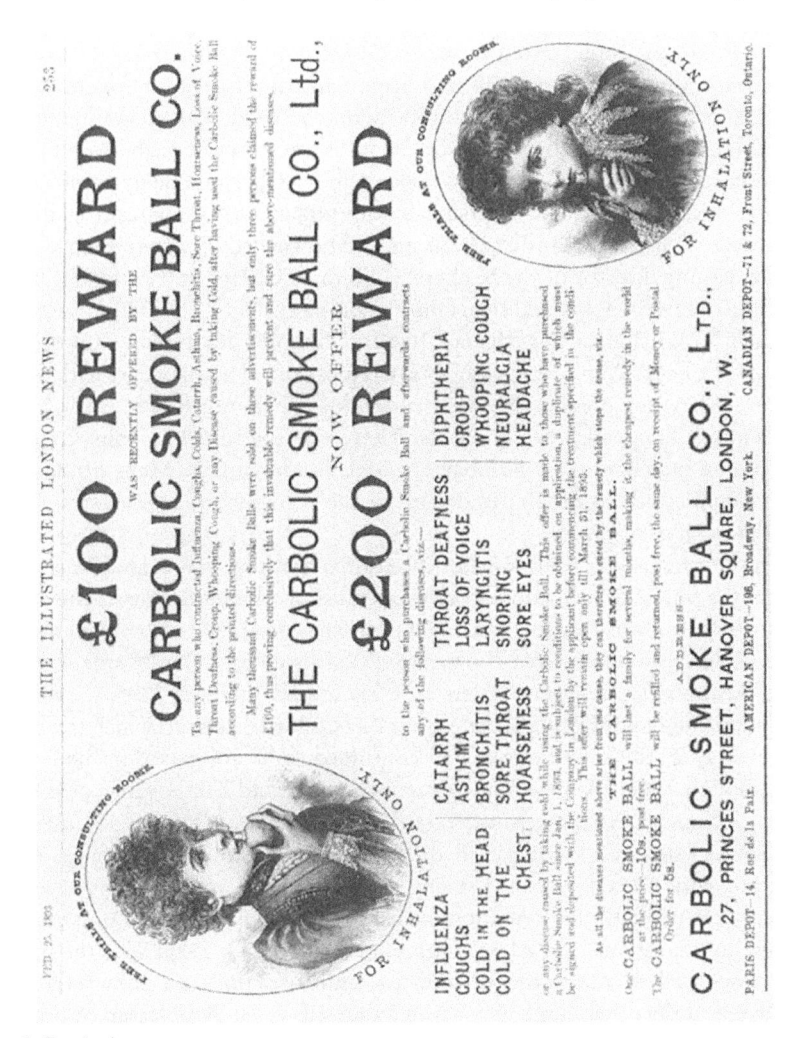

Figure 3 Roe's riposte

The text of this agreement, which had been signed on June 12, is not in the Board of Trade file, but a later agreement of July 12, which is, apparently reproduced its terms. The assets of the first company, excluding stock in trade, were to be acquired for £30,000, of which £3,500 was payable in cash and the balance in fully paid-up shares. These shares were to be allotted on the written request of the old company. The agreement was signed by Alfred Grange Shoolbred and W. Martingale,[90] directors of the

---

[90] Of 38 Lancaster Gate, London, and Woodhurst, Horley, Surrey, respectively. William or Warine Martingale was the inventor of the New Ozonic Inhaler, 'of graceful form and pleasing colour,' which received the approval of legitimate medicine by being described in 1890 (no. 1) Lancet at 354. He had premises at 10 New Cavendish Street.

new company, and Charles W. Kirk, the new company secretary, and by Frederick Roe and Henry Teasdale Turner, directors of the old company.

A summary of the capital and shareholding in the new company was later submitted to the Board of Trade, dated October 23, 1893. At that date 31,020 shares had been taken up; on 4,520 shares calls had been made of £1 each, of which £4,444-2s. had been paid. This represented new capital actually raised. The total amount agreed to be considered as having been paid on 26,500 shares was £1 each, nothing in fact having been paid. This block of shares appears to have been made up from Frederick Roe's own holding in the new company, amounting to 15,500 shares, together with 11,500 shares owned by Maurice Grant and 500 owned by his wife Frances; Grant was the managing director of the Bankers' Guarantee Company.[91] As for the block of 4,520 shares that were not issued free, Grant's company held 1,583. The largest private shareholder (1,713 shares) was Michael Joseph Connolly, described as a professor of St. Edmund College, Ware. Next came one Charles Alfred Stanley Cox with 500. The cloth was well represented by the Reverend Gilbert F. Smith Rewse (250),[92] Canon James Fleming (fifty), and several others. There was one surgeon, John Orton, and even an Indian merchant from Bombay, Devidas Vandravundas. Many holdings were extremely small, such as the shares owned by the company quartermaster, Sergeant Samuel Paterson of Gibraltar.

The result of this was both to place the company under new management and to raise from the public quite a considerable capital sum. Frederick Roe retained a stake in the business, but not control, while Henry Turner disappears from the story. How Maurice Grant became involved is obscure. Roe continued to have some connection with the business, for a surviving letter of his, dated June 22, 1895, is written on company writing paper from its premises at 219 Oxford Street, to which the business moved on May 2, 1894. The smoke ball continued to be advertised in the later part of 1893, though under the new management the scale and flamboyance of the advertisements declined.[93] A report to the Board of Trade dated October 15, 1894, notes that no shares had been by then traded. The business seems to have fallen on hard times, for on June 19, a resolution was passed to wind the company up since it could not, because of its liabilities, remain in business. The then secretary, John Fyvie, was appointed liquidator, and the job was completed by July 14, 1896. Why the company failed is obscure. A decline in the prevalence of influenza does not explain the matter, and in any event the other ailments for which the ball was sold remained common.[94] It may be that the new management had failed to grasp the fact that vigorous advertising was essential to success in the quack medicine field.

The earlier of the two companies continued to enjoy a ghostly existence for some further years. On November 1, 1893, at a symbolic meeting, held at 99 Newgate Street, a resolution was passed (and later confirmed) to liquidate the company, Frederick Roe

---

[91] Of 61 Old Broad Street. Their home was at 60 Lancaster Gate.
[92] Cox was of San Remo, Chelston, Torquay. Rewse was the rector of St. Margaret's with St. Peter's, Harleston, Norfolk, 1886–1919, rural dean and hon. canon of St. Edmundsbury and Ipswich. A handsome photograph survives.
[93] In the Illustrated London News on November 4 and December 16, 1893, and January 6, 1894.
[94] The article on influenza in the Encyclopaedia Britannica (11th ed. 1910–11) notes the deaths from influenza: 9669 in 1893, 6625 in 1894, 12,880 in 1895, 3753 in 1896.

being appointed liquidator. It was not a role in which he excelled, and some friction developed between him and the officials of the Board of Trade. The required return for 1893 was not submitted, and the officials complained to Messrs. Morton Cutler, who replied that only Roe could help. He failed to do so and a note in the file indicates that he was spoken to on December 17, 1893, and it was explained that the takeover by the new company did not absolve him from the duty to continue to make returns as required by the Companies Act. Nothing was done in 1894, but on May 11, 1895, Roe, from 219 Oxford Street, wrote to the Board to explain that he did not think that any returns were now needed, since the old company had been swallowed by the new. This did not impress the officials, and, under pressure, he swore an affidavit on June 22, 1895, that from November 17, 1892, to May 16, 1895, no assets had been received on account of the company. A similar affidavit was sworn on January 29, 1897, at 23 Great Marlborough Street; the address may signify that this was under threat of prosecution. Yet another was submitted on May 9, 1898; Roe was then back in Princes Street at a new address, number 3. No further returns were made, and on June 21, 1907, the Board served formal notice of an intention to strike the company off the register as dissolved. This notice, sent to the registered office at 27 Princes Street, was returned marked 'Gone Away years ago. Address not known.' Thus, so far as can be told from the material in the Public Record Office, did the carbolic smoke ball and its inventor vanish from recorded history. Records in St. Catherine's House show that Roe had died of tuberculosis and valvular heart disease on June 3, 1899, at his premises, 3 Princes Street; he was fifty-seven, and his occupation of 'Patent Medicine Proprietor' failed to protect him. He left a widow, but no will.

VII. THE SMOKE BALL AND CONTRACTUAL THEORY

For lawyers, and particularly for law students, *Carlill v. Carbolic Smoke Ball Co.* rapidly achieved the status of a leading case, a status which it has retained perhaps more securely in England than in the United States. Part of its success derived from the comic[95] and slightly mysterious object involved, but there were two reasons of a legal character that suggest that it deserves its place in the firmament. The first, which is not always fully appreciated, is historical; it was the vehicle whereby a new legal doctrine was introduced into the law of contract.[96] The second is that the decision could be used by expositors of the law of contract to illustrate the arcane mysteries surrounding the conception of a unilateral or one-sided contract.

So far as the first point is concerned, the so-called will theory of contract supposed that all contractual obligations were the product of the joint wills of the contracting parties, embodied in their agreement. The function of law courts, according to this

---

[95] The comic appeal is exemplified by the fact that in about 1979 the Ladies Annexe in the premises of the Law Society in Chancery Lane was named 'The Smoke Ball'; a Yorkshire solicitor won a competition for the best name. The room in question is now used as the Council Dining Room and the name has been dropped. (Information supplied by the Law Society and taken from an undated press cutting from the Daily Telegraph, about 1980.).
[96] See generally A. W. B. Simpson, Innovation in Nineteenth Century Contract Law, 91 Law Q. Rev. 247 (1975).

theory, was merely that of faithfully carrying into effect the wishes of the parties to the contract. Further reflection on the implications of this theory, which had powerful support in nineteenth-century thought, suggested that it must necessarily follow that a court should not enforce an agreement unless it was the will of the parties that it should be legally enforced. They might indeed have agreed to do something, for example go on a picnic, but be unwilling to have this agreement legally enforced. There must, it was said, be a joint intention to create legal relations before an agreement should have any legal consequences. The principal exponent of this dogma was the German jurist Savigny,[97] and some English contract writers, in particular Sir Frederick Pollock,[98] had incorporated this notion into their accounts of the law without being able to cite any case in which the doctrine had been laid down as law. It could be used to explain certain old cases in which the courts had held there to be no contract, cases in reality decided in sublime ignorance of the theories of Savigny and some long predating his birth.[99] But in legal dogmatics this retrospective reinterpretation is a normal practice, as it is in theological reasoning, which so resembles legal reasoning. But until Mrs. Carlill brought her action there was no case which had clearly recognized the requirement of an intention to create legal relations; her case did. It was indeed explicitly argued in this trial by Asquith that 'the advertisement was a mere representation of what the advertisers intended to do in a certain event. The defendants did not by issuing it mean to impose upon themselves any obligations enforceable by law.'[100] In all probability he took the idea from one of the text writers. This argument was firmly rejected by the trial judge, who relied in particular on the fact that the advertisement had stated that £1,000 had been deposited in the Alliance Bank 'showing our sincerity in the matter.' This, he argued, 'could only have been inserted with the object of leading those who read it to believe that the defendants were serious in their proposal.' In the Court of Appeal the same view was taken. Thus Lord Justice Lindley, early in his opinion said: 'We must first consider whether this was intended to be a promise at all, or whether it was a mere puff which meant nothing. Was it a mere puff? My answer to that question is No, and I base my answer on this passage: '£1000 is deposited with the Alliance Bank, shewing our sincerity in the matter.' '[101]

The fact that the judges found it necessary to make this point entailed their acceptance of the idea that without an intention to create legal relations there could be no actionable contract. In fact in the argument before the Court of Appeal little was

---

[97] This doctrine was set out in 3 Friedrich Karl von Savigny, System des heutigen römischen Rechts 309 § 140 (Berlin 1840–49).
[98] Frederick Pollock, Principles of Contract at Law and in Equity 1–2 (1876). Pollock relied on the passage referred to in Savigny, *supra* note 97, which he translated: 'When two or more persons concur in expressing a common intention so that rights or duties of these persons are thereby determined, there is an agreement.' This became his definition of a legal contract.
[99] Pollock himself did not do this; he merely treated the idea as obvious. Thus he wrote 'If people make an arrangement to go out for a walk or to read a book to-gether, there is no agreement in a legal sense. Why not? Because their intention is not directed to legal consequences, but merely to extra-legal ones; no rights or duties are to be created.' Pollock, *supra* note 98, at 2. A case often cited here is Weeks v. Tybald (1605) Noy 11, 74 E.R. 982.
[100] [1892] 1 Q.B. at 485.
[101] [1893] 1 Q.B. at 261. The leading case on 'puffs' is Dimmock v. Hallett 1866 2 Ch. App. 21. The doctrine is embodied in the maxim simplex commendatio non obligat.

made of the point, though Mr. Terrell did argue that the promise was too *vague* to be actionable, adding: 'It is like the case in which the man intended to induce a person to marry his daughter,' a reference to *Weeks v. Tybald* (1605).[102] The 'vagueness' point was picked up by other counsel engged in the case. But Lindley's opinion was so framed as to enable the case to be used as an authority for the view that Savigny's doctrine was part of English law.[103]

As for the second point, most contracts that concern the courts involve two-sided agreements, two-sided in the sense that the parties enter into reciprocal obligations to each other. A typical example is a sale of goods, where the seller has to deliver the goods and the buyer to pay for them. The doctrines of nineteenth-century contract law were adapted to such bilateral contracts, but the law also somewhat uneasily recognized that there could be contracts in which only one party was ever under any obligation to the other. The standard example was a published promise to pay a reward for information on the recovery of lost property: £10 to anyone who finds and returns my dog.[104] In such a case obviously nobody is obligated to search for the dog, but if they do so successfully, they are entitled to the reward. Such contracts seem odd in another way; there is a promise, but no agreement, for the parties never even meet until the reward is claimed. Promises of rewards, made to the world at large, will not involve an indefinite number of claims – there is only one reward offered – and the courts will uphold the claimant's right to the reward although he has never communicated any acceptance of the promise.[105] Classified as 'unilateral' contracts, such arrangements presented special problems of analysis to contract theorists, whose standard doctrines had not been evolved to fit them. Thus it was by 1892 orthodox to say that all contracts were formed by the exchange of an offer and an acceptance, but it was by no means easy to see how this could be true of unilateral contracts, where there was, to the eyes of common sense, no acceptance needed.

The analytical problems arose in a particularly acute form in the smoke ball case. Thus it seemed very peculiar to say there had been any sort of agreement between Mrs. Carlill and the company, which did not even know of her existence until January 20, when her husband wrote to them to complain. There were indeed earlier cases permitting the recovery of advertised rewards; the leading case here was *Williams v. Cawardine*,[106] where a reward of £20 had been promised by handbill for information leading to the conviction of the murderer of Walter Cawardine, and Williams, who gave such information, successfully sued to recover the reward. But this was long before the more modern doctrines had become so firmly embodied in legal thinking, and in any event the case was quite distinguishable. It concerned a reward, whereas

---

[102] Noy 11, 74 E.R. 982.

[103] Pollock had dedicated his book to Lindley. He had, so Pollock said, encouraged him to consult Savigny's works.

[104] The leading case is Williams v. Cawardine (1833) 5C. & P. 566, 172 E.R. 1101, 4 B. and Ad. 621, 110 E.R. 590, 1 Nev. & M.K.B. 418, 2 L.J.K.B. 101.

[105] Advertisements by railway companies stating the times of trains could be treated as contractual offers; see Denton v. Great Northern Railway (1856) 5 E & B. 860. In the smoke ball case Lord Justice Lindley associated the doctrine that an advertisement could constitute an offer with Willes J. The reference may be to Spencer v. Harding (1870) LR 5CP 561.

[106] See note 104 *supra*.

Mrs. Carlill was seeking compensation. There could be at most only a few claimants for this, but there is no limit on the number of those who may catch influenza. Furthermore, the Carbolic Smoke Ball Company had had no chance to check the validity of claims, of which there could be an indefinite number; much was made of this point in the argument. But the judges were not impressed with these difficulties, and their attitude was no doubt influenced by the view that the defendants were rogues. They fit their decision into the structure of the law by boldly declaring that the performance of the conditions was the acceptance, thus fictitiously extending the concept of acceptance to cover the facts. And, since 1893, law students have been introduced to the mysteries of the unilateral contract through the vehicle of *Carlill v. Carbolic Smoke Ball Co.* and taught to repeat, as a sort of magical incantation of contract law, that in the case of unilateral contracts performance of the act specified in the offer constitutes acceptance, and need not be communicated to the offeror.

Lord Justice Bowen's analysis of the facts places the moment of acceptance as the moment when Mrs. Carlill completed the three-week period of use stipulated by the directions for use. This was not the only possible view. In argument Finlay attributed the one-sniff theory to his opponents: 'According to the plaintiff, having taken one sniff at the ball, the defendant would not be at liberty to withdraw from the contract – (laughter) – because she had altered her position by sniffing.'[107] But Dickens did not agree that this was his view, though he is reported as saying that 'Here the contract arose when the plaintiff began to sniff the ball:' he thought that the contract only became binding on the defendants on completion of the course. A difficulty with Bowen and Dickens's view is that it leads to the conclusion that the offer could be withdrawn up to the moment of the last sniff, although the act of reliance by Mrs. Carlill took place earlier than this – either when she bought the ball or when she started to use it. This apparently unjust result has encouraged the further complexity of supposing there to be two contracts involved – a contract to pay the £100 if the complete course fails, and a second promise not to revoke the promise to pay the £100 once the purchaser of the ball starts the course of treatment. Other complexities somewhat inadequately dealt with in the case centered on the scope of the promise. Did it cover influenza contracted at any date in the future, or within the period of the epidemic, or while the ball was being used, or within a reasonable time thereafter? The court settled for the last possibility. And did the offer apply to any user – even one who had stolen the ball? But the judges were clearly not impressed with these problems – the defendants had not behaved as gentlemen, and that was essentially that.

VIII. ADVERTISING AND QUACK MEDICINE

Carlill v. Carbolic Smoke Ball can, however, be looked at in a completely different way, not as an incident in the doctrinal history of contract law, but rather as an incident in the shocking history of advertising and quack medicine. For as Eric Jameson puts it: 'Her case made history in the advertising world and it is said that every patent

---

[107] 40 Chemist and Druggist 843 (1892).

medicine copywriter has the words Carlill v. Carbolic Smoke Ball Company tattooed across his chest.'[108] Purveyors of quack medicines, appliances, and cures early learned the value of aggressive advertising. Since virtually all their wares were indistinguishably useless, success depended solely on promotion, and in the nineteenth century quackery was advertised on a massive scale.[109] In the early part of the century the giants were James Morrison, inventor of the Universal Pill, Herbert Ingram, purveyor of Parr's Life Pills, and Thomas Holloway,[110] though no list would be complete without a mention of Cockle's Anti Bilious Pills, which sustained Fred Burnaby on his ride to Khiva: 'And for physic – with which it is as well to be supplied when travelling in out-of-the-way-places – some quinine, and Cockle's pills, the latter a most invaluable medicine, and one which I have used on the natives of Central Africa with the greatest possible success. In fact the marvellous effects produced upon the mind and body of an Arab Sheik, who was impervious to all native medicines, when I administered to him five Cockle's pills, will never fade from my memory....'[111]

James Morison,[112] oddly self-styled 'the Hygieist,' specialized in vegetable universal medicines, and published extensively on the merits of his system; a common feature of quackery is the claim to cure all illness, or an extended list of illnesses, by a single remedy, a claim typically made for the smoke ball itself. Herbert Ingram[113] purchased the secret recipe of Parr's Life Pills from one T. Roberts and in 1842 founded the *Illustrated London News*, so it is said, in order to promote their sale.[114] The secret was said to have been passed down through the descendants of the celebrated Old Parr himself, Thomas Parr (?1483–1635)[115] whose virility was such that in 1588, at the supposed age of a hundred and five, he did public penance in a white sheet for fathering a bastard child. Thomas Holloway,[116] who founded both Holloway College and a large sanatorium for mentally deranged but curable members of the middle classes, sold his pills and ointment from premises at 244 The Strand, where the Royal Courts of Justice now stand. By the time of his death he was annually spending £50,000 on advertising and had amassed a fortune estimated at £5 million, though much of this had been given away before his death. An archetypal entrepreneur, his death inspired a long editorial in *The Times* for December 28, 1883, on the character of such a man:

> The secret is with the man himself – in his fixed, steady, unwavering purpose of making money and allowing no obstacles to come in the way of this.... Every action must be looked at from the one single point of view of the money value that may be found in it, or which it may somehow be made to bear.

---

[108] Eric Jameson, The Natural History of Quackery 62 (1961).
[109] See Henry Sampson, A History of Advertising from the Earliest Times (1875), especially chs. 14 and 15. Sampson, unrealistically, wrote as if the trade had by the time of writing become respectable.
[110] E. S. Turner, The Shocking History of Advertising 62–68 (1952).
[111] F. Burnaby, A Ride to Khiva (1877) at ch. 1. Burnaby's praises were much used in advertising the pills.
[112] (1770–1840). See the article in the DNB and an obituary in the Gentlemen's Magazine (1840) pt. 2, at 437.
[113] (1811–60). See DNB, and F. Boase, Modern English Biography (1965).
[114] The earliest advertisement published in his paper (1 (no. 1) Illustrated London News 111, June 25, 1842) has the pills as obtainable from T. Roberts and Company, London, which suggests that the standard account may not be true, unless Ingram was trading under this name.
[115] See the article in the DNB.
[116] (1800–1883); on his life see DNB; the Illustrated London News January 5, 1884; Boase, *supra* note 113; Turner, *supra* note 110, at 65–68.

As to his technique the writer continued:

> Mr. Holloway was a master in the art of advertising. The praises of his medicines have been sounded in all lands, and in all known languages. Every available place, from a London hoarding to the Great Pyramid, has been pressed into the service, and has been forced to bear testimony to their merits. Every sufferer from every conceivable disease or failing has thus been duly informed to what quarter he might look for restoration to health and strength.

Later giants in the field included Sir Joseph Beecham of St. Helen's[117] whose liver pills, 'worth a guinea a box,' and less well remembered cough medicine were advertised in the late nineteenth century on a scale rivaled only by Pear's Soap and Lipton's tea. The pills were supposed to be made up to a secret and elaborate recipe handed down from Joseph Beecham's father, Thomas Beecham (1820–1907); professional analysis suggested that they contained merely aloes, ginger, and soap.[118] By 1913 Beecham was selling fifty tons of pills a year.[119] A typical quack, Beecham at various times claimed that his pills, which were essentially laxatives, would cure Bright's disease and syphilis and procure abortions, as well as acting as a remedy for numerous less grave conditions.[120]

IX. QUACKERY AND THE LAW

From time to time quacks did come into conflict with the law. The most notable instance in the nineteenth century of such a conflict involved one John St. John Long. He specialized in the treatment of tuberculosis, a disease he confronted with a secret liniment, inhalations, and cabbage leaves, conducting his thriving practice from 41 Harley Street.[121] In 1830 Long stood trial before Mr. Justice Park at the Old Bailey for the manslaughter of one of his patients, Catherine Cashin.[122] She was an Irish girl from Limerick, and her younger sister Ellen had been treated by Long without any disastrous results. Catherine, however, died on September 17, after treatment by blistering, inhalations, liniment, and of course cabbage leaves. Although some thirty of Long's patients gave evidence in his favor at the trial, Long was nevertheless convicted; the judge imposed the light sentence of a fine of £250, no doubt a substantial sum but one which Long had no problem in paying on the spot. During the trial Long acquired a new patient, a Mrs. Colin Campbell Lloyd, wife of Edward Lloyd, a royal naval post captain. She in her turn died, and the coroner's inquest

---

[117] (1848–1916). Beecham, who had been running the business on his own since 1895, gave evidence to the Select Committee on January 13, 1913; see Norman Report (1914), *supra* note 19, questions 8964–9514. He was fairly roughly handled by the committee, which viewed him as a fraudulent rogue.

[118] *Id.*, questions 9071–78, 9133–34, 9264–65, 9426–67. The analysis was published by the British Medical Association in Secret Remedies (1909); see Norman Report, question 3510.

[119] Beecham's estimated turnover in 1913 was of the order of £340,000. He acquired a knighthood, presumably by purchase, in 1911 and a baronetcy in 1914.

[120] See Norman Report (1914), *supra* note 17, at xviii–xx; Nostrums and Quackery, *supra* note 74, at 518.

[121] (1798–1834). See Jameson, *supra* note 108, at 66–74.

[122] The trial, which took place on Saturday, October 30, is covered in the Old Bailey Sessions Papers (1830), case no. 1952 at 856.

brought in a verdict of manslaughter against him.[123] So Long again stood trial, this time before Baron Bailey, at the Old Bailey sessions on Saturday, February 19, 1831;[124] the case was considered sufficiently important for the attorney general to conduct the prosecution. Long again produced many satisfied clients, and was acquitted.[125] The hostility of orthodox doctors toward Long was intensified by his own attacks on the profession, which, in his view, principally consisted of quacks.[126] Long resumed his practice, but died young three years later, ironically enough of tuberculosis, his own specialty, presumably having caught the disease from his patients.

This was a rare incident, which had no perceptible effect on quackery. In the later nineteenth century, with the increase in flamboyant advertising, the principal criticism leveled against quackery concentrated on the extravagant claims made for medicines and appliances. A notable example of an extravagantly advertised product was Harness's Electropathic Belt, the brain child of a Cornelius Bennett Harness, President of the Electropathic and Zander Institute. As advertised, for example, in the *Illustrated London News* on February 20, 1892, this not only prevented influenza 'and all weak and languid feelings' but also cured rheumatism, gout, sciatica, lumbago, nervous exhaustion, impaired vitality, brain fag, sleeplessness, ladies' ailments, hysteria, indigestion, constipation, loss of appetite, and kidney troubles. Recommended both for weak men and delicate women as imparting new life and vigor, this appliance could be purchased from the Medical Battery Company, Ltd.[127] at 52 Oxford Street, where Harness and his colleagues maintained a considerable consulting business and engaged in alarming forms of treatment for virtually any form of disability. He also sold an electropathic corset for such women as did not feel attracted to the unisex model. In November 1893 an attempt was made to bring Harness to trial for conspiracy to defraud, together with two of his colleagues, one of whom was a deviant medical man, James Montgomery M'Cully, struck off the medical register in November 1887.[128] The prosecutor was an aged and somewhat

---

[123] The Times for November 11, 12, and 15, 1830.
[124] Old Bailey Sessions Papers (1831) at 283.
[125] Long published a defense of his system, John St. John Long, A Critical Exposure of the Ignorance and Malpractice of Certain Medical Practitioners in their Theory and Treatment of Disease ... to which is affixed a Commentary on the Medical Evidence in the case of Miss Cashin and Mrs. Lloyd (1831). Long was attacked by George Tate, M.R.C.S., in a tract published in Cheltenham in 1831, Observations upon the System of J. St. J. Long. There is also a defense of Long by an anonymous graduate of Trinity College and a member of the Middle Temple, A Defence of J. St. J. Long (1830).
[126] John St. John Long, Discoveries in the Science and Art of Healing (1830). See also S. S. Srigge, Life and Times of Thos. Wakley (1897). Wakley was the founder of the Lancet and a vigorous critic of Long's methods.
[127] The earliest such company (20909) was registered on March 10, 1885, taking over Harness's business and that of the Pall Mall Electric Association, Ltd. At this time Harness lived, appropriately, at Lavender Hill. This company was wound up in 1889, when a new company (28851) was formed; this was wound up by High Court order on November 22, 1893. A new company (58940), was registered on September 27, 1898, at which point Harness was living at 21 Baker St. This company too was wound up; one of its shareholders, William Willmott, registered a fourth such company (67755) in 1900, but this never did any business. Records in the Public Record Office include BT 31/3457/20909, 31/4432/28851, 31/8155/58940, 31/9144/67755.
[128] The hearing, which was treated as pure slapstick, may be followed in The Times for November 9, 16, 23, and 30, and December 1, 6, 7, 14, 21, 22, and 28, 1893; January 4, 11, 18, 19, and 23, and February 1 and 8, 1894. The third defendant, Charles Beavington Hollier, was a salesman. Proceedings against a fourth individual were dropped. T. E. Gatehouse, editor of the Electrical Review, had criticized the belt as useless;

decrepit military man, Colonel Jeremiah Brayser, a veteran of the seige of Lucknow during the Indian Mutiny. He had retired to live in Margate, where he suffered, so he said, from weakness of the loins; there was some ribald suggestion by counsel that he had been contemplating matrimony and had purchased the belt by way of preparation. The prosecution was handled by Thomas Terrell who had represented Frederick Roe. Horace Avory appeared for Harness. This prosecution failed at the preliminary hearing before the Metropolitan Police magistrate, James Hannah. On Wednesday, January 31, he refused to commit for trial, since no jury would have been likely to convict. Although it was possible to call medical and technical evidence to show that the belt was perfectly useless and its inventor a charlatan, the defense was able to reply with abundant evidence from satisfied customers, who were delighted with the results achieved by wearing the appliance. As Mr. Hannah commented, when dismissing the case: 'It was remarkable that although they daily saw some advertisements of quack medicines supposed to cure all sorts of diseases, no action had been taken by the Director of Public Prosecutions against the persons who issued such advertisements. He thought that if he had seen his way clear to get a conviction, the D.P.P. would undoubtedly have intervened in such cases.'[129] Hence he felt justified in refusing to commit for trial. The *Lancet*, in a leader published on February 3 under the headline 'The Immunity of Quackery' gloomily accepted the correctness of the decision, while deploring the state of the law that brought it about. In fact there was a successful prosecution in the same year; one Francis McConville, alias Thomas Kelly, alias King and Company, alias Hamilton, and alias Professor Hamilton, was convicted on March 22, at Liverpool Assizes before Justice Day for obtaining money by false pretenses. He was sentenced to five years' penal servitude. He ran the Medical Institute, posing falsely as a qualified doctor, and sold an electric belt as a cure for venereal diseases; he had previously been involved in distributing obscene literature. But this case was the exception, and had there been no pretense to medical qualifications it is unlikely that a conviction could have been achieved.[130]

The Harness case, besides serving to discourage further attempts to prosecute, also served to illustrate the uneasy line which then separated the world of the quack from that of the legitimate profession, whose members also employed various more or less absurd contraptions, including some designed to administer electrical treatment. A glance through the regular medical press of the period reveals a profession much given to the use of ludicrous appliances, such as the Vitalite Sock,[131] the New Flannel Squeezer, a contraption resembling a large garlic press,[132] the Invigorator Corset,[133] as well as numerous electrical devices, such as The Automatic Medical Battery made

---

the company had in reply circularized newsagents in September 1892 claiming that the article was libelous. Gatehouse then successfully sued the company for libel, recovering £1,000 damages in a trial before the Lord Chief Justice.

[129] The Times, January 31, 1894.

[130] See 1894 (no. 1) Lancet 826. The Harness case is discussed in the Norman Report (1914), *supra* note 19, at questions 429–37, 1056, but the Liverpool case seems to have been forgotten; it was of course distinguishable because of the claim to a medical qualification.

[131] 1891 (no. 2) Lancet 876.

[132] 1890 (no. 2) Lancet 673.

[133] 1892 (no. 2) Lancet 204.

by the H. B. Cox Electrical Company, which could be used to apply, at the physician's choice, three levels of shock to the patient.[134] And, as we have seen, one of the directors of the Carbolic Smoke Ball Company (1893) had had his New Ozonic Inhaler described and by implication recommended in the *Lancet* in 1890.[135]

But the very narrowness of the dividing line may have served to intensify the vigor with which the struggle against the quacks was pursued, and the orthodox doctors had certain substantial complaints to make. They abstained from making ludicrously inflated claims as to what they could achieve, and for some ailments they did provide either remedies or at least treatment which alleviated the symptoms. They could also argue that some quack medicines were actively harmful, and that resort to quacks could discourage those who could have benefited from scientific medicine from consulting a qualified doctor. During the early years of this century the battle against the quacks intensified, both in America and in Britain. American patent medicines and appliances exhibited a creative genius that could hardly be matched in England. In addition to the smoke ball itself, there were such products as Tiger Fat, Blessed Handkerchiefs, Hamlin's Wizard Oil, and Cram's Fluid Lightning,[136] and the appliances sold included Dr. Hercules Sanche's Oxydeno, Electropoise, Oxygenor, Oxÿpathos, Oxytonor, and Oxybon, alleged to work by the force of diaduction.[137] The generic expression in America for such products is snake oil, but I have not traced a specific reference to such a product. Public criticism of fraudulent claims was heightened by articles published by Edward Bok in the *Ladies Home Journal* and by Samuel H. Adams in *Collier's Weekly*.[138]

X. THE REGULATION OF THE TRADE

All this agitation led to legislation in the form of the Pure Food and Drugs Act, which came into force on January 1, 1907. In Britain similar agitation was expressed in two publications of the British Medical Association, *Secret Remedies* in 1909, and *More Secret Remedies* in 1912. The movement led to the establishment in 1912 of a select committee of the House of Commons, under the chairmanship of Sir Henry Norman. It reported on August 4, 1914,[139] and came out strongly in favor of introducing new legal regulation of the patent medicine industry, which it viewed as little more than licensed fraud. Naturally the committee investigated the existing state of the law, and the conclusion reached was hardly flattering to English jurisprudence:

> The situation, therefore, as regards the sale and advertisement of patent and proprietary medicines and articles may be summarized in one sentence as follows. For all practical

---

[134] 1890 (no. 1) Lancet 129.
[135] *Id.* at 354.
[136] S. H. Holbrook, The Golden Age of Quackery 188, 236 (1959).
[137] Nostrums and Quackery, *supra* note 120, at 295–309.
[138] See L. Fuller, The Muckrakers: Crusaders for American Liberalism (1939) at ch. 12; J. H. Young, The Medical Messiahs (1967) at 27–39; S. H. Adams, The Great American Fraud (1906); Collier's National Weekly from October 7, 1905–February 17, 1906, and July 14, 1906–September 22, 1906; Ladies Home Journal May 21 and July 18, 1904.
[139] See note 19 *supra*.

purposes British law is powerless to prevent any person from procuring any drug, or making any mixture, whether potent or without any therapeutical activity whatever (so long as it does not contain a scheduled poison), advertise it in any decent terms as a cure for any disease or ailment, recommending it by bogus testimonials and the invented opinions and facsimile signatures of fictitious physicians, and selling it under any name he chooses, on the payment of a small stamp duty, for any price he can persuade a credulous public to pay.[140]

It was a severe judgment on an industry which at the time was spending around £2,000,000 each year on advertising.[141] It was also a severe judgment on the judge-made law, both criminal and civil, and one which typically led to the conclusion that more direct regulation was the solution. Underlying it was a belief, not expressly articulated, that state regulation was the only appropriate reaction to the phenomenon in question: a fool and his money are easily parted. So far as criminal proceedings were concerned the impotence of the law was explained by the need to prove 'guilty knowledge' and by the fact (which of course cut both ways) that quacks could always produce satisfied customers to give evidence on their behalf.[142] As for civil law it seemed hardly worth discussing, for it was settled that mere advertising puffs could not be treated as actionable warranties.[143] But Cyril Herbert Kirby, a solicitor employed by the Chemists' Defence Union, seemed to think that there could, in theory at least, be civil liability under section 14(1) of the Sale of Goods Act of 1893, though he could only recall one case which had come to court. The risk of the occasional civil action, normally limited to the recovery of the price paid, could not of course have any substantial influence upon the conduct of a trade which could readily discount the risks involved. Kirby did, however, sing the praises of *Carlill v. Carbolic Smoke Ball Company*: 'This decision might be useful in the case of medicines advertised as definite cures for certain ailments: it would only apply to a suit by the person injured.' The chairman, surely skeptically, asked: 'Are there any other cases to illustrate that point?' And Kirby replied: 'No, I do not know of any case parallel to that, but that has always been treated as a good binding authority.'[144]

And that, so far as the Roes and Beechams of the world were concerned, was about all it was, and a good binding authority it has remained to this day. Occasionally thereafter an advertiser did, like Frederick Roe, make a specific promise of a reward, as did Elmer Shirley of 6 St. James Street in the *Daily Mail* for July 5, 1912. He claimed to be able to cure catarrh and deafness and offered to pay £500 if he failed.

---

[140] Norman Report (1914), *supra* note 19, at ix. Compare the statement, *id.*: 'By strict interpretation of existing statutes, of the precedents of Common Law, or of the authority of officials and Departments, considerable powers of prevention and prosecution may exist nominally. But we are satisfied that the difficulties of bringing the powers to successful operation are so numerous and great that for all practical purposes the sale and advertisement of secret remedies (unless they contain scheduled poisons) is unrestricted by law in this country.'
[141] Norman Report (1914), *supra* note 19, at x.
[142] *Id.* at viii, 120.
[143] See note 101 *supra*.
[144] Norman Report (1914), *supra* note 17, questions 4873–77. Kirby's evidence begins at 277.

Shirley was in fact an alias for an individual whose real name was Marr; he was also known as Professor Keith Harvey and Erasmus Coleman, and he had had at one time the distinction of employing the celebrated murderer Hawley Harvey Crippen, whom we English like to claim as one of us, though in reality he was an American.[145] Crippen too had an alias, M. Frankel.[146] He was one of the few quacks who did lose out in a conflict with the law, for reasons not directly related to his trade, though one theory explains the 'murder' of his wife as the result of an accidental overuse of hyocine as a sexual depressant.

As for the Norman Report, the outbreak of the First World War overtook it, and, as has so often happened to such reports, it accumulated dust for many years. Apart from legislation in 1917 to curb advertisements of cures for venereal diseases, it was not until the later 1930s that any further action took place to curb the trade.[147] Occasionally, however, an advertiser did burn his fingers by forgetting the case of the smoke ball. Thus in 1932 in Wood v. Letrick Ltd. the plaintiff recovered £500 against the manufacturers of the Letrik electric comb on facts very similar to the earlier case. Through an advertising agency the combs, of which some 100,000 had been sold at a price of 3/6d., had been advertised in a periodical in the following terms:

> New Hair in 72 hours. 'Letrik' Electric Comb.
>
> Great News for Hair Sufferers. What is *your* trouble?
>
> Is it grey hair? In 10 days not a grey hair left. £500 guarantee.
>
> Is it a bald patch? Covered with new hair in 72 hours. £500 guarantee.[148]

The advertisement continued in similar vein to deal with falling hair, dandruff, and straight and lifeless hair and claimed that 661,000 had been sold to all grades in society from royalty downward. The defendant's counsel attempted to argue that the promises were impossible and therefore void at law, but the judge, Rowlatt, was unimpressed and awarded the sum claimed, relying upon the smoke ball case. Five other claims were then pending and were presumably paid. But this was an isolated incident, and prudent copywriters could easily continue to deceive the public while keeping clear of the law. So although Mrs. Carlill's action has undoubtedly made a permanent contribution to legal dogmatics, it has caused only an insignificant amount of inconvenience to the likes of Frederick Augustus Roe.

---

[145] Crippen is the only murderer known to have, on arrest, replied with a metrical line: 'My name is Hawley Harvey Crippen and I come from Coldwater, Michigan, U.S.A.,' a fact exploited by Beverley Cross in writing the lyrics for the short-lived musical, 'Belle.'

[146] See Norman Report (1914), *supra* note 17, questions 5389–94, 4083–89, 4104–8, 5400–5402. Crippen, who was in fact medically qualified, had worked for the Sovereign Remedies Company as manager, then for the notorious Drouet Institute and the Aural Clinic Company, and finally became advertising manager for Munyon's Remedies. Munyon was an American quack of the worst kind; he features in Nostrums and Quackeries, *supra* note 120, at 513, 559, 590, 603. As Frankel, Crippen sold Ohrsorb, a cure for deafness. See also F. Young, The Trial of Hawley Harvey Crippen (Notable British Trials Series) (1920), at xxiv–xxv.

[147] The Venereal Disease Act 1917, the Cancer Act 1939. See Turner, *supra* note 110, at 236–37. In 1950 self-regulation began with the formulation of a code of standards.

[148] The Times, January 12 and 13, 1932. The report does not identify the periodical in which the advertisement appeared.

XI. EPILOGUE

And as for Louisa Elizabeth Carlill herself, as Figure 4 shows, she long survived her adventure with the law. After her husband died on October 6, 1930,[149] she lived in a flat in Blackheath, but by 1939 she was established in a hotel on the south coast, probably in Hastings, where she was renowned for her punctuality and her settled practice of drinking one glass of claret with her lunch. She then went to live with her daughter Dorothy Brousson at Swan House, in the village of Sellindge, near Folkestone, a lively spot to choose at the time of the Battle of Britain. There she died on March 10, 1942, at the age of ninety-six years, principally, as her death certificate records, of old age.[150]

The other cause noted by her medical man, Dr. Joseph M. Yarman, was influenza.

Figure 4 Mrs Carlill at the age of 87

---

[149] The reference is Greenwich 1d. 966 Dec. 1930.
[150] Folkestone 2a. 2703 March 1942.

6

Helby v Matthews:
The 'Great Test Case'?*

IAIN RAMSAY**

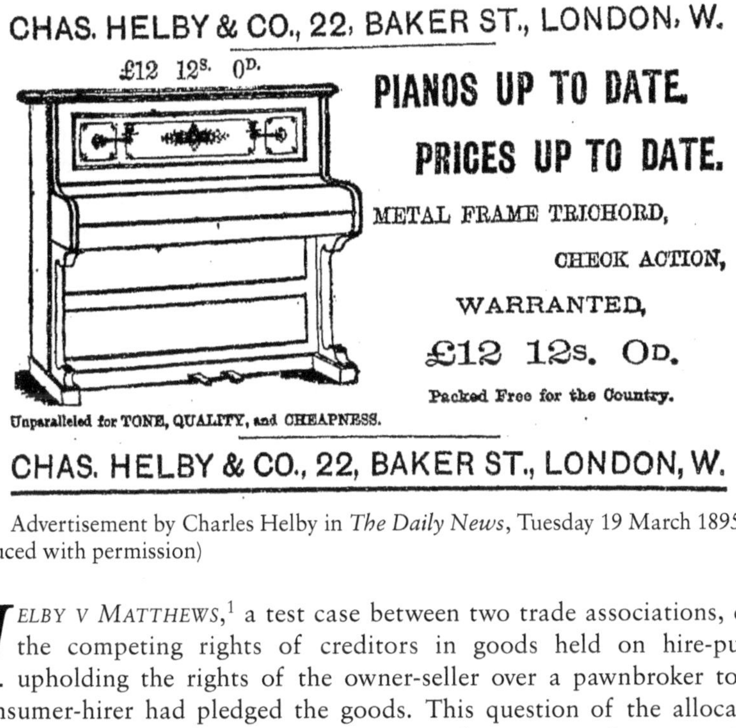

CHAS. HELBY & CO., 22, BAKER ST., LONDON, W.

£12 12s. 0D.

PIANOS UP TO DATE.

PRICES UP TO DATE.

METAL FRAME TRICHORD,

CHECK ACTION,

WARRANTED,

£12 12s. 0D.

Packed Free for the Country.

Unparalleled for TONE, QUALITY, and CHEAPNESS.

CHAS. HELBY & CO., 22, BAKER ST., LONDON, W.

Figure 1 Advertisement by Charles Helby in *The Daily News*, Tuesday 19 March 1895, 9 (reproduced with permission)

*H*ELBY V MATTHEWS,[1] a test case between two trade associations, decided the competing rights of creditors in goods held on hire-purchase, upholding the rights of the owner-seller over a pawnbroker to whom the consumer-hirer had pledged the goods. This question of the allocation of risk between commercial parties is a commonplace aspect of commercial law.[2] But the decision also legitimated hire-purchase as a contractual form, sending a

---

* The description given to *Helby v Matthews* in the Hire Traders Record in 1895.
** I would like to thank Iain Frame, Jodi Gardner, Nick Piska, Geoffrey Samuel, Joe Spooner, John Wightman, Toni Williams, and Asta Zokaityte for comments on earlier drafts of this research.
[1] *Helby v Matthews* [1895] AC (HL) 471.
[2] H Scott, 'The Risk Fixers' (1978) 91(4) *Harvard Law Review* 737.

message to lower courts which had differed in their willingness to embrace this hybrid legal form. What *Helby* did not address were the controversies at this time over the potential dangers of hire-purchase, such as high prices, excessive charges, and 'snatch-backs' where goods were repossessed immediately after an instalment became overdue. Although Lord MacNaghten briefly alluded to these issues, he viewed them as appropriate for Parliament not the courts.[3] Parliament did not enact a response until 1938, and then only through a private members Bill, sponsored by the Labour MP, 'Red Ellen' Wilkinson, and representing a consensus between social activists and the industry. Historians have puzzled over this absence of protective regulation in hire-purchase, particularly given the substantial regulation of loan financing in the Bills of Sale Act 1882, a public campaign against moneylenders in the 1890s resulting in the Moneylenders Acts 1900,[4] and the enactment of legislation in other jurisdictions.[5]

Hire-purchase became a dominant form of consumer credit for both the working and middle classes during the twentieth century,[6] notwithstanding that later commentary would criticise it as artificial, a legal fiction out of step with a more functional approach to secured credit.[7] It remains an important form of commercial and consumer credit and is regulated both by the Consumer Credit Act 1974 and under the rules of the Financial Conduct Authority.[8]

Section I sets *Helby* and the growth of hire purchase in the context of nineteenth century forms of consumer credit, and outlines the controversies over its growth, with criticism both from other trade institutions, and those concerned with its social impact. Section II discusses *Helby* and section III outlines the consequences of *Helby* and the subsequent history of regulation. *Helby v Matthews* concerned a conflict between two commercial parties but established the ground rules for twentieth-century consumer credit, permitting hire-purchase firms to set the rules for credit selling through their standard form contracts. It also illustrates the continuing theme of regulatory arbitrage in consumer credit as credit sellers seek to avoid regulation, a phenomenon illustrated by the recent exploitation by 'Buy Now Pay Later' firms of regulatory exemptions.[9]

---

[3] *Helby* (n 1) 482.
[4] See discussion in C McMahon, *Taming the Fringe: The Regulation and Development of the British Payday Lending and Pawnbroking Market* (Basingstoke, Palgrave, 2021) ch3.
[5] P Scott, 'The Twilight World of Interwar Hire Purchase' (2002) 177 *Past and Present* 195, 225; J Ziegel, 'Retail Instalment Sales Legislation: A Historical and Comparative Survey [1962] *University of Toronto Law Journal* 143: P Atiyah, *The Rise and Fall of Freedom of Contract* (Oxford, OUP, 1979) 712. German *Abzahlungsgesetz*, 1894.
[6] Scott, n 5. The Crowther Committee, *Consumer Credit: Report of the Committee* Vol 1 Tables 3.7, 3.8.
[7] See, eg, RST Chorley, 'The Hire Purchase Bill' (1938) 2(1) *MLR* 51: *Bridge v Campbell Discount* [1962] AC (HL) 600, 626–27: Ja Thornely and J Ziegel, 'Hire Purchase Reformed' (1965) (1965) 23(1) *CLJ* 59. German *Abzahlungsgesetz*, 1894.
[8] See relevant definitions in s 189(1) Consumer Credit Act 1974, The Financial Services and Markets Act 2000 (Regulated Activities) (Amendment) (No.2) Order 2013, art 60L.
[9] HM Treasury, Regulation of Buy-Now Pay-Later Response to Consultation (February 2023) www.gov.uk/government/consultations/regulation-of-buy-now-pay-later-consultation-on-draft-legislation (last accessed 22 February 2023).

I. HIRE-PURCHASE AND SECURED CREDIT IN NINETEENTH CENTURY

John Benson identifies the consumer society as one in which 'choice and credit are readily available'.[10] Different forms of credit permeated all classes of Victorian society.[11] Hire-purchase developed in England during the 1840s and 1850s for purchasing more expensive consumer goods including pianos, sewing machines, furniture, and other household goods as well as significant capital goods, such as railway wagons. One newspaper in 1849 described how newlyweds might obtain most of their furnishings on instalments through a furniture broker.[12] Women were the primary consumers, complicating legal issues, given the limited legal capacity of women in Victorian England.[13] In 1891, approximately 1 million hire purchase agreements were concluded.[14]

Sewing machines and pianos provide useful examples of the growth of hire-purchase. The Singer Sewing Machine company, a dominant multinational in the sale of sewing machines, expanded rapidly in the UK after opening its first shop in Glasgow in 1856 and a subsequent factory in Scotland in 1867.[15] Its success was built on its canvasser/collector model of direct door-to-door selling along with hire-purchase sales which allowed it to target a market of individuals with modest incomes and ensured a continuing relationship with buyers.[16] Singer may have copied the idea of hire-purchase from piano salesrooms on Broadway in New York.

In the UK the piano maker and retailer, Moore & Moore claimed to have first offered hire purchase in 1846 and the 'three year system' of payment pervaded 'all but the upper class trade' by 1895 with monthly terms from 10s to 63s a month.[17] Charles Booth in his investigations for *Life and Labour of the People of London* noted the appeal of the purchase of pianos on the hire system and the widespread advertising of wall slogans such as 'What is home without a piano?' in working

---

[10] J Benson, *The Rise of Consumer Society in Britain 1880-1980* (London, Longman, 1994) 5: M Lobban, 'Consumer Credit and Debt', in W Cornish, JS Anderson, R Cocks, M Lobban, P Polden and K Smith (eds), *The Oxford History of the Laws of England: Volume XII: 1820–1914: Private Law* (Oxford, OUP, 2010) ch V.

[11] F Trentmann, *The Empire of Things: How we became a World of Consumers, from the Fifteenth Century to the Twenty First* (London, Allen Lane, 2016) 405–08; E Rappaport, *Shopping for Pleasure: Women in the Making of London's West End* (Princeton NJ, Princeton University Press, 2001) 50. For the different forms of wage earner credit during this period see H Bosanquet, 'The Burden of Small Debts' (1896) 22(6) *The Economic Journal* 212.

[12] J Ginswick (ed) *Labour and the Poor in England and Wales 1849–51* vol ii (London, 1893), 40 cited in C Edwards, 'Buy Now Pay Later: Credit: The Mainstay of the Retail Furniture Business' in L Ugolini and J Benson (eds), *Cultures of Selling* (Abingdon, Taylor & Francis, 2006) ch 5.

[13] See S Cretney, 'The Legal Consequences of Marriage: Property Regimes' in *Family Law in the Twentieth Century: A History* (Oxford, OUP, 2005): Rappaport (n 11) 55–58, discussing *Jolly v Rees* (1864) 15 Common 628, 143 ER 931 where the court held that a husband could privately revoke a wife's agency to pledge his credit.

[14] Scott (n 5) 197.

[15] SR Fletcher and A Godley, 'Foreign Direct Investment in British Retailing, 1850–1962' (2000) 42(2) *Business History*, 43, 47.

[16] See A Godley, 'Selling the Sewing Machine Around the World: Singer's International Marketing Strategies, 1850–1950' [2006] *Enterprise & Society* 266. Singer expanded in the UK from 26 retail outlets in 1879 to 303 by 1885 with a sales growth from 30,000 in 1875 to over 90,000 in 1884.

[17] C Ehrlich, *The Piano: A History* (Oxford, Clarendon revised edition, 1990) 98.

class London.[18] Pianos were an important consumer object for Victorians. They provided entertainment and decoration, being both a musical instrument and a substantial item of furniture. Ownership of a piano conferred status, symbolic as it was of gentility, family life, taste, and wealth:[19] 'no bourgeois home was complete without it'.[20]

Sellers or lenders on credit face the problem of determining whether individuals will maintain repayments, essentially a problem of information.[21] In the nineteenth century, traders might simply wait for repayment and long term credit was a technique of maintaining continuing profitable relations with middle and upper- middle-class customers.[22] Working class consumers might obtain goods on 'tick' from local stores, a valuable source of credit if an individual fell on hard times. Hire-purchase promised a strong form of security for repayment, protecting against hirers using the goods to raise further finance through sale or pawn. Since ownership of the goods did not pass to the hirer until they exercised the option to purchase by making the last payment, under English property law of *nemo dat quod non habet*, a hirer could not pass a good title to a third party. The ability to repossess the goods in the event of non-payment also avoided the necessity of initiating court action against a debtor through the county courts, which were perceived by trade associations and creditors as slow, ineffective and debtor-friendly.[23] Assets with a long life such as sewing machines or pianos provided therefore a good security for payment.

While hire purchase as a device to sell goods on credit might be understandable to lawyers, its legal construction as a hybrid hire-and-sale, was potentially confusing. Roy Goode suggests that the distinction between a hire-purchase agreement and a sale was not always recognised 'in the early days' of hire purchase.[24] Different trades experimented with distinct forms of contract to ensure that the transaction was not interpreted as a sale, where the hirer had agreed to buy the goods. The Music Trade Society, for example, had at least two standard contracts used by its members,[25] with some of the largest firms using a simple hire contract but in practice permitting consumers to own the goods after three years.

Hire purchase as a form of instalment sale did not attract the application of the usury laws, the English courts recognising in the early nineteenth century in the context of the sale of land the idea that a seller might make an agreement

---

[18] C Booth, *Life and Labour of the People in London Third Series* (London, Macmillan, 1900) 16.
[19] F Carnevali and L Newton, 'Pianos for the People: From Producer to Consumer in Britain, 1851–1914' [2012] *Enterprise and Society* 37, 39.
[20] E Hobsbawm, *The Age of Capital* (London, Penguin, 1988) 313. The Pooters owned an upright piano 'on the three years system'. G and W Grossmith, *Diary of a Nobody* (1892) 7.
[21] J Stiglitz and A Weiss, 'Credit Rationing in Markets with Imperfect Information' (1981) 71(3) *American Economic Review* 393.
[22] See M Finn, *The Character of Credit: Personal Debt in English Culture 1740–1914* (Cambridge, CUP, 2003) 286; P Johnson, *Saving and Spending: The Working Class Economy in Britain 1870-1939* (Oxford, OUP, 1985) 147; E Ross, *Love and Toil: Motherhood in Outcast London 1870-1918* (Oxford, OUP, 1993) 52–53.
[23] See P Polden, *A History of the County Court 1846–1971* (Cambridge, CUP, 1999) 68–71.
[24] R Goode, *Hire Purchase Law and Practice*, 2nd edn (London, Butterworth, 1970) 3.
[25] See discussion in the 15 June 1894 Music Trades Review.

based partly on the present price of the land and partly its price at a future date.[26] Although hire-purchase created in substance a security interest for a purchase it was also not a loan on security and avoided the application of the Bills of Sale Acts 1882 which required registration and strict formalities,[27] and the sanction of nullity if these formal requirements were not followed. It also prohibited Bills under £30 in an attempt to protect the poorer debtor, whom it was assumed should resort to the pawnbroker rather than fall into the clutches of a moneylender. These cautionary and evidentiary techniques set precedents for future regulation,[28] and induced lenders to structure transactions as a hire-purchase. Advertisements for furniture on hire purchase stressed the 'absence of registration or publicity'.[29]

Hire-purchase might be viewed as democratising access to relatively expensive consumer goods, permitting salaried clerks with average annual incomes of £50-60 to purchase pianos.[30] Clerks were a good market for hire-purchase sales, given their relative security of income, and in the event of default, the possibility of attaching or threatening to attach their salary which was not protected by the Wages Attachment Abolition Act 1870,[31] and might also lead to their dismissal. Anecdotal evidence exists of some employees acting as agents for hire-purchase companies.[32] Figure 4 below, an advertisement for the civil service Musical Instruments Association, warns civil servants of the potential dangers associated with hire-purchase as a method of purchasing musical instruments.

Singer targeted the family market[33] as well as garment manufacturers, promising women financial independence; middle class women were encouraged by writers such as Mrs Beeton in her *Book of Household Management* to purchase a sewing machine.[34] Women's work was often a necessity for working class families and a sewing machine bought on hire-purchase permitted homeworking on dressmaking.[35] Approximately four million girls and women worked for wages in late Victorian Britain and 13 per cent of married women were in waged occupations in 1901.[36] The Select Committee of the House of Lords on the Sweating System in 1890 investigated sweating (defined as 'unduly low rates of wages, excessive hours of labour,

---

[26] *Joseph Beete v Henry Fisher Bidgood* (1827) 7 B&C 453,108 ER 792.
[27] See Report from the Select Committee on Bills of Sale Act (1878) Amendment Bill and in particular the Circular Letter, addressed, by direction of the Lord Chancellor, to the Judges and Registrars of County Courts in England and Wales respecting the Operation of the Bills of Sale Act 1878; together with their Replies thereto. (1881) Command Paper C-2859.
[28] Under the Moneylenders Acts and see now, eg, Consumer Credit Act 1974, s 127 and prior to 2006 *Wilson v First County Trust Ltd* [2003] UKHL 40, [2004] 1 AC 816.
[29] Furnish on 'The Hire Purchase System', *Standard* 5 Oct 1896, 6.
[30] J Botterill, *Consumer Culture and Personal Finance* (Basingstoke, Palgrave, 2010) 61.
[31] Report from The Select Committee on Moneylending (1898) 10.
[32] 'At Westminster' *The Times*, Tuesday 16 October 1894, 2.
[33] Godley (n 16) 281.
[34] Sewing Machines: Liberation or Drudgery for Women? www.historytoday.com/archive/sewing-machines-liberation-or-drudgery-women (last accessed 22 February 2023).
[35] See Ross (n 22) 47. 'My mother earnt a penny farthing for making [trousers] ... with a hand machine, a Singer's little one.'
[36] See H McCarthy, *Double Lives: A History of Working Motherhood* (London, Bloomsbury, 2020) 10 and sources cited.

and insanitary state of workplace') in different industries and provided dramatic examples of sweated work in shirt making such as Mrs Casey, whose husband was a dock labourer. She earned 1s 2d a day sewing shirts working from seven or eight in the morning until 11 at night, and paying instalments of 2s 6d a week (approximately £12.50 today) on a sewing machine.[37]

Middle class reformers such as Helen Bosanquet, reflecting class prejudice about the habits of the working classes,[38] probably exaggerated the extent to which working class women were taken in by the easy availability of sewing machines on credit promoted by door-to-door salesmen.[39] Helen McCarthy paints a more nuanced picture of homeworkers in the Women's Industrial Council investigation of 1897 which included examples of 'skilled and resourceful' women who liked their work (compare Figures 2 and 3).[40]

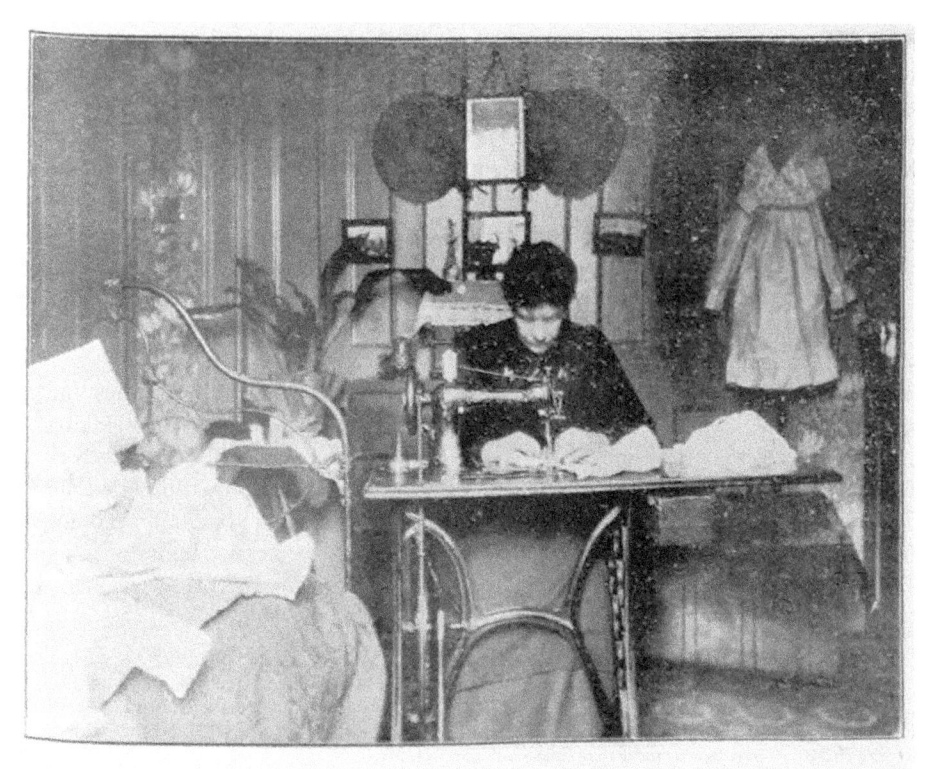

MAKING CHILDREN'S OVERALLS AND PINAFORES.

Figure 2 Making Children's Overalls and Pinafores, *Sweated industries: being a handbook of the 'Daily News' exhibition* compiled by Richard Mudie-Smith p97, University of Warwick Modern Records Centre

---

[37] Fifth Report from the Select Committee of the House of Lords on the Sweating System (1890) para 42.
[38] See P Johnson, Class Law in Victorian England' (1993) 141 *Past and Present* 147, 163.
[39] H Bosanquet, 'The Burden of Small Debts' (1896) 22(6) *The Economic Journal* 212, 220.
[40] McCarthy (n 36).

Figure 3 Seamstress at a sewing machine Berlin 1907, Courtesy Getty Images

Critics pointed to the dangers of hire-purchase, including high prices, and aggressive repossession of goods on failure of one payment.[41] A standard term used by Singer conferred power on the owner to enter the hirer's dwelling, if necessary by force, and repossess a machine.[42] Other potential concerns included the use of hire-purchase agreements to avoid the Bills of Sale Act, by structuring an agreement as a sale and leaseback,[43] and linked agreements where individuals might enter a series of agreements for different articles, with each article 'added on' to the earlier contract, so that all the articles remained as security until the last item had been paid off.[44]

Henry Tudor, a solicitor, and prominent member of the Hire Traders Protection Association, who would act on behalf of the Association in the *Helby* test case, responded to these issues in an 1888 pamphlet.[45] He defended hire-purchase from the

---

[41] See, eg, 'The Hire and Purchase System' *Daily News*, 19 October 1889 5: Bosanquet (n 11) 212. W Booth, *In Darkest England & The Way Out* (Funk & Wagnalls, 1890) 217.

[42] See, eg, the clause in *The Singer Manufacturing Company v Clark* (1879) 5 Ex D 37.

[43] See, eg, *Redhead v Westwood* (1878–88) 4 Times Law Reports 671. *Beckett v Towers Assets Company* [1891] 1 QB 638.

[44] This form of cross-collateralization occurred in the famous US case of *Williams v Walker Thomas Furniture Co*. 350 F.2d 445 (1965).

[45] See HE Tudor, *A Defence of the Hire System, based on Legal and Commercial Considerations* (London, 1888). Tudor's law firm continued a close connection with the hire-purchase community and as Tudor & Rowe acted for the Association in the development of the 1938 Hire Purchase Act.

Keep out of the Clutches of the Hire System Dealers.

How to Purchase a Pianoforte or Organ

AT

GUARANTEED WHOLESALE PRICES.

Send Post Card for Prospectus, Price Lists, and Full Exposure of the Harsh and Iniquitous Hire System.

THE SECRETARY,

The Civil Service Musical Instrument Association, Ld.

(Owned and conducted by Civil Servants).

236, HIGH HOLBORN, LONDON, W.C.

Figure 4 Thomas Farrow, *Shylock at the Bar* 1903, 2 (reproduced with permission)

standpoint of freedom of contract, and promoted the benefits of the hiring system. Higher prices were justified for the right to postpone payment, and individuals freely agreed in the contract to the right of the owner to enter and retake property. In any event reputable traders did not attempt to repossess immediately a payment was missed. In his view the courts only saw the rough side of the system which coloured their views. Competition would protect most consumers against abuse and any problems in the industry were caused by a few 'bad apples'. The system responded to popular demand from a wide group of consumers who might prefer it to cash payments, and regulation through registration of hire-purchase agreements would increase costs and restrict the availability of credit to the poor. They would be unable to purchase items of household management such as a sewing machine, essential to household survival, rather than the conspicuous consumption of a piano. As to the protection of third parties it was common knowledge that goods might be hired, and the maxim *caveat emptor* should apply: registration would be of little value to pawnbrokers who had no time to check a register.

Tudor's arguments were supported by the Musical Instrument Traders' Association which denied that it was common for traders to secure forfeiture of payments on the slightest breach of an agreement, and that it was in the interests of the dealer to treat a hirer in a considerate manner.[46]

The *Economist* concluded that although the hire-purchase system was generally beneficial if conducted with honesty and good management, 'it was capable of much abuse from the unscrupulous enforcement of harsh agreements, on the one side, or the fraudulent disposal of property on the other'.[47] The recognition that hire purchase had both benefits and costs distinguished it from the use of Bills of Sale which was associated with individuals in financial difficulties, whereas hire-purchase could be identified with the positive accumulation of assets.

Lower courts differed in their approach to hire-purchase cases. Some viewed hire-purchase as exploitative and open to abuse while others viewed the debtors as representing the feckless working class male unable to control the actions of their wives.[48] Commissioner Kerr of the City of London Court, (known for dispensing a 'rough and ready justice'[49]), gave notice in 1891 that tradesmen in London should not sell bicycles under the nomenclature of a hire and purchase, but rather 'purchase by instalments' and that if this were not done it would constitute a fraud.[50] He also characterised those using the hire system as 'foolish', advising them 'Never Buy Furniture on the hire system as long as you live.'[51] Criminal actions were sometimes brought in lower criminal courts by hirers for trespass or assault in relation to repossession of goods. Courts sometimes sustained the allegation,[52] refused costs to the defendant company,[53] permitted the return of goods on payment of arrears,[54] or rejected the claim.[55] Women, with limited contractual capacity of their own at this time, appeared in court as agents of their husband, and were often effective advocates.[56]

---

[46] 'The Hire-Purchase System' *Morning Post* (London, 8 June 1891) 8.
[47] *The Economist* (London,12 May 1894) 578.
[48] Finn (n 22) 258–59.
[49] Biography from *Vanity Fair*, 22 November 1900.
[50] According to *Cycling*, 21 February 1891, 80.
[51] 'The Hire Purchase System', *The Times* 7 November, 4.
[52] 'The Hire Purchase System', *Western Daily Press* 7 April 1885, 7.
[53] 'The Hire Purchase System', *Huddersfield Chronicle* 19 July 1892, 4.
[54] 'The Hire Purchase System and the Poor', *Daily News* 13 October 1893.
[55] 'Sewing Machines on Hire', *Daily Mail* 18 June 1896, 3.
[56] Finn (n 22) 258.

Repossessions could result in violent confrontations and some lower court judges disapproved of clauses permitting forcible entry.[57] An example is *Ellesden v Oetzmann*,[58] presided over by Judge Bacon who would decide the county court litigation in *Helby*. A piano had been bought by an elderly gentleman for £50 on the hire system and it seemed that he had got behind in payments. Oetzmann, the piano dealer, hired a 'piano inquiry agent', essentially a debt collector cum private bailiff (who claimed in court that he seized about 300 pianos a year) to recover the piano. According to one account a 'desperate struggle ensued' over a period of one hour during which the plaintiff's teeth were knocked out. The judge upheld the assault charge against the piano dealer awarding the plaintiff two guineas in damages. There were apparently 'numerous cases' where piano dealers had suffered damages for entries less violent than the particular case[59] and substantial damages could be awarded. A husband received £50 damages against the piano dealer, Mundy & Sons in 1904 for an assault on his wife during a repossession in Islington.[60] Judicial commentary suggested that owners might use a 'reasonable measure of force'[61] in attempting to recover goods, avoiding a breach of the peace. Actions might be brought for forcible entry under the Forcible Entry Act 1381,[62] although textbook authors disagreed as to the applicability of the 1381 Act to goods, rather than land.[63]

The music trade claimed that hard cases were more common in the furniture trade, and the limited evidence of newspaper reports seem to confirm this.[64] Evidence of potential public concern about repossession might be found in advertisements for furniture which indicated that 'in the event of illness, dullness of trade and non-employment etc, no forcible seizures are made'.[65]

Other credit grantors also criticised the rise of hire purchase. Trade creditors might find that if they tried to execute against a debtor's goods the return would state – 'No goods whereon to levy – Everything on hire-purchase.'[66] The ability of hire-purchase sellers to recover goods from a third party particularly irked pawn-brokers who often viewed the hire purchase system as one by which they had been

---

[57] See *Furniture Gazette*, 1 September 1886 reporting the Queens Bench division judgment in *Joseph v Davis* on 2 August 1886.
[58] Reported and discussed in the London and Provincial Music Trades Review, 15 February 1890, 25. See also the discussion in Ehrlich (n 17) 102.
[59] ibid.
[60] 'Piano causes discord', *Daily Mail* Saturday 16 April 1904. '*Wiggins v. Kent*', *The Times* Tuesday, 26 May 1895, 13 (Damages of £75 for assault).
[61] See *Blades v Higgs* (1844) 6 Man & G 142 ER 634 and the reprint of the transcript of the Shorthand notes of Lord Russell of Killowen in *Himmelspring v The Singer Manufacturing Co* (29 July 1898) reported in WH Russell and WG Earingey, *The Hire Purchase System: A practical manual of hire-trade law for lawyers and hire traders, with precedents of agreements & court forms*, 5th edn (Stevens1920) 83.
[62] Only repealed in 1977 by the Criminal Law Act 1977, ss 13(2), 65, Sch 13.
[63] See, eg, R Dunstan, *The Law relating to the Hire Purchase System: with an Appendix of Forms* (London, Sweet & Maxwell, 1910) 73: Russell and Earingey (n 61) 62.
[64] Music Trades Review 15 August 1893. See, eg, reports in *The Times*, 14 July 1893; 2 October 1893, 5 (Hirer paid £3 5s out of total of £4 7s 6d, missed two instalments, all goods seized; 7 November 1893, Norman and Stacey furniture dealers repossess furniture to recover £4 9s balance on hire-purchase of furniture.
[65] *Nottingham Evening Post* 1 January 1890, 1.
[66] Finn (n 22) 272.

'largely defrauded'.[67] A pawnbroker had to make a swift decision on the validity of a pledge: the transaction time for an average pledge at this time was approximately two minutes.[68]

The growing trade protection societies which acted as both support for debt collection and as early forms of credit reference agencies,[69] agreed that hire purchase could benefit those on limited income, but repeated the charges against hire purchase including the problem of fraudulent selling and pawning by hirers. At the annual meeting of trade associations in 1888 a resolution calling for legislation was passed with the objectives of facilitating legitimate trade, protecting poor hirers, pawnbrokers, auctioneers and the public, and punishing fraud.[70] The Associations recognised the difficulty of devising a system which would permit legitimate trade and address abuses. The solution proposed was a system of registration of hire-purchase agreements similar to that for Bills of Sale[71] and a parliamentary petition was submitted to amend the Bills of Sale consolidation Bill of 1892.[72]

The Music Trade of the London Chamber of Commerce and the Hire Traders Association vigorously opposed it as a serious threat to their trade and the clause was rejected by the then Lord Chancellor Herschell, as being too controversial for a codifying statute. Herschell noted the prevalence and potential benefits of the 'hire and sale' system, while also acknowledging strong representations from trade societies that the issue should be addressed.[73] In July 1893, the dark side of hire purchase was raised again in the Commons by Sir John Brunner, the chemical industrialist and Liberal MP who had introduced sickness insurance, shorter working hours, and holidays with pay for his employees. He reported the case of a furniture dealer who repossessed the furniture of a hirer who had paid £4 2s 6d out of £5 3s 6d due. The Solicitor General recognised that great hardships existed under the hire and sale system, that the Lord Chancellor had not been able to proceed because the Bill was contentious, but also that he was determined to take the earliest opportunity to remove abuses which are shown to exist.[74] Finally, in September 1893, an unsuccessful

---

[67] 'Pawnbrokers' Campaign' *Daily Mail*, (London, 20 January 1899) 6. Remarks attributed to Attenborough, solicitor to the Metropolitan Pawnbrokers Association. Attenborough acted on behalf of the Pawnbrokers Association in *Helby v Matthews*.

[68] McMahon (n 4) 20.

[69] See RJ Bennett, 'Supporting Trust: Credit Assessment and debt recovery through Trade Protection Societies in Britain and Ireland 1776–1992' (2012) 38 *Journal of Historical Geography* 123: Finn (n 22) 284–316.

[70] As outlined by the West Riding Trade Protection Association in 'The Hire and Purchase System', *Leeds Mercury*, 19 May 1888.

[71] Extract from *The Sewing Machine Gazette* 1 February 1888 in Appendix, Tudor (n 45) 31.

[72] See Eleventh Report of the Select Committee, Petition of the Nottinghamshire and Midland Merchants and Traders Association, Public Petitions 1833-1918. parlipapers-proquest-com.chain.kent.ac.uk/parlipapers/result/pqpdocumentview?accountid=7408&groupid=114041&pgId=ecf2cb8b-c533-48b7-a070-b4a18303 1662&rsId=17EC9432F9D.

[73] Lord Herschell's rejection of the amendment on 7 March 1893. parlipapers-proquest-com.chain.kent.ac.uk/parlipapers/result/pqpdocumentview?accountid=7408&groupid=114041&pgId=3c5aeea2-1e0f-4b74-a973-3755f0949124&rsId=17EBF00FD1C and his views on codification as a correct statement of the law at F Herschell, 'On the Amendment of the Law' (1876) 2(1) *Law Magazine and Review* 1, 5.

[74] Commons Sitting of Thursday 20 July 1893.

amendment was moved by Walter Clough to the Sale of Goods Bill which would have protected third parties such as pawnbrokers.[75]

By the early 1890s regulation of hire purchase was therefore a political issue with the trade protection societies and a few progressive Liberal MPs pressing for regulation on one side, and the hire trade on the other. It might be dangerous, however, to view the hire traders as united in their opposition to regulation. Editorials in the music trade disapproved of forcible entry to recover goods, and noted that at least one prominent firm objected to the term which gave a licence to enter premises.[76] It recognised that regulation might be inevitable and envisaged the twin objectives of legislation as protecting the 'honest but unfortunate' hirer against the 'sharks' when only a few instalments remained to be paid, and protection for the honest dealer against the dishonest hirer. Regulation might promote the interests of ethical businesses.

II. PAWNBROKERS, HIRE TRADERS AND THE FACTORS ACTS: *HELBY*

During the nineteenth century, the Factors Acts had modified the strong English common law protections for property rights under *nemo dat quod non habet*, by providing protection for good faith third parties dealing with middlemen, as part of the facilitation of commercial practices. The Factors Acts of 1889 consolidated protection for good faith third party purchasers, including those who had goods transferred or delivered to them by individuals who had 'bought or agreed to buy goods'.[77] In 1893, the Court of Appeal in *Lee v Butler*[78] addressed the case of a hirer of furniture who had agreed to make two payments for 'the hire and use' of furniture on the terms that having made the payments of £97 4s she would become their owner. The hirer disposed of the goods to a third party before making the second payment, with the assignee of the retailer now bringing an action against the third party for return of the furniture. The Court of Appeal held that the hirer had 'agreed to buy' the goods by a 'hire and purchase' agreement. Lord Esher viewed this as a 'very plain case' for the application of section 9.[79] The court did not even require the respondents' barrister CL Attenborough to reply.

The Court of Appeal judgment in *Lee v Butler* was delivered on 2 August 1893 and the Pawnbrokers Association had already communicated in June 1893 to the hire traders association that they would no longer return hired goods that were pawned.[80] It seems that on 15 August, the Hire Traders Protection Society, alarmed at the implications of this decision for the hire trade, considered supporting an appeal in *Lee v Butler* but ultimately decided to support a case being litigated in

---

[75] Amendment moved by Walter Clough MP in Committee HC Deb 14 September 1893 vol 17 cc1261-3.
[76] See *Music Trades Review*, 15 August 1893.
[77] Section 9.
[78] [1893] 2 QB 318.
[79] Esher MR at 322.
[80] According to editorial in *Hire Traders Record* no 53 (London, 1 June 1895) 1.

the county court by Charles Helby a retailer of pianos in Baker Street, London.[81] The case became therefore a test case between two rival trade associations: the Hire Traders Protection Association, and the Metropolitan Pawnbrokers Association. The Hire Traders Protection Association had been formed in 1891, for dealers in the 'easy payment and hire system', aimed at 'raising the tone of the hire system', providing standard form terms and legal assistance to members at a reduced rate, in addition to political lobbying.

Charles Helby, listed as a pianoforte maker from about 1891–1914 of 22B Baker Street, London,[82] had hired a Rass piano to Charles Brewster living at 24 Chester Street (now Chester Way) Kennington, South London on 23 December 1892. Brewster is described as a commercial traveller in the Law Times report of the county court hearing, but his death certificate in 1893 records his profession as an artist in stained glass.[83] We may speculate that he was not affluent. Charles Booth's poverty map of London indicates that Chester Street was a mix of comfortable and poor dwellings, but not well-to-do.[84] Helby did not seem to advertise credit terms in its regular advertising (Figure 1) in the Liberal *Daily News* unlike other firms of that period which would offer 'cash or … liberal terms' and '15s per month on 3 year system'.[85] The terms of the *Helby* contract were that if Brewster paid the sum of 18 guineas, (this price suggests the purchase of an upright piano at the lower end of the market) by 36 monthly instalments then he would become the owner of the piano, but until the full sum was paid the piano would continue to be the property of the owner. The contract also included a term that the hirer could terminate the hiring by delivering up the piano to Helby, but in that case would forfeit any payments and would be liable to make up any arrears. In April 1893 Brewster without the consent of Helby, pledged the piano for £7 10s to Matthews, a pawnbroker as security for an advance of £7 10s. Brewster died, aged 29, on 5 August 1893 in St Thomas Hospital. We do not know why he had pawned the piano. It is not impossible that a change in personal health or employment prospects necessitated the pawning. Matthews was also deceased so that the action was against his executor.

Matthews' executor claimed that he could take a good title to the goods under the Factors Act 1889, section 9. The initial decision by Judge Bacon in November 1893 in Bloomsbury county court[86] held that this was an agreement of hire with the provision that if Brewster paid the total amount over three years it would become the property of the hirer. Judge Bacon noted that there was no agreement to pay a lump sum as in *Lee v Butler* and this was simply an agreement of hire. Although he did not award any damages to Helby he did allow costs on a higher scale because the case was of considerable public importance. The judgment was upheld by the Divisional Court but overturned by the Court of Appeal which concluded that section 9 of the Factors

---

[81] See account in R Cranston, *Making Commercial Law Through Practice: 1830-1970* (Cambridge, CUP, 2021) 259, and fn 354.
[82] Pianoforte Makers in England, www.lieveverbeeck.eu/Pianoforte-makers_England_h.htm.
[83] Certified Copy of an Entry of Death, Charles Henry Brewster aged 29, 24 Chester Street, Kennington Road, cause of death, Aortic Disease Cardiac Syncope (on file with author).
[84] See further on Booth's classifications at booth.lse.ac.uk/learn-more/what-were-the-poverty-maps.
[85] Oetzman and Bard's pianos respectively, advertising in *The Standard* (London, 1 January 1895) 7.
[86] See Law Times 18 November 1893.

Act applied because the transaction was in substance a sale.[87] Lord Esher MR, who had little patience with technical issues – he was regarded by some as 'the epitome of good sense' and by others as 'simplistic'[88] – concluded that it is 'impossible to call such a contract simply a contract of hiring' and noted that the hirer agreed to pay 'a rent or hire instalment'. If it was a hire agreement the term 'rent' would in Esher's view have been sufficient but the addition of 'hire instalment' signified that it was an agreement for the payment of monthly instalments. The substance of the agreement was an agreement to sell by one party and an agreement to buy by the other, but with an option to the buyer to whom the property has not passed, if he changes his mind, of putting an end to the contract.

The Pawnbrokers Association commented that the judgment of the Court of Appeal 'stript hire purchase of these peculiar, and, to third parties, unfair advantages it has hitherto possessed'.[89] The Music Trades Review concluded that there could be little doubt that the *Helby* contract was in substance a contract of sale and any appeal would fail. In their view, the use of the word 'instalments' had been a hostage to fortune in the case.[90] The *Juridical Review* thought that the authoritative judgment of the Court of Appeal would 'dispel the mists' hanging about 'the ambiguous contract popularly and loosely called hire and purchase'.[91] The *Economist* approved of the decision of the Court of Appeal on the basis that the third party was at an informational disadvantage in determining the conditions of ownership of the goods and the solution lay in registration of hire-purchase agreements.[92] Provincial media concluded that the decision had dealt a serious blow to the hire system, arguing that it would reduce the availability of pianos to those on modest incomes.[93] The only silver lining, according to the *Aberdeen Weekly Journal* would be a reduction in the 'torture inflicted by the strumming of pianos in tenement houses … conferring … a great boon on a long suffering public'.[94]

Judge Bacon who had heard the case at first instance expressed approval of the Court of Appeal decision in the Law Times, because 'hire and purchase agreements were a source of great hardship to poor people'.[95] The Court of Appeal decision was followed on June 25 by Mr Justice Bruce in the Queens Bench case of *Shenstone & Co v Hilton* which held that an auctioneer to whom a hirer had delivered a piano was protected by section 9 of the Factors Act. And in October 1894 Mr Justice Bacon in Whitechapel County Court in *Payne v Wilson* rejected a claim by a piano manufacturer against an individual who had bought a piano from a hirer.[96]

The Hire Traders Association, however, supported the costs of an appeal to the House of Lords, where they were represented by Robert Finlay QC (later Viscount Finlay)

---

[87] Lord Esher MR in *Helby v Matthews* [1894] 2 QB 262, 267–68.
[88] 'Brett, William Baliol, First Viscount Esher' Dictionary of National Biography, (Steve Hedley) (2004).
[89] *The Pawnbrokers Gazette* (London, 12 May 1894) 221.
[90] *Music Trades Review* 15 June 1894, 00.
[91] (1894) 6(4) *Juridical Review* 382.
[92] *The Economist* (London, 12 May 1894) 578.
[93] *Freeman's Journal* 'A revolutionary decision' (Dublin, 17 May 1894) 5.
[94] *Aberdeen Weekly Journal* (Aberdeen, 16 May 1894).
[95] (1894-95) 98 Law Times 4.
[96] 'The Hire Purchase System: Important Test Case' *The Manchester Guardian* (Manchester, 12 October 1894) 3.

and Joseph Walton QC, both distinguished commercial barristers. The House, in a considered opinion, reversed the Court of Appeal. Lord Herschell agreed that the issue was ascertaining the substance of the transaction from a consideration of all the terms of the agreement. But having analysed the written terms of the agreement, the answer for Herschell was clear. Brewster was to obtain possession of the piano and be entitled to its use as long as he paid the rental. If he continued to make the payments for three years, the piano became his property but he could at any time return it and would no longer be liable to make any further payments.

Herschell concluded that the agreement created no legal obligation to purchase, distinguishing *Lee v Butler* on the basis that it was an agreement to buy with the purchase money payable in two instalments. He recognised that the 'parties probably thought' in *Helby* that it would end in a purchase, but that did not show that it was an agreement to buy, and that although the monthly payments were higher than one might have expected without such a clause, an individual might well be willing to pay a higher price for the use of the piano with the possibility of an option to purchase.

Jelf QC for the respondent Pawnbrokers Association had argued that the case came within the mischief of the Factors Act 1889 and that this Act ought to be construed to cover this case.[97] He argued that the Factors Acts had developed from an initial protection for agents, to protection for those in possession under a contract of sale, moving towards the civilian principle of *en fait de meubles possession vaut titre*. Lord Herschell interrupted Jelf to comment that he could not see hire purchase as a scheme for the avoidance of the Factors Acts, and disagreed with him that hire-purchase was simply a sham form of credit sale. He objected also to Jelf's seeming argument that the rules should be interpreted on a model of hire-purchase as a contract entered into by the impecunious.

The majority of the Law Lords did not comment in their opinions on the substantive fairness of the hire-purchase transaction. However, Lord Macnaghten responded sharply to what he perceived as the respondent's argument that 'dealings of this sort [were] mere traps of the extravagant and the impecunious – mere devices to tempt improvident people into buying things which they do not want and for which at the time they cannot pay'

> I do not see why a person fairly solvent and tolerably prudent should not make himself the owner of a piano or a carriage or anything else by means of periodical payments on such terms as those in question in the present case. The advantages are not all on one side. If the object of desire loses its attractions on closer acquaintance … it is something, surely, to know that the transaction may be closed at once without further liability and without the payment of any forfeit. If these agreements are objectionable on public grounds it is for parliament to interfere. It is not for the Court to put a forced or strained construction on a written document or to import a meaning which the parties never dreamed of because it may not wholly approve of transactions of the sort.[98]

---

[97] The argument is reproduced in the *Hire Traders Record* (London, 1 May 1896) 47–48.
[98] (n 2) 482.

This dictum by Macnaghten was reproduced in an early text on hire-purchase as 'a reply to critics of the hire purchase system'.[99] Macnaghten's assumption that the contract was a balanced one because of the ability to return the goods 'without further liability' would later be effectively negated by the practice of inserting 'minimum payment' clauses in standard form hire purchase contracts. The *Law Quarterly Review* in a brief note concluded that no-one could on reflection doubt that the House of Lords were right. Since Brewster could not be legally compelled to buy, there was no agreement to buy.[100]

III. AFTER HELBY

Helby v Matthews legitimated the concept of hire-purchase as a method of credit selling. The focus on the words of the written contract drawn up by the owner/seller along with limits on parole evidence posed challenges for a litigant attempting to argue that the hire purchase agreement was a sham hiding a credit sale.[101] *Helby* was an important victory for the hire trade which during this period was jostling with other creditors for a priority position in relation to the property of a debtor. The *Hire Trader Record* expressed the hope that this decision would settle the differences in approach taken by lower courts and that hire traders would be more respected by the press and the courts.[102] The Association monitored through its journal the extent to which the decision was adopted by other courts and promulgated standard form agreements based on *Helby*.

Notwithstanding the hopes of the Hire Traders Association, *Helby* did not stop complaints both about the unfairness of third parties bearing the risk of an unauthorised transfer of the hired goods, and also the fairness of the treatment of hirers.[103] In 1908 and 1912 private members Bills were introduced to amend the Factors Acts to include specifically the situation in *Helby*.[104] The Departmental Review of Bankruptcy Law in 1908 considered the issue of registration but ultimately decided on grounds of practicality that it would be difficult to operate a system for such a large number of agreements and that if small agreements (under £30) were excluded, the mischief would remain unremedied and would stimulate evasion through the use of multiple agreements.[105] In 1912 a cross-party coalition of MPs, headed by James O'Grady[106] attempted unsuccessfully to introduce greater consumer protections.[107]

---

[99] See W H Russell, *The Hire-Purchase System: A Practical Manual of Hire-Trade Law for Lawyers and Hire Traders*, 5th edn (Stevens, 1920).
[100] (1895) 11 LQR 305.
[101] See A Nicol, 'Outflanking Protective Legislation: Shams and Beyond' [1981] *MLR* 21.
[102] Hire Traders Record 1 June 1895.
[103] See, eg, 'Furniture Hire-Purchase System' HC Vol 35 Tuesday 12 March 1912.
[104] Factors Act (1889) amendment. A Bill to amend the Factors Act 1889. House of Commons. Bill no 304, Parliament 1912–13. This would have inserted 'or acquired an option to buy' into the Factors Act, s 9.
[105] See Departmental Committee on Bankruptcy Law Amendment Vol 1 Report of the Committee Appointed by the Board of Trade to Inquire into the Bankruptcy Law and its Administration (1908) Cd 4068 para 161.
[106] Trade Unionist and Labour MP, Member of the Independent Labour Party.
[107] A Bill to Amend the Law Relating to Sales on the Hire Purchase Bill 186, 1912.

One reason for the rise of hire purchase was the avoidance of the formalities and publicity of the Bills of Sale Act. In the same year as *Helby*, the House of Lords in *Mcentire v Crossley Bros*[108] held that the lease of a commercial gas engine to a lessee over nine monthly payments with the property passing to the lessee after the last payment, was not a Bill of Sale since the lessee had no property in the goods which could be secured. Herschell recognised that this contractual form conferred on the financier a similar security to a mortgagee.[109] This judgment facilitated the dominant tripartite structure of consumer financing in the UK in the twentieth century where vendors who could not finance their own credit selling, sold or assigned the contracts to a finance company which then leased the goods to the ultimate consumer. Financing of consumer purchases was therefore not through direct loans but rather through retailer financing, probably a more expensive form of financing. The British banks would not engage directly in the finance of consumer credit until the late 1960s, a fact attributed by the Crowther Committee to the 'curious legal parentage of hire-purchase' and the growth of distinct finance houses.[110]

Hire-purchase agreements increased from 1 million agreements in 1891 to 6 million in 1924, 16 million in 1928 and 24 million in 1936,[111] and Ellen Wilkinson's 1938 Hire Purchase Act represented a consensus between social activists and the industry, with regulatory techniques which survive in contemporary regulation.[112]

Hire Purchase flourished after the second world war with increasing pressures for updated regulation. Academics drew attention to the fictitious nature of hire purchase which was in substance a disguised form of mortgage – or to use the functional language of secured transactions – a purchase money security interest.[113] In 1968 the Labour Government struck the Crowther Committee to undertake a wide-ranging review of consumer credit law. Crowther proposed the introduction of a functional law of secured personal property law inspired by Article 9 of the US Uniform Commercial Code, and a Consumer Sale and Loan Act which would address the consumer protection aspects of credit lending and sales. Hire-purchase would be reconceptualised as a purchase money chattel mortgage or purchase money security interest, with associated rights and protections including a right to redeem and protection against unduly harsh forfeiture.[114] Security interests would be registered and the Bills of Sale Act abolished.

The Conservative Government of Edward Heath, in an effort to capture the consumer vote, introduced a Consumer Credit Bill incorporating only the consumer aspects of Crowther, and left in place the distinct concept of hire-purchase within the Act along with the Bills of Sale Act 1882.[115] Both this Act and hire purchase continue to exist therefore and seem resistant to reform.

---

[108] [1895] AC 457.
[109] ibid 466.
[110] *Consumer Credit: Report of the Committee* (The Crowther Report) para 9.4.4.
[111] Scott (n 5) 197.
[112] See, eg, ss 99–100, s 90 and rule book of the Financial Conduct Authority. See CONC 3 & 4 at www.handbook.fca.org.uk/handbook.
[113] See, eg, The Crowther Report (n 110) para 5.2.2: J Thornley, 'Hire Purchase Hardships and Hopes' [1962] *Cambridge Law Journal* 39.
[114] The Crowther Report, (n 110) 20–26.
[115] See I Ramsay, 'Ordoliberalism and Opportunism: The Making of Consumer Law in the UK 1950–1985' in H Micklitz (ed), *The Making of Consumer Law and Policy in Europe* (Oxford, Hart Publishing, 2021) 268.

IV. CONCLUSION

The House of Lords decided *Helby v Matthews* in 1895, a period when its decision making in contract and commercial law was characterised by a formalism linked to principles of laissez-faire. This entailed a literal reading of contracts as furthering a respect for private autonomy.[116] For Herschell the contract of hire purchase was an abstract category, with the particularities of the contracting parties removed. This may have accounted for his objection to Jelf QCs characterisation of the hire-purchase contract as one based on unequal bargaining power. Macnaghten's comments in *Helby* also did not recognise the possibility of standardised contracts drawn up by repeat-player sellers imposing terms on individuals with weaker bargaining power. It was only in 1901 that Raymond Saleilles floated the concept of the *contrat d'adhesion*, the contract whose terms were drawn up by one party with the other simply 'adhering' to the terms.

One political justification for the above approach was a concern for the legitimacy of the House of Lords. Any legislative role for the court, against the background of increasing democratic pressures, would be viewed as illegitimate. Herschell, a liberal who believed in 'one man, one vote' may have viewed formalism as a method to divert decisions from the courts to the legislature, the more democratic lawmaking body[117] for addressing the contentious and potentially complex issues around regulation of hire-purchase of which he was aware as Lord Chancellor. Yet the positive response to the Court of Appeal judgment indicates the contingent nature of the ultimate result in the House of Lords. The Court of Appeal judgment would not have brought credit selling to an end but merely shifted greater risks to sellers and resulted in different contractual forms, perhaps the conditional sale which was common in North America. However, the decision in *Helby* established a first mover advantage on hire purchase as *the* form of selling on credit even if it might not be economically or socially optimal. The subsequent growth of institutional structures and practices around this form of selling created a status quo barrier to change.

Helby illustrates therefore the role of law as both a technology of organisation and discourse of legitimation.[118] Repeat-player creditors were significant in bringing the issue of hire-purchase before the House of Lords and perhaps also in ensuring that issues such as the conduct of debt collectors in repossessions did not reach the higher courts. *Helby* illustrates the importance of these repeat-players both through selective litigation, and regulatory arbitrage.

---

[116] *Cf* the contemporary debate over contract interpretation represented by the contextual approach of Lord Hoffmann and the more literalist approach of Lord Sumption. See L Hoffmann, Language and Lawyer (2018) 134 *LQR* 553 and J Sumption, A Question of Taste: The Supreme Court and the Interpretation of Contracts, Harris Society Annual Lecture, Oxford 8 May 2017.

[117] See R Stevens, *Law and Politics: The House of Lords as a Judicial Body 1800–1976* (Weidenfeld & Nicolson, 1979) 121–22.

[118] A Fleming, 'Legal History as Economic History' in M Dubber and C Tomlins (eds), *The Oxford Handbook of Legal History* (Oxford, OUP, 2018) 216 citing to C Tomlins, *Freedom Bound: Law, Labor and Civic Identity in Colonizing English America, 1580-2010* (Cambridge, CUP, 2012).

Law students are often taught about legislative 'interventions' into the common law system, sometimes with the assumption that these are political interventions into a natural set of principles developed over the years by judges. But judges often decide whether a new technology will be recognised or a new contract form will be enforced and *Helby* demonstrates the potential long term economic and social importance of such decisions.[119]

---

[119] For a recent example see *Cavendish Square Holding BV (Appellant) v Talal El Makdessi (Respondent) ParkingEye Limited (Respondent) v Beavis (Appellant)* [2015] UKSC 67, [2016] AC 1172 where the Supreme Court legitimated the contract and business model of Parking Eye, which is now one of the largest filers of county court cases for parking penalties. See also D Kennedy, 'The Stakes of Law, or Hale and Foucault!' in D Kennedy (ed), *Sexy Dressing etc: Essays on the Power and Politics of Cultural Identity* (Cambridge, Mass, Harvard, 1993) 110: I Ramsay, 'Consumer Credit Law, Distributive Justice and the Welfare State' (1995) 15 *OJLS* 177.

7

Blacker v Lake and Elliot: (closing and opening) a Path for Injured Consumers in Tort before *Donoghue*

EMILY GORDON*

THIS CHAPTER WAS finalised during the celebration of 90 years since *Donoghue v Stevenson*.[1] However, at the risk of committing legal treason, this chapter focuses not on that famous case but instead on a tort case before *Donoghue* that shaped the path of consumer law. It is well known that, before the infamous snail's case, a consumer injured by a defective product would, in the absence of a contractual relationship, generally find it difficult to bring an action in tort against its maker.

This chapter considers another 'landmark' case, *Blacker v Lake and Elliot Limited*,[2] from 1912, which is important in two ways. First, any general duty owed by manufacturers to the ultimate consumer, outside of contract, was firmly rejected. The earlier case of *George v Skivington*,[3] it was said, could not be relied upon for such a proposition. Second, and despite the first point, it will be suggested that *Blacker* was instrumental in providing a way for injured consumers to sue the manufacturer of a product in the absence of a contractual relationship, thereby paving the way for *Donoghue*. Although a general duty was rejected, an alternative argument was flagged by the *Blacker* Court which was successfully used by injured consumers after *Blacker* and before *Donoghue*. *Blacker* may be understood as setting up conditions to precipitate the change brought about in *Donoghue* and allow tort claims by consumers against manufacturers.

---

*This chapter is based on work undertaken and submitted as part of my doctoral thesis (University of Cambridge). I would like to thank Professor David Ibbetson, my supervisor, for his invaluable guidance during the project and beyond. I would also like to thank Dr Jonathan Morgan and Dr Benjamin Spagnolo for very helpful comments on earlier versions of this research, and Professors Iain Ramsay and Jodi Gardner for the same on this chapter. All oversights or errors are my own.

[1] [1932] AC 562 (hereafter: *Donoghue*).
[2] (1912) 106 LT 533 (hereafter: *Blacker*).
[3] (1869) LR 5 Ex 1.

Of course, privity was the problem before *Donoghue*: in 1842 *Winterbottom v Wright*[4] brought the doctrine into prominence as a requirement for a duty of care in tort in situations where a contract existed. There were only limited circumstances where a duty was owed with respect to harm-causing goods outside of contractual relationships. A duty was recognised with respect to the carriage of dangerous goods.[5] However, courts seemed more reluctant to recognise liability without privity in cases of goods supplied or sold. Though it remained something of a vexed question into the twentieth century, the orthodox position by the early twentieth century seemed to be that in only two types of case was a duty recognised in relation to the supply or sale of goods to persons not party to the contract: first, where a supplier knew an item to be unsafe and fraudulently represented that it was not so; and second, in the supply of things dangerous in themselves, or *known* to be dangerous by the supplier because of some quality or defect.[6] The few cases that might be understood as suggesting that a claim may be available more generally, like *George*,[7] were not accepted as good law.

The first part of this chapter discusses the case of *Blacker* and its significance for injured consumers of the 1910s and 1920s. The second part reveals new product liability cases reported in newspapers from the same period that were hidden due to selective law reporting.[8] The third part then seeks to explain the success enjoyed by the plaintiffs in these cases which, on strict application of the privity rule, ought to have failed: it is likely that *Blacker* was instrumental in signalling the availability of a legal pathway to recovery, thereby creating pressure on the law to change in 1932. *Blacker* is deserving of treatment as a 'landmark' case for consumer actions in tort not *instead of* the famous case of *Donoghue*, but rather alongside and closely connected to it.

I. BLACKER: FACTS, FINDINGS AND SIGNIFICANCE

The plaintiff in *Blacker*, a bicycle maker, sustained serious burns through contact with ignited paraffin oil when a brazing lamp burst. The defendants were the makers of the lamp. There was no contract between these two parties, as the plaintiff had

---

[4] (1842) 10 M&W 109, 152 ER 402 (hereafter: *Winterbottom*).

[5] M Lobban, 'Personal Injuries' in WR Cornish et al (eds), *The Oxford History of the Laws of England, Vol XII: 1820-1914 Private Law* (Oxford, Oxford University Press, 2010) 958–1000, 986–87. See *Brass v Maitland* (1856) 6 El & Bl 470, 119 ER 940 and *Farrant v Barnes* (1862) 11 CBNS 553, 142 ER 912.

[6] See Lobban (n 5) 986–90; *Langridge v Levy* (1837) 2 M & W 519, 150 ER 863; *Clarke v Army and Navy Co-operative Society* [1903] 1 KB 155. See also *Donoghue* (n 1) 569.

[7] (1869) LR 5 Ex 1. See also *Heaven v Pender* (1883) 11 QBD 503. For a detailed discussion of *George*, see DJ Ibbetson, 'George v Skivington (1869)', in C Mitchell and P Mitchell (eds), *Landmark Cases in the Law of Tort* (Oxford, Hart Publishing, 2010) 69–94.

[8] Use will be made in this chapter of material reported in newspapers. This is sourced principally from the digitised collections of British newspapers available in the British Newspaper Archive (British Library, www.britishnewspaperarchive.co.uk/) and *The Times Digital Archive, 1785-2014* (Gale Cengage). Newspapers are useful for a study of this period, as law reporting in the early twentieth century was incomplete.

purchased it from a third-party vendor. The vendors, Hobday Bros,[9] were apparently not sued and receive little attention in the report. A regional newspaper notes only that 'no claim [was] … made for breach of warranty against the seller'.[10] It is unclear why this choice was made.[11]

The plaintiff's case against the manufacturers was that the lamp was a 'dangerous thing', 'either by reason of its general character or by reason of the specific condition in which it is sent out', imposing on the maker a duty to 'see that it shall be safe'[12] as far as is possible, or to take care in its manufacture and 'to provide themselves with the best knowledge in existence at the time'.[13] There had been two cases, a few years before *Blacker* and in which *George* and *Winterbottom* had been raised in argument, setting down the principle that if a chattel were inherently dangerous, or known by the vendor to be dangerous, and no warning had been given, then the vendor/supplier might be liable in negligence to any person injured.[14]

The judge at first instance, when directing the jury, had instructed that the jury might find for the plaintiff if the lamp was 'dangerous in itself', or if the defendant ought to have known it was dangerous.[15] The lamp was found to be a 'dangerous thing for the purpose for which it was intended to be used' and the plaintiff was entitled to recover.[16] It was decided that the defendants, as reasonable men, ought to have known that the lamp was dangerous.

The appeal was heard by Hamilton and Lush JJ, in the King's Bench Divisional Court. Both concluded that the judge had misdirected the jury. Hamilton J (later, Lord Sumner) referred to the various 'circumstances and conditions'[17] in which a plaintiff might recover in tort for injuries sustained by defective chattels, and said that it was a question of law, rather than fact, whether or not a certain case came within one category or another. Therefore, it was for the judge to decide if the lamp was 'a thing dangerous in itself' (and therefore belonging to that established category creating a duty).[18] The trial judge erred in leaving it to the jury to decide. Hamilton J also took the view that the lamp was not a 'dangerous' item: it had worked safely for almost a year.[19] He found that although the evidence suggested that 'more care in its manufacture might have produced a more durable article', he did not think that it brought the lamp within 'the category, so far as it has been defined, of a dangerous

---

[9] See 'Mr Blacker's Accident: Appeal Case', *The Harrow Observer*, 9 February 1912.
[10] ibid.
[11] Advertising in regional newspapers suggests that Hobday Bros were still trading later in the 1910s: see, eg, 'Situations Vacant', *The Essex Newsman*, 8 July 1916. We can only speculate as to the reason for not suing the vendors; the lack of suit may perhaps be linked to some express provision in the sale or the passage of around one year between purchase and accident: see, eg, discussion in JP Benjamin et al, *A Treatise on the Law of Sale of Personal Property*, 5th edn (London, Sweet and Maxwell, 1906) 664.
[12] *Blacker* (n 2) 536.
[13] ibid.
[14] *Clarke v Army and Navy Co-operative Society* [1903] 1 KB 155 and *Earl v Lubbock* [1905] 1 KB 253.
[15] *Blacker* (n 2) 534.
[16] ibid 534–35.
[17] ibid 535.
[18] ibid.
[19] ibid.

object, the dealing with which *per se* imposes any special legal liability'.[20] He noted that, even if it could be made stronger, this would likely be more expensive and there was no law against selling a cheap lamp. It was, Hamilton J concluded, not an item dangerous per se but only *sub modo* – that is, under some conditions. The defendants did not, he said, know that the lamp was unsafe and had no reason to believe it so. However, 'had they been wiser men or more experienced engineers they would then have known what the plaintiff's experts say that they ought to have known'.[21] That they were not so did not make them liable.

Attention turned to *George*. *George* concerned the sale by a chemist of some hair wash, which caused injury to the purchaser's wife. Mrs George's claim was successful, despite the lack of privity of contract – Mrs George, as a married woman, could not, at that time, be a party to a contract. Hamilton J said that this was a decision 'that a person who makes a hair wash owes a duty to persons for whose use he sells it to take care that the wash shall not injure those who use it'.[22] One possible view was that the judges deciding the case believed it to be a case of misrepresentation or fraud. Hamilton J went on to say that, if that were so, *George* had nothing to do with the present case. Nevertheless, a second interpretation of *George* was open: namely, that it was decided upon the ground of negligence, upon a duty owed to the ultimate user and, as such, 'an authority to which every attention must be paid'.[23] Hamilton J suggested that certain passages within the reports made it clear that the ground was *negligence*, not fraud or misrepresentation, and that the focus was upon a lack of care in preparation rather than any dishonesty.[24] He concluded that *George* was not a case that he was able to follow, it having been 'dealt with in later cases in a way which comes as near express disaffirmance as is possible without its being actually overruled'[25] and being in conflict with *Winterbottom*.[26]

The other member of the King's Bench in *Blacker* was Lush J. He opened by acknowledging that he also felt that the judge had misdirected the jury, and that this was sufficient, but wished to express his wider views given that so many 'questions of general importance ha[d] been raised'.[27] He asserted that cases like *Earl v Lubbock*[28] had established that negligence in the manufacture of ordinary chattels, not 'in themselves dangerous', could not found an action where there was no contractual duty.[29] In *Earl*, Collins MR had held the principle in *Winterbottom* to be conclusive in rejecting a duty of care by a wheelwright to the driver of a cart.[30] The privity rule and the enduring authority of *Winterbottom* were thus confirmed, in *Blacker*, also by Lush J. Commenting on *George*, he said that it was often relied

---

[20] ibid.
[21] ibid 537.
[22] ibid.
[23] ibid.
[24] ibid 537–38.
[25] ibid 538. See, eg, *Heaven v Pender* (1883) 11 QBD 503, 516–17.
[26] *Blacker* (n 2) 539.
[27] ibid 540.
[28] [1905] 1 KB 253 (hereafter: *Earl*).
[29] *Blacker* (n 2) 540.
[30] *Earl* (n 28) 256. Collins MR said that the decision in *Winterbottom* (n 4), 'since the year 1842 in which it was given, ha[d] stood the test of repeated discussion'.

upon as establishing that a party who undertakes to do work under a contract could be sued for the breach of that duty by somebody not a party to the contract if the defendant knew that the person was going to use the thing made.[31] However, this, he said, was inconsistent with *Winterbottom* and subsequent authority. He said it was now impossible to follow *George* as it could not be regarded as good law, insofar as it laid down that general proposition.

Lush J provided an overview of the situations in which a stranger to a contract could be permitted an action. He outlined three ways in which a duty might exist: first, if there was fraud on the part of the vendor as to safety; second, where the chattel was known to be dangerous and no warning was given; and, third, where the thing supplied was a public nuisance.[32] There was discussion of the rules concerning chattels of the 'dangerous' class. He commented:

> If a person ... manufactures two different articles, one being a deadly poison and the other safe, and through a careless blunder labels as safe an article which *he ought to have known was of the other category and sells it under that description*, I should be slow to say that in such a case he would not be responsible to persons who he knew would use the article (emphasis added).[33]

Lush J concluded that Blacker's case was not a case in which a dangerous article had, through negligence, been 'passed ... off' as safe.[34] He then returned to *George*, suggesting that its facts had perhaps warranted its proceeding as such a case of selling 'a thing dangerous in itself knowing that others will use it without disclosing its real character'.[35] If *George* had proceeded in this way, he did not 'think it would have been in conflict with any of the authorities ... cited'.[36] It would, he said, have been consistent with the New York Supreme Court case *Thomas v Winchester*,[37] which had been recently cited by Lord Dunedin.[38]

The outcome in *Blacker*, and the reasoning of the Court in the pre-*Donoghue* legal landscape, seems unsurprising. The privity rule was affirmed. However, the significance of *Blacker* is twofold. First, the decision renders *George* unavailable to litigants as authority for a general duty owed to consumers with respect to injuries caused by defective chattels. The Court was strong in its rejection of such a principle, finding it to be inconsistent with other authorities. To the extent that the decision in *George* could be understood as based on such a principle, and, being not overruled, potentially still available to litigants, this line of argument was effectively closed down. The Court appeared to be seizing the opportunity to make a definitive statement to this effect.

---

[31] *Blacker* (n 2) 540.
[32] ibid 540–41.
[33] ibid 541.
[34] ibid.
[35] ibid.
[36] ibid.
[37] (1852) 6 NY 397. In *Thomas*, a chemist sold a medicine which contained belladonna, but which had been labelled 'extract of dandelion' by the supplier. A third party became seriously ill, and the supplier was held liable.
[38] See *Dominion Natural Gas Company v Collins* [1909] AC 640, 646.

Second, in the judgment of Lush J we see the suggestion that the outcome in *George*, even if not described explicitly as such at the time, may be understood ex post facto as justified by the 'supply of dangerous things' exception to the privity rule. This was important for would-be plaintiffs. After *Blacker*, if a party injured by a defective product could demonstrate that the item carried a non-obvious risk of injury and there was no reasonable chance of inspection, then *Blacker* and *George* (re-characterised) suggested that a duty might be owed. This duty was owed wholly outside of contract and restricted neither by the privity rule nor, it seems, from the reasoning of Lush J, by a requirement that the defendant subjectively *knew* of the danger (if they ought to have known). A negligently-prepared hair wash is not as clearly *dangerous* as, say, the deadly poison provided in Lush J's example. Nevertheless, it was identified in *Blacker* as falling within this exception.

Blacker is a landmark decision, not because it dramatically changed the direction of the law: indeed, it confirmed, in strong terms, the applicability of a well-established doctrine. However, it signalled, in the 20 years before *Donoghue*, that any non-contractual claim against the maker of a defective product had to be formulated as one involving the *supply of a dangerous item*. This alternative mechanism allowed courts to provide compensation to injured consumers, unrestricted by the privity rule and before *Donoghue*. The next section will consider a selection of cases in which it appears that compensation was provided in these circumstances.

II. DERMATITIS AND VICTUALS: NO PRIVITY, NO PROBLEM?

Blacker apparently confirmed the strict application of the privity rule. However, alongside ostensible continuity of legal principles in the official reports, there seems to have been a proliferation of successful claims in the 1910s and 1920s for injuries caused by defective products, in circumstances where it is unlikely that there was privity of contract between plaintiff and defendant. These are reported, principally in regional newspapers, as cases in county courts and before single judges of higher courts.

How was this occurring? The brevity of reporting is unsurprising; the average newspaper reader would care little for legal technicalities. Yet this brevity means that it is often necessary to speculate about the arguments involved. The cases collated here are examples of those uncovered rather than a comprehensive sample, and there may be further examples that remain hidden. This section seeks principally to present the claims and outcomes. An explanation, along the lines foreshadowed above, will be offered in section III.

A. Fur Dermatitis

While the wearing of animal fur might, in 2022, leave you vulnerable to moral condemnation, a different concern emerged in mid-1920s Britain. Dermatitis, caused by contact with cheap, treated fur, left consumers with a debilitating rash. Fur garments were extremely popular at this time, particularly among women.[39] Fur dermatitis soon became a problem for makers and vendors. A 1923 report in *The Scotsman* noted:

> Mrs Edith Grace Norrington, of Camberwell, was awarded £12 damages at Lambeth County Court yesterday against a costumier. She bought a coat with a fur collar from the defendant ... and after wearing it three days contracted dermatitis. Dr T.C. Bull, of King's College Hospital, said between 30 and 40 cases of skin trouble, all due to wearing cheap furs, had been treated at the hospital.[40]

Claims became increasingly expensive for defendants and continued throughout the 1920s. The matter became a widespread concern and a Ministry of Health report was written on the subject.[41]

The cases concerning single women are straightforward. Miss Bertha Hart, reported as being a watercolour artist, was awarded £75 and costs in her action against the vendors of a fur-collared coat.[42] As a 'Miss', Bertha Hart was a *feme sole* and could freely contract and sue under that contract. More curious are the cases concerning married plaintiffs. Married women were less likely to be parties to the contract of sale, even if conducting the transaction. The English common law position had been, as described by the Law Revision Committee in 1934, that 'a married woman's position was merged in that of her husband'.[43] A woman's husband, during his life, was entitled to his wife's personal chattels (including her money) and wives were unable to make contracts.[44] This had been central in *George*: the injured party was not a contractual party, leading the Court in *George* to allow the wife an action in tort.[45] A married woman could only contract as agent for her husband, and in so doing bind *him*. Of course, *George* was decided in 1869 and the common law position had been gradually amended through successive Married Women's Property Acts in 1870, 1882 and 1893. These allowed married women to hold and exercise power over their 'separate property'. Every contract by a married woman was deemed to be with respect to, and to bind, her separate property, unless the contrary were demonstrated. There was therefore, at least in principle, a presumption that she was contracting to bind her separate property.[46] However, it remained likely that many

---

[39] See, eg, 'Women's Chat', *The Thanet Advertiser*, 24 October 1925: '[o]vercoats fashioned of cheaper pelts abound'.
[40] 'Skin Trouble from Fur', *The Scotsman*, 18 July 1923.
[41] *Ministry of Health Report on Public Health and Medical Subjects* (No 27, 1924).
[42] 'Skin Disease From Fur Collar: Woman Artist Awarded Damages', *The Nottingham Evening Post*, 24 March 1926.
[43] Law Revision Committee, *Fourth Interim Report*, Cmd 4770, December 1934, 4. Though, it should be noted, the wife as a separate legal person did not completely disappear: see discussion in GL Williams, 'The Legal Unity of Husband and Wife' (1947) 10(1) *Modern Law Review* 16, 18.
[44] See, eg, Williams (n 43); P Mitchell, *A History of Tort Law, 1900-1950* (Cambridge, Cambridge University Press, 2015) 72–73, 290; ACH Barlow, 'Gifts and other Transfers Inter Vivos and the Matrimonial Home' in RH Graveson and FR Crane (eds), *A Century of Family Law, 1857-1957* (London, Sweet and Maxwell, 1957) 197–226, 197.
[45] See Ibbetson (n 7), particularly at 93.
[46] See, eg, discussion in W Bowstead, *A Digest of the Law of Agency*, 7th edn (London, Sweet and Maxwell, 1924) 22.

married women were not, in fact, parties to contracts of sale. Either the married woman, or her husband, would be a party to the contract; not both.[47] The acquisition of separate property (to which the contract would attach) required something like employment, a gift, or an endowment; savings made in household expenditure remained the husband's property.[48] It remained the case (until 1935)[49] that married women did not have full contractual capacity; they were not bound personally. The common law presumption that a wife had authority to pledge a husband's credit for 'necessaries' also continued.[50] It is apparent from courts' interpretation of the Acts in cases like *Paquin v Beauclerk*[51] that the idea that women were acting as agents for their husbands was difficult to overcome.

Several newspapers reported that 'Mrs. Sarah Fox, wife of a Liverpool Corporation employee', received damages of £100 in her action against the defendant outfitter and furrier.[52] The nature of the action is not specified. The reports go on to say that the defendant's medical witness said that, after hearing the plaintiff's evidence, he did not doubt that it was a dye in the fur causing the trouble. Counsel for the defendant thereafter withdrew the defence, suggesting that any argument based on lack of privity alone was felt to be unlikely to succeed. This may be because Mrs Fox was clearly a party to the contract, bound to the extent of her separate property. However, as suggested above, there are strong reasons to discount this possibility.

The furs causing dermatitis were not expensive furs, which one might expect wealthy women to purchase with a pool of separate funds, but cheaper furs that needed chemical treatments to be saleable. It is particularly likely that these kinds of fur coats, relatively inexpensive yet still a luxury, would have been purchased by a husband for his wife, or, if physically purchased by the wife, purchased, *in law*, as agent for her husband. In many reports, the married women are also not described as having any profession or employment. While it cannot be concluded that they had none, one might contrast this with the way other cases are reported: Mrs Marion Outred, said to be 'a Croydon tailoress', would have had a pool of separate property with which to contract.[53] She might be the appropriate party to sue on the contract and in negligence. The case is less clear for married women without employment. If these plaintiffs were suing for breach of warranty, we might query their ability to do

---

[47] See, eg, WB Odgers, *Bullen and Leake's Precedents of Pleadings*, 7th edn (London, Stevens and Sons, 1915) 18–19: it is noted that it was 'now practically impossible for both husband and wife to be liable' on a parol contract made by a married woman since marriage – either the wife was agent, or she was not.

[48] See *Blackwell v Blackwell* [1943] 2 All ER 579; 'Housekeeping Money; Whether Property of Saving Wife' (1943) 196 LT 175; Barlow (n 44) 203. This position persisted until 1964: Married Women's Property Act 1964.

[49] More significant change came only with the Law Reform (Married Women and Tortfeasors) Act in 1935.

[50] See, eg, Bowstead (n 46) 23.

[51] [1906] AC 148.

[52] See, eg, 'Dermatitis From Fur: £100 Damages Against a Shopkeeper', *Northern Daily Mail*, 22 July 1926; 'Dangerous Fur Dyes: Jury Awards £100 Damages', *The Scotsman*, 22 July 1926.

[53] 'Injurious Dye in a Fur Collar', *The Scotsman*, 8 July 1924.

so given the limited contractual capacity of married women and likelihood that they were acting as agent. If, on the other hand, they were suing in negligence, we might expect lack of privity to pose a problem.

Occasionally, more detail is provided. Mr and Mrs Laceby sought damages in the Wandsworth County Court from Messrs Risman Ltd, presumably the vendors, with regard to a fur coat and resulting dermatitis.[54] The report continues:

> Plaintiffs claimed £45 and damages for breach of warranty, and 15s. 2d. for medical attendance, and Mrs. Laceby claimed £39 for personal injury sustained by the alleged breach.

The case was settled out of court. It seems that Mr Laceby might have been suing on the contract for breach of warranty, while Mrs Laceby claimed in negligence.

B. More Dermatitis: Cosmetic Products

Cheap fur was not the only product behind the many dermatitis claims of the 1920s. The manufacturer of hair dye 'Inecto Rapid', Inecto Limited, 'attained some notoriety'[55] after being successfully sued in the King's Bench by a Miss Rivette for the rash-like injuries she sustained after using the dye.[56] Miss Rivette was awarded £200 in damages against Inecto. Her claim against the hairdresser was dismissed on the basis that he had not been negligent.[57]

Another claim against Inecto (again, the hairdresser being a second defendant) was brought in the King's Bench by Mrs Lillie Pendry, the wife of a wholesale provision merchant.[58] Her claim is reported to be for breach of warranty or negligence.[59] Application of the dye caused sores persisting for several weeks. A pamphlet accompanied the product, asserting that the preparation was safe to use on healthy skin. While the evidence of the doctor who treated Mrs Pendry was that he had never seen a case of 'hair dye poisoning' before, another witness, Dr John Bunch, said that 'from the effects of Inecto which he had seen on patients he considered it a poison'.[60] It seems that, after the medical evidence was given, an 'arrangement' between the

---

[54] 'Story of a Fur Coat: Dermatitis Alleged in County Court Case', *Norwood News*, 21 June 1929.
[55] 'Compulsory Winding-Up of Hair Dye Company', *The Times*, 5 July 1922.
[56] 'Injury Caused By a Hair Dye', *The Times*, 28 February 1922.
[57] By 1955, it had been held that a contract between hairdresser and customer, involving the application of hair dye, was a contract of work and materials, and that there was an implied term in the contract, analogous to the corresponding term in the sale of goods (pursuant to s 14 of the Sale of Goods Act 1893), of fitness for purpose: *Ingham v Emes* [1955] 2 QB 366. However, that a contract of work and materials was subject to an analogous implied term seems not to have been settled before the 1930s: see *GH Myers v Brent Cross Service Company* [1934] KB 46. In *GH Myers* it was argued (in the end, unsuccessfully) for the defendant that such a contract required only the exercise of reasonable care and skill.
[58] See, eg, 'Effects of a Hair Dye: Lady's Painful Experience', *The Yorkshire Post*, 12 January 1922; 'Woman's Hair of Many Hues', *The Daily Mirror*, 12 January 1922; 'Hair Turned Green: Effect of a Poisonous Dye', *The Hull Daily Mail*, 12 January 1922.
[59] ibid.
[60] See, eg, Effects of a Hair Dye: Lady's Painful Experience', *The Yorkshire Post*, 12 January 1922.

parties was reached. Important additional information is provided in *The Chemist and Druggist*, a specialist periodical. It is reported that:

> Mr Higgins, for Inecto, Ltd, said the company took up the position that they were not liable in contract, and they were not defending the action so far as they might be liable *in tort*. He admitted, however, that there had been complaints from other people, who alleged they had suffered through using Inecto (emphasis original).[61]

The position concerning the contractual claim is understandable: the plaintiff did not purchase the dye from the manufacturer. We can speculate, plausibly, that the legal argument must have been based on privity. The settlement reached appears to have been based on the strength of the claim in tort.

Another manufacturer, Permanol Limited, was successfully sued in the King's Bench by Mrs Louise Barber.[62] The hairdresser, Madame Ennis, was also a defendant. The claim was said to be for negligence or breach of warranty.[63] It is reported that Permanol 'denied negligence or warranty, or that Permanol was a noxious and dangerous preparation'.[64] The jury found for Mrs Barber, who was awarded £300 against Permanol and one farthing against Madame Ennis. Some reports suggest that Permanol did not defend the action.[65]

In 1926, Mrs Ezme Gozney, 'wife of the stationmaster of Princes Risborough',[66] successfully sued the manufacturer of the Inecto hair dye, now Rapidol Ltd,[67] in the King's Bench.[68] A claim for breach of warranty and negligence was reported.[69] She had purchased the hair dye from a chemist[70] and alleged that she developed dermatitis, hair loss, swelling and blindness lasting several days. The manufacturer unsuccessfully argued that Mrs Gozney was to blame for failing to heed the instructions and warnings provided when she had applied the dye.[71] Mrs Gozney did not purchase the dye from Inecto, so it is difficult to see how a claim for breach of warranty would be available. This must, therefore, have been a claim in tort. Yet why was the legal point about privity not taken by the defendant, or by the court? The jury found in her favour and awarded the impressive sum of £544 in damages.

What is striking about the dermatitis claims reported in the 1920s is that the probable lack of privity seems to have posed no complication. The overall impression afforded by these cases is that these claims were generally successful – even where warnings, or instructions to test before use, had been given by the vendors and manufacturers.

---

[61] 'Hair-dye claim', *The Chemist and Druggist*, 14 January 1922.
[62] See, eg, 'Woman's Hair Dye Claim', *Sheffield Daily Telegraph*, 29 March 1924.
[63] ibid.
[64] ibid.
[65] See, eg, 'Hair Dye Action: Woman's Claim for Damages', *The Scotsman*, 28 March 1924; 'Multi-Coloured Hair', *The Daily News*, 28 March 1924.
[66] See, eg, 'Hair Dye Poison', *Leeds Mercury*, 19 May 1926.
[67] It appears that Rapidol Limited had purchased the assets, and carried on the business, of Inecto Limited after the latter was wound up in 1922: see 'Compulsory Winding-Up of Hair Dye Company', *The Times*, 5 July 1922.
[68] See, eg, 'Poisoned by Hair Dye', *The Dundee Evening Telegraph*, 18 May 1926.
[69] See, eg, 'The 'Inecto' action: £500 damages', *The Times*, 19 May 1926.
[70] See, eg, 'Woman's Hair Dye Ordeal', *Daily Mirror*, 18 May 1926.
[71] 'Hair-Dye Case', *The Chemist and Druggist*, 22 May 1926.

C. Bottled Surprises and Contaminated Food

Ginger beer seemed to pose difficulties to manufacturers and consumers in the early part of the twentieth century. In 1908, *The Times* reported a matter before Grantham J of the King's Bench, in which a young girl sued the manufacturers of ginger beer.[72] Miss Martha Oldfield had been seriously injured when a bottle exploded in her hand. The bottle had been supplied by the manufacturers to her employer. Counsel for the defendant submitted, it is reported, that there was no negligence and, more significantly, 'no duty imposed upon the defendants to confine the ginger-beer in such a way as not to cause injury to the public at large',[73] citing *Winterbottom*. It was argued that there was no case to go before the jury. Why Grantham J 'declined to withdraw the case from the jury'[74] is not explained. The case nevertheless failed, as no negligence in the manufacturing was made out.

A similar case occurred in 1913. *The Times* reported that Mr Bates 'sued both on his own behalf and on behalf of his son, a boy of 12 years old, for damages for personal injuries to the latter and expenses of his own'.[75] The defendants were, again, the manufacturers. The bottle had burst while the boy was trying to open it. However, judgment was given for the defendants, as a bottle of ginger beer was not 'in itself a dangerous thing' and they had not known of the defect in the bottle.[76]

While exploding bottles may not have been leading to successful claims, reports at the time in regional newspapers suggest that the situation and, more surprisingly, the outcome in *Donoghue* were not novel. In 1920, a seven-year-old boy, through his father, brought an action in the King's Bench against White and Sons Ltd.[77] The defendants denied liability. Several newspaper reports describe the case as one of breach of warranty, and, more reliably, so does the *Law Times*.[78] Mr Camelo had purchased bottled drinks from the defendants. His son, seeking a drink, had taken a bottle of lemon squash. The drink did not taste as it should: they discovered that it contained, as well as squash, a dead mouse. The son allegedly became ill with gastro-enteritis and was under the care of a doctor for several months.[79] Salter J found for the plaintiffs, awarding £11 7s. 6d. to the father for expenses incurred, and, curiously, £15 to the son, for 'pain, suffering, and sickness due to the defendants' negligence'.[80]

---

[72] 'Law Report, Jan 17', *The Times*, 18 January 1908.
[73] ibid.
[74] ibid.
[75] 'Injury Through the Bursting of a Bottle', *The Times*, 26 June 1913.
[76] *Bates v Batey* [1913] 3 KB 351, 353–56.
[77] See, eg, 'Mouse in Bottle of Lemon Squash', *The Evening Telegraph*, 24 June 1920; 'Dead Mouse in Lemon Squash: Bottled Shock for Thirsty Boy', *The Globe*, 24 June 1920; 'Mouse in Bottle of Lemon Squash', *The Leeds Mercury*, 25 June 1920; '£26 For a Dead Mouse Found in Lemon Squash', *The Daily Herald*, 25 June 1920' 'Dead Mouse in Lemon Squash', *The Edinburgh Evening News*, 24 June 1920.
[78] See (1920) 149 LT 397.
[79] See, eg, 'Mouse in Bottle of Lemon Squash', *The Evening Telegraph*, 24 June 1920; 'Mouse in Bottle of Lemon Squash', *The Leeds Mercury*, 25 June 1920; 'Dead Mouse in Lemon Squash', *The Edinburgh Evening News*, 24 June 1920.
[80] See, eg, 'Mouse in Bottle of Lemon Squash', *The Dundee Evening Telegraph*, 24 June 1920; 'Mouse in Bottle of Lemon Squash', *Leeds Mercury*, 25 June 1920.

We have two plaintiffs here. On a strict interpretation of the law, and as the minority in *Donoghue* saw it, the son should have no claim. The father was a party to the contract; the son was not. Mr Camelo was in the position of Mrs Donoghue's friend, who purchased her drink. Nevertheless, the son apparently received the lion's share of damages. There is no mention of this case in *Donoghue*, despite the factual similarity. Perhaps we can attribute this to a tradition in the courts of focusing only on 'higher', or Court of Appeal, decisions, at least when the King's Bench case is not properly reported.

We can contrast the *Camelo* case with the outcome in the 1929 case of *Mullen v Barr*.[81] This was properly reported and considered in *Donoghue*. In *Mullen*, children became ill after consuming ginger beer containing a mouse but the action against the manufacturers, brought through their parent, was unsuccessful. The Lord Justice-Clerk expressed his regret that no remedy could be granted but noted this was irrelevant to his decision.[82] Lord Ormidale asserted that he would have found that a duty of care existed if not constrained by authority.[83] This case demonstrates a growing tension between strict legal doctrine and acknowledgement by courts that the plaintiffs had suffered losses that would, without the support of the law, be left without remedy. It seems that, in certain cases, like that of *Camelo*, an alternative route was simply found by a court wishing to do justice. The alternative pathway is, however, unclear from the report.

Clearly, consumption of food and beverage could be a risky business in the early part of the twentieth century. Illness contracted from food was common, and sometimes fatal, even where there was no wrongdoing.[84] Even a cursory examination of regional newspapers discloses many examples of illness caused by contaminated food leading to claims for breach of warranty and negligence. This is not surprising, given food preparation and storage practices of the day. What is interesting for present purposes is the evidence of some courts' apparent willingness to award damages in the absence of a contractual relationship.

In 1911, the *Whitby Gazette* reported the 'interesting verdict' in an action between a purchaser and the vendor-manufacturer of some pork pies.[85] The plaintiff had purchased three pies, given one to his wife and divided the final pie between his three children. The entire family became ill. The plaintiff's wife had not recovered, nine months later, and one child had died. The jury found for the plaintiff, awarding just over £13 for expenses caused by the illness and £5 for the loss of his wife's services. Importantly, however, a sum of £15 was also awarded to the wife herself. The report quotes the *Medical Press* in stating:

> This case suggests that, in future, it may be a more hopeful matter to fix upon the vendor of bad food responsibility for the damage caused thereby. In the case under notice, the task of

---

[81] *Mullen v Barr* 1929 SC 461 (hereafter: *Mullen*).
[82] ibid 470.
[83] ibid 471.
[84] There are vast numbers of reports of such occurrences in the regional newspapers. See, eg, 'The Ptomaine Poisoning Case', *The West Sussex Journal*, 30 September 1902; 'The Poisoning Cases', *The Daily Derby Telegraph*, 16 September 1902 (concerning pork pies); 'Ptomaine Victims', *The Nottingham Evening News*, 17 August 1910 (pork pies, kippers).
[85] 'Damages for Meat Poisoning', *Whitby Gazette*, 3 November 1911.

bringing home the proof was rendered easier by the fact that the defendant was both maker and vendor of the [contaminated?[86]] pies.

The difficulty of suing manufacturers is thus acknowledged. However, the lack of privity between the wife and the defendant is not.

A widely-reported incident occurred in a London restaurant in 1924 involving fragments of glass in a mince pie.[87] McCardie J and a jury in the King's Bench heard how Mrs Esther Davis became aware of something sharp and gritty in her mouth after eating the pie. She claimed to experience severe internal pain and her condition became life-threatening. Mrs Davis and her husband were awarded £130. Negligence was the reported cause of action.[88] It is very likely that Mr Davis was the contracting party; Mr and Mrs Davis had gone out for lunch together. Nevertheless, Mrs Davis was able to recover for her injuries.

The privity rule had been introduced into the developing law of negligence to restrict the scope of liability.[89] The rule ought to have meant that manufacturers could rarely be sued by consumers unless they were the vendor as well. If a contract existed, married women and children were likely not to be a party and therefore strictly precluded from suing. If, instead, a husband was the contracting party, the privity rule would demand that any action to recover damages (beyond expenditure incurred by the husband) for a wife's injuries should fail. The picture we have from cases like *Donoghue* is that the privity rule in tort was strictly enforced, requiring a bold step from a majority in the House of Lords to deliver justice to otherwise remediless plaintiffs.

We would expect, therefore, that product litigation in the 1910s and 1920s would convey a uniform story of failure. Yet newspaper reports of courts' decisions from this time suggest that many plaintiffs were not remediless. There is little evidence of any complication arising from the privity rule. At least some claims were clearly brought in tort. It must be acknowledged, of course, that we are not necessarily seeing the unsuccessful claims – these are less newsworthy. Nevertheless, this survey demonstrates that results similar to that in *Donoghue* could be reached before any formal change to the rules. The next part will suggest that *Blacker* was key to this trend, and therefore key to offering consumers protection before *Donoghue*.

III. 'DANGEROUS' THINGS: A PATH TO SUCCESS FOR INJURED CONSUMERS

Questions arise upon the observation of the successful claims outlined above. How was this happening? Was there simply a practice of ignoring the privity rule? If so,

---

[86] The word is unclear on the image available from the British Newspaper Archive database.
[87] See, eg, 'Glass in a Mince Pie', *The Times*, 5 December 1924; 'Mince Pie and Glass', *The Liverpool Echo*, 4 December 1924; 'Glass in Mince Pie', *Daily Herald*, 5 December 1924; 'Glass in Mince-Pie', *Western Daily Mail*, 5 December 1924; 'Mince Pie Law Suit: Was There Glass in It?', *The Lancashire Daily Post*, 4 December 1924.
[88] See, eg, 'Glass in Mince Pie', *Sheffield Daily Telegraph*, 5 December 1924.
[89] See, eg, D Ibbetson, *A Historical Introduction to the Law of Obligations* (Oxford, Oxford University Press, 1999) 174.

why was the practice not debated and discussed? It seems incredible that legal advisers would not pursue the point that would win a case.

The early twentieth century was a period in which an unprecedented array of goods was available for purchase, and shopping was a form of leisure enjoyed by all parts of British society – not just the elite. Whatever the cause,[90] it suffices to note here there were several important developments during the nineteenth and early-twentieth centuries that encouraged and fuelled a new era of consumption. New forums for retail came into being, including emporia, co-operative stores, and department stores.[91] Unlike the smaller, specialised shops of earlier periods, these larger forums stocked a great variety of goods. By the interwar years, consumer culture had reached all parts of society; advertising expanded to target all socio-economic groups and cheap luxuries were readily available.[92] With such changes came increased separation between manufacturers and vendors; it became more likely that consumers were buying goods from a party that was not the manufacturer. Of course, the development of non-contractual actions for consumers is not a logical necessity of these developments. However, an increase in the volume of products in circulation, together with increased likelihood that consumers would not have a direct relationship with the manufacturer, is likely to have put pressure on laws restricting the availability of actions. Larger-scale manufacturers also had greater loss-spreading ability.

It is possible that, given the incomplete reporting of county court decisions, and even of matters heard in the King's Bench, some courts developed their own practice with respect to harm-causing products – out of the sight of higher courts and treatise authors. However, it was not just county courts allowing these actions: several claims outlined above were heard in the King's Bench. An explanation based on lower courts' ignoring the law altogether is not plausible. There may have been *some* level of judicial insubordination. One case shows a possible glimmer of rebellion: Grantham J refused to withdraw the case from the jury when it was argued that there was no duty of care and no viable case.[93] This could have been an instance of judicial caution, reserving the point for a higher court. Yet it is also possible that Grantham J and others may have felt sympathy for plaintiffs and a distaste for the doctrinal obstacles to consumer claims. These attitudes may have led to crude distinctions' being drawn to avoid the effects of *Winterbottom*. Nevertheless, this can also only account for some of the cases outlined above. The fact that many solicitors were drafting claims for clients injured by defective products suggests that there must have been a coherent argument available.

---

[90] See, eg, P Gurney, *The Making of Consumer Culture in Modern Britain* (London, Bloomsbury Academic, 2017); TC Whitlock, *Crime, Gender and Consumer Culture in Nineteenth-Century England* (London, Taylor and Francis, 2005) 18–19.

[91] See, eg, Whitlock (n 90) ch 1; Gurney (n 90) chs 2, 5, 6; ED Rappaport, "The Halls of Temptation': Gender, Politics, and the Construction of the Department Store in Late Victorian London' (1996) 35(1) *Journal of British Studies* 58; B Lancaster, *The Department Store: A Social History* (Leicester, Leicester University Press, 1998).

[92] See, eg, Gurney (n 90) 135–38; Lancaster (n 91) 94; C Wildman, *Urban Redevelopment and Modernity in Liverpool and Manchester, 1918-1939* (London, Bloomsbury, 2016) 96–97, 101.

[93] 'Law Report, Jan 17', *The Times*, 18 January 1908.

Another explanation is more plausible than overt and widespread judicial insubordination and concerns the decision in *Blacker*. In 1912, *Blacker* indicated to litigants and their lawyers that, to have any prospect of success, a claim similar to that in *George* must be formulated as one involving the sale of a dangerous item. The re-characterisation of *George* as a case of the 'supply of a dangerous thing', the suppression of any alternative understanding of that case and an expansive approach to what might be considered 'dangerous' together opened a pathway within the orthodox law. *Blacker* offered a route to success in tort for injured consumers.

Ideally, the plaintiff would be able to argue that the offending product was a thing 'dangerous in itself', following Lush J's description in *Blacker* of the hair wash in *George* as such an item. If that were not possible, there may still have been scope for suggesting that an item was dangerous because of a defect about which the defendant knew or *ought to have known*. It must be acknowledged that there was ongoing lack of clarity as to the precise nature of the exceptional categories identified in *Blacker*. When would something be 'inherently dangerous', rather than dangerous because of a defect?[94] Of particular trouble, too, was the knowledge requirement. Would a defendant have to have actual knowledge of the danger posed by the item supplied, or was it sufficient that they ought, if exercising sufficient care, to have known? Writing in 1929, Stallybrass noted that there was still conflicting authority:[95] Lush J in *White v Steadman*,[96] decided the year after *Blacker*, accepted as sufficient constructive knowledge. On the other hand, Horridge J in *Bates v Batey*,[97] also decided in that year, had taken the opposite view. This point of confusion had not been resolved by the time of *Donoghue*.[98]

Nevertheless, despite the continuing lack of clarity, the alternative route for injured consumers was established. Major treatises on tort at this time were amended to include consideration of *Blacker, Bates* and *White*.[99] The numerous references to this 'supply of dangerous things' principle in the *Solicitors' Journal* are the most persuasive evidence of the notion that, certainly post-*Blacker*, it was part of common legal knowledge and recognised broadly as a pathway to success.[100] This is a journal that was being read at the coal face of legal practice.

Of the successful claims identified above, the hair dye claims are most easily explained using the 'supply of dangerous things' argument identified in *Blacker*. Hair wash had, in *Blacker*, already been identified as a dangerous article to which a duty of care might attach. This categorisation required some loosening in what might be considered 'dangerous'; previously, successful claims tended to involve things like

---

[94] See discussion in WTS Stallybrass, 'Dangerous Things and Non-Natural User of Land' (1929) 3(3) *Cambridge Law Journal* 376, 387–89.
[95] ibid 388–89.
[96] [1913] 3 KB 340.
[97] [1913] 3 KB 351.
[98] See Lord Macmillan in *Donoghue* (n 1) 616.
[99] See, eg, F Pollock, *The Law of Torts*, 10th edn (London, Stevens and Sons, 1916) 529; JW Salmond, *The Law of Torts*, 4th edn (London, Stevens and Haynes, 1916) 423–24.
[100] See, eg, 'Tortious Breach of Contract' (1913) 57 *Solicitors' Journal and Weekly Reporter* 571; 'Dangerous Things' (1913) 57 *Solicitors' Journal and Weekly Reporter* 639; 'Hair-Dyes as a Dangerous Chattel' (1922) 66 *Solicitors' Journal and Weekly Reporter* 467.

poison or guns.[101] Nevertheless, this would explain why the hair dye cases appear to have moved with ease through the courts, sometimes resulting in settlement, and often resulting in significant damages awards. The contract need not supply the obligation; a duty was owed outside of it. Of course, there may have been unsympathetic courts who refused to engage in loosening, and defendants providing serious legal argument for the court to address. However, an answer must be sought for the trend. The same mechanism would have been open to those affected by dermatitis-inducing fur garments.

That *Blacker* is behind the success of these claims also involves some speculation. Many reports considered above contain little information as to the precise grounds for the claim. Occasionally, though, a more detailed glimpse is provided. Clear indication that *Blacker* and the 'supply of dangerous things' strategy was used by hair dye litigants comes from a report in *The Times* of the action by Miss Rivette, outlined above, against Inecto Limited.[102] Miss Rivette had a contractual relationship with the hairdresser; there was no contractual relationship with Inecto. The report describes the case for defendant:

> In opening the case for Inecto, Limited Mr. Giveen said he would call no evidence, but would submit that there was no contractual liability between the plaintiff and his clients. The plaintiff had to show that the company sent out, without adequate warning, a substance which was dangerous. It could not be said that this dye came within the category of dangerous things, as it had been used in thousands of cases without ill effects. He cited Blacker and Lake v. Elliot ... in support of this contention.[103]

Mr Justice Bailhache gave judgment for the plaintiff in the action against Inecto, and she was awarded £200 in damages. The warning sent out by the company had been insufficient.[104]

As noted above, Inecto was also sued by Mrs Lillie Pendry in the King's Bench. Again, the argument seems to have been that Inecto had supplied a dangerous article – it was alleged that the dye was 'poisonous and likely to give anyone who used it eczema'.[105] The plaintiff's evidence was that she was not told that the dye was dangerous. Medical evidence was given to the effect that the dye was not safe to use in 'predisposed cases'.[106] The strength of this line of argument appears to be confirmed by the fact that Inecto apparently chose not to defend the claim and settled after the first day of evidence.

Mrs Gozney's claim against Inecto was also considered above. The report in *The Times* describes the action as one in which Mrs Gozney 'sought to recover from Rapidol, Limited ... damages for alleged negligence, and breach of duty and warranty on the *sale of dangerous goods*' (emphasis added).[107] It was argued that the preparation was highly dangerous to some people and the warning provided was inadequate,

---

[101] See Stallybrass (n 94) 379.
[102] 'Injury caused by a hair dye', *The Times*, 28 February 1922.
[103] ibid.
[104] ibid. See also 'Hair-dye Injury', *The Chemist and Druggist*, 4 March 1922.
[105] See, eg, 'A woman's hair dye', *The Times*, 12 January 1922.
[106] ibid.
[107] 'The 'Inecto' action: £500 damages', *The Times*, 19 May 1926.

and evidence was given of numerous complaints about the preparation. Mrs Gozney was awarded £544 2s. However, evidence was also given that 407,000 sets of two bottles had been sold each year in the last three years, yet only three actions had resulted.[108] This does suggest a rather more liberal understanding of something that might be 'dangerous' than we might expect. Similarly, a report in the *Leeds Mercury* notes that a Dr Footner, called as a witness, had said that in the past 16 months, he had seen 16 cases of complaints about Inecto but that they were not serious cases.[109] Certainly, the defendant company knew of the risk. However, here (as in other similar cases) that risk, known but small, and only rarely serious, is treated as taking the product into the category of a 'dangerous thing'.

How, then, does this assist us to understand the prevalence of successful cases against suppliers and manufacturers of all kinds of defective goods during the 1910s and 1920s? Would we not expect the lawyers to object that the various items were hardly *dangerous*? Alternatively, an objection that the defendant did not *know* of the defect or danger? The answer must be that these objections were indeed fatal to some claims. The claims involving exploding ginger beer bottles were unsuccessful. Nevertheless, other claims did meet with success. As in *Camelo*, where a bottle contained some surprise item (there, a mouse), this might indeed ground a successful claim – at least before a single judge of the King's Bench, if not before the Scottish Court of Session in *Mullen*. It is difficult to suggest that the contents of a beverage bottle might be *inherently* dangerous, unless the same were said of all items of food and drink, which necessarily carry some risk of contamination. It is more likely that it was a case of danger by defect, and that here, as in *White*, it was found that the defendant *ought to have known*.

It is more difficult to understand how cases of unexpected objects in items of food and drink could have succeeded. Nevertheless, they seem to have done so, at least on some occasions. Given contemporary concerns with food safety (leading, amongst other things, to the enactment of legislation concerned with safety standards)[110] it is not unlikely that some courts might be prepared to find contaminated food to be sufficiently 'dangerous'.

We might, therefore, understand these claims as examples of litigants and their lawyers using an argument that had been developing in the case law but was really opened, and said to be the *only* viable argument, following *Blacker*. It was wide in scope: anything causing injury could, by reason of that fact, potentially be described as 'dangerous'. It would provide a way of side-stepping *Winterbottom* prior to *Donoghue*, in the hands of a sufficiently sympathetic judge and jury.

Blacker was a key case establishing this pathway for consumers and was certainly well-known, even if not reported outside of the *Law Times*. Frederick Pollock, it seems, would not admit it to the Law Reports.[111] This should not detract from its

---

[108] See, eg, 'Lady's Injuries from a Hair Dye', *The Bucks Herald*, 22 May 1926.
[109] 'Hair Dye Poison', *Leeds Mercury*, 19 May 1926.
[110] For example, the Sale of Food and Drugs Act 1875, and the Public Health (Regulations as to Food) Act 1907. See also J Phillips and M French, 'Adulteration and Food Law, 1899-1939' (1998) 9(3) *Twentieth Century British History* 350.
[111] See JL Barton, 'Liability for Things in the Nineteenth Century' in JA Guy and HG Beale (eds), *Law and Social Change in British History* (London, Royal Historical Society, 1984) 145–55, 154.

'landmark' status. *Blacker* was closely considered in *Donoghue*, even if the successful claims identified above were not. *Blacker* opened a tenuous pathway for consumer protection, but consumers would have to wait until 1932 for a more secure route to success.

IV. CONCLUSIONS

Blacker may be understood as a 'landmark' decision with respect to consumer protection for two reasons, both closely linked to *Donoghue*. First, it was a decision affirming, in strong terms, the application of the privity rule in the law of negligence; indeed, Lord Buckmaster used Hamilton J's formulation in *Blacker* as the 'general rule' applicable in *Donoghue*.[112] Any suggestion that there might be a general duty owed by manufacturers to the ultimate consumer, based on a line of cases including *George*, was firmly rejected. The hard line taken in *Blacker* delayed the recognition of a manufacturer-consumer duty in negligence for another 20 years. However, and perhaps somewhat paradoxically, the Court in *Blacker* was also responsible for confirming the availability of an alternative mechanism that seems to have supplied a way of providing to consumers protection in the law of tort from harm-causing products.

In many of the cases discussed, the doctrinal argument would have been rather feeble. However, it is plausible that courts were sufficiently sympathetic to those injured by defective products that they ignored the doctrinal difficulty – and even, on occasion, appear to have stopped the defendant from raising it.

Lord Macmillan's speech in *Donoghue* contains a glimmer of discontent with the practice, necessitated by the perceived gap in the law, of litigants' squeezing their claims into the 'supply of dangerous things' category.[113] This seems to have been influential in his acceptance of Mrs Donoghue's arguments for a duty in the supply of goods outside of this category.

The trend observed here, commenced or aided by *Blacker*, could be seen as undermining, or at least side-stepping the effect of, the privity rule. The more widespread such a practice becomes, the greater the pressure brought to bear upon the formal rules to avoid the incongruity. This is not something happening tucked away in the countryside; many of the decisions reported come from the King's Bench. As early as 1920, there seems to have been a King's Bench doppelgänger of *Donoghue* (albeit with a mouse and a lemonade bottle in the lead roles).

That the argument based on the 'supply of dangerous things' was rejected in *Mullen* in 1929 is likely to have brought matters to a head and meant that consumers were left with inadequate protection. With that line of argument shut down by a court at the level of the Scottish Court of Session, the need for reconsideration of the restrictive rules was more urgent than ever. The time was ripe for a snail in a bottle to precipitate a change.

---

[112] *Donoghue* (n 1) 569.
[113] ibid 611.

8

Jarvis v Swans Tours: Can Holidays be a Human Right?

JODI GARDNER**

> The idea that the poor should have leisure has always been shocking to the rich.*
>
> B Russell, *In Praise of Idleness* (1932)

I. INTRODUCTION

JARVIS V SWANS Tours is a well-known and important contract law case. It undoubtedly has landmark status, having been the first case to clearly recognise the ability of parties to claim damages for disappointment arising from breach of contract. Prior to *Jarvis v Swans Tours*, the common law of contract had no ability to award compensation for personal disappointment caused by breach of contract. Damages, even in personal/domestic contracts, were limited to the financial consequences – unless it was coupled with physical harm or inconvenience. *Jarvis v Swans Tours*, particularly the leading judgment of Lord Denning MR, changed the legal approach and provided a new head of damage in contract.

While *Jarvis v Swans Tours* is generally considered a decision on contract law damages, it additionally provides significant new consumer rights and is also a form of consumer protection. Holidays are clearly something outside of the commercial realm of contract law and are only taken by people in a 'social or domestic' context. People on holiday are, by definition, consumers: they are 'acting for purposes that are wholly or mainly outside that individual's trade, business, craft or profession'.[1] Prior to *Jarvis v Swans Tours*, consumers would not have had any clear legal right

---

** I would like to thank Devon Airey for her brilliant Research Assistant work, which was kindly funded by the St John's College Returning Carer's Scheme. I am also very appreciative of the helpful comments I received from Professors John Murphy and Iain Ramsay, and attendees at the Obligations Discussion Group at the University of Oxford. The usual caveat applies (although a special mention should go to my newborn son, Benjamin Charles, and the subsequent sleep deprivation he created).

* Reproduced by permission of Taylor & Francis Group. We also acknowledge the copyright of the Bertrand Russell Peace Foundation Ltd.

[1] Consumer Rights Act 2015, s 2(3).

to claim compensation for disappointment caused by breaches of holiday contracts. The outcome of this case is therefore another indication of the common law providing consumers with increased legal protection. It is also an early indication of the common law placing a legal value on holidays and recreation – something that has been continued in other areas of private law.

The COVID pandemic, lockdown, and travel restrictions have really brought home the value of holidays and the importance of 'getting away'. The significance placed on holidays in *Jarvis v Swans Tours* raises the question of whether holidays can and should be considered a 'human right'. The right to a holiday is included in the International Covenant on Socio-Economic Rights, where Article 7(d) states that all people should have the right to 'rest, leisure and reasonable limitation of working hours and periodic holidays with pay, as well as remuneration for public holidays'. However, the reality is that increasing numbers of people cannot afford to exercise this 'right'.

This chapter has two key parts, with the first looking at *Jarvis v Swans Tours*. It involves an outline of the facts of the case, a description of the various parties involved, a brief sketch of the High Court and Court of Appeal decisions, and a consideration of the impact of the case. The second part focuses on the socio-legal implications of the case, looking at whether the decision in *Jarvis* can be used to shine a light on an important issue – whether holidays are a human right, and if so, how this claim can be justified.

II. JARVIS V SWANS TOURS

This part of this chapter focuses on *Jarvis v Swans Tours*, highlighting the facts of the case, the different parties involved, the outcomes in the High Court and Court of Appeal, and finally the impact of the case in both the UK and around the world.

A. The Facts

Mr Jarvis booked a 15-day skiing holiday in the Swiss resort of Mörliap with Swans Tours after seeing the holiday advertised in a brochure. The brochure described the various activities of the skiing holiday, including afternoon tea, several house parties, and a performance by a yodeller. Specifically, it stated that:

> House Party Centre with special resident host … Mörlialp is a most wonderful little resort on a sunny plateau … Up there you will find yourself in the midst of beautiful alpine scenery, which in winter becomes a wonderland of sun, snow and ice, with a wide variety of fine ski-runs, a skating rink and exhilarating toboggan run … Why did we choose the Hotel Krone … mainly and most of all because of the 'Gemütlichkeit' and friendly welcome you will receive from Herr and Frau Weibel … The Hotel Krone has its own Alphütte Bar which will be open several evenings a week … No doubt you will be in for a great time, when you book this house-party holiday … Mr Weibel, the charming owner, speaks English.

The brochure also made a number of specific promises about what would be included in the holiday package, including:

> Swans House Party in Morlialp. All these House Party arrangements are included in the price of your holiday. Welcome party on arrival. Afternoon tea and cake for 7 days. Swiss dinner by candlelight. Fondue party. Yodeller evening. Chali farewell party in the 'Alphütte Bar'. Service of representative.

The holiday turned out to be very different from the one advertised. Many of the promised activities were not provided at all or were substantially different from those described in the brochure. Mr Jarvis expected house parties of around 30 people every night, but in the first week there were only 13 or so people and in the second week there were no house parties at all.[2]

The skiing was also disappointing, as it was quite far away, the hotel only provided mini-skis, and his boots rubbed. Other more 'trivial' issues included the fact that Mr Jarvis could not have the 'nice Swiss cakes which he was hoping for. The only cakes for tea were potato crisps and little dry nut cakes'.[3] The evening yodeller was a local man who arrived in work clothes and sang four or five songs only.

Mr Jarvis' work arrangement meant that he only took one holiday a year – generally at Christmas. He paid £68.45 for the holiday. He was extremely disappointed with the holiday. Mr Jarvis was a solicitor and sued Swans Tours for breach of contract to provide the holiday promised.

B. The Parties

This case is made up of some very interesting characters and institutions, and that is possibly one of the reasons why it came to court and became notorious.

i. The Claimant?

James Walter John Wallace-Jarvis was a solicitor at the time of the case. He was however suspended from practising as a solicitor on 25 January 2007 after his firm was closed in 2006 due to neglect of his clients' affairs and various complaints of misconduct. Mr Jarvis was a colourful character with a number of outside 'interests'. For example, he had a block of flats adversely possessed from him by a property company tenant as, even though he was the registered proprietor, the judge held that he ceased to pay proper attention to his duties to maintain the common parts of the property.[4] At the time of writing the chapter, Mr Jarvis lived with his wife in the colourfully named Tally-Ho!, High Lane, Stansted.

---

[2] Lord Denning emphasised the significance of this on the fact that Mr Jarvis was a 'man of about 35' but provided no further insight: *Jarvis v Swans Tours Ltd* [1973] 1 QB 233, 236.
[3] ibid.
[4] *Raj Properties Limited v James Walter John Wallace-Jarvis* [2010] EWLandRA 2009_1095.

ii. The Defendant

Swans Tours was incorporated on 2 January 1952 and was dissolved on 7 August 2012 by voluntary strike-off. The company was coming under significant financial difficulties in its final years, for example its final full accounts made up to 31 December 2010 recorded losses of around £41,000.[5]

Jarvis v Swans Tours does not capture the only occasion that the company was taken to court over the quality of its holiday packages. A similar situation arose in *Stedman v Swan's Tours*.[6] The claimant in that case made arrangements with travel agents that his party of six would be taken by air to Jersey and be provided with superior rooms with a sea view in a first-class hotel. When they arrived in Jersey, they found that the rooms reserved for them were very inferior and had no sea view. The group was unable to obtain accommodation elsewhere and as a result, the whole holiday was described as 'spoilt'.

The plaintiff was subsequently awarded damages for appreciable inconvenience and discomfort, in the amount of £63. As the original package was £207, this award was much less generous than the one in *Jarvis*, showing the significant impact of Lord Denning's approach in *Jarvis v Swans Tours*. The *Stedman* decision was referred to in the *Jarvis* case. Despite the factual similarities, Lord Denning rejected this approach, stating that 'the judge was in error in taking the sum paid for the holiday £63.45 and having it. The right measure of damages is to compensate [the plaintiff] for the loss of entertainment and enjoyment which he was promised, and which he did not get'.[7]

iii. The Hotel

Whilst Hotel Krone is still in existence,[8] there is no mention at all of the Alphütte Bar on its website. However, the Hotel did continue to provide 'cultural' events and entertainment, including Jazz evenings and a Saint Sylvester's Day party.[9] The Hotel is described on the official Swiss website of tourism as

> a turn-of-the-century building … a complete work of art intended to create a surreal atmosphere and reflect the tastes and standards of bygone eras. It plays host to the portfolio manager and the farmer's wife, the Englishwoman and the Indian, theatre lovers and storytellers, the gourmet, the lovebirds and the family. Unique in style and atmosphere, set amidst the awe-inspiring natural beauty of Central Switzerland, it offers the finest cuisine combined with an exquisite cultural programme.[10]

The Hotel continues to get poor reviews since Mr Jarvis' visit, and does not seem to have been renovated. One review (translated from German to English) stated:

---

[5] find-and-update.company-information.service.gov.uk/company/00503016.
[6] (1951) 95 SJ 727.
[7] *Jarvis v Swans Tours Ltd* (n 2) 233, 238.
[8] As at the time of writing; krone-giswil.ch/.
[9] krone-giswil.ch/Inhalt/kultur/kultur.htm.
[10] www.myswitzerland.com/en-gb/accommodations/hotel-krone-2/.

Room in the annex. Charm of the room like that in a football field cloakroom. The furnishings look to me like from the 60s, the same with the carpet, makes a dingy impression, saggy mattress, bare walls (not a single picture or decoration).[11]

Herr and Frau Weibel, mentioned in the judgment, are no longer owners of the hotel. The hotel however appears to have stayed within the family – owned later by a Mr and Mrs Ingrid and Thomi Kuster-Weibel.

C. Findings of *Jarvis v Swans Tours*

The case was first heard in the county court, which held that the claimant was entitled to compensation on orthodox damages principles. The judge took the measure of damages as the difference between what Mr Jarvis paid and the holiday he received. On that basis, Mr Jarvis was awarded only £31.72 in damages (ie, half the cost of the holiday).

Mr Jarvis appealed to the Court of Appeal claiming special damages of £68.45 for the cost of the holiday and £93.27 for two weeks' salary, together with general damages for inconvenience and loss of benefit. In a short, but dense nine-page judgment, all three members of the Court of Appeal (Lord Denning MR, Edmund Davies LJ, Stephenson LJ) rejected, either expressly or by implication, the claimant's claim for loss of salary and decided that the judge was wrong in assessing Mr Jarvis's loss at half the cost of the holiday. However, the Court was unanimous in holding that he should be compensated for his loss of entertainment and enjoyment and quantified this at £125.00.

Lord Denning MR gave the leading judgment. The underlying basis of his decision was captured in the comment: 'what is the right way of assessing damages? It has often been said that on a breach of contract damages cannot be given for mental distress or for disappointment of mind caused by a breach of contract'.[12] Previous approaches limited damages to situations where the claimant suggested 'physical inconvenience', and examples included having to walk five miles home[13] or living in an over-crowded house.[14] In a characteristically creative approach, Lord Denning decided that 'I think that those limitations are out of date'.[15] He therefore held that:

> In a proper case damages for mental distress can be recovered in contract, just as damages for shock can be recovered in tort. One such case is a contract for a holiday, or any other contract to provide entertainment and enjoyment. If the contracting party breaks his contract, damages can be given for the disappointment, the distress, the upset and frustration caused by the breach. I know that it is difficult to assess in terms of money, but it is no more difficult than the assessment which the courts have to make every day in personal injury cases for loss of amenities.[16]

---

[11] www.holidaycheck.ch/hrd/hotel-krone-giswil-laesst-zu-wuenschen-uebrig/183d54f1-4d11-33c8-9dbe-251a764b413e.
[12] *Jarvis v Swans Tours Ltd* (n 2) 233, 237.
[13] *Hobbs v London & Southern Western Railway Co* (1875).
[14] *Bailey v Bullock* [1950] 2 All ER 1167.
[15] *Jarvis v Swans Tours Ltd* (n 2) 233, 237.
[16] ibid 238.

Lord Denning then held that Mr Jarvis' holiday had been a 'grave disappointment' and was 'not what he went for'. On this basis, it was held that he was entitled to damages for the lack of facilities that had been promised and the loss of enjoyment of the holidays. This was supported by Edmund Davies LJ who held that if

> in such circumstances travel agents fail to provide a holiday of the contracted quality, they are liable in damages ... The court is entitled, indeed bound, to contrast the overall quality of the holiday so enticingly promised with that which the defendants in fact provided.[17]

On this basis, Mr Jarvis was awarded £125.00 damages, even though the holiday had only cost £68.45.

D. The Impact of *Jarvis v Swans Tours*

The traditional basis for awarding damages in contract law is inherently commercially focused: it looks ordinarily at the financial implications of a breach of contract.[18] This was later extended to include damages for physical harm and inconvenience, which is relatively uncontroversial considering the importance of bodily integrity. *Jarvis v Swans Tours* however extended this even further to include harm to mental integrity – compensation for disappointment arising from contract breaches.

The decision recognised the reality of life and the importance of holidays. As Lord Denning commented, 'Mr Jarvis only has a fortnight's holiday in the year. He books it far ahead, and looks forward to it all that time. He ought to be compensated for the loss of it.'[19] This is the starting point for the increased focus on the importance of holidays: holidays are important to what it means to be 'human'. The decision was an early indication of consumer protection for the purchase of 'package holidays' (which were starting to become more common at the time). This sector was later covered by self-regulatory approaches,[20] which were then followed by European Union (EU) statutes.[21] The case has had implications not only in UK and EU law, but has been followed in Malaysia[22] and Canada.[23] Whilst the case has been approved and applied in Australia, its application is impacted by the state-based civil liability laws.[24]

---

[17] ibid 239.
[18] *Hamlin v Great Northern Railway Co* (1856) 1 H & N 408, 411.
[19] *Jarvis v Swans Tours Ltd* (n 2) 233, 238.
[20] See, eg, ATOL (Air Travel Organisers Licence) introduced in 1973: ABTA Code of Conduct www.abta.com/about-us/code-of-conduct.
[21] Directive (EU) 2015/2302 of the European Parliament and of the Council of 25 November 2015 on package travel and linked travel arrangements; Regulation (EC) No 261/2004 of the European Parliament and of the Council of 11 February 2004 establishing common rules on compensation and assistance to passengers in the event of denied boarding and of cancellation or long delay of flights.
[22] *Malaysian Airline System Berhad v Tarn Chin Siong & Ors* [2009] 9 CLJ 435.
[23] *Keks v Esquire Pleasure Tours Ltd* [1974] 3 WWR 406 and *Elder v Koppe* (1974) 53 DLR (3d) 705.
[24] For a more detailed discussion on the interaction between holiday contracts and the CLA, see the excellent article: E Bant, K Barnett and JM Paterson, "Plain Sailing'?: Damages for Distress under the ACL and the Performance Interest in Contract' (2020) 36 *Journal of Contract Law* 272. This article highlights that the High Court's interpretation results in 'claims for more serious mental impairment or condition resulting from an equivalent failure are excluded, except in the most extreme cases, while damages for distress and disappointment are recoverable' (273).

The approach in *Jarvis v Swans Tours* and recognition of the importance of holidays has been continued in other areas of private law. For example, under the common law in the Supreme Court's generous interpretation of easements in *Regency Villas Title Ltd v Diamond Resorts (Europe) Ltd & Others*,[25] and in the statutory basis for set levels of compensation for cancelled or delayed flights.[26] It has also impacted other areas of contract law. For example, a similar factual scenario arose two years later in the context of privity of contract in *Jackson v Horizon Holidays*.[27]

III. CAN HOLIDAYS BE A HUMAN RIGHT?

It must be acknowledged that there is a class-based aspect to *Jarvis v Swans Tours* – loss of enjoyment from expensive overseas holidays is a very 'middle-class' issue to be litigating.[28] The party was a well-off solicitor who was unhappy with the quality of the international skiing holiday he had booked.

The decision can however be looked at from a different perspective. The case highlighted how important holidays are to life – to everyone's life, regardless of social or economic status. It can therefore be used to ground an argument that the ability to enjoy holidays is a legal right that should be both enforced by courts and protected in the political arena. From a socio-legal perspective at least, this is possibly the most important implication of the decision, as it raises the question of whether holidays should be considered a socio-economic human right. In this way, private law doctrines, including common law observations, can be used to shine a light on important social and political issues.

It is however important to justify the basis for protecting holidays in this manner. There are three potential justifications to be considered for grounding holidays in the language of 'human rights'– focusing on legal enforcement, political enforcement, and theoretical justifications. Each will be considered in this section.

A. Legal Enforcement

There are multiple ways in which legislation and even the courts have indicated the importance of holidays to what it means to live a meaningful and important life. In terms of international statutes, the Universal Declaration of Human Rights (UDHR), 1976 International Covenant on Economic, Social and Cultural Rights

---

[25] *Regency Villas Title Ltd v Diamond Resorts (Europe) Ltd & Others* [2018] UKSC 57, [2019] AC 553.
[26] See Regulation 261 as enforced post-Brexit by the Air Passenger Rights and Air Travel Organisers' Licensing (Amendment) (EU Exit) Regulations 2019.
[27] *Jackson v Horizon Holidays* [1975] 3 All ER 92.
[28] The same issues arose in the latter case, *Jackson v Horizon Holidays*. Again, there is a class-based aspect to the decision 'Mr Jackson is a young man, in his mid-twenties. He has been very successful in his business ... He has been working very hard [the family] is determined to have a holiday in the sun' (p 93). 'People look forward to a holiday ... When it fails, they are greatly disappointed and upset. It is difficult to assess in terms of money' (p 96).

(ICESC), and the United Nations Convention on the Rights of the Child (UNCRC) can all be seen to support the right to holidays in different yet complementary ways.

First, both the UDHR and the ICESC provide a potential legislative basis for the right to a break from work, also known as 'the right to leisure'. Article 24 of the UDHR declares that 'everyone has the right to rest and leisure, including reasonable limitation of working hours and periodic holidays with pay', and ICESC Article 7(d) states that everyone should have the right to 'rest, leisure and reasonable limitation of working hours and periodic holidays with pay, as well as remuneration for public holidays'. Rose has labelled this as 'a human right to leisure', emphasising its importance to providing equality amongst all people in her monograph *Free Time*. She comments that,

> Free time is a resource that citizens generally require to pursue their conceptions of the good, whatever those may be. Without the resource of free time, citizens lack the means to exercise their formal liberties and opportunities. In order to ensure that citizens can exercise their freedoms, a central commitment of liberal egalitarian theories of justice, citizens must be guaranteed their fair shares of free time.[29]

There are however restrictions on how effectively this Article can be used to 'enforce' a right to holidays. First, the basis is the right about workplace obligations, as opposed to general social, political, and economic rights to go on holidays. It is therefore difficult to see how a specific obligation placed generally on employers could effectively be translated into a more social right that would need to be enforced by the state. Second, there has been very little attention given to creating a framework that allows these types of socio-economic rights to be effectively enforced.[30] Ordinarily, these matters are enforceable at the behest of one state against another, but in the context of socio-economic rights of individuals, this is by no means straight-forward. Third, it is recognised that the right is focused on giving people a break from work and not specifically the right to go on holidays – although this could well be seen as a natural extension of the right to leisure.

The second international statute that seems to emphasise the importance of holidays, but specifically for children, is the UNCRC. Under Article 31(1), all children have the right 'to rest and leisure, to engage in play and recreational activities appropriate to the age of the child and to participate freely in cultural life and the arts'. Whilst it is obviously possible for children to exercise this right without needing to go on holidays, the focus on a right to play has clear connections and parallels with the argued-for right to holiday; they are both focused on the importance of giving people the right to recreation.

Similar to the restrictions of asserting the right under Article 7(d) of the ICESC, there are also issues with the enforcement of the right to play. Lott has outlined that this right is exceptionally valuable to the way children develop, but is so often 'forgotten'

---

[29] J Rose, *Free Time* (Princeton, Princeton University Press, 2017) 1.
[30] This section is largely based on the analysis undertaken in J Gardner, *The Future of High-Cost Credit: Rethinking Payday Lending* (Oxford, Hart Publishing 2022). For a more detailed analysis specifically in the context of high-cost credit contracts, see section 3.3.2 'Human Rights Approaches'.

by states when implementing regimes associated with rights enforcement.[31] She however highlights that the right to play should be seen as economic, social and cultural in nature, and of fundamental importance, arguing that there is a need to move away from viewing it as a luxury right and instead that it should be considered a right of fundamental importance and significance.[32] Lott, in arguing for an increased political and academic focus on the right to play, states

> the right to play touches upon nearly all aspects of children's economic, social and cultural rights and relates closely to some civil and political right enjoyment; its importance cannot be overstated.[33]

The courts have also implicitly protected the right to holidays in a number of decisions. For example, in *Antuzis v DJ Houghton Catching Services Ltd* the directors were found to have committed the tort of inducing breach of contract in relation to a range of employment breaches, including depriving employees of their holiday entitlement.[34] The company was subsequently ordered to pay both compensation for the annual leave and aggravated damages of 20 per cent due to the 'total and cumulative impact' of the breaches on the employees, further emphasising the courts' valuing the right to holidays and the impact of denying this right to employees.[35]

Other examples of the courts protecting holiday rights include: *Centennial Northern Mining Services Pty Ltd v Construction, Forestry, Mining and Energy Union*[36] (if an employee is paid annual leave loading during employment, they must be paid it when annual leave is paid out on termination), *Harpur Trust v Brazel*[37] (employees on permanent contracts who work for part of the year and are called in as and when required must be provided with the same holiday entitlement as full year employees), *Director, Fair Work Building Industry Inspectorate v Foxville Projects Group Pty Ltd*[38] (employer fined AUD$145,000, together with compensation of over AUD$150,000 for failure to provide adequate annual leave and keep employee records), and Australian Federal Court finding that the Commonwealth Corporation, Airservices Australia Pty Ltd, incorrectly forced its staff to take leave during the annual Christmas shutdown period. Whilst there are a number of cases where the courts have emphasised the importance of holidays by protecting annual leave and holiday pay, there are a range of access-to-justice barriers preventing the vast majority of people from asserting their legal rights in this regard.

Despite the enforcement difficulties associated with all these potential legal bases, it is essential to consider how and why socio-economic rights, in this case the right to holidays, should be enforced. The cost-of-living crisis, increased inequality,

---

[31] See N Lott, *The Right of the Child to Play From Conception to Implementation* (London, Routledge, 2023).
[32] Naomi Lott, 'Establishing the Right to Play as an Economic, a Social and a Cultural Right' (2022) 30 *The International Journal of Children's Rights* 755, 757.
[33] ibid.
[34] *Antuzis & Ors v DJ Houghton Catching Services Ltd & Ors* [2019] EWHC 843 (QB), [2019] Bus LR 1532.
[35] *Antuzis & Ors v DJ Houghton Catching Services Ltd & Ors* [2021] EWHC 971 (QB), [2021] 4 WLUK 249 at [155].
[36] *Centennial Northern Mining Services Pty Ltd v Construction, Forestry, Mining and Energy Union* [2015] FCAFC 100, 231 FCR 298.
[37] *Harpur Trust v Brazel* [2022] UKSC 21, [2023] 2 All ER 113.
[38] *Director, Fair Work Building Industry Inspectorate v Foxville Projects Group Pty Ltd* [2015] FCA 492.

and rising levels of poverty in western democracies have, however, challenged the concept that economic and social rights are of 'lesser' importance than the traditional civil and political rights. The right to food, to heat one's home effectively, and – potentially – the right to go on regular holidays, are things likely to impact an individual's day to day life to a significantly greater extent than many of the standard civil and political rights, particularly for those who are already financially vulnerable. In addition, research has increasingly highlighted the importance of providing people with both social/economic rights and civil/political rights – as Satz and Green show, the two are inherently linked.[39] The recent global financial crisis has confirmed the importance of social and economic rights, with increasing numbers of people in some of the most privileged and economically developed countries struggling to provide themselves with basic food and shelter.

B. Political Enforcement – Provision of a Social Minimum

The second approach to potentially enforcing the 'human right' of a holiday is by advocating that this is part of the state's obligation to provide a 'social minimum' to all people.[40] If holidays can be included in the identified social minimum, there are strong justifications to provide and protect this right.

The modern notion of a social minimum has been around since Rawls' *A Theory of Justice* in 1979. This concept recognises the importance of providing a level of resources to all people to ensure a minimally acceptable standard of living.[41] This has been pivotal in how we approach issues of poverty and inequality, and is linked to the provision of welfare by the state.[42] Academics and philosophers have framed the social minimum in a variety of ways.[43] For the purpose of this chapter, the focus

---

[39] D Satz, *Why some things should not be for sale: the moral limits of markets* (Oxford, Oxford University Press, 2010) 100–05; TH Green, 'Liberal Legislation and Freedom of Contract' in P Harris and J Morrow (eds), *Lectures on the Principles of Political Obligation and Other Writings* (Cambridge, Cambridge University Press, 1986); See also quote from Messer and Cohen: 'Country case studies across the developing world demonstrate that those denied civil liberties suffer disproportionately from social injustices and material deprivations, including food insecurity, hunger-related disease, malnutrition, and preventable child mortality. The significance of freedom of speech, a free press, and freedom of assembly for the protection of economic rights, including the right not to starve, connects food security to democracy and good governance': E Messer and MJ Cohen, *Approaches to Food and Nutrient Rights, 1976-2008* (2009).

[40] This section is largely based on the analysis undertaken in J Gardner, *The Future of High-Cost Credit: Rethinking Payday Lending* (Oxford, Hart Publishing, 2022). For a more detailed analysis, see ch 5 'A Social Minimum'.

[41] For a sample of the literature on this topic, see J Rawls, *A Theory of Justice* (Cambridge, MA, Harvard University Press 1971); A Sen, *Inequality Reexamined* (Cambridge, MA, Harvard University Press 1992); A Sen, *The Standard of Living* (Cambridge, Cambridge University Press, 1987); J Waldron, 'John Rawls and the Social Minimum' (1986) 3 *Journal of Applied Philosophy* 21. An excellent introductory writing by Professor Stuart White can also be found at S White, 'Social Minimum' (*Stanford Encyclopedia of Philosophy*, 2004) plato.stanford.edu/entries/social-minimum/ (accessed 22 January 2023).

[42] See discussion in T Kotkas, I Leijten and F Pennings (eds), *Specifying and Securing a Social Minimum in the Battle Against Poverty* (Oxford, Hart Publishing, 2019) in general and specifically M Alder's chapter, 'The Social Minimum in the Context of Inequality'; S Lansley and J Mack, *Breadline Britain: The Rise of Mass Poverty* (London, OneWorld Publications, 2015) specifically chs 1 and 2.

[43] The definition of protection of a social minimum is also open for debate. For example, Waldron defines it as a 'level of material well-being beneath which no member of society should be allowed to fall'

on a social minimum is identifying what is necessary for people to have a 'decent and meaningful life' in the society in which they live. This approach is largely based on Rawls' analysis[44] and supported by Nussbaum, who framed the concept of a social minimum by identifying central functional capabilities that people need to live a life which is truly 'human'.[45] There is a strong argument that the ability to have regular holidays is necessary for people to have a 'decent and meaningful life', and therefore can and should form part of the social minimum in our society.

Enforcement of the social minimum does, however, need to be justified. The provision of a social minimum requires the redistribution of assets; the state must remove property from businesses and higher-earning individuals and give it to those on a lower income.[46] This type of action therefore requires justification. Three potential explanations for the provision of a social minimum can be outlined – equality and liberal democracy, general government obligations, and the happiness of society.

The first justification builds on work by TH Marshall on citizenship, and by Satz on the importance of equal status in a functioning democracy. It advocates that a certain level of equality is needed for a functioning democratic system.[47] Satz advocates 'positive liberty'[48] as a fundamental tenet of democracy. If we believe in a democratic society, people need to be given a social minimum so that they may exercise their democratic choice as 'co-deliberants and co-participants' in that society.[49] This is further confirmed by Badger, who states 'what good is the right to vote, they ask, if you starve on the way to the ballot box? Or the right to an independent media if you can't read what it's printing?'.[50] The provision of a social minimum allows people to participate in society, and thus in government and democratic processes.[51]

The second justification is that providing a social minimum is a *duty* of the state. Political institutions must be justified – by the will, choices, or decisions of people

---

(Waldron (n 41) 21), Sen talks about the need for people to be 'happy and satisfied' (Sen (n 41)), and White states it is 'the bundle of resources that a person needs in order to lead a minimally decent life in their society' (White (n 41)).

[44] Rawls (n 41) 127–28.

[45] These are: (1) the capability for physical survival; (2) the capability for bodily health; (3) the capability for bodily integrity; (4) the capability for the exercise of imagination; (5) the capability for emotional response and exploration; (6) the capability for practical reason; (7) the capability for love and friendship; (8) the capability for connection with nature and other species; (9) the capability for play; and (10) the capability for the exercise of control over environment, including political control; M Nussbaum, 'Women and Cultural Universals' in M Nussbaum (ed), *Sex and Social Justice* (Oxford, Oxford University Press, 1999). Whilst the majority are reasonable uncontentious, the last few capabilities are clearly up for debate, particularly their application to developing countries.

[46] D Bilchitz, 'What is the Relationship between the Minimum Thresholds and Distributive Justice?' in Kotkas, Leijten and Pennings (n 42).

[47] D Satz, *Why some things should not be for sale: the moral limits of markets* (Oxford, Oxford University Press, 2010) 100.

[48] Acting in a way to have more meaningful control over one's life.

[49] Satz (n 47) 96, see also 100–05. This is not a new concept, see also TH Green, 'Liberal Legislation and Freedom of Contract' in P Harris and J Morrow (eds), *Lectures on the Principles of Political Obligation and Other Writings* (Cambridge, Cambridge University Press, 1986).

[50] E Badger, 'Are Economic Rights Fundamental Human Rights?' 2009) psmag.com/are-economic-rights-fundamental-human-rights-524ede71ed88#.3wmf7jymh (accessed 21 November 2016).

[51] This can be applied more specifically to markets for goods and services. Markets are designed to allow a person to participate in society. Intervention into the market is therefore justified if it is harmful for the standing of parties as equal citizens in a democracy; Satz (n 47) 95.

over whom they have authority.[52] The state should act for the good of its citizens, thus promoting their interests and allowing for human flourishing.[53] In a modern democracy, this equates to a state obligation to provide a social minimum to those in need. Goodin argues that the state is responsible for the consequences that its actions and choices have on those affected. Since the state's job is to protect the public interest, it must attempt to do good, or at the very least to prevent harm.[54] There is a duty to assist those who are dependent on state resources and have nowhere else to turn.[55] These people are vulnerable and dependent on the state, which has a special obligation to protect that group – this is the primary purpose of welfare.[56] More recently, O'Cinneide has linked these obligations with social and economic rights.[57]

There are two further potential reasons that the duty to provide a social minimum falls on the state. First, it is a responsibility of the moral community, and democratically elected governments are the embodiment of the moral community.[58] Second, albeit less convincingly in this age of austerity, is the 'deep pockets' theory; the government is in the best financial position to provide such assistance.[59] Others believe that the primary role of the state is to promote 'social justice'. This concept arose over 2,000 years ago from Plato's *Republic* and his enquiry into the 'true nature' of justice, including the role of the state.[60] It is generally accepted that social justice includes the provision of a social minimum.[61]

The final justification is based on the best way to ensure the happiness of all of society. A wide range of research highlights that the provision of a social minimum is beneficial not just for the recipients, but also for society as a whole. The best society maximises happiness, and the state promotes happiness more effectively than it does being left in a state of nature.[62] A natural extension of this is that the state should redistribute property and provide welfare in a way that maximises happiness in society. Analysing this concept from a basic economic perspective should indicate that people losing resources would be strongly against the concept. By extension, this would mean that the provision of a social minimum is unlikely to fulfil the utilitarian test for state regulation. Surprisingly this does not play out in practice, and societies with strong welfare systems are generally the happiest.[63]

---

[52] J Wolff, *An Introduction to Political Philosophy*, vol 3 (Oxford, Oxford University Press 2016) 35.
[53] See J Raz, 'Liberalism, Autonomy, and the Politics of Neutral Concern' (1982) 7 *Midwest Studies in Philosophy* 89, 112–13.
[54] RE Goodin, *Protecting the Vulnerable: A Reanalysis of Our Social Responsibility* (Chicago, The University of Chicago Press, 1985) 142; see also C Fried, *Contract as Promise: A Theory of Contractual Obligation* (Cambridge, MA, Harvard University Press, 1981) 106.
[55] Goodin (n 54) 147.
[56] ibid 150–51.
[57] C O'Cinneide, 'Giving Legal Substance to the Social Minimum' in Kotkas, Leijten and Pennings (n 42).
[58] Goodin (n 54) 152.
[59] ibid 152–53.
[60] NP Barry, *An Introduction to Modern Political Theory*, 3rd edn (London, The MacMillan Press Ltd 1995) 148.
[61] ibid 149–50. See also discussion at 166 on the difficulty of distinguishing between welfare and justice in the framework of western morality.
[62] Wolff (n 52) 52.
[63] When determining what makes an individual 'happy', the following aspects were considered: GDP per capita, social support available, healthy life expectancy at birth, freedom to make choices, generosity

In their book *The Spirit Level: Why Equality is Better for Everyone*, Wilkinson and Pickett argue that once a country reaches a certain level of economic achievement, further unequal financial gains do not improve happiness levels, and in fact are likely to decrease the happiness in that society.[64] The authors reviewed a wide range of indicators, including community life and social relations, trust, mental health and drug use, physical health (including life expectancy and obesity), educational performance, violence and imprisonment, and social mobility to determine what makes the happiest society. They concluded that the majority of the population benefited from increased equality, not just the recipients of the welfare.[65]

The link between equality and happiness has also been endorsed by both mainstream UK political parties. David Cameron said in 2009

> that among the richest countries, it's the more unequal ones that do the worst according to almost every life indicator … We all know, in our hearts, that as long as there is deep poverty living systematically with … great riches, we all remain poorer.[66]

The following year, Ed Miliband stated in his first speech as the leader of the Labour Party:

> I do believe that this country is too unequal and the gap between rich and poor doesn't just harm the poor, it harms us all … if you look around the world – at the countries that are healthier, happier and more secure – they are the more equal countries.[67]

The connection between happiness and equality is so strong that the 2016 Happiness Report specifically addressed that relationship.[68] The Report stated 'there are arguments both ethical and empirical suggesting that humans are or at least ought to be happier to live where there is more equality of opportunities and generally of outcomes as well'.[69] Initial research conducted by the United Nation's Sustainable Development Solutions Network highlights a number of connections between equality and happiness, including the fact that inequality reduces social trust,[70] and that there is a correlation between increased income equality and general well-being.[71]

---

and perceptions of corruption: J Helliwell, R Layard and J Sachs, *World Happiness Report 2016, Update* (Sustainable Development Solutions Network 2016) 16 (with a detailed summary of each aspect at p 17).

[64] R Wilkinson and K Pickett, *The Spirit Level: Why Equality is Better for Everyone* (London, Penguin Books, 2010) 8.

[65] ibid 275. This is particularly evident in health. In developed nations, inequality has a much bigger impact on health than the national average income. Health and social problems are closely related to inequality in more prosperous nations; they are however only weakly related to national average income in these countries: ibid 20–21. The authors note that this trend is repeated within US states: 22. These health problems are not linked to only those who are negatively impacted by the inequality, but spread across all spectrums of society, indicating that in the context of health, equality is better for everyone; ibid 175–77.

[66] Cited in Wilkinson and Pickett (n 64) 298.

[67] ibid.

[68] Helliwell, Layard and Sachs (n 63) 4–6, 9–10, 29–41.

[69] ibid 29–30. This report goes on to state 'Beyond such direct links between inequality and subjective well-being, income inequalities have been argued to be responsible for damage to other key supports for well-being, including social trust, safety, good governance, and both the average quality of and equal access to health and education, – important, in turn, as supports for future generations to have more equal opportunities': ibid 30.

[70] ibid 31.

[71] ibid 32.

Similar comments were made in the 2018 Happiness Report, indicating that it is an ongoing theme.[72]

These three justifications, equality and liberal democracy, general government obligations, and the happiness of society, provide strong justification for the provision of a social minimum, and – by extension – the right to holidays.

C. Theoretical Enforcement – Ensuring Human Flourishing

The final potential justification to consider has a more theoretical basis, and engages with McBride's novel analysis in *The Humanity of Private Law*.[73] He argues that private law (therefore, as discussed in the introduction, also consumer law), should promote 'human flourishing'. A life that is flourishing is 'a life that is going well'.[74] To determine what is included in this concept, McBride draws on John Finnis' account of human flourishing, as explained in *Natural Law and Natural Rights*. McBride however provides an extended view to the concept of human flourishing and puts forward a 'satisfaction test', stating that someone is flourishing if they have reason to be content with the way their life is going.[75] McBride also moves away from Finnis' account of flourishing in terms of the importance of positive experiences. He does not agree with the 'spartan view' that the amount of pleasure in one's life is completely irrelevant to human flourishing, stating that satisfaction and enjoyment are important aspects of human flourishing as long as they are not dependent on the suffering of others.[76]

There is considerable evidence that holidays would meet the satisfaction test, and therefore should be recognised as part of human flourishing. The Office of National Statistics, Poverty and Social Exclusion has stated that if a household is unable to go on holiday for a week once a year, it is an indication of 'severe material deprivation'.[77] It is however interesting to note that the concept of holidays being considered a 'human right' does not appear to be holding up in the court of public opinion. Approximately every 10 years in the UK, the public are asked to look at a list of experiences/items and rate whether these should be considered a 'necessity' or a 'luxury'. These surveys, called the Breadline Britain/Poverty and Social Exclusion Surveys, provide a useful and unique insight into a community-defined social minimum.[78] The results highlight that there is a notable decrease in the number of people who think that 'a holiday away from home once a year not staying with family' is part of the social minimum, down from 63 per cent of respondents in 1983 to 42 per cent in 2012.

---

[72] Helliwell, Layard and Sachs, *World Happiness Report 2018* (Sustainable Development Solutions Network 2018) 14–15.
[73] N McBride, *The Humanity of Private Law – Part 1: Explanation* (Oxford, Hart Publishing, 2019).
[74] ibid 83.
[75] ibid 86.
[76] ibid 92.
[77] Office for National Statistics, Poverty and Social Exclusion in the UK and EU, 2005–11.
[78] Lansley and Mack (n 42) specifically chs 1 and 2.

The concept of human flourishing is clearly linked with the need to provide a social minimum, but justifies the requirement on a more theoretical level than framing it as a political duty on the state.[79] McBride does however present what he calls a 'Basic Model' to determine when an obligation should be owed to another party. There are four steps:

(1) The first party is in a position where they will suffer a setback to their human flourishing if they are deprived of this 'primary good'.
(2) The second party is in a position to make a difference as to whether or not the human flourishing occurs.
(3) The law is also in a position to make a difference to whether or not the human flourishing occurs, by imposing a basic obligation on the second party.
(4) Imposing the obligation on the second party will not do more harm than the benefit provided to the first party.[80]

This model is designed to identify when a legal obligation can and should be created and/or enforced. It does however also provide a useful framework for determining when and if a state obligation should be created more generally.

First, *Jarvis v Swans Tours* highlights the importance of holidays and how the law should compensate people who have suffered disappointment and distress if they have not been provided with the promised holiday. Lord Denning emphasised that 'Mr Jarvis only has a fortnight's holiday in the year. He books it far ahead, and looks forward to it all that time.' This shows that private law believes people will suffer a setback to their human flourishing if they are deprived of the enjoyment of a holiday. Despite this importance, almost 30 per cent of families are currently unable to afford to go on holidays[81] – a nearly 50 per cent increase from pre-austerity times.

Second and third, the state is in a position to make a difference to whether or not people can take holidays, and the law is in a position to make a difference by imposing a basic obligation on the government. There are two important ways this can occur. First and foremost, the government can make a political choice to ensure that government benefits and the minimum wage are set at a level where all people can enjoy 'a holiday away from home once a year not staying with relatives'. It can also regulate conditions and legal structures of the 'gig economy' more closely so that people working in these industries are not deprived of this right due to reclassification of their employment conditions.

The second way is that policies should be initiated to encourage people to actually take holidays, and provide a scenario where they practically can take holidays. This could include mandatory recreational leave and the provision of 'leave loading'.[82] Families in particular are struggling to take holidays, due to increased

---

[79] It is however noted that McBride does discuss social minimum as part of the human flourishing, see McBride (n 73) 112–13.
[80] ibid 115–16.
[81] Office for National Statistics, Poverty and Social Exclusion in the UK and EU, 2005-2011.
[82] This involves paying people more when they take their annual leave in order to: (a) encourage them to take the leave; and (b) give them additional funds while they are on leave: www.australianunions.org.au/factsheet/leave-loading/. Leave loading is common in Australia and is the result of a labour movement in the 1970's.

financial pressures and the additional costs of holidays during school breaks (where prices invariably increase to the point of unaffordability for many families). The government could tackle this by providing more flexibility for term-time holidays or by staggering breaks for different regions at different times of the year to avoid 'peak prices'. Other potential approaches could be the provision of 'holiday vouchers' to low-income households – similar to the approach taken to encourage local tourism in the post-COVID-19 period.[83]

Finally, imposing the obligation on the state will not do more harm than the benefit provided to the first party. There is significant empirical research on the benefits of holidays, showing that they promote physical and mental well-being, encourage cultural exploration and appreciation, and can even assist with family bonding.[84] Imposing an obligation on the state would involve a small tax increase or redistribution of funds to ensure that benefits are increased accordingly, and some imaginative legislative drafting or policy development. It is therefore highly likely that the benefits will significantly outweigh the detriments, thereby meeting the requirements of McBride's 'basic model' for creating an obligation.

IV. CONCLUSION

Jarvis v Swans Tours was a landmark case that emphasised the importance of the socio-economic right of a holiday. Thanks to Lord Denning's novel take on the legal issues, the case allowed damages to be claimed for distress and disappointment arising from a breach of a contract for the provision of holiday services. This was an important change to the previous contract law approach, and provided greater protection for consumers.[85] It also opened the door for a consideration of the role that holidays, and the right to leisure, recreation and play, has in our society. If the court was happy to protect these rights so closely, does that mean holidays should be seen as a human right, and if so, what are the implications of this approach? The emphasis and outcome of *Jarvis v Swans Tours* initially comes across as a class-based decision that protects people who can both: (a) afford luxury holidays; and (b) have the ability to sue in court when the holidays do not turn out as they would like. Viewed from another perspective however, this case highlights the fundamental nature of the right of a holiday and emphasises that the law can and should protect this right for all people in society. In the words of Cranston, 'it would be a splendid thing … for everyone to have holidays with pay'.[86]

---

[83] For an academic and empirical discussion of an example of these voucher schemes, see LK Cvelbar, D Farčnik and M Ogorevcb, 'Holidays for all: Staycation vouchers during COVID-19' 2(2) *Annals of Tourism Research Empirical Insights*.

[84] HA Schänzel, KA Smith and A Weaver, 'Family Holidays: A Research Review and Application to New Zealand' (2005) 8(2-3) *Annals of Leisure Research* 105–123.

[85] There has, however, been recent calls to expand when damages can be recovered in contract for non-pecuniary loss: see Z Zlatev, 'Recoverability of Damages for Non-pecuniary Losses Deriving from Breach of Contract' (2021) 41(3) *Oxford Journal of Legal Studies* 638.

[86] M Cranston, 'Are There Any Human Rights?' (1983) 112 *Daedalus* 12.

9
The Foundations of Corporate Criminal Responsibility in Consumer Law: *Tesco Supermarkets Ltd v Nattrass* in Perspective

PETER CARTWRIGHT*

I. INTRODUCTION

THE YEAR 1969 bore witness to a number of significant events: the Apollo 11 Mission landed the first person on the moon; the bands MC5 and the Stooges released their debut albums; and a consumer named Mr Coane left the Northwich branch of Tesco, disgruntled at being charged 3s 11d for a packet of washing powder that he had seen advertised for a shilling less. While Mr Coane cannot claim to have demonstrated what was possible in space travel, nor to have laid the foundations for punk rock, his complaint to the Inspector of Weights and Measures led to a landmark decision of the House of Lords.

The case that resulted from Mr Coane's complaint, *Tesco Supermarkets Ltd v Nattrass* (hereafter '*Tesco*') is the subject of this chapter.[1] The chapter begins by explaining how *Tesco* found its way to the House of Lords before critically assessing the decision and its implications for the criminal liability of corporations. It then reflects upon the implications of the decision today in the light of more recent case law and the replacement of the Trade Descriptions Act 1968 by the Consumer Protection from Unfair Trading Regulations 2008 (CPUTRs). Next it considers the implications of the Law Commission's latest thinking before conclusions are drawn. *Tesco* is a landmark case because while it was decided in the context of statutory defences in consumer protection, the distinction it drew between those individuals who are, and those who are not, to be identified with a company for the purposes of the criminal law guides the law of corporate criminal liability to this day.

---

*Many thanks to Professors Richard Hyde and Jodi Gardner for comments on an earlier draft. The usual disclaimer applies. This chapter is dedicated to Richard Bragg. Richard was a mentor and friend as well as an authority on consumer law generally and trade descriptions in particular. Sadly, he passed away in 2021.
[1] *Tesco Supermarkets Ltd v Nattrass* [1972] AC 153.

II. TESCO v NATTRASS AND THE ROAD TO THE HOUSE OF LORDS

The facts of the case were relatively simple. A branch of Tesco Supermarkets advertised Radiant washing powder, which usually cost 3s 11d, for the reduced price of 2s 11d. A shop assistant found that none of the reduced packs were on display and put out packs with the higher price on them. However, the shop assistant did not inform the manager, who in turn did not check the stock, and the advertisement remained on display. Had the manager known of the assistant's actions he would have either removed the special offer posters or given instructions to staff to charge the reduced amount. A consumer was charged 3s 11d for a packet of the washing powder that he had seen advertised for the lower price and complained to the inspector of weights and measures in Cheshire (Kenneth Nattrass) in whose name the prosecution was brought.

Tesco were charged with an offence under (what was) section 11(2) of the Trade Descriptions Act 1968 (giving an indication likely to be taken as an indication that goods were being offered at a price less than that at which they were in fact offered). Tesco invoked the due diligence defence contained in section 24 of the Act. Section 24 stated:

... it shall ... be a defence for the person charged to prove-

(a) that the commission of the offence was due to a mistake or to reliance on some information supplied to him or to the act of default of another person, an accident or some other cause beyond his control; and

(b) that he took all reasonable precautions and exercised all due diligence to avoid the commission of the offence by himself or by any person under his control.

Although the elements of the offence had to be proved beyond reasonable doubt, Tesco were required to establish both limbs of the defence on the balance of probabilities. On the first, they claimed that the commission of the offence was due to the act or default of another person (the manager). On the second, they argued that the company had taken all reasonable precautions and exercised all due diligence by setting up an appropriate system of control and seeing that it was implemented. At first instance, the magistrates found that although the company had devised an appropriate system of control, and so far as possible ensured that it operated, the defence should fail because the manager was not 'another person' for these purposes. On appeal, the Divisional Court held that the manager was another person, but upheld Tesco's conviction on the grounds that the requirement that the defendant 'took all reasonable precautions and exercised all due diligence' referred not only to the accused (Tesco) but also to all his servants who were acting in a managerial or supervisory capacity.

Barrett noted the difficulty of reconciling this with the Divisional Court's reasoning in *Beckett v Kingston Brothers* where the employers were not liable for the acts of their manager.[2] She regarded it a matter of 'fundamental importance' that the House

---

[2] *Beckett v Kingston Brothers* [1970] 1 QB 606. Barrett suggested that the manager in Kingston Brothers may have been at the end of the chain due diligence whereas the manager in Tesco 'broke the link' in that chain. She does not, however, appear wholly convinced by that rationalisation, particularly when viewed alongside *Series v Poole* [1969] 1 QB 676. See B Barrett 'Enterprise Liability and the Guilty Employee' (1971) 34 *MLR* 220.

of Lords clarified the scope of section 24.³ However, she also sounded a note of caution: '[a] ruling by the House of Lords that these defences are of wide application would clearly weaken the enforcement of much valuable legislation by increasing the circumstances in which an enterprise may evade responsibility.'⁴

In granting leave to appeal, the Divisional Court certified the point of law of public general importance as follows:

> Whether a person charged with an offence under Section 11(2) of the Trade Descriptions Act 1968 in a retail shop owned by him would have a defence under Section 24(1) of the said Act if: —
> (a) he instituted an efficient system to avoid the commission of offences under the Act by any person under his control;
> (b) he reasonably delegated to the manager of the shop the duty of operating the said system in that shop;
> (c) the manager failed to perform such duty efficiently;
> (d) the offence charged was committed by reason of such failure
> (e) such failure by the said manager is the 'act or default of another person' relied on under Section 24(1)(a).

III. TESCO v NATTRASS IN THE HOUSE OF LORDS: IDENTIFICATION AND STATUTORY DEFENCES

Their Lordships unanimously allowed the appeal. Although there are differences of emphasis in their speeches, there was also a good deal of common ground. Like the lower courts, the House of Lords had no doubt that Tesco had prima facie committed an offence under section 11(2) by advertising the product for 2s 11d. but selling it for a higher price.⁵ However, their Lordships found that the due diligence defence in section 24 allowed Tesco to escape responsibility.

The obligation on Tesco under section 24 was to demonstrate that it had taken all reasonable precautions and exercised all diligence to avoid the commission of the offence, either by itself or by any person under its control. To understand the application of corporate liability in cases such as this, it is helpful to consider the nature of a corporation and the identity of people who constitute it. In *HL Bolton (Engineering) Co. Ltd v TJ Graham and Sons Ltd* Lord Denning famously stated:⁶

> A company may in many ways be likened to a human body. It has a brain and nerve centre which controls what it does. It also has hands which hold the tools and act in accordance with directions from the centre. Some of the people in the company are mere servants and agents who are nothing more than hands to do the work and cannot be said to represent the mind or will. Others are directors and managers who represent the directing mind and will of the company, and control what it does. The state of mind of these managers is the state of mind of the company and is treated by the law as such.

---

³ ibid 223.
⁴ ibid.
⁵ *Tesco* (n 1) 176.
⁶ *HL Bolton (Engineering) Co. Ltd v TJ Graham and Sons Ltd* [1957] 1 QB 159, 172.

A distinction was thus drawn between those employees who are the embodiment of the company and so identified with it (the 'brains' or 'directing mind and will') and those who are not (the 'hands'). Attributing the acts and minds of some employees to the company is known as 'identification'. In *Tesco*, their Lordships gave illustrations of those who, in their judgment, would be likely to be identified with the company, but their analysis differed in certain respects. Lord Reid said that it included the Board of Directors, managing director and (with a degree of circularity) 'other superior officers of the company [who] carry out functions of management and speak and act for the company'.[7] Viscount Dilhorne identified those 'who were not responsible to another person in the company' for the way in which they discharged their duties as constituting the directing mind.[8] Lord Diplock focused primarily on the company's constitution and articles of association.[9] Lord Pearson also emphasised the company's constitution.[10] Lords Diplock, Dilhorne and Pearson cited section 20, which made reference to any 'director, manager, secretary or other similar officer of the body corporate'. It became clear after the decision that it would not always be simple to identify into which category an employee fell.[11] However, categorisation is vital to determine whether a company is responsible for an employee's conduct.

Although the Divisional Court regarded Tesco as having delegated its obligation to take all reasonable precautions and all due diligence, Lord Reid concluded that the Board in Tesco did not 'delegate' their functions but 'set up a chain of command through regional and district supervisors'.[12] Tesco, he emphasised, 'remained in control'.[13] Lord Morris agreed that the manager was not a delegate: '[h]e had certain duties *which were the result of the taking by the company of all reasonable precautions and of the exercising by the company of all due diligence*' [emphasis added]. A similar approach is evident in the words of Lord Diplock:

> [i]t may be a reasonable step to instruct a superior servant to supervise the activities of inferior servants whose physical acts may in the absence of supervision result in that being done which it is sought to prevent. This is not to *delegate* the employer's duty to exercise all due diligence; it is to *perform* it.[14]

Andrews suggests that: '[t]heir Lordships did not always express themselves in a single voice as to the mechanics of the due diligence defence, but the theme was unanimous'.[15] Lord Diplock summarised the position as follows:[16]

> If the principal has taken all reasonable precautions in the selection and training of servants to perform supervisory duties and has laid down an effective system of supervision and used due diligence to see that it is observed, he is entitled to rely on a default by a

---

[7] *Tesco* (n 1) 171.
[8] ibid 187.
[9] ibid 199.
[10] ibid 191.
[11] The case was said to have opened 'a Pandoras's box of questions'. J Gobert and M Punch, *Rethinking Corporate Crime* London, (Butterworths, 2003) 64.
[12] ibid 175.
[13] ibid.
[14] ibid 203 (emphasis added).
[15] C Andrews, *Enforcement of Consumer Rights and Protections* (London, LexisNexis, 2015) 17.2.
[16] *Tesco* (n 1) 198.

superior servant in his supervisory duties as a defence under s.24(1) as well as, or instead of, an act or default of an inferior servant who has no supervisory duties under his contract of employment.

Their lordships regarded their decision as sound on the bases of statutory interpretation and policy. Whether the decision was inevitable on the basis of statutory interpretation is considered in some detail below. In relation to policy, it is helpful to draw out some of the normative conclusions from the House of Lords. There are two main issues to consider here, which relate to culpability and deterrence.

A. Culpability

First, Lord Reid argued that:

> the main object of these provisions must have been to distinguish between those who are in some degree blameworthy and those who are not, and to enable the latter to escape from conviction if they can show that they were in no way to blame.[17]

A major rationale for a due diligence defence is thus to avoid imposing guilt on the blameless. Most offences under the Act placed strict liability on traders (in that they required no proof of *mens rea*) and the defence allowed those traders to demonstrate that they lacked fault. The Act contained 'regulatory offences' which are distinct from mainstream or 'real' offences ('sins with legal definitions').[18] They have been described as 'not criminal in any real sense, but ... acts which in the public interest are prohibited under a penalty'.[19] Because no separate class of regulatory offences exists formally in the UK, we are left to identify what distinguishes them from so-called 'real' offences. Ramsay has suggested that they possess the following characteristics:[20]

1. Over-inclusive statutory standards enforced by strict liability, tempered by statutory defences and with the fine as the principal sanction;
2. A specialised bureaucracy that exercises discretion in implementing and enforcing standards; and
3. A focus on the magistrates' courts in implementing the legislation, with higher courts playing a role in developing the text of the legislation.

I have suggested two further criteria: that there is typically a requirement that the offences be committed in the course of business, and they lack the stigma commonly associated with the criminal law.[21] Despite the relative lack of stigma that regulatory

---

[17] ibid 169–70.
[18] Lord Devlin, *Morals and the Quasi Criminal Law and the Law of Tort*, Holdsworth Club Presidential Address, 17 March 1961, cited in G Borrie, *The Development of Consumer Law and Policy – Bold Spirits and Timorous Souls* (London, Stevens, 1984) 46.
[19] *Sherras v De Rutzen* [1895] 1 QBD 918, 922. In her empirical research on the prosecution of consumer protection cases, Croall found that magistrates typically treated offences as trivial and routine. H Croall, 'Mistakes, Accidents and Someone Else's Fault: The Trading Offender in Court' (1988) (15) *Journal of Law and Society* 293.
[20] I Ramsay, *Consumer Law and Policy*, 3rd edn (Oxford, Hart Publishing, 2012) 221–22.
[21] P Cartwright, 'Crime, Punishment and Consumer Protection' [2007] *Journal of Consumer Policy* 1.

offences involve, their lordships in *Tesco* showed unease with their imposing strict liability. It is interesting to note that four of the five Law Lords in *Tesco* also sat in the celebrated case of *Sweet* v *Parsley* where their concern about strict liability was particularly evident, albeit in a different context.[22] It might be argued that their Lordships scepticism towards strict criminal liability underpinned the decision, with their being particularly mindful of the injustice that strict criminal liability might produce. There have been recent examples of the courts emphasising the presumption in favour of *mens rea*, particularly in relation to 'real offences'.[23] However it is recognised to be no more than a principle of statutory construction and that consumer protection offences tend not to be regarded in this way.[24] Where it is clear that Parliament intended strict liability then strict liability will be imposed. Indeed, the existence of a due diligence defence might be taken as evidence that the offence was intended to impose strict liability.[25]

B. Deterrence

Their Lordships considered the relationship between strict liability, due diligence and deterrence. Parliament had intended to create a regime which deterred wrongdoing and incentivised compliance while, as noted above, avoiding injustice. Strict liability, coupled with due diligence, aimed to facilitate that by removing any requirement on the prosecution to establish *mens rea*, but giving an avenue of escape to defendants who demonstrated that they did all they reasonably could be expected to do to avoid the offence. Pound suggested that strict liability offences 'put pressure upon the thoughtless and inefficient to do their whole duty' and requiring traders to take all reasonable precautions and exercise all due diligence provides an opportunity to demonstrate that this duty has been discharged.[26] In the words of Lord Reid:[27]

> It is sometimes argued – it was argued in the present case – that making an employer criminally responsible, even when he has done all he could to prevent an offence, affords some additional protection to the public because it will induce him to do more, But if he has done all he can, how can he do more?

Lord Diplock similarly observed, that strict liability offences aimed to raise standards but that this 'does not extend to penalising an employer or principal who has done everything that he can reasonably be expected to do'.[28]

As a matter of logic these observations make perfect sense. A defendant who has done all he could do could not be deterred and need not be incentivised further. Lord Reid identified a suspicion on the part of some commentators that the courts

---

[22] *Sweet* v *Parsley* [1970] AC 132.
[23] See, eg, *B (A Child)* v *DPP* [2000] 2 AC 428; *R v K* [2001] UKHL 41, [2002] 1 AC 462.
[24] D Ormerod and K Laird, *Smith, Hogan and Ormerod's Criminal Law*, 16th edn (Oxford, OUP, 2021) 158.
[25] P Cartwright, *Consumer Protection and the Criminal Law* (Cambridge, CUP, 2001) 91.
[26] R Pound, *The Spirit of the Common Law* (1921) cited in *Smith Hogan and Ormerod* (n 24) 175.
[27] *Tesco* (n 1) 178.
[28] ibid 194.

did not in practice expect enough of large businesses in demonstrating that they had satisfied the defence.²⁹ Other influential commentators certainly doubted that the defence was rigidly applied. Borrie argued that it was common for an employer 'to appear to have done all he can, to point to systems and precautions and the training of staff' and suggested that 'in practice the defence is difficult to counteract'.³⁰ The judiciary also revealed itself to be mindful of such concerns. In 1976 Lord Widgery argued that unless care was taken in the application of the defence,

> we may find the administration of this Act sliding down to the sort of slipshod level at which all a defendant has to do is say in general terms that the default must have been due to something in the shop, one of the girls or some expression like that that, and thereby satisfy the onus cast upon him.³¹

However, Lord Reid emphasised that the duty on the defendants to establish the defence was significant: 'if magistrates were to accept as sufficient a paper scheme and perfunctory efforts to enforce it they would not be doing their duty – that would not be 'due diligence' on the part of the employer'.³² Thus, provided the courts did their job in requiring traders to prove that they had taken *all* reasonable precautions and exercised *all* due diligence, deterrence should be secured. On the facts of the case, the House of Lords emphasised the considerable steps that Tesco had taken to fulfil their responsibilities. Lord Morris cited the 'careful and reasonable system of selection of managers' as well as 'the various steps taken by the company in the exercise of supervision over the manager and the proper running of the store'.³³ Although a breakdown of the system had occurred this did not prevent the defence being satisfied. It could be argued that, applied properly, the defence distinguished between those deserving and not deserving of conviction, and provided optimal levels of deterrence and compliance.³⁴

C. Identification and Mens Rea

Although section 11 imposed strict liability, *Tesco* also had significant relevance for offences requiring proof of *mens rea*, such as those found in s.14 of the Act.³⁵ Section 14 stated:

> 'It shall be an offence for any person in the course of any trade or business (a) to make a statement which he knows to be false or (b) recklessly to make a statement which is false as to any of the following matters'.

---

[29] ibid 174.
[30] Borrie (n 18) 52.
[31] (1976) 140 JP 306, 310.
[32] *Tesco* (n 1) 174.
[33] ibid 177.
[34] For discussion of the concepts of optimal deterrence and compliance see A Ogus, *Regulation: Legal Form and Economic Theory* (Oxford, Clarendon Press, 1994) ch 5.
[35] Indeed, identification is most commonly discussed in the context of the liability of corporations for *mens rea* offences.

The section then listed various matters relating to services, accommodation and facilities. To establish *mens rea* against a company, it was necessary to identify someone within the company who: (a) possessed the requisite *mens rea*; and (b) was of such seniority that their actions and mind could be classed as that of the company. The doctrine of identification was thus applicable to *mens rea* offences as it was to due diligence defences.[36] This created significant challenges for enforcers. In particular, it was frequently difficult to find someone sufficiently senior who was either reckless or possessed the requisite knowledge. This sometimes led enforcers to be creative in their prosecutions. In *Formula One Autocentres Ltd v Birmingham City Council*[37] a company which might have expected to face prosecution under section 14 was instead prosecuted under section 1 so as to avoid the need to prove *mens rea*.[38] Enforcers have estimated that *mens rea* offences take twice the time of strict liability offences to investigate and so there is a significant disincentive to using them.[39] The implications of *Tesco* thus extend far beyond due diligence defences.

IV. A CRITIQUE OF TESCO V NATTRASS

The decision in *Tesco* can be criticised on a number of grounds. For example, the differences in the speeches have arguably 'failed to provide the clarity of definition that is needed in fixing the scope of criminal liability'.[40] Two key questions to consider are whether the decision was inevitable on the basis of statutory interpretation and, if not whether a different approach would have been preferable. On the first point, their Lordships appeared to regard it as such, and 20 years later Bragg suggested that 'in terms of its legal analysis, the *Tesco* decision must be correct'.[41] But it is submitted that there are ways in which the statute might have been interpreted quite differently and, perhaps produced a preferable outcome.

A. Identification and Vicarious Liability

Wells sees the result in *Tesco* as far from inevitable. In her view, the requirement under section 24 for the company to prove that the offence was caused by 'the act or default of some other person, an accident or some other cause beyond his control' points towards the defence demanding that 'some quite extraneous factor had intervened to cause the offence' rather than that an employee had erred.[42] Requiring the defendant to demonstrate that the offence resulted from someone or something outside the company (such as the act of a third party) would have meant the Act

---

[36] That the approach in *Tesco* should be used in *mens rea* offences was confirmed in *R v St Regis Paper Co. Ltd* [2011] EWCA Crim 2527, [2012] PTSR 871.
[37] *Formula One Autocentres Ltd v Birmingham City Council* (1999) 163 JP 234.
[38] P Cartwright 'Servicing and Supplying: A Judicial Muddle' [2000] *Crim LR* 356.
[39] *Formula One Autocentres* (n 37) para 15.
[40] *Smith, Hogan and Ormerod* (n 24) 265.
[41] RJ Bragg, *Trade Descriptions* (Oxford, Clarendon Press, 1991) 186.
[42] C Wells, *Corporations and Criminal Responsibility*, 2nd edn (Oxford, OUP, 2001) 97.

imposed a form of vicarious liability on companies for the acts of their employees.[43] This form of liability (typically referred to as 'extended construction' or 'attributed act') applies where there is a strict liability offence which is physically performed by an employee but is legally done by their employer.[44] Tesco recognised this to an extent; there was no doubt that the company had given the relevant indication for the purposes of the prima facie offence. But this approach did not apply it in the context of the defence.

If section 24 had been interpreted as requiring the act or default to be of someone outside the organisation in the way that Wells suggests it might have been, it would become necessary to consider who, within the company, had to take all reasonable precautions and exercise all due diligence for the defence to be satisfied. One possibility would be to say that Tesco could only escape liability where all its employees were shown to have taken all reasonable precautions and exercised all due diligence. Although this challenges the doctrine of identification (as it was drawn in *Tesco*) it could be justified on a number of grounds.

First, those employees, whether managers or shop assistants, were acting for Tesco in the course of their employment and it could be viewed as appropriate for the company to take responsibility for their actions and omissions. Indeed, such an approach might be said to better reflect what, and who, a company is. It could be argued that where a company is required to demonstrate that it has taken all reasonable precautions and exercised all due diligence by itself or anyone else under its control, this extends to requiring all its employees to take such precautions and exercise such diligence.

Second, such an interpretation may better achieve the objectives of the provision. As noted above, a key aim of the Act was to ensure compliance by deterring wrongdoing and incentivising the taking of care. Due diligence defences, interpreted as they were in *Tesco*, provide an incentive for companies to take the steps that constitute reasonable precautions and due diligence. First, by taking those steps, traders make it less likely that a contravention will occur. Second, where a contravention does occur, the trader which demonstrates that such steps have been taken will avoid liability. As their Lordships noted, if the defences are interpreted and applied properly by the courts, defendants will only be acquitted where they prove that they could not reasonably have done more. However, if the defence were interpreted as imposing a requirement for the company to demonstrate that all employees had taken all reasonable precautions and exercised all due diligence, there would still be compelling incentives for firms to take these steps at a senior level. The establishment of a robust system, thoughtfully designed and assiduously monitored by well-trained employees, should minimise the likelihood of a contravention. Liability would be stricter but not absolute, as companies would still be acquitted where the act or default was that of a third party.

---

[43] Vicarious liability applies where one person is responsible for the act of another. It might be argued that if we say that the employee is identified with the company their acts are those of the company and so the liability is not strictly speaking vicarious. However, Gobert and Punch describe identification as 'a species of vicarious liability' (n 11) 63 and Wells regards attempts to differentiate extended identification from vicarious liability as 'a distinction without a difference' (n 42) 102.

[44] See *Smith, Hogan and Ormerod* (n 24) 287.

Lord Phillips set out the principal reasons for the imposition of vicarious liability in civil law.[45] The first of these, that an employer will be better-placed to compensate a victim than an employee (in particular because they are likely to be insured) is of limited relevance in the context of criminal law (although some consumer protection cases may lead to the paying of compensation through various mechanisms). However, the others resonate. Lord Phillips observed that the action (in his example a tort) will have been committed as a result of activity being taken by the employee on behalf of the employer. Next, he pointed out that the employee's activity is likely to be part of the business activity of the employer. Furthermore, by engaging the employee to carry on the activity in question, the employer creates the risk of the harm in question. Finally, the employee is, at least to some extent, under the control of the employer. These rationales largely apply to consumer protection law. In particular, where an offence is committed, the company typically profits from that. It may therefore be appropriate as a matter of policy for the company to take responsibility for the actions of its employees. Indeed, some employers were (and no doubt are) known for doing that. In 1976, the Director General of Fair Trading's Review of the Act noted that: 'some companies trading on a national scale are willing to shoulder the blame for all offences originating within their organisation, whatever the circumstances which led to their commission'.[46] *Tesco* could have made that shouldering mandatory.

Their Lordships' reluctance to impose liability for the acts of all employees also stemmed from what they perceived to be the harshness of strict criminal liability. However, they may have overstated this harshness. As a 'regulatory offence' section 11(2) lacked the stigma commonly associated with criminal law. In *Wings Ltd* v *Ellis*, Lord Scarman described the Trade Descriptions Act 1968 as 'not a truly criminal statute' even where some *mens rea* was required.[47] Conviction for such an offence typically causes little injustice for companies, in part because of the lack of stigma generated and in part because of the low sanctions (in the forms of fines) typically imposed. These sanctions were described as 'tiresome pinpricks' by a former Director General of Fair Trading.[48] More recently, Macrory suggested that criminal convictions for regulatory offences had 'lost their stigma'.[49] Different considerations may apply where individuals are prosecuted. Ball and Friedman, writing shortly before *Tesco*, argued that 'businessmen abhor the idea of being banded a criminal'.[50] Whether that abhorrence remains is debatable, but the practical consequences of conviction for individuals do. In particular, imprisonment was available as a sanction under the Act and remains so under its replacement, the CPUTRs. However, a number of points should be noted here. Where fault is established on the part of someone who is identified with the company (under *Tesco*) there are several

---

[45] *Various Claimants v Institute of the Brothers of the Christian Schools* [2012] UKSC 56, [2013] 2 AC 1.
[46] *Review of the Trade Descriptions Act 1968* Cmnd 6628, para 54.
[47] *Wings Ltd* v *Ellis* [1985] AC 272, 293.
[48] Borrie (n 18) 56.
[49] *Regulatory Justice: Making Sanctions Effective Final Report* Nov 2006, 16.
[50] H Ball and L Friedman, 'Use of Criminal Sanctions in the Enforcement of Economic Legislation: A Sociological View' (1965) 17 *Stanford Law Review* 197, 217.

consequences. First, the company will not be able to rely on a due diligence defence as the company will not be able to say that it has, at a senior level, taken all reasonable precautions and exercised all due diligence. Second, the individual in question is likely to be guilty of the company's offence by virtue of (what was) section 20 of the Act. The prosecution would simply need to show that the offence was committed with the consent or connivance of, or was attributable to, any neglect on the part of the senior employee. There seems little objection to convicting directors and those of similar standing where there is consent or connivance, and relatively little where there is proof of neglect.

Very different issues arise where more junior employees are concerned.[51] One consequence of *Tesco* was that where a company was acquitted on the basis of the offence being due to the act or default of an employee, there was an incentive for prosecutors to pursue that employee in order to secure a conviction. This could not be achieved under section 20, but could be on the basis that the employee had, by their act or default, caused their employer to commit an offence.[52] In the absence of significant culpability on the employee's part, this appears difficult to justify. Employees do not typically benefit from the commission of an offence. They are 'locked in a system where they have to carry out a company's marketing scheme; in the case of junior employees for low wages in an uncreative environment'.[53] Rather than treat them as perpetrators, they might more accurately be viewed as 'captives of promotional practices adopted by their employers'.[54] Employees are typically not in a position to make changes to the systems under which they operate. If the principal rationale for prosecution is to improve compliance, prosecuting relatively junior employees seems to miss the target. It is the prosecution of such employees that is particularly liable to operate harshly. Holding the company to account for the acts of employees through a form of vicarious liability would reduce the opportunity to switch blame onto the employee and so the probability of more junior employees being prosecuted.

B. Extended Identification

There is a middle ground between the approach taken by their Lordships in *Tesco* and the imposition of vicarious liability for the acts of all employees which their Lordships could have taken. Wells suggests that the ambit of directing mind and will might have been interpreted in *Tesco* to include those who acted in a managerial capacity but would not usually be called the 'brains' of the company.[55] This may be referred to as 'extended identification'.[56] Williams wrote: '[t]hat a company should not be liable for an offence of negligence committed by its branch manager,

---

[51] See P Cartwright, 'Defendants in Consumer Protection Statutes: A Search for Consistency' (1992) 59(2) MLR 225.
[52] Under s 23.
[53] C Scott and J Black, *Cranston's Consumers and the Law*, 3rd edn (London, LexisNexis, 2000) 330.
[54] ibid 325.
[55] Wells (n 42) 97.
[56] See Cartwright (n 25).

who after all represents the company in a particular locality, is a considerable defect in the law.'[57] The concept of extended identification addresses this defect.

Extending identification beyond the traditional 'directing mind and will' would allow the law to regard a branch manager or employee of similar standing as being 'the company' for the purposes of the conduct in question. In the context of a due diligence defence, those employees with responsibility for particular functions would most appropriately be 'the company' and be required to have taken all reasonable precautions and exercised all due diligence for the defence to succeed. Again, this appears justifiable. *Tesco* has been criticised for requiring employees to have 'total power' before they are identified with their company.[58] This ignores the reality that in companies like Tesco with numerous disparate stores, day to day decisions have to be taken by local management. The Law Commission has emphasised that in modern corporations, strategic decision and policy making 'may be decentralised or regional rather than national'.[59] Extended identification could be both pragmatic and defensible, ensuring that companies take responsibility for the actions of those managerial employees entrusted not only with implementing the company's policies, but with making decisions about the means of that implementation. There would need to be some flexibility about when identification would be extended in this way and this is considered below. The key issue appears to be one of function rather than title. While in *Tesco* the issue was primarily concerned with the supervision of employees in a store, in other contexts it might also apply to the person who (for example) wrote a pricing algorithm or designed a marketing campaign.

In 2021 the Law Commission showed its unease with identification, suggesting that *Tesco* presented law makers with a stark choice:

> create an offence which cannot be enforced in the case of large companies or create an offence of strict liability and accept that corporations may be convicted despite blame lying with people over whom they have limited control.[60]

While this criticism is understandable, it reflects the arguably erroneous notion that it is unfair for companies to be held responsible for their own employees on the basis that they have 'limited control' of them. But by viewing those employees as (part of) 'the corporation' (which in the case of consumer protection offences seems appropriate) that criticism is significantly reduced.

V. A RETREAT FROM TESCO v NATTRASS?

In the context of consumer protection, the Act has largely been replaced by the Consumer Protection from Unfair Trading Regulations 2008 ('the Regulations'). The Regulations contain a due diligence defence extremely similar to that found in section 24. Regulation 17(1) states:

---

[57] G Williams, *Textbook of Criminal Law*, 2nd edn (London, Stevens, 1983) 973. Cited in Borrie (n 19) 52.
[58] Gobert and Punch (n 11) 65.
[59] Law Commission, *Criminal Liability in Regulatory Contexts* (Law Commission no195) para 5.85.
[60] Law Commission, *Corporate Criminal Liability: A Discussion Paper* (9-6-2021) para 2.71.

In any proceedings against a person for an offence under regulation 9, 10, 11 or 12 it is a defence for that person to prove—

(a) that the commission of the offence was due to—
  (i) a mistake;
  (ii) reliance on information supplied to him by another person;
  (iii) the act or default of another person;
  (iv) an accident; or
  (v) another cause beyond his control; and
(b) that he took all reasonable precautions and exercised all due diligence to avoid the commission of such an offence by himself or any person under his control.'

The similarity to section 24 is immediately apparent. Regulation 8(1) also contains an offence that, like section 14 of the Act, requires proof of *mens rea*. It is difficult to identify precisely how regulation 8(1) should be interpreted in the context of offences by companies, not least because of the paucity of reported cases on the provision. Cases following the doctrine of identification espoused in *Tesco* would suggest that it will frequently be difficult to find employees who possess the requisite *mens rea*, thus limiting the provision's effectiveness.[61] Furthermore, there is no compelling evidence of the courts' retreating from the orthodoxy of *Tesco* in unfair commercial practices law. However, they did make inroads into identification in related areas, creating the opportunity for a reappraisal of the law along the lines of the extended identification discussed above.

A. Identification and Defences

Where defences are concerned, inroads into the doctrine of identification as espoused in *Tesco* were made by *Tesco Stores Ltd v Brent LBC* ('*Brent*').[62] In *Brent*, Tesco were charged with supplying a video to a person under age contrary to the Video Recordings Act 1984. Section 11(2)b of that Act provided a defence where D could demonstrate that he neither knew, nor had reasonable grounds to believe, that the purchaser was under 18.

The employee supplying the video did have reasonable grounds to believe that the purchaser was under 18. The Court had to decide whether that employee's knowledge or belief could be attributed to Tesco for the purposes of the statutory defence. According to Staughton LJ: 'what mattered in terms of s.11(2)b was whether the accused (Tesco Stores Ltd.) neither knew nor had reasonable grounds to believe that ... [the purchaser] was under 18'. *Tesco* would suggest that 'the accused' did not have those grounds. A junior employee had those grounds of course but, according to *Tesco*, junior employees were not to be identified with their employers. However, the Court in *Brent* took a different approach. Staughton LJ said: 'it is her [the shop assistant's] knowledge or reasonable grounds that are

---

[61] P Cartwright, 'Unfair Commercial Practices and the Future of the Criminal Law' (2010) 7 *JBL* 618.
[62] *Tesco Stores Ltd v Brent LBC* [1993] 1 WLR 1037.

relevant. Were it otherwise, the statute would be wholly ineffective in the case of a large company'.[63]

The case demonstrated a willingness to adopt a purposive and pragmatic approach to the interpretation of the defence. Had the Court not done so, it would be virtually impossible to prosecute large companies under the provision, as they could always claim that their senior officers (those who would normally be identified with the company) neither knew nor had reasonable grounds to believe that the customer was underage. It has been pointed out that the decision was made easier than it might have been by the specific wording of the provision 'with its emphasis on knowledge of a circumstance rather than diligence in avoiding a result'.[64] This different emphasis might suggest that a clear distinction can be drawn between the case and *Tesco* with the latter remaining applicable where due diligence defences are concerned.

Another case that might be viewed as opening the door to a more flexible and purposive approach is *British Steel*.[65] V was killed when a steel platform which the defendant's sub-contractors had failed to secure appropriately collapsed. British Steel was charged under the Health and Safety at Work Act 1974. Section 3(1) of that Act stated:

> It shall be the duty of every employer to conduct his undertaking in such a way as to ensure, so far as is reasonably practicable, that persons not in his employment who may be affected thereby are not thereby exposed to risks to their health and safety.

British Steel had to prove that it was not reasonably practicable to do more than was in fact done. The company argued that, following *Tesco*, section 3(1) permitted it to escape criminal liability if it had taken all reasonable care at the level of its 'directing mind'. There is no doubt that the engineer employed by British Steel would not ordinarily be identified with the company in that way. However, the Court of Appeal concluded that *Tesco* '[did] not provide the answer'.[66] Steyn LJ said that 'it would drive a juggernaut through the legislative scheme if corporate employers could avoid criminal liability where the potentially harmful event is committed by someone who is not the directing mind of the company'.[67] The doctrine of identification did not, therefore, protect British Steel in the way that might have been expected.

It is worth noting that in *Tesco*, Lord Reid said that 'it must be a question of law whether, once the facts have been ascertained, a person in doing particular things is to be regarded as the company or merely as the company's servant or agent'.[68] While the courts have not reassessed due diligence defences in the light of these developments, cases such as *British Steel* and *Brent* suggest there is some wriggle room to depart from *Tesco* and, for the reasons suggested above, there are good policy reasons for doing so.

---

[63] ibid 1042.
[64] C Wells, 'Corporate Liability and Consumer Protection: *Tesco v Nattrass* Revisited' (1994) 57 *MLR* 817.
[65] *R v British Steel* [1995] 1 WLR 1356.
[66] ibid 1361.
[67] ibid 1362–63.
[68] *Tesco* (n 1) 170.

B. Identification and Mens Rea

When the Regulations replaced the Act, false statements about services became offences of strict liability. However, *mens rea* survived in regulation 8(1). This states:

> A trader is guilty of an offence if—
>
> he knowingly or recklessly engages in a commercial practice which contravenes the requirements of professional diligence under regulation 3(3)(a); and the practice materially distorts or is likely to materially distort the economic behaviour of the average consumer with regard to the product under regulation 3(3)(b).

I have written elsewhere about the difficulty of identifying what, precisely, has to be proved for a prosecution under regulation 8(1) to succeed.[69] On the basis of *Tesco*, it appears necessary to establish knowledge or recklessness on the part of someone who is identified with the company. The question of how widely that is to be drawn remains. As well as showing some flexibility in relation to (some) defences, the courts have also demonstrated a willingness to depart from the narrow interpretation of identification in *Tesco* where *mens rea* offences are concerned. In *Meridian Global Funds v Management Asia Ltd*[70] the Privy Council considered whether a company 'knew' that it had acquired a shareholding in a target company when two employees used funds to acquire shares in the target. It was determined that the company had such knowledge 'when that is known to the person who had authority to do the deal'.[71] In the words of Lord Hoffmann:

> It is a question of construction in each case as to whether the particular rule requires that the knowledge that an act has been done, or the state of mind with which it was done, should be attributed to the company ... Each [decision] is an example of an attribution rule for a particular purpose, tailored as it must be to the terms and policies of the substantive rule.[72]

This appeared to open the door to a more flexible approach to identification. It is consistent with the approach in *Brent* in focusing on the normative question of who should be regarded as the company for the purposes of the particular provision. On this basis, it would be possible to argue that a company should be guilty of an offence where the knowledge or reckless demanded by regulation 8(1) is demonstrated on the part of at least some employees (perhaps store managers or others with specific responsibilities) who authorise the offending conduct. Given the extent to which managers have significant discretion, this would appear to be in line with the purposes of the provision. However, it is clear that the courts will be cautious in extending identification, and recent cases suggest that this caution will be rather stronger than might have been expected.

---

[69] Cartwright (n 61).
[70] *Meridian Global Funds* v *Management Asia Ltd* [1995] 2 AC 500.
[71] ibid 511.
[72] ibid 511–12.

VI. A FALSE DAWN?

Following *Brent* and *Meridian*, it seemed that the courts might take advantage of a new freedom to interpret corporate criminal liability on the basis of the provision in question. There were some indications of caution. In *Attorney General's Reference (No.2 of 1999)* Rose LJ said that the identification theory was intended to avoid injustice and that 'it would bring the law into disrepute if every act and state of mind of an individual employee was attributed to a company which was entirely blameless'.[73] This, of course, assumes that the company is 'blameless' because the employee is not the company. While it might be a step too far to hold companies liable for the conduct and *mens rea* of the most junior employees, casting the net more widely seems appropriate for the purposes of consumer protection offences. Writing in 2010, the Law Commission still saw there as being significant room for flexibility, saying:[74]

> it is clear from the decisions in *Pioneer Concrete* and in *Meridian* that the courts now have the latitude to interpret statutes imposing criminal liability as imposing it on different bases, depending on what will best suit the statutory purpose in question.

However, the courts have not taken advantage of this latitude and the Commission's confidence now looks misplaced. Instead, the courts have recently confirmed the approach in *Tesco* while, arguably, interpreting identification even more narrowly than their Lordships did. In *SFO v Barclays PLC and ANR* ('*Barclays*') the High Court considered whether the alleged dishonesty of senior officers could be attributed to a company (Barclays) and so make it criminally liable.[75] Davis LJ said that the 'special rule of attribution' referred to in *Meridian* applied only where insistence on the primary rule (as expounded in *Tesco*) would defeat the intention of Parliament.[76] While recognising that some cases had applied *Meridian*, he argued that any expansive approach of the type heralded by the Law Commission had 'been eschewed by the criminal courts'.[77] He concluded that because the directors did not have full discretion to act independently, and were responsible to another person (namely the Board Finance Committee) for finalising any agreement, they could not be regarded as the directing mind and will for the functions in question.[78] There was some, but not full, delegation to the directors. Not even the Chief Executive Officer had the degree of autonomy that Davis LJ saw as necessary for identification to be established. In this respect, the decision in *Barclays* seems to be even more restrictive than that in *Tesco*. Where a director is particularly senior (such as a chief executive or managing director) it appears to have been envisaged by the majority in *Tesco* that such director would inevitably constitute the directing mind and will without any need for delegation.[79] However, this was not reflected by the decision in *Barclays*.

---

[73] *Attorney General's Reference (No.2 of 1999)* [2000] Cr App R 207, 211.
[74] Law Commission (n 59) para 5.103.
[75] *Serious Fraud Office v Barclays Bank plc and ANR* [2018] EWHC 3055 (QB), [2020] 1 Cr App R 28.
[76] ibid para 76.
[77] ibid para 81.
[78] ibid para 119.
[79] See discussion in Law Commission (n 60) para 2.59.

Although *Barclays* confirms the continued importance of *Tesco*, some scope to depart appears to remain. In *A Ltd*, a case heavily relied upon in *Barclays*, Sir Brian Levenson recognised that there would be instances 'where consideration of the legislation in question leads to a different and perhaps broader approach' than found in *Tesco*.[80] Indeed, even in *Barclays*, Davis LJ accepted that there might be cases where policy required a departure from *Tesco*; he just did not see *Barclays* as such a case. An important issue to establish, therefore, is when the courts will see fit to exercise their flexibility to move beyond the 'primary rule'.

When it reported in 2010, the Law Commission anticipated that the courts would adopt an approach to corporate liability that it later described as 'a purposive approach where possible; the identification doctrine only when necessarily implied'.[81] Following *Barclays*, it recognised that the law might better be described as involving 'the identification doctrine unless a special rule of attribution is necessarily implied'.[82] There remains room, therefore, for a broader approach where necessarily implied. The authors of *Smith, Hogan and Ormerod* conclude that *Meridian* 'may only be capable of applying to a small number of criminal offences which have an identifiable purpose'.[83] It is submitted that, notwithstanding the decision in *Tesco*, consumer protection is an area where a broader approach is appropriate. As explained above, the offences under the CPUTRs are 'regulatory' and lack the stigma (and *mens rea*) of mainstream crimes such as bribery. Furthermore, the rise of the digital economy and the ubiquity of online shopping mean that the consumption environment is very different from that encountered by consumers in the 1960s. It has recently been doubted whether a narrow identification principle reflects the real distribution of decision-making and knowledge within a corporation, ignoring its complexity.[84] The CPUTRs attempt to 'future proof' consumer protection law by the introduction of something approaching a general duty not to trade unfairly. To hold companies to account effectively for engaging in unfair commercial practices it is necessary to require them to take greater responsibility for the acts of their employees than *Tesco* suggested.

VII. THE LAW COMMISSION'S OPTIONS PAPER

The most recent significant contribution to the discussion of corporate criminal liability is found in the Law Commission's: *Corporate Criminal Liability: an options paper*.[85] The Commission made clear that it was not making recommendations, but was merely setting out options for reform. However, it did rule out certain options. The Law Commission discussed models which allow a corporate body to be convicted on the basis of its 'corporate culture' or systems, such as those found in Canada and Australia, but did not recommend such an approach. It also considered

---

[80] *R v A Ltd* [2016] EWCA Crim 1469, para 27.
[81] Law Commission (n 60) para 2.56.
[82] ibid para 2.56.
[83] *Smith Hogan and Ormerod* (n 25) 268.
[84] Law Commission (n 60) para 2.69.
[85] Law Commission, *Corporate Criminal Liability; an options paper* (10-6-22).

the doctrine of *respondeat superior* which is the principal model of corporate criminal liability in the federal courts (and most state courts) in the US. *Respondeat superior* makes a company criminally responsible for the activities of employees and agents of any level, provided that they commit offences within the scope of employment and with the motivation of benefiting the corporation. The similarity between this and the form of vicarious liability considered above will be immediately apparent. Indeed, the Law Commission observed that *respondeat superior* is frequently described as a form of vicarious liability, but suggested that it is instead a mode of attribution:

> [w]hen a company is convicted of a criminal offence under *respondeat superior*, it is not convicted on the basis that 'another person' did the act in question but it is expedient to convict the company, but rather that that person's acts were those of the company.[86]

However, despite this technical distinction, the Law Commission concluded that the difference between the two 'comes close to collapse at this point'.[87] Adoption of *respondeat superior* would allow companies more easily to be held to account 'where they have benefitted, or were intended to benefit, from wrongful conduct committed by people operating at more junior levels in a company's hierarchy than other attribution models'.[88] Given the arguments above concerning both the purposes of consumer protection law and the limitations of the doctrine of identification, it might therefore be an attractive model to adopt in the context of consumer protection. Nevertheless, the Law Commission concluded that there was 'insufficient evidence to support the proposition that a company should be liable for the criminal acts of any [ie, all] of its employees'.[89]

The Law Commission concluded that the principal options it could recommend were to proceed with the identification doctrine (either as it is or in an amended form) and to make further use of 'failure to prevent' offences.[90] The latter is beyond the scope of this chapter, although there are interesting arguments to be made for greater use of failure to prevent in the context of consumer protection law. On the former option, the Law Commission said that it was 'in no doubt that the identification doctrine is an obstacle to holding large companies criminally responsible for offences committed in their interests by their employees'.[91] It concluded that there was a case for extending the basis of criminal liability to cover situations where the conduct was done by, or at the behest of, a member of the 'senior management' of a corporation. The issue would then be how broadly this group is defined, as it looks in many respects little different from *Tesco*. Furthermore, the Law Commission advanced this argument in relation to offences requiring proof of *mens rea* or other fault.

It is important to ascertain precisely to what extent it would apply to offences that impose strict liability but are subject to due diligence defences, such as the

---

[86] ibid para 5.7.
[87] ibid para 5.3.
[88] ibid para 5.12.
[89] ibid para 5.53.
[90] ibid para 3.91.
[91] ibid para 3.91.

majority of those under the CPUTRs. Given its similarity to *Tesco* it is assumed that such a test would apply in such cases. The Law Commission recognised that as well as making it difficult to prosecute large companies, the doctrine of identification has failed to ensure the certainty that is sometimes claimed. In its words: 'even if the identification doctrine gives risk to a degree of certainty, we are not convinced that it gives any greater certainty than alternative models'.[92] While a restatement of the law could make matters clearer, it is difficult to conclude that it would make it significantly easier to hold large companies to account for their wrongdoing. Of course, this returns us to the question of what we understand by 'their' wrongdoing. As the Law Commission recognised, there remains a 'metaphysical' argument about what constitutes the 'real company'. It is not clear that this is answered satisfactorily by the Law Commission's paper.

VIII. CONCLUSIONS

Tesco cemented the identification principle as integral to the criminal liability of corporations, with the case's influence extending far beyond consumer protection. As a result of the decision, companies have found it (relatively) easy to escape liability. This is achieved by arguing that contraventions were the result of individuals who were not identified with the company (even when those individuals were employees with a significant degree of responsibility and discretion) and that the company had, through those who were identified with it, taken all reasonable precautions and exercised all due diligence. The decision thus made it difficult for enforcers to secure convictions for such offences. It also made it difficult for them to secure convictions against companies for offences requiring proof of *mens rea*, with that *mens rea* needing to be established on the part of someone who was identified with the company. It has been argued that *Tesco* need not have been decided in this way and that the objectives of consumer protection law are compromised by the decision.

Optimism that the courts were re-assessing *Tesco* and allowing courts greater freedom to determine when a company is responsible for the conduct of its employees appears to have been misplaced. In particular, *Barclays* seems at best to confirm that *Tesco* remains applicable except where its narrow conception of identification defeats the aim of the statute. At worst, it seems to restrict further the group of employees whose conduct (and, where appropriate, *mens rea*) are those of the company. The Law Commission has identified options for change, but it is not clear that those options would address the concerns that have been identified satisfactorily. This chapter has suggested that a broader approach could better reflect those whose actions (or states of mind) are those of the company and would be welcomed. Unless and until such a change comes about, the continued importance of the decision in *Tesco* is difficult to overstate.

---

[92] ibid para 3.78.

10

Lloyds Bank Ltd v Bundy: The Influence of the Omnibus Principle of Unequal Bargaining Power

JEANNIE MARIE PATERSON AND ELISE BANT*

I. INTRODUCTION

*L*LOYDS BANK LTD *v Bundy*[1] is a landmark case in consumer protection law. However, in contrast to many of the cases in this collection, its influence does not come directly from initiating a change in legal doctrine or principle: the impact comes from the organising theme or omnibus principle that emerged from it. *Lloyds Bank Ltd v Bundy* gave relief to an ill-informed third-party guarantor of a family member's business debt, on the basis of the undue influence of the lender bank. This approach, based on the exceptional circumstances of the case, was some years later subsumed by a more protective version of doctrine applying to non-commercial third-party guarantees in *Royal Bank of Scotland v Etridge (No 2)*.[2] In this aspect, the case falls within a family of principles concerned to protect non-commercial sureties, commonly family members who agree to mortgage their home to support a loved one's business borrowings. Lord Denning MR's broader, proposed omnibus principle of unequal bargaining power, unifying the vitiating factors of undue influence, undue pressure, duress and unconscionable dealing, has failed to find ongoing recognition in English law.[3] Yet it is that very principle that has proven

---

* This chapter was written as part of an Australian Research Council Discovery Project (DP180100932) 'Developing a Rational Law of Misleading Conduct'. Our thanks to Danielle Feng, JD candidate at Melbourne Law School, for research assistance. Our thanks also to Jodi Gardner and participants at the Landmark Cases in Consumer Law Workshop for feedback and comments.
[1] *Lloyds Bank Ltd v Bundy* [1975] QB 326 (CA).
[2] *Royal Bank of Scotland v Etridge (No 2)* [2001] UKHL 41, [2002] 2 AC 773. See also *Barclays Bank plc v O'Brien* [1994] 1 AC 180. See also R Bigwood, 'From *Morgan* to *Etridge*: Tracing the (Dis)Integration of Undue Influence in the United Kingdom' in JW Neyers, R Bronaugh and SGA Pitel (eds), *Exploring Contract Law* (Oxford, Hart Publishing, 2009).
[3] The principle has been rejected or constrained in a number of cases. See, eg, *Pao On v Lau Yiu Long* [1980] AC 614; *National Westminster Bank plc v Morgan* [1985] 1 AC 686, 708; *Alec Lobb (Garages) Ltd v Total Oil (GB) Ltd* [1985] 1 WLR 173.

most influential across a broad compass of consumer transactions. The understanding that business to consumer contracts are characterised by a profound inequality of bargaining power that reduces the ability of the weaker party to protect their own interests, undermines glib assertion of the place of 'freedom of contract', supports a generous conceptualisation and application of the doctrine of unconscionable dealing, and informs many of the interventions provided by consumer protection legislation. The omnibus principle has travelled well beyond its English village birthplace and the domestic surety context.

The principle of inequality of bargaining power may be seen as a key factor in the evolution of the doctrine of unconscionable dealing in Canada[4] and, to some extent, Australia,[5] supporting broadly framed and, at times, controversial responses to conduct that exploits a superior bargaining position. It has been less significant in respect to the English doctrine of unconscionable dealing,[6] which is arguably overshadowed by, and confused with, that of undue influence.[7] In Singapore, the principle has been met with judicial concerns about the potentially disruptive impact of granting relief in any case where the parties are not on equal terms, leading to courts adopting a 'middle ground' approach.[8] Yet, even in England, concern with unequal bargaining power, along with the influence of the EU, has informed statutory responses to unconscionable conduct,[9] unfair conduct,[10] and unfair contract terms.[11] Admittedly, the influence of traditional attitudes within the common law of contract law decrying the destabilising effect of such considerations has led to some unfortunately narrow readings of statute,[12] which is something of a theme of this collection.[13] Nonetheless, the statutory initiatives have allowed regulators to respond in a systemic manner to overreaching conduct by firms that exploit their bargaining advantage and the information asymmetries that face consumers in dealing with them. As we will see, these legislative schemes are now widespread, arguably manifesting a shared and broadly-framed statutory policy concerned to address the sorts of concerns articulated by Lord Denning MR. Looking forward, it seems likely, and desirable, that attention and resources should be focused on enabling more effective regulatory enforcement rather than continuing to debate the merits of the intervention.

In this chapter, we begin by discussing the decision in *Lloyds Bank Ltd v Bundy*. We consider the evolution of English law dealing with the discrete situation raised

---

[4] *Uber Technologies Inc v Heller* (2020) SCC 16, 447 DLR 4th 179.
[5] *Commercial Bank of Australia Ltd v Amadio* [1983] HCA 14, (1983) 151 CLR 447.
[6] YK Liew and D Yu, 'The Unconscionable Bargains Doctrine in England and Australia: Cousins or Siblings?' (2021) 45(1) *Melbourne University Law Review* 206.
[7] *Royal Bank of Scotland* (n 2) 798 [5] (Lord Nicholls); cf *Thorne v Kennedy* [2017] HCA 49, (2017) 263 CLR 85, 103–4 [39]–[40] (Kiefel CJ, Bell, Gageler, Keane and Edelman JJ) discussing the Australian authorities that consistently distinguish the doctrines. See also D Capper, 'The Unconscionable Bargain in the Common Law World' (2010) 126 *Law Quarterly Review* 403.
[8] *BOM v BOK* [2018] SGCA 83.
[9] Competition and Consumer Act 2010 (Cth), sch 2, s 21 (Australian Consumer Law).
[10] Consumer Protection from Unfair Trading Regulations 2008, pt 2.
[11] Consumer Rights Act 2015, pt 2; Australian Consumer Law, pts 2–3.
[12] JM Paterson and E Bant, 'Contract and the Challenge of Consumer Protection Legislation' in TT Arvind and J Steele (eds), *Contract Law and the Legislature: Autonomy, Expectations, and the Making of Legal Doctrine* (Oxford, Hart Publishing, 2020).
[13] See ch 1.

by the case, namely non-commercial guarantors of another's business debt. We then consider the indirect impact of the principle of unequal bargaining power in informing the equitable doctrine of unconscionable dealing in England and also in Canada, Australia and Singapore. We next turn to its manifestations in the relief given under consumer protection legislation from unfair or unconscionable conduct, as well as from unfair terms. Finally, we consider the role of statutory penalties in making this body of law effective as a deterrent to overreaching conduct and abuses of bargaining power.

II. THE DECISION

Lloyds Bank Ltd v Bundy[14] arose from an attempt by Lloyds Bank to take possession of Yew Tree Farm, which was owned by Mr Bundy. The facts of the case were 'special',[15] if not singular. The Bank had a longstanding and close relationship with the Bundy family.[16] It was intimately familiar with their financial circumstances.[17] Relevantly, the value of the farm, Mr Bundy's main asset, was £10,000. His son's business, which held an overdraft account with the Bank, was experiencing increasing difficulties. Mr Bundy had earlier used the farm as security for the overdraft facility with the Bank, initially to an amount of £1,500. Subsequently, the value of the security was increased to £7,500. On this occasion, Mr Bennett had afforded Mr Bundy proper opportunity to seek, and follow, the independent advice of his local solicitor, a reputable advisor well-known to the Bank.[18] This advice was that, given the value of the farm, this was the utmost Mr Bundy could sink into his son's affairs.[19]

However, Mr Bundy subsequently increased the secured amount to £11,000. In this final transaction, a new assistant bank manager, Mr Head, came to the farmhouse armed with the prepared guarantee and charge documents, ready for signature. The son and his wife were present and clearly anxious for Mr Bundy to sign.[20] The Bank well knew both the true, and perilous, financial condition of the son's business and the son's influence with his father.[21] Yet Mr Head did not notify Mr Bundy of the reality of the situation. The forms were signed on the spot, with no opportunity for, or recommendation to obtain, independent legal advice. Some short months later, the son's company went into receivership and the Bank made demand for repayment, followed by an attempt to exercise its rights under the mortgage and sell the farm. Mr Bundy sought an order setting aside the guarantee and charge, and an injunction restraining the Bank from selling the farm. He failed at first instance but was successful before the Court of Appeal, which ordered the charge and guarantee to be set aside and these documents to be delivered up for cancellation.

---

[14] *Lloyds Bank Ltd* (n 1).
[15] ibid 347 (Sachs LJ).
[16] ibid 339 (Lord Denning MR), 344 (Sachs LJ).
[17] ibid 344–46 (Sachs LJ).
[18] ibid 345 (Sachs LJ).
[19] ibid 335 (Lord Denning MR).
[20] ibid 345 (Sachs LJ).
[21] Ibid 339 (Lord Denning MR), 345 (Sachs LJ).

Given the relationship between the parties and the circumstances of the transaction, the result was unsurprising. The risks in the transaction for Mr Bundy were obvious. As described by Sachs LJ:

> The documents Mr Bundy [the defendant] was being asked to sign could result, if the company's troubles continued, in [the defendant's] sole asset being sold, the proceeds all going to the bank, and his being left penniless in his old age. That he could thus be rendered penniless was known to the bank – and in particular to Mr Head. That the company might come to a bad end quite soon with these results was not exactly difficult to deduce ....[22]

Mr Bundy was subject to the influence of his son, of which the Bank was well aware.[23] The assistant bank manager, Mr Head, acknowledged that Mr Bundy relied on him to provide advice about the transaction.[24] These circumstances meant that it would be quite straightforward to grant relief on grounds of undue influence.[25] Such an approach was taken by Sachs LJ, who held that the Bank owed to Mr Bundy a 'fiduciary' duty of care arising from the relationship of influence and, in the absence of an opportunity for independent advice, this duty had not been fulfilled.[26] Cairns LJ agreed with Sachs LJ. Lord Denning MR considered these factors also supported granting relief on grounds of undue influence. This was because the relationship between the Bank and Mr Bundy was one of trust and confidence, meaning the bank should not have allowed Mr Bundy to give the guarantee and mortgage without obtaining legal advice.[27]

Lord Denning MR further held that relief should be granted on the basis of a unifying principle of 'inequality of bargaining power'.[28] In developing this principle, Lord Denning MR recognised that a harsh outcome was not on its own a reason for setting aside a third-party guarantee or any contract. Yet, there were exceptions to this 'general rule' arising from 'common fairness'.[29] His Lordship noted numerous established categories of relief against a bargain in cases where there was an inequality of bargaining power between the parties that offended ideas of fairness: duress of goods, unconscionable transactions, undue influence, undue pressure, and salvage situations. Lord Denning MR considered that a single thread ran through these instances of relief, that of 'inequality of bargaining power'.[30] Relief on this ground was not open-ended. Lord Denning MR envisaged four requirements for providing relief on grounds of this principle, namely

> the English law gives relief to one who, without independent advice, enters into a contract upon terms which are very unfair or transfers property for a consideration which is grossly inadequate, when his bargaining power is grievously impaired by reason of his own needs

---

[22] ibid 345 (Sachs LJ).
[23] ibid 339 (Lord Denning MR), 345 (Sachs LJ).
[24] ibid 335–36, 339 (Lord Denning MR), 343–44 (Sachs LJ).
[25] *Allcard v Skinner* (1887) 36 Ch D 145.
[26] *Lloyd's Bank Ltd* (n 1) 344–45; see also 339, 340 (Lord Denning MR).
[27] ibid.
[28] ibid 339.
[29] ibid 336.
[30] ibid 336.

or desires, or by his own ignorance or infirmity, coupled with undue influences or pressures brought to bear on him by or for the benefit of the other.[31]

In this case, Lord Denning MR held that the guarantee was voidable owing to the unequal bargaining position in which Mr Bundy had found himself in when dealing with the bank. The relevant factors supporting this position were that the consideration moving from the bank was grossly inadequate; the longstanding relationship between the bank and the father was one of trust and confidence; the relationship between the father and the son was one where the father's natural affection had much influence on him; and there was a conflict of interest between the bank and the father.[32]

III. THE DEVELOPING LAW ON NON-COMMERCIAL THIRD-PARTY GUARANTEES

The phrase 'third-party guarantee' refers to the situation where the person who guarantees a loan is not the borrower or a person directly benefiting from the business or purpose for which the loan is obtained. Third party-guarantors are not even in a position akin to an ordinary consumer. They are assuming the risk of default on the loan transaction without receiving any tangible benefit in return. The concern over third-party guarantees in a family context, illustrated by *Lloyds Bank Ltd v Bundy*, arises from the risk that such a party has had their judgement clouded by love, loyalty, or affection. In such circumstances, the guarantor may lose out in the process by not being aware of the full extent of the legal and financial risk they are assuming.[33] As courts have recognised, this risk is present wherever the third-party guarantor stands in a close domestic relationship with the primary debtor.[34] Relief is dependent on the bank being, or being treated as being, aware of that relationship and the risk that it poses to the guarantor's free and full consent.

The relief granted in *Lloyds Bank Ltd v Bundy* was independently supported by the close, fiduciary-like quality of the relationship between the bank manager and Mr Bundy. The relevant principles applying to undue influence and third-party guarantees were restated in *National Westminster Bank plc v Morgan*,[35] with Lord Scarman rejecting any need for support from a principle of inequality of bargaining power.[36] In *National Westminster Bank plc v Morgan*, Lord Scarman said:

> The fact of an unequal bargain will, of course, be a relevant feature in some cases of undue influence. But it can never become an appropriate basis of principle of an equitable doctrine which is concerned with transactions 'not to be reasonably accounted for on the

---

[31] ibid 339.
[32] ibid 339–40.
[33] ibid.
[34] *Royal Bank of Scotland* (n 2) 813–14 (Lord Nicholls). See also *Garcia v National Australia Bank Ltd* (1998) 194 CLR 395, 404 [21]–[22] (Gaudron, McHugh, Gummow and Hayne JJ); *Kranz v National Australia Bank Ltd* (2003) 8 VR 310, 319–22 [23]–[31] (Charles JA, Winneke P and Eames JA concurring).
[35] *National Westminster Bank plc* (n 3).
[36] ibid 707–8.

ground of friendship, relationship, charity, or other ordinary motives on which ordinary men act'.[37]

Subsequently, English courts developed a different approach to third-party guarantees that does not rely on finding these kinds of 'exceptional circumstances' to give relief on grounds of undue influence.[38] In *Royal Bank of Scotland v Etridge (No 2)*, Lord Nicholls held that a lender will be put on inquiry as to the risk of undue influence in cases where the relationship between the borrower and the guarantor is one where the law presumes a relationship of trust and confidence for the purposes of the doctrine of undue influence, and in every case where the relationship between the parties is not 'commercial'.[39]

A lender put on inquiry will be required to take steps to reduce the risk of the guarantor entering into the transaction under a misrepresentation or as a result of undue influence. If these steps are not taken, the bank will be deemed to have notice that the transaction was procured by undue influence or misrepresentation on the part of the borrower and the guarantee may be set aside.[40] Typically, the bank will protect its position by ensuring the guarantor receives independent legal advice. The form and content of guarantees in consumer transactions is also now regulated by the Consumer Credit Act 1974, a consideration relied on by Scarman LJ in refusing to follow Lord Denning MR's principles in *National Westminster Bank plc v Morgan*.[41]

Royal Bank of Scotland v Etridge (No 2) aimed to find a balance between allowing parties to use domestic property as security for business ventures, and protecting the interests of third-party guarantors.[42] The motivation for intervention is clear. Granting a mortgage and guarantee over property is a useful way of securing business loans. Yet third-party guarantors are left in a highly exposed position, and may often lack understanding of this simple reality because their decision-making has been influenced by reasons of interpersonal or emotional loyalty or affection. The response in *Royal Bank of Scotland v Etridge (No 2)* was to lay down a 'clear, simple, and practically operable'[43] set of rules for lending banks taking a mortgage over land in domestic contexts where the guarantor is not benefiting from the transaction. The inevitable corollary of this position is that it does not require any substantive inquiry into whether the bank's steps to address undue influence had any real effect in liberating the guarantor from the influence of the borrower.

In Australia, the High Court has taken a different approach to the challenge of mediating the competing interesting in non-commercial third-party guarantee scenarios. The principles from the decisions in *Yerkey v Jones*[44] and *Garcia v National Australia Bank Ltd*[45] direct the courts to inquire into the range of risks of which a

---

[37] ibid 708.
[38] *Barclays Bank plc* (n 2); *Royal Bank of Scotland* (n 2).
[39] *Royal Bank of Scotland* (n 2) 813–14 [86]–[87] (Lord Nicholls).
[40] ibid 814 [87] (Lord Nicholls). For the different approach taken in Australia, see *Garcia* (n 34).
[41] *National Westminster Bank* plc (n 3) 708.
[42] *Royal Bank of Scotland* (n 2) 801 [34]–[37] (Lord Nicholls), endorsing the analysis of Lord Browne-Wilkinson in *Barclays Bank plc* (n 2) 188–89.
[43] *Royal Bank of Scotland* (n 2) 793 [2] (Lord Bingham).
[44] [1939] HCA 3, (1940) 63 CLR 649.
[45] *Garcia* (n 34).

bank should have been aware through its knowledge of the nature of the relationship between the primary debtor and the guarantor. Thus, close domestic relationships raise the risk that a guarantor may be mistaken as to the terms of the guarantee and their potential liability.[46] This is because the nature of the relationship may foster informal and inaccurate communication of information, even with the best of intentions. Likewise, a risk of undue influence may be present in cases involving a domestic surety, depending on the nature of the relationship.[47] As will be apparent, the risk of illegitimate pressure is far less likely to be apparent to a bank, absent any unusual features of the relationship or other facts known to the bank.[48] Where the bank is aware of facts that indicate a risk of vitiated consent, and the guarantor is not receiving a direct benefit from the loan transaction, then the bank must take steps to reduce this risk to a level where it is proper to proceed. Independent legal advice may be an element of that process, the appropriateness of which will be the subject of the court's active consideration.[49]

Consistently with Lord Denning MR's approach in *Lloyds Bank Ltd v Bundy*, the current approaches to third-party guarantees in both England and Australia may be understood as reflecting the institutional advantages of banks and comparative vulnerabilities (including information asymmetries and exposure to influence) of third-party guarantors. It is noteworthy that there is no requirement for the bank to ever deal directly with the domestic surety, far less for it to be aware of the reality of the guarantor's vulnerability or be seeking actively to take advantage of a grossly unfair transaction in its favour. In these respects, the guarantee doctrines stand in contrast to the more conditional approach proposed by Lord Denning MR.[50]

IV. THE WIDER PRINCIPLE OF INEQUALITY OF BARGAINING POWER

We have seen that the unifying principle of inequality of bargaining power identified by Lord Denning MR brought together doctrines of undue influence, unconscionable dealing, and duress. As outlined above, the principle of inequality of bargaining power would give relief to a party, usually a consumer dealing with a business,

i. who entered into a contract on terms which were 'very unfair' or transferred property for a consideration which was 'grossly inadequate';
ii. in circumstances were that party's bargaining power was 'grievously impaired' by reason of their 'own needs or desires', or 'ignorance or infirmity';

---

[46] ibid 404 [21] (Gaudron, McHugh, Gummow and Hayne JJ).
[47] *Liu v Adamson* (2003) 12 BPR 22,205 [22]–[23] (Macready M); *Kranz* (n 34) 319–22 [23]–[31] (Charles JA, Winneke P and Eames JA concurring).
[48] *National Australia Bank Ltd v Satchithanantham* [2009] NSWSC 21, affd [2009] NSWCA 268.
[49] *Garcia* (n 34) 408–9 [28]–[33], 408–9 [31], 411 [41] (Gaudron, McHugh, Gummow and Hayne).
[50] The doctrine in *Garcia* may also go beyond Australia's statutory prohibition on unconscionable conduct. These generally require the vitiating factor affecting the guarantor's consent to be either attributable to the bank, or the principal debtor acting for the bank: see, eg, Australian Securities and Investments Commission Act 2001 (Cth) s 12CC that prohibits unconscionable conduct including circumstances of mistake, pressure and influence on conduct of service supplier or person acting on behalf of the supplier. The National Credit Code, s 76, found in sch 1 of the National Consumer Credit Protection Act 2009 (Cth), which would otherwise avoid this limitation, does not apply to commercial borrowings: s 5.

iii. coupled with 'undue influences or pressures' brought to bear for the benefit of the other; and
iv. there was an absence of legal advice.[51]

Lord Denning MR subsequently applied the principle of inequality of bargaining power in *Clifford Davis Management Ltd v WEA Records Ltd*, an interlocutory injunction case on restraint of trade.[52] His Lordship suggested that the decision of the House of Lords in *A Schroeder Music Publishing Co Ltd v Macaulay*[53] afforded support for the principles for relief against unequal bargaining power identified in *Lloyds Bank Ltd v Bundy*.[54] Nonetheless, the principle has made little direct impact on English case law and has been expressly rejected in a number of cases. Thus, in *Pao On v Lau Yiu Long*, Lord Scarman said that any argument to the effect that agreements were voidable because they were procured by the abuse of a dominant bargaining position was 'misconceived'.[55] In *Alec Lobb (Garages) Ltd v Total Oil (GB) Ltd*, Dillon LJ referred to the principle of unequal bargaining power expounded in Lord Denning MR's judgment in *Lloyds Bank Ltd v Bundy* and read it down to apply to situations where there had been no independent legal advice.[56] In *National Westminster Bank plc*, Lord Scarman further referred to statutory protection for consumers as a reason against the common law recognising a principle of relief against inequality of bargaining power, stating:

> Parliament has undertaken the task – and it is essentially a legislative task – of enacting such restrictions upon freedom of contract as are in its judgment necessary to relieve against the mischief: for example, the hire-purchase and consumer protection legislation ... I doubt whether the courts should assume the burden of formulating further restrictions.[57]

The principle of inequality of bargaining power propounded by Lord Denning MR in *Lloyds Bank Ltd v Bundy* and its related interpretations have also been the subject of considerable criticism by scholars,[58] many of which resurfaced with the recent decision of the Supreme Court of Canada in *Uber Technologies Inc v Heller*.[59] Criticisms include that the approach would let an illusory standard destabilise the certainty of contract law,[60] and also that the value based justifications

---

[51] *Lloyds Bank Ltd* (n 1) 339–40.
[52] *Clifford Davis Management Ltd v WEA Records Ltd* [1975] 1 WLR 61.
[53] *A Schroeder Music Publishing Co Ltd v Macaulay* [1974] 3 All ER 616.
[54] *Clifford Davis Management Ltd* (n 52) 64–5.
[55] *Pao On* (n 3) 632.
[56] *Alec Lobb (Garages) Ltd* (n 3) 181–82.
[57] *National Westminster Bank plc* (n 3) 708.
[58] See, eg, LS Sealy, 'Undue Influence and Inequality of Bargaining Power' (1975) 34 *Cambridge Law Journal* 21; MJ Trebilcock, 'The Doctrine of Inequality of Bargaining Power: Post-Benthamite Economics in the House of Lords' (1976) 26 *University of Toronto Law Journal* 359. cf, in greater support of the doctrine, BJ Reiter, 'Courts, Consideration, and Common Sense' (1977) 27 *University of Toronto Law Journal* 439; P Slayton, 'The Unequal Bargain Doctrine: Lord Denning in Lloyds Bank v Bundy' (1976) 22 *McGill Law Journal* 94; SM Waddams, 'Unconscionability in Contracts' (1976) 39 *Modern Law Review* 369.
[59] *Uber Technologies Inc* (n 4).
[60] 'Uber Technologies Inc v Heller: Supreme Court of Canada Targets Standard Form Contracts' (2021) 134 *Harvard Law Review* 2598.

for the approach are not articulated.[61] It should be noted at this juncture that Lord Denning MR recognised such a risk and placed limitations around the scope of the principle.[62]

Lord Denning MR's suggested omnibus principle unifying the doctrines of duress, undue influence and unconscionable dealing has not expressly been adopted in any jurisdiction, and the relationship between these doctrines remains contested.[63] Yet the case has had an ongoing impact on this area of law. In particular, the influence of Lord Denning MR's identification of the distorting influence of unequal bargaining power on the fairness of transactions can be seen to varying extents in formulations of the doctrine of unconscionable dealing recognised in England, Australia, Singapore and Canada. Indeed, in Canada[64] and in Australia,[65] the doctrine of unconscionable dealing sets out a more contextual and less stringent set of criteria for relief than recognised by Lord Denning MR. It is to these influences of the principle of inequality of bargaining power from *Lloyds Bank Ltd v Bundy* on the equitable doctrine of unconscionable dealing that we now turn.

Concerns about a principle of relief against inequality of bargaining power represent an ongoing tension in the law of contract. On the one hand, it is clear that 'mere' inequality of bargaining power is insufficient to set a contract aside; contracting parties are rarely evenly matched.[66] Yet exploitation in the contracting process can undermine the foundations of contract with its emphasis on free consent,[67] as well as expressing profound disrespect for the autonomy of parties to contracts generally.[68]

In response to this kind of concern, courts of Equity have traditionally given relief in respect of bargains characterised by exorbitant terms entered into by 'poor and ignorant' persons who lacked the advantage of independent advice.[69] Lord Denning MR drew on this case law in framing his principle of inequality of bargaining power. However, the modern equitable doctrine of unconscionable bargain in England remains more limited in its scope than envisaged by Lord Denning MR. In *Alec Lobb (Garages) Ltd v Total Oil (GB) Ltd*, Peter Millett QC identified three elements for relief for an unconscionable bargain to be granted:

> First, one party has been at a serious disadvantage to the other, whether through poverty, or ignorance, or lack of advice, or otherwise, so that circumstances existed of which unfair advantage could be taken ... secondly, this weakness of the one party has been exploited by the other in some morally culpable manner ... and thirdly, the resulting transaction has been, not merely hard or improvident, but overreaching and oppressive.[70]

---

[61] See R Bigwood, 'Strict Liability Unconscionability in the Supreme Court of Canada: Observations on *Uber Technologies Inc v Heller*' (2021) 65 *Canadian Business Law Journal* 153.
[62] *Lloyds Bank Ltd* (n 1).
[63] See in particular *Thorne* (n 7); *BOM* (n 8); *Times Travel (UK) Ltd v Pakistan International Airline Corp* [2021] UKSC 40, [2021] 3 WLR 727.
[64] *Uber Technologies Inc* (n 4).
[65] *Amadio* (n 5).
[66] *Alec Lobb (Garages) Ltd* (n 3); *Times Travel (UK) Ltd* (n 63) [3], [25], [77].
[67] *Uber Technologies Inc* (n 4) [59]. On the rationales for relief from unconscionable bargains, see M Chen-Wishart, *Unconscionable Bargains* (London, Butterworths, 1989).
[68] On transactional exploitation, see generally R Bigwood, *Exploitative Contracts* (Oxford, OUP, 2003).
[69] *Fry v Lane* (1888) 40 Ch D 312, 322. See also *Cresswell v Potter* [1978] 1 WLR 255.
[70] *Alec Lobb (Garages) Ltd* (n 3) 94–5.

This approach requires more in all respects than Lord Denning MR's principle of inequality of bargaining power: a serious disadvantage rather than impaired bargaining power; morally culpable exploitation rather than undue influence or pressure; and a resulting transaction that is oppressive, as opposed to containing terms that are unfair or providing inadequate consideration. Unconscionability in English law classically applies where 'a poor, illiterate and unwell person is induced to enter into a disadvantageous transaction without advice and in great haste'.[71] Lord Burrows has observed, following the authority of *Alec Lobb (Garages) Ltd v Total Oil (GB) Ltd*, that it is possible the relevant weakness might be a 'very weak bargaining position', but these cases are very rare and more likely to be pleaded as economic duress.[72] This is in contrast to the position in Australia and Canada where courts recognise the possibility of not merely 'personal' disadvantage but also 'situational' vulnerability,[73] whereby the relevant inequality arises from the 'contracting circumstances' in which consumers find themselves.

In Australia, Lord Denning MR's principle of relief against inequality of bargaining power has not been expressly adopted but clear echoes of the concerns giving rise to the suggested principle can be seen in the equitable doctrine of relief on grounds of unconscionable dealing, particularly as formulated in *Commercial Bank of Australia Ltd v Amadio*, a case with not dissimilar facts to *Lloyds Bank Ltd v Bundy*.[74] Indeed, in *BOM v BOK*, the Singapore Court of Appeal thought that 'the *Amadio* formulation comes dangerously close to the ill-founded principle of "inequality of bargaining power" that was introduced in *Lloyd's Bank v Bundy*'.[75] Although not premised on inequality of bargaining power, the Australian approach to unconscionable dealing incorporates elements reminiscent of Lord Denning MR's formulation, albeit focused on the conscience of the stronger party rather than the pressure applied to the more vulnerable party. Thus, in the influential case of *Commercial Bank of Australia Ltd v Amadio*,[76] Mason J described the circumstances in which relief would be granted, focusing on the existence of a 'special disadvantage' that affected the weaker party's 'ability to act in their own best interests at the time of transacting' in circumstances where the 'other party secured the transaction with knowledge of the special disadvantage and without doing anything to redress its effect'.[77] The formulation has remained influential, although in *Stubbings v Jams 2 Pty Ltd*, Kiefel CJ, Keane and Gleeson JJ warned that the considerations should not 'be understood as if they were to be addressed separately as if they were separate elements of a cause of action in tort'.[78]

---

[71] *Times Travel (UK) Ltd* (n 63) [24], citing *Clark v Malpas* (1862) 4 De GF & J 401, 45 ER 1238.
[72] *Times Travel (UK) Ltd* (n 63) [77].
[73] *Uber Technologies Inc* (n 4) [71]. In Australia, see *Australian Competition and Consumer Commission v Samton Holdings Pty Ltd* [2002] FCA 62, (2002) 117 FCR 301, 318 [46] (French J), and more qualified discussion in *Australian Competition and Consumer Commission v CG Berbatis Holdings Pty Ltd* [2003] HCA 18, (2003) 214 CLR 51, [10] (Gleeson CJ).
[74] *Amadio* (n 5). Interestingly, this is a case that might alternatively have been pleaded on grounds of undue influence, between parent and their son, with notice and indeed involvement by the bank.
[75] *BOM* (n 8) [133].
[76] See P Ridge, 'Sir Anthony Mason's Contribution to the Doctrine of Unconscionable Dealing: *Amadio's Case*' in B McDonald, B Chen and J Gordon (eds), *Dynamic and Principled: The Influence of Sir Anthony Mason* (Alexandria, Federation Press, 2022).
[77] *Amadio* (n 5) 462, 468 (Mason J). See also *Thorne* (n 7) 103 [38]. cf *Amadio* (n 5) 474 (Deane J).
[78] *Stubbings v Jams 2 Pty Ltd* [2022] HCA 6, (2022) 399 ALR 409, 418 [39].

Mason J saw relief for unconscionable dealing as responding firmly to concerns over the unconscientious use of superior bargaining power[79] in circumstances where a special disadvantage prevented the weaker party from acting in their own best interests.[80] However, a difference in bargaining power is not on its own sufficient to give rise to relief.[81] There must be unconscionable dealing in the circumstances of the case on the part of the stronger party, which is usually associated with some form of transactional exploitation.[82] The underlying principle concerns the ability of the innocent party to make a judgment as to their own best interests.[83] Additionally, the position of disadvantage must be evident or known to the other party.[84] Under this approach, in contrast to that taken in England, there is no requirement for an improvident bargain, although such an outcome may support an inference of advantage being taken.[85]

As noted, the Singapore Court of Appeal in *BOM v BOK*[86] rejected a 'broad', Australian-style approach to unconscionable dealing, preferring instead a narrower or middle-ground approach.[87] To invoke this 'narrow' formulation of the doctrine, the plaintiff must show they were

> suffering from an infirmity that the other party exploited in procuring the transaction. Upon the satisfaction of this requirement, the burden is on the defendant to demonstrate that the transaction was fair, just and reasonable. In this regard, while the successful invocation of the doctrine does not require a transaction at an undervalue or the lack of independent advice to the plaintiff, these are factors that the court will invariably consider in assessing whether the transaction was improvident.[88]

The extent to which this differs from the Australian position remains to be seen. However, what is clear is that the Singapore Court of Appeal further rejected a unifying or umbrella doctrine of unconscionability,[89] which might be considered akin to the umbrella concept of abuse of bargaining power contemplated by Lord Denning MR in *Lloyds Bank Ltd v Bundy*.

In Canada, the doctrine of inequality of bargaining power has gained a stronger foothold. From the outset, *Lloyds Bank Ltd v Bundy* was applied in a number of decisions.[90] Canadian courts, however, quickly developed their own doctrine of

---

[79] *Amadio* (n 5) 461.
[80] ibid 462.
[81] ibid 462.
[82] *Thorne* (n 7) 103 [38].
[83] *Amadio* (n 5) 462.
[84] ibid; *Thorne* (n 7) [65] (Kiefel CJ, Bell, Gageler, Keane and Edelman JJ).
[85] *Times Travel (UK) Ltd* (n 63) [26]; *CTN Cash and Carry Ltd v Gallaher Ltd* [1994] 4 All ER 714, 717 (Steyn LJ).
[86] *BOM* (n 8).
[87] ibid [133]. See also R Bigwood, 'Knocking Down the Straw Man: Reflections on *BOM v BOK* and the Court of Appeal's 'Middle-Ground' Narrow Doctrine of Unconscionability for Singapore' [2019] *Singapore Journal of Legal Studies* 29; cf B Ong, 'Unconscionability, Undue Influence and Umbrellas: The 'Unfairness' Doctrines in Singapore Contract Law after '*BOM v BOK*'' [2020] *Singapore Journal of Legal Studies* 295.
[88] *BOM* (n 8) [142].
[89] ibid [175] ff.
[90] See, eg, *McKenzie v Bank of Montreal* (1975) 55 DLR (3d) 641; *Towers v Affleck* [1974] 1 WWR 714. See generally Slayton (n 58) 100–3.

relief from unconscionable dealing.[91] This version of a broad and plaintiff-focused principle was crystallised in *Uber Technologies Inc v Heller*.[92] In this case, the Supreme Court of Canada set aside an arbitration clause in contracts between Uber and its drivers which required all external dispute resolution processes to go through mediation and arbitration in the Netherlands. This process required an upfront fee of US$14,500. Abella and Rowe JJ affirmed a two-step test for unconscionability, requiring 'an inequality of bargaining power, stemming from some weakness or vulnerability affecting the claimant and … an improvident transaction'.[93] The justices considered that the relevant inequality of bargaining power might extend to 'cognitive asymmetry',[94] which occurs because of 'personal vulnerability or because of disadvantages specific to the contracting process, such as the presence of dense or difficult to understand terms in the parties' agreement'.[95] Additionally, the inequality relevant for relief is broadly defined to encompass transactional weakness that may be personal or circumstantial.[96] This is illustrated by the decision in *Uber Technologies Inc v Heller* itself, in which the inequality arises from the position of the drivers required to sign a 'take it or leave it' standard form contract in order to work.

The position taken by Abella and Rowe JJ does not include any requirement that the stronger party knowingly took advantage of the vulnerable position of the weaker party.[97] Such a requirement was not consistent with the focus of the doctrine on protecting the weaker party and would 'erode the modern relevance of the unconscionability doctrine, effectively shielding from its reach improvident contracts of adhesion where the parties did not interact or negotiate'.[98] As Gardner notes, the decision moves the focus of the unconscionability doctrine in Canada from targeting exploitation arising from a superior bargaining position to 'protecting weak individuals from unfair contracts'.[99] The outcome was described by Brown J as one of 'strict liability' that would erode commercial certainty.[100] As such, it may be seen as going beyond even Lord Denning MR's idea of inequality of bargaining power.

---

[91] See R Bigwood, 'Antipodean Reflections on the Canadian Unconscionability Doctrine' (2005) 84 *Canadian Bar Review* 171; R Bigwood, 'Rescuing the Canadian Unconscionability Doctrine? Reflections on the Court's 'Applicable Principles' in *Downer v Pitcher*' (2018) 60 *Canadian Business Law Journal* 124. See also P Benson, *Justice in Transactions: A Theory of Contract Law* (Cambridge, MA, Belknap Press, 2019) 167; A Swan, J Adamski and Y Na, *Canadian Contract Law*, 4th edn (Toronto, LexisNexis Canada. 2018) 986; SM Waddams, *The Law of Contracts*, 7th edn Toronto, Carswell, 2017) 379.
[92] *Uber Technologies Inc* (n 4).
[93] ibid [62]. Brown J held that the arbitration clause was invalid as contrary to public policy. Côté J would uphold the clause provided Uber advanced the funds needed to initiate the arbitration proceedings.
[94] ibid [71], quoting SA Smith, *Contract Theory* (Oxford, OUP, 2004) 343–44.
[95] ibid [71].
[96] ibid [67].
[97] ibid [84].
[98] ibid [85].
[99] J Gardner, 'Being Conscious of Unconscionability in Modern Times: *Heller v Uber Technologies*' (2021) 84 *Modern Law Review* 874, 881.
[100] *Uber Technologies Inc* (n 4) [165].

V. THE STATUTORY RESPONSE TO INEQUALITY OF BARGAINING POWER

English and Australian courts have, on more than one occasion, stated that it is for Parliament, not courts, to provide relief against inequality of bargaining power.[101] It is in legislation that Lord Denning MR's principle in *Lloyds Bank Plc v Bundy* has found its most effective expression in protecting consumers. Consumer protection regimes in England, and other jurisdictions such as Australia, provide relief against advantage-taking, typically requiring disadvantage or vulnerability on the part of the weaker party and some element of fault or culpability on the part of the stronger party. Additionally, and in this regard going further than Lord Denning's principle of inequality of bargaining power, unfair contract terms regimes focus on the problem of substantive unfairness in the bargain without proof of advantage-taking.

A. Statutory Prohibitions on Unfair and Unconscionable Conduct

In the UK, the Consumer Protection from Unfair Trading Regulations 2008 provide an avenue for relief in response to a commercial practice that is unfair.[102] A commercial practice is unfair where:

(a) it contravenes the requirements of professional diligence; and
(b) it materially distorts or is likely to materially distort the economic behaviour of the average consumer with regard to the product.[103]

In making this assessment, the prohibition directs courts that:

> 'professional diligence' means the standard of special skill and care which a trader may reasonably be expected to exercise towards consumers which is commensurate with either —
>
> (a) honest market practice in the trader's field of activity, or
> (b) the general principle of good faith in the trader's field of activity.[104]
>
> 'materially distort the economic behaviour' means in relation to an average consumer, appreciably to impair the average consumer's ability to make an informed decision thereby causing him to take a transactional decision that he would not have taken otherwise.[105]

The extent to which the prohibition on unfair trading can respond to an abuse of bargaining power depends on whether such conduct can be said to be contrary to the requirements of professional diligence. The general prohibition is also premised on the effect of the purportedly unfair conduct on an average consumer.[106] Thus, relief is dependent on whether the standard envisaged for the average consumer – that of being 'reasonably well informed, reasonably observant and circumspect' – can

---

[101] *National Westminster Bank* (n 3) 708; *Times Travel (UK) Ltd* (n 63) [3], [26], [77]. Also *Toll (FGCT) Pty v Alphapharm Pty Ltd* [2004] HCA 52, (2004) 219 CLR 165, 182–3.
[102] Consumer Protection from Unfair Trading Regulations 2008, reg 4. See also the Consumer Protection (Fair Trading) Act 2003 (Singapore), which gives a right of relief against an unfair practice: s 4.
[103] Consumer Protection from Unfair Trading Regulations 2008, reg 3.
[104] ibid reg 2(1).
[105] ibid reg 2(2).
[106] ibid reg 4.

accommodate the kind of disadvantage envisioned by the doctrine that arises from the need to transact.[107]

A more forgiving standard applies where the impugned practice is targeted at

> a clearly identifiable group of consumers ... particularly vulnerable to the practice or the underlying product because of their mental or physical infirmity, age or credulity in a way which the trader could reasonably be expected to foresee.[108]

It is unclear if this extends to situational, as opposed to certain kinds of inherent, disadvantage, such as the position of a consumer overcome with bereavement or confusion in an unusual and complex transaction.[109] The scope of knowledge requirement is also uncertain. The Regulations refer to behaviour that will 'appreciably' impair the average consumer's ability to make an informed decision. This would suggest that constructive knowledge will be sufficient – the effect needs to be appreciated but not known. It should certainly catch business systems or patterns of behaviour that, by design or operation, exploit consumers' decision-making vulnerabilities to produce outcomes that are not welfare-enhancing,[110] for example by selling products that are overly expensive, produce little utility for the consumer, or are even positively harmful.[111]

Regulation 7 prohibits aggressive conduct, which might also provide a response to overreaching conduct by a more powerful bargaining partner. Aggressive conduct is defined as involving the 'use of harassment, coercion or undue influence'.[112] This is closer to duress or actual undue influence than the use of a superior bargaining position, or unconscionable conduct by a stronger party to exploit the position of disadvantage on the part of the other.[113]

Australia takes a different approach by including a statutory prohibition on unconscionable conduct that goes beyond the concept recognised in equity,[114] at least in principle.[115] The Australian Consumer Law, section 21 contains a prohibition on conduct which is, 'in all the circumstances', unconscionable.[116] Unconscionable conduct is not defined but section 21 contains a set of interpretative principles that aim to assist in the application of the section.[117] Section 22 contains a list of factors to

---

[107] JM Paterson and G Brody, '"Safety Net" Consumer Protection: Using Prohibitions on Unfair and Unconscionable Conduct to Respond to Predatory Business Models' (2015) 38 *Journal of Consumer Policy* 331.

[108] JM Paterson and E Bant, 'Should Australia Introduce a Prohibition on Unfair Trading? Responding to Exploitative Business Systems in Person and Online' (2021) 44 *Journal of Consumer Policy* 1.

[109] For a recent application of this kind of approach see *Uber Technologies Inc* (n 4), discussed at n 92ff.

[110] E Bant and JM Paterson, 'Systems of Misconduct: Corporate Culpability and Statutory Unconscionability' (2021) 15 *Journal of Equity* 63.

[111] Paterson and Brody (n 107).

[112] Consumer Protection from Unfair Trading Regulations 2008 reg, 7(1)(a).

[113] *cf* P Cartwright and R Hyde, 'Virtual Coercion and the Vulnerable Consumer: 'Loot Boxes' as Aggressive Commercial Practices' [2022] *Legal Studies* 1.

[114] JM Paterson, 'Unconscionable Bargains in Equity and under Statute' (2015) 9 *Journal of Equity* 188.

[115] *cf* the use of the equitable formulation by the majority in *Australian Securities and Investments Commission v Kobelt* [2019] HCA 18, (2019) 267 CLR 1 and *Stubbings* (n 78).

[116] See also Australian Securities and Investments Commission Act 2001 (Cth), s 12CC.

[117] The principles confirm that the statutory prohibition is not confined by the unwritten law: Australian Consumer Law, s 21(4)(a); and also that the prohibition is capable of applying to a 'system of conduct or pattern of behaviour, whether or not a particular individual is identified as having been disadvantaged by the conduct or behaviour': s 21(4)(b).

which the court may have regard in deciding if conduct is unconscionable, including, pertinently, the 'relative strengths of the bargaining positions' of the parties;[118] whether the consumer was 'required to comply with conditions that were not reasonably necessary for the protection of the legitimate interests of the supplier';[119] and whether any 'undue influence or pressure was exerted on, or any unfair tactics were used against' the consumer,[120] as well as considerations relating to the terms and conditions of the contract.[121] Courts have reiterated that inequality of bargaining power is, on its own, insufficient to give rise to relief on grounds of unconscionable conduct under statute.[122]

The statutory doctrine is undoubtedly flexible in responding to systems of conduct or patterns of behaviour that, by design or operation, take advantage of consumers' need, inexperience or lack of understanding.[123] However, the correct relationship between the equitable doctrine and the statutory prohibition has been subject to ongoing uncertainty and debate. In our opinion, Australian courts have often been overly cautious to give effect to the full potential of the provision as represented by the statutory wording.[124] They have instead often been influenced by the requirements of the equitable doctrine and the need for a high standard of demonstrable moral culpability before giving relief.[125]

B. Unfair Contract Terms

Perhaps the statutory intervention that comes closest to Lord Denning MR's principle in *Lloyds Bank Ltd v Bundy* is the unfair terms regime in the Consumer Rights Act 2015,[126] and also in the Australian Consumer Law.[127] Remember that in *Lloyds Bank Ltd v Bundy*, Lord Denning MR identified as relevant circumstances where a party 'without independent advice, enters into a contract upon terms which are very unfair'.[128] Consistently, and giving content to the concept of 'unfairness', the unfair terms regimes confront the key consequence of unequal bargaining power, namely

---

[118] Australian Consumer Law, s 22(1)(a) and (2)(a).
[119] ibid, s 22(1)(b) and (2)(b).
[120] ibid, s 22(1)(d) and (2)(d).
[121] ibid, s 22(1)(j).
[122] See, eg, *Director of Consumer Affairs Victoria v Scully* [2013] VSCA 292, (2013) 303 ALR 168, 181 [43]; *Ipstar Australia Pty Ltd v APS Satellite Pty Ltd* [2018] NSWCA 15, (2018) 356 ALR 440, 477–8 [196].
[123] Bant and Paterson, 'Systems of Misconduct' (n 110).
[124] JM Paterson, E Bant, N Felstead and E Twomey, 'Beyond the Unwritten Law' [2023] 17 *Journal of Equity* 1.
[125] See, eg, JM Paterson, E Bant and M Clare, 'Doctrine, Policy, Culture and Choice in Assessing Unconscionable Conduct under Statute: *ASIC v Kobelt*' (2019) 13 *Journal of Equity* 81.
[126] Consumer Rights Act 2015, pt 2.
[127] Australian Consumer Law, pts 2–3. See also the Consumer Protection (Fair Trading) Act 2003 (Singapore), sch 2, pt 1 (13). Taking advantage of a consumer by including in an agreement terms or conditions that are harsh, oppressive or excessively one-sided so as to be unconscionable. See further S Booysen, 'Regulating Unfair Terms and Consumer Protection' in M Chen-Wishart and S Vogenauer (eds), *Contents of Contracts and Unfair Terms* (Oxford, OUP, 2020). Also JM Paterson, 'Regulating Consumer Contracts in ASEAN: Variation and Change' in L Nottage and others (eds), *ASEAN Consumer Law Harmonisation and Cooperation: Achievements and Challenges* (Cambridge, CUP, 2019).
[128] *Lloyds Bank Ltd* (n 1) 339.

the inability of consumers to protect themselves from harsh, overreaching and one-sided terms. The UK regime sets aside as unfair terms those which, contrary to the requirements of 'good faith', cause 'a significant imbalance in the parties' rights and obligations under the contract to the detriment of the consumer'.[129] The regime therefore addresses the issue of the substantive unfairness of the term, rather the circumstances in which consent to the agreement was made and, in so doing, represents a considerable departure from traditional common law contract doctrine.[130]

The limitation of the regime is that it does not apply to the main subject matter or core price payable[131] (provided they are 'transparent and prominent')[132] as discussed elsewhere in this collection.[133] The regime may not have assisted Mr Bundy, whose basic complaint was a misunderstanding of the overall risks inherent in the guarantee transaction, rather than a term of that guarantee. In the UK, the unfair terms regime does not apply to small businesses as opposed to consumer contracts.[134] Thus, the unfair terms regime would not have assisted in the fact situation of *Uber Technologies Inc v Heller*.[135] Nonetheless, it has had a considerable impact on 'take it or leave it' contracts in other contexts, including, pertinently, compulsory arbitration or jurisdiction clauses that work against the interests of consumers.[136] Notably, the unfair terms regime in Australia has been extended to small business contracts,[137] providing broader avenues of relief against unfair contract terms arising from an inequality of bargaining power.

VI. REDRESS AND CIVIL PENALTIES

The usual redress for consumers responding to inequality of bargaining power is to have the overly burdensome and unfair bargain set aside. This was, of course, the primary relief sought and granted in *Lloyds Bank Ltd v Bundy* itself. However, inequality of bargaining power also manifests in an absence of redress options for individual consumers. There are relatively few cases on the statutory progeny of the inequality of bargaining power principle in the UK. This cannot be purely referable to the overt reading down of the statutory provisions in cases such as *ParkingEye Ltd*

---

[129] Consumer Rights Act 2015, s 62.

[130] See M Chen-Wishart, 'Regulating Unfair Terms' in L Gullifer and S Vogenauer (eds), *English and European Perspectives on Contract and Commercial Law: Essays in Honour of Hugh Beale* (Oxford, Hart Publishing, 2014) 105; JM Paterson, 'The Australian Unfair Contract Terms Law: The Rise of Substantive Unfairness as a Ground for Review of Standard Form Consumer Contracts' (2009) 33 *Melbourne University Law Review* 934.

[131] Consumer Rights Act 2015, s 64(1).

[132] ibid, s 64(2).

[133] See ch 16.

[134] Consumer Rights Act 2015, s 61.

[135] *Uber Technologies Inc* (n 4).

[136] See, eg, R Garnett, 'Arbitration of Cross-Border Consumer Transactions in Australia: A Way Forward?' (2017) 39 *Sydney Law Review* 569.

[137] Under the Australian Consumer Law, s 23(4), the unfair contract terms law applies to standard form 'small business' contracts entered into or renewed on or after 12 November 2016.

v Beavis.[138] The relative paucity of case law is also very likely attributable to the cost of litigation for individual plaintiffs and the relatively rarity of class actions in the consumer law field. Thus, in practical terms, the statutory protection to consumers afforded by consumer protection statutes comes through the intervention of regulators.

Peter Cartwright in this collection discusses the landmark consumer cases on criminal offences.[139] Here, the objective is deterrence or the provision of incentives to comply with statutory standards. Increasingly, consumer protection statutes are making use of civil penalties as an alternative to criminal offences in allowing regulatory intervention to promote compliance with the protective provisions of the legislation. Such penalties have the attraction of carrying a civil, rather than criminal, burden of proof. They also typically are not dependent on showing the firm that contravened a statutory prohibition had the culpable state of mind required for a criminal prosecution, although this element may be taken into account in setting the quantum of the award.[140]

Civil pecuniary penalties are available under the Australian Consumer Law for contraventions of the prohibition on unconscionable conduct.[141] Currently, civil penalties or fines are not available as a response to contraventions of the UK's Consumer Protection from Unfair Trading Regulations 2008 or the Consumer Rights Act 2015. In 2019, the UK government announced a process of consultation on whether the Competition and Markets Authority should be given new powers to decide whether consumer law has been broken, without having to go through the courts, and to impose fines directly in response to such conduct.[142] There seems, however, to have been little further development on this initiative. Notably, civil penalties are available under the Data Protection Act 2018 for contraventions of its provisions and the EU's General Data Protection Right,[143] and may be imposed directly by the regulator itself.[144] The Financial Conduct Authority also has the power directly to impose penalties on financial institutions in response to unfairness or misconduct in dealing with consumers.[145] The availability of such awards gives a new 'bite' to statutory consumer protection regimes and thereby provides more effective deterrence against the offending conduct than provided by actions by individual, often relatively disempowered, consumers.[146]

---

[138] *ParkingEye Ltd v Beavis* [2015] UKSC 67; [2016] AC 1172. See also Paterson and Bant, 'Contract and the Challenge of Consumer Protection Legislation' (n 12).

[139] See ch 9.

[140] See Financial Conduct Authority, 'The Decision Procedure and Penalties Manual' (July 2022) [6.2.1].

[141] Australian Consumer Law, s 224. JM Paterson and E Bant, 'Intuitive Synthesis and Fidelity to Purpose? Judicial Interpretation of the Discretionary Power to Award Civil Penalties under the Australian Consumer Law' in P Vines and MS Donald (eds), *Statutory Interpretation in Private Law* (Alexandria, Federation Press, 2019).

[142] Department for Business, Energy & Industrial Strategy and others, 'New Powers to Fine Firms that Exploit Consumer Loyalty' (Press Release, 18 June 2019) www.gov.uk/government/news/new-powers-to-fine-firms-that-exploit-consumer-loyalty.

[143] Data Protection Act 2018, s 15.

[144] Data Protection Act 2018, s 155(1).

[145] Financial Conduct Authority, 'FCA Handbook' (1 January 2022) EG 7.1.2 www.handbook.fca.org.uk/handbook/EG/7/?view=chapterLJ.

[146] On the deterrent effect of civil pecuniary penalties see Paterson and Bant, 'Intuitive Synthesis and Fidelity to Purpose?' (n 144).

Consumers now also have rights to resolve disputes with and protect their expectations of fair treatment from financial service providers under ombudsman schemes such as the Financial Ombudsman Service in the UK[147] and the Australian Financial Services Complaints Authority in Australia.[148] These schemes respond to the very equality of bargaining power identified in *Lloyds Bank Ltd v Bundy* and also carry responsibilities to recognise and report systemic wrongdoing by financial services providers.

VII. CONCLUSION

A rather sobering reflection on *Lloyds Bank Ltd v Bundy*, and indeed the personal costs of unfair contracting, is that Mr Bundy had a heart attack in the witness box.[149] Ultimately, however, the charge and guarantee were set aside, and a costs order was awarded in Mr Bundy's favour. Census and other records suggest that Mr Bundy remained at Yew Tree farm until his death in 1981, and that his wife remained in possession after that time.[150] *Lloyds Bank Ltd v Bundy*, and in particular Lord Denning MR's principle of relief against inequality of bargaining power, has remained a key concern in the law dealing with protecting consumers. This is apparent in debates around the appropriate scope of the doctrine of unconscionable dealing and also in the development of consumer protection legislation providing responses to both procedural and substantive unfairness in consumer transactions.

---

[147] See S Williams, 'The Rise of Austerity Complaints' in *Debt and Austerity* (Cheltenham, Elgar, 2020) 227–33.
[148] See H Bolitho, N Howell and JM Paterson, *Duggan and Lanyon's Consumer Credit Law* (London, Butterworths, 2020) ch 22.
[149] *Lloyds Bank Ltd* (n 1).
[150] Research from England & Wales, Civil Registration Death Index, 1916–2007 and Salisbury District Council in possession of the author.

11

Erven Warnink Besloten Vennootschap v J Townend & Sons (Hull) Ltd: Consumer Welfarism by the Back Door?

JOHN MURPHY*

I. INTRODUCTION

IT WAS NOT until the early part of the twentieth century that any clear rationale for the tort of passing off emerged. Though the tort's origins are obscure, one useful study reveals that 'in the eighteenth century the Courts ... came to regard passing off as an action for deceit ... [albeit] a variety of deceit in which the action was not by the person who was deceived but by the person whose mark was used to deceive [the public]'.[1] Much later, it developed – perhaps surprisingly – into a tort of strict liability[2] in which the gist of the action was clearly identified as being damage to a claimant's goodwill,[3] rather than – as had been the case in the nineteenth century – damage to the 'name or trademark of a product or business'.[4]

A change in the liability basis of passing off, and the placing front and centre of goodwill do not, however, mark the only significant developments in the history of this tort. At least one other evolutionary twist is of note. This was the expansion in

---

* The micro-economic analysis in this essay benefitted from help from David Campbell, David Howarth, Lukas Jacobsen-Murphy and Lynne Pepall. I should also like to express by gratitude to those who commented on a draft at a symposium at Cambridge University.
[1] WL Morison, 'Unfair competition and passing-off the flexibility of formula' (1956) 2 *Sydney Law Review* 50, 54.
[2] See, eg, *Gillette UK Ltd v Edenwest Ltd* [1994] RPC 279, 291 (Blackburne J): 'I can see no good reason why, if damages are recoverable from the innocent infringer of a registered trademark, they should not equally be recoverable for innocent passing off.'
[3] The case that clarified its being concerned with the protection of goodwill against losses inflicted via a misrepresentation to the public was *AG Spalding & Bros v AW Gamage Ltd* [1915] 32 RPC 273.
[4] *Cadbury Schweppes Pty Ltd v Pub Squash Co Pty Ltd* [1981] RPC 429, 490 (Lord Scarman).

the concept of goodwill that allowed the tort to move beyond its classic confines of source misrepresentation, captured as follows:

> a man is not to sell his own goods under the pretence that they are the goods of another man ... He cannot therefore be allowed to use names, marks, letters, or other indicia, by which he may induce purchasers to believe, that the goods which he is selling are the manufacture of another person.[5]

In particular, in several cases involving alcoholic drinks, the concept was stretched so as to make it possible for claimants to assert that they had goodwill *in a term that is descriptive of a product*. Prior to these cases, it had only been possible to treat goodwill as a proprietary right associated with *the product itself*. The descriptions the courts recognised fell into two broad classes. First, in a trio of cases concerning Champagne, Sherry and Scotch whisky respectively, it was recognised that goodwill could attach to the particular *geographical descriptions* in issue.[6] Then, second, in *Erven Warnink Besloten Vennootschap v J Townend & Sons (Hull) Ltd*,[7] the kind of descriptive term held to fall within the compass of goodwill was one that referred to *a fixed recipe* or *certain set of ingredients*. As Lord Diplock put it:

> If a product of a particular character or composition has been marketed under a descriptive name and under that name has gained a public reputation which distinguishes it from competing products of different composition ... the goodwill in the name of those entitled to make use of it should be protected by the law.[8]

On its face, this appears but a modest extension to the concept of goodwill recognised in the earlier drinks cases. Accordingly, it is not immediately obvious why a decision designed to extend the types of descriptive terms in which one might have goodwill should be seen as a milestone in the law affecting consumers. However, as we shall see presently, what sets *Erven Warnink* apart from the other drinks cases is the fact that, in this case, the seemingly modest development in the law that was achieved was firmly anchored to a policy concern not previously expressed in the case law: the concern to protect consumers by promoting consumer welfare. Furthermore, the way this concern was articulated created conceptual room for other such developments in the future.

But here I am in danger of getting ahead of myself. Mindful that relatively few readers of this volume are likely to be familiar with *Erven Warnink*, I must first set out the facts of the case and the decision reached by the House of Lords. This is done in section II. Only against this background can we fully understand the novelty of the case and the avowedly consumer-friendly rationale for its being decided the way that it was. Thereafter, section III proffers a critique of the consumer-welfarist

---

[5] *Perry v Truefitt* (1842) 5 Beav 66, 73 (Lord Langdale MR).
[6] See *J Bollinger v Costa Brava Wine Co Ltd (No 2)* [1961] 1 WLR 277, *Vine Products Ltd v Mackenzie & Co Ltd* [1969] RPC 1 and *John Walker & Sons Ltd v Henry Ost & Co Ltd* [1970] 1 WLR 917 respectively. As regards Champagne and Scotch whisky, the relevant geographical regions are patent. Less well-known, however, is the fact that Sherry, properly so called, comes exclusively from the Jerez de la Frontera province in Spain.
[7] *Erven Warnink Besloten Vennootschap v J Townend & Sons (Hull) Ltd* [1979] AC 731, HL.
[8] ibid 735.

credentials of the decision. More precisely, the putative public interest envisaged by Lord Diplock (and signed up to by three of his brethren[9]) is examined through the lens of micro-economics. Section IV concludes with the suggestion that, although the *direct effect* of the decision in *Erven Warnink* cannot confidently be portrayed as being an unqualified victory for the consumer-welfarist cause, more confident claims about its welfarist credentials can be associated with its *indirect effect*.

II. FACTS AND DECISION

The first claimant – Warnink – was a Dutch producer of an alcoholic drink known as 'Advocaat'. Its main ingredients were eggs and a certain type of spirit known as 'brandewijn'. Despite the name of this ingredient (including as it does the Dutch word for wine) Advocaat contained no wine of any description. The second claimant was an English distributor of Warnink's beverage. Although there were various rival Dutch producers of Advocaat, Warnink had a 75 per cent share of the British market. There were certain minor differences between the competing brands of Advocaat, but they all had the same basic ingredients. It was for this reason that at first instance Goulding J held that Advocaat was a distinctive type of drink.

Warnink's competition in Britain was not, however, confined to fellow Dutch producers, for there was another alcoholic, egg-based drink that was popular among British consumers. This other type of drink was known commonly as 'egg flip'. Unlike Advocaat, the principal ingredients of egg flip were eggs and fortified wine. And although both drinks had roughly the same strength – about 30° proof – the different ingredients meant some difference in taste (albeit a difference that not all consumers were able to detect[10]). A much more profound difference – and one that could hardly be missed – was that of price. Because the excise duty levied on spirit-based drinks was significantly higher than the duty on drinks containing fortified wines, the latter could be sold at a considerably lower price.

The defendants were an English company and a partnership firm who, acting cooperatively, began producing an egg flip drink. But they did not market it as egg flip. Instead, in the words of Goulding J, 'they conceived a plan to profit from the popularity of Advocaat';[11] and this plan involved advertising their egg flip as 'Keeling's Old English Advocaat'. The lower price they were able to charge assisted the defendants in capturing a sizeable share of the British market for alcoholic, egg-based drinks. Predictably enough, their capturing this share of the market caused a loss of sales for the claimants. When litigation ensued, the question for their Lordships was whether the claimants could invoke the tort of passing off to secure an injunction to restrain the defendants from selling or distributing their drink under the name or description, 'Advocaat'. It was held that they could; and an order was duly granted to prevent the

---

[9] *Erven Warnink* (n 7) 748, 749 and 756 (Visocunt Dilhorne, Lord Salmon and Lord Scarman, respectively).
[10] This fact was adverted to by Goulding J at first instance: see [1978] FSR 1, 12.
[11] *Erven Warnink* (n 10) 12.

defendants marketing or selling as Advocaat any product which did not consist, in essence, of eggs and spirits without any admixture of fortified wine.

Although it was acknowledged to be an extension in the scope of the concept of goodwill beyond what had been previously recognised in the cases concerning copycat 'Champagnes', 'Scotch whiskies' and 'Sherries', it was nonetheless considered a justifiable development in the law. Lord Diplock was crystal clear in identifying the consumer interest as the prime justification for this extension. What he said in this regard may usefully be taken in three separate chunks. He began with the observation that:

> Parliament ... beginning in the 19th century has progressively intervened *in the interests of consumers* to impose on traders a higher standard of commercial candour than the legal maxim caveat emptor calls for, by prohibiting under penal sanctions misleading descriptions of the character or quality of goods.[12]

Shortly thereafter, he opined:

> the increasing recognition by Parliament of the need for more rigorous standards of commercial honesty is a factor which should not be overlooked by a judge confronted by the choice whether or not to extend by analogy to circumstances in which it has not previously been applied a principle which has been applied in previous cases where the circumstances although different had some features in common with those of the case which he has to decide.[13]

And ultimately, he concluded:

> Where over a period of years there can be discerned a steady trend in legislation which reflects the view of successive Parliaments as to what the *public interest demands* in a particular field of law, development of *the common law ... ought to proceed upon a parallel rather than a diverging course*.[14]

In this way, then, a concern with consumer welfarism insinuated itself into the law of passing off. It became both a key factor in setting the outer margins of the tort and, more fundamentally and controversially,[15] part of its *raison d'être* (notwithstanding the general tendency of the judiciary to leave the regulation of competition between business rivals to the legislature[16]).

Writing about the tort some years after the decision in *Erven Warnink*, Hazel Carty was emphatically of the view that 'the public interest is part of its rationale'.[17]

---

[12] *Erven Warnink* (n 7) 742–43 (emphasis added).
[13] *Erven Warnink* (n 7) 743.
[14] *Erven Warnink* (n 7) 743 (emphasis added). *Cf* Lord Fraser at [1979] AC 731, 754.
[15] The idea that rules of tort law and tort law decision making should ever be governed by policy considerations – such as the advancement of consumer interests – is a persistently tough one. I have my doubts (see J Murphy, *The Province and Politics of the Economic Torts* (Oxford, Hart Publishing, 2021) ch 6); but I leave them to one side in this chapter where I am concerned only with sketching, as an empirical matter, the consumer-welfarist credentials of the *Erven Warnink* case.
[16] For voluminous evidence, and by far the most thoroughgoing academic defence of, this abstentionist approach, see H Carty, *An Analysis of the Economic Torts*, 2nd ed (Oxford, Oxford University Press, 2010). And for a recent example, see *Times Travel Ltd v Pakistan International Airlines Corp* [2021] UKSC 40 (SC), [33] (Lord Hodge).
[17] Carty (n 16) 267.

And likewise, Christopher Wadlow – unquestionably the most authoritative scholarly voice on the subject of the tort of passing off – recognised the way that consumer interest had become pivotal in setting the boundaries of liability. He observed that the modern law 'confirms that passing off not only protects the private interests of individual claimants, but that *it is fully justified by the public interest* since it also benefits consumers and market participants generally'.[18]

Perhaps even more pertinently, endorsement of Lord Diplock's enunciation of a new rationale for the grounding of liability in passing off was not confined to academic commentators. In *British Telecommunications Plc v One In A Million Ltd*, for example, Aldous LJ remarked (in terms that were almost identical to those used in *Erven Warnink*):

> As Lord Diplock pointed out in the *Warnink* case, Parliament has over the years progressively intervened in the interests of consumers and traders ... [so] [i]t is therefore not surprising that the courts have recognised that the common law, in that particular field, should proceed upon a parallel course.[19]

Much more recently, using slightly different language in a first instance case, Pearce J held that a relevant consideration in deciding whether a claimant should be awarded a remedy for passing off is 'the public interest in allowing applicants to vindicate their legal rights'.[20] In his view, there is 'a particularly strong public interest in allowing and indeed assisting the applicants to pursue this issue ... [given] [t]he reality is that ... customers ... are, in effect, being defrauded'.[21]

Such thinking has clearly also taken root abroad. In the New Zealand case of *Tots Toys v Mitchell*, for example, Fisher J went so far as to identify the consumer's interest (as opposed to the protection of the claimant's property right) as the tort's primary *raison d'être*. He noted that while, 'there is a legitimate private interest in protecting business goodwill against the deceptive conduct of competitors. *Even more importantly*, there is a strong public interest in preserving the means of identifying the source of the products'.[22] And his understanding of the decision in *Erven Warnink* was clearly anchored to there being an infringement of *both* these interests. He observed: 'in the Advocaat case ... the combination of a deception ... with injury to the plaintiff's goodwill justified a remedy'.[23]

For all that the avowed spirit behind the *Erven Warnink* decision has certainly attracted a wide array of supporters, it is nonetheless important not to trumpet too loudly the blow struck for consumer welfarism in that case. What was clearly intended by their Lordships, and what might ultimately transpire from what was decided, *may not* be the same thing.

---

[18] C Wadlow, 'Passing Off at the Crossroads Again: A Review Article for Hazel Carty' (2011) 33 *European Intellectual Property Review* 447, 449. The confirmation was indirect. Wadlow was, strictly, commenting upon Carty's description of the modern law; but since Wadlow acknowledged the correctness of that description, it is apt to say (as I do in the main text) that he saw the modern case law as confirming the centrality of the consumer interest to this tort.
[19] *British Telecommunications Plc v One In A Million Ltd* [1999] 1 WLR 903, 913.
[20] *Domestic and General Group Ltd v Bank of Scotland Plc* [2018] EWHC 3604 (QB), [12].
[21] ibid (n 20) [12].
[22] *Tots Toys v Mitchell* [1993] 1 NZLR 325, 341 (emphasis added).
[23] ibid 359–60.

III. BENEFITS AND COSTS OF THE ERVEN WARNINK DECISION

This section of the chapter seeks to unearth the actual impact of the decision in *Erven Warnink*. It does so in three stages. It examines the extent to which it could achieve the desired beneficial effect from the consumer perspective. It then considers the various costs associated with the decision (together with some attendant limits and counterbalances to those costs). It concludes by sketching certain, further (almost certainly unanticipated) indirect benefits that may be attributed to the way that the decision in *Erven Warnink* emboldened subsequent courts in their development of the law of passing off.

A. The Perceived Beneficial Effect

English law has long since recognised and tolerated the phenomenon of sales puffery whereby false claims about products do not ground contractual liability to a person purchasing the goods in question so long as they were not seriously meant.[24] Nor do such puffs suffice to ground liability under the tort of passing off. As Lord Diplock explained in the *Erven Warnink* case: 'exaggerated claims by a trader about the quality of his wares, assertions that they are better than those of his rivals ... have been permitted by the common law as venial "puffing" which gives no cause of action to a competitor'.[25] What this means, of course, is that consumers must still be on their guard. For, in respect of at least some sorts of misleading claims, consumers can neither bring an action on their own behalf, nor firmly expect that in some circumstances certain third parties – that is, rival traders – will come indirectly to their rescue by securing an injunction for passing off. Sometimes the risks and costs associated with litigation will tip the balance against bringing a lawsuit. And sometimes, the rivals whose goods are being mimicked – especially when they are based overseas with their principal market lying elsewhere – may simply not know of the problem.

Given, then, that the maxim *caveat emptor* has life in it yet, one might think that the inroad into that principle which Lord Diplock considered to be the effect of his decision in *Erven Warnink* was reason enough to applaud it as a welcome blow for the consumer welfare lobby. But things are not quite so simple. In truth, the direct implications for consumers of that decision are very much a mixed bag. True, the case cut back the range of permissible misrepresentations that can be made with impunity in the marketplace. But the decision, nonetheless, carried with it certain costs to consumers not noted by their Lordships. Accordingly, in order to be sure that, on balance, the case was a step in the right direction (from the perspective of consumers' interests), we would need to know two key things.

First, we would have to identify *all of the effects* of this decision. Second, we would also need to know the magnitude of all of these effects. Only then could we say whether *all* the benefits – both direct and indirect – outweigh *all* the costs. Without

---

[24] See, eg, *Lambert v Lewis* [1982] AC 225.
[25] *Erven Warnink* (n 7) 742 (Lord Diplock).

such empirical information, we can at most offer only cautious applause for the consumer-welfarist credentials of the case.

Although their Lordships were right to think that an expansion in the scope of goodwill would increase the range of circumstances in which a remedy can be sought for passing off, it is important to appreciate, also, the limited practical benefit that this brings to consumers. For, in reality, there is only a limited class of misrepresentations concerning descriptions of the quality or attributes of a product that would be likely to mislead. This point requires some unpacking.

Misrepresentations about quality or attributes can be – and generally are – split into three broad categories in the false advertising literature. They are typically referred to as misrepresentations concerning 'search characteristics', 'experience characteristics' and 'credence characteristics'. Search characteristics are qualities that can be identified by cursory inspection prior to purchase. They include things such as a product's size, weight and colour. Experience characteristics are qualities – such as a food product's flavour – that become apparent to the purchaser during or after consumption. Credence characteristics are 'characteristics whose quality cannot be monitored by the nonexpert, even after consumption'.[26] An example of a credence characteristic would be the long-term health benefits of a given food product.

Some reflection on this tripartite division helps reveal the limited scope for misrepresentations that are likely to deceive customers. And an appreciation of the limited scope for consumers to be misled helps place in proper perspective the utility of any development in the law that has been introduced in order to prevent or curb such deception.

Because search characteristics are so easily discovered by consumers, false claims about such qualities are easily exposed, perhaps even obvious. For this reason there is little or nothing to be gained by making such misrepresentations. On the other hand, there is a great deal to be lost, such as the producer's trading reputation if found out.[27] Even without the assistance of a pro-consumer approach to the law of passing off, then, there is already a hefty disincentive in place to curb the use of misrepresentations about search characteristics.

Much the same can be said about false claims concerning experience characteristics.[28] There has always been a limited return for traders who make false claims about the experiential qualities of relatively cheap products that are repeatedly consumed (such as food and drink). This is because consumers will naturally adopt a 'once bitten, twice shy' attitude towards such goods. Indeed, it is only possible to perceive a genuine incentive to make misrepresentations of this kind about high value products that are typically only bought as a one-off. Yet even here, the present-day plethora of online customer review platforms makes it almost as easy to ascertain, *ex ante*, the

---

[26] ER Jordan and PH Rubin, 'An Economic Analysis of the Law of False Advertising' (1979) 8 *J Legal Studies* 427, 530.
[27] See S Naresh, 'Passing-Off, Goodwill and False Advertising: New Wine in Old Bottles' [1986] *CLJ* 97, 121.
[28] At one time it was thought that such goods 'must be consumed to be evaluated': Jordan and Rubin (n 26) 529. But personal consumption is no longer necessary in light of the volume and style of online consumer reviews.

truth about experiential characteristics as it is to discover the truth about a product's search characteristics.

The conclusion to which I think the foregoing impels us is that, in the modern era, there is – even without the decision in *Erven Warnink* – a significantly reduced facility to pull the wool over consumers' eyes.[29] Indeed, it is really only in the sphere of the misuse of hard-to-imagine descriptive names that pertain to credence characteristics that the decision in *Erven Warnink* is likely to have any immediate impact. But even here, consumer magazines and online reviews[30] can again assist the wary purchaser, subtracting yet more direct benefit from the decision in that case. Thus, without wishing to suggest that their Lordships were wrong to think that what they decided in *Erven Warnink* was beneficial to consumers, it is important to get a sense of the limited *direct benefit* that it confers.

B. Other Direct Effects

As against the limited direct positive effects of the decision in *Erven Warnink* must be weighed various (potential) costs – none of which were mentioned, or perhaps even recognised, by their Lordships. Three of these can helpfully be highlighted with the help of microeconomic analysis.

i. Loss of Consumer Surplus for Undiscerning Consumers

Loss of consumer surplus is an idea employed by economists. It refers to *a fall* in the difference between the price actually paid by consumers for a given product and the price that they would be prepared to pay (where the overall number of sales to these customers remains constant).

To appreciate the problem in play here, it is important to make two prefatory observations. The first is that all of the passing off cases concerning alcoholic drinks centre on issues associated with what economists call 'substitute goods'. The second is that, copycat drinks – whether imitations of Champagne, Sherry, Scotch whisky or Advocaat – are only substitutes for *some consumers*: those who are, for example, indifferent as between, say, a sparkling wine of no particular provenance and authentic Champagne. The significance of these two prefatory points will become clear in what follows.

In the *Erven Warnink* case, a key finding of Goulding J at first instance was as follows:

> An expert can well distinguish a wine-based drink, such as the defendants', from the traditional form of Advocaat supplied by the plaintiffs. That was successfully demonstrated by one of the plaintiffs' witnesses at a tasting attended by junior counsel on both sides, and by other evidence also. I have little doubt that a layman, if a regular drinker of one or other

---

[29] One particular deterrent of note in connection with comestibles is s 15 of the Food Safety Act 1990 which now makes it an offence to mislead as to the 'the nature or quality or substance' of any food.

[30] For other examples, see Naresh (n 27) 122.

type of beverage, could do the same. On the other hand, there is no such gross difference of taste, colour, or other qualities, as would lead the inexperienced or casual customer to regard them as different species of drink.

On the basis of this finding, it is clear that the drinks produced by the defendants and claimants respectively were only perfect substitutes in relation to the final class of consumers: the inexperienced/casual drinkers who were undiscerning. But, even so, we may reasonably assume that the number of such people was fairly large. For, in the absence of a large number of people prepared to accept the inferior drink, Warnink would not have suffered the loss of custom that occurred, and which prompted their seeking an injunction.[31] At the same time, however, it is only in relation to such undiscerning consumers, now forced to pay more for a bottle of 'Advocaat' after the injunction had been granted – that a loss of consumer surplus would be suffered. An illustration probably helps.

Assume that certain customers are happy to pay up to, say, £15 for a bottle for 'Advocaat' (whether it be genuine Dutch Advocaat or an English copycat). Assume, also, that genuine Dutch Advocaat retails at £12 per bottle, while an English egg flip (that is also marketed as 'Advocaat') sells for just £10 per bottle. For anyone indifferent as between the two – persons who regard them as substitute goods – there is a consumer surplus of £5 on the imitation drink compared to a consumer surplus of £3 per bottle on the genuine product. The removal of the facility to market the copy-cat drink by injunction results, *for these customers*, in a loss of consumer surplus when, at any future juncture, they subsequently elect to buy Advocaat. Of necessity, they would only be able to buy genuine Dutch Advocaat, and this would cost them £12. It is the granting of the injunction, and nothing else, that causes the loss (of consumer surplus) for these consumers.

But to be clear, the disbenefit is confined to just these consumers. For those consumers for whom the two drinks were *not perfect substitutes*, the *Erven Warnink* decision would in fact be doubly beneficial. It would prevent any future false labelling of the defendants' product and thereby help to build confidence among them that they were getting exactly what they expected every time they bought Advocaat.[32] Also, the injunction would help prevent the making of purchases that would produce a negative consumer surplus (ie, ones in which the discerning consumer was misled into buying imitation Advocaat at a price *above what they would be prepared to pay for the copycat drink*). That said, it seems unlikely that there would be many such customers for whom only 'the genuine article' would do. For, were this the case, the initial inroad into Warnink's market would probably have been followed by a bounce back in sales when the inferior product was later rejected by them as an inferior good.

---

[31] It is true that some sales of Keeling's egg flip will have gone to discerning consumers who did not feel that the additional cost of genuine Advocaat was justified. But there is no reason to think that these would have accounted for the vast majority of the sales. After all, even the small survey referred to by Goulding J revealed that casual drinkers and occasional purchasers were unable to tell the difference. Extrapolating from these figures would suggest that large numbers of sales went to undiscerning customers.

[32] This, in turn, might promote the making of further positive consumer surplus purchases.

Another reasonable supposition – though, of course, this cannot be known for sure – is that most purchasers of Advocaat fell into the second of the categories identified by Goulding J. After all, those in this second group were described as 'regular drinkers' of the product. But whether any benefit for these regular consumers of having the copycat drink removed from the market can be said to outweigh the loss of consumer surplus caused to consumers in the third class (ie, the irregular, undiscerning drinkers) cannot be guaranteed. For, mere membership of the second group does not translate into an automatic unpreparedness to accept the inferior product. It means only that a member of this class is able to tell the difference in taste. To know for sure, then, whether the *Erven Warnink* decision would result in a greater overall benefit (or greater overall cost) to consumers, one would require precise empirical data.

C. Monopoly Costs

There are always costs for consumers where monopolies exist. But before considering this issue in depth, we must note Goulding J's key finding that, when the litigation began, 'and for at least 12 years previously, the plaintiffs had sold 75 per cent or more of the Advocaat marketed in the United Kingdom'.[33] In other words, *Warnink* had a solid monopoly in relation to Advocaat sales in the UK, and they were therefore able to impose a monopoly price designed to maximise profits rather than maximise consumer welfare.[34] At least three significant costs to consumer welfare can therefore be attributed to the fact that the *Erven Warnink* decision helped prop up a monopoly.

The first such cost is a conversion of consumer surplus into a producer surplus: that is, the difference between the price at which a trader would be prepared to sell, and the price at which the trader is able to sell. The second cost is referred to by economists as deadweight loss of consumer welfare.[35] Such deadweight loss equates to the loss of consumer welfare caused by virtue of there being a sub-optimal – that is to say, allocatively inefficient – outcome in terms of demand and supply for a product.[36] The third is a much less technical problem associated with the loss of consumer choice and the lack of product improvement frequently associated with monopolies.

The first two costs just mentioned can be represented in diagrammatic form. They appear in Figure 1, below.

---

[33] *Erven Warnink* (n 10) 5.

[34] It is generally accepted that a trader with a 25% market share (or greater) has the ability to exert monopoly power.

[35] Where monopoly prices are imposed, there would also be a deadweight loss of producer surplus; but that is immaterial to the question of whether the *Erven Warnink* decision deserves to be seen as having credible consumer-welfarist credentials. It is also irrelevant to monopolists whose only concern is to maximise profits.

[36] It is referred to as *deadweight* welfare loss because it represents a loss of a consumer surplus that is not recovered as a producer surplus. It is lost for good!

Figure 1

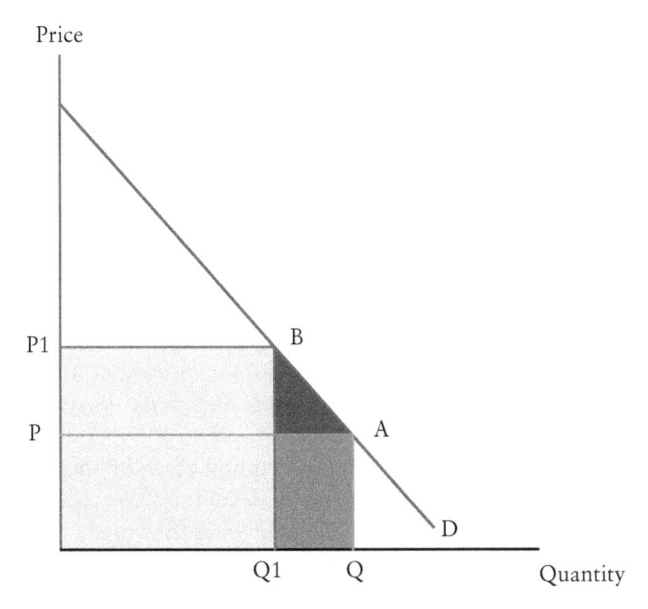

Although the representation in Figure 1 relates to a pure monopoly, in which there is a single supplier, it nonetheless serves well enough for present purposes given that the claimants had close to an entire market share. In the diagram, P represents the price that would be charged at an allocatively efficient level of production: that is, a level of production that would be achieved under perfectly competitive circumstances. However, where a monopoly exits, the supplier who dominates the market is able to fix a monopoly price that is appreciably higher than this. In the diagram, this monopoly price is given at the level P1.

The line sloping downwards from left to right is the demand curve: a linear representation of the fact that more of the product in question will be bought at progressively lower prices. At price P, the revenue generated would be P-A x A-Q (ie, price charged multiplied by the quantity sold). Visually, it would be the total area encompassed by the lower of the two yellow rectangles *plus* the area of the blue rectangle.

At the monopoly price P1, the supplier sells less of the product in order to maximise profits. This augmentation of profits is clear from the fact, although less is being sold at P1 (which would involve a lower cost of production), more revenue is being earned. The total revenue generated at the monopoly price is P1-B x B-Q1. It is captured by the totality of the yellow shading. The amount by which revenue has risen is represented by the area of the upper yellow rectangle *minus* the area of the blue rectangle.

Accompanying the supplier's profit maximisation is the more troubling phenomenon (for present purposes) of deadweight loss of consumer welfare. At price P, the total consumer surplus is captured by the combined area of: (1) the purple triangle; (2) the upper yellow rectangle, and (3) the blank triangle whose base is the line P1-B. At price P1, a great deal of the consumer surplus is lost. The upper yellow rectangle forms one part of this loss. It is the part that is transferred into a producer surplus. The second part of the loss of consumer surplus is represented by the purple triangle.

This second part of the loss of consumer surplus is the deadweight loss of consumer welfare caused by monopoly pricing. It is an overall loss in societal welfare, and it is one borne purely by consumers.

To summarise, then, when injunctions for passing off help to prop up a monopoly (as in *Erven Warnink*), there is a considerable loss in consumer welfare that can be expected via the introduction of monopoly pricing. Some of this consumer surplus is captured as producer surplus, but some of it is lost altogether as deadweight loss. These problems did not afflict the other drinks cases. There are so many genuine Champagne producers, for example, that the problems associated with monopoly power could not occur when it was held that calling one's wine, 'Spanish Champagne' amounted to passing off. It follows that Naresh goes too far in suggesting that an injunction granted in cases such as the Champagne case 'does more to protect existing producers from fresh competition than it does to protect consumers from false information'.[37] But in certain sectors of commercial activity – as was the case with Advocaat – this claim could well be grounded.

A final potential cost associated with the granting of an injunction in a case like *Erven Warnink* is that of restricted consumer choice. It will be recalled that English producers of the rival drink had historically sold what they made under the banner, 'egg flip'. The adoption of the name 'Keeling's Old English Advocaat' was a deliberate marketing strategy designed to generate sales that would come at a cost to the claimants. And the strategy succeeded. As Lord Diplock noted:

> 'Keeling's Old English Advocaat' captured an appreciable share of the English market for advocaat and, as the judge found at p 13, damage had been thereby caused to Warnink … and 'such damage would not have occurred, or would have occurred to a much smaller extent, had the defendants not used the word 'advocaat' as part of the description of their goods'.[38]

Having the freedom to advertise their drink as 'Advocaat', in other words, facilitated the defendants' ability to compete with Warnink (whose product, recall, accounted for roughly 75 per cent of all such sales in the UK). Eliminating the defendants' ability to compete in this way did not force them out of business,[39] but it might have done had their operations been more marginal.

The point, then, is that where a monopoly for a certain type of product is held by *Trader X*, an injunction of the kind granted in *Erven Warnink* serves as a barrier to competition. In some cases, it may make the difference between a prospective manufacturer being able or unable to enter the market with its own rival product. And in an extreme case it could conceivably force a marginally profitable existing competitor out of the market. In either case, the injunction will serve to bring about a restriction on substantive consumer choice and possibly, also, a disincentive on the part of the monopolist to continue to improve their product.

In short, the granting of injunctions in circumstances such as the ones with which this chapter is concerned may be said to benefit consumer choice in the sense that

---

[37] Naresh (n 27) 125.
[38] *Erven Warnink* (n 7) 735.
[39] The company is still trading today!

consumers will almost certainly be properly informed (or at least not misled) as to the provenance and quality of the goods they elect to purchase. There is, however, a price to be paid for the absence of misinformation which, to a large extent, may also be cashed out in terms of consumer choice. To be more specific: the cost of certainty as to the origins and quality of the goods that one buys may well be a restriction in the range of goods available and the quality of those goods (where a monopoly exits and there is no especial incentive constantly to improve the quality of those goods). The consumer may also be required to pay for their better informed choices in a more obvious way, namely, via the higher prices that monopolies are able to impose.

D. Indirect Beneficial Effects

Thanks largely to the growth in popularity of online shopping, together with the seemingly ubiquitous availability of accompanying consumer reviews, misrepresentations of the *Erven Warnink* variety are much less likely to deceive consumers in the present era than they were at the time that case was decided. But even so, the decision in that case may nonetheless be considered the source of two further consumer-friendly developments within the law of passing off. First, it can be seen as having played a part in the quite separate extension of the tort to cases involving supposed product endorsements by celebrities. Some commentators considered this further extension wrongheaded on the basis that it fails to fit the classical conception of goodwill, the accepted gist of the tort.[40] But for all their scepticism in this regard, it is clear from *Irvine v Talksport Ltd*,[41] that an important part of the justification for the concept of goodwill being stretched to cover cases of celebrity endorsement was the self-same consumer-welfarist desire to promote commercial honesty that was aired in *Erven Warnink*.

In *Irvine*, the defendant had distributed, as part of a promotion campaign, a brochure with a picture of the claimant on the front page. He was a well-known racing driver, not a trader with customers. The picture showed him holding a portable radio bearing the radio station's name. Laddie J granted the claimant an injunction to prevent this unauthorised use of his image. Using language that closely resembled Lord Diplock's in *Erven Warnink*, he remarked that the tort of passing off 'is a judge-made law which tries to ensure, in its own limited way, a degree of honesty and fairness in the way trade is conducted'.[42] In this way, then, he helped reduce the risk that consumers would in future be duped into making purchases of products that had not in fact been endorsed by some or other highly respected celebrity. A prominent subsequent case involved the use of an image of the popstar Rhianna on clothing popular among presumptively gullible teenagers.[43]

---

[40] The principal problem surrounding the celebrity endorsement cases centre on the goodwill requirement. For details, see M Spence, 'Passing off and the Misappropriation of Valuable Intangibles' (1996) 112 *LQR* 472, 479.
[41] *Irvine v Talksport Ltd* [2002] EWHC 367 (Ch), [2002] 1 WLR 2355.
[42] ibid, [13].
[43] *Fenty v Arcadia Group Brands Ltd (No 2)* [2015] EWCA Civ 3, [2015] 1 WLR 3291, CA.

The second positive indirect effect of *Erven Warnink* can be observed in the development of the concept of 'reverse passing off': a situation in which the defendant represents that the claimant's goods are in fact their own (rather than – as per the classic case of passing off – misrepresenting that their goods are those of the claimant). The decision in *Bristol Conservatories Ltd v Conservatories Custom Built Ltd*[44] is instructive, here. In that case, the defendants' salesmen showed potential customers a portfolio of photographs of conservatories produced by the claimant which misled them into thinking that they were the defendants' own conservatories. If a customer then ordered a conservatory from the defendants, it would be one of their own design and manufacture (and not one of the kind seen in the photographs) that would be supplied. In considering whether the law could be extended to cases of such reverse passing off, and just prior to citing the passage in Lord Diplock's speech in *Erven Warnink* in which future courts were enjoined to develop the law in ways that paralleled various consumer-friendly statutes, Ralph-Gibson LJ said:

> I see no reason to hold that their Lordships in the *Warnink* case expressly or by implication ruled that the tort of passing off outside the extended form approved and established by the actual decision in the *Warnink* case should be limited to the classic form of a trader representing his own goods as the goods of somebody else.

In other words, he interpreted *Erven Warnink* as providing a basis for an extension of the law beyond typical source misrepresentations and beyond cases involving quality misrepresentations of the kind that featured in the various drinks cases. The decision in the *Bristol Conservatories* case took the tort into pastures new. And the court identified the legitimacy of this novel development as residing in Lord Diplock's dictum in *Erven Warnink*. Reverse passing off, as a new form of the tort, was clearly seen to be a means of protecting consumers' interests by creating a legal disincentive on the part of traders to engage in a previously unregulated form of commercial misrepresentation.

IV. CONCLUSION

Lord Diplock saw the extension of the concept of goodwill in *Erven Warnink* as being a step that was consistent with the promotion of consumer interests. It would be going too far to say that this was the only, or perhaps even the main, driver behind the decision in that case.[45] Yet he was clearly of the view that the removal, by injunction, of the facility to mislead purchasers as to the true ingredients of a product was important in the interest of consumer welfare. For some (discerning) purchasers of egg-based, alcoholic drinks, the decision in *Erven Warnink* was doubtless a boon.

Yet the decision in that case was not an unqualified triumph for the consumer welfare cause. In the particular context of beverages of the kind in issue, the decision could be seen as a disappointment for those customers who were just as happy

---

[44] *Bristol Conservatories Ltd v Conservatories Custom Built Ltd* [1989] RPC 455, CA.
[45] He also made firmly the point that he found it 'impossible to draw a *rational* distinction between the instant case and the champagne case', noting also that in the previous drinks cases 'the fact that ... the descriptive name under which goods of a particular type or composition were marketed ... happened to have geographical connotations ... [was] without significance': *Erven Warnink* (n 7) 739, 745.

consuming imitation Advocaat as they were consuming the genuine article. They might not even have realised, in some cases, that they had been buying egg flip when they purchased 'Keeling's Old English Advocaat', for as Goulding J noted at first instance: '[t]he public knows of egg flip as an alcoholic drink, sold as *something different from advocaat*.'[46] For these customers the decision of the House of Lords ushered in a loss of consumer surplus.

The decision also brought with it a set of consumer costs associated with the fact that it helped prop up Warnink's monopoly. When such costs are taken into account, it is entirely possible that the aggregate direct effect of the *Erven Warnink* decision was more harmful than beneficial from a consumer welfare perspective. But there were indirect effects, too, and these must not be ignored. For Lord Diplock's general point in the case that, henceforth, the tort of passing off should be developed along consumer-welfarist lines played a significant role in the extension of the tort to two new types of case in which there exists considerable scope for consumer deception. Overall, then – and largely for reasons *other than* those that the Law Lords had in mind – *Erven Warnink* really does, on balance, deserve to be seen as landmark case in consumer law.

---

[46] *Erven Warnink* (n 10) 11.

Part II

Rethinking the Role of Consumer Law

12

Of Marginal Gains and Opportunities Missed: The Lost Landmark of *Constantine v Imperial Hotels Ltd*

TONI WILLIAMS*

An innkeeper owned two inns in the same vicinity. A traveller asked for accommodation at one of them and was refused, but he was supplied with accommodation at the other.

Held, that the innkeeper was in breach of his duty at common law.[1]

I. INTRODUCTION

THIS ABSTRACT FROM a first instance, apparently anodyne, decision suggests it is an odd choice as a landmark case in consumer law. The official Kings Bench report covers fewer than 15 pages, including the summaries of lawyers' arguments, and the case appears to have been cited rarely if at all.[2] *Constantine v Imperial Hotels Ltd.*, a case in which a Black man sued a central London hotel that refused to honour a booking he had made for himself and his family, does not appear in histories of consumer law or feature in contract, tort or consumer law casebooks and contemporaneous commentary in law journals is sparse.[3]

By contrast, the incident that led to the lawsuit, the trial of the dispute, and the judgment were covered extensively in the media in the UK and beyond.[4] Questions were

---

* My thanks to workshop participants and the editors of this book for helpful comments on earlier drafts of this chapter. Thanks also to Asta Zokaityte and Iain Ramsay for insightful conversations over many years about the ways that contract law perpetuates inequalities and injustice. Any errors or oversights are mine.

[1] *Constantine v Imperial Hotels Limited.* [1944] KB 693, 694.

[2] Westlaw indicates that 'there is no substantial judicial treatment of it' (Sept 2021).

[3] Cambridge Law Journal published a casenote (1945) 9 *The Cambridge Law Journal* 123 and the case is footnoted in a 1949 article in the *Modern Law Review*: P Hartmann, 'Racial and Religious Discrimination by Innkeepers in U.S.A.' (1949) 12 *Modern Law Review* 449. By the 1960s, the case had begun to be cited by scholars working on the Race Relations Act and similar measures, eg, BA Hepple, 'Race Relations Act 1965' (1966) 29(3) *Modern Law Review* 306–14.

[4] See sources cited in sections III and IV below.

asked about it in Parliament,[5] with one MP calling for non-renewal of the Imperial hotel's licence, another asking what the government was doing 'to prevent the exercise by hotel-keepers and others of racial discrimination which is repugnant to the traditions of this country?'[6] and a third demanding 'that racial discrimination against Colonial subjects in this country [be] made illegal'.[7] The story of Constantine's experience, as told in sporting literature, radio broadcasts and in books and articles in British history and culture, is said to have influenced the development of the UK's first Race Relations Act in the 1960s;[8] and biographers of the judge and the plaintiff's lawyers include *Constantine v The Imperial Hotels* among the more noteworthy trials in the distinguished careers of their subjects.[9] In 2022, the author of a book on law aimed at a general readership included *Constantine* on his list of the ten most significant cases to the development of modern Britain.[10]

It was this juxtaposition of invisibility to consumer law with the scale of its notoriety then and now that made *Constantine v The Imperial Hotels* stand out as, potentially, a lost landmark of the field. This chapter explores that potential, asking why was the case lost to consumer law education and scholarship and what would its rehabilitation, some 80 years after the triggering incident, contribute to the understanding of the legal regulation of consumer market relations? It investigates these questions through research into primary sources including archives, newspaper stories, parliamentary debates and law reports and secondary research of historical and cultural literature on the reception of the case and on some of its main actors. Based on this research, the chapter argues that *Constantine v the Imperial Hotels* was 'lost' for two main reasons: first, because the decision adopts the typical methodological technique of common law of suppressing information about consumer identities and about the social and political context of the disputed transaction. This technique had the effect of erasing from the official report the elemental fact that the case was brought to challenge entrenched practices of racial discrimination in British cities that denied consumers who were people of colour access to hotel accommodation (and many other markets). Absent such information, the official report is somewhat perplexing and indeed may be more likely to baffle than to enlighten the reader in search of insight into the development of consumer law.[11]

A second reason for the case being lost stems from its failure to tackle the powerful freedom of contract ideology that equates contractual sovereignty with freedom *from* contract to which other fundamental contractual freedoms – freedom *to* contract

---

[5] *Hansard* House of Commons Debates 22 September 1943 vol 392 cc189-91.
[6] ibid, MP T Driberg.
[7] ibid, MP R Sorenson.
[8] I Bing, *The Ten Legal Cases that Made Modern Britain* (La Vergne, Biteback Publishing 2022). The Race Relations Act 1965, c.73 outlawed racial discrimination in 'places of public resort' and established a Race Relations Board to oversee compliance and the resolution of difficulties when discrimination in such places occurred.
[9] H Montgomery Hyde, *Norman Birkett: the life of Lord Birkett of Ulverston* (The Reprint Society, 1965) H Heilbron, *Rose Heilbron: The Story of England's First Woman Queen's Counsel and Judge* (Oxford, Hart Publishing, 2012) H Montgomery Hyde, *Sir Patrick Hastings: His Life and Cases* (London, Heinemann, 1960).
[10] Bing (n 8).
[11] See discussion of reasons below.

and freedom to co-create contract terms – are subordinate. This ideology poses a significant barrier to justice for consumers because it fosters market environments in which providers of goods and services may deny consumers access to them for capricious or discriminatory reasons without paying compensation or being subject to any other form of accountability. In the *Constantine* case, the person denied access to the hotel of his choice was a popular celebrity and the hotel's refusal to serve him (and more generally racial discrimination across the hotel sector) had been condemned in Parliament as well as in the court of public opinion. The circumstances were therefore favourable for the court to examine freedom of contract in consumer markets and evaluate the role it plays in perpetuating exclusionary practices against minorities. But that opportunity was missed with the effect that the remedy found by the judge, though symbolically meaningful at that time, left intact the equation of contractual freedom with the power to exclude.

Notwithstanding those limitations, it is important to acknowledge that the *Constantine* decision does award a remedy to someone subjected to the indignity of racial discrimination and that this outcome was widely publicised. Whatever the shortcomings of the reported reasons, a contextualised reading of the case makes this nascent recognition of the consumer interest in dignity abundantly clear. For this reason, the chapter concludes that knowledge of this case enriches understanding of how common law has constituted consumer markets and as such *Constantine v Imperial Hotels* deserves a place amongst the landmark cases of consumer law.

The remainder of the chapter develops these claims more fully. Section II introduces the plaintiff, Mr Learie Constantine, and describes the social and historical context in which the events at the Imperial hotel occurred. Section III is an account of the incident that Mr Constantine decided to challenge and how his story was received in popular culture. Section IV summarises the litigation and section V outlines the implications of the decision for understanding how contract law, left to its own devices, enables the practice of exclusion and discrimination in consumer markets.

II. SOCIAL AND HISTORICAL CONTEXT

In an era marked by phenomena such as the cult of celebrity and the 'national treasure', it perhaps is not difficult to relate to the popular interest the case of *Constantine v The Imperial Hotels* evoked when the incident came to light in Autumn 1943 and again when the action was tried in Summer 1944. Mr (subsequently Sir and then Lord) Learie Constantine was then well-known in the UK as a highly-skilled, successful and entertaining cricketer.[12] Selected for the first ever West Indies touring side in 1923 and then the first official Test team from the Caribbean to visit England in 1928,

---

[12] Constantine later qualified as a barrister in England and then served as party chairman of the People's National Movement in Trinidad and Tobago and as a minister in the first majority government led by party founder, Eric Williams. In the early 1960s, he returned to England as an independent Trinidad and Tobago's first High Commissioner in London. He was knighted in 1962 and then in 1964 returned to legal practice together with cricket journalism after finishing his ambassadorial role, in somewhat contested circumstances. Constantine was appointed a founding member of the Sports Council in 1965 and the Race Relations Board established under the 1965 Act and awarded a peerage in 1969 when, as the first black man

he had made his mark as an allrounder with spectacular fielding skills as well as the ability singlehandedly to influence the outcome of a match with intimidating fast bowling, assertive batting, or both.[13] A famous performance at Lords, the spiritual home of first class cricket, one that Constantine himself considered his 'greatest ever against a fashionable team', showcased these skills and served to launch the cricketer in the popular imagination.[14] John Arlott, a doyen of mid-twentieth-century cricket writing, commented that 'the reports alone of [that] match established him in the imagination of thousands who had never seen him play …. [N]ext day all cricketing England accepted a new major figure'.[15]

Building on this triumph – and to fund his ambition to become a barrister after his cricketing career – at the end of the 1928 West Indies tour, Constantine signed up to join the Lancashire League club of Nelson as a professional, the first Black or West Indian cricketer to be so employed and reputedly the highest paid professional cricketer in the game.[16] During the 1930s, Constantine's fame grew with the outstanding success that he brought to the club, the attention he drew to the Lancashire League (along with a much welcome increase in funds through gate receipts and sponsorship),[17] the 1933 publication of his first book memorialising his life in cricket, *Cricket and I*,[18] and a noteworthy performance in his final test match in August 1939, which was also the last game of first class cricket played in England before the declaration of war against Germany.[19]

Although first class cricket was then suspended until May 1945, charity matches were staged to boost morale whenever organisers could assemble enough star players

to sit in the House of Lords, he became Baron Constantine of Maraval and Nelson. B Scovell, *Learie: The Man who Broke the Colour Bar* (The Book Guild Ltd, 2021). J Hill, *Learie Constantine and Race Relations in Britain and the Empire* (London, Bloomsbury Academic, 2018).

[13] He was considered the star performer on the 1928 tour and one of the few members of the team to perform to their potential. Arlott, Wisden obituary: available at: wisden.com/almanack/learie-constantine-one-of-the-first-great-caribbean-cricketers-almanack (accessed 1 February 2023).

[14] S Watts, *Sporting Witness*, BBC Sounds: www.bbc.co.uk/sounds/play/w3cszh5x (hereinafter Watts) (accessed 1 February 2023). Constantine scored 86 in less than an hour during the first innings, took 7 wickets for 57 runs and then scored 103 runs in an hour during the West Indies' second innings. See Calder for commentary on the impact of this performance on Constantine's standing in the game: A Calder, 'A Man for all Cultures: The Careers of Learie Constantine' (2003) 6 *Culture, Sport, Society* 19.

[15] Arlott (n 13).

[16] Hill (n 12); Scovell (n 12).

[17] Nelson cricket club finished top of the league in seven of the nine years in which Constantine played and was runner up in the other two years, Scovell (n 12). Calder writes about Constantine's astounding impact on Nelson's fortunes and on gate receipts across the entire league after Constantine's arrival.

> In Nelson, a town of 40,000 people, attendance might exceptionally reach 14,000 …. Rival clubs also profited from increased home gates when Constantine played against them …. [T]he president of the league in 1934 reported … that between 1929 and 1933, gate receipts in matches involving Nelson – one-seventh of the total – accounted for 75 per cent of all receipts. Note that this was a period of calamitous economic slump. Yet whereas the average number of paying spectators for Lancashire League matches had been just below 200,000 per year between 1924 and 1929, between 1930 and 1935 it was over 260,000.

Calder (n 14) 31.

[18] *Cricket and I*, (P Allan, 1933). Written with the assistance of the journalist, intellectual, fellow Trinidadian and one-time lodger, CLR James.

[19] This match, played at the Oval, which was then requisitioned, was one of Constantine's better Test match performances. Constantine took 5 wickets for 75 and on the penultimate day of the match scored 78. Watts (n 14). Calder (n 14); H Pearson, *Connie: The Marvellous Life of Learie Constantine* (Abacus, 2017).

to make an entertaining match and find a venue that had not been requisitioned for war purposes. Constantine remained active in the game as a celebrity player selected by others to appear in various all-star XIs and as an organiser of such matches through his employment as a welfare officer to West Indians working in Liverpool to support Britain's war effort.[20] Indeed, Mr Constantine's booking at the Imperial Hotel was made to give him a base in London for matches he had organised in which he was to play for a Dominions team against an England XI at grounds in Surrey and then at Lords. His play for various all-star Dominions, Empire and West Indies teams had kept Mr Constantine in the public eye during the early years of the war, so by July 1943, the date of his encounter with the hotel, Learie Constantine was a household name in English popular culture and as such was well-placed to bring attention to racial exclusion from access to consumer markets for goods and services in Britain.

By then Mr Constantine also had considerable understanding of the lived experience of racial discrimination in England, some of it personal, acquired from incidents at cricket matches, his travels and his life in Nelson, a Lancashire mill town where 'hardly any black people had ever lived'[21] before the arrival of Mr Constantine and his wife, and through miscellaneous racist encounters in hotels and at cricket clubs.[22] Subsequently Constantine deepened his knowledge (both personal and observational) of discriminatory practice in England from information shared through networks to which he belonged, such as the League of Coloured Peoples, an important mid twentieth century advocacy group for Black people in the UK,[23] and his welfare officer work in Liverpool, for which he was awarded an MBE.

In the 1940s, Liverpool, like other British west coast port cities such as Cardiff and Bristol as well as London, had a long-established Black population that pre-dated the second world war by several decades. Their experiences of racial exclusion and injury were multiple and complex and, in some respects, varied according to national origins, community histories and the interests of the British state.[24] The West African seamen employed by the Elder Dempster Shipping Company, for example, were abandoned by the state which generally chose to ignore the company's cruel exploitation

---

[20] A January 1944 newsletter of the League of Coloured Peoples records a gift in the sum of £92 10s from Learie Constantine as the proceeds of the charity matches he had organised the previous summer, likely including the fateful match for which he booked the Imperial Hotel, 52 Vol IX (January 1944) issue of *The Keys*, The newsletter of the League of Coloured Peoples, 53, available at: www.movinghere.org.uk/deliveryfiles/BL/025NWLT194401/0/2.pdf (accessed 1 February 2023).

[21] Scovell (n12).

[22] Scovell ibid ch 6 describes racist behaviour, mostly expressed as microaggressions, see also, S Hulme, *Racial Equality in Britain – Learie Constantine* (BBC, 2018); Watts (n 12). Hill offers a nuanced account of the family's relationship with the town and club in which over time the town invested the family with perceived 'white' characteristics of social mobility, ambition and local pride such that belonging, respect and eventually acclamation came to displace the racial othering and hostility they had initially experienced. Hill (n 12). See also L Constantine, *Colour bar* (S. Paul, 1954), especially 135–38.

[23] D Whittall, 'Creating Black Places in Imperial London: The League of Coloured Peoples and Aggrey House, 1931–1943' (2011) 36 *The London Journal* 225; AS Rush, 'Imperial Identity in Colonial Minds: Harold Moody and the League of Coloured Peoples, 1931–50' (2002) 13 *Twentieth Century British History* 356; D Killingray, *Race, Faith and Politics: Harold Moody and the League of Coloured Peoples: An Inaugural Lecture given by David Killingray on 23 March 1999* (Goldsmiths College, 1999).

[24] J Belchem, *Before the Windrush: Race Relations in Twentieth-century Liverpool* (Liverpool, Liverpool University Press, 2014) P Fryer, *Staying Power: The History of Black People in Britain* (London, Pluto Press, 2010).

of them except when the workers' resistance became perceived as a threat to public order.[25] Black children of mixed race relationships, by contrast, were often subjected to intensive scrutiny and control.[26]

The experiences of West Indian migrant workers of the 1940s were of particular concern to officials because of the wartime imperative to mobilise labour from across the empire and the legacies of Britain's poor treatment of their predecessors who had come to Britain to support the war effort during the First World War.[27] To avoid repeating past mistakes, the Colonial Office invested in initiatives to enhance wellbeing and development, with the dual goals of upskilling workers and inculcating positive feelings towards the UK. A comment in *The Times* about the creation in 1942 of an Advisory Committee on the Welfare of Colonial Peoples in the UK[28] illustrates Britain's sensitivity to how it was perceived. The editorial observes that if the imperial project was to evolve as desired from 'tutelage' to 'partnership', 'it is of the first importance that those who come to this country from the Colonial Empire shall feel that here too the partnership is a fact and not a phrase'.[29] Warning that '[r]acial discrimination is not always easy to avoid', the editorial advises the new committee that it 'has a task of no small importance to discharge' because those:

> who make these islands their temporary home are in a special sense representatives of their own lands; and it is a duty as well as an interest that they return with an abiding impression of the tolerance, seemliness, and good will of the English way of life.[30]

West Indian workers who answered Britain's call for assistance during the war were British subjects who had high expectations of being treated with dignity in a place they considered the 'mother country' and they made known their displeasure when they encountered discrimination at work or were excluded from accommodation and leisure facilities. According to John Carter, a Secretary to the League of Coloured Peoples, one of the main self-help and support groups for Britain's Black communities, the imported workers '[l]ike most West Indians refuse to appreciate anything that savours of colour discrimination and are never inarticulate or ambiguous in voicing their disapproval of any attempt to institute barriers'.[31] As a welfare officer, Mr Constantine's role was to provide support by advising, problem-solving, connecting the workers with local communities, organising entertainment opportunities,

---

[25] Belchem (n 24).

[26] See, eg, literature on the work of Liverpool philanthropic agencies during the 1930s purportedly aimed at improving the welfare of mixed-race children, but, as Christian and others show, much of it was inspired by eugenicist ideas and directed at limiting with a view to elimination over the longer term of the social problem perceived to be embodied by the 'half-caste' offspring of (usually) black men and white women. M Christian, 'The Fletcher Report 1930: A Historical Case Study of Contested Black Mixed Heritage Britishness' (2008) 21 *Journal of Historical Sociology* 213; Belchem (n 24).

[27] Problems include the British state reneging on commitments about repatriation and support for the workers after the First World war and its failure to protect them against the violence of race riots that broke out in many port cities in the summer of 1919. Commenting on Liverpool, Fryer labels the violence as the raging of 'an anti-black reign of terror' Fryer (n 24) 306.

[28] Hansard House of Commons Debates 28 June 1944 vol 401 cc727-8W. The Committee's documents are in the National Archives Kew, CO 876/69.

[29] 'Colonials in Britain' *The Times*, 24 September 1942, 5.

[30] ibid.

[31] League of Coloured Peoples, *Twelfth Annual Report, 1942–43* 13.

facilitating access to leisure spaces, and, through his employer the Ministry of Labour, keeping the Colonial Office informed of significant sources of unhappiness and grounds for unrest.

The 1942 arrival of American troops in the UK after the US entry into the war made a difficult situation worse for West Indian workers (and most other black men).[32] The British Government repeatedly expressed concern about the dangers of importing the US's racist 'Jim Crow'[33] policies and practices and declined to institutionalise de jure racial segregation. However, its leadership did not nothing to prevent the de facto segregation that the US military reproduced as best it could on British soil.[34] While the government could have acted to outlaw racial discrimination, for example, through licensing requirements on leisure and entertainment facilities, it chose instead to commission for American GIs pamphlets and public information films about the benign nature of 'race relations' in Britain and hope for the best.[35] Predictably enough, that educative approach had little effect on behaviour, so that the arrival of white American troops in British communities often heralded an increase in racial exclusion – and also physical violence – against their Black residents.[36]

Reporting in December 1943 on conditions in the recreational sectors in the Northwest, Arnold Watson, Mr Constantine's boss at the Ministry of Labour, recounts several incidents indicative of deterioration in access to commercial leisure facilities after the white Americans arrived, including:

> Since the first contingent [of West Indians] arrived in February, 1941, they have made use of the Grafton Dance Rooms. ... [I]n recent times [the Grafton] has degenerated on occasion into a racial fighting ground between coloured British subjects and white Americans. The Manager resented these happenings and has, therefore, barred coloured people from attending. The West Indians also frequented the Rialto, which has also been banned to them.[37] ...

---

[32] Black members of the American military (approximately 10% of American troops in the UK), by contrast, often experienced better treatment in the UK than at home, and there is evidence that in some areas, white British residents would side with Black GIs against white US military personnel, especially when the latter sought to inscribe segregation in British spaces. For an overview of this complex topic, see materials curated by the Imperial War Museum at: www.iwm.org.uk/history/they-treated-us-royally-the-experiences-of-black-americans-in-britain-during-the-second-world-war (accessed 1 February 2023); and the 2009 documentary 'Choc'late Soldiers from the USA', www.mediafusionent.com/choc-late-soldiers (accessed 1 February 2023). See also, NA Wynn, "Race War': Black American GIs and West Indians in Britain During The Second World War' (2006) 24 *Immigrants & Minorities* 324.

[33] 'Jim Crow' is the popular name given to the intricate web of state and local laws and practices that enforced racial segregation in the US (including in many parts of the country ostensibly 'lawless' violence such as lynching) after the formal abolition of slavery. Many of these laws and practices remained in effect until the second half of the 20th century. For discussions of tensions over the importation of 'Jim Crow' practice in the UK along with the white GIs, see, O Ayers, 'Jim Crow and John Bull in London: Transatlantic Encounters with Race and Nation in the Second World War' (2020) 20 *Studies in Ethnicity and Nationalism* 244 Wynn (n 32).

[34] G Schaffer, 'Fighting Racism: Black Soldiers and Workers in Britain during the Second World War' (2010) 28 *Immigrants & Minorities* 246.

[35] Eg, Welcome to Britain, 1943: www.iwm.org.uk/history/welcome-to-britain (accessed 1 February 2023).

[36] Wynn (n 32); Schaffer (n 34), 'Choc'late Soldiers from the USA' (n 32).

[37] Arnold Watson Report re: Limited Entertainment Options for West Indian Technicians and Trainees in the Northwest, 18 December 1943, LAB/26/55. Belchem, (n 24), for a detailed account of how 'colour bar' practices intensified once the Americans had arrived.

Another example in the report drew on a newspaper story about a dance hall that quoted a West Indian worker whom Watson knew to be 'a decent and self-respecting citizen, who attends regularly to his work ….'.³⁸ According to the newspaper, the manager of the Casino Dance Hall had initially operated a patriotically inclusive policy that anyone fit to contribute to the war effort was fit to use his facility and had thus advised the worker that 'as long as he paid his admission money and behaved with his usual good manners the doors would be open to him and he would be welcome'.³⁹ But the manager changed to an racially exclusionary approach after receiving a letter from a Captain of the US Army, asserting:

> it is not our intention to dictate the policies of privately-owned establishments, but in the interest of eliminating trouble in which our troops may be involved, we will appreciate your co-operation in prohibiting Negroes from attending the dances.⁴⁰

Watson comments on bitterness and resentment that such experiences understandably evoked among the West Indian workers, citing, for example, two technicians

> respectable fellows both and well-known to me [who] rang me up independently and in some distress … there was some talk of the men leaving their work, and there was a strong feeling that the Minster of Labour ought to take protective action on their behalf. Mr Constantine was able to quiet any [collective] action on the part of the men, and reported informally to the Colonial Office.⁴¹

The report is riddled with concern that the impact of such experiences on the workers would evolve into antagonism and hostility towards Britain if the country was not seen to protect men who were British subjects and contributing to the war effort. To counter damaging accusations that nothing was being done about the colour bar and 'in the hope that we may ensure that the men will go back with an undiminished faith in us', Watson proposed greater visibility to proactive initiatives to improve the lives of the West Indian workers, especially in the consumption sphere of leisure and entertainment,⁴² initiatives that included the cricket matches organised by Mr Constantine.

Additional evidence of British pandering to the segregationist demands of the US military during the war surfaces in accounts of Mr Constantine's exclusion from the Imperial Hotel but a colour bar from residential accommodation and some hotels and leisure facilities had been operational in London and other British cities since well-before the war.⁴³ Its effects were felt most brutally by students who were British subjects from African and West Indian territories in London to study for the

---

³⁸ ibid 2.
³⁹ ibid.
⁴⁰ ibid, quoting story in the *Daily Despatch*.
⁴¹ ibid (Watson Report) (n 37) 1–2.
⁴² ibid 2–3.
⁴³ Killingray (n 23); (n 24). In the early 1930s the League of Coloured Peoples led a campaign against racist exclusion of Black people from British hotels and lodging houses, which included correspondence with the Secretary of State for the Colonies. For an example of a dismayed, but not overly exercised response by the minister to a letter from Harold Moody, the head of the LCP, see P Cunliffe-Lister, *Draft of Letter from Philip Cunliffe-Lister to Harold Moody re: Treatment of Africans in England* (May 13, 1932 CO 323 – National Archives at Kew 1932). A pictorial essay by Historic Environment Scotland paints a vivid picture of the imposition of a colour bar in 1920s Edinburgh blog.historicenvironment.scot/2021/01/the-edinburgh-colour-bars/ (accessed 1 March 2023).

professional qualifications to which they had no access at home,[44] but it also ensnared famous or rich people of colour. In 1925 the chairman of the Strand Licensing Sessions used his annual report to warn hotels not to exclude customers on the basis of race, citing an incident in which a couple from 'one of our Crown Colonies', 'quite charming and cultured people', had booked a hotel in advance for their visit to see the British Empire Exhibition and were then denied the room 'solely because of their colour'.[45] In 1929, a campaign to effect change was organised by an MP, James Marley, after stories broke that Paul Robeson, the famous Black American singer, actor and intellectual, was denied service at the Savoy Hotel and Robert S Abbott, the founder of the *Chicago Defender* (then the highest circulation black owned newspaper in the world), was refused accommodation by several London hotels.[46] Similar stories were reported throughout the 1930s and early 1940s, provoking the *Observer* newspaper during the leadup to the 1937 coronation festivities to entreat 'public opinion' to reject the 'colour bar existing in some hotels and boarding houses',[47] and the Indian High Commission in 1941 to complain to the Secretary of State after Sir Hari Singh Gaur, a distinguished jurist, social reformer and parliamentarian, was refused accommodation at a London hotel.[48]

During the 1920s and 30s, much of the opposition to the colour bar was mobilised by and on behalf of Black and Indian students whose campaigns for hostel accommodation often served the purposes of political organising as well as their practical needs for shelter.[49] A 1932 county court case reported in a few newspapers, however, references one wealthy student's use of litigation in a dispute that foreshadows the Constantine case.[50] In this case, Mr Oluvole Ayodele Alakaya,[51] a graduate of Oxford University and nephew of a Nigerian leader, succeeded in an action for breach of contract against New Mansions Hotels after the hotel refused to let him use the accommodation he had prebooked. Mr Alakaya had booked the room and full board for 10 months to give him a home while he studied to become a barrister. He was initially received by the hotel and shown to a room, but while unpacking

---

[44] E Ramsden, 'Students in London', *Times*, 27 August 1938 6.

[45] 'Colour Bar at Hotels: Bench Warning to Licensees', *The Manchester Guardian*, 4 February 1925 9.

[46] 'Our London Staff. Colour Bar in London: Paul Robeson's Story 'No Admission.' Famous Hotel's Disclaimer', *The Manchester Guardian*, 23 October 1929 11; 'Colour Bar in London: Hotelkeepers Invited to Meeting', *The Manchester Guardian*, 15 October 1929 17; 'Our London Correspondence: An Hotel Colour Bar?', *The Manchester Guardian*, 29 August 1929, 8.

[47] 'The World and the Coronation: London Ready for Her Guests – Equality for All', *The Observer*, 21 February 1937 17; see also, 'Turned Away by 20 Hotels', *Sunday Mirror*, 6 May 1934 2. 'London Hotel and Indian Team', *Daily Telegraph*, 9 February 1935 14. 'Colour Bar at Swimming Pool', *Daily Telegraph*, 17 August 1935 8.; 'London's Colour Bar, Professor who Cannot go Into an Hotel', *The Manchester Guardian*, 17 December 1931 16.

[48] 'Our London Staff, the Colour-Bar: A Distinguished Indian's Experience', *The Manchester Guardian*, 19 June 1941 6. 'The Colour Bar: Policy that Makes Enemies', *The Manchester Guardian*, 14 July 1941 6.

[49] M Matera, *Black London: The Imperial Metropolis and Decolonization in the Twentieth Century* (Oakland, University of California Press, 2015).

[50] 'Colour Bar: Twelve Guineas Damages for a Law Student Against Hotel – Surprise For Clerk', *Daily Mirror*, 2 March 1932 7. 'African Student Sues Hotel 'Colour Bar' Alleged: A Prince's Nephew in English Court', *The Times of India*, 30 March 1932 5. 'Colour Bar at London Hotel', *Daily Telegraph*, 2 March 1932 5.

[51] Accounts of the case do not agree on the spelling of the plaintiff's name. Variants include: Alakya, Alakiya, Alakaya.

his luggage was told to leave because the hotel had no space for him. Since this was patently not the case, Mr Alakaya queried the decision and was then told he had been denied service because the hotel catered to white people only.[52] The judge found for Mr Alakaya, awarding him costs and 12 guineas, just over 20 per cent of the £55compensation he had claimed. Despite this finding on the specific facts of the case, the judge reinforced freedom of contract by indicating that the hotel would have been free to exclude the student had it known he was black,[53] and even considered seriously whether Mr Alakaya had an obligation to disclose his race at the time of booking to enable the hotel to deny him service.[54]

III. THE EVENTS AT THE IMPERIAL HOTEL

Like Mr Alayaka, Mr Constantine had booked his accommodation in advance. He had organised some celebrity cricket matches, in which he would play, to entertain (amongst others) the West Indian migrant workers he supported in the North West. The matches were to be played at venues in Surrey and London and, because they would take him away from home for four days, Mr Constantine decided to bring his wife and daughter with him on the trip. Personally and professionally familiar with the racial discrimination at Britain's hotels, he or his staff had checked in advance that the Imperial Hotel had 'no objection to serving coloured people'.[55] After assurances that he and his family would not be mistreated because of colour or race, Constantine concluded that the Imperial Hotel was safe and paid the deposit on two rooms for himself, his wife, and their daughter.

Upon their arrival at the hotel on 30 July 1943, however, it quickly became evident that Mr Constantine and his family were not welcome. Accounts of precisely who said what to whom and when vary across the multiple versions of the story told in books, newspapers and other media, but the common elements are that the family encountered hostility from a woman at the front desk who told them that they could not stay at the hotel for the four nights they had booked.[56] An unhappy Mr Constantine then asked to speak to the manager, with whom he insisted on the contractual nature of his rights and the hotel's obligations. The manager reiterated that the family could not stay at the Imperial hotel ostensibly to avoid upsetting the hundreds of American troops using its facilities and offered them rooms at a sister

---

[52] See above n 50.

[53] Colour Bar: Twelve Guineas Damages (n 50).

[54] 'Colour Bar at London Hotel' (n 50).

[55] The Times Law Report refers to this fact (as do Constantine's accounts of the events at the hotel) but it is not mentioned in the KB report, Law Report, 28 June *Times*, 29 June 1944 2; Constantine (n 22) 137. Constantine recounts a litany of racist micro and not-so-micro aggressions experienced by himself, his family and people he knew (n 22) 135–37, before concluding at 138: 'I could multiply these stories of personal slights indefinitely, but it would not do good. I have learned how to take them as an unpleasant part of daily life in Britain for anyone of my colour.'

[56] *The Times* reported on two days of the hearing, High Court of Justice, *Times*, 20 June 1944 2. and High Court of Justice, *Times*, 22 June 1944 2 and reported the judgment against the hotel on 29 June 1944, Law Report (n 55).

property in the vicinity. Mr Constantine stood his ground, citing his identity as a British subject as well as his contractual rights. Arnold Watson, Mr Constantine's boss from the Ministry of Labour and a white man, arrived during this conversation to find 'Mr and Mrs Constantine ... looking most disconsolate and unhappy'.[57] After speaking to the woman and finding her intransigent and noting that she referred to the Constantines using a vile racist epithet,[58] Mr Watson suggested that 'in the interests of peace and dignity they should view the alternative accommodation and accept it if it were suitable'.[59] Mr Constantine and his wife followed the suggestion and the family stayed at the Bedford Hotel, owned by the same company as the Imperial, where they were apparently 'treated very well'.[60]

The story became public about a month later when Mr Constantine gave a 'frank broadcast talk' in which he talked about his family's experiences of racism in the UK, citing specific examples from his early days in Nelson and more recently in Liverpool, commenting that 'the daily humiliations hurt and make you bitter if you are not careful'.[61] It emerged that the incident at the Imperial Hotel had been reported to the Colonial Office and that consideration of suitable responses was underway in several fora. Newspapers published letters to keep the story in the public eye,[62] discussions were held within advocacy groups and questions were asked in Parliament.[63] In response to which the Home Secretary, Herbert Morrison, affirmed in a written answer the existence of a common law obligation on hotels 'not to exercise arbitrary discrimination' and declared

> failure to accord to a British subject in this country the full equality of status and treatment to which he is entitled ... is deeply deplored and strongly condemned by responsible public opinion throughout the United Kingdom.[64]

---

[57] Law Report *Times* (n 56).
[58] ibid.
[59] 'Colour Bar: Alleged London Hotel Incident', *The Manchester Guardian*, 3 September 1943 6.
[60] Law Report *Times* (n 56).
[61] 'Colour Bar: Mr Constantine On His Experiences', *The Manchester Guardian*, 4 September 1943 6. See also G Padmore article in the *Chicago Defender*, 'Parliament To Debate Color Ban In Britain – Cricket Star On BBC Radio Blasts Hotel' 25 September 1943 and Hulme (n 22).
[62] Eg, letter from K Little, then affiliated with the University Museum of Archaeology and Ethnology at Cambridge, who in 1942 had drawn the attention of the Colonial office to the incipient racial segregation spreading across British cities and the risk it posed to its reputation in the colonies and would subsequently publish one of the first systematic studies of 'race relations' in the UK. In a letter published on 13 September, Little observed:

> it is unfortunate, perhaps, that reports of this type of incident are not circulated more widely and more often in the press. Absence of comment ... may give the impression that the experience suffered by Mr. Constantine is a rare phenomenon .... On the basis of some 700 inquiries made before the war, I have estimated that something like 60 percent of the private and commercial establishments over a large part of England, ordinarily in the habit of taking guests of good standing, were unwilling to accommodate a coloured person.

'The Colour Bar: Letter to the Editor of the Manchester Guardian', *The Manchester Guardian*, 13 September 1943 4; see also, letter from Harold Moody as Founder and President of the League of Coloured Peoples, *The Manchester Guardian*, 11 Sept 1943.
[63] *Hansard* House of Commons Debates (n 5); House of Commons Debates 23 September 1943 vol 392 cc443-4W. Rush describes extensive coverage of the story in the newsletter of the League of Coloured Peoples, Rush (n 23).
[64] *Hansard*, House of Commons Debates (n 63).

MPs and commentators debated British traditions of fair play and equality, the pervasiveness of the colour bar and the contradictions of expecting people of colour to support Britain's war effort against the racist ideology of Germany's Nazi party when the country tolerated racial discrimination against them; and there was criticism of British institutions deferring to the wishes of US military personnel.[65] What the government showed no inclination to do, however, was to take legislative or regulatory measures. In October 1943, for example, Socialist MP, Tom Driberg, asked the Minister of Food to consider withdrawal of catering licences from hotels and other businesses that discriminated amongst customers based on colour, to which the Minister responded that while sympathising with the sentiment he was not then prepared to take such action.[66]

Although litigation was just one of many avenues chosen to tackle racial exclusion, by Summer 1944, when the action was tried, it had become evident that anti-discrimination legislation was not imminent and that social sanctions such as parliamentary scolding, reprobation, and bad publicity had made little difference to the everyday practice of hotels, lodging houses and leisure facilities.[67] Harold Walduck, the managing director of the Imperial, articulated the combination of personal disinterest and commercial imperative fuelling racially exclusionary practice of hotels and leisure facilities when he stated that his hotel:

> … caters for white people, and at the present time they are largely Americans. For myself, I don't care whether they are black or white or green or yellow. I only carry on the hotel to meet the requirements of the patrons …. There is not a ban on coloured people at this hotel. We prefer to cater for white people, but there is no question of coloured people being an inferior race.[68]

For those who wished to see an end to legally permitted discrimination, considerable hope was invested in Mr Constantine's suit in which he claimed substantial

---

[65] See Hansard debates referenced above in nn 5 and 63. For other examples of coverage of public mood and discussion, see, eg, David Low's famous cartoon, 'Imperial Welcome' (*Evening Standard* 1943), available at the British Cartoon Archive at the University of Kent: archive.cartoons.ac.uk/GetMultimedia.ashx?db=Catalog&type=default&fname=DL2058.jpg (accessed 1 February 2023) and stories such as, 'What Are We Going To Do About This?' *Sunday Mirror*, 19 September 1943; 'Magistrate Says No Colour Bar Here', *The Observer*, 5 September 1943 (a magistrate's reprimand of white Canadian soldiers whose racist remarks directed at Black soldiers in a Hammersmith hotel caused a fight). 'Claim U.S. Army Officers Carry Jim Crow To London', a story by George Padmore, a radical Black journalist based in London, published in a Norfolk, Virginia newspaper, *New Journal and Guide* 02 Oct 1943. Padmore informs his American readers that:

> The incident has taken on country-wide criticism and is expected to produce governmental condemnation of the hotel management's behavior. The fact that the management had asked Constantine to leave the hotel at the instigation of U.S. Army officials living there has caused even greater gossip and complications.

[66] *Hansard*, House of Commons Debates 13 October 1943 vol 392 cc879-80.
[67] Archival documents recording continuing problems include, LN Constantine, *Extract of letter from L. N. Constantine to Arnold R. Watson, re: Racial incident with white American soldiers in the Black Horse pub, London, May 8, 1944* (LAB/26/55); Sir F Leggett, *Letter from F. W. Leggett to Sir George Gater, re: Little improvement in colour bar situation on Merseyside, June 13, 1944* ((LAB/26/55) National Archives at Kew 1944). A Watson, *Letter from Arnold Watson to J. J. Taylor, re: Colour bar issue in Merseyside will not be taken seriously by locals unless addressed by Colonial Office, May 10, 1944* ((LAB/26/55) National Archives at Kew 1944).
[68] 'Colour Bar: Mr Constantine on His Experiences', *The Manchester Guardian*, 4 September 1943 6.

(exemplary) damages for breach of contract to recognise that the hotel's denial of service had violated his – and his family's – dignitary interests.[69]

IV. THE LITIGATION

The case was tried in front of Norman Birkett J, sitting without a jury from 19–22 June 1944, in a room that doubled as a temporary air-raid shelter at the Law Courts[70] and which the *Pittsburgh Courier* reported 'was packed with Africans, West Indians and Afro-American soldiers'.[71] Learie Constantine was not the only famous person in the makeshift court room. The senior barrister on his team was Sir Patrick Hastings KC, one of the country's most eminent lawyers. Hastings was by then almost at the end of a long, high-profile career that included a short stint as Attorney-General to the first Labour Government but mostly had been spent as barrister in criminal trial courts.[72] He was known in professional circles and popular culture for outstanding advocacy skills that swayed juries, including 'a facility for plain and lucid speaking … a fine dramatic sense … [a capacity for] effective brevity'[73] and the 'power of deadly cross-examination'.[74] He was not, though, known to excel in learned argument, scholarly depth or legal imagination, which was perhaps unsurprising in a man who had no academic legal education. Constantine's second lawyer, Rose Heilbron, by contrast, had graduated with a first-class degree in law from the University of Liverpool, and had also completed a Masters degree in law, as the first woman to realise both achievements. Though still in the earlier years of what would become an exceptionally distinguished career as a barrister and judge in which she overcame many barriers to women's success,[75] by 1944 Heilbron already was well known within the profession and, as one of very few women in law, her trials were often covered by the local media in Liverpool. Like Hastings, she was primarily a criminal lawyer and together they comprised 'probably the best legal team it was possible to find in wartime'.[76]

The judge, Norman Birkett, was an extremely prominent figure in the legal profession and he had also spent time in politics. In 1935, *Daily Express* readers had voted him one of the top 20 public personalities they most enjoyed reading about.[77] As a lawyer his career overlapped with that of Hastings, and he too had

---

[69] See, eg, Hulme (n 22), where Constantine indicates that his action was inspired by his daughter's reaction and Constantine (n 22) where he writes of a wish to prevent others being similarly victimised.
[70] Hyde (n 9).
[71] 'Hotel Manager Fined; Barred West Indian', *The Pittsburgh Courier*, 8 July 1944.
[72] Biographers report that Hastings was renowned for his skill in cross-examination, Hyde (n 9).
[73] Hyde ibid 3.
[74] Birkett's foreword to Hastings biography, ibid xiv.
[75] Heilbron's many distinctions include her 1949 appointment as one of the first two women to become King's Counsel and in 1974 only the second woman to be appointed a High Court judge. See generally, Heilbron (n 9).
[76] Bing (n 8) 69.
[77] Others in the list include Winston Churchill, Lloyd George, Rudyard Kipling, Greta Garbo, Franklin Roosevelt, Mussolini, Gracie Fields and the Aga Khan. Hyde (n 9) 419 citing to the *Daily Express*, 1 February 1935.

been lauded for persuasive advocacy skills in front of juries mostly in criminal trial courts and his facility with facts, rather than expertise with the conceptual apparatus of law. The two men had frequently argued cases with or against each other, and they admired each other's skills.[78] Birkett had been appointed to the High Court in 1941, where, according to his biographer, Montgomery Hyde, he found the work challenging and anxiety-provoking.[79] One year after the Constantine decision, he accepted an appointment as the alternate British judge at the Nuremburg trials of major German War Criminals and in 1949 he was appointed to the Court of Appeal.[80]

Mr Constantine (and many press commentators) understood the dispute as a straightforward matter of breach of contract, but the hotel conceded that point at the start and there was no attempt to argue that anything other than nominal damages could be awarded for that breach. Instead, the case was litigated as a breach of the hotel's common law duty to receive and lodge a traveller. The three days of hearings presented Mr Constantine's lawyers with a platform to showcase their trial skills and gave the newspapers plenty of sensational copy on the everyday practices of racial exclusion. Mr Constantine emerged from the examination-in-chief as a bastion of respectability and a quasi-heroic figure, an impression that the hotel's lawyer was unable to shake. Ultimately, the judge found that Mr Constantine had carried himself

> with modesty and dignity, dealt with all questions with intelligence and truth, was not concerned to be vindictive or malicious, but was obviously affected by the indignity and humiliation which had been put on him and had occasioned him so much distress and inconvenience, which he most naturally resented.[81]

The hotel worker, by contrast 'cut a lamentable figure' and was exposed as a bigot and liar.[82] Once the credibility of Mr Constantine had been established and that of the hotel staff shredded, it was a relatively simple matter for the Court to find that the Imperial Hotel had breached its common law duty to receive and lodge the plaintiff.[83]

The question of remedy, by contrast, was complex and the argument convoluted. The Constantines made no claim for material loss because they had been lodged in another hotel at no extra cost. Instead, the judge was asked to award exemplary damages to recognise the circumstances of the injury and the unjustifiable humiliation and distress occasioned by the breach. Having found for Mr Constantine on

---

[78] Birkett described Patrick Hastings as 'one of the outstandingly brilliant advocates of his day and generation' in his 1961 BBC lectures, subsequently published as 'Six Great Advocates'. N Birkett, *Six Great Advocates* (London, Penguin Books, 1962). Hastings wrote to Birkett upon the latter's appointment to the Bench 'I know you will make a Judge of whom we shall all be proud, and above all one to whom we shall all be devoted, and amongst all those who may appear before you there will be none who will wish you greater happiness than Your devoted friend, Pat Hastings.' Hyde (n 9) 475.
[79] Hyde writes at 486 that for much of 1944, Birkett 'was inclined to distrust his abilities as a judge and to wonder whether he should not give up his judicial work altogether', ibid.
[80] ibid.
[81] Law Report (n 55).
[82] 'Manageress a Lamentable Figure in Witness-Box', *Dundee Evening Telegraph*, 28 June 1944 4.
[83] The hotel's lawyers tried to argue that lodging the plaintiff in a sister hotel was adequate so that there was no refusal to lodge, which argument the judge dismissed unceremoniously at 697.

the facts and conducted an extensive review of authorities on remedies for violations of common law rights through actions in defamation, maintenance, conspiracy, malicious prosecution and in protection of voting rights as well as one case on the equivalent obligation to lodge and receive in Scottish law,[84] Birkett J, held that it was not open to him to award substantial compensation for the injuries to dignity that had been incurred when the hotel caused Mr Constantine 'much unjustifiable humiliation and distress'.[85] But in recognition of the breach of a common law right to be received and lodged, he awarded Mr Constantine nominal damages in the sum of 5 guineas for violation of a common law right.[86]

V. IMPACT OF CONSTANTINE

The outcome of the case was widely publicised, appearing in local newspapers across the UK as well media outlets in other countries.[87] Commentators then and now regarded the case as marking the point at which English law finally demonstrated a capacity to acknowledge or respond to racial discrimination.[88] Certainly, a high-profile decision by a Court of Record to compensate a Black consumer for violation of a common law right supports the view that *Constantine v Imperial Hotels* is a breakthrough of some kind. And there is at least one reported instance of a case decided shortly afterwards that could potentially represent a virtuous afterglow effect, albeit that the legal issue and social problem were different.[89] That case concerned an appeal against conviction of a Black man, George Roberts, for failing to attend Home Guard duties without reasonable excuse. Mr Roberts was a West Indian worker in Liverpool; he had refused to report for duties in protest after being denied entry to a dance hall twice because of his race, once while wearing his uniform.[90] At his appeal, where Mr Roberts was defended by Rose Heilbron and supported by Constantine in his welfare officer role, the Liverpool Recorder cut the fine from £5.00 to a token sum

---

[84] *Rothfield v North British Hotel*, 1920 S.C. 805, a case that reeks of anti-semitism.
[85] [1944] KB 693 [708].
[86] Mr Constantine also recovered 'limited costs' according to the Manchester Guardian's report of the outcome, which reported that hotel had already paid 10 guineas into court '£5 5s Damages For Mr Constantine: The Hotel Case', *The Manchester Guardian*, 29 June 1944 3. So the total payment by the hotel for its racist conduct in excluding Mr Constantine is £15 guineas, or approximately £469.71 today, according to moneysorter, www.moneysorter.co.uk/calculator_inflation2.html#calculator (accessed 1 March 2023).
[87] Eg, 'Constantine Wins', *Nottingham Evening Post*, 28 June 1944 4 'Learie Gets Damages', *Trinidad Guardian B.W.I.* 29 June 1944 1. 'Constantine Awarded 5 Gns. Damages', *Derby Daily Telegraph* 28 June 1944 8, 'Hotel To Pay Damages To West Indies Cricketer', *Gloucestershire Echo*, 28 June 1944 4, 'Cricketer's Action Against Hotel', *Dundee Courier*, 29 June 1944; 'Learie Gets Damages', *Trinidad Guardian*, 29 June 1944. 'Cricketer Awarded Nominal Damages', 4 July 1944. *Guinea Gold (Papua New Guinea: 1942–1945)* 4; 'Test Player Gets Verdict', *The Sun (Sydney, NSW: 1910–1954)*, 29 June 2; 'British Court Ruling Hits Color Ban In London Hotel', *The Chicago Defender*, 8 July 1944; 'Hotel Manager Fined; Barred West Indian' (n 71).
[88] Eg, Heilbron (n 9); Bing (n 8).
[89] 'Recorder On Colour Bar', *Times*, 2 August 1944 2.
[90] This incident occurred at one of the venues referred to in Watson's report on colour bar practices in Liverpool, cited at n 37.

of one farthing and, alluding to the *Imperial Hotels* case, denounced racial exclusionary practices in trenchant terms:

> When people come here to risk their lives they are entitled to think that they are coming to conditions of decency and order .... If they find .... A noisy and intolerant minority are not prepared to give them equal rights, I think they have a right to be angry ...
>
> I think it is impertinence for any country to accept the aid of coloured people from any part of the world and then to say: 'Our laws don't enable us to deal with you on terms of complete equality. This hotel may refuse you at the expense of a nominal fine ....' If you accept aid from coloured people you should accept them as your friends and as people whose aid you are proud to receive. They should be the first to receive justice at your hands, and if they do not receive it it is a shameful business. Who is it that shuts the door of the Grafton Room to a man who comes here to fight for us, or shuts the doors of the Imperial Hotel to men like Mr Constantine?[91]

Beyond this example in which it appears that the Constantine decision emboldened a court to take account of discrimination against a Black man, it is useful to examine what the case did or did not achieve for consumers of hotel and leisure services in Britain. To start, it is worth asking to what extent the outcome was even a 'victory' for Mr Constantine? Recall that he sought substantial or exemplary damages for injury to dignity because of the hotel's offensive conduct towards him and his family. Much of the legal argument focused on this point and indeed this claim to substantial damages is cited as the reason for the case not being argued in terms of contractual damages, which the judge and both sets of lawyers agreed could not have been more than nominal.[92] But nominal damages is precisely what the judge did award for breach of the common law right despite his specific finding that 'Mr Constantine suffered ... much unjustifiable humiliation and distress'.[93] Contrary to the popular telling of the story it thus seems, first, that Mr Constantine did not get what he wanted from the law and, second, that the same result of a symbolic victory effecting little material change to the parties as ensued via the judge's complex and circuitous tour of doctrine about protecting a common law right could have been achieved more simply and coherently by reasons based on breach of contract.

That said, and because contractual damages are unavailable to those who have been denied entry to a contract, it is important to consider whether the case achieved a different goal that was a priority for Constantine, the workers he served, his boss, the Colonial Office and campaigners for change: that is, the (re)opening up of hotels and leisure facilities to people who were routinely confronted with systematic exclusion on racist grounds. On this point, a close read of the reasoning again suggests that the decision is inconclusive. True, the judgment awards a remedy on a basis that would be available to any individual who had been denied service even if they had no

---

[91] The *Guardian* version of the story 'The Colour Bar In England: Recorder's Denunciation Of A 'Noisy, Intolerant Minority'', *The Manchester Guardian*, 2 August 1944 3.
[92] Times Law Report (n 81). See J Gardner ch 8 in this volume for analysis of *Jarvis v Swan Tours* where compensation for distress and disappointment was allowed by the courts in 1972.
[93] [1944] KB 708.

contract, that is breach of the duty to receive and lodge. According to the version in the Times Law Report, however, the Imperial Hotel

> conceded that Mr Constantine was a man of high character and attainments, a British subject from the West Indies, and that although he was a man of colour no ground existed on which the defendants were entitled to refuse to receive and lodge him.[94]

This concession offers a lot to unpack, and its theme of Mr Constantine's respectability, which recurs throughout contemporaneous accounts of the trial, renders ambiguous the scope of protection against discrimination that the decision purports to offer. In other words, it invites the question: does the decision affirm a remedy for racial exclusion from hotels and lodging houses to all consumers at risk or only to those whose racialised identity intersects with indicia of their respectability that are legible to those with the power to exclude?[95]

More obviously, the extent of protection in consumer markets that the *Constantine* case offered is limited by the scope of the common law right to be received and lodged on which it focused, which evidently does not fall on recreational and leisure facilities that do not involve boarding. One might ask also whether the sanction of nominal damages was likely to change anything at all about the practices or affected businesses or if, as the Liverpool Recorder quoted above mused (and as happens so often in consumer cases), the remedy amounted to little more than a minor tax on doing business in an unjust fashion. A George Orwell editorial in the *Tribune* published in August 1944, shortly after the *Constantine* decision, with nary a mention of the case, is perhaps a reminder of its limitations in this respect. In response to yet another instance of a recent colour bar from a London dance hall, Orwell exhorted 'ordinary people' 'to be vigilant against this kind of thing and to make as much public fuss as possible whenever it happens'. With typical perspicacity he outlined the tawdry, everyday social practice by which the views of what he considered to be a minority of 'colour-snobs' would come to prevail in recreational spaces:

> The trouble always arises in the same way. A hotel, restaurant or what-not is frequented by people who have money to spend who object to mixing with Indians or Negroes. They tell the proprietor that unless he imposes a colour bar they will go elsewhere. They may be a very small minority, and the proprietor may not be in agreement with them, but it is difficult for him to lose good customers; so he imposes the colour bar.[96]

Orwell sought to mobilise the power of ordinary people to counter racial exclusion because in his view there was little popular racist sentiment at that time. Despite the currency of the Constantine case, he does not even reference law as part of the solution.

---

[94] Times Law report (n 55).
[95] AS Rush makes this point effectively, Rush (n 22) 379–81.
[96] Orwell continues: 'This kind of thing cannot happen when public opinion is on the alert and disagreeable publicity is given to any establishment where coloured people are insulted. Anyone who knows of a provable instance of colour discrimination ought always to expose it. … For this is one of those matters in which making a fuss can achieve something …. [T]he ordinary Indian, Negro or Chinese can only be protected against petty insult if other ordinary people are willing to exert themselves on his behalf.' In 'As I Please Editorial' in *Tribune* 11 August 1944, available at: www.telelib.com/authors/O/OrwellGeorge/index.html (accessed 1 February 2023).

Without stating the point explicitly, Orwell's comment exposes the ways that the concept of 'freedom of contract' functions as the institutional foundation of racial exclusion in consumer markets. Freedom of contract does this work because the dominant interpretation of the concept in common law is that freedom *from* contract has a higher social value than and prevails over other contractual freedoms, importantly freedom *to* contract as well as freedom to participate in the setting of contract terms. As a result of this conceptual choice, contract law and its offspring give permission to the providers and distributors in consumer markets to decide which consumers get access to goods and services, and it denies protections to consumers who are excluded from access on pernicious grounds such as racial identity despite their ability to pay. Notwithstanding the claims of microeconomic theory, evidence across time and places show that competitive dynamics do not reliably constrain the absolute power of freedom from contract.[97] On the contrary, one powerful effect of this embedding of freedom *from* contract into the institutional framework of consumer markets is that contract law naturalises, normalises and thus renders invisible its method of permitting systemic and structural forms of disadvantage, such as racial discrimination and market exclusion, to be practiced. Reinforcing this structural work of normalising exclusion that freedom of contract performs, consumer law has tended to reframe the discriminatory and unjust effects of structural disadvantage as the consequences of personal characteristics of 'vulnerable' individuals whom law should assist.

Constantine reveals the inadequacy of that framing. Mr Constantine was neither poor nor unsophisticated. He was fully aware of the risk that racial bigotry posed to the choices he wanted to make and sought to manage that risk by checking with the hotel in advance of his trip. Furthermore, Mr Constantine was backed by the British establishment, and he had the court of public opinion on his side. That he and his family nonetheless suffered racial exclusion and were inadequately compensated for the injury to their dignity is not a consequence of vulnerability or limited skills as a market actor, but rather exposes the failure of the construct of freedom of contract based on the primacy of freedom from contract to deliver access to markets for all. *Constantine* thus serves to illustrate how contractual freedoms 'from' and 'to' contract may collide and to remind that if consumer law is to deliver freedom, as well as equality, its model of contractual practice must embed the relational insight that 'the common-law rights of each individual are necessarily limited by the manner in which their exercise affects the common-law rights of other individuals'.[98] With its willingness at least symbolically to acknowledge the injury of racial discrimination arising from a market transaction, *Constantine v Imperial Hotels* delivers a marginal marketplace gain

---

[97] I Ayres, 'Fair Driving: Gender and Race Discrimination in Retail Car Negotiations' (1991) 104 *Harvard Law Review* 817, 817–18; LP Ambinder, 'Dispelling the Myth of Rationality: Racial Discrimination in Taxicab Service and the Efficacy of Litigation under 42 U.S.C. 1981' (1996) 64 *The George Washington Law Review* 342; DC Penningroth, 'Race in Contract law' (2022) 170 *University of Pennsylvania Law Review* 1199.

[98] *Rogers v Clarence Hotel* [1940] 3 DLR 583, 1940 *Canadian Legal Information Institute* 247 (BC CA). H Collins discusses colliding freedoms framework in 'The Vanishing Freedom to Choose a Contractual Partner' (2013) 76 *Law and Contemporary Problems* 71.

to consumers. Its non-engagement with the concepts of freedom of contract may represent a significant opportunity lost; but analysis of the case in its historical context exposes the role that contract law plays in perpetuating market inequalities and by implication the work that must be done to counteract this type of harm in consumer markets. For that reason, *Constantine v Imperial Hotels* merits a place amongst the landmark cases of consumer law.

13

Abortion and the 'Right to Choose': The Consumer Rights Implications of *Roe v Wade*

STEVIE MARTIN*

I. INTRODUCTION

ROE V WADE[1] is widely recognised as a pioneering judgment of the Supreme Court of the United States (SCOTUS) on reproductive rights. More specifically, in 1973 a majority of the SCOTUS in *Roe* held that the liberty interest safeguarded by the Fourteenth Amendment included a right to privacy which, in turn, protected the right of pregnant people[2] to access safe abortions without unreasonable obstruction by states. Whilst traditionally characterised as a pivotal constitutional law case (which it indisputably is), as this chapter will demonstrate, the majority opinion in *Roe* and its emphasis on pregnant women as patients and agents of their own reproductive autonomy is a reflection of the consumer rights movement which was gaining traction at the time the opinion was delivered. It was the first SCOTUS decision to find that the Fourteenth Amendment protected the right to choose whether to continue a pregnancy[3] and it was, then, a truly landmark case; *Roe* was an 'an event, discovery, or change marking an important stage or turning point' both politically and legally.[4] The recent overturning of *Roe* by a 6:3 majority of the

---

*I am incredibly grateful to Professor Jodi Gardner and Dr Stephanie Palmer for their very helpful comments on earlier drafts. All errors remain my own.

[1] *Roe v Wade*, 410 US 113 (1973).

[2] Save where gendered terms are used in direct quotes, or where the reference to 'women' is necessary to accurately reflect the intersection between gender and abortion (and, indeed, race), 'pregnant people' is used throughout this chapter in recognition that not all persons who become pregnant identify as female (see, for instance, *Reproductive Health Services v Strange*, 3 F.4th 1240, 1246 (11th Cir. 2021) fn 2 and D Cohen, G Donley and R Rebouché, 'The New Abortion Battleground' (2023) 123 *Colombia Law Review* 1 fn 18.

[3] This was subsequently confirmed in *Planned Parenthood v Casey*, 505 U.S. 833 (1992).

[4] Concise Oxford English Dictionary, 'Landmark', 11th edn (Oxford, OUP, 2008).

SCOTUS in *Dobbs*[5] does not alter the fact that *Roe* was a landmark decision, particularly in terms of consumer rights. Indeed, the overruling of *Roe* and the catastrophic consequences this will have for many thousands of pregnant people throughout the US, especially those living in poverty and women of colour, reaffirms the opinion's significance. The repeal of *Roe* has fundamentally altered the power dynamic between individuals, the state, and the medical profession. Following *Dobbs*, a number of US states have swiftly dismantled half a century of law recognising pregnant people as agents of their own futures and protecting consumers of abortion services.[6] As abortion clinics close and questions abound over the legality of telemedicine[7] and medical abortions as well as other reproductive services (for instance, fertility treatment), this chapter presents an opportunity to revisit the 1973 opinion and to consider its enduring significance in terms of consumer rights. Further, the overruling of *Roe* has simply pushed the legal dispute over abortion rights and access back before the state courts. As the first of those cases emerge, it is patent that the principles in *Roe* will continue to have significance for those seeking to reassert a right to abortion and to secure access to the same by reference to state constitutions. Accordingly, *Roe* remains a landmark decision of enduring importance.

It is, however, important that we resist the urge to deify *Roe*. As will be discussed in this chapter, for many pregnant people abortion has not been a true 'choice' as that term is understood in the broader consumer rights sphere.[8] Even before *Roe* was overturned, many pregnant people, especially women of colour, those living in poverty or rural settings and those whose immigration status was tenuous, simply could not exercise their constitutionally protected reproductive rights because abortion services were either non-existent or access to them was illusory. As Zeigler pithily puts it: following *Roe* 'the Constitution guaranteed only the freedom to make a decision about abortion, not the ability to actually get one'.[9] Nevertheless, a US without the fundamental right to abortion will be devastating for thousands of pregnant people.

By way of overview, this chapter will first outline the key facts and findings in *Roe* and will briefly discuss the basis for its overruling. Next, the consumerist aspects of the judgment will be examined. Section III will consider the implications of *Roe*, in particular what the judgment meant for people seeking access to abortion services. This will provide a foundation for the analysis in the final sections which will examine the implications of subsequent cases for the ability of consumers of abortion services to access such services and what the reversal of *Roe* means for such consumers moving forward.

---

[5] *Dobbs v Jackson Women's Health Organisation*, 597 U.S. 66 2022.

[6] Guttmacher Institute, 'Roe v. Wade Overturned: Our Latest Resources' www.guttmacher.org/abortion-rights-supreme-court (accessed 8 July 2022).

[7] That is, the delivery of medical treatment via various modes of technology rather than in-person or face-to-face, in particular by way of telephone and virtual consultations.

[8] C Craven, 'Reproductive Rights in a Consumer Rights Era: Toward the Value of "Constructive" Change' in C Craven and D-Ain Davis (eds), *Feminist Activist Ethnography: Counterpoints to Neoliberalism in North America* (Lanham, Lexington Books, 2013) ch 5.

[9] M Zeigler, *Reproduction and the Constitution in the United States* (London, Routledge, 2022) 46.

II. *ROE v WADE*: THE FACTS AND FINDINGS

The case involved three separate challenges to Texas legislation which criminalised the provision of abortion services to pregnant women from the date of conception, save for cases in which the abortion was provided 'for the purpose of saving the life of the woman'. Jane Roe[10] was a single, pregnant woman who wanted to obtain an abortion but did not meet the limited exception in the Texas statute. The Does – who intervened, together with Dr Hallford, in the proceedings before the lower courts – were a married couple who argued that the ban on abortion services in all bar the most extreme of cases interfered with their constitutional rights. They submitted that should they become pregnant and need to obtain an abortion, they would be unable to do so under the terms of the Texas statute. Dr Hallford was the subject of prosecutions under the Texas legislation and argued that those prosecutions were unconstitutional. Before the lower courts, Roe and Dr Hallford were found to have standing, while the Does were not given the inherently speculative nature of their case. Before the SCOTUS, the Does and Dr Hallford were held not to have justiciable claims. A majority of the Court concluded that Roe did, despite the fact that she was no longer pregnant.

In confirming the District Court's ruling, a majority of the SCOTUS (7:2)[11] held that the concept of personal liberty enshrined in the Fourteenth Amendment – which provides, inter alia, that no 'State [shall] deprive any person of … liberty … without due process of law' – protects privacy interests and the right to privacy 'encompass[es] a woman's decision … to terminate her pregnancy'.[12] In reaching this conclusion, the majority traced the treatment of abortion through several centuries of common law:

> It is … apparent that at common law, at the time of the adoption of our Constitution, and throughout the major portion of the 19th century, abortion was viewed with less disfavor than under most American statutes currently in effect [in 1973]. Phrasing it another way, a woman enjoyed a substantially broader right to terminate a pregnancy than she does in most States today. At least with respect to the early stage of pregnancy, and very possibly without such a limitation, the opportunity to make this choice was present in this country well into the 19th century. Even later, the law continued for some time to treat less punitively an abortion procured in early pregnancy.[13]

Having traced the history of abortion regulation in the US, the majority proceeded to consider the scope of the privacy interests purportedly protected by the Fourteenth Amendment. The majority concluded that the right to privacy 'founded in the Fourteenth Amendment':

> is broad enough to encompass a woman's decision whether or not to terminate her pregnancy. The detriment that the State would impose upon the pregnant woman by denying

---

[10] Whose real name was Norma McCorvey.
[11] Justice Blackmun delivered the opinion of the Court with which Chief Justice Burger and Justices Douglas, Brennan, Stewart, Marhsall and Powell joined. Chief Justice Burger and Justices Douglas and Stewart filed separate concurring opinions. Justices White and Rehnquist filed separate dissenting opinions (though Justice Rehnquist also joined with Justice White's dissent).
[12] *Roe* (n 1) 153.
[13] ibid 140–41.

this choice altogether is apparent. Specific and direct harm medically diagnosable even in early pregnancy may be involved. Maternity, or additional offspring, may force upon the woman a distressful life and future. Psychological harm may be imminent. Mental and physical health may be taxed by child care. There is also the distress, for all concerned, associated with the unwanted child, and there is the problem of bringing a child into a family already unable, psychologically and otherwise, to care for it. In other cases, as in this one, the additional difficulties and continuing stigma of unwed motherhood may be involved.[14]

In dissent, Justice Rehnquist disputed whether the right to privacy was engaged since '[a] *transaction* resulting in an operation such as this is not "private" in the ordinary usage of that word'.[15] Further, no right to access abortion could be found within the privacy interest purportedly protected by the Fourteenth Amendment given that 'when society's views on abortion are changing, the very existence of the debate is evidence that the "right" to an abortion is not so universally accepted as [Jane Roe] would have us believe'. Justice Rehnquist lamented that 'the [majority had found] within the scope of the Fourteenth Amendment a right that was apparently completely unknown to the drafters of the Amendment'.[16]

Having concluded that the Fourteenth Amendment was engaged by the Texas statute, the majority went on to consider whether the infringement of Roe's right to choose to have an abortion was nevertheless constitutional as it was necessary to support a compelling state interest. The majority accepted that there were two legitimate interests which the state could seek to protect: the health and safety of pregnant women; and, the potential of new life. Given the evidence, the majority considered that the risk to the pregnant woman's life of an abortion in the first trimester was the same as, or less than, the risk posed by childbirth, and as such, the state had no interest in restricting abortion in the first trimester. After the first trimester, the risks associated with abortion increased and the state had a corresponding interest in protecting the health of the pregnant woman. Accordingly, the state could legitimately place restrictions on access to abortion after the first trimester, provided those restrictions were 'reasonably relate[d] to the preservation and protection of maternal health'.[17] Examples of such restrictions included the qualifications of the person permitted to perform the abortion, the licensure of that person, and the facility in which the procedure was to be carried out.[18]

As to the second compelling interest – the potential of human life – the majority held that this only became a legitimate interest at the point of viability. Thereafter, the state 'in promoting [this] interest ... may, if it chooses, regulate, and even proscribe, abortion except where it is necessary, in appropriate medical judgment, for the preservation of the life or health of the mother'.[19] This finding was based on the Court's

---

[14] ibid 153.
[15] ibid 172. Emphasis added. The use of the term 'transaction' is notable in terms of the consumerist tenor of the judgment.
[16] ibid.
[17] ibid 163.
[18] ibid.
[19] ibid 164–65.

determination that the reference to 'person' in the Constitution 'does not include the unborn'.[20] However, while the 'unborn' may not have a 'right to life' from conception under the federal Constitution, a pregnant woman's privacy interest was not absolute and the state had, commensurate with the gestation of the pregnancy, an increasing interest in protecting 'potential life'.[21] And '[a]t some point in pregnancy, these respective interests become sufficiently compelling to sustain regulation of the factors that govern the abortion decision.' The majority thus concluded that 'the right of personal privacy includes the abortion decision, but that this right is not unqualified and must be considered against important state interests in regulation'.[22]

In sum, then, the majority SCOTUS in *Roe* held that:

(a) during the first trimester, the decision to abort was one for the pregnant person and their physician, 'free [from] regulation by the State';
(b) during the second trimester and prior to viability, 'the State, in promoting its interest in the health of the mother, may, if it chooses, regulate the abortion procedure in ways that are reasonably related to maternal health'; and
(c) after the point of viability, 'the State, in promoting its interest in the potentiality of human life, may, if it chooses, regulate, and even proscribe, abortion except where necessary, in appropriate medical judgment for the preservation of the life or health of the mother.'[23]

Justice Rehnquist disagreed with the majority's findings regarding the scope of the state's power to regulate the decision to abort a pregnancy. Even if the right to privacy was engaged (which, as noted above, Justice Rehnquist disputed), the majority had overstepped the proper function of the Court; by examining whether the state had a 'compelling interest' it had 'partake[n] in judicial legislation'.[24] Justice White also dissented, though the source of his dissent was based on the weight attributed to the competing interests of the pregnant person, as opposed to the principles enunciated, and relied upon, by the majority. He suggested that the majority had favoured the 'convenience, whim, or caprice of the putative mother more than the life or potential life of the fetus'.[25] A contention which would find reflection in several of the *amicus* briefs filed before the SCOTUS in support of Mississippi's ban almost five decades later in *Dobbs*.[26]

Notwithstanding the strongly worded dissents of Justices Rehnquist and White, the majority's opinion in *Roe* was indisputably a turning point in the battle over reproductive autonomy. As will be discussed in the ensuing sections, however, the emphasis

---

[20] ibid 157–58.
[21] ibid 154.
[22] ibid.
[23] ibid 114, 163–65.
[24] ibid 174.
[25] ibid 221–22.
[26] See, for instance, Brief of *Amici Curiae* the National Catholic Bioethics Center, Pro-Life Obstretricians-Gynecologists Gianina Cazan-London MD and Meslissa Halvorson MD, and Right to Life of Michigan, Inc in Support of Petitioners, which described the right to abortion as 'the morally hazardous convenience of a "right" to kill your offspring' (32) www.supremecourt.gov/DocketPDF/19/19-1392/185239/20210729121001402_19-1392%20tsac%20National%20Catholic%20Bioethics%20Center.pdf (accessed 31 July 2022).

in *Roe* on individual rights and the consumerist focus on choice has been problematic for many of the people who seek access to abortion services. Further, following the 1992 SCOTUS decision in *Casey* (which was also overturned in *Dobbs*), many states significantly eroded the protections *Roe* (at least theoretically) afforded to pregnant people. Thus, while the overturning of *Roe* and the evisceration of the constitutional right to choose whether to continue with a pregnancy is hugely problematic, particularly in terms of reproductive autonomy and equality, *Roe* was not a panacea; issues of access have existed since the opinion was delivered.

In the interests of fulsomeness, it bears noting that *Roe* was delivered together with another judgment – *Doe v Bolton*[27] – which involved a challenge to Georgia legislation restricting abortion eligibility to very limited situations. There were also procedural requirements for those cases that met the onerous restrictions including, for instance, that the procedure had to be approved by the hospital staff abortion committee. Citing the findings and principles enunciated in the more fulsome judgment in *Roe*, a majority SCOTUS in *Doe* (Justices Rehnquist and White again dissented) held that restricting access to abortion to the most extreme of cases violated the Fourteenth Amendment.[28] While the majority in *Dobbs* did not expressly overturn *Doe v Bolton*, given that that decision rested on the finding in *Roe* that there was a (qualified) constitutional right to choose whether to continue with a pregnancy and that principle *was* expressly overruled in *Dobbs*, it would be anomalous if *Doe v Bolton* withstood *Dobbs* while *Roe* (and *Casey*) did not.

A. The Basis on which Roe was Overruled

The undoing of *Roe* in *Dobbs* was not based on a determination that 'life starts at conception' or that a foetus has constitutional rights which are incompatible with a right to abortion. The majority's opinion was 'not based on any view about if and when prenatal life is entitled to any of the rights enjoyed after birth'.[29] Rather, the basis for the majority's unprecedented step of '[r]escinding an individual right in its entirety and conferring it on the State'[30] was its conclusion that the majority SCOTUS in 1973 had misunderstood the history of abortion regulation under the common law and in America at the time the Fourteenth Amendment was drafted. More specifically, the majority in *Dobbs* determined that the right to choose whether to continue with a pregnancy was not 'deeply rooted in the Nation's history and traditions. On the contrary, an unbroken tradition prohibiting abortion on pain of criminal punishment

---

[27] *Doe v Bolton*, 410 US 179 (1973).
[28] An attempt in the mid-2000s by Mary Doe – Sandra Cano – to have the courts reconsider (and, ultimately, overturn) *Doe v Bolton* was unsuccessful (*Cano v Baker*, 435 F.3d 1337 (11th Circuit Court, 2006) law.justia.com/cases/federal/appellate-courts/ca11/05-11641/200511641-2011-02-28.html (accessed 27 July 2022). The SCOTUS refused to hear an appeal from the Eleventh Circuit's decision (Supreme Court Docket No 05-11641). It should also be noted that Jane Roe similarly unsuccessfully sought to have *Roe v Wade* overturned (*McCorvey v Hill*, 385 F.3d 846 (5th Cir. 2004) (the SCOTUS similarly refused to hear an appeal from the Fifth Circuit's decision (Supreme Court Docket No 04-967)).
[29] *Dobbs* (n 5), Opinion of the Court, 38.
[30] *Dobbs* (n 5), Dissenting Opinion of Breyer, Sotomayor and Kagan JJ, 54.

persisted from the earliest days of the common law until 1973.'[31] Thus, it could not be said that the liberty interest in the Fourteenth Amendment included a right to abortion. As a result of the *Dobbs* majority's overturning of the 'egregiously wrong' judgment in *Roe* (and, indeed, *Casey*), states are now free to ban abortions from the point of conception provided there is a 'rational basis on which the legislature could have thought that it would serve legitimate state interests'.[32]

III. ROE THROUGH THE CONSUMERIST LENS: THE CENTRALITY OF 'CHOICE'

The constitutional significance of *Roe* is indisputable. It confirmed that the Fourteenth Amendment enshrined a right to privacy which has proven invaluable in protecting rights in myriad other scenarios including, for instance, legal recognition of same-sex relationships and medical decision-making.[33] And, it recognised that that right to privacy incorporated a qualified right to choose to terminate a pregnancy. In the subsequent SCOTUS decision of *Casey*,[34] *Roe* was characterised as a 'watershed decision'.[35] In resisting a call to overturn *Roe*, the majority in *Casey* described the 1973 decision as 'rare' and unlike 'normal cases'.[36] Such was the significance of *Roe* that, from the decision onwards, 'the Supreme Court's abortion cases ... established (and affirmed, and re-affirmed) a woman's right to choose an abortion before viability'.[37] The concept of 'choice' played a central role in the judgment. Indeed, Justice White in dissent lamented the majority's judgment as placing pre-eminent weight on the ('capric[ious]') *choice* of pregnant women, particularly in the first trimester. The majority also made reference at various points to the pregnant woman's 'decision' and 'choice'.[38] The emphasis on 'choice' in *Roe* is illustrative of the consumerist tenor of the judgment. Choice is, after all, 'the most consumerist idea of our time'.[39]

---

[31] ibid 25. As the Opinion in *Roe* itself demonstrates, this reading of history is not undisputed (see, for instance, *Dobbs* (n 5), Opinion of the Court, fn 34). Further, as the strongly worded dissent of Justices Breyer, Sotomayor and Kagan makes clear, even if this historical account were valid (which the dissenting justices dispute), interpreting the Fourteenth Amendment 'just as the ratifiers did' is also open to criticism (*Dobbs* (n 5), Breyer, Sotomayor and Kagan JJ dissenting, 13–14).

[32] *Dobbs* (n 5) 77.

[33] See, for instance, M Ziegler, *Beyond Abortion: Roe v Wade and the Battle for Privacy* (Cambridge, MA, Harvard University Press, 2018). As Karst observed in 1977, citing *Roe*, 'In the last dozen years, the Court has ... invented (or reinvented) a right of privacy' (KL Karst, 'The Supreme Court, 1976 Term' (1977) 91 *Harvard Law Review* 1, 43). Indeed, Justice Thomas in his separate concurring opinion in *Dobbs* (n 5) considered that the SCOTUS should not stop at abortion rights but, rather, should 'reconsider all of this Court's substantive due process precedents ... Because any substantive due process decision [including, for instance, those opinions recognising the rights of same-sex couples to have their relationship legally recognised] is "demonstrably erroneous", we have a duty to "correct the error" established in those precedents' (3).

[34] *Casey* (n 3).

[35] ibid 867.

[36] ibid.

[37] *Jackson Women's Health Organisation v Dobbs*, United States Court of Appeals for the Fifth Circuit, No 18-60868, 13 December 2019, 1.

[38] See, for instance, *Roe* (n 1) 153, 163–64. See, also, Justice Stewart's concurring opinion at 168 and 169.

[39] Rickie Solinger cited by Ziegler (n 33) 38.

Subsequent abortion jurisprudence has continued to focus on the 'choice' of the pregnant person. During oral arguments in *Dobbs*, Justice Breyer characterised the decision in *Roe* as 'laying down a constitutional principle, in this case, women's choice'.[40] Indeed, in their dissenting opinion in *Dobbs*, Justices Breyer, Sotomayor and Kagan referred to the 'constitutional ... right to choose' and noted that it 'situate[d] a woman in relationship to others and to the government'.[41] However, as will be discussed below, for many pregnant people abortion is not, in truth, a choice:

> [T]he concept of choice masks the different economic, political, and environmental contexts in which women live their reproductive lives. Choice ... disguises the ways that laws, policies, and public officials differently punish or reward the childbearing of different groups of women as well as the different degrees of access women have to health care and other resources necessary to manage sex, fertility and maternity.[42]

In addition to its protection of choice, the majority's limitation of the state's 'supervisory role' in *Roe* was consistent with the broader consumer rights movement which was gaining traction at that time. Ziegler has suggested that *Roe* 'seemed to echo newfound optimising about market-based solutions ...'.[43] Indeed, following *Roe*, private facilities providing abortion services (and other pregnancy and gynaecological services) proliferated, and the overwhelming majority of abortions today are performed in non-hospital settings.[44] Further, in recent years, there has been a significant increase in the rates of self-managed abortions (primarily by way of medication abortion which takes place outside of the hospital/clinical setting) which is in line with the wider shift to direct-to-consumer medical services and the rise in popularity of telemedicine and self-management of medical care.[45] Similarly, the majority's emphasis on viability as the point at which the state's interest in protecting potential human life became relevant also provided protection for the rights of pregnant people as consumers of abortion services; prior to viability, the individual rights of pregnant people to choose prevailed subject to restrictions necessary to protect *their* health.

While *Roe* significantly curtailed the ability of states to restrict access to abortions, particularly in the first trimester, subsequent SCOTUS authority paved the way for states to place increasingly onerous restrictions on the provision of abortion services. Indeed, even before *Roe* was overruled, many pregnant people were either unable to access such services in their own state or confronted considerable difficulties in doing so.

---

[40] *Dobbs v Jackson Women's Health Organisation*, Supreme Court of the United States, No 19–1392, Oral Arguments, 1 December 2021, 9.

[41] *Dobbs* (n 5), Breyer, Sotomayor and Kagan JJ dissenting, 52.

[42] LJ Ross and R Solinger, *Reproductive Justice: An Introduction* (Oakland, University of California Press. 2017) 47.

[43] Ziegler (n 33) 38.

[44] See, for instance, JD Forrest, C Tietze and E Sullivan, 'Abortion in the United States, 1976–1977' (Sep–Oct 1978) 10 *Family Planning Perspectives 5*, 271. Approximately 95% of all recorded abortions are provided at clinics as opposed to hospitals (E Nash and J Dreweke, 'The U.S. Abortion Rate Continues to Drop: Once Again, State Abortion Restrictions Are Not the Main Driver' (Guttmacher Institute, 18 September 2019) www.guttmacher.org/gpr/2019/09/us-abortion-rate-continues-drop-once-again-state-abortion-restrictions-are-not-main (accessed 19 January 2022)).

[45] Y Lindgren, 'When Patients Are Their Own Doctors: Roe v. Wade in an Era of Self-Managed Care' (2022) 107 *Cornell Law Review* 151 cornelllawreview.org/wp-content/uploads/2022/04/Lingren-PDF-final-1.pdf (accessed 27 July 2022).

And, in many cases, such restrictions had little if anything to do with the protection of the health of the pregnant person. Further, these difficulties

> disproportionately impact[ed] those [with] limited resources to overcome financial and logistic barriers. This includes young people, people with disabilities, LGBTQ+ people, people with low incomes and those in rural areas, as well as Black, Indigenous and other people of color.[46]

The focus in *Roe* on 'choice' and individual rights was itself problematic in terms of securing equitable access to abortion services; without addressing the factors that lead pregnant people to seek abortions including, importantly, poverty, the 'right' to 'choose' abortion has, for many, been illusory. Nevertheless, while we should be realistic in our appreciation of *Roe*, a US without the constitutional protections afforded by the landmark decision will be catastrophic for many thousands of pregnant people. It was predicted that in the year after *Dobbs* was delivered, between 93,546 and 143,561 pregnant people would be prevented from accessing abortion care.[47]

IV. THE POSITIVE IMPLICATIONS OF ROE

To fully appreciate the implications of *Roe's* overruling, it is necessary to consider the impact the judgment has had on reproductive autonomy. Before *Roe*, 'estimates of the number of illegal abortions in the 1950s and 1960s ranged from 200,000 to 1.2 million per year'.[48] *Roe*, thus, heralded a significant improvement in the standard of treatment pregnant people could receive when accessing abortion services. Research in the years immediately following the judgment revealed that 'legalization of abortion [was] accompanied by a sharp decline in abortion deaths – almost entirely due to the drop in illegal abortion, from 39 in 1972 to just three in 1975'.[49] Rates of illegal abortions were estimated to have declined from approximately 130,000 to 17,000 over the same period.[50] Clearly, the judgment had a profound impact on the ability of many pregnant people to safely assert their reproductive autonomy.

Indeed, today it is more dangerous to carry a pregnancy to term and to give birth than it is to obtain a legal abortion. Research has revealed that the risk of death during childbirth is 14 times higher than the risk posed by legal abortion.[51] 'Approximately 700 women die in the United States each year as a result of pregnancy

---

[46] www.guttmacher.org/article/2021/11/resources-journalists-15-things-consider-when-covering-abortion-supreme-court-and (accessed 19 January 2022).
[47] C Myers et al., 'Predicted changes in abortion access and incidence in a post-Roe world' (2019) 100 *Contraception* 5, 373.
[48] RB Gold, 'Lessons from Before Roe: Will Past be Prologue?' (2003) 6 *The Guttmacher Report on Public Policy* 1, 8 www.guttmacher.org/sites/default/files/article_files/gr060108.pdf (accessed 19 January 2022).
[49] W Cates Jr and RW Rochat, 'Illegal abortions in the United States: 1972–1974' [1976] *Family Planning Perspectives* 86, 87 www.jstor.org/stable/pdf/2133995.pdf (accessed 19 January 2022). See, more recently, Zane et al., 'Abortion-related mortality in the United States 1998–2010' (2015) 126 *Obstetrics & Gynecology* 2, 258–65.
[50] Cates and Rochat (n 49) 87.
[51] EG Raymond and DA Grimes, 'The comparative safety of legal induced abortion and childbirth in the United States' (2012) 119 *Obstetrics and Gynecology* 2, 215–19.

or its complications, and significant racial/ethnic disparities in pregnancy-related mortality exist.'[52] In fact, such research has indicated that restrictive abortion policies *contribute* to maternal mortality:

> a recent study found that the enactment of gestational age limits for abortion was associated with a 38% increase in maternal mortality, and a 20% reduction in Planned Parenthood clinics was associated with an 8% increase in maternal mortality.[53]

In contrast to the approximately 700 pregnant people who die each year as a result of pregnancy or its complications, during the period from 1998–2010, of the approximately 16.1 million abortion procedures that were carried out, 108 women died, resulting in a mortality rate of 0.7 deaths per 100,000 procedures (which can be contrasted with the maternal morality rate of 17.4 per 100,000).[54]

In addition to improving the safety of abortion services, *Roe* empowered pregnant people, especially pregnant women, to choose the direction of their lives and this, in turn, has had significant consequences in terms of gender equality. As the respondent's brief in *Dobbs* observed:

> That the right guaranteed by *Casey* and *Roe* is critical to women's equality is clear from the impact on those who make the decision to end a pregnancy but are denied the ability to do so. Women who are denied an abortion:
>
> - must endure the comparatively greater risks to their health of continued pregnancy and childbirth;
> - may lose educational opportunities;
> - face decreased opportunities to pursue their full career potential and take an active role in civic life;
> - are more likely to experience violence from the man involved in the pregnancy;
> - are more likely to experience economic insecurity and raise their existing children in poverty;
> - are more likely, as pregnant women and mothers, to experience economic harms, despite modest changes to workers' protections.[55]

The consequences for people denied access to abortion services provide an insight into the complexity of the reasoning that underpins a decision to abort a pregnancy.

---

[52] EE Peterson et al., 'Racial/Ethnic Disparities in Pregnancy-Related Deaths – United States, 2007–2016', *Morbidity and Mortality Weekly Report*, 6 September 2019 www.cdc.gov/mmwr/volumes/68/wr/mm6835a3.htm#suggestedcitation (accessed 19 January 2022). See, also, D Vilda et al., 'State Abortion Policies and Maternal Death in the United States, 2015–2018' (2021) 111 *American Journal of Public Health* 9, 1696–1704.

[53] Vilda et al., (n 52) 1697.

[54] S Zane et al., 'Abortion-Related Mortality in the United States 1998–2010' (2015) 126 *Obstetrics and Gynecology* 2, 258; D Hoyert and A Miniño, 'Maternal mortality in the United States: changes in coding, publication, and data release, 2018' (2020) 69 *National Vital Statistics Reports* 2.

[55] *Dobbs v Jackson Women's Health Organisation*, Supreme Court of the United States, No 19-1392, Brief of Respondents, 38–39 (footnotes omitted) www.supremecourt.gov/DocketPDF/19/19-1392/192267/20210913143126849_19-1392bs.pdf (accessed 19 January 2022). Indeed, as Justices Breyer, Sotomayor and Kagan observed in dissent, 'women must take their place as full and equal citizens. And for that to happen, women must have control over their reproductive decisions' (*Dobbs* (n 5), Breyer, Sotomayor and Kagan JJ in dissent, 47).

Contrary to Justice White's contention in *Roe* that those seeking access to abortion services are merely motivated by whim or caprice, research has repeatedly demonstrated that the decision to abort a pregnancy is, typically, a considered judgement based on a number of factors. Data collected from over 1,000 women who attended at more than 30 abortion clinics across the US revealed that 'among the primary reasons for wanting an abortion were: feeling not financially prepared (40%), not the right time (36%), and having a baby now would interfere with future opportunities (20%)'.[56] On the latter point, research has revealed that pregnant women who are denied access to abortion services are 'significantly less likely to have vocational goals compared to women who obtained an abortion, likely because employment-related goals felt unattainable while parenting a newborn'.[57] Other research has confirmed that the most common reasons for wanting to end a pregnancy are financial 'in particular, not having enough money to raise a child or support another child'.[58] The intersection between poverty and abortion will be discussed below but, for now, it suffices to note that 75 per cent of women who access abortion services are living below the federal poverty level.[59] And research has found that 'when poor women have children, both they and their children are likely to stay poor'.[60] Women who are denied abortions face greater economic hardship than women who receive abortions and these difficulties persist over time. Amongst women who were refused access to abortion services, in the five years after the refusal, they were more likely than those who were able to access such services to report 'not having enough money to cover basic living expenses'.[61] In this context, it must be acknowledged that 59 per cent of women accessing abortions already have a child/children.[62]

In addition to the financial implications of not being able to access abortion services, research in the US has consistently revealed a relationship between a lack of access and negative health outcomes. For instance, an examination of restrictive abortion policies between 2005 and 2015 found that in most regions, 'increases in abortion restrictions were associated with adverse birth outcomes'.[63] There are many reasons for this but, fundamentally, abortion is a safer option than pregnancy and childbirth: 'compared with legal induced abortion, pregnancy and childbirth are markedly less safe and associated with more pregnancy-related morbidities and mortality'.[64] In fact, childbirth is approximately 14 times more likely to result in death than legal abortion and, in Mississippi, which enacted legislation banning abortions after 15 weeks'

---

[56] UD Upadhyay et al., 'The effect of abortion on having and achieving aspirational one-year plans' (2015) 15 *BMC Women's Health* 102, 2 citing MA Biggs et al., 'Understanding why women seek abortions in the US' (2015) 13 *BMC Women's Health* 1, 29.

[57] Upadhyay et al., (n 56) 9.

[58] DG Foster et al., 'Socioeconomic Outcomes of Women Who Receive and Women Who Are Denied Wanted Abortions in the United States' (2018) 108 *American Journal of Public Health* 3, 407.

[59] Guttmacher Institute, 'Induced abortion in the United States', September 2019 www.guttmacher.org/fact-sheet/induced-abortion-united-states (accessed 19 January 2022).

[60] M Oberman, 'Motherhood, Abortion, and the Medicalisation of Poverty' (2018) 46 *The Journal of Law, Medicine & Ethics* 665, 669.

[61] Foster et al., (n 58) 411.

[62] Guttmacher Institute (n 59).

[63] SK Redd et al., 'Variation in Restrictive Abortion Policies and Adverse Birth Outcomes in the United States from 2005 to 2015' (2021) Women's Health Issues (18 November 2021) 1.

[64] ibid 2.

gestation and which was the focus of the proceedings in *Dobbs*, it is about 75 times more dangerous to carry a pregnancy to term than to have an abortion.[65] That risk is disproportionality borne by Black women.[66]

Structural inequalities in the health system including the 'lack of insurance coverage, shortages of primary care and obstetric providers, and [an] inability to access affordable, comprehensive, and culturally appropriate care',[67] further compound the risks faced by pregnant people who are refused access to abortion services. In fact, states that have significant restrictions on access to abortion services 'generally have fewer policies supporting the health and wellbeing of pregnant people, their children, and their families'.[68] The lack of effective access to abortion services, coupled with the absence of sufficiently supportive programmes and policies for pregnant people and parents, has consistently been linked with adverse health outcomes for pregnant people and infant mortality.[69] Given the significant consequences of pregnancy, childbirth and childrearing, the finding in *Roe* that the Fourteenth Amendment protects the right to choose whether to continue with a pregnancy had profound consequences for the one in four people of reproductive age who have an abortion in their lifetime.[70] As the ensuing section discusses, however, prior to its reversal in *Dobbs*, '*Roe v. Wade* [was] hobbled.'[71]

V. THE LIMITATIONS OF ROE AND ITS FOCUS ON 'CHOICE'

A. 'Choice' for Whom?

While *Roe*, and subsequent abortion jurisprudence, was couched in the consumerist notion of 'choice', for many of the pregnant people accessing abortion services, it is not so much a 'choice' – understood as the 'preferential determination between things'[72] – as the only option. And, for many pregnant people for whom abortion services are not accessible, it is not even a choice, however conceptualised. As Oberman has observed:

> For the past half-century, the U.S. has fought over abortion in rhetorical terms that, upon scrutiny, are hollow. We speak of 'choice' and 'life' as if they reflect women's actual experiences when opting for or against having an abortion ... What we learn from those who seek abortions is that the decision to terminate a pregnancy is not so much a choice as a response to the ways in which poverty inscribes itself onto our bodies.[73]

---

[65] *Whole Women's Health v Hellerstedt* 579 US 582 (2016) 30; *Dobbs* (n 55) 28. See, also, research set out in n 51. See, also, *Dobbs* (n 5), Breyer, Sotomayor and Kagan JJ in dissent, 41.
[66] *Dobbs* (n 55) 28; Peterson et al. (n 52).
[67] Redd et al. (n 63) 2.
[68] ibid. See, also, *Dobbs* (n 5), Breyer, Sotomayor and Kagan JJ in dissent, 42.
[69] Redd et al. (n 63) 2.
[70] R Jones and J Jerman, 'Population group abortion rates and lifetime incidence of abortion: United States, 2008–2014' (2017) 107 *American Journal of Public Health* 12, 1904–09.
[71] I Panich-Linsman and L Kelley, 'Before Roe', *The New York Times* (21 January 2022) www.nytimes.com/interactive/2022/01/21/opinion/roe-v-wade-abortion-history.html (accessed 19 January 2022).
[72] Oxford English Dictionary, 'Choice' www.oed.com/view/Entry/32111?rskey=PrFV8t&result=1#eid (accessed 19 January 2022).
[73] Oberman (n 60) 670.

The difficulty of considering abortion access through the lens of individual rights and choice is that '[t]he ideology of choice is rooted within a binary construct' and '[i]n this formulation of individual choice, a distinction needs to be made between decisions based on a lack of viable alternatives versus optimal reproductive freedom.'[74] The overwhelming majority of people who access abortion services live in poverty.[75] For such individuals, the decision to obtain an abortion is rarely an exercise of 'optimal reproductive freedom'. Further, when employing the nomenclature of 'choice', it is important to appreciate just what 'choices' we are talking about: 'the abortion "choice" is not between having an abortion and not having one, but between having an abortion and carrying a pregnancy to term' and '[w]omen's social and economic situations may in fact give them no real choice at all if they face poverty, loss of family support, or the threat of violence in connection with their pregnancy.'[76]

B. No Right to Access

For many pregnant people the 'choice' promised by *Roe* has been entirely illusory. In understanding why, it is necessary to consider several key cases which substantially eroded the protections (however theoretical) conferred by *Roe*. In the years immediately following delivery of the *Roe* opinion, the SCOTUS twice upheld restrictions on funding for abortions. In both cases – one concerned state legislation in Connecticut which restricted Medicaid reimbursement to abortions which were deemed medically necessary (ie, it did not cover non-therapeutic abortions)[77] and the other centred on the Hyde Amendment which was passed by Congress in 1976 and prohibited the use of federal funding for abortions except in cases of rape, incest, or medical necessity[78] – the SCOTUS reiterated that despite the fact that the principal impact of such restrictions fell 'on the indigent' 'that fact alone [did] not render' the legislation unconstitutional.[79] As Justice Brennan in dissent in *Harris* (which concerned the Hyde Amendment) observed, such legislative restrictions had the effect of 'injecting coercive financial incentives favouring childbirth into a decision that is constitutionally guaranteed to be free from governmental intrusion' such that these restrictions 'deprive[d] the indigent woman of her freedom to choose abortion over maternity, thereby impinging on the due process liberty right recognised in *Roe v Wade*'.[80]

Almost two decades after *Roe* a majority SCOTUS in the matter of *Casey*[81] reaffirmed *Roe's* central finding that the Fourteenth Amendment protected a right to abortion. However, the majority rejected the *Roe* court's reliance on trimesters and, instead, focused on the point of viability, developing and applying a lower standard of

---

[74] I López, *Matters of Choice: Puerto Rican Women's Struggle for Reproductive Freedom* (New Brunswick, Rutgers University Press 2008) 142.
[75] Guttmacher Institute (n 59). See, also, Jones and Jerman (n 70) 1906.
[76] FH Stewart et al., '*Keeping abortion legal: a look beyond Roe v. Wade*' (2003) 68 *Contraception* 307.
[77] *Maher v Roe*, 432 U.S. 464 (1977).
[78] *Harris v McRae*, 448 U.S. 279 (1979).
[79] ibid 323.
[80] ibid 333.
[81] *Casey* (n 3).

review to determine whether restrictions on abortion both before and after that point were constitutional. Following *Casey*, states could regulate access to abortion services throughout the entirety of a person's pregnancy 'so long as they [did] not impose an undue burden on the woman's right, but they [could] not ban abortions [prior to viability]'.[82] An undue burden existed if a regulation's 'purpose or effect [was] to place a substantial obstacle in the path of a woman seeking an abortion before the fetus attains viability'.[83]

Applying this standard, states have been able to place increasingly onerous restrictions on access to abortions without falling foul of *Roe*. Since *Roe* 'states have constructed a lattice work of abortion law, codifying, regulating and limiting whether, when and under what circumstances a person may obtain an abortion'.[84] Since 1973, 'over 1,000 legal restrictions [on abortion access] have been adopted in the states'.[85] In the lead-up to *Dobbs*, such restrictions proliferated; '... more laws restricting abortion access were enacted between 2011 and 2015 than in any previous five-year period since 1973'.[86]

> [A]s of 2020, 29 states demonstrate[d] hostility to abortion rights, and 58% of women of reproductive age [were] living in states considered hostile or very hostile to abortion services, meaning they had four or five (hostile), or six (very hostile) abortion restrictions in effect.[87]

Many states had also introduced Targeted Regulation of Abortion Providers (TRAP) laws, which are alleged to further pregnant people's health interests but, on closer inspection, 'do little or nothing for health, but rather strew impediments to abortion'.[88] Examples of TRAP laws include:

- waiting periods of up to 72 hours between appointments;
- mandatory ultrasounds in which physicians must describe results in real-time;
- bans on certain, medically preferable abortion procedures;
- the required provision of inaccurate medical information; and
- parental consent and notification requirements for minors.[89]

Bearing in mind the intersection between abortion and poverty, TRAP laws further 'constrict poor women's reproductive health decisions'.[90] For instance, in addition

---

[82] *Jackson Women's Health Organisation v Dobbs* (n 37) 1–2.
[83] *Casey* (n 81) 837.
[84] Guttmacher Institute, 'An Overview of Abortion Laws', 16 July 2022 www.guttmacher.org/print/state-policy/explore/overview-abortion-laws (accessed 31 July 2022).
[85] L Shepherd and HD Turner, 'The Over-Medicalization and Corrupted Medicalization of Abortion and Its Effect on Women Living in Poverty' (2018) 46 *Journal of Law, Medicine and Ethics* 3, 672.
[86] NR Bhardwaj, 'Traveling for rights: Abortion trends in New Mexico after passage of restrictive Texas legislation' (2020) 102 *Contraception* 2, 115.
[87] Redd et al. (n 63) 2.
[88] *Planned Parenthood of Wisconsin Inc v Schimel*, 806 F. 3d 908 (CA7 2015) 921, cited with approval by Justice Ginsburg in *Whole Women's Health v Hellerstedt* (n 65) 2.
[89] Shepherd and Turner (n 85) 672.
[90] ibid 668.

to the cost of the procedure itself (which is, on average, US$593),[91] in states with extended waiting periods, pregnant people seeking to access abortion services bear the additional costs associated with travel, childcare, missed work and accommodation.[92] And this assumes that there is an abortion provider within the pregnant person's state; '[i]n 2017, 89% of U.S. counties did not have a clinic facility that provided abortion care, and 38% of women aged 15–44 lived in these counties.'[93] Thus, while there may have been an 'unbroken' jurisprudential line from *Roe* confirming that pregnant people had a constitutional right to choose whether to continue with a pregnancy, many people simply could not access those services. As the late Ruth Bader Ginsburg observed:

> There's a sorry situation in the United States, which is essentially that poor women don't have choice. Women of means do. They will, always. Let's assume *Roe v. Wade* were overruled and we were going back to each state for itself, well, any woman who could travel from her home state to a state that provides access to abortion and those states never go back to old ways … So if you can afford a plane ticket, a train ticket or even a bus ticket you can control your own destiny but if you're locked into your native state then maybe you can't. That we have one law for women of means and another for poor women is not a satisfactory situation.[94]

Further, such restrictions have profound implications for those pregnant people who are able to access abortion services notwithstanding the considerable hurdles. The mandating of ultrasounds is inimical to the right of patients to refuse treatment, while the provision of inaccurate medical information arguably negates informed consent and fundamentally weakens the trust between doctor and patient.[95]

Thus, even before *Dobbs*, for many thousands of pregnant people in the US, especially women of colour and those living in poverty and/or in rural areas, while they might have had a constitutional right to choose to abort their pregnancy, they were unable to access the services necessary to act upon that choice. And, even when they could access such services, their rights as consumers of medical services were, in many states, very significantly curtailed or, indeed, violated. While the post-*Dobbs* surge in restrictive abortion legislation in a significant number of US states[96] illustrates the

---

[91] And, given the absence of federal funding ('In 1976, Congress passed the Hyde Amendment, which prohibited the use of federal dollars for abortions except in cases of rape, incest, or medical necessity' Oberman (n 60) 667), if pregnant people 'do not qualify for government-sponsored health insurance like Medicaid, they must pay out of pocket the full cost of their own health care-including reproductive health care services like … abortion care', T O'Neill, 'What Does the Minimum Wage Have to Do with Reproductive Rights' (2016) 49 *Akron Law Review* 319, 323.

[92] ibid. See, also, Redd et al. (n 63).

[93] RK Jones et al., 'Abortion Incidence and Service Availability in the United States, 2017', September 2019, 7 www.guttmacher.org/report/abortion-incidence-service-availability-us-2017 (accessed 26 January 2022).

[94] S Lachman, 'Ruth Bader Ginsburg Calls "Choice" An Empty Concept for Poor Women,' HuffPost, 30 July 2014 www.huffpost.com/entry/ruth-bader-ginsburg-reproductive-rights_n_55ba42c9e4b095423 d0e0716 (accessed 26 January 2022).

[95] Lindgren (n 45) 181–83.

[96] One month after the delivery of *Dobbs* '11 states – all in the South and Midwest – had either banned abortion completely (Alabama, Arkansas, Mississippi, Missouri, Oklahoma, South Dakota and Texas) or implemented a ban on abortion starting at six weeks of pregnancy (Georgia, Ohio, South Carolina and Tennessee)', M Kirstein, 'One Month Post-Roe: At Least 43 Abortion Clinics Across 11 States Have

primordial importance of a constitutional right to choose, it is imperative that state governments that are inclined to protect reproductive autonomy also take proactive steps to ensure that consumers are able to access the services necessary to give meaningful effect to the right to choose.

VI. THE POST-ROE REALITY: THE ENDURING LEGACY OF ROE'S PRINCIPLES AND THE CHANGING NATURE OF ABORTION

While it may no longer be binding precedent, as the first of the challenges to state bans on abortions make their way through the state courts, it is clear that the principles enunciated in *Roe* are going to play a significant role in deciding whether state constitutions protect the right of pregnant people to abort their pregnancies. For instance, in *EMW Women's Surgical Center v Daniel Cameron*, Judge Mitch Perry of the Jefferson Circuit Court granted a temporary injunction preventing a ban on abortion after six weeks of pregnancy from taking effect.[97] In reaching his decision, Judge Perry observed that:

> The Six Week Ban will have wide ranging effects on family planning decisions that are traditionally protected from governmental imposition. It not only compromises a woman's right to self-determination protected in Section 2 of the Kentucky Constitution by taking away the choice to have an abortion in many instances, but also undercuts a woman's choice to have children at all ... Women have legitimate concerns about their ability to receive adequate care, and the possibility their health and safety will be deemed subordinate to the life of a fetus. Already, laws similar to the ones at issue here, are creating confusion and concern in healthcare settings as doctors, in order to avoid incurring civil and criminal liability, are forced to wait until women are in dire medical conditions before interceding ....[98]

The references to 'family planning decisions', 'self-determination' and the 'choice to have an abortion' are redolent of the majority's opinion in *Roe*. It is highly likely that similar arguments will feature in the numerous challenges being lodged to other state bans.[99] Judge Perry's explicit mention of concerns regarding access to adequate care is also significant. Only time will tell how successful such arguments are going to be. However, it does bear noting that state constitutions may offer greater protection than

---

Stopped Offering Abortion Care', Guttmacher Institute, 28 July 2022 www.guttmacher.org/article/2022/07/one-month-post-roe-least-43-abortion-clinics-across-11-states-have-stopped-offering (accessed 28 July 2022).

[97] *EMW Women's Surgical Center v Daniel Cameron*, Jefferson Circuit Court, Division Three, No 22-CI-3225 fingfx.thomsonreuters.com/gfx/legaldocs/zgpomxldjpd/07222022abortion_kentucky_ruling.pdf (accessed 27 July 2022). That injunction was dissolved on appeal. A similar injunction was granted in *Planned Parenthood of Southwest and Central Florida v State of Florida*, Judge Cooper, Circuit Court of the Second Judicial Circuit in and for Leon County, Florida, Case No 2022 CA 912 www.aclu.org/legal-document/order-granting-pls-injunction (accessed 27 July 2022). This injunction was automatically revoked following the lodgement of an appeal.

[98] *Daniel Cameron* (n 97) 14.

[99] Indeed, the arguments outlined in the increasing number of motions filed by the American Civil Liberties Union against state bans on abortion following *Dobbs* clearly demonstrate the centrality of the consumerist concept of choice to such challenges: ACLU, 'All Cases' www.aclu.org/court-cases?pages=1#all_content (accessed 27 July 2022).

the federal Constitution in terms of the right to privacy and the concomitant protections afforded to reproductive autonomy. In *EMW Women's Surgical Center*, Judge Perry noted that the 'Kentucky Constitution has been held to "offer greater protection for the right to privacy than provided by the Federal Constitution as interpreted by the United States Supreme Court."'[100] While it is open to the state governments and legislatures to amend state constitutions to preclude a right to abortion,[101] the fact that such arguments (as well as others that were referenced, if not fully considered, in *Roe* including those concerning equality) are being relied upon to challenge state bans on abortion is a testament to the enduring significance of the 1973 decision.

Again, however, it is important not to view *Roe* through rose-tinted glasses. The judgment in *Roe* was based on a medical gatekeeper model of abortion services which did not reflect the reality of abortion then and most certainly does not reflect the nature of most abortions today.[102] The majority in *Roe* placed the doctor-patient relationship front and centre, holding that in the first trimester, the decision whether to abort a pregnancy was one for the patient in consultation with their doctor. As Lindgren notes, *Roe* has long been criticised for foregrounding the role and judgement of the physician on the basis that this had the effect of 'subordinating the pregnant person's constitutional rights to the judgment of the relevant healthcare provider' (it also further restricted access to abortion services, as most pregnant women were unable to afford private physicians and, instead, where reliant on state services with the attendant restrictions on funding).[103]

Today, most abortions in the US take place in the first trimester and occur by way of medical abortion; that is, the ingestion of two drugs, mifespristone and misoprostol.[104] Subject to state restrictions,[105] it is entirely possible (and safe) for a medication

---

[100] *EMW Women's Surgical Centre* (n 97) 13.
[101] As was proposed in Kentucky during the recent midterm elections, where a majority of voters responded 'No' to the question 'Are you in favor of amending the Constitution of Kentucky by creating a new Section of the Constitution to be numbered Section 26A to state as follows: To protect human life, nothing in this Constitution shall be construed to secure or protect a right to abortion or require the funding of abortion?', Kentucky General Assembly, HB 67, 2020 Regular Session apps.legislature.ky.gov/recorddocuments/bill/20RS/hb67/bill.pdf (accessed 31 July 2022). See, E Nash and I Guarnieri, 'In the US Midterm Elections, Resounding Victories for Abortion on State Ballot Measures', *Guttmacher Institute*, November 2022 www.guttmacher.org/2022/11/us-midterm-elections-resounding-victories-abortion-state-ballot-measures (accessed 11 November 2022). In early August 2022, voters rejected an attempt to amend the Kansan |Constitution to restrict abortion following a 2019 finding by the Kansas Supreme Court that the Kansan Constitution protected the right of personal autonomy which included the ability to control one's own body and to make decisions about whether to continue a pregnancy: Hodes & Nauser, *MDs v Schmidt* (Supreme Court), No 114, 153 (26 April 2019) www.kscourts.org/Cases-Opinions/Opinions/Published/Hodes-Nauser,-MDs-v-Schmidt-(Supreme-Cour (accessed 15 August 2022). See, for instance, M Smith and K Glueck, 'Kansas Votes to Preserve Abortion Rights in its Constitution', *The New York Times*, 2 August 2022 www.nytimes.com/2022/08/02/us/kansas-abortion-rights-vote.html (accessed 15 August 2022).
[102] Lindgren (n 45).
[103] ibid, 156, 166 and 175.
[104] RK Jones et al., 'Medication Abortion Now Accounts for More Than Half of All US Abortions', Guttmacher Institute, 24 February 2022 www.guttmacher.org/article/2022/02/medication-abortion-now-accounts-more-half-all-us-abortions (accessed 27 July 2022).
[105] As with regulation of abortion services more generally, many states have singled out medication abortion and subjected it to more onerous restrictions than other forms of medical treatment. Discussing

abortion to occur at home, without any involvement of a physician. Such a practice of safe, self-managed medical abortion would have been entirely alien to the justices ruling on *Roe* in 1973 when self-managed abortions carried significant risks and frequently resulted in injury or even death.[106] During the COVID-19 pandemic, the Food and Drug Administration (FDA) temporarily suspended the requirement that mifespristone be dispensed in person and, in December 2021, the FDA permanently removed that requirement.[107] Such changes reflect the growing prevalence of direct-to-consumer medical treatment and telemedicine. Indeed, in a post-*Roe* reality, telemedical abortions are likely to be the source of significant interstate dispute as abortion-restrictive states attempt to limit the ability of their residents to access abortion services online and over the phone and abortion-supportive states takes steps to insulate providers within their borders from being prosecuted for providing telemedical abortion services to residents in abortion-restrictive states.[108] In recognition of the growing prevalence – and importance – of medical, including telemedical, abortions in a post-*Roe* US, the US Congress has passed the Women's Health Protection Act of 2022 which 'prohibits governmental restrictions on the provision of, and access to, abortion services', and notes in particular that state governments 'may not limit a[n] [abortion] provider's ability to':

- prescribe certain drugs;
- offer abortion services via telemedicine; or,
- immediately provide abortion services when the provider determines a delay risks the patient's health.[109]

The Act further addresses (and limits) the ability of states to put in place TRAP laws.[110] While the Act was defeated in the Republican-controlled Senate, the contents

---

the continued requirement that mifespristone be prescribed in-person during the COVID-19 pandemic notwithstanding the additional risks face-to-face contact posed, Justice Sotomayor in her dissenting opinion (with which Justice Kagan agreed) observed in *Food and Drug Administration v American College of Obstetricians and Gynecologists* 141 S.Ct. 578, '[t]his country's laws have long singled out abortions for more onerous treatment than other medical procedures that carry similar or greater risks … Like many of those laws, maintaining the FDA's in-person requirements for mifepristone during the pandemic not only treats abortion exceptionally, it imposes an unnecessary, irrational, and unjustifiable undue burden on women seeking to exercise their right to choose' (585). In December 2021, the FDA determined to remove the requirement that mifespristone be prescribed in-person (see n 107), though this has not prevented states from maintaining such a requirement: see, for instance, G Donley, 'Medication abortion exceptionalism' (2022) 107 *Cornell Law Review* 627.

[106] Lindgren (n 45) 167–70.
[107] American College of Obstetricians and Gynecologists, 'Understanding the Practical Implications of the FDA's December 2021 Mifespristone REMS Decision', 28 March 2022 www.acog.org/news/news-articles/2022/03/understanding-the-practical-implications-of-the-fdas-december-2021-mifepristone-rems-decision#:~:text=On%20December%2016%2C%202021%2C%20the,dispense%20mifepristone%20must%20be%20certified (accessed 27 July 2022).
[108] Cohen et al. (n 2).
[109] Women's Health Protection Act of 2022, s 4132, 117th Congress (2021–2022), Summary www.congress.gov/bill/117th-congress/senate-bill/4132#:~:text=Introduced%20in%20Senate%20(05%2F03%2F2022)&text=This%20bill%20prohibits%20governmental%20restrictions,and%20access%20to%2C%20abortion%20services.&text=immediately%20provide%20abortion%20services%20when,delay%20risks%20the%20patient's%20health (accessed 27 July 2022).
[110] ibid.

of the legislation nevertheless reflect an appreciation that abortion services today are, in most cases, very different to those which were at the forefront of the justices' minds in *Roe*. The 2022 Act also demonstrates that *Roe's* emphasis on the doctor as gatekeeper is clearly inapt to deal with modern abortion services and reflects an appreciation of the significant issues regarding access.

VII. CONCLUSION

It is difficult to think of a case that has evoked more controversy in the US than *Roe v Wade*. In finding that the Fourteenth Amendment protected the right (albeit qualified) to abort a pregnancy, the majority SCOTUS opinion was patently a landmark decision: it fundamentally altered the landscape surrounding reproductive rights and drastically improved the safety of abortions. In the almost fifty years that passed between the date of the opinion and its reversal in 2022, hundreds of thousands of pregnant people were able to exercise safely their reproductive autonomy. While *Roe* is frequently discussed in the context of constitutional law, the consumer protection aspects of the case – which are, arguably, of equal importance as the constitutional implications – are often overlooked.

Roe placed the 'choice' of pregnant women to abort their pregnancy (and, thus, their right to access abortion services) front and centre, and this emphasis on the consumerist idea of choice continues to be a feature of abortion jurisprudence today, including in post-*Dobbs* state-based litigation. This emphasis on choice has undoubtedly proven vital for tens of thousands of pregnant people who have been able to exercise that choice. However, in the interests of achieving equality of access to abortion services (and obstetric and gynaecological services more generally) it is important not to overstate the success of *Roe*. For many thousands of pregnant people, the decision to abort a pregnancy is not truly a 'choice' but, rather, the only option and for many other pregnant people, impediments to access to abortion services render the 'right' to choose entirely academic. By focusing on 'choice' we 'overlook vast historical and contemporary disparities in women's access to maternity care in the United States'.[111] The reasons why pregnant people seek access to abortion services and the inability of thousands of pregnant people to do so is illustrative of the 'racialized and class-based tensions' that permeate access to reproductive services more generally.[112]

When we frame abortion through the rubric of consumer protection and 'choice', we ignore the roles poverty and race play in the decision to abort and in the ability (or inability) of people to exercise that choice. In addition to the terminological difficulties of *Roe*, we must also appreciate that in the almost 50 years since the opinion was delivered, many states (emboldened by a series of subsequent SCOTUS decisions, most notably the 1992 opinion in *Casey*) significantly curtailed the ability of pregnant people to exercise their right to choose whether to continue with a pregnancy. The

---

[111] C Craven, 'Reproductive Rights in a Consumer Rights Era: Toward the Value of "Constructive" Change' in C Craven and D-Ain Davis (eds), *Feminist Activist Ethnography: Counterpoints to Neoliberalism in North America* (Lanham, Lexington Books, 2013) 8.
[112] ibid.

use of TRAP laws resulted in the closing of hundreds of abortion providers, thereby forcing pregnant people to travel significant distances often at considerable expense to exercise their constitutional right to reproductive autonomy. And, for those who could not travel, there were the 'options' of illegal and potentially unsafe abortions or the compelled carrying of a pregnancy and childbirth which are far more dangerous than legal abortions.

Framing *Roe* in terms of consumer protection does, however, offer a powerful indication of the catastrophic implications of the decision's reversal. As the rates of illegal abortions prior to the 1973 decision demonstrate – and, indeed, as research from countries in which abortion is illegal but which, nevertheless, have rates of abortion commensurate with rates in countries where it is legal reveals[113] – the illegality of abortion does not mean it does not occur. Rather, overturning *Roe* will force many pregnant people further into poverty because of the costs associated with travelling to states that allow abortion. If travel is not an option, pregnant people may resort to telemedical abortion or to self-managed medical abortions with medication sourced online or elsewhere with the attendant risks of criminal sanction such activities carry under the restrictive abortion legislation being enacted in many US states. Thus, while the focus on 'choice' in *Roe* and the subsequent abortion jurisprudence has its limitations, a United States without a constitutionally protected right to choose will be devastating for tens, if not hundreds, of thousands of pregnant people and, as is the case with health services more generally in the US, those effects will most acutely be felt by 'women without money'.[114]

---

[113] See, for instance, G Sedgh et al., 'Abortion incidence between 1990 and 2014: global, regional, and subregional levels and trends' (2016) 388 *The Lancet* 10041, 265.

[114] *Dobbs* (n 5), Breyer, Sotomayor and Kagan JJ in dissent, 50.

14

Virginia State Board of Pharmacy v Virginia Consumer Citizens Council, Inc: Commercial Speech: Advancing the Rights of Consumers or Enhancing the Rights of Corporations?

MARY SPECTOR*

I. INTRODUCTION

The subject of this chapter, *Virginia State Board of Pharmacy v Virginia Citizens Consumer Council, Inc.*,[1] squarely held that 'commercial speech' is entitled to protection under the First Amendment of the US Constitution. That provision states that Congress 'shall make no law … abridging the freedom of speech'. The case also paved the way for decades of successful challenges to state laws around the country that restricted advertising by professionals, such as pharmacists, doctors and lawyers. Although not necessarily intended by the attorneys for the plaintiffs in the case, it also opened the door to challenges to state laws and federal regulations *requiring* certain types of disclosures in commercial advertising, all in the name of consumer protection.[2] Consumer protection policies were the foundation of the *Virginia Board of Pharmacy* decision, and the Court's application of the First Amendment clearly furthered those policies.

Yet, over time, market changes affecting distribution and pricing of prescription drugs as well as an expansive application of the First Amendment in commercial and

---

* I would like to thank the editors of this volume and the participants in the September 2021 workshop who took the time to read, comment and discuss an early outline of the chapter. Special thanks go to Professor Jodi Gardner for her patience and support (and friendship), and Professor Iain Ramsay for his careful reading and helpful comments that contributed to my thinking and the completion of the chapter.

[1] *Virginia State Board of Pharmacy v Virginia Citizens Consumer Council, Inc.* 425 U.S. 748 (1976) (hereinafter '*Virginia Board of Pharmacy*').

[2] AB Morrison, 'No Regrets (Almost): After Virginia Board of Pharmacy' (2017) 25 *William and Mary Bill of Rights Journal* 949 (essay written by attorney representing plaintiffs in the case challenging the statute).

non-commercial contexts suggests that protection of consumers' interests in receiving information have yielded to the speakers' right to deliver information in a particular way, such as the placement and size of point-of-sale cigarette advertising.[3] Some scholars contend, however, that all consumer speech is not alike and that analysis under the First Amendment in a way that is consistent with consumer protection policies expressed in *Virginia Board of Pharmacy* should lead to a less expansive application of the First Amendment in some cases.[4] Scholars may differ on whether courts apply or should apply the First Amendment broadly or narrowly in a particular case and there is a rich literature exploring the many views of the subject. This chapter takes a different approach in its examination of *Virginia Board of Pharmacy* by exploring the practical effects the case has had on consumers attempting to obtain information necessary for informed decisionmaking about their healthcare. It finds that any impact the case may have had (or still has) on promoting pricing transparency, is far outweighed by the impact it has had on expanding the rights of corporations within the marketplace in the US. At the same time, its impact on the development of the law relating to freedom of expression in Europe and Canada has progressed in a way that one can imagine the original advocates would approve.[5]

After providing historical context in section II regarding the advertising and regulation of prescription drugs, in section III, I will focus on the case itself and the consumer advocates' use of the First Amendment as a means to protect the public's right to know. As I explore the Court's opinion, I will consider some of the prevailing policy justifications for engaging in consumer protection. In section IV, I will explore some of the broader effects the case has on the expansion of protection for commercial speech and the rights of corporations in the US and abroad. In section V, I will return to explore the practical impact of the case on prescription drug advertising in the US and in section VI, I will consider the cost of that advertising to consumers. I will conclude with thoughts about what I believe is the legacy of the case and for some, its lost promise for American consumers, particularly in terms of advertising in the healthcare industry.

II. HISTORICAL CONTEXT

A. Advertising of Medications: Prescriptions v Nonprescription

In the US, prescription medications and advertising related to them are regulated by the federal government through the United States Food and Drug Administration. The agency's responsibility for prescription drugs dates only to the 1906 Pure Food

---

[3] See, eg, *Lorillard Tobacco Co. v Reilly*, 533 U.S. 525, 566 (2001) (holding that restrictions on size and placement of point of sale cigarette advertising violated manufacturer's first amendment rights to advertise its product); see also *Expressions Hair Design v Schneiderman*, 581 U.S. 37 (2017) (case challenging statute's prohibition against advertising credit card prices as including a 'surcharge'). See also, Morrison (n 2) 949 (2017); F Wu, 'Commercial Speech Protection as Consumer Protection' (2019) 90 *University of Colorado Law Review* 31.
[4] See Wu (n 3) 631.
[5] See below, section IV.B.

and Drugs Act (1906 Act), which focused on accurate drug labelling and the disclosure of certain ingredients such as alcohol and cocaine; it did not regulate advertising about the effectiveness of the drugs.

Before 1906, the United States Pharmacopoeia (USP) compiled a list of standard drugs considered 'ethical'.[6] By 1905, the American Medical Association's Council on Pharmacy and Chemistry set standards for ethical drugs and urged doctors to avoid prescribing drugs not on the list, or so called 'patent' or 'proprietary' drugs that were marketed directly to consumers. In contrast to the ethical drugs, the patent drugs contained ingredients that their manufacturers considered secret and marketed them with broad claims about effectiveness for a variety of ailments. Passage of the 1906 Act required disclosure of patent drugs' ingredients like alcohol, an ingredient common in many of them. Amendments to the 1906 Act attempted to prohibit false and deceptive claims about effectiveness.[7]

The 1938 Food, Drug and Cosmetic Act, required that drugs' safety and effectiveness have FDA approval before they could be made available to consumers. Although the FDA considered prescription drugs potentially harmful for use by consumers without the supervision of a physician, it nevertheless required disclosures regarding the drugs be made only to the physicians who prescribed the drugs and pharmacists who dispensed them and not to the consumers who used them. As a result, pharmaceutical companies directed their promotional efforts and advertising dollars to doctors and other health professionals and did not advertise directly to consumers.

Until the 1970s, the only direct-to-consumer advertising of medications were for over-the-counter medicines, such as common pain relievers, that were not regulated by the FDA. Any regulation related to their advertising was left to the Federal Trade Commission, with its broad authority to protect consumers from false and deceptive acts and practices, particularly where health and safety are involved.[8]

B. Enter the Consumer Movement

By the late 1960s, a growing consumer movement led to a number of laws at both the federal and state levels designed to protect the safety of consumers and promote fairness and access to truthful information about consumer goods and services. At the federal level, they included the Truth in Lending Act, first passed in 1968,[9] which utilised disclosure to promote fair lending practices, the Fair Credit Reporting Act first enacted in 1970,[10] which placed limits on the reporting of consumers' credit information to protect privacy and promote accuracy, the Equal Credit Opportunity Act of

---

[6] J Donohue, 'A History of Drug Advertising: The Evolving Roles of Consumers and Consumer Protection' (2006) 84 *The Millbank Quarterly* 659, 666 (2006).
[7] One such patent drug is Lydia Pinkham's Vegetable Compound, first sold in the 1870s and aggressively marketed to women to relieve a wide variety of problems ranging from menstrual cramps, to post-partum depression, to menopause. See ibid.
[8] See FTC, *Division of Advertising Practices*, www.ftc.gov/about-ftc/bureaus-offices/bureau-consumer-protection/our-divisions/division-advertising-practices.
[9] 15 U.S.C. §§ 1601–07.
[10] 15 U.S.C. §§ 1681–81x.

1974[11] designed to prevent discrimination on the basis of race or marital status, and the Fair Debt Collection Practices Act first passed in 1978[12] to prohibit deceptive and unfair practices in the collection of consumer debts.

Just as consumers sought and obtained greater rights and protections in the marketplace, patients sought greater rights and protections in connection with the delivery of healthcare.[13] Indeed, the same consumer advocates who were fighting for fairness with respect to lending, credit and debt, were also calling for greater recognition of individual's rights with respect to health care. They included Public Citizen, then led by Ralph Nader, whose 1965 book, *Unsafe at Any Speed*, detailed car manufacturers' lack of attention to safety and eventually led to laws requiring seat belts in all passenger vehicles and the creation of the National Highway Safety Transportation Administration (NHSTA).[14]

Public Citizen's focus on safety expanded to consumer products and its impact was far-reaching. It contributed to the creation of federal agencies like the federal Consumer Product Safety Commission and worked with Congress to ban harmful drugs and pesticides on the market.[15] Its work eventually led to the FDA's requirement that prescription labels be provided to patients/consumers as well as to their doctors.[16] It also sought greater transparency in prescription drug pricing, which it saw it as the first step of a much broader litigation strategy to end advertising bans in the professions, particularly among doctors and lawyers, and ultimately increase the availability of affordable legal services.[17] Central to securing both patients' and consumers' rights was the availability of information necessary to make important purchasing and healthcare decisions.

C. Parallel Expansion of First Amendment Protections

Public Citizen's strategy was to continue and expand an approach begun in the 1930s that began to chip away at municipal bans on the distribution of printed matter in public. The availability and distribution of information was at the core of plaintiffs' challenges to a municipal ordinance from New Jersey, which banned the distribution of printed matter of any kind on city streets.[18] Finding the ordinance unlawfully prohibited the distribution of political or religious materials on public streets, the Court invalidated it as over broad, cautioning that its holding did not preclude municipal regulation of commercial advertising or the reasonable regulation of the hours in which political and religious materials could be distributed.[19]

---

[11] 15 U.S.C. §§ 1691–91f.
[12] 15 U.S.C. §§ 1692–92p.
[13] See Donohue (n 6) 672.
[14] See C Jensen, '50 Years Ago, 'Unsafe at Any Speed' Shook the Auto World', *NY Times* (26 November 2015).
[15] See Public Citizen interactive timeline www.citizen.org/victories/.
[16] Donohue (n 6) 672.
[17] See Morrison (n 2) 949-50.
[18] *Schneider v New Jersey*, 308 U.S. 147 (1939).
[19] ibid 165.

Three years later, in *Valentine v Chrestenson*,[20] the Court considered a challenge to a more narrowly drawn ordinance brought by Chrestenson, the owner of a former US Navy submarine docked at a pier in New York City owned by the State of New York. When police informed him that only distribution of political or religious material was permitted, Chrestenson revised the content of his original handbill to remove information about the admission fee, and also included a protest against New York City's refusal to allow him access to a city-owned pier. Based on its rulings in the prior cases, the Court acknowledged that municipalities could not unduly burden speakers use of public places 'for the exercise of the freedom of communicating information and disseminating opinion', but held that the First Amendment did not protect speakers in similar circumstances for communicating information of a 'purely commercial nature.' Finding that Chrestenson's second handbill was nothing more than an attempt to 'evade' the ordinance, the Court let it stand.

Over the next 30 years, the Court considered a number of cases challenging government practices that had the effect of limiting or prohibiting speech related to some form of commercial activity. Some limits were invalidated,[21] others were found to be reasonable.[22] As the cases chipped away at government attempts to limit commercial speech the Court also seemed to reject a determinative view of the commercial nature of the speech and focused instead on the content of the speech, its truthfulness and its utility to the listener.[23]

III. VIRGINIA BOARD OF PHARMACY: ADVANCING CONSUMERS' INTEREST IN RECEIVING INFORMATION

A. The Statute

With its strategy designed to end advertising bans for the professions, the Public Citizen Litigation Group turned to Virginia. The statute at the centre of *Virginia Board*[24] was enacted in 1969 as part of a comprehensive regulatory scheme that controlled the licensing and discipline of pharmacists.[25] It made licensed pharmacists subject to discipline by the State Board of Pharmacy for engaging in the price

---

[20] *Valentine v Chrestenson* 316 U.S. 52 (1942).
[21] Eg, *Martin v City of Struthers*, 319 U.S. 141 (1943) (municipal ordinance preventing door-to-door distribution of religious literature); *Thomas v Collins*, 323 U.S. 516 (1945) (invalidating Texas law as applied to prevent paid union organizer from delivering speech); *Bigelow v Virginia*, 421 U.S. 809 (1975), (striking ban on advertising availability of abortion services lawful in other states).
[22] Eg, *Pittsburgh Press Co. v Pittsburgh Comm. on Hum. Rel.*, 413 U.S. 376 (1973) (holding anti-discrimination statute validly applied to restrict placement of advertisements).
[23] See generally, *Griswold v Connecticut*, 381 U.S. 479 (1965) ('The right of freedom of speech and press includes not only the right to utter or to print, but the right to distribute, the right to receive, the right to read.'); *New York Times v Sullivan*, 376 U.S. 254 (1964) (holding First Amendment protects corporate entity from liability in libel action unless it acted with malice).
[24] *Virginia Board of Pharmacy* (n 1).
[25] See RP Bezanson, 'Speech Stories: How Free Can Speech Be?' *The Pharmacist* 158 (NY University Press, 1998).

advertising of prescription drugs. Such discipline could include a monetary fine, licence suspension or revocation.[26]

Previous challenges to an advertising ban on dentists in Oregon,[27] and a ban on advertising related to eye examinations in Oklahoma,[28] on equal protection grounds had failed. Indeed, the Virginia statute at the heart of *Virginia Board* survived a similar challenge on equal protection grounds just a few years before in the western district of Virginia.[29]

B. In the District Court

This time the approach was different. Lynn Jordan, a Virginia resident, and the Virginia Citizens Consumer Council who, together with the Virginia affiliate of the AFL-CIO labour union, represented more than 200,000 members initiated the case challenging the statute. Alan B Morrison of the Public Citizen Litigation Group represented them. They sought a declaration that the provision violated the First Amendment to the US Constitution's guarantee that Congress and the states 'shall make no law ... abridging the freedom of speech'. They also sought an injunction preventing its enforcement.[30]

In an 'interesting twist of irony', the pharmacists who were prevented from advertising under the statute were not present in the case.[31] Instead, the plaintiffs, individually, and on behalf of their members – consumers – claimed that the statute denied them the right to receive truthful price information to enable informed decisions about matters of great importance.

The Commonwealth of Virginia maintained that the statute, including the provision at issue, was a reasonable exercise of its police power to regulate the state's pharmacies and pharmacists. In particular, it maintained that the speech it prevented was wholly commercial, and therefore not entitled to the protection of the First Amendment under *Chrestenson*, the 1942 case upholding the municipal ban on distributing advertising on city street.

A three-judge district court agreed with the plaintiffs, stating as follows:

> The right-to-know is the foundation of the First Amendment; it is the theme of this suit. Consumers are denied this right by the Virginia statute. It is on this premise that we grant the plaintiffs the injunction and the declaration they ask.
>
> Why the customer is refused this knowledge is not convincingly explained by the State Board of Pharmacy and its members. Enforcement of the ban gives no succor to public health; on the contrary, access by the infirm or poor to the price of prescription drugs would be for their good. This information 'serves as a tool to educate rather than deceive.'[32]

The State of Virginia appealed directly to the Supreme Court.

---

[26] Vir. Code Ann. § 54-524.35(3) (1974).
[27] *Semler v Oregon St. Bd. of Dental Examiners*, 298 U.S. 604 (1935).
[28] *Williamson v Lee Optical of Oklahoma*, 348 U.S. 483 (1955).
[29] *Patterson Drug Co., v Kingery*, 305 F. Supp. 821 (W.D. Va, 1969).
[30] See, *Virginia Citizens Cons. Council, Inc., v Virginia Bd of Pharm.*, 373 F. Supp. 683 (E.D. Va. 1974).
[31] See Bezanson (n 25) 157.
[32] 373 F. Supp. 683.

C. In the Supreme Court

The State of Virginia filed its brief in the Supreme Court on 2 June 1975. It framed its issue on appeal as 'Whether the First Amendment grants consumers an independent 'right-to-know' thus allowing invalidation of a statute which validly prohibits the (sic) dissemination(sic) of commercial advertising.'[33] Again, relying on *Chrestenson*,[34] it argued that First Amendment protection did not extend to purely commercial speech that 'simply seek[s] to induce consumers into purchasing the services offered'.[35] The state also relied on the cases in which the Court had upheld state regulation of dentists,[36] and opticians[37] on equal protection grounds, not on the basis of the First Amendment.

In contrast the consumers framed the issue this way:

> Can the State of Virginia constitutionally prohibit the dissemination of drug price information and thereby deny consumers the facts that they need to make informed decisions about where to purchase the drugs that their doctors prescribe for them?[38]

The American Association of Retired Persons, the National Association of Advertisers and retailer Osco Drug, Inc., submitted amici briefs, all in support of the appellees. No amici wrote in support of the State of Virginia.

On 24 May 1976, Mr Justice Blackmun delivered the Court's opinion affirming the district court's decision to find that the statute's prohibition of truthful prescription price advertising violated the First Amendment. Chief Justice Burger and Justice Stewart concurred in separate opinions and Mr Justice Rehnquist dissented.

The first order of business was the matter of the plaintiffs' standing to assert a First Amendment right, if any existed. As noted above, no pharmacists were among the group of plaintiffs challenging the statute. To determine standing, Justice Blackmun turned to a string of decisions in which the Court had recognised that First Amendment protection extended to citizens' right to receive information that a statute or government official otherwise prevented them from receiving. They included a citizen's right to receive foreign political mail,[39] and a married couple's right to receive information about contraception.[40] In each of these cases, the intended recipient was permitted to receive the information without interference from the state. Justice Blackmun reasoned that if First Amendment protection is afforded to a willing speaker, and to the communication, there was a 'reciprocal right' to receive the information, and that right could be asserted in the case before it by consumers and those representing them who sought the information the statute prohibited.[41]

---

[33] Appellant's Br. At 2.
[34] 316 U.S. 52 (1942).
[35] Brief for Appellant at 2, *Virginia State Board of Pharmacy v Virginia Citizens Council, Inc.*, (No 74-895).
[36] *Semler v Oregon State Board of Dental Examiners*, 294 U.S. 608 (1935).
[37] *Williamson v Lee Optical of Oklahoma* (n 28).
[38] Appellee's Br.
[39] *Lamont v Postmaster General*, 381 U.S. 301 (1965).
[40] *Griswold v Connecticut* (n 23).
[41] *Virginia Board of Pharmacy* (n 1)756.

Next, Justice Blackmun turned to the state's primary argument, that 'commercial speech' was not entitled to First Amendment protection. He turned a critical eye toward the cases decided in the years after *Valentine v Chrestenson* denied protection to 'purely commercial advertising'. The first post-*Valentine* case he considered was *Breard v Alexandrea*,[42] in which the Court rejected a First Amendment challenge to a conviction under a Louisiana statute that prohibited door-to-door sales of magazine subscriptions, and noted that just nine years after that decision it struck a conviction under a similar statute where the door-to-door conduct involved religious materials.[43] Justice Blackmun reasoned that the Court had begun to move away from its prior holdings that the economic interest of the speaker determined whether or not First Amendment protection attached to the speech. He noted that publishers in the business of making money, such as the *New York Times*, were routinely entitled to First Amendment protection[44] and distinguished those cases in which the Court had upheld restrictions on commercial speech after *Breard* on the grounds that the challenged statutes permissibly restricted only the *manner* in which advertising content could be distributed and not its content.[45]

Turning next to the consumer's interest in receiving the information, Justice Blackmun wrote that the 'interest in the free flow of commercial information ... may be as keen, if not keener, by far, than his interest in the day's most urgent political debate'.[46] Although he did not provide a precise definition of commercial speech, one scholar has since explained that 'what makes commercial speech commercial is its role in communicating commercial information in order to facilitate commercial transactions'.[47] Acknowledging that states could regulate the content of speech by prohibiting deceptive or false advertising, Justice Blackmun distinguished the Virginia statute from anti-deception legislation on the basis that it prevented the advertising of truthful information, which he described as 'simply', 'I will sell you the X prescription drug at the Y price.'[48]

With the *consumer's* interest at the forefront, the Court invoked a number of now familiar approaches to the analysis of commercial practices that are common in the field of consumer law. For example, he considered the imbalance of power and information that existed. On one side were pharmacists and medical professionals with knowledge of the market and power to set prices. On the other side were consumers, left in the dark without easy means to obtain critical information necessary to their daily life. He saw the balance as even more striking among consumers most affected by price, the 'poor, the sick, and particularly the aged'. He also considered empirical evidence from a number of sources demonstrating wide variations in drug prices for a single prescription within a single city or market[49] without means for consumers to

---

[42] *Breard v Alexandrea* 341 U.S. 622 (1951) (discussion post-*Valentine* cases).
[43] *Virginia Board of Pharmacy* (n 1) 758.
[44] ibid 761 (citing *New York Times v Sullivan* (n 23).
[45] *Pittsburgh Press Co. v Human Relations Comm'n*, 413 U.S. 376 (1973) (upholding statute banning restrictions on the manner of publishing employment advertisements it was designed to prevent illegal discriminatory hiring).
[46] *Virginia Board of Pharmacy* (n 1) 763.
[47] Wu (n 3) 631.
[48] *Virginia Board of Pharmacy* (n 1) 762.
[49] ibid fn 11.

identify differences in a ready fashion, and evidence of significantly higher per capita spending on prescription for those over 65.[50]

Justice Blackmun saw the advertisement of drug prices as an important factor that could help to balance the power and information scales in much the same way that financial and other types of disclosure were being used in other areas of consumer law.[51] He rejected justifications for the law that rested on maintaining professional standards, holding that the state was free to impose standards on its professions, but 'may not do so by keeping the public in ignorance'.[52] The bottom line, according to Justice Blackmun, was that a state may not prohibit the dissemination of advertising that contains 'concededly truthful information about an entirely lawful activity'.[53]

The decision was not a unanimous one. Justice Stevens did not take part in the decision and both Chief Justice Burger and Justice Stewart concurred. The Chief Justice wrote to express his view that advertising of 'professional services carries with it quite different risks from the advertisement of standard products', and to highlight that Court's opinion did not extend First Amendment protection to advertising by 'traditional learned professions of medicine or law'. Justice Stewart wrote separately to emphasise that it was truthful advertising that the Court protected and that the decision did not limit state's ability to limit deceptive or untruthful advertising.

Justice Rehnquist dissented. He was not convinced of the plaintiffs' standing, nor was he convinced that the interests of the consumer should override the determination by the state that pharmacists should not advertise. The primary danger he saw in the Court's opinion was the slippery slope on which he believed the Court had embarked by adopting a rule that could not be limited to truthful price advertising, but would eventually extend to promotional drug advertising and 'the active promotion of … liquor, cigarettes, and other products the use of which it has previously been thought desirable to discourage' as well as advertising by lawyers, doctors and other professionals.[54]

For better or worse, he was right. The chapter will explore the slippery slope about which Justice Rehnquist worried in sections IV and V below.

IV. BROADER EFECTS

A. Breadth of Virginia Board Narrowed by Central Hudson

Prior to *Virginia Board*, commercial speech enjoyed virtually no protection under the First Amendment. Although the architects of the case focused their strategy to protect the rights of the listener to receive truthful information important to a

---

[50] ibid fn 18. This is still true today, although the numbers referred to in the opinion seem small in comparison to today's numbers.
[51] Eg, Truth in Lending Act, 15 U.S.C. § 1601(a) (finding 'economic stabilization would be enhanced' and competition among lenders would be 'strengthened' by 'informed use of credit').
[52] *Virginia Board of Pharmacy* (n 1) 748. Cf, *Jones v Westside Buick Co.*, 93 S.W.2d 1083 (Mo. Ct. App. 1936) (court rejecting industry's common practices as legitimate reason for keeping consumers in the dark).
[53] ibid 772.
[54] *Virginia Board of Pharmacy* (n 1) 781 (Rehnquist J dissenting).

commercial transaction, it did not take long before the speakers, that is, the sellers, used the First Amendment to protect their own rights to provide information regardless of whether it was helpful to the listener.[55] Indeed, the four-part test announced in the Court's 1980 decision in *Central Hudson v Public Serv Comm'n*,[56] starts with the premise that the content of the speech 'must concern lawful activity and not be misleading' and then determines whether the government's interest is substantial and balances the effect of the state's action against the rights of the speaker. Specifically, the Court states:

> For commercial speech to come within that provision, it at least must concern lawful activity and not be misleading. Next, we ask whether the asserted governmental interest is substantial. If both inquiries yield positive answers, we must determine whether the regulation directly advances the governmental interest asserted, and whether it is not more extensive than is necessary to serve that interest.[57]

By the early 1990s, the Court used the *Central Hudson* test to protect the rights of a corporate speaker seeking to avoid government limits on its ability to advertise[58] and one after another, corporate speakers succeeded in challenging limits on advertising they claimed abridged their First Amendment rights to engage in protected commercial speech.[59] Although a number of cases decided in the years after *Virginia Board of Pharmacy* recognised the importance of informed consumers, it can be argued that by striking down laws limiting information relevant to consumers' purchasing decisions, courts did so 'at the expense of other societal values'.[60] Some scholars describe this approach to First Amendment law as an anti-paternalistic approach that is not found in other areas of constitutional law but that was 'born' in *Virginia Board of Pharmacy*.[61]

In an essay looking back on the legacy of the case, Alan B Morrison, attorney for the plaintiffs in the case, wrote that by invoking the First Amendment to protect the rights of an electric company to promote electricity usage rather than conservation,[62] or the rights of casinos[63] or liquor stores to advertise,[64] courts have given 'undue weight to the interest of the advertiser and too little weight to whether the information was useful to the listener',[65] suggesting that the anti-paternalistic approach may have gone too far.

---

[55] See, eg, *Lorillard Tobacco Co.*, 533 U.S. 525 (*Rubin v Coors Brewing Co.*, 514 U.S. 476 (1995) (brewers' successful challenge to ban on advertising alcohol content of beer).
[56] *Central Hudson Gas & Elec. Corp. v Public Serv Comm'n*, 447 U.S. 557 (1980).
[57] ibid 566.
[58] *Bolger v Youngs Drug Prod. Corp.*, 463 U.S. 60 (1983) (striking ban on unsolicited mailings of pamphlets regarding contraceptives as impermissible regulation of commercial speech).
[59] *City of Cincinnati v Discovery Network, Inc.*, 507 U.S. 410 (1993) (commercial publishers' successful challenge to ordinance banning news racks containing advertising where ban did not apply to news racks containing traditional newspapers); *Liquormart, Inc. v Rhode Island*, 517 U.S. 484 (1996) (holding state could not ban liquor price advertising).
[60] See Wu (n 3) 640.
[61] Eg, D Carpenter, 'The Antipaternalism Principle in the First Amendment' (2004) 37 *Creighton Law Review* 579.
[62] *Central Hudson Gas & Electric Corp. v Public Serv Comm. of New York*, 447 US, 557 (1980).
[63] *Greater New Orleans Broadcasting Assn v United States*, 527 U.S. 173 (2014).
[64] *Liquormart, Inc. v Rhode Island*, 517 U.S. 484 (1996) (successful challenge to ban on advertising liquor prices).
[65] Morrison (n 2) 949 (2017).

While Alan B Morrison also acknowledges the view that *Virginia Board* enabled the expansion of First Amendment rights of corporate entities, he denies full responsibility for the expansion of corporations' civil rights.[66] He notes that the speaker in *New York Times v Sullivan*,[67] which he calls the most important libel case under the First Amendment, was a corporation. He also points out that the Court did not cite *Virginia Board of Pharmacy* in one of its most notorious corporate rights cases under the First Amendment, *Citizens United v Federal Election Comm'n*.[68] Somewhat reluctantly, however, he must acknowledge the Court's reference to it in *First Nat. Bank of Boston v Bellotti*,[69] in which the Court struck a Massachusetts law limiting corporations' ability to make political expenditures,[70] and upon with the *Citizens United* decision relied.[71]

A recent case brought by a sports magazine and gun manufacturers challenging a California ban on advertising of firearms directed to minors may test the limits of *Central Hudson*.[72] In the last months of 2022, a federal district judge upheld the ban in *Junior Sports Magazines, Inc. v Bonta*, but the plaintiff immediately appealed to the Supreme Court. As of the writing of this chapter, no decision has been made but the plaintiff immediately appealed to the United States Court of Appeals for the Ninth Circuit. The case was argued and submitted to the court for decision on 28 June 2023, but no decision has been made as of the publication of this chapter.

B. Commercial Speech Outside the United States

Virginia Board of Pharmacy is considered 'central' to the development of commercial speech doctrine outside the US, in both Canada and Europe[73] where 'freedom of expression' is guaranteed. Both Article 10 of the European Convention for Protection of Human Rights and Fundamental Freedoms[74] and the Canadian Charter of Rights and Freedom[75] have been interpreted to provide protection to commercial expression.[76] Yet, in contrast to their American cousin, the First Amendment, both documents expressly provide that the right to expression will give way as may be necessary in a 'democratic society'.[77]

---

[66] ibid 957.
[67] *New York Times Co. v Sullivan* (n 23).
[68] *Citizens United v Federal Election Comm'n* 558 U.S. 310 (2010).
[69] *First Nat. Bank of Boston v Bellotti* 435 U.S. 765 (1979).
[70] Morrison (n 2) 957.
[71] See generally, CE Schneider, Free Speech and Corporate Freedom: A Comment on *First National Bank of Boston v Bellotti*' (1986) 59 *Southern California Law Review* 1227.
[72] *Junior Sports Magazines Inc. v Bonta*, 2022 WL 14365026, Case No 2:22-cv-04663-CAS (C.D. Cal., 22 November 2022).
[73] See RA Shiner, *Freedom of Commercial Expression* (Oxford, OUP 2003) 324.
[74] Council of Europe, *European Convention for the Protection of Human Rights and Fundamental Freedoms, as amended by Protocols Nos. 11 and 14*, 4 November 1950, ETS 5, available at www.refworld.org/docid/3ae6b3b04.html [hereinafter *European Convention on Human Rights*].
[75] Canadian Charter of Rights and Freedoms, Part 1 of the Constitution Act, 1982, being Schedule B to the Canada Act 1982 (UK), 1982, c 11.
[76] See Shiner (n 73) 70-110.
[77] See *European Convention on Human Rights* (n 74) Art 10 (2); *Canadian Charter of Rights and Freedoms*, s 1 and 2(b).

In Canada – as in the US – many of the first cases involving commercial speech were brought by members of the professions who sought to challenge advertising bans.[78] Although early cases examining the Charter appeared to be somewhat more deferential to government limits on expression than US courts, over time there has come to be 'considerable overlap in the kind of case decided and manner of deciding'.[79]

In contrast, the European Court of Human Rights and the European Court of Justice, both charged with considering challenges to freedom of commercial expression, demonstrate less 'individualtist hostility to government regulations', than their counterparts on the other side of the Atlantic.[80]

V. IMPACT OF THE CASE ON PRESCRIPTION DRUG ADVERTISING, PRICE TRANSAPARENCY AND THE PROFESSIONS

In the Introduction to this chapter, I promised to explore whether the practical goals of *Virginia Board of Pharmacy* have been achieved, that is, to provide consumers with price transparency in an effort to bring down costs of prescription drugs and to promote broader access to lawyers and healthcare. I do so in this part, by first looking at the growth of prescription drug advertising and the continuing challenges consumers face in the prescription drug market as well as with respect to availability of healthcare and access to the professions.

A. Growth of Prescription Drug Advertising and Consumer Spending

The immediate effect of the case was to protect commercial speech that provides truthful information on the theory that receipt of truthful information helps consumers make rational purchasing decisions. In the short run, as those involved in the litigation had hoped,[81] the case paved the way for greater advertising within the professions by eliminating barriers to advertising by lawyers and doctors.[82]

It also paved the way for today's staggering amount of prescription drug advertising, although the growth was not immediate and virtually none of the advertising is about price. Today, more than 20,000 prescription drug products are approved by the US Food and Drug Administration (FDA) for advertising.[83]

---

[78] See Shiner (n 73) 73, 77.
[79] ibid 91.
[80] ibid 107.
[81] See nn 24 to 32 above and accompanying text.
[82] *Zauderer v Office of Disciplinary Counsel of Supreme Court of Ohio*, 471 U.S. 626 (1985).
[83] Oversight of prescription drug advertising is handled in the FDA's Office of Prescription Drug Promotion (OPDP) whose mission is to protect 'the public health by helping to ensure that prescription drug promotion is truthful, balanced, and accurately communicated. This is accomplished through comprehensive surveillance, compliance, and education programs, and by fostering better communication of labeling and promotional information to both healthcare providers and consumers.' Of course, the regulation comes at a cost as well. And, today, up to 45% of that cost is borne by the companies whose products it regulates through the payment of application fees and other charges. today.uconn.edu/2021/05/why-is-the-fda-funded-in-part-by-the-companies-it-regulates-2/.

In the first ten years after the decision, a handful of pharmaceutical companies dipped their toes in the advertising waters and did so with mixed results. In the early 1980s one high profile campaign resulted in the manufacturer pulling the drug off the market after media outlets exaggerated the effectiveness of a drug's ability to treat arthritis.[84] Over time, however, pharmaceutical companies began to see the value in direct-to-consumer (DTC) advertising as a complement to traditional promotional campaigns directed to doctors and other health professionals. Budgets for spending on DTC advertising of US$55 million in 1991 grew to US$363 million in 1995.[85]

Just over 20 years later, the numbers have grown even more. In May 2021 the General Accounting Office (GAO) reported that pharmaceutical companies spent US$17.8 billion in DTC of prescription drugs from 2016 to 2018.[86] Approximately 67 per cent of those advertising dollars were spent to advertise 39 brand-name drugs. Although pharmaceutical industry sources report that after overall advertising expenditures dropped in 2019, pharmaceutical DTC advertising exceeded US$6.58 billion in 2020.[87] The bulk of the advertising was spent to advertise drugs to treat chronic conditions such as arthritis, diabetes and depression.[88]

Although the GAO found that DTC advertising dollars were associated with the increased use and consumer spending on those drugs, it was reluctant to place all of the blame for increases in spending on DTC advertising. Instead, it found that such advertisements were just one of several factors that lead to increases in spending on the drugs prescribed.[89] Notably, during roughly the same period covered by the GAO report, another federal agency, the Congressional Budget Office (CBO), found that average net price of brand-name prescription drugs increased substantially, in some cases more than 100 per cent for some brand-name drugs over the period from 2018 to 2021.[90]

B. Price Transparency Remains Elusive

Even with billions spent on prescription drug advertising, transparency in prescription drug pricing remains elusive in the US. Instead, the initial promise that transparency in drug pricing would lower costs for consumers has given way to a robust industry for the advertising of drugs situated in a complex system of prescription distribution and pricing.

One explanation for the lack of transparency in prescription drug pricing is the stunning complexity of the American pricing system for pharmaceuticals. In its January 2022 report, the CBO describes the process for getting prescription drugs

---

[84] Donohue (n 6) 675.
[85] ibid 683.
[86] General Accounting Office, 21-380, Prescription Drugs; Medicare Spending on Drugs with Direct-to-Consumer Advertising, May 2021 [hereinafter GAO-21-380].
[87] www.fiercepharma.com/special-report/top-10-ad-spenders-big-pharma-for-2020.
[88] See GAO-21-380 (n 86).
[89] ibid 20 (discussing other reports that came to similar conclusions).
[90] ibid.

to market and just how 'the concept of 'price' differs depending on the entity that is receiving payment – or paying – for a prescription'.[91]

Distribution and pricing begin with the manufacturer or pharmaceutical company who sells to a wholesale distributor. The distributor then sells to a pharmacy at a price that is often negotiated by a middle person such as an insurance company's pharmacy benefit manager, and the pharmacy then sells it to the ultimate user. But how much the consumer pays ultimately depends on whether they are uninsured or insured through private insurance (and which one), or publicly available insurance schemes such as Medicare (for people over 65), Tricare (most military personnel, their families and survivors), or Medicaid (very low-income or disabled). What is more, the US Department of Health and Human Services estimates that 8 per cent of Americans are without health insurance.[92]

To be sure, in the post-*Virginia Board of Pharmacy* world, pharmacies advertise. They utilise a variety of media that include newspaper inserts, direct mail, television, and digital. For example, Walgreen's, which operates approximately 9,000 stores[93] in all 50 states, and CVS with more than 9,800 stores nationwide,[94] routinely advertise special pricing on a number of over-the-counter medicines, as well as cosmetics, personal care, household cleaning supplies, food and wine.[95]

Although neither company routinely advertises prescription drugs, they acknowledge the difficulties consumers face in finding the best prices for the prescription medications. On its website, CVS states 'Search for Rx savings can be confusing. So, we do it for you. We search coupons, insurance and discount codes to help find you savings.'[96] Clicking a link takes consumers to a page where they must sign in or 'create an account to start searching for savings',[97] and provide personal information that can be used for more marketing and advertising.

Recent years have seen the development of technological tools developed by third parties that are promoted as a way to comparison shop for prescription drugs. Pharmacy or prescription discount cards and technology-based services can provide consumers some relief when navigating the system by comparing drug prices offered within a certain geographical area. Services such as ScriptSave, Well Rx and GoodRx offer consumers traditional or electronic cards that can be presented to the pharmacist to obtain the discounts. Although these services can mean lower prices paid to pharmacies, they also bring consumers into stores where they may also be likely to spend on non-prescription items when buying their prescriptions. And while the benefit to consumers in terms of lower prices is clear, there may be hidden costs of trading

---

[91] Congressional Budget Office, *Prescription Drugs: Spending, Use, and Prices* 6-7 January 2022, available at www.cbo.gov/publication/57050.
[92] Health and Human Services, *New HHS Report Shows National Uninsured Rate reached All-Time Low in 2022* (August 2022), www.hhs.gov/about/news/2022/08/02/new-hhs-report-shows-national-uninsured-rate-reached-all-time-low-in-2022.html.
[93] news.walgreens.com/fact-sheets/frequently-asked-questions.htm.
[94] www.scrapehero.com/location-reports/CVS%20Pharmacy-USA/.
[95] www.cvs.com/weeklyad/?icid=cvsheader:weeklyad.
[96] ibid.
[97] ibid.

personal information for the possibility of lower prices.[98] Unfortunately, the promise of lower prices also requires the disclosure of personal identifying information with little to no information about how the private facts may be used or who will use them.

Regulatory efforts to rein in costs whether through advertising or disclosure continue to face challenges under the First Amendment. In 2019 the Centers for Medicare and Medicaid, a division of the Department of Health and Human Services (HHS) promulgated a Disclosure Rule requiring disclosure of prescription drug prices in television advertisements.[99] Pharmaceutical companies challenged the rule, maintaining that agency had exceeded its statutory authority in promulgating the rule and, somewhat ironically, that it violated their First Amendment rights. In June 2020, the US Court of Appeals for the District of Columbia agreed, but never reached the First Amendment argument, deciding that the department lacked the authority to promulgate the rule, in part because of the complicated pricing mechanism of prescription drugs.[100]

In a second case decided the same year, the same Court came to a different conclusion with respect to a different regulation promulgated by HHS pursuant to the Affordable Care Act (a.k.a. Obamacare) that required hospitals to provide a list of standard charges. The American Hospital Association and others challenged the regulation on a number of grounds, including under the First Amendment's application to commercial speech. Because of the complex way in which Americans pay for healthcare, plaintiffs argued that disclosure would not be helpful, an argument reminiscent of the one made by the state in *Virginia Board of Pharmacy*.[101] In December 2020, the D.C. Circuit Court of Appeals rejected the argument and found that requiring hospitals to disclose prices prior to delivering services was a reasonable regulation of commerce that did not violate the First Amendment.[102] A stronger rule was set to go into effect in 2021, but a year after the intended effective date, studies showed that fewer than six per cent of hospitals were complying.[103]

C. Advertising and the Professions

The architects of *Virginia Board of Pharmacy* planted the seeds for a transformation of the business of prescription drugs advertising with a promise of greater consumer choice and lower prices. As described above, much of the promise has gone unfulfilled. With similar goals, they paved the way for widespread lawyer[104]

---

[98] O Hilas, 'A Pharmacist's Primer on Prescription Discount Cards', *US Pharmacist*, 15 October 2021.
[99] See 42 C.F. R. Part 403 (2019).
[100] *Merck & Co. v Health and Human Services*, 962 F.3d 532 (D.C. Cir. 2020).
[101] *American Hospital Association v Azar*, 983 F.3d 528, 541 (D.C. Cir. 2020).
[102] ibid.
[103] P Sullivan, 'US Health Spending Rose to Over $4 Trillion in 2020 Amid Pandemic Response', *Fortune*, 15 December 2021, fortune.com/2022/01/14/one-year-on-hospital-price-transparency-is-still-a-work-in-progress-compliance-rules-biden-care-cost-cynthia-fisher/.
[104] See *Bates v State Bar of Arizona*, 433 U.S. 350 (1977) (finding Arizona State Bar rule prohibiting lawyer advertising violated First Amendment); see also *Zauderer v Office of Disc. Counsel of Supreme Court of Ohio*, 471 U.S. 626 (1985) (holding that lawyer advertising is protected commercial speech).

and doctor[105] advertising as a means to increase access to the justice and healthcare systems. Whether advertising has brought about greater access to legal services or healthcare is a separate question.

With a national average of about 40 lawyers for everyone 10,000 Americans, the National Center for Access to Justice (NCAJ) estimates that even for those who are 'comfortably middle class', the cost of a private lawyer is beyond their means.[106] NCAJ estimates that 25 lawyers are needed for every 10,000 American at or below 200 per cent of the federal poverty level, yet only six states had more than two attorneys for each 10,000 people at that level.[107] Legal Services Corporation estimates that 92 per cent of low-income Americans do not receive any or enough legal help for 92 per cent of their serious legal problems.[108]

Despite widespread lawyer advertising in the US, one study of lawyer advertising in Florida, New York and Texas found a 'dearth' of information relating to the cost of legal services.[109] Indeed, only 6.39 per cent of the advertising reviewed contained exact prices of legal services offered.[110] The research also suggested that lawyer advertising did not necessarily encourage historically under-represented groups to seek legal assistance.[111] Noting that 50 per cent of US adults do not read above an eighth grade level and approximately 20 per cent read below a fifth grade level, the researchers found that much of the lawyers' internet advertising they examined had a readability level of 10.97, well above the reach of at least half of the adult population.[112]

The demand for doctors, like the demand for lawyers, also outpaces the supply. Statistics regarding the number of doctors are even more troubling than those relating to lawyers. One source reports that there are fewer than five general practitioners for each 10,000 Americans.[113] The shortage of doctors exists despite widespread advertising, much of which is in the form of 'Top Doctors' 'Best Doctors', which are a ubiquitous feature of popular magazines.[114] As with prescription drug advertising, virtually none of the advertisements contain information about pricing. This is particularly troubling in a climate of reduced access to health care in the US, where, according to The Center for Disease Control and Prevention, 'unmet needs for healthcare are often the result of cost-related barriers'.[115]

---

[105] American Medical Association, Code of Ethics, Opinion 9.6.1 (There are no restrictions on advertising by physicians except those that can be specifically justified to protect the public from deceptive practices).
[106] National Center for Access to Justice, ncaj.org/state-rankings/justice-index/attorney-access.
[107] ibid.
[108] Legal Services Corporation, The Justice Gap: The Report, (April 2022), available at lsc-live.app.box.com/s/xl2v2uraiotbbzrhuwtjlgi0emp3myz1.
[109] Jim Hawkins and R Knake, 'The Behavioral Economics of Lawyer Advertising: An Empirical Assessment' (2019) University of Illinois Law Review 1005, 1030.
[110] ibid.
[111] ibid 1032.
[112] ibid 1035.
[113] D Thompson, 'Why America Has so Few Doctors?', *The Atlantic* (14 February 2022) (data provided by the Niskanen Center).
[114] See, eg, '2022 Best Doctors', *D Magazine*, available at directory.dmagazine.com/search/?sections=Doctors&awards=Best+Doctors+%3E+2022.
[115] Center for Disease Control and Prevention, National Center for Health Statistics, *Reduced Access to Care* (July 2022) www.cdc.gov/nchs/covid19/pulse/reduced-access-to-care.htm#print.

VI. CONCLUSION: DOES FREE SPEECH COST US CONSUMERS?

Twenty-first century advertising of prescription drugs is a far cry from Justice Blackmun's suggestion that 'I will sell you X drug at Y price.' Rather than advertising price, much of the focus is often on improved lifestyle after taking the drugs, highlighting people engaging in social or recreational activities, precisely the situation that Justice Rehnquist anticipated in his *Virginia Board of Pharmacy* dissent.[116]

That begs the questions: does more information help consumers make better decisions? That is the theory at the root of modern disclosure laws. Disclosure statutes such as the Truth-in-Lending Act require disclosure of complex financial information in addition to cost on the theory that providing consumers with information helps them make better choices. Some experts maintain, however, that disclosure of complex information such as this may serve only the speaker and not the consumer, and in some cases may actually harm the consumer.[117]

Physicians and healthcare providers have been ambivalent on the value of direct to consumer advertising of prescription drugs. On the one hand, some maintain that the advertisements motivate consumers to seek more information about their health, including medical attention. Indeed, research has shown that some patients seeing a doctor about a condition may do so for the first time after seeing an advertisement. Others see the advertisements as biased and misleading by emphasizing the use of medications over diet, exercise or other approaches to wellness.

One thing is certain in the US: the debate over the extent to which broad protection for commercial speech actually benefits consumers is not over.

---

[116] Virginia Board of Pharmacy (n 1) 781 (Rehnquist J, dissenting).
[117] See Penn Regulatory Review, *Is Mandatory Disclosure Helping Consumers* (collected essays) (2015).

15

A v National Blood Authority: An Experiment in Radical Consumer-centric Strict Liability for Products

JACOB EISLER

I. INTRODUCTION

A v National Blood Authority (NBA)[1] is a lonely pillar in the landscape of consumer protection through product liability. It addressed if patients exposed to blood transfusions that infected them with Hepatitis C could claim the blood itself was defective (that is to say, less safe than they could reasonably expect), even where technology to evaluate if the blood was contaminated was still in development and there were no alternative products. It was the first major case to offer an exhaustive treatment of the meaning of 'defect' under the Consumer Protection Act 1987. In concluding that contaminated blood was defective, Judge Burton took the instruction that liability for defective products under the CPA should not take fault into account seriously – and thereby advanced a legal standard equivalent to strict liability. As such *NBA* advanced a robustly pro-consumer vision of product safety, and prevented producers from invoking the difficulty or costliness in preventing harm or their own lack of fault to avoid liability.

Yet despite the rigour and thoughtfulness of Burton J's analysis, his decision has not brought meaning of defect under the CPA in line with strict liability in the UK jurisprudence. Instead, it has been eroded by subsequent case law, in particular the cases *Wilkes v DePuy*[2] and *Gee v DePuy*.[3] These cases asserted that factors such as risk-benefit analysis and the costs to producers of preventing harm should be part of a defect analysis, and thereby introduced a more producer-friendly, less consumer-protective understanding of defect. Subsequent developments since *NBA* thus show the challenges facing a truly strict and thus fundamentally consumer-oriented approach to products liability: there is a strong impulse among legal thinkers to conceive of

---

[1] *A v National Blood Authority* [2001] EWHC QB 446, (2001) 65 BMLR 1.
[2] *Wilkes v DePuy* [2016] EWHC 3096 (QB), [2018] QB 627.
[3] *Gee v DePuy* [2018] EWHC 1208 (QB), [2018] Med LR 347.

defect analysis as reflecting a balance of risk and benefits of a product, and thus operating as a form of reasonableness analysis familiar from negligence. After working through the statutory context of the CPA, *NBA*'s own facts and reasoning, and *Wilkes* and *Gee*, this chapter elaborates on this analytical struggle at the foundation of the definition of defect under the CPA.

Product liability and tort law doctrine generally are closely interwoven. The gateway of the modern negligence regime is *Donoghue and Stevens*,[4] in which the manufacturer of a bottle of ginger beer which carelessly contained a snail (the most famous snail of all time, it has been quipped)[5] was found to owe a duty of care to the person who drunk the beer, even though that person was not the purchaser. *Donoghue* established that duty of care tracks reasonably foreseeable harm to other persons generally. Prior to *Donoghue*, duty of care was restricted to specific contexts such as medical negligence, and in the case of a harmful products, liability would only follow privity in contract.[6]

Yet while *Donoghue* may be linchpin of tort law generally, it is, in terms of its doctrinal domain, a product liability case: the product was unequivocally defective because of the presence of an unwanted, harmful substance in the bottle. As such, *Donoghue* established that where a product is carelessly manufactured, liability travels with the product to any reasonably foreseeable end user. In one sense, the innovation of *Donoghue* exemplifies a historical pattern in tort law: social and technological innovations (such as industrial machinery, cars, and railroads) create new risks and new patterns of risk distribution, inspiring legal innovation. *Donoghue* reflects the emergence of a new regime of risk to consumers thanks to the development of mass manufacturing and distribution of products.

However, the unlike most modern product liability regimes, the *Donoghue* regime still requires fault, that is, breach of duty of care. Where a product is harmful even in the presence of reasonable care in its design and production by the manufacturer, the unlucky consumer who suffers harm from its appropriate use has, in effect, lost a 'lottery' 'played' by all consumers of the product.[7] Such allocation of harm to a presumptively random set of persons in the world contravenes principles of fairness that underlie tort law.

The result is that the development of the modern product liability tort regime has been marked by the emergence of liability based on defectiveness of the product. This occurred through a variety of mechanisms. As Jonathan Goldberg and Benjamin Zipursky note, both prevalent advisory scholarship and case law began moving towards defect-based liability, rather than proof of typical negligent carelessness.[8] The concern was frequently allocation of risk to a consumer who was worse-positioned,

---

[4] *Donoghue v Stevenson* [1932] AC 562.
[5] The Commercial Court of England and Wales, 'James Richard Atkin, Baron Atkin of Averdovey (1867-1944)', www.commercialcourt.london/jr-atkin (describing the notoriety of *Donoghue v Stevens* on and a plaque in Paisley, Scotland that memorialises 'history's most famous snail').
[6] See S Green and J Gardner, *Tort Law* (Oxford, Hart Publishing, 2021) 14.
[7] Such reasoning of lotteries and just distributions is one foundational idea of *A. v National Blood Authority* itself.
[8] JCP Goldberg and BC Zipursky, 'The Strict Liability in Fault and the Fault in Strict Liability' (2016) 85 *Fordham Law Review* 771–72.

both in terms of wealth and in terms of risk avoidance, as is famously reflected in the reasoning of Judge Traynor of the California Supreme Court:

> Those who suffer injury from defective products are unprepared to meet its consequences. The cost of an injury and the loss of time or health may be an overwhelming misfortune to the person injured, and a needless one, for the risk of injury can be insured by the manufacturer and distributed among the public as a cost of doing business.[9]

The result of such a regime is to shift the core of the product liability test from one of *carelessness* to one of *defect*. The critical question is if the product is less safe (however that is assessed) than it should be, regardless of the carefulness or carelessness of the manufacturer.

There is a long-running scholarly debate, however, if even a defect-based test can be truly strict, or merely serves as a cloak (or perhaps an unhelpful intermediate test) for a rigorous negligence regime. William Prosser, in the Second Torts Restatement, famously declared product liability to fall upon manufacturers even where they have taken 'all possible care'[10] – a clear statement of strict liability. However, the identification of defect itself requires some substantive test, even if that test examines the product rather than the processes that generate it. Many products must be inherently dangerous in some sense to function – for example, a functional knife must be sharp, and a functional car must be able to move at a high rate of speed – and the question is when it becomes so dangerous so as to be defective. Some have argued that the defectiveness analysis must also become a reasonableness analysis that parallels the fault test of negligence. Zipursky and Goldberg have argued that the apparently strict liability regimes of product liability simply 'define wrongdoing on demanding or unforgiving terms'.[11] Jane Stapleton is even more specific, and argued that strict liability is simply a more easily satisfied negligence test.[12]

One result has been a struggle between statutory regimes that seek to create product liability tests that provide complete protection to consumers, that is, are truly strict, and the claim that such product liability regimes are nothing but enhanced negligence regimes. Without further elaboration, declaring defect to be the *sine qua non* of a product liability regime can easily just interpolate a step into an analysis of manufacturer fault. Some have identified such defect tests as 'empty vessels' that must be filled with some other moral reasoning, thus prospectively lending themselves to such fault-based analysis.[13] One question facing any deliberate statutory attempt to forge a product liability regime is if it can truly produce consumer protecting strict liability rather than identify, in some form or another, manufacturer carelessness.

---

[9] *Escola v Coca Cola Bottling Co.*, 150 P.2d 436, 441 (Cal. 1944).
[10] W Prosser, *Restatement (Second) of Torts*, § 402A (American Law Institute, 1977).
[11] Goldberg and Zipursky (n 7) 773.
[12] J Stapleton, *Product Liability* (London, Butterworths,1994) 236.
[13] See D Nolan, 'Strict Product Liability for Design Defects' (2018) 134 *LQR* 176–81, 181, discussed in Green and Gardner (n 6) 212.

II. BACKGROUND TO THE CPA

One possible understanding of the CPA – at least as animated by Burton J's interpretation – is an attempt to decisively make product liability strictly consumer-centric rather than ultimately dependent on manufacturer fault. Such a move followed from tragic circumstances. Following perhaps the most notorious failure of product safety, the worldwide pharmaceutical thalidomide tragedy that caused birth defects in several thousand children,[14] product liability underwent a distinctive transformation with the passage of the Consumer Protection Act 1987 (CPA),[15] which establishes that producers are strictly liable for physical harm attributable to defective products. A threshold requirement for liability under the CPA is that the product be defective.[16] Under the CPA a product is defective and thus there is strict liability for producers, 'if the safety of the product is not such as persons generally are entitled to expect'.[17] When a product is defective, even if that defect cannot be attributed to negligence or other misconduct by a producer, the strict liability regime is activated and the producer will be liable for any physical harm it causes.[18] Where, however, any harm caused by a product cannot be attributed to a defect in the product, the core condition of the CPA is not satisfied, and the special no-fault tort regime does not apply.

Because defect is a threshold requirement for application of the CPA, how judges determine whether a product is as safe as users expect, and thus, whether it is defective, is of great significance. This seemingly straightforward requirement of product defect, however, opens an analytic and conceptual quagmire, particularly when the nature of a product defect is an intrinsic risk that may only be solved by compromising other desired features (such as cost or wide availability). The CPA defines defect as the failure of a product to be as safe as persons are entitled to expect.[19] While this definition has been criticised as circular,[20] it is defensible, and perhaps inevitable. Since the virtues of a product, including its safety, are a function of social construction,[21] it seems impossible to exclude users' expectation from any assessment

---

[14] PJ Lachmann, 'The Penumbra of Thalidomide, the Litigation Culture and the Licensing of Pharmaceuticals' (2012) 105 *QJM* 1179.

[15] The CPA implemented the European Directive on Product Liability, Council Directive 85/374/EEC of 25 July 1985 ('the Directive') on the approximation of the laws, regulations and administrative provisions of the Member States concerning liability for defective products. [1985] OJ L210/29.

[16] CPA, s 3.

[17] CPA, s 3.1.

[18] D Fairgrieve and G Howells, 'Rethinking Product Liability: A Missing Element in the European Commission's Third Review of the European Product Liability Directive' (2007) 70 *MLR* 967.

[19] CPA, s 3.1.

[20] Stapleton (n 12) 234; Fairgrieve and Howells (n 18) 967, cites this assessment with approval.

[21] Treatises broadly hint at this socially constructed character, but it has received little formal exploration. See, eg, WE Peele and J Goudkamp, *Tort* (London, Sweet & Maxwell, 2014) 312–13 (observing that defect in standard products turns on a 'value judgment' regarding the product, while in the previous paragraph breaking down the need for a non-standard product to suggest producer fault); CJ Miller and RS Goldberg, *Product Liability* (Oxford, Oxford University Press, 2004) 354 (observing that the circularity criticism raised by scholars is inherent in a law that attempts to protect safety). ibid 367 observes that safety is meant to track the diffuse 'general public expectation' and observes some attendant difficulties. This is a general problem of all ontology, however, not just law. JR Searle, *The Construction of Social Reality* (St. Ives, Penguin, 1995) 14.

of product defect. Moreover, its philosophical virtues aside, the expectation test has been memorialised by statute, so it is likely here to stay.

III. FACTS AND FINDINGS *A v NBA*

The judiciary struggled, and has continued to struggle, over how to best address the defect query.[22] In the 2002 *A v National Blood Authority*,[23] however, Burton J was ready to grasp the nettle, and offered the first systemic and theoretically rich account in response to a situation of both great legal and social importance.

The facts and context of *NBA* clarify why the case comprised such a dramatic entry into the previously thin judicial analysis of strict product liability under the CPA. The case was a group action by 114 claimants who were infected with Hepatitis C through blood transfusions between 1 March 1988 (the date when the CPA came into effect) and 1 April 1991 (when effective testing for Hepatitis C was put into effect for the national blood supply in England and Wales).[24] The infected persons were infected by receiving transfusions supplied by the National Health Service and its subsidiaries, who were under a statutory obligation to provide the blood.[25] Two critical facts intersected to complicate the analysis. First, it had been known since at least the 1970s that some percentage of transfused blood in the UK was infected with Hepatitis C, though this was common knowledge only among medical professionals and was not communicated to blood transfusion patients.[26] Secondly, however, there was no effective direct test available until 1990, though there were 'surrogate' tests that could be used to identify potential donors who posed a higher risk of being infected with Hepatitis C (though adoption of such surrogate tests by national blood testing systems was uneven as a policy matter).[27] The context of blood transfusions thus comprised a context in which a product inevitably had to be offered to consumers (both by law, and because of the preferability of even risky blood donation to none at all) but where the risk of the blood being infected by Hepatitis C could not be eliminated (though consumers were not informed of this risk). It thus comprises a classic 'hard case' in the Dworkinian sense, because it reflected a conflict between two foundational values and how they could be reconciled as a matter of legal and

---

[22] Some opinions have resorted, directly or indirectly, to case-by-case intuition. *Abouzaid v Mothercare* [2000] EWCA Civ 348, [2000] All ER (D) 246 characterises the defect enquiry as 'a question of fact' [at 40]. In *Tesco Stores v Pollard* [2006] EWCA Civ 393, (2006) 150 SJLB 537, Laws LJ indicated it was impossible to offer a more precise standard for a childproof bottle to be adequately safe other than it be more difficult to open than an ordinary screwtop [at 18], an almost impossibly non-generalisable conclusion. Strangely enough, *Tesco Stores* did not engage with the reasoning of *NBA*, or cite the case at all. While it is possible to frame the issue in *Tesco Stores* narrowly (that is, wholly about the question of if the CPA defect standard incorporates regulatory safety standards automatically) and thus place it beyond the scope of the defect analysis in *NBA*, given *NBA*'s status as a leading case, failure to discuss it is certainly a peculiar omission.

[23] *A v National Blood Authority* (n 1).
[24] ibid [11].
[25] ibid [42].
[26] ibid [30]; G Howells and M Mildred, 'Infected Blood: Defect and Discoverability A First Exposition of the EC Product Liability Directive' (2002) 65 *MLR* 95, 97.
[27] *A v National Blood Authority* (n 1) [122].

community norms. Namely, the urgent need to ensure blood was supplied for medical use for the welfare of all patients; and the right of individual patients not to be exposed to blood that was contaminated.

Doctrinally, Burton J had to resolve a number of thorny questions regarding interpretation of the CPA.[28] His Honour rejected that: 1) the unavoidability of harmful characteristics; 2) the impracticability of measures that would eliminate the harm; and 3) the benefit of the product to society, ought to be factors in assessing if a product is less safe than consumers can legitimately expect.[29] To support this analysis, he advanced a distinction between 'standard' and 'non-standard' products,[30] and indicated that infectious bags of blood were non-standard products. Standard products perform as expected; even if that involves risks of harm, they are intrinsic to the product (sharp knives can cut, and cars have the capacity of going dangerously fast). Non-standard products, conversely, behave in a manner that consumers would not expect (a knife splinters or the brakes of a car fail to reduce its speed). No consumer – particularly in light of the failure to disclose to patients or the public at large the specific widespread risk of Hepatitis C – expected their particular bag of blood to be infected.[31] Thus it was determined that the bags of blood received by the infected claimants were non-standard. This classification is particularly important because it circumvents any efforts by producers to point to the difficulty of avoiding the occasional 'lemon' in a generally sound class of products, or the need or benefit to bringing an entire class of product to market even if some of them will, by bad luck, fail to perform as expected. A final doctrinal conclusion by Burton J was to reject the defence available to a producer under the CPA that where a defect could not have been discovered due to the state of scientific and technical knowledge, given the defendants had general knowledge of it.[32] Thus, His Honour concluded the bags of blood were defective and the defendants were liable for the harm caused.

This analysis, running to over 100 pages and drawing widely from other jurisdictions (Burton J himself acknowledges the influence of law from France, Germany, Spain, Portugal, Sweden, Denmark, Belgium, Italy, Holland, Australia and the US),[33] comprised the first extensive treatment of defect under the CPA, and provided the preliminary indications of how the statutory strict liability regime would transform product liability more generally. Burton J's approach provides a framework that is, above all else, focused on protecting consumers. In identifying the bags of blood as non-standard and rejecting the relevance of contextual factors related to their production, he firmly asserted that the polestar of product liability is what consumers

---

[28] In his opinion, Burton J treats the relevant provisions of the CPA as interchangeable with the mandating EU directive, though this does not affect the technical analysis.
[29] *A v National Blood Authority* (n 1) [68].
[30] The standard/non-standard distinction stands in opposition (as Burton J notes, ibid [39]) to the well-established US distinction between manufacturing and design defects, which treats design defects by 'what amounts to a thinly designed negligence standard', Howells and Mildred (n 26) 98. Some have criticised Burton J's reasoning as identifying defect too broadly, perhaps even by default. J Stapleton, 'Bugs in Anglo-American Products Liability' (2002) 53 *South Carolina Law Review* 1230, 1250.
[31] *A v National Blood Authority* (n 1) [65].
[32] CPA, s 4(1)(e); *A v National Blood Authority* (n 1) [84].
[33] *A v National Blood Authority* (n 1) [17].

expect in terms of safety. It is, above all else, a consumer-centric vision. In such a context, defect will be identified and producers will (absent an applicable defence) be liable wherever the characteristics of a product cause harm that a consumer would not anticipate from use. This is the case even if the defence could not be identified or addressed *and* the producer was under a legal obligation to provide the product.

While the consumer-centrism of *NBA* is in line with strict liability in the statutory language, it is at odds with the typical treatment of identifying strict liability with a loosened version of a negligence test.[34] This may explain why Burton J's analysis also excludes traditional law and economics touchstones for allocating risk, such as risk-benefit utility analysis, in favour of robust assurances that consumers could expect their products not to harm them. This approach is at odds with the dominant understandings of common law tort as either advancing efficiency or serving to track the moral standing of parties. But it does serve the statutory purpose, and moreover, the broader balance of social power, in protecting consumers where a product causes them unexpected harm (regardless of any other context).

NBA, with its expansive conception of defect and adoption of an analysis that suggests consumers generally expect all products they use to be non-harmful, indicated an approach to product liability that prioritised consumer protection. Burton J's analysis was committed to a robust conception of product liability as strict (as formally articulated in the CPA), and his approach would tend to find producers liable where products were less safe than consumers might expect – even if the product behaved as designed and the harmful characteristics could not be avoided.

IV. RESPONSE TO A v NBA

Scholarly reaction to *NBA* was, on the whole, hostile, as the decision was seen as one-sidedly favouring consumers over producers, and prospectively imposing liability too widely. Christopher Hodges criticised Burton J for (in declaring avoidability by the producer irrelevant for a finding of defect) failing to appropriately 'evaluate and balance all circumstances' to decide when a product is unsafe.[35] Jane Stapleton described its reasoning as 'very strange', 'preferr[ing] the heroic rhetoric of the claimants' cause'.[36] Even the somewhat more sympathetic Howells and Mildred characterise the decision as 'strong stuff', but speculate it could be the basis for 'a radical product liability regime which takes risk-spreading seriously.'[37]

This subtle contrast between the reaction of Stapleton compared with Howells and Mildred draws out the deeper structural issue at stake in the approach of *NBA*. Stapleton critiques the decision's pro-consumerist stance for 'ignor[ing] the overall social utility of the standard product',[38] fundamentally because it fails to consider society-wide costs and benefits to risk allocation. Invoking such society-wide benefits

---

[34] Stapleton (n 12) 236; Howells and Mildred (n 26) 98.
[35] C Hodges, *Compensating Patients* (2001) 117 *LQR* 528, 530.
[36] Stapleton (n 30) 1250.
[37] Howells and Mildred (n 26) 101.
[38] Stapelton (n 30) 1251.

of a product and how its development and distribution will be shaped by the product liability regime is the touchstone for traditional cost-benefit analysis.[39] Yet as Howells and Mildred observe, *NBA*'s consumer-focused reasoning, in concerning itself entirely (as a formalist approach to strict liability might be expected to) with the position of the user, could form the basis for radical change. This radical change might not be welcome to those who use utility balancing to identify optimised regimes.[40] But *NBA*'s approach and spirit, broadly applied, would radically shift the allocation of risk as well as the moral character of the product liability regime, upending the traditional focus on economic maximisation in favour of consumer certitude.

As the leading opinion in the application of the CPA, *NBA* thus could have been a sea change in product liability, consumer law, and tort law more generally. Yet judges are often preservers of the status quo rather than reformers, and such a radically onerous test for defect and prospective subsequent changes in allocation of risk created hesitancy in the adoption of *NBA*. As Fairgreave and Howells note, the cases that followed on the heels of this landmark decision either ignored it, or, even where they cited it with approval, did not seem to cleave to its spirit.[41]

V. THE LEGACY OF A v NBA

Despite being such a landmark case, the consumer-focused approach to defect in *A v NBA* has not been followed by the courts. A pair of recent cases throw the legacy of the case into doubt, and suggest that it may be increasingly confined to history. *Wilkes v DePuy*[42] and *Gee v DePuy*[43] both queried if artificial hip implants joints which caused harm to the patient-recipients should be classified as 'defective'. Though the specific nature of the harms and the procedural postures of the *Wilkes* and *Gee* cases differ, the two cases both challenge the adamantly consumer-protectionist view of product liability advanced by *NBA*. In particular, both suggest that an appropriate understanding of defect must be 'holistic',[44] and use this premise to reject Burton J's explicit disregard of certain producer-exonerating factors and shift defect analysis towards a utilitarian risk-benefit balancing. They thus erode *NBA*'s firmly consumer-protectionist approach to strict liability.

Wilkes was the first case to critically engage with *NBA*. It involved a single claimant whose artificial hip joint fractured for reasons, because of the causal complexity, could not be precisely determined,[45] and brought suit under the CPA on the grounds the implant was defective. In finding for the defendant by declining to identify a defect, Hickinbottom J examined (as the leading, 'monumental' authority on defect analysis

---

[39] See, eg, G Calabresi, 'First Party, Third Party, and Product Liability Systems: Can Economic Analysis of Law Tell Us Anything About Them?' (1984) 69 *Iowa Law Review* 833.
[40] For an aggressive position, see RA Epstein, 'Products Liability as an Insurance Market' (1985) 14 *Journal of Legal Studies* 645.
[41] Fairgrieve and Howells (n 18) 968.
[42] *Wilkes* (n 2).
[43] *Gee* (n 3).
[44] *Wilkes* (n 2) [78]; *Gee* (n 3) [165].
[45] *Wilkes* (n 2) [112]–[113].

under the CPA)[46] the reasoning of *NBA*. While refraining from a general oversight or rejection of *NBA*'s conclusions of law, Hickinbottom critiqued certain analytic categories. Two points are of particular importance: the rejection of Burton J's distinction between standard and non-standard products;[47] and rejection of the conclusion that certain factors (particularly avoidability of the harm) ought to be excluded from defect analysis.[48] Given there was no indication that the particular joint at issue was outside design specifications,[49] this in effect turned the evaluation of defect into a risk-benefit assessment of the product being made available to users.

Wilkes was the first case to articulate clear disagreement with Burton J's approach in *NBA*. The procedural context of *Wilkes*, however, can be contrasted to *NBA* in that *Wilkes* considered a single claimant, whereas *NBA* was a group action. While this should not affect doctrinal analysis of defect, *Wilkes* might be seen as addressing a more individuated set of circumstances, as well as the resolution of a less authoritative dispute. Hickinbottom J's scepticism, however, only prefigured that of Andrews J in *Gee v DePuy*, which incorporated and extended the critiques of *NBA* articulated in *Wilkes*. *Gee* involved 312 hip implant recipients who had experienced dispersion of metal particles into their bodies, due to the friction between the joint components, and suffered subsequent pain and medical complications. The entry of particulate debris into the body from such an implant is inevitable;[50] the question is if the implant at issue was defective in being less safe than the recipients of the implants were entitled to expect.[51]

In denying the defectiveness of the implants, Andrews J's opinion, which rivals *NBA* in its length and the depth of its analysis, roundly rejects Burton J's analytic approach, and explicitly rejects claimants' counsel reliance upon it.[52] He criticises the approach to identification of defect in *NBA* as 'self-evidently circular' for correlating a characteristic in a product that causes harm with the presence of a defect.[53] In rejecting this circularity, Andrews J declares 'safety is inherently and necessarily a relative concept', and that no product 'can be absolutely safe'.[54] This serves as a point of entry for Andrews J's decision to incorporate 'all circumstances', including avoidability and risk-benefit into his consideration of defect, explicitly contra *NBA*.[55] Andrews J's overall tone is to reject *NBA*'s approach as excessively likely to identify defect, and to respond by noting there is no entitlement to an 'absolute level of safety' from any product.[56] Unsurprisingly, after so aggressively pruning *NBA*'s consumer-protectionist stance, Andrews J declined to find the hip implants defective, in short

---

[46] ibid [55].
[47] ibid [94].
[48] ibid [87]–[89]; see also at [124] (taking into account regulatory compliance).
[49] *Wilks* (n 2) [115].
[50] *Gee* (n 3) [23].
[51] The model was ultimately withdrawn from the market, having been replaced by technically superior alternatives and apparent difficulties with the implants. [225]–[229].
[52] *Gee* (n 3) [108].
[53] ibid.
[54] ibid.
[55] ibid [154], [160].
[56] ibid [96].

because it did not fall below the standard that could be expected of such a product at the time it was on the market given technical and scientific knowledge at the time.[57]

There are multiple layers to the divergence between *NBA* and *Gee*. The most immediate question is what the aim is, narrowly speaking, of the CPA, and, broadly speaking, of strict liability. While Andrews J is scrupulous to explicitly commit to the no-fault nature of product liability under the CPA,[58] he re-introduces factors into the assessment of defect that bear on producer conduct. His Honour denies that this switch contravenes the no-fault nature of strict product liability stating that

> Inquiring whether there was fault or absence of fault on the part of the producer is not the same thing as considering whether, as a matter of fact, the risk of injury could have been eliminated or reduced, and whether that has any impact on what the public generally was entitled to expect in terms of its safety.[59]

Whether or not[60] this turns the strict product liability test into a particularly easy to satisfy negligence test (as some scholars have suggested)[61] may be a question of semantics (or at least of how one parses negligence and strict liability at the margins of their definitions). What is incontestable is that it shifts the nature of the test for defect from one wholly concerned with protecting consumers when they are harmed by a product into one that also takes into account the character of producers' conduct. Whether or not this is appropriate by the terms of the CPA itself is contestable; it is possible to incorporate it by asserting that what consumers are entitled to expect in terms of safety is shaped by these producer-considering factors.

This clarifies the aim of Burton J's reasoning, and in particular his decision to exclude avoidability, elimination of risk, and benefit to society from his consideration of defect. Burton J's aspiration – which Hickinbottom and Andrews JJ reject – is to establish a definition of defect that is wholly delineated by user protection. The most evident basis for this is that section 3(1) of the CPA defines defect by reference to consumer expectation alone. As Burton J notes, quoting Howells J,[62] this does not mean the liability is absolute, but it does mean that insofar as a product can cause harm, that harm must be a function of users' own autonomy in choosing to use the products and taking on evident downsides and risks, rather than because of some consideration based on collective social utility or the appropriate conduct of the producer. Such a view is eminently consumer-centric.

Recognising *NBA* as such makes it a striking (if short-lived) experiment in consumer protection, product liability, and the extent of strict liability. This is not merely because *Wilkes* and *Gee* turned against it, but because in doing so these subsequent cases fall in line with a vast and diverse academic scholarship. This attack has come from multiple sides. The rawest attack is that the definition of defect, at least

---

[57] ibid [484]–[500].
[58] ibid [66], [146], [154].
[59] ibid [146].
[60] See J Eisler, 'One Step Forward and Two Steps Back in Product Liability: The Search for Clarity in the Identification of Defect' (2017) 76 *CLJ* 233, 235 (characterising the multi-factor cost-benefit analysis advanced by *Wilkes* as 'an inverted assessment of breach in negligence').
[61] See n 30 above.
[62] *A v National Blood Authority* (n 1) [28].

under the CPA, necessarily is 'very little different from the common-law test of negligence because, in essence, it requires the court to conduct a cost-benefit analysis'.[63] This critique is a particularisation of the claim that, as an analytic matter, the strict liability test is a negligence test with different parameters for identifying fault. The challenge to the viability of genuine strict liability in products liability has also faced fierce normative critiques from both major approaches to tort. Champions of a deontological understanding of tort have argued either that strict products liability that disregards producer conduct contravenes the relationship of tort liability to moral responsibility,[64] or that, despite being typically described as no-fault, products liability remains necessarily fault-based.[65] Law and economics theorists, meanwhile, have argued that strict liability is frequently inefficient,[66] in particular because it shifts the burden of bearing costs and changing behaviour to avoid harm entirely on to the producer. Burton J in *NBA*, in other words, takes the mandate of the CPA seriously despite having to face down a scholarly tradition that has frowned upon strict liability in the context of product safety,[67] and, at least in the Anglophone world, taken a broad turn against it.[68]

One particular development of the law and economics argument against truly consumer-focused strict liability is worth exploring, because it appears to underlie much of the anxiety that *Wilkes* and *Gee* expressed towards Burton J's reasoning in *NBA*.[69] Some have argued that the type of regime advanced by *NBA* is socially destructive, insofar as it exposes producers to excessive risks levels and thus distorts incentives for proper cost-benefit analysis in bringing products to market.[70] The concern is not merely that a wholly consumer-focused definition of defect will be morally unfair to producers, but that it will ultimately harm consumers by distorting appropriate incentives for innovation, marketing, and consumer uptake. This concern

---

[63] P Cane, *Atiyah's Accidents, Compensation, and the Law* (Cambridge, Cambridge University Press, 2013) 102. Interestingly, Cane does not discuss Burton J's attempt to resist this in *NBA*.

[64] E Weinrib, *The Idea of Private Law* (Cambridge, MA, Harvard University Press, 1995) 178–81. In a related vein, R Stevens, *Torts and Rights* (Oxford, Oxford University Press, 2007) 99–100, intimates that the type of 'absolute duty' created by product liability is not philosophically tenable.

[65] Goldberg and Zipursky (n 7) 743.

[66] See, eg, RA Posner, 'Strict Liability: A Comment' (1973) 2 *Journal of Legal Studies* 205; A Schwartz, 'Proposals for Products Liability Reform: A Theoretical Synthesis' (1988) 97 *Yale Law Journal* 353, 355; WV Viscusi, *Pricing Lives: Guideposts for a Safer Society* (Princeton, Princeton University Press, 2018) 85 (arguing that satisfying certain safety benchmarks should exonerate producers from products liability).

[67] Interestingly the UKSC has been more balanced in their treatment of vicarious liability. Following a spate of cases that expanded the ken of vicarious liability (*Mohamud v WM Morrison Supermarkets plc* [2016] UKSC 11, [2016] AC 677 in the context of the requirement of a relationship between employment and act, and *Various Claimants v Catholic Child Welfare Society* [2012] UKSC 56, [2013] 2 AC 1 in the context of identifying employment-like relationships as satisfactory to satisfy the traditional requirement of employment), the Court has recently indicated limits to the extent of vicarious liability in these areas (*WM Morrison Supermarkets plc v Various Claimants* [2020] UKSC 12, [2020] AC 989 and *Barclays Bank plc v Various Claimants* [2020] UKSC 13, [2020] AC 973). This back-and-forth shows an attempt to strike a balance between protecting those harmed by vicarious agents and ensuring fairness towards non-negligent actors, whereas product liability, as this chapter described, has been marked by more of an about-face.

[68] See J Henderson and A Twerski Jr., 'Closing the American Products Liability Frontier: The Rejection of Liability without Defect' (1991) 66 *NYU Law Review* 1263, 1269–73 (observing the turn against the expansion of strict liability in the US).

[69] *Wilkes* (n 2) [73]; *Gee* (n 3).

[70] See Epstein (n 40) 664.

is particularly acute where a product may prove beneficial to many users – and thus collective welfare as a whole – but may cause harm beyond what would be expected from a 'safe' product to some unlucky recipients. As *NBA* notes, extensive use of warnings and disclosure may alleviate identification of defect, as can some of the defences available under section 4 of the CPA, most notably the developmental risks defence. Burton J intimates, but does not clearly state, that warnings given directly to patients that every bag of blood carried a risk of infection might have alleviated identification of defect.[71] However, given the structure of Burton J's analysis, this would have been hard to track through to the standard/non-standard product distinction, and made *every* bag of blood – included infected bags – a 'standard' product, where the standard product has a risk of infection. This would have fundamentally altered his classification of infected bags.[72] In *generally* refusing to engage in risk-benefit analysis, particularly by classifying the instances of products that were harmful as non-standard, *NBA* declined to allow consideration of collective social welfare of the availability of a product to be a meaningful factor in defect identification.

The essence of the shift in *Wilkes* and *Gee*, beyond rejecting *NBA*'s formal framework, was to return to the collective social welfare of the availability of products to the centre of defective analysis. One of the core innovations the cases reject, the standard/non-standard product distinction, serves to advance this. By identifying products that are harmful as non-standard, *NBA* farms them out into a separate category whose harm to users cannot simply be classified with the overall social effect of the availability of the product. Rather, it is specifically *harmed* users who are prioritised in Burton J's analysis. Rejecting the standard/non-standard distinction, as *Wilkes* and *Gee* do, facilitates a return to risk-benefit analysis, by contemplating how each user, before knowing if the product they received was harmful, would find it preferable to use the product, or not (a position *NBA* specifically rejects in its declaration that users are not 'entitled to expect a form of Russian roulette'[73]). This allows for another framing of the defect analysis – if the aim of defect analysis under the CPA is to identify if the product behaved as expected across the entire group of users (including those who suffered no harm), or to consider if it behaved as expected only with regards to those who were harmed by the product. The former approach conceives of defect as an average function of welfare across all users; the latter only considers the post-harm posture of an individual who has been harmed. Much of *NBA*'s analysis is designed to support defect identification from the posture of the unlucky individual, regardless of how unlikely the harm was and how beneficial the general product availability may be.

NBA's analysis thus might be critiqued for failing to appropriately weigh society-wide impact of products – and this lies at the core of the critiques offered by *Wilkes* and *Gee*. Yet the conclusion that *NBA*'s consumer-protectionist view is insufficiently concerned with social welfare must face at least two further arguments. The first is that the face of the statute makes no reference to considering the society-wide benefit

---

[71] *A v National Blood Authority* (n 1) [108].
[72] ibid [65].
[73] ibid.

of the product, even as it defines other factors that either should be disregarded as indicative of defect (ie, the availability of safer product that becomes available later[74]), and the defences available to producers that allow them to exonerate identification of defect.[75] While this does not explicitly favour limiting what persons are entitled to expect only to harmed persons, the absence of failing to identify total welfare either in the statute or, apparently, in the underlying Directive or other legally dispositive materials, while including these other factors, could be taken to suggest that cost-benefit analysis is not a factor that should influence user expectations of safety. At a minimum, it suggests that the meaning of defect under the CPA is a contestable 'hard' (in the Dworkinian sense) question.[76] It thus becomes the moral responsibility of judges to adopt the approach that is most conducive to the morality of the community.

Much scholarly analysis is dedicated to showing why, from various perspectives, legal and social values would be better served by using risk-benefit analysis as the touchstone of product liability. But this view disregards a critical feature of product liability as it relates to consumers: the greater social power held by producers, and the role of law (both statutory and judge-made) to correct this balance. This power differential is typically understood as primarily relating to information[77] – producers possess information that consumers do not, and ensuring that consumers have this information (or can reasonably access it) is costly. Yet the greater power held by producers goes beyond their superior possession of information. Producers – particularly in an economic environment of increasing economic centralisation and surveillance capitalism – typically have greater power than any individual consumer. The nature of this power is diverse, from the capacity of producers to draw off greater economic resources held through the corporate form to their ability to influence governmental decision-making through concerted lobbying.[78] Ultimately much of this power, whether in the typically recognised form of information differentials, or the less frequently recognised forms of greater economic and political resources, can be attributed to the durability and flexibility corporate form, even if this does not traditionally enter into product liability analysis. There is an admitted irony in the particular case of *NBA* in that the tortfeasor was a public body that does not necessarily have the corporate features that typically create this power differential; this does not, however, change the fact that Burton J's analytic approach would favour users and consumers over producers who are usually corporate.

---

[74] CPA, s 3(2).
[75] CPA, s 4.
[76] R Dworkin, *Law's Empire* (Oxford, Hart Publishing, 1998).
[77] Epstein (n 40) 650; Goldberg and Zipursky (n 7) 773. For a critique of this focus, see J Henderson and A Twerski Jr., 'Doctrinal Collapse in Products Liability: The Empty Shell of Failure to Warn' (1990) 65 *NYU Law Review* 265.
[78] The scholarship on the disproportionate power held by corporations is vast. See, eg, D Nyberg, 'Corporations, Politics, and Democracy: Corporate political activities as political corruption' (2021) 2 *Organization Theory* 1 (reviewing literature on corporate influence in democratic decision-making and offering a unifying theory); M Galanter, 'Why the 'Haves' Come out Ahead: Speculations on the Limits of Legal Change' (1974) 9 *Law & Society Review* 95 (offering an account of why litigation favours corporate defendants over individual harmed claimants).

The power held by producers means that typical cost-benefit analysis will have several effects. It will, structurally and holistically, tend to favour producers, by homogenising the analysis of the social effects of harm by products and thus ignoring the unique position held by firms.[79] Furthermore, such cost-benefit analysis will tend to replicate the existing distribution of social power, by considering maximisation of wealth rather than justice of distribution.[80] Therefore, the greater power held by producers compared to consumers casts Burton J's willingness to advance a consumer-centric view, and his decision to disregard certain producer-exonerating factors, in a new light. The primary resource of consumers – who are also rank-and-file citizens – against the greater power of producers is the state, as expressed through law. In advancing a consumer-protecting view, *NBA* served to counterbalance the power held by producers in its conception of strict liability. Faithful to the text of the CPA (if not to its drily technical underlying legislative motivation in harmonising the product liability regime in the EU), it looked only to the interests and expectations of harmed persons. It thus could serve to make strict product liability a mechanism for progressive change, rather than a mechanism for reproducing the status quo. This moral quality runs throughout the opinion, from the decision to refuse to consider factors that might exonerate producers but would not be part of users' decision-making, to the decision to classify a uniquely harmful instance of a product as non-standard, to the refusal to conclude that users should be posited to expect to be playing a 'harm' lottery. The end result of the landmark decision *NBA* as an analytic model is to return power to consumers, even if it comes at the apparent economic welfare of producers.

Such favouring of consumers also provides an instance of reconceptualising the understanding of the moral end of tort law. As noted above,[81] deontological theorists of tort have typically criticised the idea of consumer-centric strict liability as deviating from tort as typically serving the end of human dignity by assigning liability without culpability. Yet conceiving of product liability's broader position in the socio-legal order points to a way that strict liability might serve 'the moral end of maintaining just relationships'.[82] These moral relationships are maintained not merely by individual relationships between tortfeasors and victims, nor by a homogenised conception of social welfare as utility maximisation, but by considering the power relationships that a given legal rule maintains or alters. When intervention in such a power relationship is indicated by statute, judges might have justification in hewing to the logic of the statute, even where it defies typical understandings. Thus, the consumer-centric view of products liability, and the subsequent shifting of power to consumers in *A v NBA*, is supported not only by Burton J's reading of the text, but

---

[79] One prominent law and economics accounts, in a detailed technical analysis of liability by firms, wholly disregards the greater social power held by firms, and goes so far to relegate the observation that catastrophic injuries may be existentially destructive to consumers to a footnote, where it is then dealt with via an abstraction. S Shavell, *Foundations of Economic Analysis of Law* (Cambridge, MA, Harvard University Press, 2004) 184, fn 11.
[80] R Korobkin, 'The Endowment Effect and Legal Analysis' (2003) 97 *Northwestern Law Review* 1227, 1276.
[81] See n 64.
[82] J Eisler, 'The Limits and Promise of Instrumental Legal Analysis' (2020) 47 *Journal of Law and Society* 499, 505.

by a consideration of the statutory enactment of a strict products liability regime in the context of the power balance between corporations and consumers.

VI. CONCLUSION

NBA is a landmark case because it shows the radical potential of products liability, and in particular how judicial interpretation of a seemingly straightforward statutory provision (the definition of defect) could accomplish this. It also demonstrates, however, the suspicion or hostility with which such radicalism might be met. Whilst *NBA* is generally considered a tort case looking specifically at the interpretation of obligations under the CPA, it clearly has an important consumer protection angle. *NBA* asserted that the welfare of consumers – and specifically the most vulnerable consumers, though who have suffered harm – should stand at the centre of legal analysis. In doing so it challenged the status quo of both legal rules and the power structure, and has been met by scepticism from both. The result has been that *NBA* has been undermined, even as it continues to stand as a landmark case for how strict liability could have truly protect consumers.

16

Failure to Protect the Vulnerable: *Office of Fair Trading (Respondents) v Abbey National Plc and Others (Appellants)*

CHRISTINE RIEFA*

BANKS HAVE GENERATED staggering amounts of money (some £2.56 billion) by applying charges notably for unauthorised overdraft. This case tried to challenge their legitimacy but ended up focussing on a relatively narrow point of law, namely whether those charges could be assessed for fairness under the Unfair Terms in Consumer Contracts Regulations 1999 (UTCCRs). Following both the High Court[1] and Court of Appeal[2] concluding that they could, the Supreme Court overruled their decisions. While the Supreme Court did not rule the charges were fair, it precluded their assessment for fairness under Regulation 6(2) UTCCRs. This decision dealt a huge blow to many thousands of consumers who had started proceedings to seek reimbursement of the charges. Despite leading to some positive albeit slow changes in the law and practice of the banks, the case continues to represent the propping up and continuation of the prevalent 'free in credit' banking model in the UK, under which consumers in debit subsidise those in credit.

I. BACKGROUND TO THE CASE

In March 2006, Which?, the UK consumer association campaigned to end the levying of charges on customer accounts for unauthorised overdraft. The practice of banks at the time was to charge interest on authorised overdraft and interest as well as a fixed fee for unauthorised overdrafts. Which? argued that the UTCCRs[3] (which implemented

---

* The author wishes to thank Roma Randeria for her assistance in the preliminary research for this case commentary.
[1] *The Office of Fair Trading v Abbey National Plc & Others* [2008] EWHC 875 (Comm), [2008] 2 All ER (Comm) 625.
[2] *Abbey National Plc & Others v The Office of Fair Trading* [2009] EWCA Civ 116, [2009] 2 WLR 1286.
[3] SI 1999/2083.

Directive 93/13/EEC) made it unlawful for banks to impose charges for unauthorised overdrafts which are disproportionate to their costs or use charges as a deterrent or profit stream.[4] Bank customers sought refunds by filing individual claims. The sheer volume of claims in the county courts (estimated over 53,000, from March 2006 to August 2007)[5] attests for the high level of dissatisfaction felt by many thousands of customers affected by the charges.[6] Amidst the uncertainty resulting from the thousands of individual cases,[7] the Office of Fair Trading (OFT), the main enforcer at the time,[8] started an investigation prompted by the complaints it had received.[9] In parallel it began a market study[10] which considered the competitive landscape of banking provision.[11] At the early stages of these investigations, the banks raised objections based on Regulation 6(2) UTCCRs, a point that was also raised by individual litigants in front of the county courts. In July 2007, in agreements with the banks,[12] the OFT initiated a test case seeking a declaration that Regulation 6(2) did not apply to the relevant bank terms and thus they could be assessed for fairness by the OFT. Most of the individual actions were stayed, pending the outcome of the test case, resulting in long delays as the case worked its way up to the Supreme Court.

II. THE NARROW ISSUE AT STAKE AND ITS PRACTICAL IMPORTANCE[13]

In *Abbey National*, the Supreme Court did not have to decide if the system of charging personal current account customers adopted in the United Kingdom (UK) was

---

[4] R Mulheron, 'The case for an optout class action for European Member States: a legal and empirical analysis' (2009) 15(3) *Columbia Journal of European Law* 409–53.

[5] R Mulheron, 'Recent milestones in class action reforms: a critique and a proposal' (2011) 127 *LQR* 288, 298–99.

[6] *Office of Fair Trading (Respondents) v Abbey National Plc & Others (Appellants)* [2009] UKSC 6, [17].

[7] Note that county court judgments are not binding and thus it would have been possible for courts to arrive at different outcomes, damaging legal certainty.

[8] The OFT has now been replaced by the Competition and Markets Authority. Note that Financial Services in the UK come principally under the remit of the Financial Conduct Authority, but powers are exercised concurrently with the CMA. See FCA, CMA, *Memorandum of Understanding between the Competition and Markets Authority and the Financial Conduct Authority on the use of concurrent powers under consumer protection legislation* (July 2019) www.fca.org.uk/publication/mou/fca-cma-consumer-protection-mou-2019.pdf (accessed 4 October 2022).

[9] *Abbey National* (n 6) [18].

[10] Market studies are ex ante enforcement tools examining the causes of why particular markets may not be working well. They can precede full market investigations where the enforcer can impose remedies to fix market failures without the need for establishing firms' liability for breaches of competition or consumer law. See CMA, *Market Studies and Market Investigation: Supplemental Guidance on the CMA's Approach* (2014, revised 2017) 20. The CMA inherited the OFT's powers in this area under the Enterprise and Regulatory Reform Act 2013 (ERRA).

[11] The OFT launched a market study into personal bank accounts in 2007.

[12] *Abbey National* (n 6) [19]. There were 8 banks involved in the test case: Abbey National, Barclays Bank, Clydesdale Bank, HBOS, HSBC Bank, Lloyds TSB Bank, Nationwide Building Society, The Royal Bank of Scotland Group.

[13] The OFT also claimed that the fees charged (not in line with the actual costs incurred by the banks) equated to the were akin to default charges. It is not an aspect we develop in this chapter as it did not succeed in the lower courts and this position was endorsed by the Supreme Court (see *Abbey National* (n 6) [82] (Phillips SCJ).

fair.[14] The system is based on the principle of 'free-if-in-credit' meaning that less well-off customers who need credit facilities subsidise better-off customers, a state of play that Lord Mance had qualified as a 'reverse robin hood exercise'.[15] Instead, the point looked at by the Supreme Court was rather narrow. It was limited to determining whether the charges levied in respect of unauthorised overdrafts could be challenged by the OFT as excessive in relation to the service supplied to consumers.[16] Lord Walker explained that the package of services that pertained to the opening of a current account was essentially composed of interests and charges on authorised and unauthorised overdrafts and specific charges for particular non-routine services (such as expedited or foreign money transmission services) and interests foregone by consumers whose current accounts are in credit because they receive a relatively low interest on this balance (if any at all).[17] To this, Lord Philips added the collection of cheques drawn in favour of the customer and honouring of cheques drawn by the customer and the use of credit or debit cards and cash distribution facilities.[18]

The case that came to the Supreme Court was limited to examining the nature of the exclusion contained in Regulation 6(2) which implements into UK law, Article 4(2) of Directive 1993.[19] The Court had to decide if the relevant terms in the consumers' contracts for personal bank accounts concerned the 'price or remuneration in exchange for the services supplied' by the bank and thus falling within the scope of Regulation 6(2) UTCCR.[20] Any terms within its scope could avoid scrutiny. Any terms outside of its remit would not and the Court would be free to assess if they were fair or not. According to the legislation in place, a term found to be unfair could then be set aside,[21] which would have resulted in bank customers not having to pay unfair bank charges and potentially clawing back those already paid, to the tune of £2.56 billion.[22]

III. THE DECISION ON THE SCOPE OF REGULATION 6(2) UTCCRS

The case concerned four main relevant bank charges: (1) an unpaid item charge (when instruction is declined for insufficient funds); (2) a paid item charge (when instruction

---

[14] *Abbey National* (n 6) [1] (Walker SCJ).
[15] ibid [2] (Walker SCJ).
[16] ibid [3] (Walker SCJ).
[17] ibid [42] (Walker SCJ).
[18] ibid [53] (Philips SCJ).
[19] Directive 93/13/EC of 5 April 1993 on Unfair Terms in Consumer Contracts, OJ L95/29.
[20] The issue was linked with looking also deciding if the scope of Reg 6(2) led to excluding terms from assessment altogether or simply assessment regarding the adequacy of the price. This may appear as being a fairly abstract point, but the Supreme Court as did the Court of Appeal noted that it was likely to be a great practical importance before favouring the excluded assessment route, meaning the term remained subject to the Regulations but could not be assessed with regards to its adequacy. See *Abbey National* (n 6) [29] (Walker SCJ) citing [60] and [61] (Phillips SCJ).
[21] Art 6 Directive 93/13 states that unfair terms are not binding on the consumer and the contract shall continue to bind the parties upon those terms if it is capable of continuing in existence without the unfair terms. Reg 8 UTCCRs 1999 states: '(1) Any unfair term in a contract concluded with a consumer by a seller or supplier shall not be binding on the consumer. (2) The contract shall continue to bind the parties if it is capable of continuing in existence without the unfair term.'
[22] *Abbey National* (n 6) [36] (Walker SCJ).

is honoured but there are insufficient funds); (3) a guaranteed paid item charge (for payment of cheques when funds are insufficient); and (4) an overdraft excess charge (where an account goes overdrawn in the absence of an overdraft facility and/or goes above the limit of an existing overdraft facility).[23] Those terms where included in the contracts consumers entered into with the banks. They were not individually negotiated. The terms were also deemed to be in plain and intelligible language.[24]

Under the UTCCRs, 'a contractual term which has not been individually negotiated shall be regarded as unfair if, contrary to the requirement of good faith, it causes significant imbalance in the parties' rights and obligations arising under the contract, to the detriment of the consumer' (as per Regulation 5(1)). However, there are some exceptions to the fairness test so provided, laid out in Regulation 6(2) UTCCRs 1999 which states:

> In so far as it is in plain intelligible language, the assessment of fairness of a term shall not relate– (a) to the definition of the main subject matter of the contract, or (b) to the adequacy[25] of the price or remuneration, as against the goods or services supplied in exchange.

A. Ancillary and Core Terms

Both the High Court and the Court of Appeal held that the charges did not fall within Regulation 6(2) of the UTCCR because they were not part of the essential bargain between the parties. The charges were not imposed as a consequence of the application of a 'core' term but rather in the operation of an ancillary price term (charges for unauthorised overdrafts) that a typical consumer would not recognise as part of the price.[26] In reaching this conclusion the Court of Appeal considered the case of *Director General of Fair Trading v First National Bank Plc*[27] where the House of Lords decided on an injunction to restrain the Bank from using a term under which interest on an overdue debt continued to accrue even after judgment. In this case, the term in the contract only kicked in once the consumer was in default leading to the term being considered subsidiary and thus subject to the fairness test.[28] In *First National*, the House of Lords agreed with the Court of Appeal on the scope and the fact that the clause could be assessed for fairness as it was not 'core' but disagreed as to the fairness element.

---

[23] *Abbey National* (n 6) [24].
[24] ibid [95] (Mance SCJ) explaining that this was the case expect in the case of four banks in certain specific and minor respects.
[25] Adequacy is meant to mean appropriateness, as per *Director General of Fair Trading v First National Bank plc* [2001] UKHL 52, [2002] 1 AC 481, [64]. Mance SCJ in *Abbey National* (n 6) [94] also adds reasonableness (in amount).
[26] Note by contrast, the case of *OFT v Foxtons Ltd* [2009] EWHC 1681 (Ch), [2009] CTLC 188. See also *Office of Fair Trading v Ashbourne Management Services* [2011] EWHC 1237 (Ch), [2011] ECC 31 concluding a core terms' fairness could nevertheless be assessed because it did not relate to the fairness of the bargain but to the consequences to members of early termination (at [102]).
[27] *Director General of Fair Trading* (n 25). The case concerned the application of Reg 3(2) now Reg 6(2) bar a few changes in text.
[28] This is an analysis the Supreme Court seems to endorse, *Abbey National* (n 6) Lord Walker, [32].

Lord Walker in the Supreme Court warned that ancillary meant 'subservient, subordinate and ministering to something else' and that in considering services the notion of ancillary needed to be treated with caution.[29] Indeed, the Supreme Court conceptualised the charges as a 'service' that was part of a package of services which made up a current account[30] and viewed the 'price or remuneration' as including the customer's potential liability for charges rather than the payments actually made.[31] In doing so, Lord Walker found the observation in *First National* that in a broad sense all terms of the contract are in some way related to the price or remuneration[32] persuasive although it acknowledged that some will be subject to the fairness test (notably if included in Schedule 2). The Court also conceded that while an assessment on price was precluded by Regulation 6(2)[33] it would be possible to challenge and assess fairness on other grounds for those terms that are deemed core.[34]

B. Price or Remuneration for Services Supplied in Exchange

The Supreme Court went on to consider if the charges for overdraft were a 'price paid in exchange for this package of services',[35] concluding that the term fell within the scope of Regulation 6(2) and thus could not be assessed for fairness. There the Court distinguished the terms in question with *First National* where the term was a default provision[36] which was not the case in *Abbey National*. This was because in interpreting Regulation 6(2) the Court ought to objectively determine if the price is in exchange for a package of services. Lord Mance explained that whether a term constitutes the price or remuneration is to be objectively considered and the Court should adopt the view which a hypothetical reasonable person would take to the nature and terms of the contract.[37]

The High Court had reasoned that the relevant charges could be assessed for fairness because they were not charged in exchange for anything. The charges were not imposed by way of payment for the services. They also would not be recognised by consumers as such and were not presented by the banks in their terms or other documentation.[38] The Court of Appeal followed the same line, but it did so having acknowledged that the substance of the contract had to be analysed as a package and

---

[29] *Abbey National* (n 6) [46] (Walker SCJ); [102] (Mance SCJ) explained citing Lord Hope of Craighead ([43] in *First National*) that the term in question in *First National* was concerned with the consequences of the borrower's breach of contract and not directly with the price charged for the loan or its adequacy.
[30] *Abbey National* (n 6) [47] (Walker SCJ).
[31] ibid [98] (Mance SCJ) citing the Court of Appeal's decision [97].
[32] *First National* (n 25) [34] (Steyn LJ); *Abbey National* (n 6) [42] (Walker SCJ).
[33] This is referred to as the 'excluded term' construction, whereby the term escapes all scrutiny so long as it relates to price. This is to be contrasted with the excluded 'assessment construction' whereby the term can still be considered but its fairness cannot be tested against its price. Other factors can be considered instead, as per *Abbey National* (n 6) [60] (Philips SCJ); [95] (Mance SCJ).
[34] ibid [60] (Philips SCJ).
[35] ibid [57] (Philips SCJ).
[36] Traders ought not to be able to outflank consumers by drafting themselves into a position where they can take advantage of a default provision; see *Abbey National* (n 6) [43] (Walker SCJ).
[37] *Abbey National* (n 6) [113] (Mance SCJ).
[38] ibid [67] (Philips SCJ).

not a series of individual services. This package of services could be divided into 'core or essential bargain' and 'incidental or ancillary' services, the latter falling outside the scope of Regulation 6(2).

The Supreme Court questioned how to consider if a charge is part of a payment or price for services. It ventured that the exercise could be done from the vantage point of what the customer knows, or if it was more constructive, to approach the matter from the viewpoint of the bank or no viewpoint at all, by the application of an objective test.[39]

The Court of Appeal privileged the viewpoint of the consumer, reflecting on whether or not a 'typical' consumer would understand this price to be in exchange for a service (the overdraft), leading to the conclusion that they would be unlikely to have anticipated the charge or would not have attached importance to it at the time they entered into the contract.[40] Indeed, free-if-in-credit bank customers open current accounts expecting to be in credit and would not have regard for the consequences of unforeseen events[41] leading to going overdrawn or having insufficient funds for a cheque to be drawn. The Court of Appeal viewed the purpose of the Directive to protect consumers as weaker parties from unfair contract terms, except where those terms reflect a true exercise of their contractual autonomy, that is, a genuine choice.[42]

The Supreme Court acknowledged that to consider the role played by the charges it should 'have regard to all the facts that are relevant to the operation of the contractual adventure and not just to those that are, or reasonably should be, within the knowledge of the customer'.[43] In doing so, it preferred to assess the case from the vantage point of the supplier of the goods or services.[44] It went on to consider that 'charges for unauthorised overdrafts are monetary consideration for the package of banking services supplied to personal account customers' noting that those charges constituted more than 30% of the banks' revenue[45] coming from personal current accounts and that they were an important part of the bank's charging structure as a result.[46] Lord Walker had little sympathy for the fact that the charges are in fact contingent and were not incurred by many customers, a fact he classed as 'irrelevant'.[47] Besides, Lord Phillips who had agreed that individually, it was difficult to see a price being paid for some of the relevant charges, as a package, it was clear that a price or remuneration was given in exchange, a point, the Court of Appeal had conceded.[48]

Lord Phillips also focussed on the fact that

> if it is possible to identify a price or remuneration being paid in exchange for services, even if the services are fringe or optional extras, Reg 6(2) will preclude an attack on the

---

[39] ibid [72] (Philips SCJ).
[40] ibid [69] (Philips SCJ).
[41] ibid [79] (Philips SCJ).
[42] S Whittaker, 'Unfair Contract Terms, Unfair Prices and Bank Charges' (2011) 74(1) *MLR* 106, 113.
[43] *Abbey National* (n 6) [73] (Philips SCJ).
[44] *Whittaker* (n 42) 116.
[45] Although the charges were incurred by only 20% of customers; see *Abbey National* (n 6), Lord Phillips, [87].
[46] *Abbey National* (n 6) [47] (Walker SCJ).
[47] ibid.
[48] ibid [75] and [77] (Philips SCJ).

price or remuneration in question if it is based on the contention that it was excessive by comparison to the services for which it was exchanged.[49]

He added that if the banks did not receive the relevant charges they would not be able to provide services profitably to customers in credit.[50]

IV. ANALYSIS OF THE SUPREME COURT'S DECISION

Many commentators agree that the Supreme Court failed to protect consumers against unfair surprises notably by emphasising the impact this decision would have on banks, rather than consumers.[51] There were in addition procedural failings, such as not referring the case to the European Court of Justice (ECJ) or taking a purposive approach, which would have been beneficial to consumers,[52] points to which we now turn.

A. No Referral to the European Court of Justice

Despite the opacity surrounding the interpretation of the notions of price and remuneration and the disagreements in interpretation of Regulation 6(2) derived from Article 4(2) of the Directive, between the High Court, Court of Appeal and Supreme Court, the Supreme Court declined a referral to the ECJ. The Supreme Court conceded that the interpretation of the UTCCRs, which implements the Unfair Terms Directive, was a question of European law.[53] Yet, it felt it was not necessary to refer the matter to the ECJ. This went

> against the logic of minimum harmonisation which requires that a national court of last instance must refer a question to the ECJ for a preliminary ruling whenever the national court would resolve the question in a way that is detrimental to the social group the Directive aims to protect.[54]

---

[49] ibid [78] (Philips SCJ). The Court of Appeal had avoided the application of Reg 6(2) because it considered the charges for overdrafts were ancillary.

[50] *Abbey National* (n 6) [88] (Philips SCJ).

[51] P Siciliani, C Riefa and H Gamper, *Consumer Theories of Harm, an Economic Approach to Consumer Law Enforcement and Policy Making* (Oxford, Hart Publishing 2019) 45–46. See contra, J Montague, 'Office of Fair Trading v Abbey National Plc: Contract – Bank Levies Unfair Terms – Office of Fair Trading' 14 (2009) 2 *Coventry Law Journal* 44–45 who argues albeit briefly that the decision has been misunderstood and should not be generally viewed, as it has been 'as further proof of the establishment's protection of the banks' profits'. See also S Brown, 'Using the Law as a Usury Law: Definitions of Usury and Recent Developments in the Regulation of Unfair Charges in Consumer Credit Transactions' (2011) 1 *Journal of Business Law* 91–118, arguing that the court missed an opportunity to discuss interest rates as part of price.

[52] D Barry, QC E Jenkins, C Sumnall, B Douglas-Jones and D Lloyd, *Blackstone's Guide to the Consumer Rights Act 2015* (Oxford, Oxford University Press, 2016) 109.

[53] *Abbey National* (n 6) [96] (Mance SCJ).

[54] M Schillig, 'Directive 93/13 and the Price Term Exemption: A Comparative Analysis in the Light of the Market for Lemons Rationale' (2011) 60 *International & Comparative Law Quarterly* 4, 933, 962.

Lord Walker's view was that because all Supreme Court judges unanimously agreed that the appeal should be allowed, the point was thus *acte clair*.[55] In EU parlance, where there has not yet been a preliminary ruling, nor clarification of a point of EU law by other case law, a national court may refrain from a reference only where the correct interpretation is so obvious as to leave no reasonable doubt.[56] However, this requires that the national court must be convinced that the matter is equally obvious to the courts of the other Member States and to the ECJ.[57]

Yet, the Supreme Court refrained from a reference because Lord Walker and Lord Mance[58] explicitly considered the matter to be *acte clair*. Lord Phillips disagreed but thought that a referral under Article 234 was not appropriate because the fairness of the relevant terms had not yet been challenged.[59] Lord Neuberger would have reluctantly concluded that a reference was required, if interpretation had been necessary and the ECJ could have interpreted the point differently from the Court of Appeal, which he agrees it was likely to.[60] This alone ought to have hinted towards the need for a reference. In the reasoning of the judges there is reluctance to defer to another court. In addition, the German Federal Supreme Court's arrived on a similar term at a largely different solution and thus, it was not obvious that courts in other Member States would deem the matter *acte clair*.

Ultimately, only the ECJ could guarantee the EU-wide uniform interpretation and application of the Directive by clarifying the meaning of the price term exemption under Article 4(2). The fact that the ECJ may not arrive at a satisfactory result for UK customers or that fairness was not yet challenged when it was in fact subject to elucidating if the terms were exempt seemed hollow arguments. Part of the reasons for not referring the matter to the European Court also stemmed from a concern for efficiency.[61] Lord Walker expressed the view that prevailed that even though the point may not be *acte clair*, avoiding further delays ought to take precedence over EU interpretation even though this may be regarded as unprincipled.[62]

B. Failure to Protect?

In *Abbey National*, the Supreme Court had a perfect opportunity to protect 'disadvantaged consumers finding it hard to make ends meet',[63] but whether directly or indirectly, decided to favour the banking regime. This was in spite of the fact that 12

---

[55] *Abbey National* (n 6) [49] (Walker SCJ).
[56] ECJ Case 283/81 *CILFIT v Ministry of Health* [1982] ECR 3415.
[57] ibid.
[58] *Abbey National* (n 6) [115] (Mance SCJ). At [96] Mance SCJ opined that the proper interpretation of Reg 6(2)(b) was a matter of EU law while whether the relevant charges fall within the scope of the regulation, properly interpreted was not involving a question of European law (as it concerned the application of the law, a matter for domestic law).
[59] *Abbey National* (n 6) [91] (Philips SCJ).
[60] ibid [120] (Neuberger SCJ). Lord Mance also raised this point, at [115] explaining that he though the ECJ's likelihood of accepting the Court of Appeal's interpretation was remote.
[61] *Abbey National* (n 6) [48] (Walker SCJ).
[62] ibid [50] (Walker SCJ).
[63] ibid [2] (Walker SCJ).

million customers who were regularly charged for unauthorised overdrafts subsidised some 42 million who were in credit.[64] The Supreme Court was more persuaded by the fact that if the banks did not receive the relevant charges they would not be able to provide services profitably to customers in credit.[65] The fact that other countries have a functioning banking system that relies on all customers contributing to its operation[66] left the Court unmoved and unwilling to explore a way to influence its structure. It was also possibly influenced by the context at the time, taking the financial crisis into consideration and concerned that a requirement to repay all the bank charges wrongly charged may lead to even more economic damage.[67] In addition, the Court did hint at the fact that it believes that the banks succeeding on the narrow issue did not close the door on the OFT's investigations and may well not resolve the myriad cases stayed at the time pending decision.[68] It was indeed accepted that while assessment of fairness of the term was barred because it was part of the price, the term could still be assessed on other grounds.[69] The fact that the OFT may be discouraged from doing so in light of the decision in *Abbey National* did not weigh on the judgment.

In any event, the route travelled in *Abbey National* may have less to do with statutory interpretation and more to do with the use of discretion by judges to choose between several competing options.[70] But the blame for an unequal banking structure in the UK and the failure to intervene when the opportunity presented itself may not solely be laid at the UK Supreme Court's door. Instead, the Court was also propped by a system that is structurally not designed to protect vulnerable consumers at its core.[71] The Supreme Court did in any event suggest that the matter was one for the legislator, flagging hence that reforms were to be welcome. Lord Walker was aware of the significance and controversy of the decision. He recognised the inequity of the situation[72] but ultimately determined that it was out of the Court's jurisdiction and explicitly invited ministers and Parliament to consider the matter further[73] and potentially revisit the decision to transpose the Directive in an era of so-called light touch regulation rather than conferring a high degree of consumer protection.[74]

---

[64] ibid [1].
[65] ibid [88].
[66] Eg, Lord walker mentions France operating a different form of cross-subsidy concentrating the charges on processing standing order and debit card transactions, as per [1].
[67] M Kenny and J Devenney, 'A Comparative Analysis of Bank Charges in Europe: *Abbey National plc* Through the Looking Glass' in M Kenny and J Devenney (eds), *Consumer Credit, Debt and Investment in Europe* (Cambridge, Cambridge University Press, 2012) 217.
[68] *Abbey National* (n 6) [61] (Philips SCJ).
[69] ibid [60] (Philips SCJ).
[70] O Amao, 'Judicial Discretion and Doing between the Banks and their Customers: A Critical Analysis of the Supreme Court Decision in *Office of Fair Trading v Abbey National Plc and Others*' (2011) Web JCLI, webjcli.ncl.ac.uk/2011/issue5/amao5.htm (accessed 4 October 2022).
[71] See notably, J Gardner, *The Future of High Cost Credit, Rethinking Payday Lending* (Oxford, Hart Publishing, 2022) which concludes that the system (political and financial) on payday lending does not adequately protect the vulnerable.
[72] *Abbey National* (n 6) [52] (Walker SCJ) explaining: 'If the Court allows this appeal the outcome may cause great disappointment and indeed dismay to a very large number of bank customers who feel they have been subjected to unfairly high charges in respect of unauthorised overdraft ....'
[73] *Abbey National* (n 6) [52] (Walker SCJ), [118] (Mance SCJ) endorsing Lord Walker's position.
[74] ibid [52] (Walker SCJ). Point endorsed at [93] (Hale SCJ), although she warned that it may not be easy to find a satisfactory solution.

In any event and although over a million bank customers suffered as a direct result of the decision, the overall economic assessment of the decision may be somewhat kinder to the Supreme Court than scholarly assessments have been. The majority of customers who rarely or never incur bank charges were arguably victorious as they would likely have lost 'free' banking had banks been ordered to return the estimated £10 billion in past charges and lower their future fees.[75]

C. Legislation Structurally Deficient to Protect Consumers in Need

'One of the main deficiencies of the unfair term regime is that it starts from the premise that competition and market pressures will lead to the right outcomes for consumers and that therefore what needs to be controlled is effectively the transparency and prominence of terms.'[76] Indeed, if a term is clear, it will not be assessed for fairness.[77] On this point, Collins notes that the directive which is implemented by the UTCCRs,

> does not require consumer contracts to be substantively fair, but it does require them to be clear. Clarity is essential for effective market competition between terms. What matters primarily for EC contract law is consumer choice, not consumer rights.[78]

The UK legislation, as well as the Directive made the distinction between core and ancillary terms whereas the former cannot be assessed for fairness. Indeed, the UTCCRs leave out terms that pertain to the 'price' and 'subject matter' of the contract. The rationale for this exclusion was that allowing courts some say into the potential striking out or revision of terms concerning the price or the main essence of the contract would be encroaching on freedom of contract. Legislation was thus set to ensure that a 'consumer cannot allege unfairness merely because he has made a bad bargain'.[79] Core terms were carved out to ensure the statute could not become an instrument to alter agreements already made. Yet the notions of 'price' (and accessorily 'subject matter') remain quite difficult to define as the case of *Abbey National* illustrates.

Another key deficiency can be found in the exclusion from the protection of the Directive and UK implementation of any individually negotiated terms. The original proposals for the Unfair Terms Directive were more ambitious and contemplated applying to individually negotiated terms, although this was dropped during

---

[75] Law Commission and Scottish Law Commission, *Unfair Terms in Consumer Contracts: a New Approach?* Issues paper (25 July 2012) [5.68], 43. Following *Kleinwort Benson*, money which is paid by mistake of law may be recovered for up to six years from the date when the mistake could have been discovered. This meant that if the Court had found the charges to be unfair, customers would have had six years to seek repayment of any unfair charges they had paid. It would have been a significant liability for UK banking – the banks' charges income for 2006 alone was put at £2.56 billion. It could also have resulted in a significant liability for the state as a shareholder/guarantor of some of the banks involved.
[76] Siciliani, Riefa and Gamper (n 51) 43.
[77] ibid.
[78] H Collins, 'Good Faith in European Contract Law' (1994) *OJLS* 229, cited in *OFT v Abbey National* [2010] 1 AC 696, [44].
[79] Woodroffe & Lowe, *Consumer Law and Practice* (London, Sweet & Maxwell, 2016) 197.

negotiations. In the Supreme Court judgment, Lords Walker and Mance highlight[80] an article by Brander and Ulmer[81] which had an influence in the Directive's development. They suggested that Article 4(2) reflects a double purpose: first, to ensure the Directive does not interfere with free market operation and second, to ensure consumers have genuine choice regarding price and the main subject matter of the contract. To this end, they argued that the Directive's application to individually negotiated terms would drastically restrict an individual's autonomy. A compromise was reached whereby only non-individually negotiated terms would fall within the Directive's ambit, and a 'fairly high threshold' was set for meeting this test. The Unfair Terms Directive thus follows a general pattern at EU level where consumer rights have therefore been overridden by consumer choice[82] a fact acknowledged by the Supreme Court. Lady Hale commented that 'consumer law in this country aims to give the consumer an informed choice rather than to protect the consumer from making an unwise choice'.[83] She did however question if the real problem was that we do not have a real choice because the suppliers offer all much the same product and do not compete on some of their terms.[84]

D. An Unrealistic View of the Average Consumer

The case resolutely sides with the view that average consumers are able to strike good bargains and guard themselves against unfair terms. Indeed, Lord Walker comments that the question of fairness of the bank charging system does depend partly on 'whether one's perception of the average customer who incurs unauthorised overdraft charges is that he is spendthrift and improvident, or that she is disadvantaged and finding it hard to make ends meet'.[85] The Court of Appeal had deliberated on the 'typical customer'. For clarification, assessing unfair terms does not have to be done by reference to an 'average consumer' which is the standard developed by the ECJ and that became enshrined in the regulation of unfair commercial practices. It was therefore not an issue for the Supreme Court to decide, but it would have inevitably tainted the understanding of the UTCCRs themselves.

Lord Mance indeed does allude to the fact that there is no requirement to interpret the contract and terms by attempting to identify a 'typical consumer' or conjecture on the matter they would be likely to focus on when entering the contract.[86] Instead, the consumer is to be assumed to be capable of reading the relevant terms and identifying whatever is objectively the price and remuneration under the contract.[87] The Law

---

[80] *Abbey National* (n 6) [6] (Walker SCJ); [109] (Mance SCJ).
[81] Brandner and Ulmer, 'The Community Directive on Unfair Terms in Consumer Contracts: Some Critical Remarks on the Proposal Submitted by the EC Commission' (1991) 28 *CML Review* 647.
[82] R Norbert, 'Protection of Consumers' Economic Interest by the EC' [1992] *Sydney Law Review* 23, 25.
[83] *Abbey National* (n 6) [93] (Hale SCJ).
[84] ibid. For an account of this problem, see J Gardner, *The Future of High Cost Credit: Rethinking Payday Lending* (Oxford, Hart Publishing, 2022) para 2.2.2., 33–35.
[85] *Abbey National* (n 6) [2] (Walker SCJ).
[86] *Abbey National* (n 6) [113] (Mance SCJ).
[87] ibid [113].

Commission on this point notes that unfair terms legislation assumes that consumers are rational but busy and do not have the time or resources to plough through standard form contracts. The legislation however assumes that when told about price or subject matter, these terms will factor into their decision making and thus will be subject to competition. This is the rationale for those terms not being assessed for fairness.[88]

However, the evidence uncovered after the decision in *Abbey National* shows that there is limitation to rationality.[89] Scholars have also argued that it is indeed rational to abstain from reading terms in a contract.[90] As a result, the expectations placed on consumers to account for price and exclude those term from scrutiny may no longer be justified.

Indeed, we have seen in recent years more concern for 'vulnerable consumers'[91] because it has been widely acknowledged that the notion of the average consumer developed by the ECJ was not reflective of actual consumer behaviour and thus not sufficiently protective. The work of Caplovitz[92] in this area has been instrumental in acknowledging that the poor pay more, and the bank charging system is a case in point. Vulnerable consumers, those who due to personal circumstances are especially susceptible to harm,[93] have become a point of regulatory focus in the financial industry. This is a welcome change of direction as just under half of the UK adult population is known to display characteristics of vulnerability.[94]

V. THE LONG ROAD TO PROTECTION – MAPPING THE IMPACT OF THE SUPREME COURT DECISION IN ABBEY NATIONAL

The decision in *Abbey National* had a chilling effect on public enforcement actions.[95] However, while it might have put a restraint on public intervention in front of the courts and the running of test cases, it did prompt the exploration of alternative

---

[88] Law Commission (n 75) [3.54].
[89] Siciliani, Riefa and Gamper (n 51) 46.
[90] Siciliani, Riefa and Gamper (n 51) 42; C Riefa and H Gamper, 'Economic Theory and Consumer Vulnerability, Exploring an Uneasy Relationship' in C Riefa and S Saintier (eds), *Vulnerable Consumers and the Law, Consumer Protection and Access to Justice* (Abingdon, Routledge, 2021) 24; See also M Chen-Wishart, 'Transparency and Fairness in Bank Charges' (2010) 126 *LQR* 157, 160 explaining that consumer law should be mindful that rational consumers do not read lengthy and complicated standard form contracts, whether in plain intelligible language or not, thus, debunking Lord Mance's assumption that the typical consumers will read and seek to understand all contractual terms *prior* to entering contracts as unrealistic.
[91] See, eg, European Commission, 'Consumer Vulnerability across Key markets in the European Union' (2016); Riefa and Saintier (n 90); P Cartwright, 'The Vulnerable Consumer of Financial Services: Law, Policy and Regulation'; FCA, *Treating Vulnerable Consumers Fairly* (2020) /www.fca.org.uk/firms/treating-vulnerable-consumers-fairly (accessed 4 October 2022).
[92] D Caplovitz, *The Poor Pay More* (Free Press, 1967).
[93] FCA, *Guidance for Firms on the Fair Treatment of Vulnerable Customers* (2021) www.fca.org.uk/publications/finalised-guidance/guidance-firms-fair-treatment-vulnerable-customers (accessed 4 October 2022).
[94] FCA *Financial Lives Survey 2020*, reported in FCA, *Financial Lives, the Experience of Vulnerable Consumers* (2020) 9-10.
[95] Siciliani, Riefa and Gamper (n 51) 42.

routes, some of which leading to an improvement in the charging structure relating to unauthorised overdrafts.

A. 'Voluntary' Actions by the Banks

Following the decision, the OFT stopped its investigation into unarranged overdraft charges. Instead, it changed strategy and opted for persuading the banks to reform their practices.[96] While seemingly optimistic, banks did in fact reduce their charges for services during the investigation and after the legal proceedings, producing a long-term benefit for all consumers.[97] No doubt the publicity surrounding the case would have helped sway the position, the banks being aware the OFT was not going to pursue matters further.

The banks agreed to introduce 'transparency measures' which included providing customers with annual summaries of the cost of their accounts; making charges prominent on monthly statements; and producing illustrative scenarios showing unarranged overdraft charges, giving consumers an idea of the costs for different patterns of use. Many banks revised their charging structures, such that the average unpaid item charge fell from £34 in 2007 to £14 in 2010.[98]

B. Governmental Intervention and Reforms

Legislative activity came in the aftermath of the *Abbey National* decision. In the wake of the commitments obtained by the OFT and a change in banking practice, government intervened to strengthen consumer protection launching the Consumer Credit and Personal Insolvency Review and publishing a formal Response on Consumer Credit in November 2011. In addition, a package of further commitments was announced, including giving consumers the option to receive text or email notification when balances fall below a certain level; giving a grace period to credit funds without incurring a charge; offer a buffer to avoid hefty charges on small overdrafts.[99] Those reforms came into force between 2012 and 2013. Further reforms took place further down the line: The Consumer Rights Act 2015 and intervention from the Financial Conduct Authority in 2019.

The decision in *Abbey National* hurried along an already much-needed reform of unfair terms in the UK. The decision had left in its wake some confusion. There were indeed, as the Law Commission noted, some contradictions in the Supreme Court decision as to what may qualify as price and concerning what and how those price terms could be reviewed.[100]

---

[96] Law Commission (n 75) [5.68], 51; Montague (n 51) 44–45.
[97] Montague (n 51) 44–45.
[98] Law Commission (n 75) [5.69], 52.
[99] ibid [5.71], 52.
[100] ibid [5.84], 55.

The positions adopted were not always easy to reconcile, allowing for differing interpretations of the decision. One of the key factors responsible for the introduction of the Consumer Rights Act 2015 (CRA) was thus the need to clarify uncertainty surrounding the scope of UTCCRs Regulation 6(2). Some of the Law Commission's revised recommendations in 2013[101] were implemented in Part 2 of the CRA.

The CRA maintains an exemption for core terms. It however provides for a slightly different test under which we can wonder if *Abbey National* would likely have been decided differently. Under section 64, a term is excluded from fairness if it is: (a) the main subject matter of the contract; or (b) an assessment of the price payable. The term will however only be excluded from a fairness assessment if it is 'transparent' and 'prominent'.

This is a narrower exception to the fairness assessment. Indeed, Freeman believes that the terms in question may not fall within the definition now.[102] Specifically, it is likely that the fact that the sums are an important part of the trader's charging structure, amounting to over 30 per cent of their revenue stream, especially where the revenue is levied without providing a service in exchange[103] is unlikely to fall within the exception under the CRA.[104] Similarly, sums that the trader relies on to be able to be profitable are unlikely to be exempted.[105] But the issue remains regarding the interpretation of the services provided and whether or not they need to be regarded as stand-alone or as part of a package of services that come bundled together when opening a current account with a bank. For this reason, it is quite possible that *Abbey National* continues to be good law and hence, will provide no relief to consumers. Indeed, for some scholars, the introduction of 'prominence' may not have any effect on interpretation[106] especially when calibrated against the notion of the average consumer that is now featured in section 64 CRA 2015.[107] The expectation would remain that consumers are able to understand the terms and would thus be bound by them regardless of their actual situation and vulnerabilities.

VI. CONCLUDING REMARKS – THE FUTURE OF ABBEY NATIONAL

In 2019, the Financial Conduct Authority made changes to fix the overdraft market banning extortionate overdraft fees and increasing the transparency of charges.[108]

---

[101] Law Commission (n 75).

[102] J Freeman, 'Unfair Contract Terms', in Kirk and Lewin (eds) *Consumer and Trading Standards, Law and Practice 2022*, 10th edn (London, Lexis Nexis, 2022) 609.

[103] In case C26/13 Kàsler and Kàslerné Rábai [57], 58.

[104] Freeman (n 102).

[105] ibid.

[106] Siciliani, Riefa and Gamper (n 51) 46 explain that it seems questionable whether the outcome would differ much under the new prominence test, because vulnerable consumers who are most reliant on this expensive form of short credit do not respond positively to the introduction of message alerts warning about an imminent move to an unarranged overdraft. Many indeed are unable to avoid the charge needing to go overdrawn to pay for necessities.

[107] Prior to this, the High Court used this standard in the case of *Office of Fair Trading v Ashbourne Management Ltd* (n 26).

[108] FCA, Overdraft Pricing and Competition Remedies, Policy Statement PS19/25 (2019), www.fca.org.uk/publications/policy-statements/ps19-25-overdraft-pricing-remedies-competition (accessed 4 October 2022).

It made rules to simplify the pricing of all overdrafts and to end higher prices for unarranged overdrafts. This was done by a series of measures, notably, a ban on higher prices for unarranged overdrafts compared to charges for arranged overdrafts; a ban on fixed fees for borrowing through an overdraft; mandating a single annual interest rate instead of fixed daily or monthly charges; extending the ban on fixed fees to include overdraft facility fees for arranged overdrafts up to £10,000. Banks will also be required to advertise arranged overdraft prices increasing transparency (this includes the display of a representative Annual Percentage Rate (APR) to aid comparison). This is coupled with some action aimed at assisting vulnerable consumers, notably issuing guidance to reiterate that refused payment fees should reasonably correspond to the costs of refusing said payments and requiring banks to do more to identify customers who are showing signs of financial strain or are in financial difficulty, and develop and implement a strategy to reduce repeat use of overdraft facilities.[109]

Unfortunately, while banks stopped using those fees, there is evidence that instead they are charging high interest rates, in some instances up to 40 per cent.[110] Transparency is a useful tool in some circumstances, but unable to truly sway consumer behaviours and encourage them to walk away. Many are trapped in bank accounts as their arrears and credit status makes them undesirable customers to other banks. In any event, the retail banking market remains dysfunctional, with major banks having a major competitive advantage on others[111] and evidence that major banks were earning high yields on overdrafts.

With this in mind, the UK bank account pricing structure appears to remain safe, with those who are unable to meet their financial commitment continuing to subsidise those who can.[112] Indeed, in 2016, more than 50 per cent of firms' unarranged overdraft fees came from just 1.5 per cent of customers. People living in deprived neighbourhoods were more likely to incur these fees.[113] Yet, and in spite of reforms, the FCA itself acknowledged that the 'free-in-credit' banking is unlikely to disappear as a result of changes to overdraft rules, although it is hopeful it might be following interventions in other areas.[114] What has changed is the focus on vulnerable consumers. However, the roll out of reforms so far does not seem to have yielded the intended results. The views expressed in the Supreme Court Decision of Abbey National in 2009 sadly therefore still hold true today and the poor continue to pay more.[115]

---

[109] FCA, High Cost Credit Review: Overdrafts Policy Statement, Policy Statement PS19/16 (June 2019) www.fca.org.uk/publication/policy/ps19-16.pdf, [1.8] (accessed 4 October 2022).

[110] V McKeever, 'HSBC Hikes Overdraft Charge to 40% for UK Customers', www.cnbc.com/2019/12/05/hsbc-hikes-overdraft-charge-to-40percent-for-uk-customers.html (accessed 4 October 2022).

[111] FCA, Strategic Review of Retail Banking Models, final report (December 2018) www.fca.org.uk/publication/multi-firm-reviews/strategic-review-retail-banking-business-models-final-report.pdf, [1.5] (accessed 4 October 2022).

[112] FCA (n 109) [1.2].

[113] ibid.

[114] FCA (n 111) [1.17].

[115] See for recent examples the work of Fairness by Design, a not-for-profit fighting to end the poverty premium, notably fairbydesign.com/insurance-poverty-premium/ (accessed 4 October 2022).

17

Bankruptcy, Housing, 'Have Nots', and the Limits of Legal Landmarks: *Places for People Homes Ltd v Sharples*

JOSEPH SPOONER*

I. INTRODUCTION

GIVEN THAT BANKRUPTCY law protects an insolvent individual from creditor debt recovery actions, can a tenant in rent arrears rely on bankruptcy to prevent their eviction? In the case of *Places for People Homes Ltd. v Sharples*,[1] the English Court of Appeal provided a negative answer to this question, effectively holding that bankruptcy's protection does not extend to saving renters from losing their homes. This is a perplexing decision on several levels. First, a central feature of bankruptcy law is the freezing or 'staying' of all creditor debt collection activities and processes against an insolvent individual on commencement of insolvency proceedings (the 'stay of enforcement'). This is prior to (most of) the individual's debts being 'discharged' or cancelled at the end of the bankruptcy process (the 'debt discharge'). So, it seems contrary to this basic principle for a court decision to allow a landlord to continue with eviction proceedings on the grounds of rental debt (under English law terminology, a 'possession order' procedure) while a tenant is under bankruptcy protection. Second, contemporary understandings of bankruptcy law emphasise the centrality of the 'fresh start' policy, the idea that many important economic and social objectives can be advanced by providing over-indebted households with relief from unpayable debt.[2] A court decision which permits a landlord to evict a bankrupt tenant seems to conflict patently with this idea of offering insolvent individuals a fresh start.

---

*I thank Mr Richard Holland for agreeing to be interviewed as part of this piece. I thank Professor Iain Ramsay, Professor Jodi Gardner, Dr Irina Domurath, and Dr Jacob Eisler for comments on earlier drafts. All errors and omissions are mine.

[1] *Places for People Homes Ltd v Sharples; A2 Dominion Homes Ltd v Godfrey* [2011] EWCA Civ 813, [2011] HLR 45.

[2] J Spooner, *Bankruptcy: The Case for Relief in an Economy of Debt* (Cambridge, Cambridge University Press 2019) ch 3.

The *Sharples* case is perhaps an unusual landmark in consumer law. Rather than marking an expansion of consumer protections, the Court of Appeal decision extends landlord rights in the face of an eminently plausible pro-debtor reading of the relevant legislation.[3] I have written elsewhere on the weakness of the substantive reasoning of the Court, and its negative policy consequences in the context of a housing crisis and mass household over-indebtedness.[4] This chapter reflects on what the *Sharples* story tells us about the challenges of realising landmark litigation in favour of low-income groups. The case was a dispute between a 'Repeat Player' and a 'One-Shotter', between representatives of the 'haves' and 'have nots' – its story illustrates how structural features of the legal system limit the ability of society's 'have nots' to advance their interests in the courts.[5] A failure of our legal system to facilitate cases 'with precedent-setting potential', means that legal development 'remains worryingly haphazard'.[6] Obstacles to strategic litigation on behalf of the poor, however, mean that this haphazard trend is not random – it skews against the likelihood of legal landmarks on behalf of lower-income groups such as consumers. This chapter draws extensively on an interview I conducted with Mr Richard Holland, the debt advisor who advised Ms Sharples and who was responsible for initiating the central legal arguments ultimately raised before the Court of Appeal.[7] After setting out key features of the case and the Court of Appeal's decision, the chapter continues to discuss theories of dispute resolution, which illustrate the challenges to bringing strategic litigation on behalf of low-income consumers. Mr Holland's fascinating insight into the reality behind the Court decision then illustrates how the case represented a creative defence of a client's interests in the face of a desperate emergency. The result was a legal campaign born of necessity, rather than one developed under ideal conditions for strategic litigation in the pursuit of legal landmarks.

II. SUMMARY OF THE CASE

The Court of Appeal decision in *Sharples* opened promisingly with an acknowledgement that the case raised 'important issues of general principle' about the interface between housing and bankruptcy or personal insolvency law.[8] A functionalist account would see as inevitable the intersection of bankruptcy with social policy areas such as housing, given that many legal systems understand consumer bankruptcy laws as a form of social insurance.[9] In providing relief and a 'fresh start' to financially troubled households who fall through gaps in welfare state provision, bankruptcy can

---

[3] Insolvency Act 1986, s. 251G.

[4] J Spooner, 'Seeking Shelter in Personal Insolvency Law: Recession, Eviction, and Bankruptcy's Social Safety Net' (2017) 44 *Journal of Law and Society* 374.

[5] M Galanter, 'Why the 'Haves' Come out Ahead: Speculations on the Limits of Legal Change' (1974) 9 *Law & Society Review* 95.

[6] L Mulcahy, 'The Collective Interest in Private Dispute Resolution' (2013) 33 *Oxford Journal of Legal Studies* 59, 60.

[7] Interview conducted on 5 November 2021.

[8] '*Sharples*' (n 1) [5].

[9] Spooner (n 4) 378–79; I Ramsay, 'Comparative Consumer Bankruptcy' (2007) 2007 *University of Illinois Law Review* 241.

be seen as a social safety net of last resort, but also as an ultimate consumer protection mechanism.[10] Irrespective of an ability to establish firm liability or consumer defences, bankruptcy law initially protects individuals unable to repay their debts from creditor enforcement, before subsequently discharging or cancelling those debts. This is how the bankruptcy system operates for debt advisers such as Mr Holland, who each day see clients like Ms Sharples invoke bankruptcy to obtain respite from over-indebtedness. From the point of view of English legal institutions, perhaps more used to dealing in abstractions of contractual enforcement and property rights, bankruptcy law however seems to hold a dual identity. Sometimes the law appears to emphasise the aim of household debt relief, but at other times it seems to operate as a tool of creditor wealth maximisation.[11] The *Sharples* case raised the question of which of these views of bankruptcy should take priority.

The Court of Appeal heard joined appeals in two cases where housing associations sought to evict tenants who had fallen behind on rent and sought insolvency protection. The two cases differed in the form of insolvency procedure used by each tenant. Ms Sharples had entered the Bankruptcy procedure,[12] a mechanism existing for centuries through many amendments and policy evolutions, which essentially involves the freezing of all debt collection activity against an insolvent individual; the pooling of their non-essential assets (into a 'bankruptcy estate') and the liquidation of their estate for the benefit of creditors; and finally, the discharge of their debts. Mr Godfrey entered the Debt Relief Order (DRO) procedure, a form of 'bankruptcy light' for 'no income, no assets' cases introduced by 2007 legislation.[13] This mechanism involves the freezing of debt collection and the discharge of debt, but no seizure or distribution of debtor assets. Distinctions between the two procedures are limited due to the reality that most individuals entering Bankruptcy are now consumers with low incomes and few assets, meaning that in most cases there is no 'bankruptcy estate' and no distribution of assets to creditors. One key difference lies in the condition that access to the DRO procedure is limited to individuals owing debts of less than £30,000. The DRO was introduced specifically to deal with modern problems of over-indebtedness among low-income groups, and courts have recognised it as serving the sole purpose of providing 'unadulterated debt relief'.[14] This makes the DRO procedure resemble bespoke 'consumer bankruptcy' laws of the types enacted in many European countries to address the emergence of a problem of mass household over-indebtedness.[15] In contrast, the Bankruptcy procedure has existed for centuries,

---

[10] WC Whitford, 'The Ideal of Individualized Justice: Consumer Bankruptcy as Consumer Protection, and Consumer Protection in Consumer Bankruptcy' (1994) 68 *American Bankruptcy Law Journal* 397.
[11] Spooner (n 2) ch 3.
[12] In this chapter, 'Bankruptcy' refers to the specific personal insolvency procedure under English law, while 'bankruptcy' refers more broadly to the concept of a law which addresses the insolvency of an individual, whether that law falls under the label of personal insolvency, bankruptcy, debt settlement, debt restructuring etc.
[13] I Ramsay, 'The New Poor Person's Bankruptcy: Comparative Perspectives' (2020) 29 *International Insolvency Review* S4.
[14] *R (Cooper and Payne) v Secretary of State for Work and Pensions* [2010] EWCA Civ 1431, [2011] BPIR 223 [85].
[15] See, eg, I Ramsay, *Personal Insolvency in the 21st Century: A Comparative Analysis of the US and Europe* (Oxford, Hart Publishing, 2017).

from a time when it was first primarily used as a debt collection tool against debtors who actually held assets capable of constituting a 'bankruptcy estate'. This historical baggage means that some courts and lawyers persist in seeing Bankruptcy as serving an aim of debt collection or maximising returns to creditors, embracing only partly (if at all) the aims of debt relief and the 'fresh start' policy.[16]

Given the lack of other material differences between the two appeals, this chapter focuses on the dispute between Ms Sharples and her landlord, Places for People Homes Limited. Places for People is the largest housing association in the UK. Its status seems emblematic of how recent decades have seen the commercialisation of social housing under a 'business ethos', alongside the consolidation of the sector among a small number of large firms.[17] According to its promotional material, it 'provide[s] and manage[s] every kind of housing, plans and builds new developments, manages leisure facilities and offers customer-friendly financial products'.[18] Only approximately half of its business activity is now in the area of 'affordable housing'. The company's turnover in 2021 reached over £800 million, with profits exceeding £200 million, reserves over £700 million, and fixed assets of almost £5 billion.

In December 1997, Ms Sharples rented Denbigh Place from Places for People under an assured tenancy.[19] The next details in the court judgment are that Ms Sharples fell into difficulty paying rent, apparently after almost eight years at Denbigh Place. In September 2005, Places for People commenced possession proceedings against Ms Sharples at Salford County Court, having previously served on her a notice seeking possession. The court adjourned these proceedings on terms that Ms Sharples would pay current rent and a weekly amount towards her arrears, but reinstated them in early 2009 after this repayment plan broke down. A possession order hearing was listed for 19 May 2009, but on 14 May Ms Sharples filed a bankruptcy petition in Salford County Court and was declared bankrupt. The possession order hearing proceeded on 19 May and District Judge Hovington awarded the possession order to Places for People, finding that a mandatory ground for a possession order was established (the ground being at least eight weeks' unpaid rent).[20] Ms Sharples appealed this decision to Judge Tetlow, who rejected the appeal on 28 August 2009. Ms Sharples then took her case to the Court of Appeal.

The Court of Appeal answered negatively the central question raised of 'whether a bankruptcy order … preclude[s] the making of an order for possession of a dwelling let on an assured tenancy on the ground of rent arrears'.[21] The Court held, first, that

---

[16] Spooner (n 2) 65–77.

[17] D Cowan, C Hunter and H Pawson, 'Jurisdiction and Scale: Rent Arrears, Social Housing, and Human Rights' (2012) 39 *Journal of Law and Society* 269, 282–86.

[18] placesforpeople.co.uk/about-us/who-we-are/what-we-do.

[19] The assured tenancy is the standard form of tenancy in both the private and social housing sectors, and the principles of this case apply to all main forms of tenancy: see, eg, Insolvency Service, 'Insolvency Service Technical Manual, Part 4: Tenancies' (18 July 2012) para 30.70; Cowan, Hunter and Pawson (n 17) 283–88.

[20] Housing Act 1988, Sch 2, Ground 8.

[21] *Sharples* (n 1) [5].

bankruptcy's stay of any creditor's 'remedy in respect of a debt'[22] did not apply to a possession order claim. Etherton LJ stated that:

> An order for possession is not obtained with a view to payment of arrears of rent at all. Its object is to restore to the landlord the right to full possession and enjoyment of the landlord's property ....

Second, the Court held that this finding was not undermined by a legislative amendment introduced under the Housing Act 1998 which had removed an insolvent individual's tenancy from the bankruptcy estate.[23] Rejecting the idea that this amendment had been designed specifically to clarify that bankruptcy protection encompasses eviction, Etherton LJ held that the amendment simply ensured that a court could be confident that in ordering eviction it was not depriving an insolvent individual's creditors of an asset otherwise available to them. The Court found for Ms Sharples on the point that rent arrears constituted debts included in the bankruptcy, and so were discharged. The result is that while Bankruptcy cancelled Ms Sharples' rent arrears, it did not prevent a court from making an order evicting her based on those no-longer-existing arrears.[24]

Figure 1 Denbigh Place – image from Google Maps

---

[22] See Insolvency Act 1986, ss 285, 251G(2).
[23] Insolvency Act 1986 (1986 c. 45), s 283(3A), inserted by Housing Act 1988 (c.50), s 117(1).
[24] Mr Holland notes here that local authorities and housing associations also tend to treat a housing applicant's rent arrears from a former tenancy as an 'indelible black mark' against an application, even if the former arrears are now 'non-existent' due to an applicant's discharge through personal insolvency.

III. STRUCTURAL INJUSTICE OF CONSUMER LITIGATION AND THE LIMITS OF LEGAL CHANGE

The story of the *Sharples* case offers insight into the structural injustice of consumer litigation, which can tilt the law against the interests of the poor and reduce the odds of consumers achieving landmark change through the courts. Galanter's flagship piece on the why 'haves' tend to win over 'have nots' in battles of adjudication offers a useful frame for exploring the challenges for pursuing progressive change through law.[25] Legal advances for consumers must come at the expense of firms, and landmark cases usually involve a contest for favourable precedent between 'One Shotters' and 'Repeat Players'. 'Repeat Players' are well-resourced and organised parties who frequently use the court system. These actors can structure transactions in legally favourable ways, develop expertise and establish informal relations with institutional actors, and approach litigation strategically. Tactical approaches to litigation involve 'playing the odds' and maximising gains over a series of cases rather than focusing on just one case; as well as litigating to produce long-standing rules rather than solely concentrating on the outcome of a given case.[26] In contrast, 'One-Shotters' are individuals who may take part in litigation once in a lifetime, for whom the stakes in one particular dispute are too large and the financial value too low for such claims to be managed strategically (or to be managed at all – often the One-Shotters have no representation). When focusing on court decisions as legal landmarks, we must remember that fundamentally 'courts are passive' and the potential for legal progress only arises when proceedings are 'triggered by parties'.[27] Repeat Players hold 'superior opportunities … to trigger promising cases and prevent the triggering of unpromising ones', and so can shape precedent and legal development.

One way in which One-Shotters might tilt the litigation and legal development imbalance is through intermediaries – most notably lawyers but also other advisers and campaigners – who could 'bring well-planned and strategized test cases'.[28] In this way, a One-Shotter may be converted into something resembling a Repeat Player. This element of strategy may be unavailable, however, to groups advocating on behalf of the poor. In the context of debt, housing, and related issues in the UK, clients will generally be assisted by debt advice agencies.[29] These agencies 'must take cases as they come', depriving them of the ability to select the most promising cases, which is arguably a process 'central to the success of test cases'.[30] While a Repeat Player can approach all litigation from a strategical perspective, there is necessarily

---

[25] Galanter (n 5).
[26] ibid 98–101.
[27] ibid 103.
[28] C Menkel-Meadow, 'Do the Haves Come Out Ahead in Alternative Judicial Systems: Repeat Players in ADR' (1999) 15 *Ohio State Journal on Dispute Resolution* 19, 29.
[29] For informative discussions of the advice sector, see, eg, S Kirwan, *Advising in Austerity: Reflections on Challenging Times for Advice Agencies* (Bristol, Policy Press, 2016); D James and S Kirwan, '"Sorting out Income": Transnational Householding and Austerity Britain' (2020) 28 *Social Anthropology* 67.
[30] T Prosser, *Test Cases for the Poor: Legal Techniques in the Politics of Social Welfare* (Child Poverty Action Group 1983) 40.

a certain degree of randomness in litigation brought on behalf of the poor.[31] Much research in this tradition has focused on consumers and low income litigants as *claimants*, and explored how these groups can(not) transform a wrong or grievance into a legal claim.[32] A majority of people experiencing grievances will not progress them through the legal system, and mostly this is 'rational inaction'[33] – where, for example, a party decides that the costs of legal action outweigh the significance of a dispute. Advisors of clients such as a tenant or homeowner facing eviction, however, do not have the option of suggesting that a client 'lump it' and abandon a legal claim.[34] A One-Shotter *claimant* faces no worse consequences than the status quo when they decide not to pursue their claim, but a One-Shotter *defendant* may lose everything unless they can raise a defence.[35] A legal defence must sometimes be pursued even if it is not the perfect test case or part of a long-term strategy, and even against the odds of it producing a positive outcome or useful precedent. While an adviser might usually evaluate the merits of a grievance and dissuade a client from pursuing a weak *claim*,[36] an adviser may have little option but to try to mount a *defence* where the alternative outcomes for the client are severe. The litigation battle must then be fought on the terms of the Repeat Player who has chosen to pursue this matter. The defendant must accept the claimant's definition of the legal problem, while the claimant has the power 'to make crucial choices about parties, timing, posture, forum, relevance, and relief'.[37] Ideally a campaigning group might identify and compile evidence of harmful practices of certain firms or landlords, before strategising as to the optimum time, case, and theory of harm/cause of action for mounting a legal attack against such practices.[38] In reality, advisors of low income defendants cannot follow such an approach and must fight fires where they spark – 'the emphasis in advice provision tends to be geared towards disaster management'.[39]

This raises the further dichotomy in legal advice for the poor between 'service and impact',[40] or between offering advice to individual clients and pursuing campaigns

---

[31] M Feldman, 'Political Lessons: Legal Services for the Poor' (1994) 83 *Georgetown Law Journal* 1529, 1534–42.

[32] WLF Felstiner, RL Abel and A Sarat, 'The Emergence and Transformation of Disputes: Naming, Blaming, Claiming …' (1980) 15 *Law & Society Review* 631; SE Merry, *Getting Justice and Getting Even: Legal Consciousness among Working-Class Americans*, 2nd edn (Chicago, University of Chicago Press, 1990); A Buck, P Pleasence and NJ Balmer, 'Do Citizens Know How to Deal with Legal Issues? Some Empirical Insights' (2008) 37 *Journal of Social Policy* 661.

[33] P Pleasence and N Balmer, 'How People Resolve 'Legal' Problems: A Report to the Legal Services Board' (Legal Services Board, 2014) 100.

[34] Galanter (n 5) 124–25.

[35] EST Poppe, 'Why Consumer Defendants Lump It' (2019) 14 *Northwestern Journal of Law and Social Policy* 149, 156.

[36] E Rose, 'Getting from the Story of a Dispute to the Law' in S Kirwan (ed), *Advising in Austerity: Reflections on Challenging Times for Advice Agencies* (Bristol, Policy Press, 2016) 142–43.

[37] Feldman (n 31) 1545.

[38] ibid 1546. For example, since the Court of Appeal seemed to place weight on Places for People's status as a social landlord, one wonders whether a case involving a private landlord might have removed at least one strand of pro-creditor policy argument from the court's decision.

[39] H Genn, *Paths to Justice: What People Do and Think about Going to Law*, UK edn (London, Bloomsbury Publishing, 1999) 255.

[40] Feldman (n 31) 1537–39.

for legal change on behalf of client groups.[41] In contemporary conditions of advice, the bulk of advice work will focus on the individual client. From the zenith of poverty lawyering in the 1960s and 1970s,[42] changes in philosophies of poverty activism may subsequently have moved away from litigation strategies and towards community-focused efforts.[43] Policy developments, such as the decimation of legal aid in the UK,[44] may have reduced the viability of such litigation strategies. Questions arise as to whether the removal of legal aid funding may have 'delegalised' problems of the poor, suggesting that policymakers prefer to cast these as non-legal problems, apparently not 'deserving' legal advice.[45] Among the money and debt advisers who now shoulder the burden of supporting clients, debate exists as to the extent to which their work involves *legal* advice. Advisers clearly hold legal knowledge, and some describe their work as involving legal diagnostics, communicating the law to clients, and 'framing the law in terms of possible courses of action'.[46] There appears to be considerable dispute, however, as to extent to which debt advisers can engage in legal strategising and 'get involved in the tactics'.[47] Certain debt advice agencies may also take organisational positions not to raise legal issues on behalf of debt clients, preferring to admit liability and work on negotiating repayment plans.[48]

While lawyers for 'Repeat Players' can play the 'long game' and trade off losses on some cases for gains on others, duties to individual clients mean that advisers of One-Shotters must strive for the best outcome in each individual case.[49] Where a client has multiple debt problems, bankruptcy is an option which offers relief against (almost) all debts. This is of course more advantageous to a client than raising legal

---

[41] See, eg, Prosser's discussion of internal debate on this point in the Child Poverty Action Group: Prosser (n 30) 19–22.
[42] M Galanter, 'Reflections on Why the 'Haves' Come Out Ahead' in A Hinshaw, AK Schneider and SR Cole (eds), *Discussions in Dispute Resolution: The Foundational Articles* (Oxford, Oxford University Press 2021) 317.
[43] SL Cummings and IV Eagly, 'A Critical Reflection on Law and Organizing' (2000) 48 *UCLA Law Review* 443.
[44] J Robins and D Newman, *Justice in a Time of Austerity: Stories From a System in Crisis* (Bristol, Bristol University Press 2021) ch 9.
[45] Barrister and Conservative member of the House of Lords, Edward Faulks, stated that 'the question that arises out of social welfare law is whether it is always necessary for everybody who has quite real problems to have a lawyer at £200-odd an hour, or whether there are better and more effective ways of giving advice'. 'Legal Aid, Sentencing and Punishment of Offenders Act 2012: Question' publications.parliament.uk/pa/ld201516/ldhansrd/text/150610-0001.htm#15061054000331 (accessed 24 November 2022). This overstated the fees of legal aid lawyers almost fourfold: Robins and Newman (n 43) 16.
[46] Rose (n 36) 139.
[47] S Kirwan, '"Advice on the Law but Not Legal Advice so Much": Weaving Law and Life into Debt Advice', in *Advising in Austerity: Reflections on Challenging Times for Advice Agencies* (Bristol, Policy Press 2016) 150.
[48] As Mr Holland notes, in the context of the forced instalment of home energy prepayment meters during the energy crisis of 2022-23, similar dilemmas arise for organisations as to whether to build campaigns around legal (human rights) challenges or negotiations with industry. For an outline of relevant issues, see, eg, Department for Energy Security and Net Zero and G Shapps MP, 'Energy Companies Halt Forced Installation of Prepayment Meters' (*GOV.UK*) www.gov.uk/government/news/energy-companies-halt-forced-installation-of-prepayment-meters (accessed 4 April 2023).
[49] Galanter (n 5) 117.

defences in respect of all their debts,⁵⁰ but militates against clients pursuing points of importance in consumer law. In other situations, advisors may wish to settle a claim even where there is a valid legal point at issue, due to limitations on resources, or uncertainty about how a court might decide an unclear legal point.⁵¹ Even where an advisor has the time and resources to identify a potentially strong legal defence, questions arise as to whether a client will wish to continue with a legal action which may involve considerable stress,⁵² or even stigmatisation,⁵³ in a legal process which is often alienating and disempowering.⁵⁴ Surveys of public attitudes to legal problems have found that when 'faced with a justiciable event most people simply want to solve the problem'.⁵⁵ In this context, 'the One-Shotter has nothing to gain by trying to "make law" when what is needed is an immediate resolution of their problem'.⁵⁶ Some have lamented a reduced willingness of poverty lawyers to 'fight' for their clients by refusing settlements and taking cases to court.⁵⁷ Others see this as a natural rebalancing of the client-lawyer relationship – a move beyond criticisms of lawyers 'disempowering clients by controlling litigation strategies', towards ensuring the primacy of clients' ability to determine their own interests.⁵⁸ Indeed, some consider 'money advice to be the most complicated of advice areas given the extent to which the adviser must allow the client to make their own decisions'.⁵⁹ Tensions might arise between strategic litigation goals and client empowerment – one housing law strategy in 1970s New York considered that it had to expand from a focus on 'resolving individual problems in the narrowest possible manner' in order 'to develop a political strategy that could improve the legal position of all tenants'.⁶⁰ This occasionally involved risky tactics for individual tenants, such as encouraging them to withhold rent and force landlords to court.⁶¹ The pressure to settle and the risks of litigation raise tension between producing best results for each client and fighting the tendency of repeat players to 'buy off' defendants in order to avoid unfavourable precedent and legal change.⁶² In contrast, the *Sharples* case illustrates that in certain situations the fight for the best outcome for a client leaves no option but to mount a potentially landmark legal action.

---

⁵⁰ Whitford (n 10).
⁵¹ Feldman (n 31) 1549.
⁵² Rose (n 35) 143–34.
⁵³ Tensions might arise between individual and group interests, where an individual does not wish to see themselves as part of a stigmatised group such as 'the poor': K Summers, 'For the Greater Good? Ethical Reflections on Interviewing the 'Rich' and 'Poor' in Qualitative Research' (2020) 23 *International Journal of Social Research Methodology* 593.
⁵⁴ Genn (n 39) 254; Cummings and Eagly (n 43) 455.
⁵⁵ Genn (n 39) 254.
⁵⁶ C Alkon, 'Galanter's Analysis of the 'Limits of Legal Change' as Applied to Criminal Cases and Reform' in A Hinshaw, AK Schneider and SR Cole (eds), *Discussions in Dispute Resolution: The Foundational Articles* (Oxford, Oxford University Press, 2021) 313.
⁵⁷ Feldman (n 31) 1548–49.
⁵⁸ Cummings and Eagly (n 43) 458–60.
⁵⁹ Kirwan (n 47) 149.
⁶⁰ M Lazerson, 'In the Halls of Justice, the Only Justice Is in the Halls' in RL Abel (ed), *Politics of Informal Justice: The American Experience v.1* (First Printing edition, New York, Academic Press Inc, 1982) 129.
⁶¹ ibid 130.
⁶² Prosser (n 30) 84.

IV. THE SHARPLES STORY AND LITIGATION FOR THE 'HAVE NOTS'

The challenges to progressive legal change posed by the structural inequalities of the legal system are evident in the story of the *Sharples* case, and particularly the insight offered by my interview with Richard Holland. This case was not a consumer law test case in the usual sense – it did not arise from a deliberate strategic campaign,[63] or did not represent the culmination of a series of cases at lower court levels.[64] While the case certainly tested a new point of law, its origins were in a debt advisor's creative and determined efforts to assist an individual client in desperate need. Once Ms Sharples approached the debt advice office for assistance, her case was quickly chosen for casework due to factors such as the levels of her debt, the nature of her financial problems, and the high stakes involved in her situation (the imminent threat of eviction). From the beginning, the odds seemed stacked against Ms Sharples. It became clear that her financial position meant petitioning for Bankruptcy was the appropriate option for her, but the substantial costs of presenting a petition were an obstacle – in England and Wales, bankruptcy petitioners must now present up-front fees of almost £700.[65] After a period of delay, the debt advice office managed to obtain a grant from charitable funds to cover the costs of the Bankruptcy petition. Ms Sharples was declared Bankrupt and so was protected from creditor collection efforts, but the possession order hearing was still due to take place in the days following her Bankruptcy. Requests were then made to Places for People to abandon the possession claim due to Ms Sharples' Bankruptcy. Often housing associations will work with debt advisors and agree to abandon claims for rent arrears and possession due to the insolvent tenant's confirmed inability to pay, allowing cases to be settled. In this instance Places for People, which did not have the kind of working relationship with local debt advice services which might have facilitated settlement, continued to pursue its claim.

At the possession order hearing, Mr Holland first raised the argument which was to be central to the Court of Appeal case – that since Bankruptcy provides that creditors shall not have any remedies against the insolvent individual in respect of their debts, it should prevent a possession order from being pursued and made against the tenant availing of Bankruptcy protection. Mr Holland's argument was born of necessity and creativity. He knew that something had to be done to assist this client in keeping her home if possible. He also remembered reading a piece in the Money Advice Association journal, *Quarterly Account*, which had suggested that the stay of enforcement in Bankruptcy could operate to protect insolvent tenants from eviction.[66] Mr Holland considered that the argument could work on the facts of the case, and decided that 'we're going to have a go at this'.

For the debt advisor, this was an unusual step into the unknown. Often resourcing issues, individual client needs, and the demands of following set procedures and timelines under Money and Pensions Service (MAPS) funding contracts, mean

---

[63] *R v Lord Chancellor, ex parte Lightfoot* [2000] QB 597 (Court of Appeal (England and Wales)).
[64] *McGuffick v Royal Bank of Scotland plc* [2009] EWHC (Comm) 2386, [2010] 1 All ER 634.
[65] On the costs of accessing Bankruptcy, see Spooner (n 2) ch 4.
[66] J Kruse, 'The Impact of Bankruptcy on Rent Arrears' (2003) 70 *Quarterly Account* 9.

that often legal challenges on behalf of clients are not fully explored. Mr Holland noted that cases still arise in which legal issues can be pursued, often in consultation with second-tier specialist advice agencies, but that legal challenges were more common in the past than under current conditions. Mr Holland sees it as part of a debt adviser's remit to raise a challenge in cases where a client's legal liability to pay a debt is in doubt. Where a client owes multiple debts, however, the 'broader picture' must be considered and a liability challenge 'might not be worth it'. The wiser solution might be to ignore this legal issue and instead opt for insolvency. Negotiated arrangements regarding debt repayment, or entry into an insolvency remedy, offer a means of tackling a client's multiple debts as far as possible, while a legal challenge may address one problem while leaving other debts unresolved. So, while a few 'pioneering' debt advisors remain open to bringing legal challenges, the abovementioned factors mean that they now resemble a 'dying breed' – something has been lost in this side of debt advice. Where legal defences are still pursued, for example in mortgage possession proceedings, often a debt advisor will follow well-trodden paths relying on widely used precedent, rather than seeking to construct a new landmark.[67] In Mr Holland's words, the *Sharples* case was 'unproven ground', and it is a rare experience for a debt advisor to raise a defence based on a previously untested point of law. As he explains

> So, it was a kind of a novel thing … it was like well, we've got to try this, because if I don't defend it, she's out. And the whole purpose of this is that we would try to make a difference to her situation. It would be unfortunate if she ended up losing her debts but also losing her home. So, we had to do it, simple as that.

Despite her extremely difficult situation, Ms Sharples was in a comparatively fortunate position among possession order defendants, in that she had the representation of Mr Holland at her hearing before District Judge Hovington. This allowed her to avoid attending in person to present her own defence, unlike the many tenants who are 'often scared witless' as they are forced into possession order hearings with no greater representation than 'last-minute emergency advice' from a court duty solicitor.[68] Often the only resolution for which a tenant might reasonably hope in eviction proceedings is a postponement due to paperwork errors or the striking of a deal between the duty solicitor and relevant housing officer over an arrears repayment schedule.[69] This contrasts with the hour-long hearing in which Mr Holland presented the previously untested legal point, which would have prevented eviction outright for Ms Sharples and potentially many more insolvent tenants in the future. After the hearing, the District Judge decided that while Bankruptcy discharged the rent arrears owed by Ms Sharples, it did not prevent the court from issuing a possession order, which the judge duly made. It became clear to Mr Holland at this point that Ms Sharples would require legal representation to appeal this order, and he

---

[67] The conditions under which a court will exercise its discretion to suspend a mortgage possession order are established in *Cheltenham & Gloucester Building Society v Norgan* [1995] EWCA Civ 11, [1996] 1 WLR 343 (EWCA (Civ)).
[68] Robins and Newman (n 44) 9–11.
[69] ibid 11.

subsequently referred the case to Glaisyers solicitors and ultimately barristers Jan Luba QC and Ben McCormack. Legal aid was required to fund further stages of the litigation and the ultimate Court of Appeal challenge. Again raising this funding was an uphill struggle, as the Legal Aid Board initially refused aid and Ms Sharples' representatives were forced to bring a successful judicial review of the Board's decision in order to obtain funding.[70] Even where an important and novel legal point regarding the scope of bankruptcy protection had been raised, not to mention the pressing need to challenge the imminent loss of the defendant's home, significant obstacles remained in getting the case to court.

V. JUDICIAL REASONING AND THE EXCEPTIONALITY OF LOW-INCOME LITIGATION

The above discussion might support a 'user theory of law', which understands law 'as being made and changed by the cumulative efforts of its users', and 'moved in a particularly evolutionary direction by the dominant users'.[71] In this 'market-based development of law', 'lawyers and court personnel are devoted disproportionately to identifying, articulating, analysing, defining, understanding, and sometimes expanding the law serving those with economic power'.[72] This means that those lacking power are 'systematically excluded from this law-making process, resulting in doctrinal voids'. The under-representation of lower-income groups in litigation may mean that judges do not see poor people's problems as the kinds of issues appropriate for legal resolution.[73] As a stark example, the Court of Appeal once held that the 'benign administrative process' of bankruptcy raises no issues for judicial determination, such that no right of access to justice arises for those seeking to enter bankruptcy.[74] A life-changing matter for an individual may be seen by court officials as one of many 'garbage' cases of little legal significance.[75] Claims to enforce contracts or evict tenants can come to be viewed less as legitimate disputes calling for scrutiny and adjudication, and more as a 'nuisance',[76] items for 'routine processing' to be cleared from dockets,[77] under 'conveyer belt justice',[78] or 'assembly-line' litigation.[79] As factors such as the reduction of legal aid provision lead to fewer cases of low-income litigants

---

[70] Indeed, Mr Holland has explained that the *Sharples* case did not proceed beyond the Court of Appeal because funding was unavailable to allow Ms Sharples and Mr Godfrey to appeal further Etherton LJ's decision.

[71] L Nader, 'A User Theory of Law' (1984) 38 *SMU Law Review* 951, 952.

[72] KA Sabbeth, 'Market-Based Law Development' (*LPE Project*, 21 July 2021) lpeproject.org/blog/market-based-law-development/ (accessed 27 July 2021).

[73] Prosser (n 30) 84.

[74] *Lightfoot* (n 63) 609; For the US counterpart, in which the US Supreme Court rejected a constitutional right of access to court to petition for bankruptcy, see H Rose, 'Denying the Poor Access to Court: United States v Kras (1973)' in MA Failinger and E Rosser (eds), *The Poverty Law Canon: Exploring the Major Cases* (Michigan, University of Michigan Press, 2016).

[75] Merry (n 32) 43.

[76] Lazerson (n 60) 151.

[77] Galanter (n 5) 121.

[78] Robins and Newman (n 44) 10.

[79] D Wilf-Townsend, 'Assembly-Line Plaintiffs' (2022) 135 *Harvard Law Review* 1704.

appearing before judges, there is a risk 'that whole categories of legal claims will quickly disappear from the docket', heightening the danger of judges becoming unfamiliar with specialist legal areas impacting the lives of low-income groups.[80] A risk develops of a spiral of judicial indifference, as judges become increasingly 'unversed in and desensitised to the underlying factual issues that affect lower-income groups'.[81]

One way this might manifest is through a judicial 'commitment to formalism', which allows courts to avoid both the 'human stories' behind the law,[82] and the political questions involved in disputes between groups such as consumers and firms, and landlords and tenants.[83] The decision of Lord Justice Etherton relies heavily on formalistic technical distinctions: first, between a particular court procedure (an application for a possession order), and the statutory concept of a 'remedy in respect of a debt'; and second between a legal process for enforcing property rights, and a process for the collection of rents representing the fruits of such property rights. This approach is indicative of how formalistic approaches to adjudication can hinder legal activism on behalf of the poor.[84] Based on 'intellectual orderliness, with identified categories, fixed boundaries, and clear resolutions', formalistic approaches miss 'complexity and a discussion of other social processes', including the complex intersecting legal problems of low-income groups.

A further formalistic aspect of Etherton LJ's reasoning is a textualist approach to legislative interpretation, in which he rejects consideration of relevant policy concerns. Etherton LJ had no regard to apparent legislative intent that insolvent tenants should be protected from losing their homes.[85] The Court similarly considered that 'no assistance' could be offered from the 'policy underlying' the Pre-action Protocol for Possession Claims by Social Landlords. It thought that the DRO procedure's acknowledged aim of providing 'relief from debt [to] those with limited means and limited debts' could not be used to give an 'artificial meaning' to the legislative text.[86] This adjudicative method excludes the policy context in which the law exists, as well as creating a disconnect between abstract legal principle and contemporary lived realities.[87] The 'human stories' are missed as formalist accounts of case law reduce clients to 'mere caricatures, fashioned from the highly truncated facts of heavily edited appellate opinions'.[88] This commitment to formalism also stifles the extent to which such context might drive progressive legal outcomes. Under this perspective

---

[80] Prosser (n 30) 28, 37.

[81] M Gilles, 'Class Warfare: The Disappearance of Low-Income Litigants from the Civil Docket The 2015 Pound Symposium: The War on the U.S. Civil Justice System: Articles & Essays' (2015) 65 *Emory Law Journal* 1531, 1561.

[82] C Gearty, 'In the Shallow End' (2022) 44 *London Review of Books* www.lrb.co.uk/the-paper/v44/n02/conor-gearty/in-the-shallow-end (accessed 20 February 2022).

[83] Griffith argued that 'when faced with the realities of a genuine political conflict', judges have often 'retreated hastily behind the barricades of legal ... formalism' JAG Griffith, *Politics of the Judiciary*, 5th edn ((Reissue), Fontana Press, 2010) 303.

[84] Feldman (n 31) 1586–91.

[85] HL Deb 11 October 1988 vol 500, 725, per Lord Malcolm Sinclair, Earl of Caithness.

[86] *Sharples* (n 1) [77].

[87] Prosser notes that in a series of social welfare test cases in the 1970s/80s, English courts tended to ignore arguments about the social consequences for claimants of their decisions: Prosser (n 30) 32.

[88] Feldman (n 31) 1588; Etherton LJ reduces Ms Sharples' eight years of home life at Denbeigh Place to a single sentence: 'She fell behind with her rent.' *Sharples* (n 1) [6].

'change is orderly and incremental ... the vantage point is retrospective; the conclusion inevitable'. Therefore, legal change, 'like law more generally, is impersonal and disembodied ... how and why clients and lawyers went about seeking change remains unaddressed'.[89]

Etherton LJ's rejection of 'artificial meanings' reverts to the 'plain meaning' method of statutory interpretation, which sees the court's role as giving legislation the meaning its words would 'ordinarily mean for reasonable people'.[90] While this approach continues to operate as a starting point for interpretation in English law, its limitations are well-recognised. In an appellate case, in which both sides present convincing arguments for conflicting interpretations of a statute, it becomes artificial for a judge to rely only on a single 'plain meaning'. Recognising this potential lack of clarity, textualism usually relies on 'canons of construction', which offer rules for interpreting text.[91] A problem long recognised, however, is that these various 'canons' can be deployed in support of opposing conclusions, meaning that a party's argument must 'be sold, essentially, by means other than the use of the canon'.[92] Indeed, it appears that Etherton LJ was required to look beyond legislative wording and ultimately invoked policy arguments to justify his decision. First, Etherton LJ held that the objective behind bankruptcy's freezing of debt collection activities was not to protect debtors from enforcement, but rather to preserve assets for distribution among the pool of creditors.[93] From this perspective, the court could allow a landlord to obtain a possession order since this would not impact other creditors, without need to consider whether this outcome is compatible with the 'fresh start' policy. Second, Etherton LJ appealed to the potential negative consequences for landlords if Ms Sharples was allowed to win her case. While not considering the policy benefits of debt relief, the judge endorsed a past court decision which explains how a possession order 'affords relief to the landlord from being saddled with a defaulting tenant'.[94] Similarly silent regarding the catastrophe of eviction and housing insecurity,[95] Etherton LJ warned that it

> could be financially catastrophic for [social] landlords to be unable to recover possession from persistent non-payers and could threaten the availability of social housing to meet the great demand from the large number of people who are economically disadvantaged and seek suitable and affordable permanent accommodation.[96]

Thus, we reach the position under which Etherton LJ swore that loyalty to literalism requires rejection of pro-debtor policy objectives as expressed in legislative history

---

[89] Feldman (n 31) 1587.
[90] N Duxbury, *Elements of Legislation* (Cambridge, Cambridge University Press, 2012) 140.
[91] A Marmor, 'The Immorality of Textualism Symposium: Theories of Statutory Interpretation' (2004) 38 *Loyola of Los Angeles Law Review* 2063, 2063; see also R Doerfler, 'Late-Stage Textualism' (2022) 2022 *Supreme Court Review* 267.
[92] KN Llewellyn, 'Remarks on the Theory of Appellate Decision and the Rules or Canons about How Statutes Are to Be Construed Symposium on Statutory Construction' (1949) 3 *Vanderbilt Law Review* 395, 401.
[93] *Sharples* (n 1) [30], [70].
[94] *Razzaq v Pala* [1997] 1 WLR 1336.
[95] M Desmond, *Evicted: Poverty and Profit in the American City* (New York, Allen Lane, 2016).
[96] ibid [71].

and official documents such as Pre-Action Protocols, only then to justify his decision through pro-creditor and pro-landlord policy considerations. This approach chimes with the argument that there is often a 'hidden story' behind textualist approaches to legislative interpretation, which may betray a conservative preference that 'unresolved interpretative issues ought to remain unresolved by judges', so that 'unregulated disputes ... remain unregulated'.[97] In other words, formalism and textualism often work hand-in-hand with protecting extant market incumbents such as landlords, while rejecting regulation of market activity. When speaking of the financial impact on landlords and invoking the classic conservative argument that pro-consumer policies may hurt consumers,[98] Etherton LJ's 'opinion doesn't read much differently than a congressional committee report recommending legislation to a chamber divided on partisan lines'.[99]

Of course, judicial political ideas may align with prevailing political moods – general pro-market and pro-property sentiments may dominate politics outside of the courtroom also (even a local paper styled the *Sharples* test case as a threat to landlords countrywide[100]). Nonetheless the asymmetrical invocation of policy arguments evident in Etherton LJ's judgment seems of a piece with judicial tendency to refuse expansive interpretations of consumer protection measures. While enforcing property rights and contracts represents business as usual for courts, the rarity of low-income litigation may contribute to a judicial view of its exceptionality. Consumer protections and progressive bankruptcy laws, which threaten the traditional dominance of property rights and market allocations, may fall within a certain judicial 'abhorrence for 'redistributive' "class legislation"',[101] persistently viewed as distorting interventions in the 'neutral and rational principles of the common law [of property and contracts]'.[102] One review of the attempts of 1970s welfare rights advocacy commented that campaigns must overcome 'ideology of the judges, the legal profession more generally and legal education'.[103] One wonders whether these challenges have become any less daunting four decades later.

VI. CONCLUSION

The *Sharples* story exemplifies challenges of achieving landmarks of legal change in the interests of consumers and low-income groups. Structural inequalities mean that the legal process is tilted against One-Shotters such as Ms Sharples, who must

---

[97] Marmor (n 91) 2066.
[98] AO Hirschman, *The Rhetoric of Reaction: Perversity, Futility, Jeopardy* (Cambridge, MA, Harvard University Press, 1991) 11; D Kennedy, *A Critique of Adjudication [Fin de Siecle]* (Cambridge, MA, Harvard University Press, 1998) 149.
[99] Kennedy (n 98) 149.
[100] 'Landmark rental case', *Salford Advertiser*, 8 April 2010, 4.
[101] RW Gordon, 'Afterword' in M Galanter (ed), *Why the Haves Come Out Ahead: The Classic Essay and New Observations* (New Orleans, Quid Pro, LLC, 2014) 113–14.
[102] I Ramsay, 'Consumer Credit Law, Distributive Justice and the Welfare State' (1995) 15 *Oxford Journal of Legal Studies* 177, 196.
[103] Prosser (n 30) 84.

compete against well-resourced institutions who can afford to pick the battles they are confident they will win. Once deciding that a case raises an opportunity to create favourable precedent, 'Repeat Players' can draw on tools of formalism and textualism, as well as classical understandings of the sanctity of property and contract, to fight off progressive legal development which might be demanded by contemporary socio-economic conditions and pressing public policy concerns. The case shows that litigation in the law of the poor – consumer law, bankruptcy, housing law – is seldom a fair fight.

Various conclusions could be drawn from this story. One approach would be to adopt 'scepticism toward law as a vehicle for social change', and to focus progressive reform efforts on community organising and political campaigning.[104] Money advice work in organisations such as Citizens Advice has long combined client service with policy campaigns built on evidence of problems collected in local offices.[105] Even this campaigning function is under 'threat', now that government grant agreements specify that funds cannot be used to influence politics.[106] On the other hand, emerging grass-roots independent campaigning organisations are making their presence felt.[107] A further approach might be to rest hopes on regulatory enforcement of consumer law and Alternative Dispute Resolution mechanisms.[108] Regulatory redress mechanisms have recently produced great victories for consumers,[109] most spectacularly in the £50 billion Payment Protection Insurance (PPI) compensation scheme.[110]

These alternative strategies offer little immediate assistance, however, to a consumer defendant faced with the sharp end of the law's enforcement machine. Therefore, other perspectives keep faith in law and see the necessity of trying, even sometimes in vain, to invoke the legal system as a means of achieving social change. 'Repeat players' will continue to use the legal system against low-income groups, and defences must be mounted by those who refuse to accept that 'our society is necessarily better off if judges merely passively support the powerful'.[111] Invocation of law's procedural fairness and creative use of its technicalities may remain 'the best defences of the subordinate classes, even if these rules were the instruments by which the dominant classes came to power'.[112]

This chapter has shown that taking a client's problems from a debt advice office to the Court of Appeal can alone be seen as a remarkable achievement. A debt advisor's

---

[104] Cummings and Eagly (n 43) 451, 460.
[105] M McDermont, 'Citizens Advice in Austere Times' in S Kirwan (ed), *Advising in Austerity: Reflections on Challenging Times for Advice Agencies* (Bristol, Policy Press, 2016) 32.
[106] ibid 40.
[107] wearedebtadvisers.uk/news/a-huge-relief-but-now-maps-must-now-be-changed-for-good (accessed 14 September 2022).
[108] WC Whitford, 'Structuring Consumer Protection Legislation to Maximize Effectiveness' (1981) 1981 *Wisconsin Law Review* 1018.
[109] S Williams, 'The Rise and Rise of Affordability Complaints' in M Gray, J Gardner and K Moser (eds), *Debt and Austerity* (Cheltenham, Elgar, 2020).
[110] 'Monthly PPI Refunds and Compensation' (*FCA*, 29 April 2021) www.fca.org.uk/data/monthly-ppi-refunds-and-compensation (accessed 14 September 2022).
[111] S Macaulay, 'Private Legislation and the Duty to Read--Business Run by IBM Machine, the Law of Contracts and Credit Cards' (1965) 19 *Vanderbilt Law Review* 1051, 1121.
[112] Lazerson (n 60) 159.

commitment to clients may nonetheless leave an abiding sense of disappointment and unfairness at the ultimate result in this case. Mr Holland pointed out the injustice of a situation in which possession proceedings could be reintroduced on what was effectively a non-existent, discharged, debt. As he put it, a tenant can 'make one mistake [in falling into arrears] and [end up] paying for that for a long time'.[113] This risk, that a tenant who is paying current rent could be evicted based on historic arrears, achieved judicial recognition in a subsequent case.[114] For the debt advisor, there was a sense of disappointment at not achieving a true 'fresh start' for the client:

> ... why I don't talk about it too much ... is that it didn't work ... we had a go but it didn't work and unfortunately that's what can happen. But it's important to underline that there was no alternative for her ... we had to push that otherwise she would have been out a lot sooner ... and she did get to stay there for another two years.

The outcome of the case highlighted the vulnerability of tenants even when they avail of bankruptcy protection,[115] and gave landlords immunity to evict tenants on becoming aware of their bankruptcy.[116] Campaigners for social and economic change through law have accepted, however, 'that there would be as many unsuccessful cases as there would be successes'.[117] The losing cases can themselves raise the profile of important issues, highlighting injustice, exposing inconsistency, and supporting campaigns for reform. Test cases can 'politicise issues by forcing them into the arena of political debate'.[118] The *Sharples* struggle was surely a more valuable approach than an alternative of passively accepting the silent and routine enforcement of possession orders against insolvent tenants. It is difficult to measure 'success' in campaigns for social change – 'what looks like failure at one point, turns into success at another', and 'struggle is an unending process in which wins must be defended and extended over time'.[119] In this way, highlighting the obstacles to achieving change through law may help develop strategies and paths to future reform. Some landmarks may take time to reveal themselves along a march towards change.

---

[113] Here Mr Holland reminds us that past rent arrears can be held against an individual in an application for public or social housing.

[114] *Irwell Valley Housing Association Limited v Docherty* [2012] Court of Appeal, England and Wales [2012] EWCA Civ 704 CA The judge nonetheless allowed a possession order to proceed.

[115] It is now accepted in debt advice that bankruptcy offers little assistance to tenants facing eviction for rent arrears, and that bankruptcy may actually damage a tenant's credit history such as to limit their future ability to rent in the private sector, if evicted: '25.02.22' (*The Debt Advice Diaries*) debtadvicediaries.blogspot.com/2022/02/250222.html (accessed 28 February 2022).

[116] Citizens Advice Bureau (CAB), *Cutting Our Losses: The Need for Good Debt Collection Practice for People with Debt Relief Orders (2015)* 17.

[117] Prosser (n 30) 22.

[118] ibid 85.

[119] S Cummings, *An Equal Place: Lawyers in the Struggle for Los Angeles* (Oxford, Oxford University Press, 2021) 489–90.

18

European Integration after *Mohammed Aziz*

IRINA DOMURATH AND HANS-W MICKLITZ

I. INTRODUCTION

THE CASE OF Mohammed Aziz,[1] the defaulted mortgagor from Spain who lost his house after the financial crisis, has probably received most scholarly and political attention in the field of EU consumer law since *Cassis de Dijon*.[2] More than ten years have passed since the Court of Justice of the European Union (CJEU) turned upside down Spanish Procedural Law for the sake of the effectiveness of European consumer law and it continues impacting subsequent national legislation not only in Spain but also elsewhere.

What more is there to say about the case?[3] What we intend to do in this chapter is to 'stand and stare' at the legal developments and academic commentary ever since 2013, when the judgment was passed, trying to bring forward a broader analysis of the case's impact on European integration. First, we summarise the facts of the case and highlight the impact it has had in European consumer law. Second, we analyse *Aziz* and subsequent case law from the perspective of the 'Jack in the Box' of European Private Law (EPL) as the new driver for European integration. In the course of this argument, we offer a re-interpretation of the principle of procedural autonomy and highlight the way in which different Member States courts have dealt with a new sense of empowerment, however limited it may be.

---

[1] Case 415/11 *Mohamed Aziz v Caixa d'Estalvis de Catalunya, Tarragona i Manresa (Catalunyacaixa)* [2014] ECLI:EU:C:2013:164.

[2] Case 120/78 *Rewe-Zentral AG v Bundesmonopolverwaltung für Branntwein* [1979] ECLI:EU:C:1979:42.

[3] Just to mention a few analyses of the case: Hans-W Micklitz 'Comment to Case C415/11, Mohamed Aziz V Caixa D'Estalvis de Catalunya, Tarragona I Manresa (Catalunyacaixa), NYR' in *Landmark Cases of EU Consumer Law – In Honour of Jules Stuyck* (Cambridge, Intersentia, 2013) 633–52; Hans-W Micklitz, 'Mohamed Aziz – sympathetic and activist, but did the Court get it wrong?' in A Sodersten and JHH Weiler (eds), *Where the Court got it Wrong* (Publications of ICON, www.ecln.net/florence-2013.html); SI Sánchez 'Unfair Terms in Mortgage Loans and Protection of Housing in Times of Economic Crisis: Aziz c. Catalunyacaixa' [2014] *CMLR* 955–74.

II. MOHAMMED AZIZ AND EUROPEAN CONSUMER LAW

A. The Case

The *Aziz* case is emblematic for the financial crisis in Europe since 2008 and for the struggle of debtors in a context of the implosion of the Spanish mortgage system and the downfall of the Spanish savings banks. The *caixas* had been at the centre of a construction-driven boom and had competed fiercely with commercial banks to offer real estate loans, encouraged to sell previously unwanted land and venture beyond their regions. More than 4.2 million homes were constructed in the first decade of the new century, and in the five years after the system's implosion in 2008, about half a million people had lost their homes.[4] In order to seek protection, many of the mortgage debtors went to the courts, which have continued to send references to the CJEU.

Mohammed Aziz is the most prominent of these debtors. In July 2007, he concluded a loan agreement secured by a mortgage with Catalunyacaixa. €138,000 were to be reimbursed in close to 400 instalments for a period of more than 30 years. Mr Aziz had a fixed monthly income of €1,341. The monthly instalments amounted to more than half of his monthly salary. Mr Aziz paid off the loan for ten months before losing his job as a construction worker and being unable to continue paying the monthly instalments. After trying unsuccessfully to make Mr Aziz continue the payment of the monthly instalments, the bank instituted enforcement proceedings. In a judicial auction in July 2010, no bid was made. The court consented to the vesting of the property at 50 per cent of its value. Mr Aziz was evicted from his home and, according to Spanish law, remained liable for the payment of the outstanding credit amount including interests.

A few months before the eviction, Aziz had applied to the Juzgado de lo Mercantil No 3 in Barcelona for a declaration seeking the annulment of clause 15 of the mortgage loan agreement, on the ground that it was unfair and that, as a consequence the enforcement proceedings could not be based on this clause. At the time, Art 698 Spanish Code of Civil Procedure precluded the possibility to object to the enforcement proceedings based on a declaratory assessment of unfairness of the underlying contract terms. So, the process before the Barcelona court could not stop the enforcement procedure.

The Juzgado referred basically two main questions to the CJEU. The first one concerned Article 698 Spanish Code of Civil Procedure and its compatibility with Council Directive 93/13/EEC of 5 April 1993 on unfair terms in consumer contracts (UCTD). Under Article 698 of the Code of Procedure, any claim of the debtor concerning the clauses of the underlying credit agreement must be settled by judgment and does not have the effect of staying or terminating the eviction procedure.

The CJEU answered that this clause, which led to the irreversibility of the eviction, was not compatible with the UCTD in so far as it prohibited the Court hearing the declaratory proceedings concerning the unfairness from granting interim relief

---

[4] AQ Pastrana 'A garantía da vivenda digna e accesible Crise económica e sustentabilidade', *PhD Thesis*, Universidade de Santiago de Compostella (on file with one of the authors).

in terms of staying/terminating the mortgage enforcement.[5] The CJEU elaborated that granting compensation to Mr Aziz would be 'insufficient' and would neither constitute an adequate nor effective means of preventing the continued use of that term. Here, it also mattered that any compensation would not prevent the definite and irreversible loss of the 'family home'.[6] Therefore, the CJEU found Article 698 to be contrary to Article 7(1) UCTD.[7] In conclusion, the CJEU stated that Spanish law hinders or makes excessively difficult the protection sought for by the UCTD and, thus, violates the principle of effectiveness.[8]

The second issue concerned the interpretation of 'unfair term' in Articles 3(1) and (3) UCTD with regard to the assessment of specific terms, such as an acceleration clause which allowed the bank to call in the total loan in case of arrears, the fixing of default interests, and the unilateral determination by the lender of the amount of the unpaid debt. Based on the AG opinion, the CJEU gave the following guidelines for interpretation. The fairness of acceleration clauses depends on whether there is a 'sufficiently serious' non-compliance with the obligation to repay the loan.[9] The fairness of fixing of the default interests depends thus on the difference between the default interest laid down in the contract and the statutory interest rate and whether any discrepancy is appropriate to secure Member State objectives. The fairness of the unilateral determination by the lender of the amount of the unpaid debt, which was linked to the possibility of initiating mortgage enforcement proceedings, depends on the rules applicable in the absence of an agreement between the parties and the procedural means at the consumers' disposal to take legal action in their defence.

B. The Social Impact of EPL

The discourse in academic commentary right after *Aziz* was that the CJEU acts as a social actor or an actor of social change, for which it has received both acclaim and critique. Some foresaw the development of a genuine European Social Mode through judicial activism, as it was already in the making in consumer and anti-discrimination law.[10] *Aziz* opened up this possibility also for housing matters. *Aziz* was seen as a gate-opener to accommodate the right to housing into the field of EU law.[11]

The Court referenced the importance of the 'home' when stating that the existence of interim relief in mortgage contract enforcement procedures was indispensable, because ex post compensation would not be able to make good the damage of losing

---

[5] *Aziz* (n 1) [55]–[57].
[6] ibid [61].
[7] ibid [60].
[8] ibid [63].
[9] ibid [73].
[10] Eg, Hans-W Micklitz 'Judicial Activism and the Development of a European Social Model in Anti-Discrimination and Consumer Law', in Neergard et al (eds), *The Role of Courts in Developing a European Social Model – Theoretical and Methodological Perspectives* (Chicago, Djoef, 2010) 25–63.
[11] Eg, J Rutgers 'The Right to Housing (Article 47 of the Charter) and Unfair Terms in General Conditions' in H Collins (ed), *European Contract Law and the Charter of Fundamental Rights* (Cambridge, Intersentia, 2017) 125–37; also R Albanese 'Within the Public-Private Divide. Right to Housing and Consumer Law in Recent European Private Law Trends' (2019) 2 *Global Jurist* 19, 1.

the family home. In the follow-up cases to *Aziz*, the CJEU went further and gave the consumer-debtor constitutional protection: in *Sánchez Morcillo* based on Article 47 ChFR and in *Kušionová* based on Article 7 ChFR.[12] In *Sánchez Morcillo* the CJEU acknowledged that the 'final vesting of mortgaged property in a third party is always irreversible' and that the 'special features of the mortgage enforcement proceedings' have to be 'taken into account'.[13] The fact that the mortgaged home is the primary residence of the debtor mattered however only as a reinforcing argument, and the statements on the role of the primary residence of the debtor were still blurry. In *Kušionová*, the CJEU clarified that the right to housing of Article 7 ChFR needs to be taken 'into account' in eviction procedures due to outstanding debt. The CJEU highlighted – in line with previous ECtHR case law (a not very common reference in the CJEU case law[14]) – that the loss of the home is the most extreme interference with the right to a home and that the occupier therefore has the right to have the proportionality of the eviction reviewed.[15] So, by the mentioning of 'family home' in *Aziz*, the CJEU arguably opened the door for the right to housing in European Private Law.[16]

However, despite these developments,[17] it is questionable to what extent the CJEU case law since *Aziz* really has had a concrete social impact in the cases in question. The reality is that Mohammed Aziz, like many others, did lose his home in the end. In Spain alone, more than 2 million people have lost their homes in more than half a million evictions since the 2008 financial crisis; despite seemingly 'activist' national courts and intense law reform (see below). It seems that the 'social progress' might be for the next generation of house owners only.

The reason for this lack of social effect might simply be that EU Law is a misfit for housing (or other social) matters. What the CJEU did since *Aziz* is to subsume housing matters into EU consumer law, which is arguably not about protection but about access to the internal market.[18] Even though the CJEU confirmed that remedies in the sense of Article 6 UCTD must be proportionate (inter alia),[19] this does not imply the assessment of the proportionality of the eviction itself, but merely of the proportionality of the remedy and the breach of EU law, that is the effectiveness of the UCTD. As Perriello rightly points out, the CJEU confines the right to housing to a transparency test.[20] In line with its more general approach to consumer

---

[12] F Della Negra 'The Uncertain Development of the Case Law on Consumer Protection in Mortgage Enforcement Proceedings: Sánchez Morcillo and Kusionová' (2015) 52 *CMLR* 1009.

[13] Case 169/14 *Juan Carlos Sánchez Morcillo und María del Carmen Abril García gegen Banco Bilbao Vizcaya Argentaria SA* [2014] ECLI:EU:C:2014:2099, [38].

[14] Eg, *Rousk v Sweden* App no 27183/04 (ECtHR, 25 July 2013), [137].

[15] Case 34/13 *Monika Kušionová v SMART Capital* [2014] ECLI:EU:C:2014:2189, [63]–[65].

[16] Eg, Rutgers (n 11); S Sánchez, 'Unfair Terms in Mortgage Loans and Protection of Housing in Times of Economic Crisis: Aziz c. Catalunyacaixa' (2014) 51 *CMLR* 955–74.

[17] See also N Reich and Hans-W Micklitz, 'The Court and the Sleeping Beauty: the revival of the Unfair Contract Terms Directive (UCTD)' (2014) 52 *CMLR* 771.

[18] Hans-W Micklitz, 'The Expulsion of the Concept of Protection from the Consumer Law and the Return of Social Elements in the Civil Law: A Bittersweet Polemic' (2012) 35 *Journal of Consumer Policy* 283–96.

[19] Case 565/12 LCL *Crédit Lyonnais SA v Fesih Kalhan* [2014] ECLI:EU:C:2014:190, [44].

[20] L Perriello 'Right to housing and unfair contract terms' [2017] *Journal of European Consumer and Market Law* 101.

law, the actual social issue – eviction and the right to a home – is nothing but a matter of the proportional effectiveness of EU Law. EPL is not the level playing field for social justice.[21] Rather it leads to a proceduralisaton of justice, concerned with procedural rights and remedies.[22] The assertion that the CJEU prefers to avoid questions of social justice is reflected in the continuous reference to national default rules, which are presumably already striking a balance in terms of contractual justice in the respective national legal orders.[23] Ironically, the CJEU brought about a situation in which it is actually better for the consumer if there is just one unfair term, because in the respective case, it will not be enforced against them, whereas in cases of having to avoid nullity of the whole contract, the national law remains applicable, irrespective of its consequences for the consumer.[24] Certainly, any possible social outlook of the CJEU is always mediated through Member States' laws and national courts.

So, what emerges is a differentiated picture. Notwithstanding its undoubted social dimension and the importance of the UCTD in post-crisis litigation, it remains to be seen whether the CJEU will step up and use it for furthering the EU's social dimension. But what the *Aziz* case does show is that European consumers are at the intersection of EU Law, private law, and procedural law. The enforcement of consumer mortgage contracts and the procedural rules in one country are reviewed under EU Law and, in this way, can have broad implications beyond national borders. It touches upon issues of financial inclusion and exclusion and evictions from a mortgaged home as a matter of consumer protection.[25] It has caused many more cases, especially follow-up references from Spain and references on loans in foreign currencies in Central and Eastern European (CEE) Member States which had undertaken intense reforms of national law. It has sparked political controversy and touched upon the issue of fundamental rights in horizontal relations. So, even without a direct social impact, EU law is – as Lord Denning said – like an 'incoming tide' that goes 'into the estuaries and up the rivers'.[26]

---

[21] See in detail: Hans-W Micklitz, *The Politics of Justice in European Private Law* (Cambridge, CUP, 2018) 119–51.

[22] For further debate Negra (n 12); van Duin 'Metamorphosis? The Role of Article 47 of the EU Charter of Fundamental Rights in Cases Concerning National Remedies and Procedures under Directive 93/13/EEC' (2017) 6 *Journal of European Consumer and Market Law* 190; I Domurath *Consumer Vulnerability and Welfare in Mortgage Contracts* (Oxford, Hart Publishing, 2017) 172 et subs.

[23] Recently: Case 81/19 *NG, OH v SC Banca Transilvania SA* [2020] ECLI:EU:C:2020:532, [26], where the CJEU departed from a more consumer-friendly reading presented by AG Kokott; in line with Case 92/11 *RWE Vertrieb AG v Verbraucherzentrale Nordrhein-Westfalen eV* [2013] EU:C:2013:180 and Case 51/17 *OTP Bank Nyrt. and OTP Faktoring Követeléskezelő Zrt v Teréz Ilyés and Emil Kiss* [2018] EU:C:2018:750, [53]; also: P Nebbia 'Unfair contract terms' in Twigg-Flesner (ed), *The Cambridge Companion to European Private Law* (Cambridge, CUP, 2010) 216.

[24] M Józon 'Unfair Contract Terms Law in Europe in Times of Crisis: Substantive Justice Lost in the Paradise of Proceduralisation of Contract Fairness' (2017) 4 *Journal of European Consumer and Market Law* 163.

[25] For a discussion see G Comparato, *The Financialisatioon of the Citizen – Social and Financial Inclusion through European Private Law* (Oxford, Hart Publishing, 2018).

[26] *HP Bulmer Limited and Showerings Limited v J Bollinger SA and Champagne Lansonpére et fils* [1974] 3 WLR 202, [1974] 2 All ER 1226, [1974] Ch 401, [1974] EWCA Civ 14.

III. AZIZ AND THE 'JACK IN THE BOX' OF EPL

A. EPL as the New Driver of European Integration

Aziz occupies a crucial position in the ongoing process of EU integration. It showcases the importance of private law in European legal integration. What we can see now is that the enforcement of consumer contract law and the UCTD are the drivers of economic integration in the EU, with Spain and the CEE Member States taking the lead. While the EU free movement rules were arguably the driver of European integration in a line of cases such as *Van Gend en Loos, Simmenthal, Cassis de Dijon* and others, this integration through market freedoms has somewhat come to a halt. The CJEU has become more deferential to Member States authorities.[27] The academic debates about partial and minimum or maximum harmonisation,[28] their (doubtful legal) basis in the rules on the distribution of competences,[29] and their effects on national legal orders have lost impetus.

But this does not mean that the EU has ended its integrative process. Rather, the focus of European integration has shifted: towards the somewhat blurry field of EPL, which cuts across almost every field of law. Through consumer law, EPL reaches into standard contracts, which are concluded in all imaginable fields, ranging from labour to banking relations. And then, *Aziz* connected the unfairness of contract clauses not only to human and fundamental rights but also to procedural law. Likewise, the focus of integration has shifted from the old to the 'newer' Member States, Spain in the West and Hungary, Poland Rumania, Slovakia in the East.

This is yet another proof that EU Law really is a 'Jack in the Box' as Wilhelmsson claimed already in the late 1990s.[30] One of the reasons for the huge impact the UCTD has had on European integration might be its openness. A short Directive of 11 openly worded articles is necessarily a fertile ground for judicial interpretation and a gateway for what could be perceived as judicial activism. The introduction of EPL into national decision-making, be it legislative or judicial, has created a certain indeterminacy for national courts. Proof of this uncertainty is the quantity of preliminary references which national courts have sent to the CJEU in order to clarify legal issues that arose in the aftermath of *Aziz*.[31] More often than not, the CJEU has taken the possibility to elucidate some of the issues, such as the role of human rights in eviction proceedings, contract law, and procedural law. In doing so, it has enabled a

---

[27] J Zgilinski, *Europe's Passive Virtues: Deference to National Authorities in EU Free Movement Law* (Oxford, OUP, 2020).

[28] Eg, J Stuyck 'European Consumer Law after the Treaty of Amsterdam: Consumer Policy in or Beyond the Internal Market?' (2000) 37 *CMLR* 367; S Weatherill, *EU Consumer Law and Policy* (Cheltenham, Elgar, 2005) 61 et subs; Ma Loos, 'Full Harmonisation as a Regulatory Concept and its Consequences for the National Legal Orders. The Example of the Consumer Rights Directive' [2010] *Centre for the Study of European Contract Law Working Paper Series* 10/03.

[29] S Weatherill, *Contract Law of the Internal Market* (Cambridge, CUP, 2016).

[30] T Wilhelmsson, 'Jack-in-the-box theory of European Community law' in Krämer, Micklitz and Tonner (eds), *Law and Diffuse Interests in the European Legal Order: Liber Amicorum Norbert Reich* (Baden-Baden, Nomos, 1997) 177.

[31] B Kas and Hans-W Micklitz, 'Rechtsprechungsübersicht zum Europäischen Vertrags-und Deliktsrecht (2014–2018)' [2018] *EWS* 181, 241 (Parts I and II).

new path that is not much concerned with the distribution of competences between Member States and the EU, but promoting a genuine EPL which combines substance and procedure. Whether and to what extent the Member States courts are ready to seize the opportunity and use newly developed concepts and remedies is a matter for further investigation. In the Aziz saga, it seems that – after consistent pressure from the CJEU – the Spanish courts have accepted the challenge.

B. Effectiveness as the Integrative Principle for EPL

The guiding principle in Aziz and subsequent case law was the principle of effectiveness. In this section, we offer a new reading of the principle of procedural autonomy in the light of effectiveness as employed by the CJEU. The hypothesis is that the CJEU re-interpreted procedural autonomy of the Member States as procedural autonomy of the national courts for the further integration of EU law through EPL. This means that national courts are invited, if not obliged, to be activist when it comes to challenging national law. However, while they are to 'free' themselves from the 'constraints' of national law, they are mere vassals of the CJEU serving the effectiveness of EU law. In the end, we draw attention to the differentiated effects of CJEU jurisprudence concerning EPL in the Member States, which points at a higher 'burden' of EPL integration for CEE countries (and Spain) than for older Member States.

i. A New Interpretation of Procedural Autonomy Through Effectiveness

Procedural law is no longer a closed door for European integration. The principle of procedural autonomy of the Member States, which obviously includes their exclusive competence for procedural law, has been changed to fit EU law goals. Of course, this procedural autonomy has never existed in an unlimited way: equivalence and effectiveness have been its inherent limitations from the outset.[32] In view of Article 19 I 2 TEU, the CJEU interpreted it more and more openly, from not only making impossible to obtain redress for the violation rights derived from EU law to not making excessively difficult the reparation for breaches of EU law.[33]

Through equivalence and effectiveness, the CJEU ensured that national procedural law would not help to circumvent EU law. Already in 1990, the CJEU made it clear that in order to bring EU Law into full effect, interim relief must be available under national procedural law.[34] Then ex officio came, the doctrine through which the CJEU encroached upon the procedural autonomy of the Member States in the

---

[32] As for the limitations of the principle of procedural autonomy: D-U Galetta, *Procedural Autonomy of the Member States: Paradise Lost?* (Berlin, Springer, 2010) 7–32; for a critical assessment: M Bobek, 'Why There is no Principle of Procedural Autonomy of the Member States' in de Witte and Micklitz (eds), *The European Court of Justice and the Autonomy of the Member States* (Cambridge, Intersentia, 2011).

[33] Joined Cases 46/93 and C-48/93 *Brasserie du Pêcheur SA v Bundesrepublik Deutschland and the Queen v Secretary of State for Transport, ex parte: Factortame Ltd and others* [1996] ECLI:EU:C:1996:79, [83].

[34] Case 213/89, *The Queen v Secretary of State for Transport, ex parte: Factortame Ltd and others* [1990] ECR I-2433, [19]–[23].

1990s and early 2000s.³⁵ The CJEU significantly expanded the doctrine to a guiding principle in consumer law. First it allowed³⁶ and then obliged³⁷ national courts to check standard contracts for unfair terms under EU Law. Later, in *Banco Primus*,³⁸ the CJEU clarified that the ex officio doctrine also applies to (all) other contract terms, including those on which the court has already ruled in previous decisions that have become final, at least in cases where the court does not have to engage in own fact-finding in order to assess the fairness of standard terms. Here, the Court – for better or worse – arguably disregarded the role of national courts within the national judicial culture.

And in *Aziz*, the CJEU used the 'principle of effectiveness' of EU law, despite or maybe because of its contourlessness and all-encompassing effect,³⁹ to connect EU contract law with national procedural law. In fact, by stating that the enforcement procedure cannot proceed without taking into account the result of the declaratory proceedings concerning the unfairness of the underlying contract, the CJEU went beyond merely stating that interim relief must exist, but it effectively created a procedural interim remedy.⁴⁰ So, even though ex officio control did not play any role in *Aziz*, the CJEU went beyond, opening the door for the connection between the UCTD and national procedural law by stating that the principle of effectiveness also extends to national procedural provisions.⁴¹ Effectiveness of the UCTD was impaired through Spanish procedural law, because eviction could proceed even if a term in the underlying mortgage agreement was unfair.⁴² Effectiveness now seems total – there is no escape for Member States and their courts; there is no issue it will not touch.

This has understandably caused a lot of academic commentary, which has followed the decades-old criticism on the increasing violation of the procedural autonomy of Member States. True, the ex officio doctrine did encroach upon Member States' procedural autonomy.⁴³ Arguably not much is left of it. And Member States legislation which does not know ex officio review for interim measures, for example in

---

³⁵ The case law was still ambiguous at that time. Dismissive cases: Joined Cases 430/93 and C-431/93, *Jeroen van Schijndel and Johannes Nicolaas Cornelis van Veen v Stichting Pensioenfonds voor Fysiotherapeute* [1995] ECLI:EU:C:1995:441; Case 72/95 *Aannemersbedrijf P.K. Kraaijeveld BV e.a. v Gedeputeerde Staten van Zuid-Holland* [1996] ECLI:EU:C:1996:404; Joined Cases 222/05 to 225/05 *J. van der Weerd and others* [2007] ECLI:EU:C:2005:797; permissive: Case 312/93 *Peterbroeck, Van Campenhout & Cie SCS v Belgian State* [1995] ECLI:EU:C:1995:437.

³⁶ Case 237/02 *Freiburger Kommunalbauten GmbH Baugesellschaft & Co. KG v Ludger Hofstetter und Ulrike Hofstetter* [2004] ECLI:EU:C:2004:209.

³⁷ Case 243/08 *Pannon GSM Zrt. gegen Erzsébet Sustikné Győrfi* [2009] ECLI:EU:C:2009:350; Case-137/08 *VB Pénzügyi Lízing Zrt. v Ferenc Schneider* [2010] ECLI:EU:C:2010:659.

³⁸ Case 412/14 *Banco Primus SA v Jesús Gutiérrez García* [2017] ECLI:EU:C:2017:60.

³⁹ For example: Bobek (n 32); U Sadl, 'The Role of Effet Utile in Preserving the Continuity And Authority of European Union Law: Evidence from the Citation Web of the Pre-Accession Case Law of the Court of Justice of the EU' (2015) 8(1) *European Journal of Legal Studies* 18; N Reich, *General Principles of EU Civil Law* (Cambridge, Intersentia, 2017). For a positive view: P Rott, 'The Court of Justice's Principle of Effectiveness and its Unforeseeable Impact on Private Law Relationships' in Leczykiewicz and Weatherill (eds), *The Involvement of EU Law in Private Law Relationships* (Oxford, Hart Publishing, 2013) 181.

⁴⁰ Hans-W Micklitz and B Kas 'Overview of Cases Before the CJEU on European Consumer Contract Law (2008–2013) – Part I' (2014) 1 *European Review of Contract Law* 10, 26, 1–63.

⁴¹ *Aziz* (n 1) [46].

⁴² ibid [50]–[51].

⁴³ If one agrees that procedural autonomy ever existed; to the contrary Bobek (32).

Poland or Slovenia,[44] will probably be struck down at some point as hindering the effectiveness of EU Law.

We want to argue that procedural autonomy of the Member States is not only being more and more limited, but that the effectiveness principle is changing its very nature. We think that the CJEU might have invited – if not obliged, for the sake of the effectiveness of EU law – national courts to be autonomous from the national legislator and national procedural law. This means that national courts must not only, irrespective of the procedural rules in place in their national legal system, control by their own motion whether any of the contract terms contains unfair clauses, by setting aside any possible contradictory national procedural provisions. Since *Aziz*, this also means that they have to apply the new remedy of interim relief that halts eviction proceedings while the declaratory proceedings on the unfairness of contract terms is pending. Member States' procedural laws do not have any say in this. For the CJEU, this might not even have anything to do with procedural autonomy of the Member States, but rather with the exercise of its judicial power to ensure the effectiveness of EU Law,[45] for which it puts in charge national courts. Willingly or not, it does not put procedural autonomy as a variable into the interpretation of the issue at hand. Discrepancies with national procedural laws are of no interest. In this sense, one could say that procedural autonomy of the Member States vis-á-vis EU Law became reinterpreted as procedural autonomy of national courts vis-á-vis Member States' procedural law.

This procedural autonomy of national courts from national legal orders is not absolute. Default rules of national law are the limit. The wide discretion that the courts had since *Freiburger Kommunalbauten* was concretised (and gradually narrowed) making sure that the ultimate yardstick for the unfairness assessment are the default rules of national law.[46] By making the default rules of national law the yardstick for the unfairness assessment, the CJEU basically turned the unfairness assessment from a question of fact into a question of law.[47] So far, the ECJ has not yet had the opportunity to decide on what kind of equivalent a common law court would have to refer to. If there is one at all, it might be 'precedence'. In more conceptual terms, the ECJ seems to promote private law being understood as civil law.[48]

ii. National Courts as Activists?

It looks as if at least some national courts have readily assumed this new empowered role in order to deal with national legislative measures or the lack thereof. The following examples from Spain and Hungary evidence an interplay or maybe even a struggle

---

[44] Roadmap to European effective Justice Casebook, *Effective Justice in Consumer Protection, Judicial Training Project: Roadmap to European Effective Justice: Judicial Training ensuring Effective Redress to Fundamental Rights Violations*, 117–18.

[45] In this vein also: V Trsenjak and E Beysen, 'European Consumer Protection Law: Curia semper debit remedium' (2011) 48 *CMLR* 119.

[46] Józon (n 24) 162. The cases are: Case 92/11 *RWE Vertrieb AG v Verbraucherzentrale Nordrhein-Westfalen eV* [2013] EU:C:2013:180, [28], Case 51/17 (n 23); Case 81/19 (n 23) [26].

[47] Józon (n 24) 162.

[48] Reich (n 39).

between national courts and the legislator that emerged in the aftermath of *Aziz*, with the courts challenging legislative inertia or new legislative packages that were to bring national law in line with the CJEU specifications.

Gómez and Lyczowska confirm the activist role of Spanish courts. They point at the Spanish academic commentary that underlines that 'somebody had to do something', providing reason for the courts to step in; they even talk of 'preferred policies' of the courts.[49] So one of the explanations for the tide of preliminary references from Spain is that courts tried to find judicial response to the social emergency in Spain after the 2008 financial crisis.[50] The argument in favour of such activism of lower instance courts is that the Spanish Government was committed to a 'low protection' regime and that the CJEU had sent signals that it was prepared to review substantive and procedural terms of national law as it did in *Aziz*. Also Barral-Viñals observes that the CJEU judgments enabled a kind of 'social engineering' at the national level, in the sense that especially the lower courts were pushing the EU principles of consumers protection as established by the CJEU, while the Spanish legislator and the Supreme Court were reluctant to engage in this 'social policy'.[51] In fact, the Supreme Court and the Constitutional Court of Spain highlighted that as long as the eviction took place in accordance with Spanish law, there was no abuse of rights in initiating enforcement procedures.[52]

What ensued was a lively back and forth between the Spanish legislator and national courts, with the CJEU 'in between'.[53] The Spanish legislator responded to *Aziz* and *Banif Plus Bank* with Law 1/2013 concerning measures to protect mortgage debtors and provide for debt restructuring and social rents. *Sanchez Morcillo I* challenged the part of the law that concerned a new procedural law allowing the bank to appeal against the staying of the enforcement proceedings without granting the same right to the consumer debtor. It led to the adoption of Royal Decree 11/2014 and *Asturcom* and *Banesto* led to the adoption of Law 42/2015, which reformed Civil Procedural Law in order to reduce the statute of limitations for personal actions. Finally, the Mortgage Credit Directive was transposed into Spanish Law in 2019.[54] In Spain, there was a 'call-and-response' between legislator and courts

---

[49] FG Pomar and K Lyczowska, 'Spanish Courts, the Court of Justice of the European Union, and Consumer Law' [2014] *InDret* 22.

[50] J Mayoral and AT Pérez, 'On Judicial Mobilization: Entrepreneuring for Policy Change at Times of Crisis' (2018) 40 *Journal of European Integration* 719.

[51] I Barral-Viñals 'Aziz Case and Unfair Contract Terms in Mortgage Loan Agreements: Lessons to be Learned in Spain' (2015) 1 *Penn State Journal of Law & International Affairs* 4, 69, 70. Also: F de la Rosa 'The Treatment of Unfair Terms in the Process of Foreclosure in Spain: Mortgage Enforcement Proceedings in the Aftermath of the ECJ's "Ruling of the Evicted"' [2015] *Zeitschrift für Europäisches Privatrecht* 366; TJ París, 'El incidente de oposición en la ejecución hipotecaria por existencia de cláusulas abusivas y las SSTJUE de 17 de julio de 2014 y 21 de enero de 2015' [2015] *Revista Crítica de Derecho Inmobiliario* 982/1004, 985.

[52] For a discussion: A van Duin, *Effective Judicial Protection in Consumer Litigation Article 47 of the EU Charter in Practice* (Cambridge, Intersentia, 2022) with reference to: Tribunal Supremo Judgment no 681/2006, ECLI:ES:TS:2006:681 and Tribunal Constitucional Order no 113/2011, ECLI:ES:TC:2011:113A.

[53] For a discussion: T García and D Suárez (2016) 'Crónica sobre la aplicación judicial del derecho de la UE en España' *Revista Electrónica de Estudios Internacionales* Nr. 31. Also: see van Duinibid.

[54] Ley 5/2019, de 15 de marzo, reguladora de los contratos de crédito inmobiliario establece las normas de protección para las personas físicas que sean deudoras de préstamos hipotecarios.

with national courts sending references to the CJEU and with the CJEU judgments leading to law reform.

The situation in Hungary was similar. Continuously sending references to the CJEU, Hungarian courts seemed to be receptive to CJEU 'signals' of their empowerment.[55] When a new legislative package dealing with consumer loan agreements raised new problems with regard to its compatibility with EU Law, it was challenged by Hungarian courts.[56] Józon argues that the Hungarian courts were 'left on their own' to deal with the mass impacts of unfair terms in foreign currency loans,[57] which might have led them to turn to CJEU to clarify certain issues on the interpretation of the UCTD. One question the CJEU was called upon to clarify in *Kásler* – which concerned foreign-currency consumer loans – was whether a clause establishing a mechanism for the calculation of instalments was exempt from unfairness control under Article 4(2) UCTD. Another concerned the question whether Article 6 (1) UCTD means that all clauses of the contract have to be examined individually.[58] Thus, Hungarian courts were arguably searching for 'far-reaching economic, political, and social solutions' by addressing gaps in national private and procedural law, and clarifying the role of the courts vis-á-vis the legislator in the enforcement of the UCTD.[59]

This might be a position that Hungarian courts were involuntarily put into.[60] Nevertheless, they became policy framers in the field of consumer contract justice by testing the regulatory space given by the UCTD in conjunction with procedural autonomy to shift responsibility to the national legislators.[61] There was, in fact, a lively exchange between the highest Hungarian courts, the Constitutional Court and the Supreme Courts and the legislator – maybe not unsimilar to the interplay between legislator and judiciary in Spain. In 2014, after the *Kásler* ruling, the Hungarian Supreme Court – not the legislator – standardised the legal interpretation of standard terms with regard to foreign-currency loans, stating that the term assigning the risk of exchange risk fluctuations remain outside of the unfairness assessment as they form part of the main subject matter of the contract; however, they are subject to transparency review.[62] The Constitutional Court, upon a motion by the Hungarian Government to provide interpretation of Hungarian Law concerning 'abuse of power' and consumer protection in economic competition, stated that – because courts can only interfere in individual cases and therefore not adequately deal with the issue of large-scale foreign-currency loans and their adverse economic, systemic effects – the legislator can apply the principle of *clausula rebus sic stantibus*. The legislator

---

[55] *Pannon GSM* (n 37); Case 34/18 *Ottília Lovasné Tóth v ERSTE Bank Hungary Zrt* [2019] ECLI:EU:C:2019:764; C-26/13 *Árpád Kásler, Hajnalka Káslerné Rábai v OTP Jelzálogbank Zrt* [2014] ECLI:EU:C:2014:282.
[56] Case C-438/16 *Zsolt Sziber v ERSTE Bank Hungary Zrt.*, ECLI:EU:C:2018:367; C-51/17 (n 23).
[57] Józon (n 24) 160.
[58] Case C-511/17 *Lintner Györgyné v UniCredit Bank Hungary Zrt.* [2020] ECLI:EU:C:2020:188.
[59] Józon (n 24) 160.
[60] ibid 160.
[61] ibid 159.
[62] As to this issue: J Fazekas 'The Consumer Credit Crisis and Unfair Contract Terms Regulation – Before and after Kásler' (2017) 3 *Journal of European Consumer and Market Law* 99, 104–05.

followed suit and retroactively replaced the exchange rate spreads with the official exchange rate of the Hungarian National Bank, thus presuming the unfairness of clauses that allow unilateral increases of interests, fees or charges in foreign-currency loans.[63] Against this specific backdrop, it might be correct to talk of courts as exercising regulatory functions.[64]

To be sure, other courts are less active in exercising the procedural autonomy granted to them by the CJEU. The Polish Supreme Court is rather reluctant to refer cases to CJEU. No cases have been referred to the CJEU since 2009, maybe because national law covers many aspects of the possible disputes, thus 'shielding' the Supreme Court from having to apply EU law.[65] This lack of engagement of Polish courts with the CJEU and the preliminary reference procedure could be a sign of 'ignorance' about EU law and maybe even 'disregard' of EU law rules.[66] The latter would be in line with the Polish Constitutional Court and its concern with Polish 'sovereignty' vis-à-vis the EU generally.[67]

So there is an uneven spread between courts which refer cases to Luxemburg. Much of the *Aziz* discourse remained within the Spanish – CJEU silo and did not reach the legal orders in other Member States, except for similar experiences in Hungary. Despite the irregular readiness of national courts to send preliminary references to the CJEU, when they do send references, there is a new element in this arguably not new dialogue between the judiciary and the legislative:[68] The normative framework for assessing national law does not come from the national Constitution but from EU Law.

iii. National Courts as Vassals of the CJEU: Questioning Judicial Dialogue

Irrespective of the question whether national courts actually accept the procedural autonomy granted to them under EU Law and by the CJEU, the fact is that the CJEU – through the ex officio doctrine – has obliged national courts to emancipate from their national legal orders as far as consumer contracts are concerned. The examples of Spain and Hungary show that the newfound autonomy of national courts could indeed be seen as an emancipation of national courts, who can give fruitful impetus

---

[63] ibid 105.

[64] M Józon 'Judicial Governance by Unfair Contract Terms Law in the EU: Proposal for a New Research Agenda for Policy and Doctrine' (2020) 4 *ERPL* 909.

[65] R Mańko 'The Impact of EU Membership on Private Law Adjudication in Poland: A Case Study of the Polish Supreme Court's Case Law on Unfair Terms in Consumer Contracts' in Bobek (ed), *Central European Judges Under the European Influence: The Transformative Power of the EU Revisited* (Oxford, Hart Publishing, 2015) 73.

[66] ibid.

[67] Just recently, and most famously, in the tug-of-war concerning supposed political control of judicial power in Poland, the Constitutional Court in case K 3/21 declared unconstitutional Articles 1, 2 and 19 TEU inasmuch as they require that national judges to discard Polish Legislation on the organization of the judiciary.

[68] This dialogue is one of the well-studied phenomena in democratic legal systems, see eg, J Waldron, 'Some Models of Dialogue between Judges and Legislators' (2004) 23 *Supreme Court Law Review* 7; J Waldron, 'The Core of the Case against Judicial Review' (2005) 115 *Yale Law Journal* 1346; LB Tremblay, 'The Legitimacy of Judicial Review' (2005) 3 *I-CON* 617.

to the case law of the CJEU, even joggling back and forth legal issues and challenging different legal solutions. Against this backdrop, the question emerges to what extent the national courts are fully empowered and emancipated not just from national legislators but also from the CJEU.

An in-depth discussion of the arguments is outside of the scope of this contribution, but the main assumption of the dialogue literature seems to be that there is theoretically room for and actually a practice of judicial dialogue among different courts in different Member States and on different institutional hierarchies.[69] However, seen from the perspective of procedural autonomy of national courts, the judicial dialogue in the EU seems much less developed than commonly claimed, at least in the field of EPL. For a true dialogue between the CJEU and national courts or even among national courts we think that at least three requirements should be satisfied: first, the courts need to be autonomous from each other and from their Member States; second, there must be at least some overlapping competence as concerns the legal issues at hand; third, there must be mutual references to the other court's case law.

As to the first requirement, autonomy, we have argued above that national courts have indeed become more autonomous from Member States' legal orders because of the re-interpreted procedural autonomy of courts based on effectiveness and ex officio. However, it is one thing for national courts to decouple themselves to a certain extent from their national legislators and quite another to engage in actual dialogue with the CJEU. Since the procedural autonomy of national courts flows from the sought-after effectiveness of EU Law, this effectiveness is also the main limitation for the national courts to exercise their new empowered role. National courts are not only empowered but also made responsible for the effective implementation of EU law. Clearly, the ex officio doctrine serves the integration of the UCTD into national legal orders, may it be contract or procedural law. But what happens if the national court infringes its ex officio duty? Is the Member State liable under the Francovich doctrine for consumer harm? The emancipation from national legal 'constraints' is only desirable if it serves further legal integration in the EU.

Moreover, neither the second nor the third requirement are fulfilled. As to the second, from the outset, the European judicial system is not designed in a way to allow for overlapping competences. The division is obviously quite simple: the CJEU has the sole competence to interpret EU law; national courts are to implement the CJEU specifications in the individual cases. And the 'principle' of effectiveness of EU law is to ensure the correct implementation. The EPL case law has not reached a level of density similar to the one on market freedoms, where the CJEU – after initial tightening of rules – now leaves the Member States courts more leeway in the interpretation of EU law.

---

[69] A few seminal discussions of judicial dialogue are: T Tridimas 'The ECJ and the National Courts: Dialogue, Cooperation, and Instability' in Chalmers and Arnull (eds), *The Oxford Handbook of European Union Law* (Oxford, OUP, 2015) 403; F Caffaggi and S Law, *Judicial Cooperation in European Private Law* (Cheltenham, Elgar, 2017); Hans-W Micklitz 'The Transformation of Enforcement in European Private Law. Preliminary Considerations' (2015) 23 *ERPL*, 491.

Third, mutual references in the case law of the different courts do not exist, at least not in the EPL and EU consumer protection law. Even in cases similar to the ones in other Member States, national courts – rather than referring to other Member States' legal orders – seem to want to make sure about their interpretation of the UCTD by sending the case to the CJEU, which then in turn refers to the cases from other countries.[70] For example, in *Addiko Bank*, the referring Slovenian court asked the CJEU a question that should already be clear from previous case law. The fact the Slovenian court in that case decided to refer to the CJEU instead of, for example, assuming the existing case law in order to solve the underlying issue or even refer to the jurisprudence of other Member States' courts, shows that the CJEU is an important sounding board for national courts. Instead of backing up its solution of the case with comparative work, the national court probably looked for support from the CJEU concerning Slovenian procedural law. So, horizontal interaction takes a backseat to authoritative guidelines on national law.

If anything, there might be legal transplantation from the 'core' to the 'periphery' (and maybe back to the 'core').[71] In practice, the CJEU's interpretation has a very limited 'horizontal effect' on judicial dialogue. Maybe the CJEU has to answer similar or even identical questions from different national courts, before its ruling gains a status which becomes evident beyond the referring courts.

What is more, in the aftermath of *Aziz*, the CJEU has given quite precise 'guidance' to national courts concerning the interpretation of unfairness under the UCTD. National courts have to exclude the application of an unfair term,[72] but cannot modify the contract by revising the content of that term.[73] If the contract cannot continue to exist without the unfair term, the courts can replace it with a supplementary provision of national law instead of annulling the contract in its entirety.[74] This means that substitution is fully justified in order to restore the formal balance between rights and obligations of the parties. Thus, if it is 'particularly unfavourable' for a consumer if a term, for example, indicating an index on the basis of which a variable interest rate is calculated, is considered unfair, the national court can replace this term with a reference to a statutory index.[75]

---

[70] *Addiko Bank* was remarkably similar to cases from Spain and Poland (*Aziz, Banesto, Profi Credit Polska* and *PKO Bank Polski*).

[71] R Mańko, 'Legal Transfers in Europe Today: Still "Modernisation Through Transfer"'? in Bieś-Srokosz et al (eds), *Mutual Interaction between Contemporary Systems and Branches of Law in European Countries*, (Czestochowa, 2017) 139.

[72] See *Pannon GSM* (n 37) [35]; Case 618/10 *Banco Español de Crédito, SA v Joaquín Calderón Camino* [2012] EU:C:2012:349, [65]; Joined Cases 618/10 and 179/17 *Abanca Corporación Bancaria SA v Alberto García Salamanca Santos and Bankia SA v Alfonso Antonio Lau Mendoza and Verónica Yuliana Rodríguez Ramírez* [2019] EU:C:2019:250, [52].

[73] *Banco Español*, ibid [73]; Case 26/13 *Árpád Kásler and Hajnalka Káslerné Rábai v OTP Jelzálogbank Zrt* [2014] EU:C:2014:282, [77], and *Abanca and Bankia*, ibid. [53].

[74] See to that effect *Kásler* ibid [80] to [84], and, concerning a statutory index for calculating variable interests: *Abanca* and *Bankia* (n 72) [56] and [64], also: Case 260/18 *Kamil Dziubak and Justyna Dziubak v Raiffeisen Bank International AG, prowadzący działalność w Polsce w formie oddziału pod nazwą Raiffeisen Bank International AG Oddział w Polsce, anciennement Raiffeisen Bank Polska SA* [2019] EU:C:2019:819, [48].

[75] Case 125/18, *Gómez del Moral Guasch v Bankia* [2020] ECLI:EU:C:2020:138, [62].

So, instead of dialogue we rather see a situation of vertical emission from one active end, the CJEU, towards the receiving end, Member States courts (or, horizontally, from 'core' Member States to 'peripheral' Member States). At least the national courts which send preliminary references to the CJEU probably might not mind about this. They sent the reference in order to get an authoritative interpretation about an EU law issue. This allows the further integration of EPL. It also means that there is no court-driven 'voluntary bottom-up approximation of private law'.[76] While procedural autonomy of national courts would certainly further the approximation of private law – as for example in cases of legislative inertia like in Spain and Hungary – the ex officio doctrine is more than an invitation: national courts must check for unfair contract terms by their own motion. In this sense, the procedural autonomy of national courts is inherently limited and might even lead to national courts being regarded as mere vassals to the CJEU in its mission to further the integration of EU law, having to follow its 'guidance'.

iv. The Changing Character of (Some?) Member States' Private Law Systems

It is noteworthy that the effects on Member States' private legal orders have been differentiated, to say the least. Many of the preliminary references come from Member States which had not fully aligned their private laws to EU Law prior to the financial crisis, mainly CEE countries. In Poland, for example, the Article of the Code of Civil Procedure that provided the third-party effect of a declaration of unfairness in abstracto was now overtaken by an administrative fairness review.[77] Also the post-*Aziz* (and *Kásler*) developments in Hungary are exemplary. Hungarian law now allows the retrospective substitution of contractual exchange rates with the official exchange rates (in application of clausula rebus sic stantibus). Other Member States such as Croatia, Poland or Slovenia, for example, followed this controversial model.[78]

These are also the Member States that have been especially struggling with the large-scale social and economic effects of the financial crisis. In those countries, Józon observes, initial resistance to the integrative power of EPL has given way to a welcome acceptance of measures of crisis management.[79] Incidentally, with the exemption of Spain, these are also rather the newer Member States. It was, thus, especially courts of those countries that engaged in market regulation by using the ex officio doctrine. In contrast, older Member States such as Germany and France are largely absent from these European judicial and legal debates. It is hard to find out whether and to what extent the CJEU case law is taken into account in the judicial practice. The role in which the CJEU put national courts – the one of market supervisory authorities having to

---

[76] See Józon (n 24).
[77] Re-jus Casebook (n 44) 105.
[78] E Miščenić 'Currency Clause in CHF Credit Agreements: A Small Wheel in the Swiss Loan Mechanism' (2020) 6 *Journal of European Consumer and Market Law* 226 with reference to Opinion of the European Central Bank of 18 July 2019 on the conversion of Swiss franc loans (CON/2019/27).
[79] Józon (n 24) 161.

balance national 'consumer justice' and sectoral economic policies against the values of internal market – lies therefore with the national courts of the new Member States. This new 'multi-level governance' as a process in which Member State courts use preliminary reference procedures as a 'tool of domestic judicial policy'[80] is thus not visible in all Member States. It also means that the 'instrumentalisation'[81] or 'publification'[82] of private law hits Member States private law systems in different ways.

IV. CONCLUSION

We have seen that *Aziz* and its subsequent cases are a prime study for European integration. The principle of effectiveness of EU law weighs heavily in those cases and poses questions as to European integration, its actors, and its limits. *Aziz* & Co have made EPL the new playing field of European integration, after the free movement rules have lost impact. The connection of EPL with procedural remedies has had a systemic impact on national legal orders. In the integrative process that was kicked off through the connection of unfair terms control with procedural remedies 'anchored'[83] EU law in national private law systems, which have to adjust during the enforcement stage. So national procedural law had to change for the sake of the effectiveness of EPL. This is especially the case for Spain and the newer Member States, which had not yet aligned their civil codes fully with the requirements of the open-worded UCTD. So, especially the CEE countries are facing the integrative power of secondary legislation and EPL.

Effectiveness of EU Law coupled with the ex officio doctrine leads to a multifocal picture. From the viewpoint of the Member States, procedural autonomy has never existed or has been extremely limited. National courts (at least some of them), in turn, might feel empowered vis-á-vis national legislators, openly challenging national legislation even for political or social reasons. To that end, the CJEU has vested them with procedural autonomy *from* Member States through the ex officio doctrine. For the CJEU, all that matters is the effectiveness of EU Law. If Member States cannot deliver it, because of ignorance or disregard, the national courts must step in. For the CJEU, national courts might be mere vassals of EU Law, transporting EPL into evermore fields of national law.

In the larger story of European integration this means that different Member States have had different encounters, or 'integrative wake-up calls', with the 'tidal wave' of EU law. For Germany this was *Cassis*, for the UK *Sunday Trading*, for Italy *Dreiglocken*.[84] For Spain and the CEE countries it is *Aziz*. The European integration

---

[80] Józon (n 24) 159.
[81] C Schmid, *Die Instrumentalisierung des Privatrechts durch die Europäische Union* (Baden-Baden, Nomos, 2010).
[82] W Leisner, *Privatisierung des Öffentlichen Rechts: von der Hoheitsgewalt zum gleichordnenden Privatrecht* (Berlin, Duncker & Humblot, 2007).
[83] Józon (n 64).
[84] Case 145/88 *Torfaen Borough Council v B & Q plc* [1989] ECLI:EU:C:1989:593; Case 407/85 *3 Glocken GmbH and Gertraud Kritzinger v USL Centro-Sud and Provincia asutonoma di Bolzano* [1988] ECLI:EU:C:1988:401.

has differentiated, maybe even biased effects, it unfolds differently with regard to market freedoms and European private law. The potential consequence might be an increasing tension between the old Member States and the new Member States, or more resistance between new Member States and the EU's integrative force; the older benefiting from the CJEU's deferral in the field of market freedoms, the newer Member States dealing with strong intervention into their private law orders.

19

Plevin v Paragon: Undisclosed PPI Commissions Give Rise to an Unfair Credit Relationship

NICOLA J HOWELL*

I. INTRODUCTION

THIS CHAPTER DISCUSSES a 2014 decision of the UK Supreme Court – *Plevin v Paragon Personal Finance Limited*[1] (*Plevin*). The matter involved the sale to Mrs Plevin of a payment protection insurance (PPI) policy as part of a personal loan transaction, and the main legal arguments focused on the 'unfair relationships' provisions in the Consumer Credit Act 1974 (CCA). The CCA gives courts very wide powers to remedy an unfair credit relationship between a debtor and a lender, however, at the time of writing, *Plevin* represents the only occasion on which the Supreme Court has examined their application in a substantive way.[2] This alone might be sufficient to designate *Plevin* as a landmark case in the consumer credit arena. However, *Plevin* also has significance for broader consumer law issues, including open-textured rules and clarity, regulator and ombudsman roles, disclosure and consumer empowerment, and access to justice.

This chapter has three substantive parts; in section II, I set out the relevant facts of the case. In section III, I discuss the litigation in more detail and explain the contrasting approaches taken by the Court of Appeal and Supreme Court to the arguments that the relationship between Mrs Plevin and the lender (Paragon Personal Finance Ltd ('Paragon')) was an unfair relationship. The Supreme Court found in Mrs Plevin's favour on the basis of the first argument only, Paragon's failure to disclose the PPI commission. In section IV, I explain the many reasons why *Plevin* is landmark decision.

---

* Thanks to Jodi Gardner, Christine Riefa and Amandine Garde for their valuable feedback on an earlier presentation based on this article.
[1] *Plevin v Paragon Personal Finance Limited* [2014] UKSC 61, [2014] 1 WLR 4222 (*Plevin*).
[2] The Supreme Court has agreed to hear an appeal from *Smith v Royal Bank of Scotland plc (Burrell v Royal Bank of Scotland plc)* [2021] EWCA Civ 1832; [2022] 1 WLR 2136; [2022] WLR(D) 69, so further Supreme Court guidance on s 140A CCA may be forthcoming through that appeal.

II. THE FACTS OF PLEVIN v PARAGON

The relevant facts in this case were quite simple. In 2006, in response to an unsolicited invitation in her letterbox, Mrs Plevin contacted LLP Processing (UK) Ltd (LLP) (a credit broker and loan introducer), about a loan to repay her existing (unsecured) debts and fund some home improvements. LLP suggested that Mrs Plevin borrow £34,000 from Paragon, for a 10-year term, with the loan secured over her home, and also purchase PPI (with a term of five years) from Norwich Union. The premium for the PPI (£5,780) was added to the loan amount, resulting in a total sum borrowed of £39,780. Paragon was one of the lenders with which LLP had existing introducer arrangements, and Norwich was the insurer designated to underwrite PPI policies for Paragon's loans.[3]

LLP then sent Mrs Plevin the proposal, disclosure documents for the loan and PPI, and a loan application form. She completed the application form and returned it to LLP for submission to Paragon.[4] The only direct contact that Mrs Plevin had with Paragon was in a telephone call, designed for Paragon to ensure compliance with its money laundering obligations. Paragon approved the loan, and sent Mrs Plevin a copy of the credit agreement, the PPI certificate, and cheques for her creditors and herself.[5]

The disclosure documents noted that 'commission is paid by the lending company'. However, there was no disclosure of the amount or recipients of any commissions in relation to the PPI sale. In fact, commissions to LLP (£1,870) and Paragon (£2,280) made up 71.8 per cent of the PPI premium, and only £1,630 was remitted to Norwich (the insurer) by Paragon.[6] Mrs Plevin also claimed that neither LLP nor Paragon considered or advised on the suitability of the PPI.

III. THE LITIGATION AND OUTCOMES

A. Summary of the Outcomes of the Litigation

In 2009, Mrs Plevin commenced legal proceedings against both LLP and Paragon but the claim against LLP was settled in 2010 for £3,000.[7]

The proceedings against Paragon continued. Although several different claims were initially introduced,[8] by the time of the first appeal, the proceedings were reduced to an argument that Mrs Plevin's relationship with Paragon was unfair because of: (i) the non-disclosure of the amounts of the commissions; and (ii) the failure of anyone involved to assess and advise on the suitability of the PPI.

---

[3] *Plevin* (n 1) [3].
[4] ibid [4].
[5] ibid [5].
[6] ibid [6].
[7] *Plevin v Paragon Personal Finance Limited* (Manchester County Court, 4 October 2012) (*Plevin 2012*) [1].
[8] ibid [12].

Mrs Plevin relied on sections 140A–140C of the CCA. Relevantly, section 140A(1) gives the court a discretionary power to:

> make an order under s 140B in connection with a credit agreement if it determines that the relationship between the creditor and the debtor arising out of the agreement (or the agreement taken with any related agreement) is unfair to the debtor because of one or more of the following:
>
> …
>
> Any other thing done (or not done) by, or on behalf of, the creditor (either before or after the making of the relevant agreement or any related agreement).

If a court finds that a relationship is unfair to the debtor, it can make a range of orders, including an order requiring the creditor to repay monies paid by the debtor, to set aside a duty owed by a debtor, or to alter the terms of the agreement.[9]

Mrs Plevin's initial claim was dismissed in the county court,[10] and she appealed to the Court of Appeal.[11] This appeal was conjoined with another matter where a similar argument about the PPI commission was being made (involving the parties Conlon and Black Horse Limited).[12]

In the Court of Appeal, Mrs Plevin was unsuccessful on the non-disclosure argument: the Court of Appeal considered that it was bound by the earlier Court of Appeal decision in *Harrison v Black Horse*.[13] However, the Court of Appeal did accept Mrs Plevin's argument that LLP's failure to advise on the suitability of the PPI product was conduct 'on behalf of' Paragon, and that this created an unfair relationship between Mrs Plevin and Paragon.

Paragon appealed to the Supreme Court.[14] In the Supreme Court, Mrs Plevin was again successful, but this time on the first argument (non-disclosure of the PPI commission), but not the second (failure to advise on suitability). The matter was remitted to the County Court to determine the appropriate redress: HHJ Platts ordered that Mrs Plevin be relieved of the obligation to pay any of the PPI commission (a total of £4,115).[15]

B. Mrs Plevin's Successful Argument – Non-disclosure of PPI Commissions

Mrs Plevin first argued that Paragon's failure to disclose the PPI commissions created an unfair relationship. In the Court of Appeal, the detailed analysis of this first argument was provided in the discussion of Conlon and Black Horse (the conjoined

---

[9] Consumer Credit Act 1974, s 140B(1).
[10] *Plevin 2012* (n 7).
[11] *Plevin v Paragon Personal Finance Limited* [2013] EWCA Civ 1658, [2014] Bus LR 553 (*Plevin 2013*).
[12] ibid [1].
[13] *Harrison v Black Horse Limited* [2011] EWCA Civ 1128, [2012] Lloyd's Rep IR 521 (*Harrison*).
[14] *Plevin* (n 1).
[15] NA Chowdhury, 'Plevin Bound/Unbound' [2016] *Butterworths Journal of International Banking and Finance Law* 220, 221. Mrs Plevin was also involved in subsequent litigation on the costs of her matter, see *Plevin v Paragon Personal Finance Limited* [2017] UKSC 23, [2018] 1 All ER 292 (*Plevin 2017*).

matter). On this issue, the Court of Appeal regarded itself as being bound by the authority of *Harrison*.[16]

In *Harrison*, the lender's commission on PPI was 87 per cent of the premium, an amount which Tomlinson LJ described as 'quite startling'.[17] However, it was relevant that there was no regulatory prohibition on charging such a commission, nor any regulatory obligation to disclose such a commission. Tomlinson LJ saw the regulatory rules operating as a bound for the unfairness test, observing:

> It would be an anomalous result if a lender was obliged to disclose receipt of a commission in order to escape a finding of unfairness under s 140A of the Act but yet not obliged to disclose it pursuant to the statutorily imposed regulatory framework under which it operates.[18]

In the Court of Appeal decision, Briggs LJ found that there was nothing in the facts of the matter to distinguish the circumstances of Mrs Plevin (or indeed Mrs Conlon) from those in *Harrison*, and that he was bound to come to the same conclusion as in *Harrison*, albeit reluctantly.[19] The other judges agreed.[20]

The Supreme Court, however, found that *Harrison* was wrongly decided.[21] Lord Sumption (with whom the other judges agreed) was satisfied that Paragon's failure to disclose the PPI commissions created an unfair relationship between Mrs Plevin and Paragon. Specifically, although Mrs Plevin might be taken to have known that some commission would be payable, there was a point at which the commission was so large that a failure to disclose the commission would be unfair because it prevented her from shopping around or from considering whether the insurance represented value for money and the transaction was worth entering into. Although this tipping point was not identified, a commission of 71.8 per cent was 'a long way beyond' that point.[22] The fact that there was no obligation to disclose commissions did not prevent the non-disclosure from giving rise to an unfair relationship.

C. Mrs Plevin's Unsuccessful Argument – Duty to Advise on Suitability

In a reversal of the fortunes of her first argument, Mrs Plevin's argument based on suitability advice was initially successful in the Court of Appeal, but then overturned in the Supreme Court. At the relevant time, there was an obligation in the Insurance Conduct of Business (ICOB) Rules to advise on the suitability of insurance products, but in the fact scenario in *Plevin*, this obligation was imposed on LLP and not Paragon.[23] The question was then whether the alleged failure of LLP to comply with

---

[16] *Plevin 2013* (n 11) [25]–[26].
[17] *Harrison* (n 13) [58].
[18] ibid [58]. The Harrisons choose not to appeal the decision because Black Horse repaid the Harrisons in full in respect of the PPI: *Plevin 2013* (n 11) [18].
[19] *Plevin 2013* (n 11) [25] (in relation to Mrs Conlon), [45] (in relation to Mrs Plevin).
[20] ibid [80] (Beatson LJ), [81] (Moses LJ).
[21] *Plevin* (n 1) [16].
[22] ibid [18], [20].
[23] ibid [23].

this obligation was something done (or not done) 'on behalf of' Paragon for the purposes of section 140A(1)(c) CCA.

In the Court of Appeal decision, Briggs CJ concluded that the phrase 'on behalf of' should be given a broad interpretation, such that it could extend beyond traditional agency relationships, and could cover any conduct beneficial to the creditor or contributing to bringing about the transaction, irrespective of the person's relationship with the creditor.[24] On that interpretation, a failure of LLP to comply with the relevant obligations was done 'on behalf of' Paragon, and thus could create an unfair relationship between Mrs Plevin and Paragon.[25]

However, the Supreme Court took a different approach. Lord Sumption confined the phrase 'on behalf of' in section 140A(1)(c) to its natural meaning, with application only to agents and deemed agents of the creditor, and in relation to Paragon, LLP was neither. Indeed, LLP was actually Mrs Plevin's agent.[26] LLP's failure could not therefore be sheeted home to Paragon, and LLP's conduct had no relevance to the relationship between Mrs Plevin and Paragon for the purposes of section 140A(1)(c) CCA.

Lord Sumption also considered whether Paragon's own failure to advise on suitability created an unfair relationship. However, he found that, in circumstances where there was a duty to assess suitability imposed on LLP, Paragon could not reasonably have been expected to undertake that task. As a result, Paragon's own failure to assess suitability also did not create an unfair relationship.[27]

IV. THE SIGNIFICANCE OF PLEVIN v PARAGON

Despite being a relatively new case, *Plevin* clearly deserves its reputation as a 'landmark' consumer law decision. This section outlines the significance of the decision as it relates to consumer law legislation, regulation and regulators, and policy approaches.

A. Legislation: Clarifying the Scope and Application of Section 140A CCA

A key contribution of *Plevin* is that it provides much needed guidance on several aspects relating to the scope and application of the unfair relationships provisions in the CCA.

Guidance on the unfair relationships test is important because the test is an open-textured one. It relies on an imprecise concept of 'fairness' without even a binding list of 'matters to have regard to' or other form of statutory guidance as is the case

---

[24] ibid [49], [51].
[25] The case was remitted for rehearing on the question of whether LLP had complied with its ICOB obligations: ibid [64], [79] (Briggs LJ).
[26] *Plevin* (n 1) [33].
[27] ibid [26].

for some other open-textured standards in the UK[28] and in other jurisdictions.[29] Open-textured standards, using terminology such as 'unfair', 'unconscionable' or 'unjust' are common in the financial services and consumer legislation.[30] Such standards facilitate flexibility and consideration of the individual circumstance of the consumer who relies on these provisions. However, they have also been criticised as lacking clarity and certainty in application.[31] For example, writing on the unfair relationships test in 2010, Howells explained:

> The Act provides little guidance on what amounts to unfairness. It simply states 'the court shall have regard to all matters it thinks relevant (including matters relating to the creditor and matters relating to the debtor). This vagueness was deliberate to promote flexibility, but it also creates uncertainty with the potential for undermining the confidence in contractual certainty creditors need.[32]

The decision to leave the test without statutory guidance was a deliberate policy choice to 'give the courts a wide discretion to consider unfairness on a case-by-case basis'.[33] As explained by Lord Sumption in *Plevin*, for section 140A, 'It is not possible to state a precise or universal test for its application, which must depend on the court's judgment of all the relevant facts.'[34]

Regulator guidance can also help to understand open-textured standards.[35] The unfair relationships provisions were initially accompanied by a requirement, in section 140D, for the then regulator (the Office of Fair Trading) to publish its views on the interaction between sections 140A–140C CCA and Part 8 of the Enterprise Act 2002.[36] However, section 140D was repealed in 2013.[37] The Financial Conduct

---

[28] The Consumer Protection from Unfair Trading Practices Regulation 2008, SI 2008/1277, prohibits 'unfair commercial practices' (see reg 3(1)), and provides statutory guidance on the circumstances in which a commercial practice will be unfair.

[29] Eg, in Australia, financial services businesses are prohibited from engaging in unconscionable conduct (s 12CB(1), Australian Securities and Investments Commission Act 2001 (Cth)). To support the application of this provision, the legislation also provides a set of interpretative principles (s 12CB(4)), and a non-exclusive list of matters to which the court *may* have regard for the purpose of determining whether there has been a contravention of the provision (s 12CC).

[30] Examples in the UK include the prohibition against unfair terms (see Unfair Terms in Consumer Contracts Regulation 1999, SI 1999/2083, reg 5) and the treating customers fairly principle (FCA Handbook PRIN 2.1.1 (Principle 6)).

[31] Eg, for s 140A CCA, see Financial Conduct Authority, *Review of Retained Provisions of the Consumer Credit Act: Final Report* (March 2019) (*CCA Review*) 38 (para 5.53).

[32] G Howells, 'The Consumer Credit Litigation Explosion' (2010) 12 *Law Quarterly Review* 617, 638.

[33] *CCA Review* (n 31) [5.53].

[34] *Plevin* (n 1) [10]. This statement has also been cited in Australian cases where the court has been asked to apply an open-textured standard: see for example, *ACCC v Chrisco Hampers Australia Limited* [2015] FCA 1204 239 FCR 33 (AU) [39].

[35] However, Brown notes that the regulatory guidance is provided for the regulator, not for the courts: S Brown, 'The Unfair Relationship Test, Consumer Credit Transactions and the Long Arm of the Law' [2009] (Feb) *Lloyd's Maritime and Commercial Law Quarterly* 90, 98.

[36] Office of Fair Trading *Unfair Relationships: Enforcement Action under Part 8 of the Enterprise Act 2002* (OFT854Rev, May 2008, updated August 2011) 4. For a discussion of this guidance document, see generally Brown (n 35).

[37] See Financial Services and Markets Act 2000 (Regulated Activities) (Amendment) (No.2) Order 2013 (SI 2013/1881), Art 20(40).

Authority (FCA) has acknowledged industry concerns about the lack of clarity in the unfair relationships test, but has not identified a need for regulator guidance.[38]

In the absence of legislative or regulator guidance, case law plays a crucial role in understanding the scope and application of open-textured standards. However, there has been relatively little litigation on the unfair relationships provisions. In 2019, the FCA reported that there were fewer than 50 reported cases on unfair relationships;[39] and *Plevin* is the first instance of this test being considered by the Supreme Court.

There are three key aspects of this contribution of *Plevin* that are applicable more broadly. First, *Plevin* clarifies the relationship between the unfair relationships test and other, often more prescriptive, or bright-line obligations that are imposed on lenders. Prior to *Plevin*, some commentators expected that courts would be reluctant to find an unfair relationship if that would result in the debtor receiving greater remedies than would be available under common law or other regulatory principles.[40] And in the specific issue under consideration in *Plevin*, the earlier decision of *Harrison* had determined that, in the absence of a regulatory obligation to disclose commission, a failure to disclose the commission could not give rise to an unfair relationship.[41]

However, the Supreme Court in *Plevin* took a different view, clarifying that a relationship could be unfair even if the lender had complied with all regulatory obligations imposed on it. The fact that the law does not require the creditor to do a particular act does not preclude the failure to do that act from creating an unfair relationship, and this is the case even where the rule-maker had explicitly decided against imposing a rule on that point (as was the case here).[42] According to *Plevin*, the test in section 140A can be *influenced* by the standard of commercial conduct reasonably expected of a lender (as might be demonstrated by a regulatory requirement), but such standards cannot be determinative of whether or not the unfairness test is satisfied.[43]

Second, *Plevin* clarifies the circumstances in which failing to do something can create an unfair relationship. It can be conceptually straightforward to identify a positive act for the purpose of assessing the existence of an unfair relationship.[44] However, it is more difficult to identify whether a something that should have been done but was not done is relevant. *Plevin* articulates a test to assist: a failure to do something can create an unfair relationship where the creditor fails to take such steps as: (i) it would be reasonable to expect the creditor or someone acting on their behalf to take in the interests of fairness; and (ii) would have removed the source of that

---

[38] *CCA Review* (n 31) 38 (para 5.53).
[39] ibid 110 (para 202). Creditors also noted that judgments have been inconsistent: 38, para 5.53.
[40] E Lomnicka, 'Unfair Credit Relationships: Five Years On' (2012) 8 *Journal of Business Law* 713, 729. However, see also the discussion in *Scotland v British Credit Trust Limited* [2014] EWCA Civ 790, [2014] Bus LR 1079 [72] (confirming that the existence in the CCA of a remedy for specific misrepresentations did not preclude the misrepresentation being relevant for s 140A claim).
[41] *Harrison* (n 13) [58].
[42] *Plevin* (n 1) [15]. The Office of Fair Trading had also expressed a similar view: OFT (n 36) 21, para 3.32.
[43] *Plevin* (n 1) [17]. See also the discussion in *Kerrigan v Elevate Credit International Ltd (t/a Sunny) (In Administration)* [2020] EWHC 2169 (Comm), [2020] CTLC 161 [48].
[44] *Plevin* (n 1) [19].

unfairness or mitigated its consequences so that the relationship as a whole can no longer be regarded as unfair.[45]

This test was applied in relation to the two unfairness arguments in *Plevin*. In relation to commission disclosure, it *was* reasonable to expect Paragon to disclose the commissions (paid to itself and to LLP) in the interests of fairness, because Paragon was the only party that knew of both commissions, and the decision in relation to obtaining the PPI policy from Norwich (or at all) was a significant one. In addition, the disclosure of the commissions would have removed the source of the unfairness, 'because Mrs Plevin would then be able to make a properly informed judgment about the value of the PPI policy'.[46]

However, applying this test in relation to the suitability argument led to a different result. The Supreme Court found that it *would not* be reasonable for Paragon to assess and advise on the suitability of the PPI policy. This was because the ICOB rules *did* impose a duty to assess suitability, but that duty was assigned to LLP, and it would not be reasonable to expect Paragon to perform a function that was expressly assigned to someone else.[47]

Of course, it is likely that this approach does not completely eliminate the uncertainty associated with identifying when failing to do something can create an unfair relationship.[48] However, the concept of reasonableness in law is a familiar one, and the test articulated in *Plevin* does set some boundaries around this issue.

Finally, *Plevin* confirms the circumstances in which a person will do (or not do) something 'on behalf of' the creditor. In contrast to the expansive interpretation in the Court of Appeal, the Supreme Court found that, for the purposes of section 140A(1)(c), the phrase 'on behalf of' did not extend beyond agency relationships and deemed agency relationships. There was no special statutory or contractual context that necessitated a wider interpretation of the phrase 'on behalf of' than the ordinary and natural meaning as importing agency,[49] an interpretation that will have given some comfort to creditors.[50]

The three contributions of *Plevin* discussed above are applicable to a range of factual circumstances. However, *Plevin* also makes an important contribution to the understanding of how the unfair relationships test applies in the context of PPI commissions. The case confirms that a failure to disclose a PPI commission may create an unfair relationship if the amount of commission exceeds some 'tipping point', albeit without identifying the tipping point. Some post-*Plevin* commentary suggested that the court's reluctance in *Plevin* to specify a tipping point might lead lenders to err on the side of always disclosing commission.[51] However, any such

---

[45] ibid.
[46] ibid [20].
[47] ibid [26].
[48] P Skinner, 'Caveat Creditor: Difficulties in Unfair Relationship Claims' [2015] *Butterworths Journal of International Banking and Finance Law* 555, 556.
[49] *Plevin* (n 1) [30].
[50] GoughSquare Chambers (2014) 'Plevin v Paragon: A summary of the decision' (12 November 2014) goughsq.co.uk/publication/summary-supreme-court-decision-plevin-v-paragon/ (accessed 11 December 2021).
[51] G Standing, 'The Supreme Court rules on unfair relationships – where does that leave us? gowling-wlg.com/en/insights-resources/articles/2014/the-supreme-court-rules-on-unfair-relationships/ (accessed 11 December 2021).

concern is likely to have been ameliorated by the FCA's response to the *Plevin* decision, discussed in section IV.B below.

The above discussion illustrates how *Plevin* has provided some clarity on the application of sections 140A–140C CCA. These points have been relied upon in subsequent decisions of the Court of Appeal and the lower courts, confirming their continued value and relevance.[52]

B. Regulation and Regulators: Setting Standards and Influencing Firm Practices

Section B.i explains how *Plevin* is relevant to our understanding of the scope and application of the CCA. However, *Plevin* has also influenced regulator policy making and consumer dispute resolution outside of the litigation context.

i. Making New Rules to Respond to a Court Decision

Plevin is a significant decision because it provided an impetus for new FCA guidance and rules relevant to PPI complaints, published in Policy Statement 17/3 (*PS 17/3*).[53] This policy statement was one of several responses of the FCA and its predecessors to concerns about the mis-selling of PPI, widely regarded as the largest mis-selling scandal in the UK financial services sector.[54] The post-*Plevin* package of measures was introduced to reduce the 'significant new uncertainty' that *Plevin* introduced into 'an already uncertain landscape',[55] and to help 'bring the PPI issue to an orderly conclusion'.[56] Most relevant for this chapter is the updated Handbook rules and guidance on dealing with PPI complaints. The rules reflect a complaints-led approach; the FCA did not use its powers to establish a consumer redress scheme.[57]

The *PS 17/3* changes required firms to implement a two-step process for dealing with individual PPI complaints. In the first step, a firm in receipt of a complaint must consider whether it had failed to comply with PPI sales obligations, and, if so, whether

---

[52] Eg, *UBS AG (London Branch) & Anor v Kommunale Wasserwerke Leipzig GmbH* [2017] EWCA Civ 1567, [2017] 2 Lloyd's Rep 621 (16 October 2017); *McMullon v Secure the Bridge Ltd (Rev 1)* [2015] EWCA Civ 884 (5 August 2015).

[53] Financial Conduct Authority, *Policy Statement: Payment protection insurance complaints: feedback on CP16/20 and final rules and guidance* (PS 17/3, March 2017) (PS17/3).

[54] With over 32.4 million complaints and more than £38 billion of redress paid to consumers between 2011 and 2019, the FCA has described the PPI process as 'by far the largest consumer redress exercise in the UK's history': Financial Conduct Authority, *Payment protection insurance complaints deadline – Final report* (April 2020) 3. For a summary of key regulatory responses to PPI, see YY Park, 'Regulator-led Resolution in Mass Finance Mis-selling: Implication of the UK PPI Scandal' (2019) 12(2) *Journal of East Asia and International Law* 321, 323–329.

[55] *PS 17/3* (n 53) 6 (para 1.8).

[56] ibid 6 (para 1.9). A subsequent policy statement dealt with other issues, including recurring non-disclosure of commissions: Financial Conduct Authority, *Previously rejected PPI complaints and further mailing requirements – Feedback on CP18/33 and final rules and guidance* (Policy Statement PS 19/2, January 2019).

[57] See discussion of the FCA's powers under s 404 of the Financial Services and Markets Act in *PS 17/3* (n 53), 36. The impact on FOS of taking this approach (instead of a consumer redress scheme), was considered in R Lloyd, *Independent Review of the Financial Ombudsman Service* (2018) 38–39.

the consumer should be given any redress (because, for example, the consumer would not have purchased the PPI in the absence of that breach or failing).[58] This first step focused on mis-selling concerns, and largely reiterated the FSA's 2010 guidance.[59]

The second step was introduced as a direct response to *Plevin*.[60] In this step, if a firm did not disclose in advance the commission (and anticipated profit share[61]), it must consider whether it can satisfy itself on reasonable groups that the failure to disclose did not give rise to an unfair relationship under section 140A.[62] All relevant matters must be considered, including 'whether the non-disclosure prevented the complainant from making a properly informed judgement about the value of the payment protection contract'.[63]

The FCA also created a more certain and objective standard for assessing fairness in this context. This was done through setting a *presumption* that a firm's failure to disclose the commission would give rise to an unfair relationship if the anticipated or reasonably foreseeable commission and anticipated profit share was more than 50 per cent of the amount paid for the policy.[64] Conversely, an amount that was lower than this 50 per cent 'tipping point' would give rise to a presumption that the relationship was *not* unfair.[65]

Examples of factors that may contribute to the rebuttal of a presumption that a relationship was, or was not, unfair are also given as guidance, and include where disclosure would have made no difference to the complainant's view of the value of the PPI product.[66]

Also in step two, if an unfair relationship is found, redress is to be calculated by paying the consumer the commission and deducting 50 per cent of the amount paid by the consumer.[67] In other words, the consumer will receive a refund of the commission to the extent that the amount of the commission exceeds 50 per cent of the product's cost.

With the exception of the factors that may rebut a presumption, the Handbook provisions are evidential provisions, and contravention can be relied upon as tending to establish a contravention of DISP 1.4.1R (the obligation to assess complaints fairly and offer redress where appropriate).[68] Consumers that are not happy with a firm's response to a PPI complaint can refer the matter to the Financial Ombudsman Service

---

[58] *FCA Handbook* DISP App 3.1.2G; 3.1.3G.
[59] Financial Services Authority, *The Assessment and Redress of Payment Protection Insurance Complaints: Feedback on the Further Consultation in CP10/6 and Final Handbook Text* (Policy Statement 10/12, August 2010).
[60] *FCA Handbook* DISP App 3.1.4A.
[61] Reference to profit share in the assessment was added after the case of *Brookman v Welcome Financial Services Ltd* (County Court Cardiff, 6 November 2015). For simplicity, the remainder of this chapter will refer to the commission only.
[62] *FCA Handbook* DISP App 3.3A.2.
[63] ibid.
[64] *FCA Handbook* DISP App 3.3A.4(1). There are different approaches for single premium payment protection contracts and regular premium payment protection contracts.
[65] *FCA Handbook* DISP App 3.3A.4(2).
[66] *FCA Handbook* DISP App 3.3A.5, 3.3A.6.
[67] *FCA Handbook* DISP App 3.7A.3. A different approach is used if the relationship is unfair despite the commission being less than 50%: DISP App 3.7A.4.
[68] *FCA Handbook* DISP App 3.10.3.7A.3.

(FOS), which is required to make decisions based on what is fair and reasonable in all the circumstances of the case, taking into account the law and regulations; regulators' rules, guidance and standards; industry codes and (where appropriate) good industry practice at the time.[69] In relation to non-disclosure of PPI commissions, the influence of the FCA's rules is apparent in the advice of FOS to firms:

> In cases we've seen where a consumer's credit falls within these dates[70] and the consumer wasn't told they were paying more than half the premium in commission, our ombudsmen have typically decided that the fair answer is to give back the bit of the commission that was over half the premium.[71]

FOS must consider the individual circumstances of a complainant. However, my review of a selection of ombudsman decisions suggests that decisions that rebut the presumptions as to the relevant 'tipping point', or that take a different approach to calculating the appropriate redress may be rare. I reviewed a selection of 181 ombudsman decisions that were published between June 2019 and October 2021, and that discussed PPI commissions.[72] Of these, 139 decisions explicitly considered whether the non-disclosure of commission gave rise to an unfair relationship,[73] and in each of these cases, the ombudsman applied the FCA's approach and required the firm to compensate the consumer in an amount that reflected the amount of commission that exceeded 50 per cent of the premium.[74] There were only nine decisions where no repayment was required because the commission was less than 50 per cent (although the actual amount or percentage was not specified). Another three decisions noted that an appropriate amount of commission had been repaid by the firm, without specifying whether the commission was above or below 50 per cent of the premium.

Consumers also have a right to institute legal proceedings based on section 140A CCA and. the implication of possible divergence between the FCA guidance, FOS decisions and litigation outcomes is explored in the next section below.

ii. Resolving the Tension between Open-textured Standards and Certainty

As discussed above, open-textured standards are sometimes criticised as lacking clarity and certainty in application. In contrast, more prescriptive, bright line, or 'hard-edged'[75] standards can give firms greater confidence in the steps they need to take to comply with their obligations.

---

[69] See Financial Services and Markets Act 2000, s 228; *FCA Handbook* DISP App 3.6.1, DISP App 3.6.4.
[70] These are the relevant dates for the application of s 140A CCA.
[71] Financial Ombudsman Service, 'PPI' (26 January 2021) www.financial-ombudsman.org.uk/businesses/complaints-deal/ppi (accessed 28 January 2022).
[72] The published Ombudsman decisions on PPI were searched using the keyword 'commission' and the dates (i) dates 1/10/21–5/10/21 (43 decisions), 1/6/20–15/6/20 (37 decisions), and 1/6/19–15/6/19 (101 decisions). The reason for not using decisions from June 2021 was that the vast majority in this time period were decisions where the ombudsman found that the unfair credit relationship provisions did not apply.
[73] The remaining 42 decisions reviewed did not consider the *Plevin* rules because the ombudsman found that the PPI was mis-sold (and therefore that the whole of the premium should be repaid) or the unfair credit relationship provisions were not applicable.
[74] See, eg, FOS *Decision DRN3532010* (14 June 2019); *Decision DRN-1886455* (15 June 2020); *Decision DRN-3029312* (5 October 2021).
[75] *Plevin* (n 1) [17].

The use of both bright line and open-textured standards is common in consumer protection law, but, as Lord Sumption explained, these different types of rules (referring specifically to the ICOB Rules and section 140A CCA) are 'doing different things'.[76] As bright line or 'hard-edged' rules, the ICOB rules impose a minimum standard of conduct on insurers and intermediaries, applicable in a wide range of circumstances, and advised of in advance. In contrast, section 140A CCA 'does not impose any obligation and is not concerned with the question of whether the creditor or anyone else is in breach of a duty'.[77] It imposes a test of fairness that is applied to a particular debtor-creditor relationship and requires the court to make its own assessment, as a matter of judicial discretion, and forensic judgment. As Lord Sumption explained:

> ... the question whether the debtor-creditor relationship is fair cannot be the same as the question whether the creditor has complied with the ICOB rules, and the facts which may be relevant to answer it are manifestly different.[78]

Firms therefore are required to navigate through a regulatory regime that requires consideration of these different types of standards.

One potential way to manage this uncertainty is for the regulator to set a quasi-bright line rule or rules for an open-textured standard as it applies in a particular context. The FCA's post-*Plevin* rules are an example.

However, there is not necessarily consistency between the rules set by the FCA and the outcomes of litigation on PPI commissions and unfair relationships, including in *Plevin*. For example, the tipping point of 50 per cent was not derived directly from *Plevin* (where the commission was 71.8 per cent of the premium). And in other cases involving undisclosed PPI commission, courts have expressed concerns about commissions that were higher (for example, 87 per cent) or lower (for example, more than 40 per cent) proportions of the costs than was the case in *Plevin*.[79]

The FCA explained that it considered the figure of 50 per cent:

> to be appropriate in the context of our regulatory judgement concerning PPI complaints, based on what the Supreme Court said in *Plevin* about undisclosed commission of 71.8% being a 'long way beyond' the 'tipping point' for unfairness. Further, whilst we are aware that it is only one of a number of approaches that may have been taken in the county courts, we have also taken account of the approach adopted by Mr. Justice Platts (sitting in the Manchester County Court) in *Yates and Lorenzelli v. Nemo Personal Finance* (14 May 2010) who considered that a commission of over 50% should be disclosed.[80]

---

[76] ibid.
[77] ibid.
[78] ibid.
[79] For some examples of the range of PPI commissions considered in relevant cases, see: *Harrison* (n 13), where the commission was 87% of the PPI premium (see [4]); *Conlon v Black Horse*, reported in *Plevin* 2013 (n 11), (commission more than 40%, see [10]); *Canada Square Operations Ltd v Potter (Rev 2)* [2020] EWHC 672 (QB), [2020] 4 All ER 1114, [13] (commission more than 95%, see [2]); *McWilliam v Norton Finance (UK) Limited* [2015] EWCA Civ 186, [2015] 2 BCLC 730 (commission 62.6%, see [4]); and *Smith v The Royal Bank of Scotland PLC* [2021] EWCA Civ 1832, [2022] 1 WLR 2136, [2022] WLR(D) 69 (commission more than 50%, see [5]). See also D Galeza, 'How to Pursue a Plevin Claim When Time Runs Out' (2022) 37(5) *Journal of International Banking Law and Regulation* 207, 212.
[80] Financial Conduct Authority, *Rules and guidance on payment protection insurance complaints* (Consultation Paper CP15/39, November 2015), 52 (para 5.53); see also *PS 17/3* (n 53) 85–86.

The FCA's rules on redress also differ from the outcome in *Plevin*, where Mrs Plevin was awarded the whole of the PPI commission (but not the full amount of the premium).[81] A later case, *Doran v Paragon Personal Finance*, took an even more generous approach. Here the 'gross commission' was 76 per cent of the premium,[82] and the court awarded repayment of the full amount of the premium, explicitly rejecting the FCA's approach to calculating redress in such cases.[83]

This potential disparity between the FCA's rules and the actual decision in *Plevin* (and in other court cases) has been criticised.[84] As most court cases have involved commissions above 50 per cent (where the relationship would be presumed unfair under the FCA's rules), it is the redress aspect where the disparity is likely to have the most impact. Very few cases will proceed to litigation, and the redress component of the FCA's rule provides little deterrence to high commissions if firms know that they will only rarely be asked to repay any commission that is less than 50 per cent of the premium.

FOS has also acknowledged the potential for different outcomes in litigation. For example, in one decision, the ombudsman explained:

> I accept that if Mr S went to court and it was decided there was an unfair relationship under section 140A of the Consumer Credit Act, he might be awarded a full refund of the premiums he paid – this would be a remedy available. And this is a route that's available to Mr S if he doesn't accept my decision. In this case I think CBS's offer [to repay an amount reflecting the amount of commission above 50% if the premium] is a fair way to resolve this case.[85]

Acknowledging that there is some nuance in the FCA's rules (for example, in the ability to rebut the presumption),[86] in practice, the FCA's decision sets a quasi-bright-line rule to explain the application of an open-textured standard to PPI commission disclosure. Taking a uniform approach like this can be an effective way to deal with low value mass claims,[87] and can provide a speedier, cheaper and more straightforward

---

[81] Chowdhury (n 15) 221.

[82] *Doran v Paragon Personal Finance Limited* (26 June 2018, Manchester County Court, unreported) [3(g)] (*Doran*).

[83] ibid [71]–[75]. The court also chose not to the follow the FCA's suggested approach to the interest calculation, awarding a lower amount: [76]–[78]. See also the discussion in R Rosenburg, 'Consumer Credit – PPI – Commission – Unfair Relationship' [Summer 2018] *Quarterly Account* 36. Other decisions taking a more generous approach to redress are *Martin-Smith v Welcome Finance Limited* (Manchester County Court, 18 December 2019), see St John's Buildings, 'James Martin-Smith v Welcome Finance Limited' (19 December 2019), stjohnsbuildings.com/news/james-martin-smith-v-welcome-finance-limited (accessed 16 May 2022); and *Verrin v Welcome Financial Services Ltd* [2017] ECC 7 (referred to in *Doran* ibid [62]).

[84] For example, *PS 17/3* (n 53), 85; Chowdhury (n 15) 223. See also P Lewis, 'FCA is wrong on Plevin Redress' (*Paul Lewis Money*, 4 October 2015) paullewismoney.blogspot.com/2015/10/fca-is-wrong-on-plevin-redress.html (accessed 27 January 2022). More recent discussions have noted that the post-*Plevin* cases confirm that consumers are likely to obtain more in litigation than would be granted under the FCA's approach, see, eg, I Weatherall and J Bates, 'Finance Litigation – the latest cases and issues – September 2018' (*Gowling WLG*, 12 September 2018) gowlingwlg.com/en/insights-resources/articles/2018/finance-litigation-september-2018/ (accessed 11 May 2022).

[85] FOS, *Decision DRN3040152* (23 March 2019).

[86] *FCA Handbook* DISP App 3.3A.5.

[87] Park (n 54) 335. In 2020, the FCA reported that the average redress for unfair relationships complaints was £740: FCA 2020 (n 54) 8 (para 2.32).

outcome for consumers than litigation.[88] However, avoiding the costs of litigation equally benefits firms, and it is not immediately obvious why a non-litigious approach should set expectations for firms (in terms of disclosure and redress) that are likely *lower* than what might be expected of them by a court. This critique applies also to FOS decision making: it seems counter-intuitive that a 'fair and reasonable' approach would award less than what would be awarded by a court relying on a statutory provision.

For many consumers, FOS is the *only* practical mechanism for challenging a firm's decision, even though litigation may achieve a more favourable award. Even consumers who might otherwise be prepared to litigate will often prefer to pursue matters through FOS. However, since August 2019, firms and FOS have not been required to accept complaints about PPI mis-selling.[89] This may see more cases litigated[90] and potentially magnify the divergence between the approaches of the FCA and FOS and litigation outcomes.

C. Policy Approaches: Common Themes in the Design of Consumer Law

Finally, *Plevin* is significant in the way that it illustrates themes that should be kept in mind in the design and development of consumer law – the extent of regulatory complexity, the appropriate reliance on disclosure obligations and consumer empowerment, and the challenge of access to justice in consumer disputes.

i. Highlighting the Complexity of Consumer Protection Regulation in Financial Services

Plevin highlights the complexity of consumer protection regulation in credit and financial services more broadly, and the reality that courts, regulators and firms often have to grapple with overlapping duties, rights and remedies. For example, although *Plevin* focused on section 140A CCA, there were several other claims initially included in the Particulars of Claims. These included various breaches of statutory and/or fiduciary duties by LLP, of which Paragon had actual or constructive knowledge; the PPI agreement being an improperly regulated agreement and therefore unenforceable; breaches of fiduciary duty and misrepresentation; unfair contract terms; and breaches of various codes of conduct.[91] Other commentary has suggested that the issues raised in *Plevin* and/or other unfair relationships cases might overlap with the FCA Handbook's High Level Principles and/or the prohibition against unfair trading practices.[92] These various and overlapping regulatory obligations and statutory

---

[88] The FCA also noted that 'having the fair alternative of our rules and guidance may help avoid an increase of cases to the courts, with all the challenges and costs that might involve for consumers and firms.' (See *PS 17/3* (n 53) 34).
[89] *FCA Handbook* DISP 2.8.9R.
[90] See also FCA 2020 (n 54) 10 (para 2.47).
[91] *Plevin* 2012 (n 7) [12]. In the first instance decision, Recorder Yip suggested that the claim had been 'grossly over-complicated' ([11]).
[92] Skinner (n 48) 557.

rights have also been 'superimposed on relationships that were already primarily governed by obligations law: contractual, tortious and fiduciary'.[93] A complex set of rules, obligations and rights of different types apply to consumer credit and financial services transactions, with redress and enforcements options that vary across the different sources of rules.[94]

Such complexity in the regulatory framework is difficult to avoid in markets that are inherently complex. Consumer protection regulation is not a fixed entity, but is built, modified and renovated over time, reflecting different triggers (for example, court cases), changes in the market (for example, the implications of electronic transactions, artificial intelligence and automated decision making), and changes to regulatory sensibilities, understandings of consumer behaviour, and attitudes to risk.[95] Complexities can also derive from the existence of dual levels of legislative power (for example, national and regional), and of industry codes, with different approaches to enforceability.[96]

Regulatory complexity is costly for regulators, firms and consumers,[97] and *Plevin* reminds us of the need to focus on the extent of coherence and consistency of rules, principles and regulation within and across the different parts of the framework for regulating consumer transactions when introducing new rules, and also the importance of regular reviews of the framework that consider coherence and consistency.[98]

ii. Illustrating Two Key Consumer Protection Themes

Plevin also illustrates several themes common to consumer protection regulation more generally, including the continued reliance on disclosure as a consumer protection mechanism and the challenge of ensuring access to justice.

Traditionally, consumer protection laws have emphasised disclosure obligations. It is argued that pre-contractual disclosure gives consumers information on which they can base their decisions and empowers consumers to choose the option that best

---

[93] E Lomnicka, 'The Impact of Rule-making by Financial Services Regulators on the Common Law: The Lessons of PPI' in L Gullifer and S Vogenauer (eds), *English and European Perspectives on Contract and Commercial Law: Essays in Honour of Hugh Beale* (Oxford, Hart Publishing, 2013) 51.

[94] See the comparison of the remedies and sanctions under consumer credit and financial services laws in E Lomnicka, 'The Future of Consumer Credit Regulation: A Chance to Rationalise Sanctions for Breaches of Financial Services Regulatory Regimes?' (2013) 34(1) *Company Law* 13.

[95] In the Australian context, see generally the discussion on the changing approaches to risk in financial services in Australian Law Reform Commission, *Risk and reform in Australia's financial services* law (Background Paper FSL5, March 2022).

[96] Eg, on the difference between the enforceability of industry codes in England and Ireland, see D McIlroy and J Freeman 'The Actionability of Codes of Conduct in English and Irish Law' (2021) 32 *Journal of Banking and Finance Law and Practice* 74. See also the discussion of the role of financial services codes in *Plevin* (n 1) [39].

[97] For a summary of why legislative complexity matters in financial services law, see Australian Law Reform Commission, *Complexity and legislative design* (Background Paper FSL2, October 2021) 2–7, 2–8.

[98] A recent example of a review focusing on coherence and consistency was the FCA's review of the retained CCA provisions: *CCA Review* (n 31). Reducing complexity and improving coherence are also a focus of the current Australian Law Reform Commission Review of the legal framework for corporations and financial services regulation: see Australian Law Reform Commission *Financial Services Legislation: Interim Report A* (November 2021) 29–31, paras 1.1–1.6 (on the scope of the inquiry. The second interim report of the Inquiry focuses on the coherence of regulatory design: Australian Law Reform Commission *Financial Services Legislation: Interim Report B* (September 2022).

meets their individual needs and preferences. Firms that offer products and services that meet the preferences of consumers will do well, and poorly designed or poor value products will be effectively driven out of the market by the lack of demand.

This (over)reliance on disclosure has a long history of academic criticisms.[99] However, in *Plevin*, the non-disclosure of commissions was explicitly tied to the potential for consumer empowerment: without disclosure, Mrs Plevin's ability to shop around or properly consider the value of the product was impeded. Reliance on the evidence that Mrs Plevin would 'certainly have questioned' the commission if she had known of it is also consistent with this emphasis on consumer empowerment, as was Mrs Conlon's evidence that she would not have purchased the PPI policy if she had known of the amount of the commission.[100] The link between disclosure and consumer empowerment was also highlighted in the later case of *Nelmes v NRAM*, where the Court of Appeal found that there was no need to give further relief (apart from accounting for the commission) because, in contrast to *Plevin*, the non-disclosure did not affect the consumer's ability to assess value for money.[101]

The emphasis on disclosure and consumer empowerment in the context of PPI commissions is replicated in the factors that might rebut the presumptions,[102] and in the decisions of FOS. For example, in one case, the ombudsman explained:

> I hope I have clarified the point that it isn't the actual level of commission that is unfair, it is the fact if over 50% commission is paid and not disclosed it creates an unfair relationship. Ms S now knows what commission level she is paying and so can make an informed choice as to whether keeping the PPI in place is worth the cost of the premiums, knowing that between 56% and 62% of what she pays may be for commission.[103]

However, disclosure may not be of much assistance to a consumer if all commissions are at a similarly (high) level,[104] if the consumer is focused on the primary product (the loan), or if the consumer does not understand the significance of the commission(s) in the sales process.[105] Also, many consumers will not be in the more advantageous

---

[99] See generally, J Gardner, *The Future of High Cost Credit: Rethinking Payday Lending* (Oxford, Hart Publishing, 2022) 3.4.2.

[100] *Plevin* (n 1) [18], [20]. See also the discussion in Brown arguing that although the decision 'hints at an essential role for transparency', it also expresses a protective ethic, given the court's confirmation that other factors may also be relevant: S Brown, 'Vulnerable consumers in financial services and access to justice: The regulatory response' in C Riefa and S Saintier (eds), *Vulnerable Consumers and the Law: Consumer Protection and Access to Justice* (Abingdon, Routledge, 2021) 241. Disclosure was also important in *Doran* (n 87) [42]–[47].

[101] *Nelmes v NRAM PLC* [2016] EWCA Civ 491, [2016] CTLC 106 [34]–[35].

[102] See *FCA Handbook* DISP App 3.3A.5(3). The FCA also explicitly stated that the rules were focused on disclosure and were not trying to address high prices in an uncompetitive market: *PS 17/3* (n 53) 86.

[103] FOS *Decision DRN1671473* (5 June 2020). For another decision focusing on the relevance of disclosure to the purchasing decision, see FOS Decision DRN-3029132 (5 October 2021).

[104] In the review of ombudsman decisions for this chapter, only nine of 139 FOS decisions that applied the 50% rule found that the commission was less than 50% of the premium.

[105] The problem of remuneration structures facilitating a mis-alignment of incentives for consumers and lenders in the context of PPI is considered in OO Cherednychecnko and JM Meindertsma, 'Irresponsible Lending in the Post-crisis Era: Is the EU Consumer Credit Directive Fit for its Purpose?' (2019) 42 *Journal of Consumer Policy* 483, 497.

position of Mrs Plevin, who potentially had an alternative to PPI through life insurance, sick leave and redundancy entitlements.[106]

The FCA's approach therefore potentially privileges the informed, engaged consumer, but it may be of little assistance to consumers who are disengaged, or operating under restrictive constraints and options. These consumers may in fact be more vulnerable and in need of protection from the costs associated with high commissions.[107] Further, an approach focused on disclosure does little to address the distorting impact that high commissions have on sales practices. In its explanation, the FCA expressly noted that its approach in relation to PPI complaints and *Plevin* was not designed to address the issue of high prices per se.[108] However, given the above comments about the limitations of disclosure, this may be an issue for future policy consideration in the UK.

A contrast is seen in the Australian context, where commissions for selling the equivalent product (consumer credit insurance) must generally be disclosed in pre-contractual statements for credit if the commission is financed by the loan agreement,[109] and commissions cannot exceed 20 per cent of the premium.[110] This gives similar protection to empowered, disengaged and vulnerable consumers. Other protections and recommendations restricting product design and distribution have also been implemented through legislation, regulator guidance, and industry codes, in recognition of the limitations of commission disclosure as a consumer protection tool.[111] As a result, Australian consumers do not have to rely on an open-textured standard, such as an unfairness test, to protect them from high or undisclosed commissions associated with the sale of CCI.

Plevin also highlights the issue of access to justice for consumer disputes, something which is discussed further in by Dgegling, Gardner and McGeechan in their chapter on class actions. As I explain above, for open-textured standards, the courts play a key role in helping consumers, firms and regulators to understand the scope and application of the standards and, as such, litigation continues to be important.[112] However, the financial barriers for consumers to access justice through litigation are often prohibitive. In *Plevin*, the value of the dispute – at its highest – was in the order of £5,000, and Mrs Plevin was ultimately awarded £4,115 plus interest. However, this amount was dwarfed by the legal costs of pursuing the matter to the Supreme Court, assessed at £751,463.84.[113] Even in the original County Court decision, the costs were estimated to be £320,000.[114]

---

[106] As alleged in *Plevin* 2012 (n 7) [31].
[107] For a discussion on vulnerability in consumer credit, see also generally Brown (n 100).
[108] PS 17/3 (n 53) 86.
[109] National Consumer Credit Protection Act 2009 (Cth), sch 1 ('National Credit Code') s 17(15).
[110] ibid s 145.
[111] See generally, Australian Securities and Investments Commission, *Consumer credit insurance: Poor value products and harmful sales practices* (REP 622, July 2019).
[112] Brown (n 100) 82–83, 84. For a discussion on this issue in the Australian context, see N Howell 'Shutting the Courts Out: Developing Consumer Credit Law in the Shadow of Alternative Dispute Resolution and the new Australian Financial Complaints Authority' (2020) 30(2) *Journal of Banking and Finance Law and Practice* 57.
[113] *Plevin* 2017 (n 15) [2].
[114] *Plevin* 2012 (n 7) [11].

Other measures, including collective action,[115] and the use of claims management companies and conditional fee agreements may sometimes assist in increasing access to litigation, but are clearly not complete (or efficient) solutions. Alternative dispute resolution options, such as FOS, also play a key role in facilitating access to justice, and – like the courts – can consider individual circumstances. However, where FOS relies on FCA rules for dealing with open-textured standards, it is arguably even more important that any presumptive rules mirror closely the outcomes known to be likely in litigation.

V. CONCLUSION

This chapter has explained the decision in *Plevin*, where the Supreme Court found that the failure to disclose high commissions associated with the sale of a PPI policy created an unfair relationship between the lender and Mrs Plevin. A short time after Mrs Plevin purchased her PPI policy, new rules came into play that prohibited the sale of this type of PPI policy. This and other regulatory changes meant that PPI policies had largely stopped being sold by late 2010.[116] However, other policies can be used by consumers to address the risk of loan defaults, and some of the features of the PPI mis-selling scandal may also arise in selling of these other products.[117] The features that make *Plevin* worthy of the description as a landmark case are therefore likely to have relevance to credit and consumer law beyond the specific example of PPI sales.

---

[115] The UK Government has recently decided not to implement additional options for collective consumer redress: Department for Business, Energy and Industrial Strategy, *Reforming competition and consumer policy: Government response to consultation* (CP 656, April 2022) 99–100.

[116] Comres, *Payment Protection Insurance Research* (Analytical Report, November 2015) 65.

[117] Financial Conduct Authority, 'Income and Payment Protection' (17 July 2020) www.fca.org.uk/consumers/income-payment-protection (accessed 21 January 2022).

20
Cake, Conflict and Consumer Law: The Significance of *Masterpiece Cakeshop v Colorado Civil Rights Commission* and *Lee v Ashers Baking Company Ltd*

SARAH BROWN*

I. INTRODUCTION

TWO RECENT LANDMARK cases have generated heated debate around consumer law and LGBTQ+ rights. Sometimes referred to as the 'gay cake cases', they concern the refusal of a bakery to provide a cake to a homosexual individual/couple, due to the owners' religious beliefs. The nub of both actions lay in whether the customer had been unlawfully discriminated against on the basis of sexual orientation, specifically in the context of same sex marriage. These cases are the United States (US) case *Masterpiece Cakeshop v Colorado Civil Rights Commission* ('*Masterpiece*')[1] and the United Kingdom (UK) case *Lee v Ashers Baking Company Ltd and Others* ('*Ashers*').[2] After a string of appeals, neither case resulted, ultimately, in victory for the customer. To some this has been a travesty and a missed opportunity to send a clear message that there is no place for discrimination, on the basis of sexual orientation, in provision of goods and services.[3]

Questions arise from these judgments, primarily regarding the application of rights under discrimination laws and the balancing of these with rights of free speech and the exercise of religious conviction. The decisions underscore uncomfortable questions in relation to compelled speech, conscience claims (including commercial conscience) and the appropriateness of morality, dignity and competing rights

---

*The author would like to thank Professors Iain Ramsay and Jodi Gardner for their very helpful comments on previous drafts of this chapter. Any omissions, misunderstandings or misconceptions are the author's own.
[1] *Masterpiece Cakeshop v Colorado Civil Rights Commission* 584 US (2018).
[2] *Lee v Ashers Baking Company Ltd and Others* [2018] UKSC 49, [2020] AC 413.
[3] C McCrudden, 'The Gay Cake Case: What the Supreme Court did and didn't Decide in *Ashers*' (2020) 9 *Oxford Journal of Law and Religion* 238 (McCrudden sees some of these arguments as over inflated).

in the public accommodations space.[4] The *Ashers* decision has had support,[5] but there is a feeling that the UK Supreme Court engaged in some neat footwork to come to a conclusion that, whilst legally correct, did not result overall in the appropriate normative result.[6] Commentary has inter alia covered theories of indissociability and/ or associative discrimination in establishing direct discrimination, and substantive equality.[7] The US Supreme Court's approach in *Masterpiece*, whilst again receiving support[8] primarily centred on the view that the Court sidestepped the real issues with a narrow ruling that lacked empathy for the complainants and concentrated on procedural justice, with predictions of a flood of discriminatory practices.[9] There has been discussion of the extent to which 'places of public accommodation [can] discriminate against protected classes',[10] whether denying a free exercise exemption can be justified,[11] 'procedural animus',[12] the role the concept of 'mere civility' may or may not have in regulation of markets,[13] and identity politics.[14]

---

[4] Eg, K McK Norrie, 'Lee v Ashers Baking Company Ltd [2018] UKSC 49: Comment by Professor Kenneth McK Norrie, Strathclyde Law School' [2019] *Jur Rev* 88; JA Campbell, 'Compelled Speech in Masterpiece Cakeshop: What The Supreme Court's June 2018 Decisions Tell Us About The Unresolved Questions' (2019) 19 *Federalist Soc'y Review* 142; R Ahdar and J Giles, 'The Supreme Courts' Icing on the Trans- Atlantic Cakes' (2020) 9 *Oxford Journal of Law and Religion* 219; R Moon, 'Conscientious Objection and the Politics of Cake Making' (2020) 9 *Oxford Journal of Law and Religion* 329; MDC van der Tol, 'Conscience and Cakes: Reaffirming the Distinction between Institutional Duties and Individual Rights' (2020) 9 *Oxford Journal of Law and Religion* 372; for discussion pre-*Masterpiece* on the corporation's ability to claim free exercise rights: RK Vischer, 'Do For Profit Businesses have free exercise rights? (2013) 21 *Journal of Contemporary Legal Issues* 369.

[5] Eg, McCrudden (n 3); EV Ibarra, 'Lee v Ashers Baking Company Ltd and Others: The Inapplicability of Discrimination Law to an Illusory Conflict of Rights' (2020) 83 *MLR* 190.

[6] McCrudden (n 3) 259, although this is not his view.

[7] McCrudden (n 3) 259–67; S Fredman 'Tolerating the intolerant: Religious Freedom Complicity and Rights to Equality' (2020) 9 *Oxford Journal of Law and Religion* 305; D Capper, 'Free Speech is Not a Piece of Cake' in RL Weaver and others (eds), *Free Speech and Media Law in the Twenty First Century* (Durham, NC, Carolina Academic Press, 2018); KK Waggoner, 'Mastering Masterpiece' (2019) 68 *Catholic University Law Review* 699.

[8] 'State v. Arlene's Flowers, Inc. Washington Supreme Court Limits Masterpiece Cakeshop to the Context of Adjudications' (2019) 133 *Harvard Law Review* 731 (case note); K Crowley 'The Many Layers of Masterpiece Cakeshop (2020) 100 *Boston University Law Review* 301 (case note).

[9] G Seaquist, M Barken and A Bramhandkar, 'Discrimination at Places of Public Accommodation After Masterpiece Cakeshop Ltd v Colorado Civil Rights Commission' (2019) 38 *North East Journal of Legal Studies* 103; EJ Schoen, 'Masterpiece Cakeshop: A Case Study Brought to You by the US' [2019] *Rohrer College of Business Faculty Scholarship* 40, rdw.rowan.edu/business_facpub/40 (accessed 20 January 2022); MR Killenbeck, 'Pandora's Cake' (2020) 72 *Arkansas Law Review* 4, 769.

[10] Seaquist (n 9); P Barker, 'Religious Exemptions and the Vocational Dimension of Work' (2019) 119 *Columbia Law Review* 169; Killenbeck (n 9).

[11] LD Weeden, 'A Functional Free Exercise Clause Analysis Requires a State to Prove a Compelling Interest Before Interfering with an Individual's Faith-based Same-Sex Marriage Participation Objections' (2018-19) 18 *Appalachian Journal of Law* 113.

[12] KA Macfarlane 'Procedural Animus' (2020) 71 *Alabama Law Review* 1185; see also M Pearson 'Empathy and Procedural Justice in Clash of Rights Cases' (2020) 9 *Oxford Journal of Law and Religion* 350.

[13] JD Tedesco, 'Masterpiece Cakeshop and the Foundations of Free Speech and Toleration (2020) 9 *Oxford Journal of Law and Religion* 271; JM Oleske Jr, 'The Mere Civility of Equality Law and Compelled Speech Quandaries' (2020) 9 *Oxford Journal of Law and Religion* 288 discussing T Bejan, *Mere Civility Disagreement and the Limits of Toleration* (Cambridge, MA, Harvard University Press, 2017).

[14] JA Ho, 'Queer Sacrifice in Masterpiece Cakeshop (2019) 31 *Yale Journal of Law and Feminism* 249.

The cases raise these issues in the context of access to goods and services and it is here they demonstrate their consumer law credentials. Consumer protection legislation is commonly recognised as protecting the consumer in relation to transactional procedure and substance. In its most obvious form these laws govern how and upon what terms the consumer-trader relationship is entered into and provides protection against exploitation, lack of transparency and dangerous products. However, the cases show that this is not the only legislative regime that contributes to consumer protection and that guarding against discrimination is an extremely important aspect of consumer law. Treatment of these issues, and the legislative regimes used to address them, translate across the Atlantic. *Masterpiece* and *Ashers* reflect differences, yet in essence have much in common. They emphasise the right to be treated fairly is not just about protection against exploitation and dishonesty; inequalities in the consumer-trader relationship are not just about economic power, but also involve respecting human dignity and ensuring access to goods and services. This is not just about competitive markets, but also a form of social justice that is Micklitz's 'access justice' ('justice through access').[15]

This chapter will explore the principles that emerge from these two cases as aspects of consumer law and how they demonstrate approaches in both the US and the UK to protecting consumers accessing goods and services. The chapter will begin with analysis of the cases and the judgments. It will then provide a brief overview of how consumer law, and the importance and concept of consumer protection has developed over the years across the Atlantic.[16] Discussion will move on to how the cases are highly significant in the context of consumer law, before concluding.

II. THE CASES

A. Masterpiece Cakeshop v Colorado Civil Rights Commission 584 U.S. (2018)

Originating in the US State of Colorado, *Masterpiece* centred on a decision by the Colorado Civil Rights Commission (CCRC). A cake shop owner (Jack Phillips) refused to sell a wedding cake to a homosexual couple, citing his religious opposition to same sex marriages.[17] The couple filed a complaint with the CCRC, which ruled the shop's refusal to make the cake was a violation of the Colorado Anti-Discrimination Act 1957 which prohibits discrimination based on sexual orientation in a 'place of business engaged in any sales to the public and any place offering services … to the public'.[18] The CCRC held the bakery had discriminated against these potential customers because of their sexual orientation, and ordered Phillips to 'cease and desist from discriminating against … same-sex couples by refusing to

---

[15] This is not the form of social justice understood in redistributive terms – Hans-W Micklitz – 'Social Justice and Access to Justice in Private Law' (EUI Working Papers Law 2011/12) 2. dx.doi.org/10.2139/ssrn.1824225 (accessed 21 January 2022).
[16] In the context of transactional protection rather than safety/product liability.
[17] Note: Colorado did not recognise same sex marriages at the time this took place.
[18] Colo Rev Stat § 24-34-60(2).

sell them wedding cakes or any product [they] would sell to heterosexual couples'.[19] Phillips appealed to the Colorado Court of Appeals on, inter alia, two constitutional bases.[20] His position was that requiring him to make a cake for a same sex wedding would violate his First Amendment constitutional rights, namely his right to:

(a) free speech – he would be compelled to express a message with which he disagreed, through his artistic talents in creating the cake; and
(b) the free exercise of religion (Free Exercise Clause).[21]

Separately there was a disparity in treatment by the CCRC compared to other similar cases, which, together with language used by some Commissioners, demonstrated a hostility to his belief.

The decision of the CCRC was upheld by the Colorado Court of Appeals, which found that the CCRC's order was not unconstitutional: the order did not compel Phillips to convey 'a celebratory message about same-sex marriage'.[22] The Free Exercise Clause did not allow an individual to sidestep compliance with a 'valid and neutral law of general application'.[23] On the matter of neutrality the Court distinguished the cases that Phillips asserted showed hostility towards his religion. Phillips had engaged in sexual orientation discrimination even though he would sell any other cake to those in the protected class. Phillips appealed to the US Supreme Court ('SCOTUS').

The Supreme Court reversed the Colorado Court of Appeal's decision by a 7-2 majority. The rationale of the decision did not lie in a fundamental disagreement with the finding that there had been discrimination on the part of Phillips. The reason for the reversal was a finding that the CCRC had violated Phillip's rights under the First Amendment because the CCRC's decision and subsequent cease and desist order were 'inconsistent with the State's obligation of religious neutrality'.[24] SCOTUS stated that homosexual individuals must be protected in the exercise of their rights, yet at the same time religious objections to same-sex marriage are protected views, and may indeed be protected forms of expression. What swung the Supreme Court in Phillips' favour was the approach of the CCRC. Whilst Colorado law can protect homosexual persons in acquiring products and services on the same terms and conditions as are offered to other members of the public, the law must be applied in a manner that is neutral toward religion. However, they found there was a more than palpable hostility in the Commission's decision towards Phillips' beliefs, and that there was

---

[19] *Masterpiece* (n 1) 1726.
[20] 370 P 3d 272 (2015). Other points of the appeal related to a) denial of two motions to dismiss, b) that the court had erred in finding CADA had been violated. These arguments were rejected by the Court of Appeal.
[21] 'Congress shall make no law … prohibiting free exercise of religion' US Const. Amend. 1.
[22] Phillips' conduct would not be 'expressive' for the purposes of free speech in providing the cake because a reasonable observer would think he is merely complying with Colorado's public-accommodations law 370 P 3d 272 (2015) [44]–[45], [66] (Judge Taubman).
[23] ibid [77]–[101]. This law is broad and does not single out any particular activity. The Court's rationale was that the law in question passed a rational basis review – applying this law would not interfere with religious practice or belief (applying *Employment Div, Dept of Human Resources of Ore v Smith* 494 US 872 (1990) (superseded on other grounds by statute).
[24] *Masterpiece* (n 1) 1723.

therefore some doubt over whether the deliberations of the Commission were fair and impartial. This was exacerbated by seeming inconsistency in relation to other recent cases of a similar nature brought before the Commission (where three bakeries refused to produce cakes with anti-same sex marriage messages for a customer, William Jack).[25] As such the Commission had violated Phillips' First Amendment rights by demonstrating a lack of neutrality in considering his religious objections when applying the law, as was required by the Free Exercise clause. This is where the crux of the dissenting opinion of Ginsburg and Sotomeyer JJ lay. They disagreed with the view that the CCRC had been inconsistent in relation to these other cases, which in their view were not comparable. Phillips had refused to provide actual goods (a wedding cake) due to the customers' sexual orientation. The other bakeries however had not refused to provide goods to Jack because of his characteristics (religious belief) but because of the message on the cake.

There have been a number of cases since the SCOTUS decision both in Colorado and across the US on this issue in relation to other goods and services. In *Telescope MediaGroup v Lucero* in Minnesota a pre-enforcement challenge in relation to wedding videos was pursued.[26] In New Mexico, the owner of Elane Photography refused service to a same sex couple on the basis it was contrary to her religious beliefs. She was found to have contravened the New Mexico Human Rights Act.[27] In *Arlene's Flowers v Washington*[28] the Washington Supreme Court narrowed *Masterpiece* as relevant to adjudicatory bodies only (on the neutrality point) – and upheld the claims against the flower shop. SCOTUS declined to hear an appeal.[29] Phillips has also been embroiled in further court action, seen by some as a crusade by Colorado officials.[30] There is also a separate lawsuit ongoing in Denver with an initial judgment, in part, against Phillips from the District Court.[31] Phillips is now appealing to the Court of Appeals. However, the most impactful decision since *Masterpiece* is the SCOTUS judgment in *Creative LLC v Elenis*, ('*Creative*')[32] on appeal from the Tenth Circuit Appeals court (which had upheld the Colorado Anti- Discrimination Act as against a pre-enforcement challenge). It was held, on a majority of 6-3,[33] that a web designer could refuse to offer wedding website services for same-sex marriages. This was on the basis that the website designer's First Amendment right to free speech would be violated, if required to offer the service, as the design of the website constituted 'pure speech'.[34] Her refusal was not on the basis of protected characteristics of a customer,

---

[25] *Jack v Gateaux, Ltd*, Charge No P20140071X (24 March 2015); *Jack v Le Bakery Sensual Inc*, Charge No P20140070X (24 March 2015); *Jack v Azucar Bakery*, Charge No P20140069X (24 March 2015).
[26] 936 F3d 740 (8th Circ 2019).
[27] *Elane Photography LLC v Vanessa Willock* 309 P3d 53 (NMSC 2013).
[28] 441 P3D 1203 (Wash 2019).
[29] www.supremecourt.gov/orders/courtorders/070221zor_4gc5.pdf (accessed 22 January 2022).
[30] www.dailysignal.com/2021/06/25/the-crusade-to-destroy-jack-phillips-continues/; thehill.com/opinion/civil-rights/402114-colorado-end-your-crusade-against-masterpiece-cakeshop/ (accessed 20 May 2022).
[31] *Scardina v Masterpiece Cake Shop Inc* 19CV32214 (D Colo 2019).
[32] 600 U. S. ____ (2023).
[33] Gorusch J., delivered the opinion of the Court, in which Roberts, C. J., Thomas, Alito, Kavanaugh, and Barrett, JJ. joined. Sotomayor, J., filed a dissenting opinion, in which Kagan and Jackson, JJ., joined.
[34] 600 U. S. ____ (2023), 9.

but because it would constitute a message that violated her beliefs.[35] The decision has prompted condemnation, including from President Biden.[36]

B. Lee v Ashers Baking Company Ltd [2018] UKSC 49

This case involved different facts, although in the context of baking and same sex marriage. The events took place in Northern Ireland. Here Gareth Lee, who was homosexual, ordered a cake from Ashers Baking Company asking for the cake to be decorated with a message that stated 'Support Gay Marriage'. The bakery is a small business owned by the McArthur family (husband, wife and son). Initially Mrs McArthur took the order but then having consulted with the other family members rang Lee and refunded his money, stating they could not make the cake in all conscience because of its message. This was because they believed that same sex marriage was inconsistent with the bible and its teachings, and therefore contrary to their profoundly held beliefs.[37]

Lee consequently brought a claim again the bakery and its owners for breach of statutory duty, asserting discrimination on the grounds of sexual orientation and/or grounds of religious belief or political opinion contrary to the Equality Act (Sexual Orientation) Regulations (Northern Ireland) Order 2006 (under which it is unlawful to discriminate in the provision of goods, facilities or services to the public or section of the public on the basis of sexual orientation) and the Fair Employment and Treatment (Northern Ireland) Order 1998 (which covers discrimination on grounds of religious belief or political opinion).[38] There were a number of issues at stake:

(a) whether there had been a breach of the regulations;
(b) whether the regulations were compatible with the European Convention on Human Rights (ECHR) – more specifically the McArthurs' rights under Articles 9 and 10 (freedom of religion and freedom of expression);[39] and
(c) issues in relation to devolution (which are less relevant to the context of the discussion here).

At first instance the district judge found that there had been direct discrimination on the grounds of sexual orientation. There had also been direct discrimination on the grounds of Lee's religious belief or political opinion. The court confirmed that the

---

[35] ie, there was a distinction between status and message. Gorusch J referred to *Ashers*. However, these cases are arguably not directly comparable: in *Ashers* the message was distinct from the goods (in that the cake could have been sold without the message) – in *Creative* it was accepted the goods (the website) and message were, in essence inseparable.

[36] www.whitehouse.gov/briefing-room/statements-releases/2023/06/30/statement-from-president-joe-biden-on-supreme-court-decision-in-303-creative-llc-v-elenis/.

[37] Note: same sex marriages were not yet allowed in Northern Ireland at this time.

[38] Equality Act 2010, s 10 (England and Wales) protects religion or belief and belief includes any philosophical belief; a lack of belief is also a protected characteristic. Political opinion is only protected if it comes within the definition of philosophical belief.

[39] Human Rights Act, s 3 requires primary and secondary legislation to be interpreted in a way that is so far as is possible, is compatible with ECHR rights. Section 6 provides that it is unlawful for public authorities to act in a way which is incompatible with a Convention right.

pleaded legislation was compatible with the defendants' rights under Articles 9 and 10. The limitation to the McArthurs' rights was necessary and proportionate in the commercial sphere.[40] The defendants appealed to the Court of Appeal of Northern Ireland on the basis they would have (and indeed had) provided other goods to Lee and any customer regardless of their sexual orientation, but anyone ordering a cake with this message would have been refused. They had a right to live their lives and pursue their trade consistently with their conscience and religious identity. The Court of Appeal found however that there had been associative direct discrimination against Lee.[41] Furthermore there was no compelled speech and therefore no breach of Article 10 by requiring the cake to be supplied.[42] Through a process of appeals, complicated by the devolution issues, the case finally reached the UK Supreme Court.

The question for the Court was whether there had been unlawful discrimination in refusal to supply the cake, and if so, was the refusal nevertheless protected under Articles 9 and 10 of the ECHR. The Supreme Court unanimously held that there was no breach of the relevant regulations and that there was no less favourable treatment due to sexual orientation. The rationale for the decision was that the bakery's objection was to the message on the cake not the provision of the cake itself. Anyone ordering a cake with this message would have been refused and the refusal was not on the basis of the customer's protected characteristic; there was therefore no breach of the Equality Act (Sexual Orientation) Regulations (Northern Ireland) Order 1998. Separately, although there was potential for Lee to have been discriminated against for his political opinion, as here there was a closer association with the 'man and the message', the Court also found that, when engaging the Article 9 and 10 rights of the bakers, and on balancing competing rights of the parties, the bakers could not be compelled to express a message with which they disagreed unless there was justification for doing so. There was not the requisite justification here. In the judgment the Supreme Court referred to *Masterpiece*. The message they took from that decision was that there is a difference between refusing to provide a cake because of the message it conveys, whoever orders it, and refusing to provide a cake to a specific customer because of their protected characteristics.

Lee took his case to the European Court of Human Rights. He claimed that the UK Supreme Court failed to give appropriate weight to his rights under the Convention, namely Articles 8–10 and 14 and that the Court's approach was not 'proportionate'. His application was denied in January 2022 on the basis he had failed to exhaust all domestic remedies in relation to such a complaint as he did not invoke these rights during the domestic proceedings.[43] The ECtHR stated

---

[40] *Lee v Ashers Baking Company Ltd* [2015] NICty 2; [2015] 5 WLUK 483.
[41] By virtue of his association with the homosexual and bisexual community *Lee* [2016] NICA 39; [2016] 12 WLUK 629 [58]. The question here is, broadly, whether the action is so closely related to the protected ground (cannot be disassociated from it) that it in essence is action taken on the basis of the protected characteristic.
[42] ibid [67].
[43] Whilst Lee's rights may have been discussed in substance, the problem was that his specific rights under the convention were not balanced directly against the McArthurs' Convention rights – rather the balance he advanced at the time was against the specific rights granted under the national discrimination legislation.

> Given the heightened sensitivity of the balancing exercise in the particular national context, the domestic courts were better placed than [the European Court] to strike the balance between the competing Convention rights of the applicant, on the one hand, and the McArthurs, on the other ....[44]

Needless to say, this has drawn condemnation as a denial of rights based on a technicality, and that it leaves uncertainty.[45] There has even been talk of a fresh case being brought back to the domestic courts.[46]

III. DEVELOPMENT OF CONSUMER PROTECTION ACROSS THE ATLANTIC

Consumer law has been described as 'an instrumental form of law, organised around achieving the goals of efficient and fair consumer markets'.[47] Whilst rights based in common law still may have relevance, the development of consumer law tends to be identified with market behaviours, and as primarily framed in regulatory initiatives.[48] Consumer protection has long been a key policy initiative across the Atlantic. Beyond ensuring product safety,[49] rights to be treated fairly and not exploited are key. Regulation in this respect, however, is based in the competitive market agenda with rights of choice based in confident and empowered consumers (in the sense of rational decision-making). Protection of the consumer against detriment has been primarily equated with transparency and consumer autonomy, promoting entrepreneurism of the self[50] and 'enablement' of consumers.[51] US President Biden's Executive Order in July 2021 states 'A fair, open, and competitive marketplace has long been a cornerstone of the American economy … for consumers, it means more choices, better service, and lower prices.'[52] In the UK, the consumer is viewed by the current government as the 'focus of the competitive market'.[53]

US consumer protection is based in both federal and state laws. Protection has been seen as providing a bridge between free enterprise and the public's stake in society.[54]

---

[44] *Lee v United Kingdom* App no 18860/19 [2022] IRLR 371 (ECtHR, 7 December 2021) [76].
[45] See, eg, Stonewall and The Rainbow Project statements, bbc.co.uk/news/uk-northern-ireland-59882444 (accessed 22 January 2022).
[46] www.bbc.co.uk/news/uk-northern-ireland-59882444 (accessed 6 May 2022).
[47] I Ramsay, 'Consumer Law, Regulatory Capitalism and the New Learning in Regulation' (2006) 28 *Sydney Law Review* 9, 9.
[48] I Ramsay, *Consumer Law and Policy*, 3rd edn (Oxford, Hart Publishing, 2012) 1.
[49] For comparative analysis of product liability law see G Howells and DG Owen, 'Products Liability in America and Europe' in G Howells and others (eds), *Handbook of Research on International Consumer Law* (Cheltenham, Edward Elgar, 2010).
[50] D Marron, *Consumer Credit in the United States: A Sociological Perspective from the 19th Century to the Present* (Basingstoke, Palgrave Macmillan, 2009) 72.
[51] See, eg, Department for Business Energy and Industrial Strategy, *Modernising Consumer Markets* (Green Paper, Cm 9595, 2018).
[52] Presidential Executive Order on Promoting Competition in the American Economy (9 July 2021). www.whitehouse.gov/briefing-room/presidential-actions/2021/07/09/executive-order-on-promoting-competition-in-the-american-economy/ (accessed 21 January 2022).
[53] Department for Business Energy and Industrial Strategy ('BEIS') 'Reforming Competition and Consumer Policy Driving Growth and Delivering Competitive Markets that Work for Consumers' (CP488 2021) 11.
[54] L Cohen, 'The New Deal State and the Making of Citizen Consumers' in S Strasser, C McGovern and M Just (eds), *Getting and Spending European and American Consumer Societies in the Twentieth Century* (Cambridge, CUP, 1998) 115.

Even before the Great Depression and the pursuant New Deal, a point at which the consumer started being more of a focus,[55] 'consumer society' already existed,[56] matured within the context of mass production and consumption.[57] Although the New Deal has been criticised for being relatively ineffective in relation to the championing of consumer interests, the goal of increasing purchasing power together with increasing pressure from consumer groups precipitated federal interest in consumer protections.[58] It was at this time that consumer oriented policies and consumer interest agencies started to appear with a new interest in legislative intervention.[59] The first 'federal drive' for consumer protection properly emerged with President Kennedy's Consumer Bill of Rights in 1962,[60] continuing with the Johnson administration.[61]

Writers, such as Cohen and McGovern, give detailed accounts of the rise of the political relevance of the consumer and the notion of consumer citizenship.[62] Consumption was seen as a vehicle for 'agency and self-determination'.[63] It was 'entitlement to a decent standard of living',[64] the tangible expression of the 'American Way of life', and American nationality – of being a 'good' American.[65] Post WWII the economic importance and rights of the consumer became intimately associated with consumers' political and constitutional rights[66] and party politics. Yet inequalities existed, particularly in relation to race.[67] Cohen describes in detail, following WWII, the African American community's frustration with the discrimination they encountered, whether for example through exclusion from public accommodations, or higher prices through lack of enforcement of price controls.[68] This included discrimination in real estate sales and mortgage lending (including low-cost mortgages), manifested through the practice of redlining. The resultant push for equality demanded 'full citizenship in [the emergent] Consumer Republic'[69] and equality in rights to consume. Ostensibly, in subsequent years Democratic policies have equated

---

[55] ibid 114.

[56] C McGovern, 'Consumption and Citizenship in the United States 1900–1940' in Strasser et al (n 54) 37.

[57] K Mouré, 'Prosperity for All? Britain and Mass Consumption in Western Europe after World War II' in E Rappaport, ST Dawson and MJ Crowley (eds), *Consuming Behaviours: Identity, Politics and Pleasure in Twentieth-Century Britain* (Abingdon, Routledge, 2015) 218.

[58] McGovern (n 56) 55; Cohen (n 54) 120, 124.

[59] Cohen (n 54) 120, 123.

[60] SW Waller and others 'Consumer protection in the United States An Overview' [2011] *European Journal of Consumer Law* 1.

[61] With pressure from activists such as Ralph Nader.

[62] McGovern (n 56); Cohen details a developing and shifting 'consumer Republic' in L Cohen (ed), *A Consumer Republic: The Politics of Mass Consumption in Postwar America* (New York, Vintage, 2004).

[63] McGovern (n 56) 57.

[64] V de Grazia, 'Changing Consumption Regimes in Europe 1930-1970: Comparative Perspectives on the Distribution Problem' in Strasser et al (n 54) 61.

[65] Particularly pushed by advertisers in the 1930s-40s McGovern (n 56) 48, 50, 55, 57.

[66] Cohen (n 62) 111, 112.

[67] Also gender, delegitimising 'the civic authority women had gained during WWII, ibid 135.

[68] Cohen (n 62) 87–89; David Caplovitz's study of low-income families in New York in the 1960s, highlighted the cost of participation for these families (many being black or Puerto Rican), through higher prices and predatory practices – see *The Poor Pay More: Consumer Practices of Low-Income Families* (Free Press New York, 1963). For discussion in the context of current policy see I Ramsay and T Williams 'Peering Forward 10 Years After: International Policy and Consumer Credit Regulation' (2020) 43 *Journal of Consumer Policy* 209, 219–220.

[69] Cohen (n 62) 174, 200–27. For the full discussion see 83–100, ch 4, 201–40.

consumer protection and access to markets with social equality and defence against exploitation, unfairness and discrimination,[70] whilst Republican discourse has primarily championed de-regulation, and autonomy.[71] This political partisanship is observable in *Masterpiece* itself: with visible Republican support for Phillips and Democrat support for the CCRC decision.[72]

There is a wide basis to legal rules in the US that underpin consumer protection in fairness and market practices, but essentially it is decentralised with each state having some form of consumer protection law that deals with unfair and deceptive practices, including provision for enforcement and remedies.[73] Many state laws mirror, at least to some extent, Federal laws on these issues. The Uniform Commercial Code provides a set of rules for sale of goods covering the formation of the contract, unconscionability and implied terms of merchantability and fitness for purpose. The Code is not enforceable Federal law but again most states have adopted some form of it into their own legal systems.[74] The government agency with the primary task of ensuring consumer protection outside financial services is the Federal Trade Commission (FTC). Its regulatory supervisory and enforcement remit covers unfair competitive practices and deception/abuse of consumers.[75] Enforcement of state laws is by the state's Attorney General.[76]

In the UK the position is a little less complicated although protections are delivered across a number of regulatory instruments. Much current consumer legislation is based on, or transposes EU Directives. Following Brexit this, mainly, will remain as 'retained EU law' (unless there is repeal or reform).[77] Future planned EU consumer protection regulation will not impact UK law, unless the UK Government decides to introduce similar national provisions.[78] Basic consumer rights in relation to the purchase of goods and services and unfair terms are now contained in the Consumer Rights Act 2015. Other statutory regulations deal with general unfair

---

[70] Eg, during the Clinton era with espousal of 'Third Way' political philosophy, also Obama's fight on wealth and income inequality – S Brown, *Regulation of Consumer Credit: A Transatlantic Perspective* (Cheltenham, Edward Elgar, 2019) 32; in contrast with Trump's policies, Biden's commitment to the Consumer Financial Protection Bureau (CFPB) www.nbcnews.com/politics/white-house/cop-beat-again-biden-looks-reassert-consumer-watchdog-agency-sidelined-n1261586 (accessed 24 January 2022).

[71] See, eg, Reagan and Bush administrations, Brown (n 70) 32; *cf* Keller and Kelly who argue there is evidence financial regulatory policy has, in fact converged since the 1980s in E Keller and NJ Kelly 'Partisan Politics, Financial Deregulation, and the New Gilded Age' (2015) 68 *Political Research Quarterly* 428.

[72] Via support from Member of Congress in filed amicus briefs. Similar things are happening in other cases.

[73] Waller (n 60) 17–20. Pre-emption of state law may however apply. There are FTC cooling off rules for certain contracts, repeated in many states.

[74] See also the Magnuson Moss Warranty Federal Trade Commission Improvements Act 1975, 15 USC §§2301-2312 (Supp. 1975) as amended.

[75] www.ftc.gov/enforcement/statutes/federal-trade-commission-act (accessed 22 January 2022).

[76] Together with some federal laws, in collaboration with federal consumer protection agencies Brown (n 70) 102; National Association of Attorneys General 'Interjurisdictional Collaboration' www.naag.org/issues/consumer-protection/interjurisdictional-collaboration/ (accessed 26 October 2022).

[77] European Withdrawal Act 2018, ss 2–4.

[78] For an informative overview see L Conway, *Brexit: UK consumer protection law* (House of Commons Library Briefing Paper 9126, 21 May 2021).

and misleading practices and cooling off periods.[79] The supervisory authority is the Competition and Markets Authority (CMA) which, like the FTC, is an independent agency that covers competition and consumer issues.[80] The regulator of financial services is the Financial Conduct Authority (FCA), its equivalent, to most intents and purposes, in the US being the Consumer Financial Protection Bureau (CFPB). Current strategic goals of the CMA include protecting consumers from unfair behaviour, and the vulnerable from breaches of competition and consumer law.[81] The FCA's general vision is 'a well-functioning market that works for consumers'.[82] This includes working towards protection of the vulnerable, inclusion and fairness.

UK development of targeted consumer protection legislation began in earnest the 1960s–70s following the Molony and Crowther Committee Reports, with concerns based in consumer/supplier inequality and unfair practices.[83] This, however, was not the beginning of interest in the 'consumer'. During the inter war years the working classes in the UK were 'embraced as integral to mass consumption',[84] – by the 1950s there was mass consumption of manufactured goods in Europe.[85] Whilst the 'consumer citizen' is a concept that developed from the early 1900s,[86] it was during the 1930s and 1940s that a Conservative party vision created the consumer citizen as, collectively, a national tool of support for the Empire, 'whose first duty was to the nation'.[87] However in the 1950s a more individualised notion of the consumer took hold in the political imagination of both Labour and Conservative thought, opening the way for a 'competitive model of consumption', so marginalising the co-operative movement which underpinned the notion of the consumer (particularly working class consumers) as an organised body.[88] This continued through the Thatcher years which embraced neoliberal, de-regulatory initiatives and New Labour with 'their espousal of the Third Way'.[89] Ramsay has pointed to responsibilisation of consumers in more recent UK consumer strategy, where consumers are framed as 'citizen consumers' – a regulatory subject within a 'decentered model of regulation 'crucial to achieving national goals'.[90] This is the consumer

---

[79] The Consumer Contracts (Information, Cancellation and Additional Charges) Regulations 2013, SI 2013/3134; Consumer Protection Amendment Regulations 2014, SI 2014/870; Consumer Protection from Unfair Trading Regulations 2008, SI 2008/1277.
[80] Small Business, Enterprise and Employment Act 2015, s 37.
[81] CMA 'Competition and Markets Authority Action Plan 2021-22' (2021, CMA 137) 11–12.
[82] FCA 'FCA Mission: Approach to Consumers' (FCA 2018). See also FCA 'Our Strategy 2022-2025' (FCA 2022).
[83] G Borrie, *The Development of Consumer Law and Policy – Bold Spirits and Timorous Souls* (Stevens, 1984); Micklitz (n 15) 7.
[84] ST Dawson, 'Designing Consumer Society: Citizens and Housing Plans during World War II' in Rappaport (n 57) 180.
[85] ibid 190; Mouré (n 57) 217.
[86] J Davies, 'Entrenchment of New Governance in Consumer Policy Formulation: A Platform for European Consumer Citizenship Practice? (2009) 32 *Journal of Consumer Policy* 245.
[87] E Rappaport, 'Drink Empire Tea: Gender, Conservative Politics and Imperial Consumerism in Inter-war Britain' in Rappaport (n 57) 142.
[88] P Gurney, 'A House Divided: The Organized Consumer and the British Labour Party, 1945–60' in Rappaport (n 57) 238, 247.
[89] P Gurney, *The Making of Consumer Culture in Modern Britain* (London, Bloomsbury Publishing, 2017).
[90] Ramsay (n 47) 13.

as the 'guardian of the public interest',[91] involved in developing consumer policy.[92] Subsequent Conservative governments, whilst increasingly recognising vulnerability as a headline in consumer detriment, still base policy in the empowered and confident consumer, providing the individual with competition and informed choice.[93]

The characterisation therefore of 'consumer as citizen' has gained prominence, marking the role of the consumer as something beyond a simple participant in markets as a purchaser of goods and services.[94] Certainly in the UK the perception of the consumer has moved beyond the 'consumer as shopper' to a 'political subject' encompassing policy areas of, for example, healthcare and social services.[95] The consumer is seen as having an inherent influence on society, supporting both the pursuit of choice and collective wellbeing.[96] In the US, as Cohen sets out in describing the link between consumer and democratic citizen by Roosevelt; being a consumer covers not only being an advocate for the general good, and a participator in mass consumption, but also a need to be protected against exploitation.[97] Exploitation is linked with vulnerability and exclusion.[98] Discussions around exclusion have tended to concentrate on social exclusion as a by-product of financial exclusion, particularly in the US[99] but there are other manifestations beyond the financial context.[100] As Ramsay has argued 'the role of consumer policy in achieving equitable goals is illuminated by the modern concept of social exclusion'.[101] It is, of course, exclusion that was the primary issue in *Masterpiece* and *Ashers*.

IV. THE SIGNIFICANCE OF MASTERPIECE AND ASHERS

An initial comparison of these two cases, and their impact, speak to the difficulties in balancing parties' legal rights, whether national, state or constitutional.[102]

---

[91] F Trentmann, 'Knowing Consumers Histories Identities Practices: An Introduction' in F Trentmann (ed), *The Making of the Consumer: Knowledge Power and Identity in the Modern World* (Oxford, Berg, 2006) 7, 11.

[92] M Coppack, F Jackson and J Tallack, 'Involving consumer in the development of regulatory policy' (UKRN 2014) www.ukrn.org.uk/wp-content/uploads/2018/06/20140728-InvolvingConsumersInRegPolicy.pdf (accessed 22 January 2022).

[93] Eg, Department for Business Innovation and Skills 'Enhancing consumer confidence by clarifying consumer law: Consultation on the supply of goods, services and digital content' (URN 12/937 2012).

[94] From early as the 18th century – N McKendrick, J Brewer and JH Plumb, *Birth of a Consumer Society* (Edward Everett Root. 1982) 1.

[95] Trentmann (n 91) 11.

[96] M Eagleton-Pierce, 'Historicising the NeoLiberal Spirit of Capitalism' in S Springer, K Birch and J Levy (eds), *The Handbook of Neoliberalism* (Abingdon, Routledge, 2016); F Trentmann, 'Introduction' in F Trentmann (ed), *The Oxford Handbook of the History of Consumption* (Oxford, OUP, 2012) 4–5.

[97] Cohen (n 54) 124.

[98] CMA 'Competition and Markets Authority Annual Plan 2018-19' (CMA 75 2018) [2.21]–[2.24].

[99] See MN Browne and others, 'Protecting Consumers from Themselves: Consumer Law and the Vulnerable Consumer' (2015) 63 *Drake Law Review* 157. Protection of the economically vulnerable has been a primary aim of the CFPB. The FTC has also referenced vulnerable consumers in recent policy – FTC 'Annual Highlights' (2020) www.ftc.gov/reports/annual-highlights-2020 (accessed 22 January 2022).

[100] Eg, from digital markets BEIS (n 51) and in relation to energy – Ofgem 'Consumer Vulnerability Strategy' (OFG 1161, Ofgem 2019).

[101] Ramsay (n 47) 29.

[102] The balance in the US on the basis of state regulation and constitutional rights, in the UK on the basis of equality legislation and the ECHR.

In finer points the cases diverge: whilst *Ashers* involved an express message on a cake, *Masterpiece* involved an implicit one. In the latter, the baker refused to supply the product itself because of what it represented; in the former the bakers refused to supply a product because of the message on it, rather than the product itself. Yet in essence the cases are very similar in terms of principle in one important respect: the importance of safeguarding a right to access to goods and services. Rights of consumers to be treated fairly encompass not only being treated with respect and dignity in the provision of goods and services but also access to those goods and services. Whilst the decisions went against the consumers in both cases, this essential principle was articulated within the judgments. In *Masterpiece* Justice Kennedy – in writing for the majority – said 'these disputes must be resolved with tolerance, without undue disrespect to sincere religious beliefs, and without subjecting homosexual persons to indignities when they seek goods and services in an open market'.[103] In the words of Lady Hale in *Ashers*, 'it is deeply humiliating, and an affront to human dignity, to deny someone a service because of that person's race, gender, disability, sexual orientation or any of the other protected personal characteristics' – although, according to the court, such denial had not occurred here.[104]

Certainly, protection against inequality has long played a part in the creation and interpretation of rules and principles of consumer protection law and its reform.[105] Unfair commercial practices regulation, and control of unfair terms, including via the common law[106] are directed towards addressing inequality in bargaining power and ensuring all consumers are treated fairly; access on fair terms to goods and services is seen as key.[107] However the extent to which the underlying ethos of consumer protection regulatory initiatives assists with wider, more pervasive inequalities which may manifest in consumer markets, is debatable. Whilst, unless the supplier has a monopoly,[108] denial is not to the market as a whole, denial of access to goods and services even by one supplier does not just make the bargaining power of the consumer unequal, it removes it altogether in relation to that particular transactional relationship. This demonstrates what Ramsay terms the 'unavoidable conflict between freedoms embedded in the legal construct of freedom of contract'.[109] Whilst freedom of contract is identified with individuals' liberty to contract on whatever terms they wish, and the corresponding freedom *to* contract, it also encompasses the freedom *not* to contract (freedom from contract).[110] Discrimination by a supplier illustrates this conflict.[111]

---

[103] (n 1) 1732.

[104] (n 2) [35].

[105] Indeed, consumer law originally developed from the problems of unequal bargaining power: Ramsay (n 47) 9.

[106] Eg, unconscionability and good faith.

[107] See CMA (n 99); CFPB 'Kraninger Marks Second Year as Director of the Consumer Financial Protection Bureau' (Press Release, December, 2020) www.consumerfinance.gov/about-us/newsroom/kraninger-marks-second-year-director-consumer-financial-protection-bureau/ (accessed 22 January 2022).

[108] The Colorado Court of Appeals Tenth Circuit in fact held this was the case in relation to the creation of a wedding website in *Creative* 6F.4th 1160 (10th Circ 2021), 1179–1180.

[109] I Ramsay, 'Productive Disintegration and the Law of Contract' (2004) *Wisconsin Law Review* 495, 503–04 discussing T Rakoff, 'Is Freedom from Contract Necessarily a Libertarian Freedom?' (2004) *Wisconsin Law Review* 477.

[110] Ramsay (n 109) 501–03.

[111] ibid drawing on the example of the Canadian case of *Christie v York Corp* [1940] SCR 139 1939 CanLII 39 (SCC) (racial discrimination by a tavern owner).

The regulatory aspects of consumer law, narrowly conceived, are primarily driven by neoliberal concerns of the competitive market. In such context, consumer rights are framed in terms of economic choice and economic freedoms, rather than moral questions of unacceptable social exclusion. As the UK CMA itself states, whilst it is committed to ensuring access and fairness in markets 'addressing inequality in society is a policy matter for government and politicians and outside our statutory remit'.[112] Laws based in equality create exception to freedoms in the contractual context as there is recognised social value in protection.[113] The *Masterpiece* and *Ashers* cases concern access for a specific section of the community, from a moral perspective, where proscriptive rules that attach to the transactional relationship go beyond contractual rights and remedies to questions of civil and political rights. This is why they are landmark cases.

Consumer protection principles in Europe have been distinguished as 'pre-interventionist, interventionist and post-interventionist'.[114] Discrimination law as a form of consumer law reflects this interventionist approach. Macneil has argued that law supports the 'accomplishment of co-operation'[115] and whilst his theory primarily deals with the process of engagement and contracting rather than whether the engagement takes place at all, the aim of discrimination laws reflect this. They require a degree of co-operation, establishing external norms and values which 'foster co-operation by reducing the choice of the recalcitrant party'.[116] Ensuring a fair free market for consumers is the aim of both UK and US consumer policy, therefore this co-operation from suppliers is key. Here however is where the particular difficulties arise – the basis upon which non-co-operation could be justified. In the recent UK employment case of *Forstater v CGD Europe*[117] the court explained a belief is capable of protection under Article 9 of the ECHR if it does not seek to destroy the rights of others.[118] On this basis it is arguable that the beliefs of the bakers in *Ashers* and *Masterpiece* deserved the weight they were given. Whilst the refusal to provide the services/goods did in fact seek to destroy the availability of choice for the customer, whether this amounted to destruction of rights altogether, that is, those of access, is a different matter.[119]

The meaning of a free market in this context engages questions of commercial morality beyond dishonesty and exploitation, to those of 'commercial conscience'.[120] The concept of commercial conscience is controversial. Markets have been described

---

[112] CMA 'Competition and Markets Authority Annual Plan 2019/20' (CMA 97 2019) [2.22].
[113] N Busby 'Lee v Ashers Baking Company' [2019] *Emp LB* 149, 2–5.
[114] N Reich, 'Diverse Approaches to Consumer Protection Philosophy' (1992) 14 *Journal of Consumer Policy* 257, 267–68.
[115] D Campbell 'The Social Theory of Relational Contract Macneil as the Modern Proudhon' (1990) 18 *International Journal of the Sociology of Law* 75, 79.
[116] ibid. Macneil here was specifically signposting trade custom ie, norms/values beyond the law.
[117] *Forstater v CGD Europe* [2022] ICR 1 [79]; [2021] IRLR 706.
[118] Belief would only be excluded if the expression would be akin to Nazism or totalitarianism.
[119] McCrudden is dismissive of possible third-party effects (n 3) 266 – with few reports of denial of service and no monopoly Lee could have easily got (and indeed did) the cake elsewhere.
[120] D Romney, 'Ramifications of the 'gay cake' case' (2019) *Counsel Magazine*. www.counselmagazine.co.uk/articles/ramifications-of-the-gay-cake-case (accessed 22 January 2022).

as 'conscience free zones' – beyond the basic question of fairness 'morality has no place'.[121] Suppliers act in self-interest and only to maximise profits,[122] therefore business cannot claim conscience rights. Sepinwall sees this as far too simplistic.[123] She is not alone in arguing markets are not amoral,[124] and certainly it is more difficult to separate the small business owner from their business, when considering belief and personal freedoms.

The consumer may have power to influence policy and engage in 'consumer citizenship practice',[125] as discussed above. However, the consumer is not the only 'citizen'. Suppliers are also participants. However, whilst the law recognises they, as individuals, also have rights, they may have to accept compromise as the 'price of citizenship';[126] '[a] multicultural, pluralistic society, ... demands no less'.[127] Indeed Crowley argues this is the guidance that can be taken from the *Masterpiece* decision,[128] although the controversial SCOTUS decision in *Creative* has arguably moved the US position away from such compromise. Across the Atlantic the law is clear: discrimination on the basis of a protected characteristic is not allowed in the provision of goods and services.[129] This in essence confirms rights of access to these consumers. What, it is argued, that has been left unclear by the judgments of *Ashers* and *Masterpiece*, and indeed *Creative*, is what constitutes discrimination and on what basis, if at all, exemptions can or should apply.[130]

The *Masterpiece* and *Ashers* cases have been expensive, both in monetary terms and personally.[131] Yet the significance of these challenges cannot be over-stated, and the SCOTUS decision in *Creative* demonstrates the partisan politics, particularly in the US that these challenges attract. These cases are confronting extremely important questions that reflect how we live and interact as a community from moral and legal standpoints, which continue to be debated and tested in the courts (certainly in the US) both in consumer markets and beyond. They expose a struggle between individualism and communalism, consumer welfarism and market individualism, politics, power and morality. Albeit unsuccessful from the claimants' perspective, *Masterpiece*

---

[121] A Sepinwall, 'Conscience in Commerce: Conceptualising Discrimination in Public Accommodations' (2021) 53 *Connecticut Law Review* 1, 10.

[122] ibid 15. *Cf* A Walsh and A Lynch, 'Can Individual Morality and Commercial Life Be Reconciled?' (2004) 16 *Journal of Interdisciplinary Studies* 80.

[123] Sepinwall (n 121) 18 although she argues the logic of anti-discrimination law does not allow for exemption.

[124] Walsh (n 122).

[125] Davies (n 86). *Cf* M Hilton, 'The Death of a Consumer Society' (2008) 18 *Transactions of the RHS* 211.

[126] *Elane* (n 27) [92] (Judge Richard Bosson).

[127] ibid [91].

[128] Crowley (n 8).

[129] Note-in relation to sexual orientation and gender identity legislation is only at state level, and not in all states.

[130] Eg, R Reyes, 'Masterpiece Cake Shop and Ashers Baking Company: A Comparative Analysis of Constitutional Confections' (2020) XVI *Stanford Journal Of Civil Rights and Civil Liberties* 113, 114; ML Movsesian 'Masterpiece Cakeshop and the Future of Religious Freedom' (2019) 42 *Harvard Journal of Law and Public Policy* 3, 711.

[131] Although the parties have been supported: Ashers by the Christian Institute, Lee by the Equality Commission for Northern Ireland, Phillips by The Alliance Defending Freedom.

and *Ashers* also highlight the fact that 'consumer law' encompasses far more than specific consumer statutes, and that consumer's access to goods is enshrined in other important statutory mechanisms beyond 'traditional' consumer protection laws. Some see the law as 'imperfect', exposed by the dilemmas created in *Masterpiece* and by correlation *Ashers*.[132] If consumer protection law is based in purely competitive free market thinking, this same argument of imperfection has some force – rights of access as 'choice' is not being delivered to all. As Sunstein argues, '[competitive] markets will not cure discrimination'.[133] A combined legislative approach however may provide some relief.

V. CONCLUSION

Across the Atlantic, consumer protection legislation, narrowly conceived, has aimed to deliver protection through 'transparency', increased consumer rationality,[134] individual responsibility and consumer empowerment in protecting consumers in their relationships with other market participants. This, however, is only one aspect of legal protection for the consumer, based, as it is, in economic choice and freedoms rather than the moral question of unacceptable social exclusion. Real consumer empowerment goes beyond simply a tool for a consumer for rational choice and self-interest but should also represent positive rights to access to goods and services as a form of social justice.[135] Indeed the idea that consumer rights can be conflated with moral, civil and social rights is nothing new.[136] This is where discrimination law is vital.

Masterpiece and *Ashers* have arisen in the context of discrimination law, yet the cases show that whilst legislation labelled as 'consumer' protects against unfairness in harmful terms and practices regarding the consumer trader relationship, it does not safeguard against exclusion from the relationship altogether. In contrast anti-discrimination rules are concerned with the unfairness of denial of access altogether. As Ramsay says, 'a central role of consumer law is to affect the norms of the marketplace'.[137] The cases highlight the importance of protection against discrimination in public accommodation, and how constitutional rights and human rights should be balanced in this context. Across the Atlantic the cases demonstrate the social and communal significance of consumer access to goods and services, more particularly in the context of LGBTQ+ rights. They have highlighted awareness of the importance of human dignity within consumer markets.[138] Hilton has observed that individual

---

[132] Crowley (n 8) 333 in relation to *Masterpiece*.
[133] CR Sunstein, *Free Markets and Social Justice* (Oxford, OUP, 1997) ch 6.
[134] Reich (n 114) 272.
[135] In the context of the EU, it is argued this already an enforceable right vis-à-vis services of general economic interest -Micklitz (n 15) 25.
[136] For detailed discussion see I Benohr and H-W Micklitz, 'Consumer Protection and Human Rights' in Howells (n 49).
[137] Ramsay (n 47) 35.
[138] Crowley (n 8) 338.

choice over access has become the 'benchmark' to measuring the success of consumer society – but this can change.[139] The use of anti-discrimination and human rights legal frameworks shows it is possible to affect change for the better for *all* consumers. What the cases of *Masterpiece* and *Ashers* demonstrate however is that, in balancing competing rights, the courts have a difficult task in navigating application of the law, in order to affect that change.

---

[139] Hilton (n 125) 234.

21
Small Claims, Big Challenges: *Merricks v Mastercard*

SIMONE DEGELING, JODI GARDNER AND JOSH McGEECHAN

I. INTRODUCTION

As THIS COLLECTION highlights, laws designed and implemented to protect consumers cover a wide variety of legal areas. These areas clearly go beyond any view of consumer law that limits its ambit to 'consumer protection statutes'.[1] However, whilst the substantive legal issues raised in consumer cases may vary significantly, such cases are characterised by underlying practical and relational similarities. Consumers in general have inherent power and resource imbalances when dealing with businesses, which makes vindicating their legal rights difficult. Consumers may be unable to afford to commence an action against an offending business or the value of their claim may be relatively insignificant when compared to the cost of litigation. Moreover, consumers face barriers in the non-financial burdens of the carriage of the litigation, the need to make weighty legal and financial decisions and their potential unfamiliarity with the legal system and legal processes. Substantive consumer law rights are thus only valuable to the extent that the legal system facilitates the enforcement of those rights against businesses. One of the means by which these difficulties may be overcome is via collective civil procedures. This chapter briefly considers the pathway to consumer redress provided by participation in collective proceedings brought before the Competitions Appeal Tribunal (CAT) under section 47B of the Competition Act and the initial, albeit as yet incomplete, experience of that procedure in *Walter Hugh Merricks CBE v Mastercard* (*Merricks*).

As a general matter, collective civil procedures permit the claims of many to be aggregated and brought by a representative on behalf of all. These procedures offer the promise of a more financially viable avenue of redress for consumers to commence and conduct their claim. Collective procedures also have the advantage of potentially reducing the cost of litigation overall for both consumers and businesses by eliminating the need to try the same issue in separate claims. There are also other potential benefits to the businesses in question, as they obtain res judicata on the common

---

[1] See ch 1 in this volume.

questions before the decision maker and therefore obtain protection from the risk of multiple suits and inconsistent findings. Finally, there are correlative benefits to the justice system in being saved court time and other resources. Given it has only recently been introduced, there is little evidence of the efficacy of the CAT collective procedure on which we focus. Nonetheless, in this chapter we highlight some of the potential benefits and risks of that procedure.

This chapter uses *Merricks* as a focus for discussion. At the time of writing, there has been no substantive hearing of the legal merits and the proceedings have not concluded via settlement or judgment. Regardless, the case is clearly landmark in the certification of the claim via the issuing of a Collective Proceedings Order (CPO) on 18 May 2022[2] following the UKSC decision to remit certification back to the CAT, the number of consumers potentially bound by the proceeding and the overall legal significance of the case. As discussed below, *Merricks* also reaffirms the role of competition law to enhance consumer welfare and protect consumer rights and highlights the difficulties of court-based litigation for small value claims and the complexities of collective actions for rights enforcement.

II. MERRICKS V MASTERCARD – FACTS AND HISTORY

This second section outlines *Merricks*, highlighting the background, facts and history of the case. In the development of this section, we had the benefit of discussing the case with the class representative, Walter Merricks, and thank him for his insight into these issues.

A. Facts of the Case

Merricks concerns a 'gargantuan'[3] class action brought against Mastercard Incorporated, Mastercard International Incorporated and MasterCard Europe S.P.R.L (collectively 'Mastercard'). The claim is estimated to be on behalf of 46.2 million individuals in the UK for losses valued at circa £14 billion.[4] The alleged losses arise from customers being overcharged for goods and services from merchants who participated in the Mastercard payment scheme.

Mastercard payments are ubiquitous in consumer transactions. Consumers' banks issue Mastercard cards which permit consumers to purchase goods and services from merchants. Mastercard set a fee to be paid by the merchant's bank to the consumer's bank for each transaction paid by the use of a Mastercard card, the 'multilateral interchange fee' (MIF), which applied unless otherwise agreed. This fee was debited

---

[2] CPO made by Mr Justice Roth on 18 May 2022, Case No 1266/7/7/16.
[3] *Walter Hugh Merricks CBE v Mastercard and others* [2020] UKSC 51, [2021] 3 All ER 285 ('*Merricks*') at [175].
[4] Although this figure is likely to be an over-estimate – see *Walter Hugh Merricks CBE v Mastercard Incorporated Mastercard International Incorporated and Mastercard Europe SPRL* [2017] CAT 16, [2017] 5 CMLR 16 ('CAT Decision') at [2].

from the payment made by the consumer's bank to the merchant's bank for each purchase. The setting of the MIF has been (and continues to be) the subject of extensive litigation.[5] In 2007 the European Commission found that the intra-EEA MIF set by Mastercard breached Article 101 of the Treaty on the Function of the European Union (TFEU).[6]

The Commission determined that setting the default MIF had the effect of 'inflating the base on which [merchants' banks had] set their lower merchant service charge ('MSC') charged to merchants, thereby restricting competition between [merchants' banks] to the detriment of merchants (and subsequent purchasers)'.[7] Importantly, the Commission stated:

> A further consequence of this restriction of price competition is that customers making purchases at merchants who accept payment cards are likely to have to bear some part of the cost of MasterCard's MIF irrespective of the form of payment that customers use. This is because depending on the competitive situation merchants may increase the price for all goods sold by a small margin rather than internalising the cost of them by a MIF.[8]

Setting the MIF was anti-competitive because it limited the pressure that merchants could exert on their banks to lower the MSC.[9] The interchange fee was passed on to merchants through the MSC by their banks. The question of who may have suffered a loss because of the interchange fees depends on how merchants respond to the imposition of the MSC. The CAT in *Sainsbury's Supermarkets Ltd v Mastercard*[10] noted four options available to a merchant to respond to the increased cost: (1) do nothing and suffer a corresponding reduction of profits; (2) reduce discretionary expenditure by, for example, reducing its marketing or advertising budget; (3) reduce its costs by negotiation with other suppliers; or (4) raise its prices and thereby pass on the costs

---

[5] A helpful summary of some of the relevant litigation is set out in [12] to [36] of *Sainsburys Supermarkets Ltd and others v MasterCard Incorporated and others; AAM v MasterCard; Sainsbury v Visa* [2018] EWCA Civ 1536, [2019] 1 All ER 903. The decision of the Court of Appeal was appealed to Supreme Court. The Supreme Court's decision was handed down on 17 June 2020 *Sainsbury's Supermarkets Ltd v Visa Europe Services LLC and others; Sainsbury's Supermarkets Ltd and others v Mastercard Incorporated and others* [2020] UKSC 24, [2020] Bus LR 1196.

[6] Decision C (2007) 6474 in Cases COMP/34.579 – MasterCard, COMP/36/518 – EuroCommerce, and COMP/38/580 – Commercial Cards ('Commission Decision'). Appeals against the Commission decision were dismissed by the General Court (Case T-111/08 *MasterCard and others v Commission* EU:T:2012:260) and by the Court of Justice (Case C-382/12P, EU:C:2014:2201) ('CJEU Decision').

[7] CAT Decision (n 4) at [13]. The Commission found that compared with other methods of operating the payments scheme, the MIF reduced price competition between merchants and acquiring banks by inflating the base on which acquiring banks set charges to merchants (at [408]–[410]).

[8] Commission decision at [411].

[9] '... As the Commission rightly points out, the judgment under appeal is not based on the premiss that high prices in themselves constitute an infringement of article 81(1) EC. On the contrary, as is apparent from the wording of para 143 of the judgment under appeal, high prices merely arise as the result of the MIF which limit the pressure which merchants could exert on acquiring banks, with a resulting reduction in competition between acquirers as regards the amount of the MSC' CJEU decision (n 6) at [195]. The Commission found that: '[t]he decisive question is whether in the absence of the MIF the prices acquirers charge to merchants would be lower. This is the case, because the price each individual bank could charge to merchants would be fully determined by competition rather than to a large extent by a collective decision among (or on behalf of) the banks' Commission Decision (n 6) at [448].

[10] *Sainsbury's Supermarkets Ltd v Mastercard* [2016] CAT 11, [2016] Comp AR 33.

to consumers.[11] It is only where the merchants adopt option 4 that consumers are harmed. Whether or not this occurred in Merricks is a question yet to be determined.[12]

Merricks, as the class representative, commenced proceedings to recover losses caused by merchants passing on the cost of the MSC to consumers through raising prices for goods and services. The class was defined to be individuals who had, between 22 May 1992 and 21 June 2008, purchased goods and services from businesses selling in the UK that accepted Mastercard cards.[13] The class was therefore not limited to consumers who had used Mastercard cards. Rather, it captured consumers who had purchased goods and services from merchants who had during the relevant period accepted Mastercard cards for payment.[14]

The proceedings commenced by Merricks were brought on a 'follow-on' basis. That is, the claim was based on the earlier decision of the European Commission that Mastercard had breached Article 101 of the TFEU.[15] At the time the Merricks proceeding was commenced, decisions of the European Commission were 'infringement decisions' for the purposes of sections 47A and 58A(2) of the Competition Act. The effect of those provisions were that persons could make a claim for damages in UK courts relying on decisions of the European Commission and the decisions of the European Commission were binding. The ability of consumers to bring 'follow-on' actions in respect of decisions of the European Commission issued after 1 January 2021 has been substantially altered following Brexit.[16]

The question for the Supreme Court in Merricks was whether these proceedings should have been certified by the CAT.

B. Background to Collective Proceedings Orders Through CAT

The UK Government's response to the consultation paper on Private Actions in Competition considered that a 'strong process of judicial certification' in relation to

---

[11] At [434] and [455] and referred to in the Supreme Court's decision in *Sainsbury's Supermarkets Ltd v Visa Europe Services LLC and others; Sainsbury's Supermarkets Ltd and others v Mastercard Incorporated and others* [2020] UKSC 24 at [205].

[12] This question is not only a decision for *Merricks*. Other proceedings have also commenced before the CAT in relation to the operation of the Mastercard payment scheme, including the extent to which MIF was passed on to consumers. In recognition of this connection, or potential connection, between proceedings, in *Dune Group Ltd v Mastercard Inc* [2022] CAT 14 (order 20) the tribunal ordered that the proceedings are to be tried by reference to a series of issues, including causation. In *Re the Merchant Interchange Fee Umbrella Proceedings* [2022] CAT 31 (order 61) further guidance was given on what evidence was required to be adduced by the parties in demonstrating that the MIF was or was not passed on.

[13] *Merricks* (n 3) at [125]. Class members are additionally required to have been aged 16 years or over and to have been resident in the UK for a continuous period of at least three months at the time of purchase.

[14] As discussed further below, the CPO was granted on both an opt-out and opt-in basis. Opt-out applies to those meeting the class description who were living in the UK on 6 September 2016. These class members are automatically included in the claim. However, if particular individuals desire not to join the class action, they must follow the specified steps to exclude themselves and opt-out by 2 March 2023. Correlatively, those meeting the class description who were living outside the UK on 6 September 2016 are not automatically included, but are able to join the class action by taking affirmative steps to opt-in by 2 March 2023.

[15] *Merricks* (no 3) at [13].

[16] See for example, the amendments of the Competition Act effected by the *Competition (Amendment etc) (EU Exit) Regulations* 2019 (SI 2019/93) and the guidance published by the Competition and Markets Authority concerning the Brexit transition period 'Guidance on the functions of the CMA after the end of the Transition Period' 1 December 2020 CMA125.].

collective proceedings (particularly opt-out proceedings) was important to protect against 'frivolous or unmeritorious cases being brought'.[17] Section 47B of the Competition Act provides for collective proceedings to be brought before the CAT. Before collective proceedings can be continued, the CAT must make a collective proceedings order (CPO).[18]

The CAT may make a CPO only

> if it considers that the person who brought the proceedings is such a person who, if the order were made, the [CAT] could authorise to act as the representative in those proceedings ... in respect of claims which are eligible for inclusion in collective proceedings.[19]

Claims are 'eligible for inclusion' if they satisfy two conditions: the CAT considers that the claims: (1) raise 'the same similar or related issues of fact or law'; and (2) are 'suitable to be brought in collective proceedings'.

Rule 79 of the Competition Appeal Tribunal Rules 2015 ('CAT Rules') provides that the CAT may certify claims as eligible for inclusion where the CAT is satisfied that the proceedings:

(i) are brought on behalf of an identifiable class of persons;
(ii) raise common issues; and
(iii) are suitable to be brought in collective proceedings.

Rule 79(2) provides that in determining whether claims are 'suitable' to be brought in collective proceedings the CAT 'shall take into account all matters it thinks fit' including a number of issues enumerated by the Rules. One of the factors specified to be considered by the CAT is 'whether the claims are suitable for an aggregate award of damages'. The certification procedure is a means of balancing the 'substantial legal advantages' conferred on plaintiffs by the collective proceedings regime and is designed to ensure that those advantages are only conferred in appropriate cases.[20] It is however clear from *Gutmann v South Western Trains Limited* that the CAT can consider the deterrent impact of litigation in determining whether the matter should be certified.[21]

C. Tribunal Decision

In the initial hearing, the CAT refused to make a CPO pursuant to section 47B(4) of the Competition Act for two reasons: (1) the claims were not suitable for an aggregate award of damages;[22] and (2) Merrick's proposal for the distribution of any aggregate

---

[17] See Department for Business Innovation & Skills *'Private Actions in Competition Law: A consultation on options for reform – government response'* January 2013 (publishing.service.gov.uk) at [5.52]–[5.55].
[18] Competition Act 1998, s 47B(4).
[19] ibid s 47B(5).
[20] *Merricks* (n 3) at [98]–[101].
[21] *Gutmann v South Western Trains Limited* [2021] CAT 31 at [177].
[22] Collective proceedings are within the exclusive jurisdiction of the CAT and are subject to the Competition Appeal Tribunal Rules 2015 (SI 2015/1648) ('Rules'). Rule 79 provides that the CAT may certify claims eligible for inclusion in collective proceedings where, having regard to all the circumstances, are, amongst other things, 'suitable to be brought in collective proceedings'. In determining whether claims

award did not respond to the compensatory principle.[23] In refusing to make a CPO, the CAT considered whether Merricks had put forward a

> sustainable methodology which can be applied in practice to calculate a sum which reflects the aggregate of individual claims for damages, and (2) a reasonable and practicable means for estimating the individual loss which can be used as the basis for distribution.[24]

The key issue for the claimants in *Merricks* to overcome was whether sufficient evidence could be obtained to allow them to reach an estimate weighted average of MIF that had been passed through to consumers. After considering the expert report provided on behalf of the claimants, the CAT concluded that although the process for determining the weighted average pass-through was methodologically sound, there was insufficient data for the methodology to be applied without an unacceptable risk of error. Accordingly, the CAT was not satisfied that the claims were suitable for an aggregate award of damages.[25] The CAT further held that the claims were unsuitable for certification because the method for distribution of the aggregate award of damages proposed by Merricks was not connected to the compensatory principle that claimants should be put in the position they would have been but for the breach.[26]

D. Court of Appeal

The CAT determination was appealed to the Court of Appeal, which allowed the appeal and made a CPO. Following a discussion of relevant Canadian authorities[27] the Court of Appeal held that the CAT had 'demanded too much' at the certification stage.[28]

The Court held that, at the certification stage, the question for the CAT was not what the possible sources of evidence identified in the expert report could prove at trial. The CAT had effectively carried out a 'mini-trial' and subjected the application for certification to a 'more vigorous process of examination than would have taken place at a strike-out application'.[29] Accordingly, the Court held that the CAT's decision was vitiated by an error of law because they misdirected themselves as the correct test to be applied. At the certification stage, the applicant should not 'be required to demonstrate more than that he has a real prospect of success'.[30]

The Court also held that the CAT erred by refusing certification by reference to the proposed method of distribution. Distribution was said to be a matter for the trial

---

are suitable the Tribunal can take into account all matters it thinks fit, including *'whether the claims are suitable for an aggregate award of damages'*.
[23] See *Merricks* (n 3) at [30] and [83].
[24] *Walter Hugh Merricks v Mastercard Incorporated and Ors* [2017] CAT 16 at [67].
[25] ibid at [77]–[78].
[26] ibid at [88]–[89].
[27] Various Canadian territories had adopted a certification regime which was similar to the system introduced in the UK.
[28] *Merricks v Mastercard Incorporated & Others* [2019] EWCA Civ 674, [2019] Bus LR 3025 at [48].
[29] ibid at [52]–[53].
[30] ibid at [54].

judge and an aggregate award of damages does not need to be distributed in accordance with individual loss.[31]

E. Supreme Court

Mastercard appealed the decision to the Supreme Court. The appeal was heard before Lords Kerr, Briggs, Sales, Leggatt and Thomas. Due to the untimely passing of Lord Kerr, the Court was divided 2:2, however, given Lord Kerr had indicated that he agreed with the reasons of Lord Briggs, the appeal was ultimately dismissed.[32]

There were two issues before the Supreme Court in determining whether the CAT was correct to refuse a CPO. First, the claims were not suitable to be brought in collective proceedings and second, Merricks did not propose to distribute damages in a way which reflected the class members' individual losses. All the judges of the Supreme Court agreed that the CAT's second reason for refusing certification was unsound.[33]

The central point of disagreement between the judgment of Lord Briggs (with Lord Thomas agreeing) and the joint dissenting judgment of Lords Sale and Leggatt was how 'suitability' should be construed, reflecting a difference in the emphasis of the purpose of collective proceedings and certification. Lord Briggs held that the question of suitability was a relative one. That is, are collective proceedings 'suitable' when compared to the relevant alternative of individual proceedings.[34]

Lord Briggs considered the relevant Canadian authorities and the purpose of the UK collective proceedings regime. His Lordship noted that collective proceedings were introduced as an alternative to individual claims. Accordingly, when determining whether claims are 'suitable' to continue as a collective proceeding, it is relevant to consider how – if it all – individual claims may be brought.[35]

In determining that the question of suitability is a relative one, Lord Briggs emphasised that the collective proceedings are a 'special form of civil procedure for the vindication of private rights, designed to provide access to justice for that purpose where ordinary forms of individual civil claim have proved inadequate for the purpose'.[36] His Lordship also referred to the fact that the refusal to make a CPO would likely

> make it certain that the rights of consumers arising out of a proven infringement will never be vindicated, because individual claims are likely to be a practical impossibility. The

---

[31] ibid at [61]–[62].
[32] As Lord Kerr agreed with the reasons set out by Lord Briggs prior to his retirement on 30 September 2020 and Lord Kerr was recorded as agreeing with the reasons of Lord Briggs in the draft judgment circulated to the parties' legal advisers. Lord Kerr passed away three days before the judgment was due to be handed down. In those circumstances Lord Briggs, Lord Thomas, Lord Sales and Lord Leggatt all agreed that the appeal should be dismissed notwithstanding the 2:2 split – *Merricks* (n 3) at [82] and [83].
[33] *Merricks* (n 3) [77] and [83].
[34] ibid at [56].
[35] ibid at [55].
[36] ibid at [45].

evident purpose of the statutory scheme was to facilitate rather than to impede the vindication of those rights.[37]

Lord Briggs accordingly held that the CAT's refusal to make a CPO was vitiated by errors of law and the appeal should be dismissed. The fact that quantifying the loss may be very difficult or expensive was not, in and of itself, a reason to refuse certification.[38]

In their joint dissenting judgment, Lords Sales and Leggatt emphasised the substantive role of the CAT as providing a 'control mechanism' for collective proceedings.[39] Given the emphasis on the CAT's role as guarding against potentially oppressive or unfair proceedings, their Lordships disagreed that the test of 'suitability' requires only a relative comparison between collective proceedings and individual claims. They considered that: (a) the words of the Act did not establish a relative test;[40] and (b) collective proceedings confer substantial advantages on claimants which 'are capable of being exploited opportunistically' and in the absence of clear wording, simply demonstrating that members of a class would face greater difficulties pursuing their claims individually is not sufficient to justify claims being brought as a collective proceeding.[41] To the extent comparisons are relevant, Lords Sales and Leggatt opined that the choice is not whether some form of collective proceeding is preferable to individual proceedings. Rather, it is whether the claims for which certification is sought are suitable to be combined. Their Lordships commented that 'answering that question in the negative does not mean that there is no other class of claims which is suitable to be brought as collective proceedings'.[42]

Lords Sales and Leggatt preferred a construction of suitability which asked whether the claims are:

> suitable to be grouped together and determined collectively in accordance with the regime established by the Act and the CAT Rules ... This includes consideration of whether collective proceedings offer a reasonable prospect of achieving a just outcome. It also calls for an assessment of proportionality: is combining these claims and determine them collectively in accordance with the collective proceedings regime likely to achieve the fair determination of the claims at proportionate cost.[43]

Their Lordships took a similar approach to the construction of whether a claim is 'suitable' for an aggregate award of damages – identifying the relevant test as whether 'claims are suitable to be grouped together as unit for the purpose of proving and assessing loss, justly at proportionate cost'. This requires an assessment of the method available which can be used 'to assess loss suffered by the class as a whole with a reasonable degree of accuracy'.[44] Accordingly, their Lordships held that it was appropriate that, at the certification stage, the CAT required the class representative to demonstrate that there is a 'method capable of establishing loss in a reasonable

---

[37] ibid at [54].
[38] ibid at [74].
[39] ibid at [99].
[40] ibid at [117].
[41] ibid at [118].
[42] ibid at [119].
[43] ibid at [116].
[44] ibid at [121].

and just way, and at proportionate cost, on a class-wide basis'.[45] They agreed with the Court of Appeal that the task before the applicant was to 'satisfy the CAT that the expert methodology was capable of assessing the level of pass-on to the represented class and that there was, or was likely to be, data available to operate that methodology'.[46]

Lords Sales and Leggatt disagreed with the Court of Appeal's criticism that the CAT wrongly required Merricks to establish more than a reasonably arguable case. Merricks had to satisfy the CAT that the proposed methodology 'offered a realistic prospect of establishing loss on a class-wide basis'. In this case, that question turned on whether there is likely to be sufficient data to operate that methodology.[47] Their Lordships also disagreed with Lord Briggs' criticism of the CAT for treating the question of whether the case was suitable for an award of aggregate damages as if it were a hurdle rather than simply another factor for consideration. Importantly, it was noted that the position taken by the CAT did not 'undermine the efficacy of the collective proceedings regime'. It would be open for applicants to seek a CPO for a more limited set of proceedings where they could be more confident that there was sufficient data to apply the proposed methodology.[48]

The certification regime is designed to balance these competing interests by deferring to the CAT's judgment. However, as is demonstrated by *Merricks*, like most areas of the law, there is room for substantial differences of opinion about how certification decisions should be made. It is obvious that the higher the burden placed on representatives at an early stage, the more likely CPOs will not be made. As Lord Briggs emphasised, where a certification order is not made, it is unlikely that individual consumers will have the ability or desire to pursue their claim.

Lords Sales and Leggatt observe that it is somewhat illusory to compare the certification of collective proceedings with individual claims being pursued – it is plausible that a different form of collective claim may be 'suitable' to be pursued. In *Merricks*, it is not clear that is the case. As their Lordships noted, there is likely to be significant variation in the pass-on rates within the businesses operating in the different sectors of the economy identified in the expert report. As such, it is likely that Mastercard could have made similar arguments about a lack of data to operate the proposed model even if the claim was drawn more narrowly to focus on particular sectors.[49]

F. Progress Since Supreme Court

At the time of writing this chapter, over two years have passed since the Supreme Court remitted the issue of certification in *Merricks* back to the CAT. There have been multiple procedural steps, but the substantive matters have not yet been litigated and there is no indication of a settlement agreement being reached. The next

---

[45] ibid at [123].
[46] ibid at [155].
[47] ibid at [158].
[48] ibid at [175].
[49] As suggested by their Lordships in *Merricks* at [175].

significant step is for class members to either opt-in or opt-out of the proceedings. The CPO was granted on an opt-out basis. As set out above, the class comprises individuals who between 22 May 1992 and 21 June 2008: (a) were aged 16 years and over; (b) were resident in the UK for a continuous period of at least three months; and (c) purchased goods or services from businesses selling in the UK that accepted Mastercard cards, irrespective of the form of payment tendered for the particular transaction. Individuals meeting the class description living in the UK on 6 September 2016 are automatically included in the class but may choose to opt-out by completing the opt-out form either online or in paper format and posting to the address specified.[50] Class members who were living outside the UK on 6 September 2016 are not automatically included, but may similarly join the class action by completing the opt-in notice online or in paper format and posting to the address specified.[51] The form and content of opt-out and opt-in notices are required to be approved by the CAT[52] when authorising the class representative. Obviously for opt-out or opt-in processes to reach as many eligible group members as possible the class action must be widely publicised. The need to notify class members is also of intense concern for the CAT which must consider the representative's proposed method for notifying the class members of the proceeding when authorising that representative.[53] Although a publicity campaign has yet to commence in *Merricks* it will soon be activated intending to reach class members both in the UK and also offshore.

III. FIRST LESSON – COMPETITION LAW AS CONSUMER LAW

As outlined in many of the other chapters in this collection, consumers are often protected by legal claims that we do not traditionally view as 'consumer law'. *Merricks* provides another area of law inherently linked with protection of consumers, namely competition law. The connection between these two areas are clearly intricate and complicated,[54] and this case only provides a single case study. There is, however, substantial global consensus that one of the key purpose of competition law is enhancing consumer welfare.[55] Effective competition within a market can therefore give consumers a choice of products at the lowest possible prices. In this sense,

---

[50] www.mastercardconsumerclaim.co.uk/Content/Documents/Opt%20Out%20Form.pdf (accessed 15 December 2022).
[51] ibid.
[52] Competition Appeal Tribunal Rules 2015 ('CAT Rules') r 78(3)(c) which requires the class representative to 'prepare a plan for the ... proceedings that satisfactorily includes (i) a method for bringing the proceedings on behalf of represented persons and for notifying represented persons of the progress of the proceedings'.
[53] ibid. See also Competition Appeal Tribunal *Guide to Proceedings* at [6.30].
[54] See, eg, KJ Cseres, *Competition Law and Consumer Protection* (Kluwer Law International, The Hague, 2005).
[55] See International Competition Network discussion document '*Competition Enforcement and Consumer Welfare*' (2011) which found that more than 50 national competition authorities identified increasing consumer welfare as the primary or at least one of the goals of competition law enforcement. OECD Policy Roundtable 'The interface between Competition and Consumer Policies' 2008. For a general discussion see Ezrachi 'Sponge' (2017) 5(1) *Journal of Antitrust Enforcement*'.

competition law and consumer law are, in many ways complementary, a key goal of both being the promotion consumer welfare. The complementarity of these areas of law is reflected in the fact that many national authorities charged with regulating competition law also have a consumer law remit.[56]

While there is a broad agreement that competition law should focus on consumer welfare, there is 'deep disagreement' about what 'consumer welfare means and especially about what policies [are] best to promote it'.[57] Despite the complementarity between these areas of law, it must be recorded that there are certain areas of tension. For example, some consumer protection policies, such as mandatory product standards which inhibit the entry of new competitors, may adversely impact competition (and ultimately reduce long term consumer welfare). Similarly, opening new areas to competition by removing regulations may raise issues for consumer protection.[58]

Regardless of the disagreements about how the consumer welfare should be defined, there is little argument that one of the results of ensuring healthy competition within an economy is enhanced consumer welfare. Effective competition within a market ultimately results in consumers having a choice of goods and services at the lowest possible prices. While promoting effective competition increases consumer welfare it is not the same as 'consumer protection'. Consumer protection also enhances welfare by ensuring that consumers can intelligently and efficiently exercise the choices provided by competition law.[59] Competition law primarily seeks to enhance consumer welfare through protecting and promoting competition generally on the presumption that a competitive market tends to promote consumer welfare. As well as generally promoting competitive markets, competition law also seeks to address harm that may be caused to end-product consumers. For example, companies which provide roofing installation and repair services in a particular region may agree to cooperate when providing quotes to customers to ensure that certain companies win contracts. Such cooperation between companies results in consumers paying more for services than they would have if the companies had not cooperated.[60]

Such anti-competitive cooperation between companies causes loss to consumers. Such loss is actionable as a breach of statutory duty.[61] Suspected breaches of competition law may be investigated by authorities charged with enforcing competition law. In addition, persons who have suffered loss due to the anti-competitive practices of others, may commence proceedings to vindicate their rights. It has long been recognised that such actions make 'an important contribution to the maintenance of effective competition'.[62]

---

[56] See International Competition Network discussion document '*Competition Enforcement and Consumer Welfare*' (2011) 21–23.

[57] G Werden, 'Essays on Consumer Welfare and Competition Policy' (2009). See also *Competition Enforcement and Consumer Welfare* stating, 'Many authorities have not adopted a formal definition of consumer welfare.'

[58] OECD Policy Roundtable 'The interface between Competition and Consumer Policies' 2008, 17–20.

[59] OECD Policy Roundtable 'The interface between Competition and Consumer Policies' 2008.

[60] See, eg, 'Felt and single ply roofing contracts in Western-Central Scotland: anti-competitive practices' – GOV.UK (www.gov.uk).

[61] In the example, it would be breach of the Competition Act 1998 UK, s 2(1).

[62] *Sainsbury's Supermarkets Ltd v Visa Europe Services LLC* [2020] UKSC 24 at [185] citing *Courage Ltd v Crehan* (Case C-453/99) [2002] QB 507 at [26]–[27].

While consumers who suffered loss due to anticompetitive practices can commence proceedings for compensation, such actions face significant hurdles. First, consumers may not know they have been harmed. The nature of anti-competitive agreements are that they are often secretive and difficult to prove. Absent a competition law regulator undertaking an (often lengthy) investigation, a consumer may not be aware they have suffered any loss. Second, even if retail consumers are aware they have suffered loss, the amount of loss they have suffered may not justify any single consumer taking action.[63]

The UK has seen significant movement on that front in less than a decade. In January 2013, the UK Department of Business Innovation & Skills released the government's response to a consultation paper on private actions in competition law.[64] That paper recognised that 'the legal costs and complexity remained an insuperable barrier for the vast majority of SMEs and consumers' to bring private actions.[65] A key reform identified in that paper was to introduce a regime for commencing opt-out collective actions for breaches of competition law.[66]

As a result, the ability to commence an opt-out collective proceedings regime was introduced by the Consumer Rights Act 2015 which amended the Competition Act 1998. Section 47B of the Competition Act was amended to allow collective proceedings to be commenced but only allows such proceedings to continue if the CAT makes a collective proceedings order. *Merricks* is a landmark case in the sense that it will be the first significant test of the effectiveness of the competition law-based collective action regime in allowing a representative to commence opt-out proceedings on behalf of consumers.

Allowing consumers to commence collective actions to vindicate their rights was one the key purposes behind the CAT opt-out process. However, in terms of ensuring both consumer law and competition law purposes, collective enforcement of consumer welfare through competition law mechanism is only as effective as the procedures that allow enforcement of the substantive rights. This leads us onto the second lesson from *Merricks*.

IV. SECOND LESSON – CHALLENGES AND OPPORTUNITIES OF COLLECTIVE ACTIONS

As outlined in the introduction, the cases in this collection highlight that it is uncommon for an 'everyday' consumer to take on a business and create a landmark case.[67]

---

[63] However, where the relevant 'consumer' is a corporate entity located higher up the distribution chain (for example a large retailer) they may have both the means and the incentive to take action to recover the losses caused by the anticompetitive conduct.

[64] This was effectively the end of lengthy debate about the role of private actions in competition law which began with discussion published by the Office of Fair Trading in April 2007 '*Private actions in competition law: effective redress for consumers and business*'. In April 2012, the UK Government issued a consultation on options for reform (*Private actions in competition law: a consultation on options for reform*).

[65] See Department for Business Innovation & Skills '*Private Actions in Competition Law: A consultation on options for reform – government response*' January 2013.

[66] The paper noted that 'breaches of competition law, such as price-fixing, often involve very large numbers of people each losing a small amount, meaning it is not cost-effective for any individual to bring a case to court. Allowing actions to be brought collectively would overcome this problem, allowing consumers and businesses to get back the money that is rightfully theirs – as well as acting as a further deterrent to anyone thinking of breaking the law'.

[67] See section I above.

Given the asymmetries of resources between the parties, and the relative cost of proceedings, consumer cases are fertile ground for group action to be pursued via a collective civil procedure. UK law provides for various mechanisms for collective actions including via a Group Litigation Order,[68] a representative action[69] or a CAT collective action pursuant to section 47B of the Competition Act 1998. Alternatively, a matter could be pursued by a regulator on behalf of consumers, such as that brought by the Financial Conduct Authority (FCA) against Wonga[70] for breach of responsible lending obligations. This resulted in the company entering into an agreement with the FCA to provide redress to over 350,000 customers, at a cost in excess of £220 million, as well as making significant changes to their lending guidelines and criteria.[71] This chapter only discusses CAT collective actions and does not further consider these other procedures.

CAT collective actions may be brought by class members or another legal person who is not a class member, subject to meeting a 'just and equitable' standard and obtaining the authorisation of the CAT.[72] This may open the gateway for consumer representative groups to bring a claim, or for a special purpose vehicle to be formed to be the representative entity. Solicitors are unlikely to be permitted to bring the action as the solicitor would have a 'material interest ... in conflict with the interests of class members'.[73] CAT collective actions may be brought either on an opt-in or an opt-out basis subject to certification by CAT.[74] For opt-out actions, this means that the claim is brought on behalf of a defined group. Individuals are automatically part of the group by meeting the group description. It is not necessary individually to identify group members or value their individual claims. Non-UK domiciled claimants may nonetheless opt-in to the (otherwise opt-out) claim. Alternatively, the action may be conducted on an opt-in basis. For persons domiciled in the UK, *Merricks* was brought on an opt-out basis. CAT collective actions raise at least two issues for consumers which run alongside the potential for redress provided by the regime. These relate to two interconnected decisions consumers will likely face in relation to their participation in the class action: (1) whether or not to opt-out or into the proceedings; and (b) the possible need to acquire litigation funding.

Turning first to the decision by consumers as to whether or not to opt-out or into the proceeding. The class representative is required to give notice of the CPO to class members 'in a form and manner approved by the Tribunal'.[75] Relevantly, the notice must explain to class members that judgment on the common issues obtained in the class action will bind those represented in the class action and also explain what

---

[68] These were introduction into English civil procedural rules introduced in April 1999. A GLO is made under Civil Procedure Rules, 19.10 and 19.11 for claims which 'give rise to common or related issues of fact or law'.

[69] Actions that are made by or against one or more persons who have the '"same interest' in a claim (CPR 19.6); see for example, *Lloyd v Google* [2019] EWCA Civ 1599, [2020] QB 747.

[70] Financial Conduct Authority, *Media Release: Wonga to Make Major Changes to Affordability Criteria Following Discussions with the FCA* (2014).

[71] See J Gardner, *The Future of High-Cost Credit: Thinking Payday Lending* (Oxford, Hart Publishing, 2022) 7.

[72] CAT Rule 78.

[73] CAT Rule 78(2)(b).

[74] CAT Rule 79.

[75] CAT Rule 81.

the class member must do, and by when, to opt-out. Failing to opt-out is therefore attended by serious legal consequences. Res judicata applies on the common issues to those who remain in the class. Consumers may well need to obtain independent legal and financial advice before making the decision to opt-out (or in). The opt-out or opt-in processes next in view in *Merricks* are described above. Whilst the content of notices and the attendant publicity campaign to reach class members is supervised by the CAT, as a general matter the efficacy of opt-out or opt-in notices is unclear. For example, as standard form documents which relate to the exercise or relinquishment of legal rights of action it has yet to be demonstrated the extent to which they are truly understood and consented to by those who sign them. Moreover, we cannot know how many class members decline to opt-out or opt-in by reason of a failure to comprehend the terms.

Second, participation in a class action *may* involve the need to acquire a financial product. Whilst improved access to justice is a goal of most class actions regimes, justice is not free. The need for a financial product arises both for the representative party and also, potentially, for group members. The representative party will incur legal costs, the costs of experts, and bears the risk of an adverse costs order and the requirement to pay security for costs. The CAT, in determining whether a party is an authorised representative, considers whether the proposed representative is able to pay the defendant's recoverable costs if ordered to do so and whether the representative has sufficient financial resources to fairly and adequately represent the class.[76] In *UK Trucks Claim Ltd v Fiat Chrysler Automobiles*[77] the CAT reviewed the Litigation Funding Agreements (LFA) of two potential representatives in rival class actions. The CAT held that the terms of neither LFA provided a ground for refusing to authorise the relevant applicants as a class representative.[78] In relation to individual class members, the LFA structure in the *UK Trucks Claim* seems to contemplate, at least in relation to one of the rival class actions, that whilst the representative party would sign the LFA, individual class members would sign a 'litigation management agreement' with the representative party which carried obligations about opt-in such that:

> the 'Claimants' as defined includes not only [the representative party] but also the individual members of the class who have entered into a separate litigation management agreement with the [representative party], and that they themselves become parties to the [LFA]. Clause 9.8 of the [LFA] provides:

> 'The Claimants (other than the [representative party]) hereby agree with [the funder] that, in the event that a CPO is made, they shall use their best endeavours to opt-in to the Collective Proceedings.'[79]

Whilst we may distinguish this case on the basis that it did not concern 'consumers'[80] but those involved in the road haulage industry, the above facts nonetheless illustrate a

---

[76] CAT Rules 78(1)(b); 78(2)-(3). CAT Tribunal's *Guide To Proceedings* (2015) at [6.30] and [6.33]. The *Guide to Proceedings* has the status of a Practice Direction per CAT Rules 115(3).
[77] *UK Trucks Claim Ltd v Fiat Chrysler Automobiles* [2019] CAT 26.
[78] *Competition Act* 1998, s 47B.
[79] *UK Trucks Claim Ltd v Fiat Chrysler Automobiles* NV [2019] CAT 26 at [57].
[80] At least, a consumer as defined by the Consumer Rights Act 2015, s 2(3) to be 'an individual acting for purposes that are wholly or mainly outside that individual's trade, business, craft or profession'.

more general problem. All of the known risks which attend the formation of contracts for financial products are potentially implicated in a class member's interactions with a litigation funder. For example, the contract may be vitiated by misrepresentation, undue influence, unconscionability or duress. The class member may not truly understand the nature of the product or consent to the terms. Whilst there is a voluntary code of conduct for litigation funders (the 'ALF Code')[81] which also speaks to the content of litigation funding agreements, the ALF Code has no legal force[82] and provides limited protection for class members.[83] It contains various provisions requiring the litigation funding agreement to state to what extent the funder is liable to meet any liability for adverse costs, to provide security for costs and to meet any other financial liability.[84] The funding agreement is also required to set out the extent to which the funder is empowered to influence or direct decisions in the class action and in relation to settlement.[85] Whilst the Code requires the funder to take reasonable steps to ensure that class members receive independent legal advice on the terms of the funding agreement prior to its execution, and not to take any steps that cause or are likely to cause the claimant's solicitor or barrister to act in breach of their professional duties,[86] this advice may apparently be given by the a lawyer instructed in the dispute.[87]

Finally, there is the pervasive issue of the financial return to the funder. Litigation funding is a commercial activity and market participants expect a return in exchange for assuming significant legal risk. Prior to agreeing to fund an action, a litigation funder will conduct extensive due diligence on the claim and will likely seek correlative mechanisms of control, both formal and informal, over the progress of the claim and the terms of any agreed settlement. A potential disadvantage to class members is therefore that a significant proportion of the overall recovery will be required to be paid to the litigation funder. However, this must be balanced against the cost and burdens of litigation if pursued on an individual basis.[88] The CAT must approve any payment out of an award of damages or approved settlement.[89] It remains to be seen how intensively the CAT will scrutinise and potentially vary the contractual entitlement of funders to a proportion of the recovery.

---

[81] Association of Litigation Funders of England and Wales, Code of Conduct for Litigation Funders (January 2018) ('ALF Code').
[82] A court could potentially seek an undertaking from a funder that the funder would abide by the Code.
[83] See S Degeling and M Legg, 'Undue Influence, Litigation Funding and Group Proceedings' [2023] 42 *CJQ* 237.
[84] ALF Code at [10].
[85] ALF Code at [11]–[13].
[86] ALF Code at [9].
[87] ALF Code at [9.1].
[88] Which may in any case no longer be available. In *Merricks* the limitation period for individual action has expired so that those who opt-out or fail to opt-in will not be able to pursue an individual claim.
[89] CAT Rules 93 (Distribution of Award) and 94(3) (Collective settlement where a collective proceedings order has been made: opt-out collective proceedings).

V. CONCLUSION

The authors recognise the irony of *Merricks* as a landmark case; the substantive legal principles of this case are yet to be heard. At the time of writing, it is unclear whether the case will settle or proceed to court and, if the latter, there is no indication of whether it will succeed. The case is however worthy of its status as a landmark case, as it shines an important and illuminating light on the challenges, risks and opportunities of collective actions. In many ways, this also helps us see the future of consumer law. Rising court costs and the lack of legal aid provision for civil cases means that collective actions are likely to become an increasing feature of consumer law enforcement. Whilst these provide the potential to address some of the inherent power imbalances that exist in consumer law cases, they come with their own risks. The complex role of opt-out and opt-in processes, the risk of lack of informed consumer consent and the asymmetries of power and information which exist between litigation funders and lawyers on the one hand, and consumers on the other,[90] raise new and difficult challenges, something that is clearly worthy of future consideration.

---

[90] See generally S Degeling and M Legg, 'Fiduciaries and Funders' (2017) 36 *CJQ* 47.

Index

abortion rights   245–64
access to justice   12–15, 367–8
adulteration of foods   50, 145–7
advertising
   and consumer law   9
   prescription drugs   265–9, 276–7
   professions   279–80
   and quack medicine   106–8
   unfair   10, 52
Association of Litigation Funders of England and Wales, Code of Conduct for Litigation Funders (ALF code)   401
attorneys   35, 36
automobiles   16

banking   2, 12–13, 299–313
bankruptcy   6, 315–31
bargaining power, inequality of   5, 189–90, 192–3, 195–206
bottomry bonds   30
breach of trust   35

catching bargains   28, 30–3
caveat emptor   8
Chancery and fraud   28, 29, 30–3
class actions   13–15, 388–396
collective civil procedures   387–8, 398–401
Collective Proceedings Orders (CPOs)   388, 390–6
commercial speech   9–10, 265, 269, 271–6, 279
common carriers   58–61
competition law   10, 396–8
   Competition and Markets Authority (CMA)   379
   Competitions Appeal Tribunal (CAT)   387–8, 391–6, 399–401
conditional sales   132
consumers   4–7
   consumer choice   10–11, 251–3, 256–7
   consumer citizens   379–80
   consumer contracts   15, 51
      exemption clauses in   52
   Consumer Council   51–2
   consumer credit   117–26, 131
   consumer culture   148
   Consumer Financial Protection Bureau (CFPB)   379

consumer litigation, structural injustice of   320–3
consumer protection   13, 50, 376–80
consumer society   57–8
consumer surplus, loss of   214–16
consumer welfare   208–9
contrats d'adhesion   132
corporate criminal liability   184–7
cosmetic products   141
Court of Common Pleas   64
cozenage   28
credence characteristics   213
credit   117–26
credit cards   1, 6
credit selling   132
credulous consumers   5–6
Crook, Japhet   35–8
Crowther Committee   131

dangerous goods   136–40, 147–52
defective product claims   140–7, 149–52
defective products   283, 284–5
dermatitis   140–4, 150
disappointment, damages for   153–68
due diligence defence   182

egg flip   209–10
European Convention on Human Rights (ECHR)   374–6
European integration   333–49
European Private Law (EPL)   333, 335–48
exemption clauses in consumer contracts   52
experience characteristics   213–14
experiential damages   18
extended identification   179–80

Federal Trade Commission (FTC)   378
Financial Conduct Authority (FCA)   379
financial products   16–17
fitness for purpose   51
food contamination   50, 145–7
fraud
   catching bargains   28, 30–3
   and Chancery   28, 29, 30–3
   cozenage   28
   marriage brocage contracts   33–4

presumption of   34–8
six badges of   28–9
undue influence   34–5
freedom of contract   7–8, 11, 226–7, 242–3
fur dermatitis   140–3, 150

Gabell, Alverstone   56, 65
Gardner, Robert   42
'gay cake cases'   369–76, 380–4
ginger beer   145–6
goodwill   207–8, 210, 219
Group Litigation Orders   399
guarantees   51

hair dye   141, 149–51
hair wash   138
Hire Purchase Act (1938)   50
Hire Purchase Act (1964)   52
hire traders   126–30
hire-purchase
contracts   132
as disguised form of mortgage   131
growth in   131
regulation of   125–30, 131, 132
repossessions   121–5
and secured credit   117–26
third party purchasers   126, 130
holidays   154–168
horse sales   43–4
housing   315–31, 333–49
human flourishing   166–8
human rights law   11–12, 374

identification   172, 175–6, 176–80, 181–3
identity   5
implied terms   51
implied warranties   41, 43–9
inequality of bargaining power   5, 189–90, 192–3, 195–206
influenza epidemics   79–82, 86–8

Janssen, Abraham   24
judicial decisions and consumer law   2, 17–18
judicial insubordination   148

Law Commission   185–7
Corporate Criminal Liability: an options paper   185–7
legislative interventions in common law   133
limitations of liability   58–77
Litigation Funding Agreements (LFA)   400
low-income litigation   326–9

manufacturer liability   16
Marlborough (Sarah Churchill, Duchess of)   23–7

marriage brocage contracts   33–4
medicine
advertising and regulation   266–9, 276–7
patent medicine industry   106–13
merchant service charge (MSC)   389–90
merchantability   41, 47, 49, 51, 52
mince pies   147
misrepresentations about quality or attributes   213–14
Molony Committee   50–2
monopoly costs   216–19
mortgage debt   333–49
multilateral interchange fee (MIF)   388–9

New Deal   377
nisi prius reports   39–40
no-fault compensation   16
non-commercial sureties   189–206

Office of Fair Trading (UK)   13
European Court of Justice, no referral to   305–6
failure to protect customers   306–8
future of   312–13
impact of   310–12
issue at stake   300–1
legislation, deficiency   308–9
Supreme Court decision   305–10
impact of   310–12
One-Shotters (OSs)   12–13, 320–3
one-sided contracts   105–6
overdraft charges   299–313

package holidays   18
passing off   10–11, 207–21
patent medicine industry   106–13
pawnbrokers   126–30
Payment Protection Insurance (PPI)   13–14, 351–68
pianos   117–18, 124, 126–30
prescription drugs, advertising and regulation   266–9, 276–7
price transparency   277–9
privacy, right to   247–9, 251, 261
privity rule   136, 138, 140, 144, 147
product endorsements by celebrities   219
product liability   16, 283–97
product litigation   147
professions, advertising   279–80

quack medicine   106–11

racial discrimination   7, 11, 226–7, 229–34, 377–8
railways
cloakrooms   61–8
as common carriers   58–61

and consumer society   57–8
  limitations of liability   58–77
recreation   154
religious neutrality   372–3
Repeat-Players (RPs)   12, 320–3
reproductive rights   245–64
retail forums   148
reverse passing off   220
risk of innovation   15–17

saleable quality   39–40
sales puffery   212
search characteristics   213
security interests   131
sewing machines   117, 119–20
sexual orientation discrimination   369–76, 380–4
sexuality, discrimination on the grounds of   7, 369–85
silk waste   42–3
social exclusion   380
Spencer, John   23–7
standard form contracts   73–4
Star Chamber   28–30
Statutes of Fraudulent Conveyances   28
Statutes of Usury   29–30
strict liability   16, 285, 287, 292–3, 296
structural injustice of consumer litigation   320–3
substitute goods   214–15
sweated work   119–20

Targeted Regulation of Abortion Providers (TRAP) laws   258
technology   15–17
terms and conditions of contracts   15, 73
Thalidomide scandal   16
third-party guarantees   189–206
transaction costs   2

UCTD (Directive on unfair terms in consumer contracts)   334–5, 336–8, 340, 343, 345–6
unconscionable bargains   24–5, 31
unconscionable conduct   202–3
unconscionable dealing   190
undue influence   34–5, 192
unfair advertising   10, 52
unfair competition   10
unfair conduct   201–2
unfair terms   203–4, 333–49
Uniform Commercial Code (USA)   5, 378
usury   24–5, 29–30

vicarious liability   176–9

warranties   15, 41, 43–9, 50
weakness of consumers   5
will theory of contract   103–5
women, as consumers   5–6
Wonga   399

Milton Keynes UK
Ingram Content Group UK Ltd.
UKHW050608110124
435758UK00007B/60